SUPPLY CHAIN ARCHITECTURE

A Blueprint for Networking the Flow of Material, Information, and Cash

The St. Lucie Series on Resource Management

Titles in the Series

Applying Manufacturing Execution Systems
by Michael McClellan

Back to Basics: Your Guide to Manufacturing Excellence
by Steven A. Melnyk and R.T. "Chris" Christensen

Basics of Supply Chain Management
by Lawrence D. Fredendall and Ed Hill

Collaborative Manufacturing: Using Real-Time Information to Support the Supply Chain
by Michael McClellan

Enterprise Resources Planning and Beyond: Integrating Your Entire Organization
by Gary A. Langenwalter

ERP: Tools, Techniques, and Applications for Integrating the Supply Chain
by Carol A. Ptak with Eli Schragenheim

Handbook of Supply Chain Management
by Jim Ayers

Integral Logistics Management: Planning and Control of Comprehensive Supply Chains, Second Edition
by Paul Schönsleben

Integrated Learning for ERP Success: A Learning Requirements Planning Approach
by Karl M. Kapp, with William F. Latham and Hester N. Ford-Latham

Introduction to e-Supply Chain Management: Engaging Technology to Build Market-Winning Business Partnerships
by David C. Ross

Inventory Classification Innovation: Paving the Way for Electronic Commerce and Vendor Managed Inventory
by Russell G. Broeckelmann

Lean Manufacturing: Tools, Techniques, and How To Use Them
by William M. Feld

Lean Performance ERP Project Management: Implementing the Virtual Supply Chain
by Brian J. Carroll

Macrologistics Management: A Catalyst for Organizational Change
by Martin Stein and Frank Voehl

Restructuring the Manufacturing Process: Applying the Matrix Method
by Gideon Halevi

Supply Chain Management: The Basics and Beyond
by William C. Copacino

The Supply Chain Manager's Problem-Solver: Maximizing the Value of Collaberation and Technology
by Charles C. Poirier

Supply Chain Networks and Business Process Orientation: Advanced Strategies and Best Practices
by Kevin P. McCormack and William C. Johnson

The St. Lucie Series on Resource Management

SUPPLY CHAIN ARCHITECTURE

A Blueprint for Networking the Flow of Material, Information, and Cash

William T. Walker, CFPIM, CIRM

CRC PRESS

Boca Raton London New York Washington, D.C.

Cover art courtesy of Ralph J. Walker, AIA, RA

Library of Congress Cataloging-in-Publication Data

Walker, William T.
Supply chain architecture: a blueprint for networking the flow of material, information, and cash/William T. Walker
p. cm. — (The St. Lucie Press series on resource management)
Includes bibliographical references and index.
ISBN 1-57444-357-7 (alk. paper)
1. Business logistics. I. Title. II. Series.

HD38.5.W345 2004
658.5—dc22 2004051922

Direct all inquiries to CRC Press LLC, 2000 N.W. Corporate Blvd., Boca Raton, Florida 33431.

Visit the CRC Press Web site at www.crcpress.com

International Standard Book Number 1-57444-357-7
Library of Congress Card Number 2004051922
Printed in the United States of America 1 2 3 4 5 6 7 8 9 0
Printed on acid-free paper

About the Author

William T. Walker, CFPIM, CIRM is an expert in supply chain architecture and an accomplished practitioner. Bill's 33 years of experience with Hewlett-Packard and its spin-off, Agilent Technologies, included the design, operation, and optimization of global supply chain networks. His work involved new product development, commodity sourcing, import/export logistics, operations outsourcing, inventory risk management, product line transfers, new product distribution, and reverse supply chains.

Bill is the St. Lucie Press Resource Management Series Editor for CRC Press. He is a respected thought leader for Achieving Supply Chain Excellence through Technology (ASCET). Bill is a senior fellow with the University of Dayton Center for Competitive Change. He is a member of the Council of Logistics Management (CLM). Bill has led seminars on competitive supply chain networks around the world in Southeast Asia, the Americas, Western Europe and South Africa. He was named among the "Top 20 Logistics Executives of 2000" by The Logistics Forum and e-Supply Chain Forum. Bill was a contributing author to *Supply Chain Networks and Business Process Orientation*, CRC Press (2003) and was coauthor of *Supply Chain Management: Principles & Techniques for the Practitioner*, APICS (1998).

Bill co-developed the principles of supply chain management taught through APICS, the international professional society for resource management education. He authored the APICS principles courseware "Build a Competitive Infrastructure" and coauthored the APICS principles courseware "Leverage Worldwide Logistics." Bill was the event developer for the interactive supply chain game show, "You Are the Middle Link," first presented at the 2003 APICS International Conference in Las Vegas. As a past president of the APICS Educational & Research Foundation, Bill directed research grants to expand the APICS body of knowledge. As a past APICS vice president of Education for Specific Industry Groups (SIGs), Bill held oversight on APICS educational development for aerospace and defense, process, remanufacturing, repetitive, small manufacturing, and the textile and apparel industry groups. Bill is APICS certified at the fellow level, and holds BSEE and MSIE degrees both from Lehigh University.

You can reach Bill at: billwalker@primeisp.net
www.supplychainarchitecture.com

This work is dedicated to Elise, my granddaughter, and to her generation.

Table of Contents

Appendix A
The Network Blueprint 381

Preface

Immediately upon graduating from Lehigh University with a bachelor's degree in electrical engineering, I went to work for a small division of Hewlett-Packard—and never looked back until being "workforce managed" into retirement from Agilent Technologies, the HP spin-off, some 33 years later. I learned the intricacies of supply chain architecture through a progression of job rotations, business-related world travel, cross-industry work experiences, attainment of APICS certification and subject matter expertise, volunteerism alongside colleagues from academia, and the authorship of books and published articles. I had the honor of meeting both Bill Hewlett and Dave Packard early in my career while still a product development engineer.

Some executives do not want to be burdened with the details. After all, they are the senior management, and they employ others to perform the work. Bill Hewlett was down-to-earth. He was comfortable with detail and especially comfortable with basic principles. Yet Bill had an uncanny ability to cut through the clutter right to the chase. I can remember giving Bill a new-product briefing while he sat atop my lab bench. I was going on and on about how the lab was struggling to hold down product costs. After a minute Bill simply asked, "What is this product's value to the customer that it should have to be so large and cumbersome?" He was thinking in a completely different, much more customer-centric context.

Dave Packard was a towering individual and a consummate businessman. Dave instilled a sense of urgency everywhere. A favorite Packard legend is a speech Dave is reported to have given to his senior staff early in 1974. Packard had recently returned from a tour of duty as the U.S. deputy secretary of defense. Apparently, the HP management team had let Dave down while he was away in Washington. An unofficial transcript of Packard's speech was widely circulated within the company; its message had two themes. The first theme was that managers were forbidden to cut prices in order to buy market share. HP's reputation was built on creating value for its customers and stakeholders, which chasing market share fails to do. The second theme was that HP was awash in inventory. Dave simply told his general managers to cut inventory, or he would find someone else who could. Packard was forcefully stating the obvious. His company had lost sight of its business fundamentals, and was out of control.

Bill and Dave brought their vision and shared values together in building Hewlett-Packard into a great company. They also instilled a set of basic business rules and guiding principles. Our future was based on growth fueled by profit.[1] One piece of wisdom was that profits are ensured by growing revenue faster than expenses. We developed annual targets, with quarterly forecasts. During the times that revenue exceeded the plan, we were not allowed to spend more than the total expense dollars in the target. During the times that revenue was short of the plan, we were not allowed to spend more than the expense percentage in the target. This scheme drove honest targets and conservative spending.

A second piece of wisdom was that a steady stream of new products that include technological contributions and bring value to customers ensures growth. One-half of each year's total revenue came from products that had been introduced within the past three years. This kept the contribution high and the product lines fresh, but it also meant that HP had an enormous catalogue to manufacture.

A third piece of wisdom was that you do not buy what you cannot afford. HP had one of the strongest balance sheets in the industry because it had no debt. Hiring, advertising, travel, and consultants were each carefully scrutinized as discretionary purchases. The cash flow of HP was funded by turning orders into deliveries and deliveries into cash, and not by borrowing. These maxims are as true today as they were back then. My work site grew from 350 employees to 1,200 employees by following these wisdoms.

The New Jersey Division of Hewlett-Packard, later known as the Power Products Division, was a vertically integrated manufacturing site producing a full-line catalog of low-volume, high-mix electronic power supplies, electronic loads, and AC sources. Our final assembly and test, printed circuit assembly, printed circuit board fabrication, sheet metal fabrication, magnetic components fabrication, and warehousing operations were all housed under one roof. The site was organized under a general manager with oversight for human resources, marketing and sales, finance, research and development, manufacturing operations, and materials management.

When profitability first became an issue, the division reacted with the decision to outsource nonessential building services and the cafeteria. Then a harder transfer pricing decision was made to stop fabricating printed circuit boards in New Jersey and to buy boards from a sister division at a lower cost by consolidating the higher volume. Later there was a decision to outsource the internally captive sheet metal fabrication operation to a local third-party supplier. The employee skills and machinery assets were deemed to be a low-technology commodity that could be bought more competitively from the outside. Also, information technology operations were decentralized, then centralized, then decentralized, and finally centralized again.

Consideration of revenue growth issues at the division was disconnected from any consideration of the supply chain. Life cycles of high-margin products were extended, whereas those of low-margin products were cut short. Although focused advertising campaigns helped to create customer awareness that HP was in the power products business, the division experimented with starting several new businesses, making a series of quick investments that were not well-integrated with their target markets. Each of these attempts failed within the first three years.

Return on investment was poor for another reason. The division's products had such a long product life cycle that there was considerable mismatch between the life cycles of the components used to manufacture the products and the products themselves. A disproportionate amount of engineering dollars had to be invested in supporting existing products, compared to new product development. Later the product catalog was broadened by licensing some new product designs from HP in Seoul, South Korea, and by licensing an existing product design from a third party on the West Coast.

As years passed, the division reinvented itself many times to ensure continuous profit and reasonable growth. My job responsibilities progressed from product development engineering to production engineering, to project management, to operations, to inventory control, to purchasing management, to materials management, to supply chain architecture, to Asian transfer program management. During one three-year period, my software project team developed more than a million lines of source code for an instrument networking application.

A colleague suggested that I consider becoming Certified in Production and Inventory Management (CPIM) through an international professional education society called APICS. I joined APICS, became certified, and quickly ascended through many volunteer leadership positions as chapter president, region staff, society vice president of the New York and New Jersey region, society vice president of Educational Development for Specific Industry Groups (SIGs), treasurer of the APICS Educational and Research Foundation, and president of the APICS Educational and Research Foundation. My volunteerism provided exposure to a rich body of knowledge that encompassed materials requirements planning, just-in-time supply processes, the Theory Of Constraints, lean manufacturing, and enterprise resource planning, as well as purchasing, logistics, quality, and service industry concepts. My SIG contacts with practitioners and consultants and my professional relationships with dozens of operations management academicians applying for research grants helped me build a unique practitioner's understanding of networks.

Fast-forward 30 years. Bill Hewlett and Dave Packard were gone. Agilent Technologies had been spun off from Hewlett-Packard as a startup company with $6 billion in revenue and 44,000 employees. The Test and Measurement Group alone represented more than half the new company's revenue. From the start Agilent Technologies positioned itself to the investment community as a growth company, in contrast to HP's historical positioning as a value company. The Agilent leadership quickly learned that the market price of their stock depended upon their ability to predict earnings and to communicate those predictions to the stock analysts. It was to be a rocky road.

HP was a decentralized organization with many independent divisional clusters of cross-functional expertise. Agilent's Test and Measurement Group quickly became a centralized organization with geographically distributed functions. Agilent's legacy systems were too numerous and too interwoven with those of HP. Agilent decided to undertake an ambitious multiyear, multiphase enterprise resource planning implementation to replace its legacy systems. It was Oracle's largest ERP implementation ever.

As Agilent pulled away from HP, Agilent learned that its manufacturing base was United States-centric and no longer global, as it would need to be to sell worldwide. Whole product lines had to be transferred and rebalanced among four international locations chosen to be Agilent manufacturing centers, in Malaysia, California, Colorado, and Scotland. The decision was made to transfer all manufacturing from New Jersey to Penang, Malaysia, to realize significant cost savings from lower labor rates, lower material costs, and a more favorable tax environment. This transfer was made in two phases, with assembly and test transferred to the Agilent facility in Penang and component fabrication outsourced to third parties elsewhere in Asia. Over years of organizational change, the vertical integration in New Jersey had been stretched, molded, and radically transformed into a supply chain network.

Disaster struck when the telecom market bubble burst, shortly followed by the economic disruption of September 11, 2001. Telecom represented the majority of the clients of Agilent's Test and Measurement Group. The overcapacity in fiber optics and the shortfall in demand for cell phone handsets rippled through the supply chain, bringing down wireless service providers, operating companies, handset manufacturers, base station manufacturers, equipment manufacturers, electronic component manufacturers, and raw materials suppliers. It was as though an entire industry had been caught up in a giant bullwhip effect. The crush of business began to swirl, and the largest companies reacted by expunging employees representing millenniums of combined knowledge and experience. After exercising the obvious spending restraints, hiring freezes, and draconian cost-cutting measures, Agilent had no choice but wave after wave of workforce reductions. Ultimately these resulted in 15,000 layoffs by the end of 2003.[2] Following the upheaval, my work site shrank to 85 employees. The world had changed forever, and we had not yet learned how to survive and flourish in a networked environment.

This book begins from the premise that no firm, even one with the resources of a Hewlett-Packard, can succeed alone. Every manufacturing and service firm needs customers, channels of distribution, value-added manufacturing, logistics and information support, financial services, and a supply base to survive. Every manufacturing and service firm lives or dies within a networked context. This book presents the rules for networking success in terms of five principles: *Velocity, Variability, Vocalize, Visualize*, and *Value*.

Bill Walker
August 14, 2004

NOTES

1. David Packard, *The HP Way: How Bill Hewlett and I Built Our Company*, HarperCollins, New York, 1995, p. 83.
2. Agilent Technologies, 2003 Annual Report to Stockholders, 2003, p. 1.

Acknowledgments

I wish to acknowledge the love and unswerving support of my wife, Linda, and my family Stacy, Andy, Elise, Ralph and Nicolle. I also wish to pay a debt of gratitude to my late parents, Betty and Bill, and my late parents-in-law, Dot and Marrel, for the exceptional formal education and business education they provided me. Special thanks go to my son Ralph, a licensed architect, who created the kitchen blueprint artwork.

I wish to acknowledge the contributions of my publisher, Rich O'Hanley, and my editors and reviewers, Claire Miller, Robert Vokurka, and George Wells.

Finally I wish to salute my professional colleagues worldwide, who gave me opportunities to learn and challenged my thinking along the way, especially: Karen Albers, Fred Barrie, Trevor Barrows, Bob Beecy, Greg Beers, Jane Biddle, Jon Blokker, Raghu Boppanna, Lynn Boyd, Cecil Bozarth, Ed Brorein, Al Bukey, Tim Buntin, Scott Burchell, Jorge Calaf, Brian Cargille, Ernie Carnicelli, Doug Charlton, Jim Chisolm, Mike Clark, Gary Cokins, Jim Cox, Art Darbie, Terry Dekalb, Oscar DeVries, Rick Elder, Dennis Faerber, Sherrie Ford, Howard Forman, Don Frank, Jill Franze, Karen Wynn Freeman, Bill Gaines, Jeff Galuten, Jack Gips, Tom Golden, Jonathan Golovin, Bill Grauf, Dan Guide, Pat Hanley, Mike Harding, Roger Harris, Safdar Hasan, Norm Heilweil, Don Hons, Dan Hudson, Yvonne Huertas, Radin Ikram, Anna Jeliazkov, Steve Kahl, Eng Lok Khoo, Mary Holmgren King, Andrew Ko, Barbara Kobryn, Gene Kobryn, Guenter Krause, Greg Kreger, Bruce Krueger, Tom Krupka, Barry Jacobs, Bill Johnson, Dan Kamas, Doug Kelly, Hank Kowalla, Kip Krawl, Andre Kuper, Jennifer LaJoie, Ross Lampshire, John Langley, Bill Latham, Keith Launchbury, Barrie Leigh, Chee Beng Lim, Derrick Lim, Mickey Linn, Archie Lockamy, Rick Looper, Al Low, Rhonda Lummus, Terry Lunn, Mike Lythgoe, Harvey McChesney III, Kevin McCormack, Jim McKim, Daniel Mak, Barry Markus, Sal Massulli, Eugene Micek, Juan Montermoso, J.T. Montgomery, Connie Munson, Andrew Musliner, Rich Myers, Sue Neff, Barry Newland, Dan Oldfield, Jong Soek Oh, Grace Ooi, Maarten Oosten, Steve Parkoff, Martin Perazza, Greg Petras, John Petriano, Alan Pfeffer, Frank Polizzi, Jim Pope, Cash Powell, Lisa Prats, Frank Prevete, Itzhak Priel, Carol Ptak, John Quense, Frank Quinn, Renu Ramnarayanan, Diego Ramos, Betty Rausch, Suzanne Richer, Dave Rivers, Boyd Runyon, Georg Ruof, Jochem Rupp, Rene St. Denis, Dianna Sacke, Doug Sage, Brooke Saladin, Greg Schlegel, Bob Schmelzer, Arvil Sexton, Aznul Shahrim, Carol Shaw, Joe Shedlawski, Arthur Shulman, Suhel Siddiqui, Bruce Skalbeck, Wu Soo Soo, Paul Sprunken, Jean Steele, David Steven, Paul Stevens, Markus Stauss, Keith Summers, Werner Teichroeb, Siow Khiang Teoh, Sam Tomas, Spencer Ure, Ben Veldboer, Dave Vennard, Virginia Vogel, Martin Waigh, Joe Walden, Jim Wallin, Alex Watson, Fred Wendt, Patricia Wickham, Blair Williams, Mark Williams, Ann Willis, Francisco Folch-Winter, Chon Leong Yoon, Shane York, Amy Zeng, John Zoller and Herman Zwirn.

About This Book

When the doorbell rang, there was a FTD florist delivery truck parked at the curb and a smiling delivery person standing on the stoop holding out a fresh bouquet of pink and yellow roses. The card read simply "For Elise." The thoughtful sender had only learned of my granddaughter's birth the day before. How did it happen that these delicate flowers, auctioned at 4 a.m. that morning in Amstelveen in the Netherlands and flown from Schiphol Airport to Newark, New Jersey, should arrive on my doorstep? How did it happen that Del Duca's Florist picked up their standing order for pink and yellow long stemmed roses after the shipment cleared Customs at the Port of Newark and drove them back to their Springfield Avenue shop? How did it happen that the sender selected the bouquet from an electronic catalog, entered a personalized greeting, placed the order, and paid for the service with MasterCard over the Internet during her lunch break?

Competition today is between geographically distributed networks of organizations separate by distance and time.

Consider a global manufacturing company competing for a customer order in Eastern Europe. A contract manufacturer in Khuala Lumpur, Malaysia, employing Chinese laborers, exports assemblies to fulfill an order from a manufacturing center in New Jersey. Twenty-five hours later, these assemblies arrive in New York City as cargo on a Korean airliner. Final production and testing of the product is completed at a factory in northern New Jersey by a Hispanic labor force, and the product is exported through JFK Airport, this time on a German aircraft. The goods are held in a customs-bonded warehouse in Frankfurt for ten days, and then re-exported to fulfill a customer order in London. The cash payments are transacted in pounds sterling, European Euros, U.S. dollars, and Malaysian ringgits through a bank with headquarters in Hong Kong.

Both examples represent complex, international supply chain networks where the flow of material, information, and cash among participating organizations works to the advantage of the customers and stakeholders. They reflect how the rules of business have changed. Business success is now largely determined by conditions outside the four walls of any one company. Because of the accelerating rate of change and the incredible demands on their time, many business executives and practitioners simply do not understand these new networks. The information systems used to run the networks have grown so massively complex that no one person in the organization understands what is going on below the surface. The reality is that practitioners must learn how to design and operate a competitive, value-adding network that beats the competition in getting to the customer. The bottom line is that executives must learn how to manage risk across a network in order to protect the return on their investment.

TAKING A NETWORK PERSPECTIVE

There is a rich diversity of supply chain management perspective rooted in the individual business backgrounds and experiences of people in manufacturing. People having had work responsibility in a single function, at one site, for a unique product or service, tend to view the world with an operational perspective centered on physical distribution within the four walls of their own company. They tend to think "inside the box." However, the frame of reference for this book is much broader. It is like a Rubik's Cube that integrates all facets of the network's organization, the network flows, and the network's competitive results, see Figure I-1. The key to supply chain architecture is thinking "outside the box."

Respect for the perspectives of others is essential when people work together to build and operate competitive supply chain networks. For example, teammates who are professionals in Purchasing tend to view the supply chain primarily toward the upstream supplier base. Other teammates who are professionals in Marketing tend to view the supply chain primarily in terms of downstream channels of distribution. Logisticians come close to an integrated view of supply chain networks that considers material flow and information flow, but the logisticians usually do not concern themselves with the cash flow. The focus of production and inventory control planning professionals lies primarily inside the boundaries of their immediate organization. Chief Executive Officers and other C-Level executives favor the financial and value view of a supply chain, see Figure I-2. This book presents an end-to-end, totally integrated view of the design and operation of a supply chain network, which enables all team members to see and understand the perspectives of everyone who is an essential partner of the network.

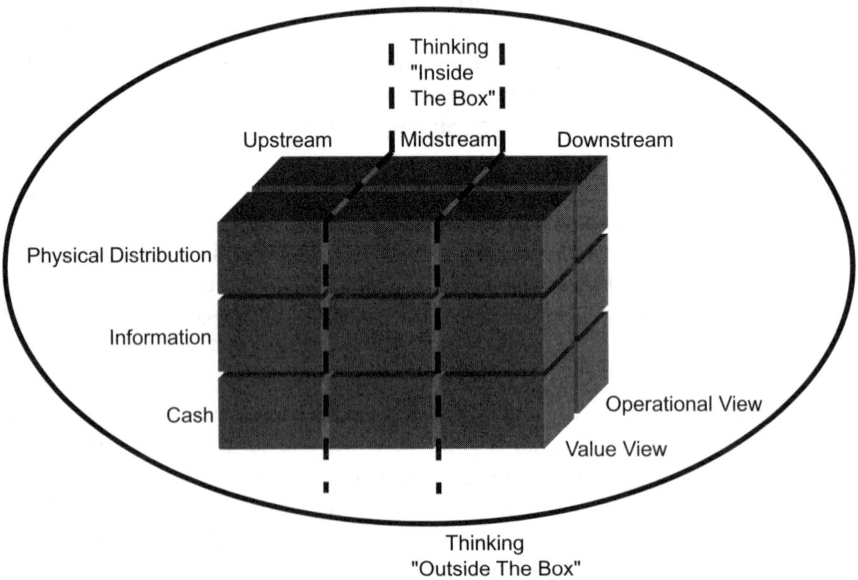

FIGURE I-1 A frame of reference.

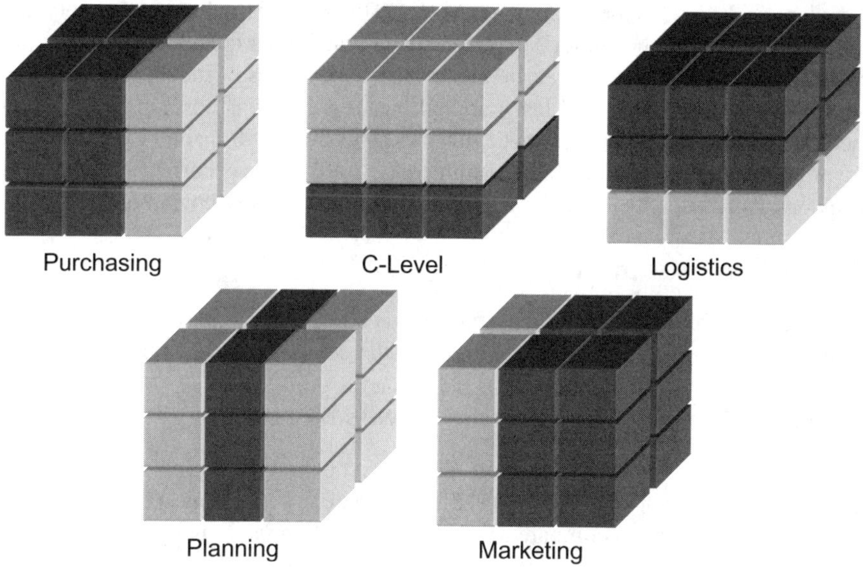

FIGURE I-2 Team members come from a diversity of perspectives.

This book is written for three primary audiences:

- *Practitioners*—This book is a *blueprint* for the competitive design and operation of global supply chain networks that deliver products and services. Manufacturing, distribution and service industries are represented in concept and by example.
- *Teammates*—This book shows teams *how to integrate* by providing a common vocabulary, a comprehensive explanation and a common vision for the competitive design and operation of global supply chain networks. Team diversity is valued and integrated.
- *Executives and Managers*—This is a *risk management* book for business executives and managers, from every functional area, who recognize that their business success depends on the competitive design and operation of global supply chain networks.

This book is about problem solving by people who must work together in teams separated by geography, time, and diversity of perspective to deliver products and services of great value. Its common-sense solutions come from proven industrial application and the real-life experiences of practitioners.

HOW THE BOOK IS ORGANIZED

Supply Chain Architecture reveals five business principles that have broad application, across all industries, in manufacturing and adjacent service sectors, including logistics services, information services, and financial services. These principles—*Velocity, Variability, Vocalize, Visualize*, and *Value*—simplify the design and operation of complex, real-world supply chain networks. This book is a blend of theory and practice forged from the author's experience as a practitioner collaborating with other practitioners, consultants, and academicians in various types of industries around the world. It is a blueprint for taking marginal business relationships and transforming them into exceptionally competitive networks. This book will inspire executives and practitioners alike to see beyond the immediate walls of their current organizations to unlock the competitive energy within an end-to-end supply chain network.

Chapter 1: A False Start

A picture of a failing and internally focused, cost driven company. The story opens with an economic jolt that threatens to drive the company into bankruptcy.

Chapter 2: Conceptualizing a New Business Model

The blueprint for competitive network design and operation begins with a business model. This blueprint can also be used to compare a network design with a competitor's network, and to compare a proposed network improvement with the current design. It becomes easier to think outside the box when the entire network is taken into consideration.

Chapter 3: Collaborating Network Relationships

Different organizations participate in different kinds of network relationships. Many of the organizations are related to the network through a product Bill Of Materials (BOM). The network is optimized by rationalizing trading partners to a network zone and echelon. The Chapter concludes with an example Partnership Agreement.

Chapter 4: Designing a Competitive Network

Trading partners are selected to optimize landed cost versus supply chain length. Nominal trading partners complete the information, material and cash flows. The order-to-delivery-to-cash cycles that interconnect the trading partners are designed for competitiveness. This is done by optimizing the process steps to maximize velocity while minimizing variability. Improvement in competitiveness is measured using a value circle technique.

Chapter 5: Overcoming Information Boundaries

Real networks are partitioned by geography, import/export boundaries, time zones, business cultures and legal entities. Information systems help to overcome these internal boundaries. Techniques to transform the order-to-delivery-to-cash cycle from a serial to a parallel arrangement are presented relative to the product BOM.

Chapter 6: Leading Change in Performance Measurement

The trading partners learn to move from a cost-oriented view of the network to a throughput-oriented one by applying Business Process Orientation. The trading partners educate, negotiate, collaborate, and communicate around a set of global performance measures that align their behavior to the business strategy.

Chapter 7: Operating a Competitive Network

The push/pull boundary separates the demand-driven build-to-order portion of a network from the forecast-driven build-to-stock portion of a network relative to the product BOM. Vocalizing throughput and visualizing system inventory among the trading partners optimizes network operations. Broadcast demand and synchronous operations are used to defeat the bullwhip effect. Improvement in competitiveness is measured using a value circle technique.

Chapter 8: Planning for Network Operations

Physical inventories and cash "inventories" must be planned for the network. Planning capacity and buffer stock to support synchronized operations in a pull environment is different from forecasting demand and risk pooling safety stock in a push environment. The planning interfaces between push and pull network zones are defined.

Chapter 9: Generating Top Line Growth and Bottom Line Profit

A competitive supply chain network generates more revenue opportunities with higher profit margins and provides higher service levels using smaller inventory and cash asset investments. There is a direct cause-and-effect relationship between supply chain network decisions and the value created for stakeholders and the customer. Return On Invested Capital combines improvements to the income statement and balance sheet to realize stock value appreciation.

Chapter 10: A New Start

The story of a growing and externally focused, customer driven network. The book ends with some consideration of the dynamics of change that cause trading partners in a supply chain network to learn how to become more responsive, flexible, and adaptive.

Appendix A: The Network Blueprint

Presents the integrated steps for the design and operation of a competitive supply chain network. This blueprint is applicable to product-delivery, service-delivery, and reverse supply chains.

Appendix B: Bibliography

Additional influential book titles.

HOW TO GET THE MOST FROM THIS BOOK

Each Chapter begins with two stories. The first story line progresses from Chapter to Chapter and describes the renovation of the kitchen space in an older home. The home belongs to a supply chain architect and his wife. The supply chain architect is always surprised to learn something of value about networks from the house architect renovating the kitchen. The second story line also progresses Chapter to Chapter and describes the struggles of a manufacturing company making the transition from being cost-focused to being throughput-focused. In each scenario, the architect takes something learned from the home project and applies it to team problem solving at the office. Both story lines serve to introduce the main focus of the text that immediately follows them.

Each Chapter also ends with a story. The third story line tells of the competitiveness issues the wife faces in her service company. The architect is able to help the wife formulate service business solutions from a deep understanding of the supply chain network used in manufacturing. Valuable insights about both manufacturing and service businesses are gained from each topic. The kitchen-renovation and the manufacturing-business stories, together with the service-business story, are bookends for each Chapter. They point to and apply the main lessons of this book.

The central content of each Chapter consists of text with tables and figures that present a comprehensive, integrated blueprint for designing competitive networks and tying their operations together through the product BOM. Concepts are organized and developed in a practical, common-sense way that progresses from the more basic to the more advanced. The examples are very detailed and complete; it is best to read them quickly for their concept, and then return to study the ones of interest for their technique. In the author's business experience, many trading partners have failed to shift to a network perspective and have failed to master network basics. Detailed practical examples from a variety of industries and settings are used to illustrate major points. By the conclusion of this book, *you and your team* will be able to apply the five principles—*Velocity*, *Variability*, *Vocalize*, *Visualize* and *Value*—to improve your own supply chain network situation. The Network Blueprint, in the Appendix, integrates all the detail of this book.

1 A False Start

The house had been built in 1895 on an open tract of farmland a mile from the center of town. It was a two-story frame construction sitting on a sturdy field-stone foundation and was finished in clapboard. The house was unique in its appearance and layout, as none of the neighboring houses had been built by the same carpenter. A tall oak tree graced the property, protecting it from the afternoon sun.

A century later, the house was firmly entrenched in the suburbs. The size of its lot had shrunk to an eighth of an acre, the oak tree was gone, and the aluminum siding on many of the surrounding houses gave a sameness to the properties along the street. However, this house sat higher than its neighbors and commanded the view up and down the street.

It was a quiet evening in June. The temperature was mild, there was no humidity, and it was too early in the season for many insects. The supply chain architect and his wife sat on the wide porch of the house drinking beer and watching the taillights of an occasional passing car as it slowed to take the corner turn. The wife was the owner and president of a small corporate education and training service. The fortunes of her service company depended on the spending plans of several local manufacturing firms. There was some house work still to be done this evening, but it was too early and felt too good to get started on that. The couple simply sipped their beers, letting their minds and the conversation wander…

As the fourth owners of the house, they had quickly realized that it had become a little neglected over the years. The previous owners, in order to cut costs, never saw fit to change the faded wallpaper or replace the worn rugs. The smallest of the three upstairs bedrooms had a leaky roof and was closed off from the rest of the house in the winter to conserve the heat generated from the small gas-fired furnace in the basement. The most modern appliance in the whole house was the two-year-old replacement water heater.

The idea that this old house, their house, was a complex system of integrated components intrigued them. The heating system kept the pipes in the plumbing system from freezing. The cold water pipe in the plumbing system grounded the electrical system and the telephone. The electric sump pump kept water out of the basement and away from the crumbling furnace. The wife wondered what the blueprint for the old house must have looked like back then, or whether the builder had even had a blueprint.

The supply chain architect could certainly use some kind of blueprint at work. He was responsible for designing and optimizing new product supply chains. Whenever a new product was to be introduced, its bill of materials would be reviewed against the existing supply base to see whether any new supplier relationships were needed. A cost analysis would be developed to explore any outsourcing opportunities, and the capability of the existing sales channels to distribute the new product to its target market would be analyzed. All of this required expertise in a variety of areas including operations, production and inventory planning and control, logistics, import/export, purchasing, process design, product design, finance, and information systems. It was very interesting work because each product introduction was a little different.

But lately it felt as though business in general was making less and less sense. The sales forecast was no longer useful in predicting future sales. This was partially because they had seen 80% turnover in their customer base. The bosses were scrambling for every order and for every dollar of profit that they could find. The focus in every department was to cut costs. Discretionary spending for advertising, travel, training, and consultants had been stripped away. All hiring had been stopped, and when people left, they were not replaced. This reduction in resources put incredible pressure on the product development team to produce and to produce quickly! Rumors were running rampant that layoffs were to be announced very soon.

Friday, June 7

The conference room was chaotic when the supply chain architect arrived. The sales manager and the general manager were huddled in a far corner of the room. Members of the project team were just arriving, taking their coffees and selecting seats at the long, wide conference table. The architect waved at Hector Morales, vice president of manufacturing, and Dana Hoffmann, the chief financial officer. A speakerphone resting on the center of the table was being used to patch in some executives who were offsite visiting with a key customer. People were booting up their laptops in preparation for the meeting. The screen at the far end of the room and the two flip charts were each blank for now.

The general manager called the meeting to order a few minutes late. "Ladies and gentlemen, I'd like to welcome each of you here today and especially those of you on the road. When we look back, we may find that this meeting was a turning point in our company's history. We cannot afford to allow the situation to deteriorate any further. The bad news is that we are losing market share, our profitability is eroding, our costs and our inventories are going through the roof, and our stock price has plummeted. The good news is—well, there is no good news." Income statement, balance sheet, and cash flow numbers from the last quarter and the projections for the next quarter briefly flashed across the screen behind the G.M. "Now let me turn the meeting over to our C.F.O."

"Good morning, and thanks for taking time from your busy schedules to be here today," said Dana as she walked to the head of the table. "Our G.M. has done an excellent job of summarizing our recent business performance. I want our lack of performance to be underscored by one of our key customers. Joining us this morning on the speakerphone is Adam Stone, president and chief executive officer of Colonial Distributor, our third-largest customer. Good morning, Adam, and thank you for being with us!"

"Yes, well. Can you hear me alright? Good morning," said Adam Stone through the speakerphone.

"Yes, we can all hear. Go ahead," replied Dana.

Adam continued, "What I'm about to say will not be pleasant for you to hear. I wanted to attend your meeting to be able to deliver this message to you face-to-face, but the scheduling was just not possible. Anyway, my company has decided to pull its account and to go with one of your competitors."

Faces around the table looked stunned.

"Please—please let me continue," said Adam. "It's not fair to you to make this kind of an announcement without explaining why Colonial Distributor is taking this extraordinary action."

Someone began taking notes on one of the flip charts.

"Your product quality has been steadily slipping. Your order processing has been making an excessive number of entry mistakes, and our product returns to your company now exceed 14 % of your shipments," he continued. "We provided defect details to your sales people and asked your company in April and again in May to clean up your act. Then you really pushed us over the edge when you announced, last week, your across-the-board price increase of 6%. Colonial Distributor has worked at being a good customer, but this is unacceptable."

The person at the flip chart wrote furiously.

"I've thought about your situation for some time. Based on my experience I've come to the following conclusions: First, your organization appears, to me, to be too internally focused rather than being focused on your customer. It is no longer fun to do business with your company. Second, there is too much friction in the flow of orders, products, and cash between us. You seem to have lost much of your earlier competitiveness," Adam concluded.

The conference room was silent.

"I wish you the best of luck, and thank you for allowing me some time at your meeting this morning."

The speakerphone went dead.

"We knew his issues, and we didn't address them?" asked Hector incredulously. "What were our sales and customer service people thinking?"

"Yeah!"

Dana jumped in, "Hold on everyone! Please! This morning's meeting is not meant to be a witch-hunt. This management team has serious issues to face, perhaps about our very survival, and we have just been handed a gift in the form of an open and honest appraisal by a key customer. Now, let's work as a team to figure out what we are going to do about it."

Turning to the person at the flip chart, Dana asked, "Now look at the specific issues listed by the customer. Let's see whether we can focus our collective wisdom today on assessing the probable causes of our dilemma? We will then need to go back and use real data to sort out and validate the appraisal of the root cause."

The words stared back at the group from the flip chart as a great silence filled the room:

- Quality defects unresolved for over two months
- Repeated ordering errors
- Customer returns 14% of product shipments
- Customer balks at 6% price increase
- #1 Too internally focused
- #2 Too much friction to do business

"Maybe we're looking at this the wrong way," Hector finally said. "Maybe we don't really understand how to face our customer."

Several side conversations broke out around the table.

"Wait, I'm serious," said Hector. "If there is some kind of core competency involved in listening to customers, selling products, and taking orders, then maybe some other people know how to do it a lot better than our company does."

"I resent that you would think such a thing," huffed the sales manager.

Hector continued, "I'm going to go way out on a limb here, but what if my own organization lacked the competency in manufacturing to be competitive in what we are asked to do. Don't you see? There are many aspects of the business where this company excels. But we should be open to consider that there may be some aspects of our business where we don't even know what we don't know."

"I still think you are way out of line," said the sales manager. "We have been able to book a 22% increase in orders this past quarter relative to the same quarter one year ago. You heard Adam Stone. Now sales will have to find probably three new customers to replace the one we just lost! I think the problem is that you can't build the product to their quality standard. They just said that they return one seventh of everything you ship."

Dana stepped back into the conversation. "When you are able to take the emotion out the conversation, I think a couple of important points have been made. First, what does a business need to do well and succeed? Second, which parts should this organization do, and which parts might someone else do better?" Dana wrote her two questions on the flip chart. "Can anyone think of other points or questions that have come up so far? Let's brainstorm for a few minutes."

Yes, there's got to be a better way," someone volunteered.

For the rest of this book, imagine that *you and your team* are supply chain architects. What would *you* do?

You are probably working harder than you ever have before in your life. If you are employed, you put so many hours into being on the job that the balance between work life and personal life is a significant issue. Hundreds of e-mails, dozens of voicemails, endless meetings, and team teleconferences have invaded your personal time. If you are employed in manufacturing, you are straining under an increasing workload. If you are employed in a service industry, you find yourself working very long hours for a very low wage. There is no time for family, for extra activities, or for understanding why the world feels so interconnected. Whole industries are restructuring. Manufacturing jobs and certain kinds of service jobs are being outsourced internationally. If you are unemployed, you are working hard to compete for a limited number of high-paying jobs like the one you used to have, or else you are contemplating a career change.

Revenues have shrunk, profits are down, excess inventory abounds, new product introductions are late, coping with the latest system implementation has taken over every waking hour, and the company stock price is in the tank. You are learning that everything is linked to everything else without really understanding how. Your boss wants to talk with you about taking on more responsibility for the same, or less, pay. What's in this book for you?

Simply how to survive and make order out of chaos.

This book is about working smarter rather than harder. This book is about using some fundamental principles to understand how things are interconnected and then making those things better—better in the sense of being more competitive by being simpler, smarter, faster. This book is viewed through the mind of an accomplished practitioner, someone who has "been there and done that."

Too many company employees have little or no understanding of the business fundamentals required to win in their industry. This lack of understanding is not their fault. The information systems that employees must use have become so huge, so complex, and so functionally segmented that they mask the basics of how to succeed in the business. For example, a buyer has a programmatic choice of eight different lot-sizing algorithms but cannot see the sales forecast. The planner has a graphical representation of work center capacity but does not know how many retail stores are driving the demand. The chief financial officer can close the books in record time but cannot determine the committed cash position two months into the future. Business today cannot function without information technology, but the success of the business still hinges on solid business relationships and on every employee's knowledge of business basics.

THE NETWORK CONTEXT

Context is used to define what something is and what it is not. Sometimes it is easier to describe the "is not" part then the "is" part. This book is not about functional cost minimization. Nor is it an Enterprise Resource Planning (ERP) installation checklist. It is not about any specific information systems technology, nor does it endorse any particular vendor's solution. It is not call for the status quo.

This book is about learning in a fundamentally different way how supply chain networks are designed and operated to improve their competitiveness and reduce risks. The network context described here is the material flow, information flow and cash flow for a fully integrated supply chain. It is a principles-based view of capacity and inventory planning and control among the organizations that makeup the network. It is about the end-to-end performance measurement and global optimization of the network. It is a complete architectural blueprint for change that has broad applicability across most manufacturing and service industry sectors.

Defining the Customer's Context

Although your organization may never interact with the end-customer, the end-customer is a key stakeholder in your supply chain network. The end-customer interacts with the following three fundamentally different classes of networks:

- *Manufacturing networks*—Accept the end-customer's orders for products, deliver those products, and take the customer's cash in payment for those products. A manufacturing network delivers value-added products to the end-customer.
- *Service networks*—Accept the end-customer's orders for services, deliver those services, and take the customer's cash in payment for those services. A service network delivers value-added services to the end-customer.
- *Reverse networks*—Acknowledge the end-customer's request to return a product, accept the customer's return of those products, and refund the customer's cash in payment for those returns. A reverse network accepts product returns from the end-customer to perform its value-subtracting work.

In the most general sense, the end-customer buys products from manufacturing networks, buys services from service networks, and sells returns to reverse networks, see Figure 1-1. It is also common for two or more network classes to be integrated

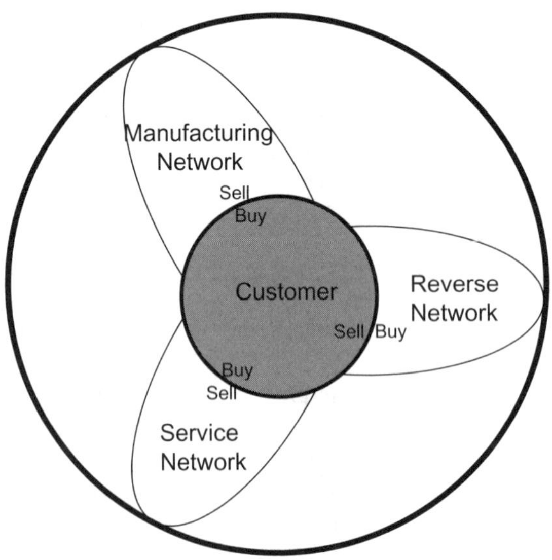

FIGURE 1-1 The customer context.

into a single network. For example, the same network may deliver both products and services, or the same network may provide both forward and reverse functionality. However, in the context of this book, manufacturing networks are designed and operated differently than service networks, which are designed and operated differently than reverse networks.

Defining the Value Context

Each class of network represents an opportunity to integrate a product design for a manufactured good or a service, a network design, and a network operation within an environment of a business strategy, an information system, and organizational change in order to bring value to the stakeholders. The primary emphasis of this book is on the optimal architecture that integrates product design, network design, and network operation. Secondarily, this book addresses how the optimal architecture should connect with the business strategy, with the information system, and with change management in the organization. Figure 1-2 shows the relationship of these elements at a very high conceptual level. This book uses a set of guiding principles to turn these conceptual relationships into practical, competitive networks.

Primary emphases:

- *Product design*—How the product design of the manufactured good or service interacts with network design and network operation
- *Network design*—How network design interacts with product design and network operations
- *Network operation*—How network operations interact with product design and network design

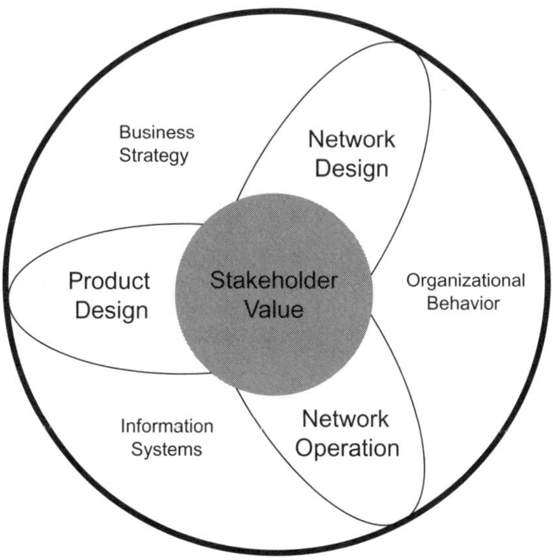

FIGURE 1-2 The value context.

Secondary emphases:

- *Business strategy*—How the network system aligns with the business strategy
- *Information systems*—How the network system is enabled through information technology
- *Organizational behavior*—How the network system is enabled through changes in behavior

A manufacturing network, a service network, and a reverse network each require the integration of these same factors to be competitive. The approach is to identify the class of network being developed and to keep with that perspective throughout the application of the blueprint. Where a single network comprises multiple classes, the approach is to work through the network blueprint for each class separately.

The Threshold of Competitiveness

When a buyer faces a choice of products from two or more sellers, the two sellers are in a competitive situation. Buyers will make a purchase decision based on their perception of the product's value. Product value is determined from how its functionality, quality, price, availability, and delivery fit with the buyer's needs. When a shareholder faces a choice of investments from two or more brokers, the brokers are in a competitive situation. Shareholders will make a decision based on their perception of the investment's return versus risk. Relative to the magnitude of the amount invested, return is determined from the interest, dividends, or capital gains generated; the timing of the return cash flow; and the risk probability that the full principal amount can be recovered.

Some examples of value to end-customers:

- The network provides a range of high quality products and services.
- The network prices products and services competitively.
- Product availability is competitive, and product delivery is predictable and reliable.
- The network supports alternative methods of payment.
- Product returns, if necessary, are no hassle.
- The customer's interaction with the network is frictionless.

Some examples of value to shareholders:

- The network demonstrates consistent earnings growth.
- The network generates free cash flow.
- The network provides a competitive return on investment at an acceptable level of risk.

The *competitiveness threshold* determines the value seen by a customer and the reward versus risk potential seen by the shareholder. Although it is true that information systems technology is the enabler that makes a global supply chain network possible, it is false that this technology investment defines the network's competitiveness threshold. If the underlying architecture of a network is noncompetitive, no amount of technology investment will tip the scale. This is a hard lesson to learn.

Barriers to Success

You are probably working for a business organization that believes it is largely in control of its own destiny. The myth is that the vertically integrated firm can reach from raw materials to the end customer within its own legal structure. The reality is that even the vertically integrated firm operates from within a networked context to build and deliver its products and services. Making the transition to a network perspective can be painful. In addition, there are many myths that prevent organizations from realizing the maximum potential of supply chain management. The following ten statements are representative of the folklore that gets in the way:

1. The benefits of supply chain management come only from Enterprise Resource Planning.
2. The investment required for ERP is too large and the return too low.
3. Information systems that large companies can afford are too expensive for small companies.
4. Supply chain management is only for large companies.
5. A network is too complex to understand.
6. Companies have to clean their own house before joining a network.
7. Networks fail because of greed by one of the trading partners.
8. Networks fail because of a lack of trust among the trading partners.
9. Networks fail because people at all levels resist change.
10. Every organization has to be an equal for the network to function.

IN SUMMARY

This book replaces such myths with practical, workable solutions to real business problems. Just as it is the architect, rather than the plumber or carpenter or electrician, who designs and builds a house as an integrated whole, it can be *you and your team* who are the architects for a competitive supply chain network. The set of network principles in this book is your blueprint for success.

2 Conceptualizing a New Business Model

Monday, June 10

Monday promised to be intense. The calendar entries on the supply chain architect's Palm Pilot read: "Meet with architect @ home—7:30 a.m.," "All day meeting @ Building 1—8:30 a.m. start," "Dinner @ home—8:00 p.m.," "Call team in Singapore—10:00 p.m."

The house renovation was going to be spectacular! He and his wife had decided to spend some real money, gut the interior of the kitchen, and rebuild it to suit their life style.

Tom, the house architect, arrived right on time with a tray of three cups of steaming coffee. "Good morning. I've brought the coffee. It's going to be another great day weatherwise. I wanted to show you and your wife the layout for the new kitchen space."

"Thanks, Tom, come on inside. I wouldn't know about the weather. I'll be stuck inside in a conference room all day," he said. Taking a coffee, he would have burnt his hand had it not been for the corrugated cardboard wrapper Starbucks always placed around its cups. "My wife won't be joining us this morning."

"That's too bad." Tom spread fresh blueprints over the old table. The table and two chairs were the only furniture left in the gutted cavity of the original kitchen. The back of the house was exposed, with only a sheet of heavy plastic keeping out the elements. "I think you're going to like this design. It really meets your wife's needs for more cabinet space without the added cost of extending the room beyond its original footprint. Here, let me show you on the blueprint."

As Tom began to review the plans, the supply chain architect thought back to how he and his wife had gotten to the decision of undertaking such a major renovation. Although they had lived in the house for a considerable time, the house was uncomfortable. The kitchen, in particular, was cold and dark and lacked the necessary workspace.

"Now, as I was just saying, over here your new counterspace integrates the dishwasher, the sink, and the range. Above the counter are the microwave, multiple-purpose cabinets, and—"

Over the years, he had tinkered with obvious remedies. He had installed new fluorescent lighting on the ceiling and over the sink, but there was no daylight in the room. He had replaced the dripping faucets on the sink with a shiny, single-handle Moen fixture, but the water pressure was still low. He had installed insulated ceiling tile in the cellar underneath the kitchen, but the kitchen floor remained cold.

"A small table will easily seat two people right here for meals," Tom said, pointing again to the plans. "The new bay window will bring in daylight until the sun sets."

"That's really great!" The supply chain architect could visualize the sunny room and a comfortable breakfast with his wife. The project was getting exciting now.

It had not taken him long to realize that he lacked the carpentry and plumbing skills to do the renovation work himself. As the supply chain architect grew older and traveled extensively for his job, he never devoted much time to the house—that is, until his wife finally declared that one day it was going to fall down on their heads.

"Speaking about plans—there's one additional requirement my wife has for the kitchen design. This is something new that was not possible with the old kitchen, but now that the room is gutted and we can see the new space, she wants something more, Tom."

"What does your wife have in mind?"

"Well, I hope my explanation will do it justice. My wife was planning to be here this morning. However, as you know, her business is conducting on-site seminars for her clients. Last night one of her instructors called in sick, and she had to leave very early this morning to be at the client's site."

"Being the president of your own company can be a challenge."

"Okay, so here's what we want you to accomplish. We want to eliminate the beam supporting the back wall that breaks that part of the room in half. We want to be able to seat six people comfortably around a table in the new space."

"You know that the present load-bearing beam is 18 feet across right now. The new building codes just won't allow more than 12 feet without additional support," replied Tom.

"Please see if you can figure out a way around the design issues. This is really important for us. Maybe you can grandfather something in because of the age of our house."

Tom was quiet for a few moments, "I'll have to consult with my structural engineer and get back to you. This is difficult, and I won't make any promises that it can even be done."

"You mean that with all the money I'm paying you for these plans, you have to consult with someone else on the structure?"

"Oh sure. It's my seal on your plans, and I need to be completely thorough. I learned a long time ago that structural engineers are worth their weight in gold. One of the keys to success in my business is knowing when to bring in specialists. You can't really expect me to be equally competent in every aspect of design and construction," Tom said.

The supply chain architect finished up with the house architect a little before 8:00 a.m. and then raced out of the driveway, headed for work. His commute normally took 35 minutes, and he was going to have to move it along. Fortunately, traffic was light.

*****

Hector Morales, vice president of manufacturing, called the staff meeting to order at 8:30 a.m. sharp. Four others were seated around the conference table besides Hector and the supply chain architect. Roberta Perez, the operations manager, Gus Lopez, the master scheduler, and William Smith, the purchasing manager, each reported directly to Hector. In addition, Ray Smith, the cost accounting manager, generally attended these meetings.

Hector lost no time in getting started. "Let's get right to the point. We will need to overproduce the master schedule in July and August to make up for the sales we lost from Colonial Distributor in June. I just hope sales can sell the heck out of what we have in the pipeline. William, how long will it take to ratchet up material purchases?"

Gus, who had not been to work on Friday, was just catching up to the others. He broke in, "From what I hear the loss of Colonial Distributor is a complete disaster, boss! They have a lot of special orders in process with us."

"Colonial broke their deal with us. They will have to pay us for any unique material committed to their open orders," responded Hector. He turned towards William.

"I've already got Carlos Gonzalez, our best buyer, and the others talking discreetly with our longest lead-time suppliers. I should have some numbers for you by this afternoon," replied William.

"Good, I'm glad somebody is competent around here." Hector was still steamed from Friday's news. "Roberta, which lines are tight on capacity right now?"

"We'll be okay for about the next six weeks. I have a number of employees planning to take vacations during August. We might have to bring in some temp workers to cover for them."

"That can get expensive fast," said Hector. "Work with Alice in human resources and see whether some of those vacations can be postponed. We are facing a crisis. What about restarting a second shift? Do we need a second shift again?"

"I can't answer that question until Gus has a chance to analyze adjustments to the master schedule."

"It will take two days to input a new plan and run some what-if scenarios. I should be able to turn that around by Wednesday afternoon," Gus replied hopefully.

Hector turned his head toward the architect, "You're being awfully quiet."

"We're missing the whole point."

"What did you say?"

"We're missing the whole point. This is not business as usual. This is not an operations problem we can fix with some tweaks to the master schedule."

The others around the table waited for an explosion from Hector. Instead, he said firmly, "Go on."

"Look, our company just encountered a major shift in demand with some of the highest quality customer feedback we've ever gotten. Demand for our products has just fallen off a cliff; building inventory and substituting a few new small orders is not going to fix the situation. At the same time, we have been handed some insight about how to proceed, but we don't know how to process this information organizationally. It is a huge mistake to think that manufacturing is going to solve an enterprise problem."

"That's your opinion?" asked Hector.

"That's my opinion," replied the architect.

"Well, I happen to think you're right," said Hector. A long silence descended upon the table.

Ray spoke up first. "Maybe we could reprioritize some production engineering work to take some cost out of our highest-volume products. If we could improve the contribution margin on certain products, we could make up some lost profit."

"That's good thinking," said Roberta.

"I can't help but think that sales is in a position to sell more," said Gus. "Every month I have to adjust the master schedule during the last three days of the month because sales suddenly 'finds' all kinds of new orders. Sales lost this customer, and sales can find new customers. This is primarily a sales problem."

"If quality control had been paying more attention, we would not have shipped those defective products," said William.

"We're getting off track again—" began the architect.

Hector spoke, "I like the direction Ray was going, to cut costs. I've been thinking, for some time now, that maybe we should be outsourcing our lowest-technology assemblies. Like Ray said, if manufacturing can figure some ways to cut costs, it would take some of the pressure off sales. We should try to approach this as a team."

"Where were you thinking about outsourcing?" asked William.

"I know a guy who is the V.P. of operations at a twin plant in Mexico, near Nogales. I could ask him for a quote on some of our assemblies. William, can I ask you and Roberta to pick a sample of our products and prepare a request for quote that I can forward to this guy?"

"Sure, I guess so," said William. "Roberta, when can you let me know which products to include in the RFQ?"

"Not so fast—We need to form a couple of teams to review our product catalogue. It would be good to identify a couple of additional suppliers to RFQ so we know when we're getting a competitive deal. The team members should come from production engineering, purchasing, and cost accounting," said Roberta.

"I agree," said Hector.

"We'll also need a good project manager who can speak his mind," Roberta finished, looking squarely at the supply chain architect.

Significant external events and internal mandates can trigger change in a supply chain network. A shift in demand, such as the one in the story line, the bankruptcy of a supplier, or an inventory valuation discrepancy revealed by a Sarbanes-Oxley audit are example of external event triggers. New initiatives to cut the cost of goods sold by 4%, to reduce the inventory investment by 5 million dollars, or to introduce a new product family in six months are examples of internal triggers.

The first step is to understand the big picture of the business. A supply chain network is only as good as its fit with the business strategy. When someone is standing outside looking in, the business strategy and its supporting network usually appear quite nebulous. There needs to be a top-down way of identifying the dominant players and understanding their primary relationships. The details will come later. This chapter presents techniques to reveal the highest structural level of a supply chain network. It establishes a baseline from which to conceptualize new business models in order to improve competitiveness. Such new business models will require an organization to think outside the box in terms of its customer requirements, its core competencies, and its ability to add value to the business.

THE NETWORK BIG PICTURE

We often become aware of a business for the first time through the purchase of its products. We might stumble across some of its other customers, competitors, or even suppliers. However, it is rare to think about a business as a network. Nonetheless, each business exists in the context of a supply chain network. The network connects to raw materials, adds value during the manufacture of the product, and delivers the product and services to the end-customer. Other networks compete against this network. Moreover, some portion of the network may interconnected with other, potentially competing, networks.

The network blueprint in this book includes everything necessary to design and operate a supply chain network from the ground up. The techniques throughout this book are useful for both analyzing a competitor's network and reengineering your own network. The tools in this book help unravel complex organizations and network flows to reveal their underlying structure. Understanding the network big picture begins with an understanding of the following:

- A definition of "supply chain"
- A positioning framework of zones and echelons
- A technique for tracing the physical distribution flow
- A review of interwoven networks

SUPPLY CHAIN DEFINITION

The *APICS Dictionary*, 10th Edition, defines a supply chain as "the global network used to deliver products and services from raw materials to end-customers through an engineered flow of information, physical distribution, and cash." The network is global in a geographic sense, extending outside the four walls of any single legal organization. The network delivers both physical products and nonphysical services. The network provides a continuous path from dirt to the paying end-customer and operates through the integration of its three flows. A consideration of cash flow, the

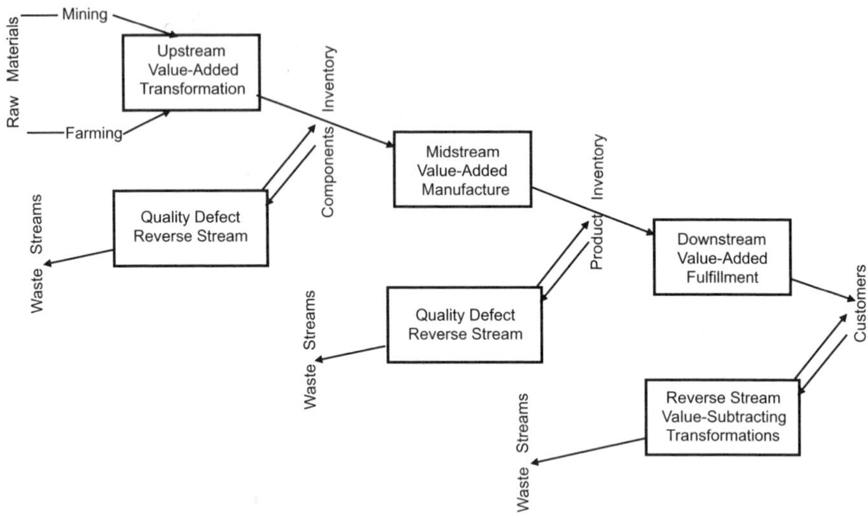

FIGURE 2-1 The four supply chain network zones.

third flow, is what differentiates the study of supply chain management from that of logistics and of lean manufacturing.

Four *zones* provide an easy framework for describing an organization's position within a supply chain network. The rectangles in Figure 2-1 identify each zone. Notice that any zone in the forward supply chain can have a reverse stream zone. There may be a series of organizations stretching from one zone boundary to the next. For example, a downstream zone might start at the midstream/downstream boundary and pass through a distribution center, a wholesale warehouse, and a retail store before reaching the downstream/customer boundary. Each of these serially intermediate organizations represents an *echelon* in that zone.

- *Upstream zone*—Connects each raw material with the network and provides the value-adding transformation of raw materials into components. The upstream zone may have multiple echelons.
- *Midstream zone*—Provides the value-adding manufacture of components into products. The midstream zone may have multiple echelons.
- *Downstream zone*—Provides the value-adding fulfillment of orders for products and services and connects the network with each customer. The downstream zone may have multiple echelons.
- *Reverse stream zone*—Provides the value-subtracting transformation of products and components into raw materials and remanufactures product and component cores for reuse. There may be a reverse stream associated with any portion of a forward supply chain because of quality defect returns. The reverse stream zone may have multiple echelons.
- *Echelon*—A level of nodes in the supply chain network. When a zone is missing from the network, there are zero echelons in that zone. When a

zone is present in the network, count the highest number of serially connected, independent organizations required to cross between the zone boundaries to determine the number of echelons in that zone.

The first step in understanding a supply chain network is to place one of the network organizations into its proper zone, based upon the physical distribution flow. Locating an organization in one of the zones makes it easy to locate other organizations in the remaining zones by considering who sells to the first organization and who buys from the first organization. Because this is a high-level analysis, each network organization will be an independent legal entity. For example, upstream contract manufacturer Solectron feeds midstream factory Hewlett-Packard, which feeds downstream distributor CompUSA, which reaches the end consumer. Notice that two organizations appearing to have the same name may, in fact, be different legal entities when they are located in different geographic regions or provide unrelated functions. For example, the parent company for electronics distributor Arrow maintains different legal entities for each of the super regions it serves, such as Arrow-North America and Arrow-Europe. As another example, the ASTEC factory in Kuantan, Malaysia, is a different legal entity than the ASTEC service and repair facility in Carlsbad, California.

The Upstream Supply Chain Network

The upstream zone adds value by transforming raw materials into components. This includes the conversion of raw materials extracted from the ground through mining or grown in the ground through farming into self-contained components. For example, a 4 × 8-foot sheet of aluminum is considered a raw material to an electronics industry supply chain, but this sheet aluminum has already been mined, smelted, forged into ingots, rolled into strips, and cut into sheets. In this example, the aluminum primary metal industry is a separate supply chain network that delivers aluminum sheets to its customer, the sheet metal distributor. This sheet metal distributor connects with both the downstream of the aluminum industry network and with the upstream of the electronics industry network. The sheet metal distributor is the upstream edge of the upstream zone for the electronics industry supply chain network.

Normally the upstream edge of the upstream zone begins beyond the conclusion of any mining or farming processes. However, there may be strategic reasons to include some part of a mining or farming process within the network model. For example, the smelting operation at a forge may be the capacity constraint that limits the throughput of an entire supply chain network. At the other end, component inventory locations establish the downstream edge of the upstream zone. Here are the common configurations of supplier organizations found in the upstream zone:

- *Sole source*—Only one supplier in the world has the technology or the process to provide the component.
- *Single source*—Two or more suppliers have the technology and the process to provide the component, but the network chooses to purchase from only one source for business reasons.

- *Spot source*—A seller's market that comes together at a point in time to provide a one-time supply of the component through an auction.
- *Multiple source/distributed source*—The component is a commodity that is easily provided by any number of substitutable suppliers and distributors.
- *Tier—One supplier*—When a component has its own lower-level BOM, a Tier-One supplier is used to coordinate the upstream echelons that source the raw materials required to build that component.

The upstream zone must be competitive in the following core transformation competencies: materials technology, process technology, process quality, capacity management, logistics, capital investment, innovation, and forecasting. When a network organization is not competitive in one or more of these competencies, it will seek a partner. For example, the upstream zone might include independent network organizations such as plating, secondary welding and painting operations, or material engineering consultants.

The supply base can be located anywhere in the world. The upstream zone connects the geographical location of each supplier with the midstream network. Components display their Country Of Origin on information labels. It is often difficult to know whether a particular component enters the midstream directly from the supplier or through additional layers of supply distribution. The upstream zone of one supply chain network is often the downstream zone of another supply chain network. The breadth of geographical locations of the customer base for a component determines the type of distribution used for that component. For example, Intel microprocessors are purchased by many customers worldwide and by a few customers in very high volume. The design of Intel's downstream distribution channels must reach out to both low-volume, high-mix customers and to high-volume, low-mix customers.

The Midstream Supply Chain Network

The midstream zone adds value by manufacturing components into products. In general, the product Bill Of Materials (BOM) type defines the organization of manufacturing within the midstream zone. The parent is the top level of a BOM tree. Children items are related to the top-level parent in the next level of the BOM, just like in a family tree. A BOM tree may have several high level branches, as we will see below. Each child on an upper level becomes the parent of the children on the next lower level, and so on down the tree. Finally, a child terminates each of the tree roots at the bottom of the tree.

Inventory locations define the boundaries of this zone. Finished-goods inventory locations establish the downstream edge of the midstream zone. Component inventory locations establish the upstream edge of the midstream zone. Four common BOM types define the configuration of organizations within the midstream zone:

- *A-type bill of materials*—A large number of child items feed a small number of parent items. For example, an electronic instrument (parent) is manufactured from hundreds of resistors, capacitors, integrated circuits, etc. (children).

- *I-type bill of materials*—A number of child items feed into a small number of common subassemblies, which become children that feed into a number of parent items. I-type manufacturing also represents continuous-flow manufacturing. For example, orange juice (parent) is manufactured from concentrate (child).
- *T-type bill of materials*—A number of child items feed into a small number of common parent subassemblies, which feed into a larger number of parent items. For example, tens of thousands of automotive product options (parents) are manufactured from combinations of a limited number of frame, seat, motor, transmission, and tires subassemblies (children/parents), which are manufactured from thousands of components and dozens of raw materials (children).
- *V-type bill of materials*—A small number of child items feed into a large number of parent items. For example, screws with dozens of thread sizes and shank lengths (parents) are manufactured from a few bar stocks (children).

The midstream zone must be competitive in the following core manufacturing competencies: logistics, import/export, manufacturing processes, production engineering, capacity management, inventory management, planning and forecasting, material handling, lot tracking, procurement, materials engineering, quality management, information systems, and product development. When a network organization is not competitive in one or more of these competencies, it will seek a partner. For example, the midstream zone might include independent network organizations for contract manufacturing, process subcontracting, or international procurement.

Visual inspection of the product catalog, product packaging and labeling, and the product itself can provide clues to the organization of the midstream zone. The product catalog indicates the range of product options and the degree of product customization (parents). Disassembling the product and counting the number of different parts indicates the range of components (children). The product packaging and labeling includes Country Of Origin information and sometimes the company names of suppliers. Physically large components inside the product can yield additional Country Of Origin and supplier information.

The Downstream Supply Chain Network

The downstream zone adds value through fulfillment of orders. This zone of the supply chain network is easy to identify because it is customer-facing. The term *customer-facing* means that this portion of the network is in direct contact with the end-customer to take the order and deliver the product. This is where the product changes hands from the seller (network) to the buyer (end-customer) and where the buyer pays the seller. This also is where the network delivers services to the end-customer.

The end-customer is the downstream edge of the downstream zone. Network organizations holding finished-goods inventory define the upstream edge of the downstream zone. *Finished goods inventory*, in this book, means a single, unpackaged unit of a completely manufactured product. There can be extensive transportation and warehousing logistics of finished goods inventory within the downstream zone. The downstream zone boundaries blur when product manufacture and product packaging are completed within the zone. Three common configurations of a downstream zone include the following:

- *Direct channel*—The midstream factory ships finished goods directly to the end-customer, effectively eliminating the downstream zone.
- *Postponement channel*—The midstream factory ships a mostly complete product. The distribution organization customizes and packages the product before delivering it to the end-customer.
- *Indirect channel*—The product passes through multiple echelons of Distributors, such as wholesalers and retailers, before reaching the end-customer.

The downstream zone must be competitive in the following core fulfillment competencies: marketing, selling, demand management, customer service, order taking, order processing, transportation, warehousing, packaging and repackaging, postponement, quality, financial services, payment processing, and information technology. When a network organization is not competitive in one or more of these competencies, it will seek a partner. For example, the downstream zone might include independent network organizations for wholesale distribution, retail sales, or third-party logistics services.

Customers reside in local, regional, or worldwide markets. The downstream zone must reach out geographically and touch each end-customer location. One complication is that large customers have multiple locations that place orders, take deliveries, and make payments. Some types of products also require the delivery of a range of product consumables through the distribution channel or through a separate supply chain network. Common examples include the batteries, film, and paper consumables required to operate radio, camera, and printer products. The customer needs easy access to these consumables to enable product use.

The Reverse Stream Supply Chain Network

The reverse stream zone accepts returned products for repair, remanufacture, or recycling. Recycling subtracts value by transforming product into various raw material waste streams. The reverse stream zone is also a customer-facing zone. The customer seeks a no-hassle return of the unwanted, defective, or spent product. Either the customer returns the product to a collection point, or the network arranges to pickup the return at the customer's site. In some cases, the customer is given a replacement, or *loaner*, product. The customer expects to receive a cash credit for a return and no-cost coverage on a warranty repair.

The customer-installed base defines the upstream edge of the reverse stream zone. When there is remanufacturing, aftermarket customers are a second upstream edge of the reverse stream zone. Spare component inventory defines the downstream edge of the reverse stream zone for repair and refurbish operations. Waste streams going back into the ground define the downstream edge of the reverse stream zone for recycling operations.

Here are six common organizational functions performed in a reverse stream zone:

- *Defective-item return*—Products, components, and raw materials re-turned anywhere within a supply chain network because of a defect.
- *Product return*—Customer product is returned to a collection point. The returned product is dispositioned as "new" or "used." New product is returned to stock, and used product is refurbished or recycled.
- *Repair and recalibration*—Customer product is returned to a repair depot for repair or recalibration. A loaner product may be lent to the customer for the duration. The reverse stream network must be able to track serial numbers, warranty periods, and the return of loaners flawlessly.
- *Recall*—Customer product is recalled by the manufacturer to fix some significant defect.
- *Remanufacture*—Used or spent original equipment "cores" are gathered into a collection point. The cores are sorted according to wear, defective components, and missing components. The remanufacturer rebuilds or refurbishes usable cores into remanufactured products. The remanufactured product is sold under different terms and conditions to aftermarket customers.
- *Recycle*—Used or spent customer product is returned to a collection point, where it is disassembled and processed into various waste streams. An attempt is made to recover significant economic value from the recycling waste streams. The recycling is environmentally responsible.

The reverse zone must be competitive in the following value-subtracting core competencies: customer service, returns collection, return credit, warranty tracking, inventory management, disassembly, troubleshooting and repair, calibration, component separation, hazardous materials transport, and environmentally responsible recycling. When a network organization is not competitive in one or more of these competencies, it will seek a partner. For example, the reverse stream zone might include independent network organizations such as collection centers, hazardous materials logistics specialists, or primary-material smelters.

Upstream, the reverse stream zone must reach the geographical location of every installed base and aftermarket customer. Downstream, the zone extends to the geographical locations of the raw materials for the spare component suppliers and the waste-stream termination points of the recyclers. Address information on warranty claims and credit refunds can provide clues to the locations of the reverse stream network organizations. Recycling paths are difficult to follow from the outside because of the identification destruction that occurs within the product disassembly and component separation processes.

Follow the Physical Distribution Flow

Understanding a supply chain network is like reading a roadmap. The destination city is located first on the map. Then the alphabetical city listing is used to reference the grid coordinates to locate intermediate, minor cities. Once the string of cities on the route has been identified, the major highways that connect one city to the next are located. Finally, the driving route is determined by following the connecting highways from the city of departure to the city of destination.

In a like manner, the zone edges are a grid to the map of a supply chain network. Each of the independent network organizations is positioned within their upstream, midstream, downstream, or reverse-stream zones and relative to the product flow within the zone. Even at such a high level, some organizations are so large and geographically dispersed that it is helpful to divide them into smaller pieces. For example, an Asian manufacturing hub and its East Coast U.S. distribution center might be called out separately on the network map. The major highways that connect the cities on the roadmap are analogous to logistics connections between network organizations.

The purpose of tracing the physical distribution flow is to identify a complete set of value-adding network organizations. This flow runs completely across the network, from the downstream edge of the downstream zone to the upstream edge of the upstream zone. It encompasses the end-to-end value-adding order fulfillment, manufacturing, and raw-materials transformation in the forward supply chain. It encompasses the end-to-end value-adding remanufacturing transformations and value-subtracting recycling transformations in the reverse supply chain. Because a business serves many customers, the downstream portion of a network will have many branches. Because a product BOM tree has parallel paths, the upstream portion of a network will have many roots. A typical supply chain network looks like a tree turned on its side with many branches, a thick trunk, and many roots. Follow the steps described in Table 2-1 to trace the physical distribution in a network from the highest dollar-value fulfillment step, through the highest dollar-value manufacturing step, to the highest dollar-value raw-materials transformation.

How do you determine the main branches for a business with hundreds of customers and thousands of stock keeping units (SKUs), such as a large distributor? Ask who is a preferred customer and which products are preferred products in terms of revenue. How do you determine the main roots for a product with hundreds or thousands of parts? Determine the where-used connection of high value components and raw materials to the highest revenue SKUs. Relative contribution margins are approximately given as follows:

For a SKU: Contribution Margin = Revenue – Cost of Goods Sold
For a component: Contribution Margin = Price – Variable Cost

SEPARATING INTERWOVEN NETWORKS

At this point you have a good idea of the major organizations that compose the supply chain network and how physical distribution flows from the raw material to the end-customer. You probably have developed a sense of how this network competes in the marketplace. However, maybe some pieces do not seem to fit. This is because you are beginning to realize that the supply chain network you are studying is interwoven with one or more other supply chain networks. The following lists some helpful ways to separate your network from a set of interwoven networks. A network definition must be properly bounded to be useful.

TABLE 2-1
Seven Steps for the High-Level Mapping of a Network

Step	Analysis
1	Focus on a single major product line rather than total revenue.
2	Draw pictures of the packaged physical product in trucks, containers, pallets, or cartons as they move through the network; ask where does distribution take place, where does packaging take place, and where does manufacturing take place?
3	Assign one or more legal entity organizations to each supply chain zone.
4	Label each organization on the network map; break huge organizations apart where it is known that each part is located in a separate geography or provides an unrelated function.
5	Connect the organizations with lines that indicate the physical product flow. Continue sketching the network until a string of organizations connects end-customers with raw materials without any breaks. When the lines intersect more that one organization crossing a zone, there are multiple echelons within that zone.
6	• For a forward supply chain: Start with the end-customer and follow the physical distribution flow of the product to its raw material origin along the path of highest value from product to component to raw material. • For a reverse supply chain: Start with the end-customer and follow the physical distribution flow of the return to repair or remanufacture, and then continue the flow to the recycling of waste streams. Remanufacturing will include a separate fulfillment flow to aftermarket customers.
7	Use a different color to highlight different main branches and different main roots that connect with the network trunk. Select main branches and main roots based on a descending order of contribution margin. • Which customer or customer site drives the highest contribution margin or revenue? • Which SKU yields the highest contribution margin or revenue? • Which component supports the highest contribution margin or revenue?

- *Serial networks*—It is possible that the network is one of several self-contained networks arranged in a series. Each network feeds the next. You may have inadvertently defined either the end-customer or the raw material supplier too far downstream or too far upstream because they fall in the adjacent network. This makes your network too long and too complex to understand. For example, who are the end-customers to a 5-speed transmission manufacturer? Is it Ford, General Motors, and Daimler-Chrysler; is it their franchised distributorships; or is it the consumer? Who is the raw material supplier to a teenager buying a cell phone? Is it the Intel microprocessor foundry or is it the synthetic silicon-crystal grower? The answers depend on the purpose of your analysis.
- *Tangential networks*—Sometimes the customer end of one network is tangential to the midstream zone of another network. Capital equipment manufacturing is a good example. The demand for the capital equipment product is really the capacity required by an independent supply chain network. The capital equipment network feeds tangentially into some

other network; the capital equipment provides the means for that network to operate, but it is no longer physically connected through the physical distribution flow.

- *Crisscrossed networks*—This is very common. One or more organizations in your network may buy and sell out-of-network as part of other, totally unrelated networks. For example, the machine screw supplier in your network also sells hardware fasteners to the automotive industry, the aircraft industry, the construction industry, and the durable goods industry. If none of these out-of-network connections relates to your business, they can be ignored.
- *Competing networks*—There will always be other supply chain networks competing with your network. Sometimes this is only evident at the most downstream customer-facing echelon of your network. However, it is possible for another organization to both collaborate in your network and compete against your network. Your relationship with the two roles of such an organization must be kept separate.

NETWORK MAPPING

The following three network-mapping examples translate theory into practice. In the first example, a competitor's supply chain network is analyzed from public information made available through a variety of sources. In the second example, internal company data is analyzed in both tabular and graphical form to reveal the basic network. The third example describes a network map for a reverse supply chain.

Analyzing a Competitor's Network

A large amount of public data is available today from company Web sites on the Internet, through product catalogs, and in Form 10-K financial reporting for investors. It is usually possible to sketch a competitor's downstream and midstream network from such public data. Discovering a competitor's upstream network is harder and may require some reverse-engineering of its products. Table 2-2 outlines the relevant information sources for a supply chain competitive analysis focused on physical distribution.

Purchasing a men's dress shirt through a mail-order catalog distributor provides a good example of how to use public information to map a competitor's network. The merchandiser's catalog describes the downstream network. Once a shirt is ordered, a Midwestern U. S. distribution center picks and packs the shirt within 24 hours. The shirt ships directly to the customer. The customer is given a downstream transportation choice of free UPS Ground delivery, which can take up to four days, or UPS Next Day Air service at a premium price. Customers can order their initials embroidered on the shirtsleeve with no delivery-time penalty. The embroidery is done at the distribution center as a postponement operation. The downstream zone is a single echelon of distribution built around the merchandiser.

The company has a long-standing policy to accept any catalog returns with no questions asked. The customer is instructed to use UPS and the preprinted address

TABLE 2-2
Information Sources to Follow a Competitor's Physical Distribution Flow

	Downstream
Product branding	• Check the Web site and catalog for product brands and product family groupings. • Check the product itself for brand labels such as "Intel Inside." • Gather competitive data at industry trade shows.
www.companyname.com look for a "product" tab	• Within a brand and a product family, check the Web site and catalog for the range of products, options, customization, etc.
Significant customers	• If the supplying echelon is a public company, the Form 10-K financial report will list significant customers and important business risks.
Delivery logistics	• Note the carrier delivering the product. Examples include UPS, FedEx, DHL, Airborne, U.S. Postal Service, etc.
Multi-echelon distribution	• Look for evidence of multi-echelon distribution, such as wholesale and retail. Ask the store where the warehouse is located. Ask about drop shipping the product.
	Midstream
www.companyname.com look for the "investor relations" tab	• If the company is public, the 10-K and 10-Q financial fine print often mentions key manufacturing and distribution locations. • If the company is private, consider purchasing a Dunn & Bradstreet credit report.
Product bill of materials	• If the manufacturer is a public company, the Form 10-K financial report may discuss aspects of the technology. • If the product is inexpensive, buy one and disassemble it. • If the product is expensive, buy one to inspect and return.
Country of origin	• Check carton labels and outside product labels for the COO.
Logistics look for freight forwarder labels	• Motor freight, if the origin and destination are land connected. • Rail freight, if the origin and destination are land connected and the product's volume and weight are excessive. • Airfreight or ocean freight, if the origin and destination are not land connected. • Consult an atlas for land connections and distances.
	Upstream
Product bill of materials	• Consult encyclopedias, industry handbooks, or trade publications for "how it works" articles.
Country of origin	• Check internal component labels for the COO.
Logistics look for freight forwarder labels	• Motor freight, if the origin and destination are land connected. • Rail freight, if the origin and destination are land connected and the product's volume and weight are excessive. • Airfreight or ocean freight, if the origin and destination are not land connected. • Consult an atlas for land connections and distances.

(*Continued*)

TABLE 2-2 (Continued)

	Reverse Stream
www.companyname.com look for the "company policy" tab	• Check the Web site and catalog for warranty, returns policy, and the collection point.
Return logistics look for freight forwarder labels	• Note the carrier specified for product returns; examples include UPS, FedEx, DHL, Airborne, U.S. Postal Service, etc. • Check the return packaging and return labels provided. Check ship-to addresses and maintenance schedule information in the owner's manual.
Loaner units	• Check product warranty fine print regarding loaner units.
Recycling	Check the Web site, the owner's manual, and product labels for evidence of recycling programs. Determine whether the raw materials that make up the product have significant economic value.

label on the packing slip to ship the return back to the central distribution center. The merchandiser inspects, cleans, and repackages these returns. The merchandiser operates a limited number of outlet stores where these returns are resold at a discount. The reverse stream zone includes a central collection point plus a few outlet stores.

Specific public information is more tenuous as one moves the analysis upstream. When the shirt arrives, its tag reads, "60% Cotton/40% Polyester/Assembled in Honduras out of U.S.A. components." The number of shirt styles, sizes, and colors made from a single fabric indicate that the midstream is organized around a V-type bill of materials. The apparel manufacturer is a cottage industry located in Honduras, chosen for the benefit of its low-cost labor market. Duty and import quotas imposed by the Country Of Origin are important cost considerations for manufacturers of textile and apparel goods. The textile mill is located close to a source of raw materials, cotton in this case, maybe in North or South Carolina. Sometimes it is possible to read in the trade press about a specific mill doing business for a specific brand; the textile mill is a single source supplier.

Because the seasonal volume of fabric could fill many containers, transportation into and out of Honduras consists of a motor-freight or rail-freight land bridge coupled with a leg of ocean freight. Smaller volumes of fabric can be rushed into and out of Honduras by more expensive airfreight. The midstream and upstream zones remain an educated guess until they can be refined from actual data. Figure 2-2 shows a sketch of the forward supply chain for this men's dress shirt.

Analyzing a Network from Internal Company Data

Data is more readily available when analyzing a network from inside the supply chain. Start by selecting the right level of product data aggregation (see Table 2-3). If product lines and product families are commingled, focus the analysis on the highest revenue product.

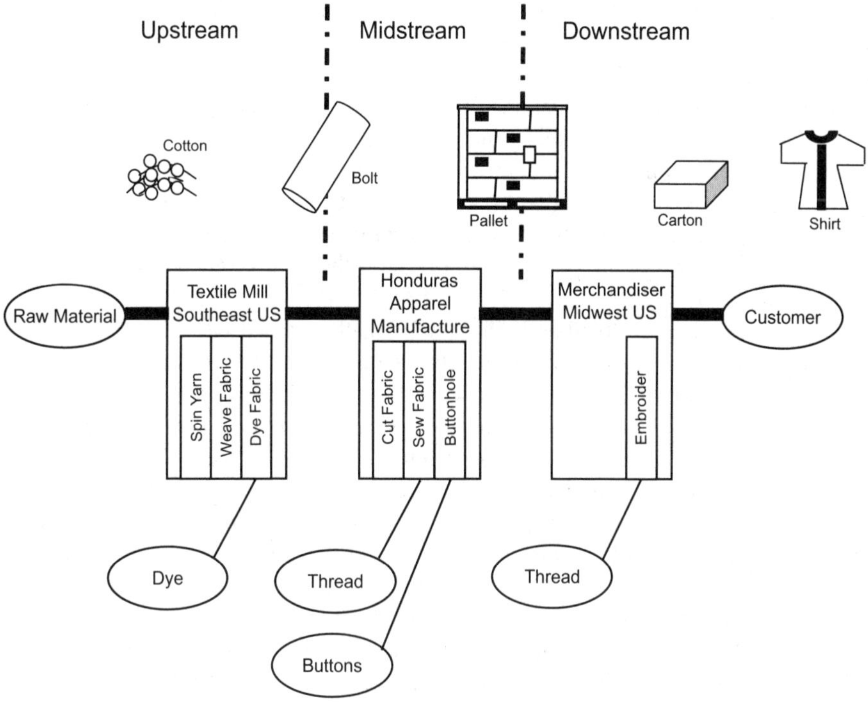

FIGURE 2-2 Mapping a competitor's network from public information.

A review of internal company sales data reveals that the top 79% of product line revenue comes from customer demand in the following nine customer account–geography pairs: Customer A in Japan—17%, Customer B in Hong Kong—5%, Customer C in Singapore—8%, Customer D in Germany—19%, Customer E in Texas—7%, Customer F in France—12%, Customer G in the U.K.—14%, Customer H in California—14%, and Customer I in Malaysia—4%. Likewise, a review of internal company purchasing data reveals that 82% of purchase orders go to the following eight commodity–geography pairs: semiconductors from Japan—21%, unloaded printed circuit boards from Oregon—15%, integrated circuits from Thailand—14%, passive

TABLE 2-3
Levels of Revenue Aggregation

Level	Characteristic	Use to Analyze
Corporation	Top line revenue aggregates several business units	No
Business unit	Business unit revenue aggregates two or more supply chains	No
Brand	Brand names often aggregate very different product types	No
Product line	Right level of aggregation for a consistent network	Yes
Product family	Can be used when the individual products are similar	Yes
Product option	May represent only a partial product	No

components from South Carolina—10%, sheet metal from New Jersey—16%, fans from Germany—8%, molded plastic parts from Taiwan—9%, and passive components from California—7%.

Picture the product at the customer receiving dock. Then imagine how the product looks packaged in the warehouse and in transport for shipment to the customer. Connect the geographies of demand with the finished-goods inventory of the manufacturing process. Next, imagine how the product looks as it is disassembled into its component parts, and how the component parts are packaged for shipment to the factory. Connect the geographies of supply with the component inventories of the manufacturing process.

The product is assembled and individually packaged at a factory in New Jersey. The packaged units are shipped on pallets, factory-direct, to customers worldwide, using airfreight and motor-freight connections. A single loaded printed circuit assembly (PCA) is the highest-value component inside the product. The PCA represents about 65% of the material cost of this product. The PCA is assembled in Colorado, packaged six to a carton, and shipped cross-country by motor freight. Other physically large commodity parts are packaged in cartons and shipped by motor freight. The remaining, physically small commodity parts are bulk-packed and shipped by airfreight. Sheet metal, plastic parts, and the fan are consumed by the factory in New Jersey. All the other parts are consumed by the PCA assembler in Colorado.

Table 2-4 is a tabular description of the supply chain network derived from this information. The column for "Latin America" and the row for the "Reverse Stream" are included for completeness but are not relevant in this example. In the "Upstream Supply" rows of the table, components shipped to the PCA assembler have their supply percentages shown on the left, whereas components shipped to the factory have their supply percentages shown on the right.

The tabular information presented in Table 2-4 is shown graphically as a network in Figure 2-3. The relative size of each demand circle indicates the percentage of downstream demand by geography. The relative size of each supply circle indicates the percentage of upstream supply by geography. The logistics lines connect the points of supply to the points of demand. The supply chain network is the concatenation of a downstream direct channel, a midstream A-type BOM manufacturer, and an upstream combined sole source and distributed source supply base.

Analyzing a Reverse Supply Chain Network

A manufacturer of portable monitoring devices used in pharmaceutical research laboratories offers a line of products with built-in battery backup. A Sealed Lead Acid (SLA) battery powers the device for up to two hours should a laboratory's main power fail. The SLA battery has a three-year shelf life, and the monitoring device manufacturer says the battery is not field replaceable. The monitoring device is designed to automatically discharge and recharge the battery once a month to keep the battery functional. The product carries a five-year manufacturer's warranty.

When the battery's lifetime passes, the product is returned under warranty to a centralized repair facility. The repair facility immediately ships an equivalent replacement unit back to the customer. The warranty period for the product is tracked by customer

TABLE 2-4
A Supply Chain Network Derived From Internal Data

	Asia/Pacific	North America	Latin America	Europe
Reverse Stream				
Downstream Demand	17%-Japan Customer A 8%-Singapore Customer C 5%-Hong Kong Customer B 4%-Malaysia Customer I 34% Total	14%-California Customer H 7%-Texas Customer E 21% Total		19%-Germany Customer D 14%-UK Customer G 12%-France Customer F 45% Total
Midstream Manufacture		100%-Factory New Jersey PCA Assembler Colorado		
Upstream Supply	Taiwan-9% Molded Plastic 21%-Japan Semiconductors 14%-Thailand Integrated Circuits 35% Totals 9%	New Jersey-16% Sheet Metal 15%-Oregon Printed Circuit Bd 10%-S. Carolina Passives 7%-California Passives 32% Totals 16%		Germany-8% Fans 0% Totals 8%

account and not by product serial number. The repair facility replaces the worn battery with a new one, refurbishes the product, and stocks the refurbished product for its future use as a warranty replacement unit. New SLA batteries are shipped to the repair facility by a common carrier and are considered nonhazardous material. Spent SLA batteries are classified as hazardous material (HAZMAT) for transport and disposal.

In this example the path taken by the SLA battery defines the physical distribution flow of the reverse supply chain network. There are two main flows in this network. The first follows the new replacement battery from the battery manufacturer through the repair facility into the refurbished product shipped as a warranty replacement unit. The second flow follows the spent battery from the customer's returned product through the repair facility to its environmentally responsible disposal. This reverse stream network combines repair with recycling. Figure 2-4 shows the two flows running in opposite directions and intersecting within the repair facility. Notice that it requires three SLA battery units to complete one exchange: First, the spent battery is returned from the customer under warranty; second, a new battery is installed in a previously returned unit shipped as this replacement; and third, a new battery is used to refurbish this unit and to be stocked in distribution for a future replacement.

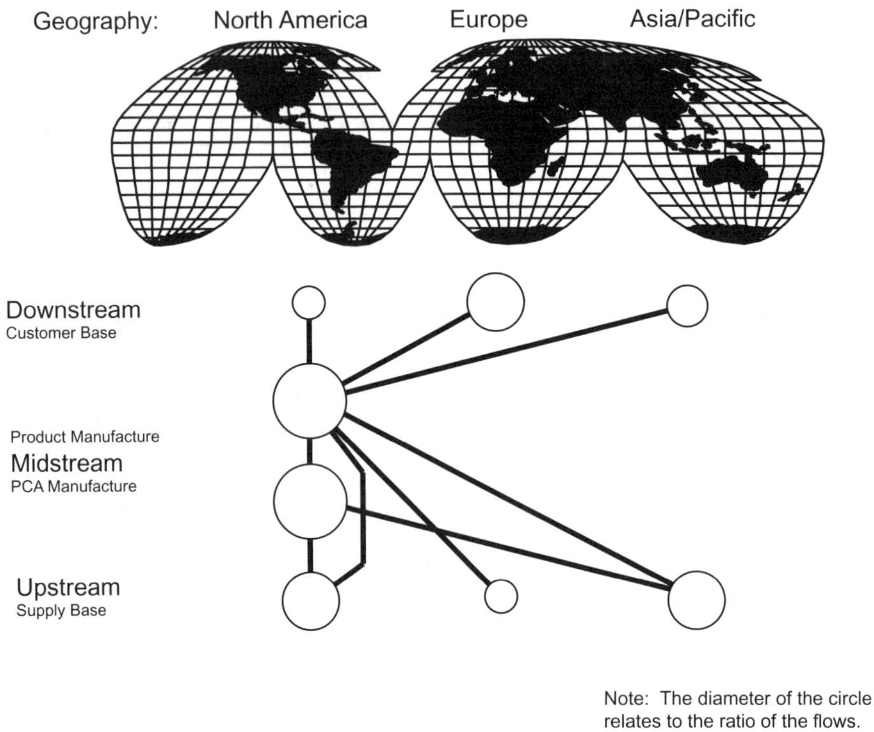

FIGURE 2-3 A supply chain network mapped from internal data.

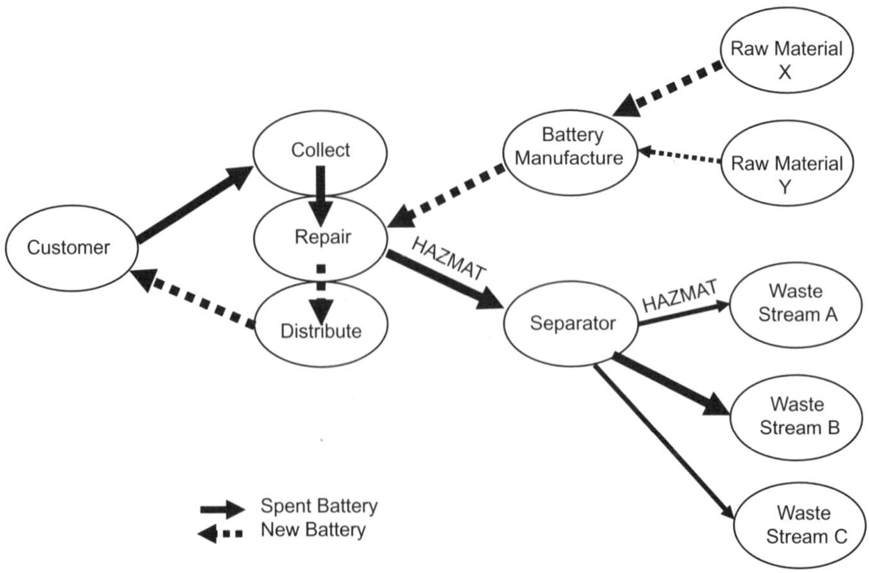

FIGURE 2-4 Mapping a reverse supply chain network.

FOCUS FIRST ON THE CUSTOMER

The *APICS Dictionary,* 10th Edition, defines competitive advantage as "an edge, e.g., a process, patent, management philosophy, or distribution system that a seller has, that enables the seller to control a larger market share or profit than the seller would otherwise have." What makes an organization competitive? Competitiveness can be debated either from an external customer perspective or from an internal management perspective. The customer perspective is the more valuable of the two because the customer pays for the product and services. When two organizations are selling essentially the same product, the buyer will gauge the competitiveness of each company against a common yardstick. Then the customer will buy the product with the highest perceived value.

Retail customers judge value using eight criteria: brand, fashion, service, range, quality, convenience, availability, and price. Not only does the product have to be on the shelf with the best price, but the product has to be the right brand, in fashion, of the highest quality, easy to buy and return, etc. A supply chain network must consistently do all of this to be considered competitive in the customer's eyes and to win the sale.

Most customers are very vocal when they have a problem. However, few customers are able to vocalize a solution to their problem. Here is where the competitive competency of the supply chain network comes into play. When the supply chain network is able to focus some combination of product and service on providing an economic solution to the customer's problem, the customer will buy from that network. In addition, though a supply chain network delights in providing a volume of the same product, customers have come to expect customization for their specific requirements. A competitive supply chain network learns how to customize the product downstream while manufacturing generic components upstream.

COMPETITIVE COMPETENCIES

Organizations strive to improve their ability to compete within cost and against time. There is top line revenue growth and bottom line profitability. If the organization cannot sustain top line revenue growth with bottom line profitability, then it is not competitive. There are also productivity gains, asset utilization, and time-to-market. If the organization cannot do more with less, with less inventory and cash in less time, then it is not competitive.

The following three competencies, singularly or in combination, lie at the core of an organization's ability to compete in the market:

- *Technological core competency*—The organization adds value through a technology. Competing organizations cannot access this technology or have not learned how to make the technology work. The organization has learned how to apply this technology to its competitive advantage.
- *Process core competency*—The organization adds value through a process. Competing organizations are less mature in their process knowledge, process consistency, and process quality. The organization has learned how to apply this process to its competitive advantage.

- *Relationship core competency*—The organization adds value through access to a relationship. Competing organizations are not trusted or lack an introduction to this relationship. The organization has learned how to nourish this relationship to its competitive advantage.

It is a common, but false, belief of senior management that it should be easy to transplant a competitive organization into a different geographical location and a different culture. In one example, a lower-cost group of recently hired engineers with limited product knowledge replaced a team of long-term employees designing product enhancements from deep technology knowledge. Soon afterwards, the customer stopped making purchases. When asked, the customer said that even though the price point on product enhancements had dropped, the manufacturer was no longer competitive.

THINKING OUTSIDE THE BOX

Conceptualizing a new business model is hard work, especially for companies with long histories of growth and profitability. However, over time companies stumble and lose their way. Once-successful companies become internally focused and fail to see how remaining externally focused is essential to their business survival. The supply chain network needs to align with the business strategy. For some companies, fixing a growth problem through a new distribution partnership leads to an unexpected profitability crisis. This is because the new channel expects a deep discount on its purchases. For other companies, fixing a profitability problem through outsourcing can lead to an unexpected cash crisis. This is because the longer supply chain requires additional inventory investment. It is like lying on the beach under a blanket that is too small. You pull the blanket over your right shoulder to keep from getting sunburned, but your left ankle is exposed. Pulling the blanket down to cover your ankles exposes your neck.

WHO'S KEEPING SCORE?

Four stakeholder groups get to vote on the competitiveness of your business. Your owners are constantly asking themselves whether your business is still giving a competitive return on their investment. Your customers are constantly asking themselves whether your business is still providing the most competitive product, pricing, delivery, and service solutions to meet their needs. Your employees are constantly asking themselves whether your business is still providing fair pay with competitive benefits. Your suppliers are constantly asking themselves whether your business still values their goods and is still capable of paying their invoices. When you can drive your supply chain network to exceed the expectations of all four constituents while lowering their risk, your business will win their votes. The four groups are not equals, however. The needs of customers and owners outweigh the needs of suppliers and employees. Table 2-5 summarizes stakeholder rewards and risks.

Changing your business model requires an investment. Like any other investment, there will be tradeoffs between returns and risks. The risk of implementing a

TABLE 2-5
Stakeholder Rewards and Risks

Owners	Customers	Employees	Suppliers
• Asset return • Growth • Profits • Investment risk	• Price • Delivery risk • Quality risk • Service	• Fair pay • Benefits • Employment risk	• Supply value • Payment risk

single growth strategy in an evolutionary plan is much lower than the risk of implementing two or more growth strategies in a revolutionary business makeover. The ultimate test for determining whether any of the growth strategies shown in Table 2-6 will result in a better business model is the answer to the following questions:

- Will the new business model grow value within an acceptable level of risk?
- Will the new business model grow revenue within an acceptable level of risk?
- Will the new business model grow profitability within an acceptable level of risk?

Imagine a Different Way of Doing Business

For years the textile and apparel industry has had the dream of being able to transact the customer's cash from the point of sale all the way to the gray-goods mill before any part of the garment is sewn. This dream is shaped by the characteristics of the industry. This business is highly seasonal, and sales depend on the latest fads, fashions, and colors. Customers come in an infinite variety of shapes that don't always fit into the limited number of standard sizes. Customers also have learned to wait for sales, when markdowns can drive prices below 20% of the original hanger price. The industry is flush with inventory and returns. The mills still groove on large production runs to control setup costs, whereas the distributors and retail outlets flirt with the latest advances in technology.

Against this background, suppose you are a regional distributor for a specialty mail-order apparel business. You are in the business of selling men's and women's work shirts through catalogs targeted at the industrial workforce. The business is profitable because it is not very seasonal; it does not follow trendy fashions. You forecast future sales including the expected mix of colors and sizes once a quarter. The work shirts are purchased in lots by the dozen through an apparel supplier in Hong Kong. The apparel supplier buys textiles of the color and grade of fabric required from textile suppliers. The fabric is cut, kitted, and shipped with your order to a cottage industry for sewing in the Peoples Republic of China, across the border from the New Territories. The sewn work shirts are transported back to Hong Kong and exported to your distribution warehouse in the United States. Figure 2-5 shows the network diagram.

TABLE 2-6
Growth Strategies

Value Growth Strategy

Move up the value chain by in-sourcing part of the customer's process.

Network alignment	The downstream zone must be aligned with this strategy to deliver the right level of product integration and a full range of customer focused services.
Risk	The customer base shrinks because products and services become more customized.
Return	The customer is willing to pay top dollar to outsource a part of its process.

Value Growth Strategy

Create new value by orchestrating the formation of a virtual network.

Network alignment	The upstream, midstream, and downstream zones are primarily linked through relationships agreements and information technology.
Risk	The network unravels if any of the partners fail to share the common vision.
Return	There are no boundaries with this strategy. Bold, new businesses can be created.

Value Growth Strategy

Grow through post-sales services.

Network alignment	The reverse stream zone must be aligned with this strategy to provide new value through repair, recalibration, remanufacturing, and recycling.
Risk	Requires investment in capacity, inventory, and cash. Tends to yield lower profit margins because of the low-volume, high-mix nature of this business.
Return	Adds to top-line revenue. Leverages opportunities to sell service contracts.

Revenue Growth Strategy

Lead the competition in new product introduction.

Network alignment	The upstream zone must be aligned with this strategy to ensure access to technology and sole source component suppliers.
Risk	Extended life cycles of older products slow the investment in new product development. Accelerated component life cycles require significant investment in engineering support.
Return	New products better meet customer needs and can create new market opportunities.

Revenue Growth Strategy

Grow the product catalog through horizontal product licensing.

Network alignment	The midstream zone must be aligned with this strategy to fully integrate the licensed products prior to entering the distribution channel.
Risk	A mismatch of business cultures and product quality can lower the customer's view of the base brand value.
Return	An economical solution to one-stop shopping for every need. Provides revenue growth without corresponding balance sheet investment.

Revenue Growth Strategy

Grow through acquisition.

Network alignment	Network support functions are centralized while the networks of trading partners remain decentralized.
Risk	The acquisition may have no synergy or strategic alignment with the rest of the business. Valuable human resources are spent integrating the acquisition.
Return	Gain both new revenue and new assets.

TABLE 2-6
(Continued)

Revenue Growth Strategy	
Grow the market by adding new sales channels.	
Network alignment	The downstream zone must be aligned with this strategy to support customers in all geographies, 24 hours a day, 7 days a week.
Risk	Need to manage channel conflict, for example between a commission-based sales force and customer self-service through an Internet virtual store.
Return	Attracts customers from different market segments to expand product demand.
Revenue Growth Strategy	
Vertically integrate to become the lowest cost producer.	
Network alignment	The midstream zone must be aligned with this strategy to minimize supply chain length. This strategy works best for high-volume, low-mix commodity products.
Risk	Labor and material cost inflation built up over time can negate the benefit.
Return	Grow market share. Highly responsive to small changes in customer demand.
Profitability Growth Strategy	
Rationalize and consolidate to reduce costs.	
Network alignment	Upstream supply and downstream distribution are rationalized under this strategy while all support functions, like information systems, are consolidated.
Risk	Loss of some capability through consolidation.
Return	Reduces business complexity and operating costs by consolidating transaction volume.
Profitability Growth Strategy	
Divest unprofitable lines and refocus.	
Network alignment	Unprofitable upstream, midstream, downstream, and reverse stream operations are unbundled from the business.
Risk	Critical support functions may be lost through divestiture. Valuable human resources are consumed while preparing to sell part of the business.
Return	Unprofitable lines are eliminated from the income statement. Nonproductive assets are removed from the balance sheet. The working capital position improves.
Profitability Growth Strategy	
Outsource domestically to upgrade a core competency.	
Network alignment	This strategy can be applied to all zones in the supply chain network.
Risk	It is difficult to recover a function once it is outsourced. The network is lengthened and becomes dependent on additional organizations.
Return	Opportunity to restructure assets on the balance sheet. Provides workforce flexibility.
Profitability Growth Strategy	
Outsource manufacturing internationally to change the Country Of Origin.	
Network alignment	The midstream zone must align with this strategy to take advantage of the cost restructuring.
Risk	The network is lengthened and becomes dependent on additional organizations. The total supply chain network requires more inventory and cash for operations.
Return	Provides opportunity to restructure assets on the balance sheet and costs on the income statement. Provides workforce flexibility.

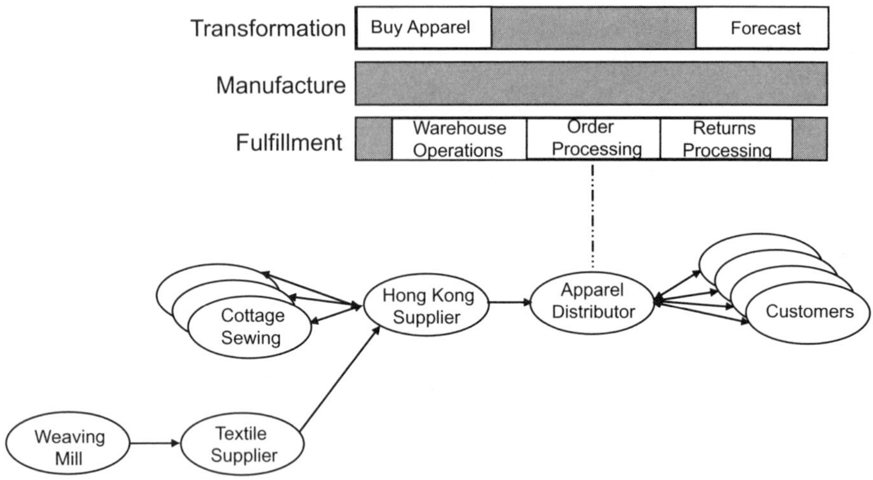

FIGURE 2-5 The starting point as a high mix, low volume distributor.

The stock is on your shelf and the Hong Kong apparel supplier is paid before you receive any orders or payment checks by mail from your customers. Each customer order is processed first-in, first-out and sent to warehouse operations for packaging and shipping. The warehouse also handles returns sent back by customers. When you think about your current business model, you realize that its core competencies include planning, apparel procurement, order processing, and warehouse operations. Your profit margin is thin.

Like any other business, this one has many problems and opportunities. Although the Hong Kong connection keeps the basic price of the work shirts low, logistics costs are expensive, and you worry how U.S. Customs might change apparel import quotas and duties in the future. The lead-time with Hong Kong is 12 weeks, and you have interest expense for your letters of credit. Once the shipment arrives, you have a large amount of cash tied up in inventory until it can all be sold. Your forecasts never get the right mix of colors and sizes to match actual customer demand. You hope to get returns under better control because a significant number of shirts come back due to problems with their fit. The forecast error and the 7% return rate forces you to write-off inventory twice a year. This reduces the bottom line. Additionally, some new competitors are starting to take notice of your niche market.

How else might you organize the business? Which value growth strategy, revenue growth strategy, or profitability growth strategy might apply to your business situation? Would a different business model be more or less risky than your current business model? Table 2-7 is an example of how the set of growth strategies from Table 2-6 could be applied and prioritized to imagine a new business model.

You determine that the new model could work like this: Instead of using mail-order catalogs, customers would order their work shirts from an interactive Web site on the Internet. This provides customers a more convenient way to place their orders 24 hours per day, 7 days per week. It eliminates the expense of printing and distributing

TABLE 2-7
Prioritize Growth Strategies To Formulate Potential New Solutions

Strategy	Applicable (Yes/No)	Priority (1,2,3)	Comment
Value growth Move up value chain	No		
Value growth Form virtual network	Yes	2	Replace mail and phone with Internet information technology to tie the network together.
Value growth Post sale service	No		
Revenue growth New products	Yes	2	Use computer technology to solve the returned-for-fit problem.
Revenue growth License products	No		
Revenue growth Acquisition	No		
Revenue growth New sales channel	Yes	1	Use of Internet for faster ordering through a virtual store; use of credit cards to increase working capital.
Profitability growth Vertical integration	Yes	1	Move from distribute-from-stock to build-to-order reducng lead-time and the inventory asset investment. Offset increase in cost of goods sold with savings from discontinued catalog printing and distribution.
Profitability growth Rationalize/consolidate	Yes	3	Shorten the total supply chain length and reduce the number of planning interfaces.
Profitability growth Divest	No		
Profitability growth Domestic outsource	No		
Profitability growth International outsource	No		Current business model.

catalogs because a single electronic catalog is available online. You have decided to experiment with a new computer imaging technology that produces a perfect-fit shirt pattern. The algorithm determines a cutting pattern from four customer body measurements, supplemented by four garment measurements from the customer's "most comfortable" shirt. The eight measurements will be entered through the Web site and stored for future purchases. It is expected that this will cut returns by 80%. The customer's credit card will be charged at the time the order is taken. Cash generated through credit card transactions will be used to purchase the labor and textiles to produce the work shirts.

The space inside the current distribution center will be reorganized into textile receiving and storage, a cutting floor, flexible sewing lines, and a small shipping/

logistics area. Every six hours the backlog of customer orders will be grouped by size against a set of sizing standards. Then sets of paper patterns will be computer generated for each sized lot. Bolts of textiles will be unrolled and stacked according to the fabric and colors of the customer orders. Then high-pressure water knives will be used to cut the stacks of textiles, tracing around the customized paper patterns. The cut fabric will be moved to the next available sewing line, where the sewing machines are easily reconfigured in a job-shop environment. Once the fabric is sewn, the nearly completed shirt will be sent to the button-hole department. In this postponement operation, the buttons will be limited to a few diameters and to a few colors and styles. The shirt will be ironed, folded, and packaged for shipment to the end-customer.

You will manufacture product only when you have a paid customer order. Although the manufacturing is labor-intensive and uses a workforce that is expensive relative to that in China, this workforce is highly flexible and sews only shippable customer orders. Purchasing will now buy textiles directly from the textile supplier instead of buying finished goods from Hong Kong. The textile supplier still deals with the mill. Figure 2-6 shows the network diagram for the proposed new way of doing business. The required set of core competencies has changed under the new business model to include textile procurement, pattern making, sewing, e-retailing (electronic retailing over the Internet), and logistics. This will require reskilling your workforce.

A deeper understanding of the relationship between business strategy and supply chain opportunities has led to a radical rethinking of your business. Table 2-8 summarizes the investments, possible risks, and expected returns for the new business model. A side-by-side income statement and balance sheet analysis would be an essential part of the due diligence leading up to a final decision for change. At this point it is unclear whether the new model can be profitable without the benefit of low-cost labor.

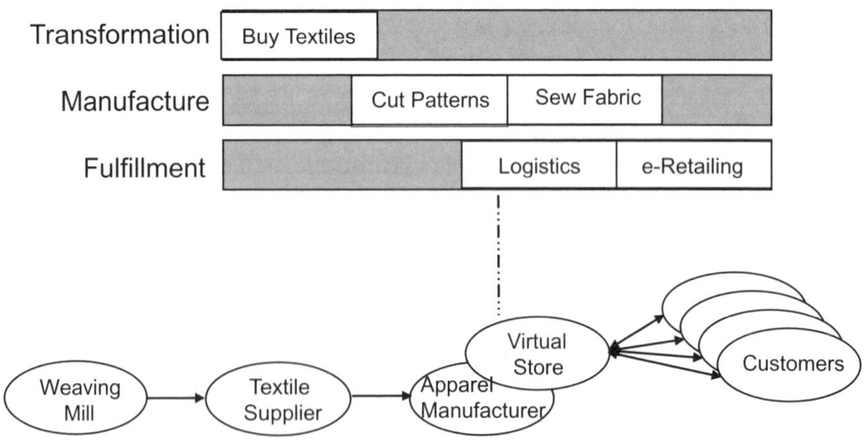

FIGURE 2-6 The ending point as a high-mix, low-volume manufacturer.

TABLE 2-8
A Risk-Return Analysis of the New Business Model

Investment	Risks	Return
Adopt e-retail Implement selling through a virtual retail store channel.	• Ability to develop awareness for the Web site. • Customers comfortable with mail order may not be comfortable with a Web site.	• Save the high cost of printing and distributing catalogs. • 24 × 7 convenience for customers.
Upgrade pattern technology Customers provide body measurements and "best-fit" garment measurements.	• Customer confusion over entering garment measures. • Customer privacy issues over saving measurements.	• Cut returns by 80%.
Re-skill the workforce Acquire new skills, train for similar skills, release unneeded skills.	• Managing employee relations. • Timeframe to convert the workforce.	• Transition from pick-from-stock distribution to sew-to-order manufacture. Operate the supply chain with less total inventory and cash investment.
Direct purchase of textiles Transition from purchasing apparel to purchasing textiles.	• Loss of low-cost labor. • Ability to convert the Purchasing department. • Customs quotas on imports.	• Shorten the supply chain to gain responsiveness.

IN SUMMARY

This chapter has presented a technique for mapping a supply chain network. This is a high-level analysis, by definition, and considers only the physical distribution flow. This chapter has raised three fundamental questions:

- Is your organization focused on the end-customer?
- Does your organization know the boundaries of its core competencies?
- Are you thinking outside the box to align your supply chain network with your business strategy?

In Chapter 3, customer needs and business strategy are used to define requirements for network relationships and core competencies. The supply chain network uses these embedded relationships and core competencies to sustain a competitive advantage over time and through changing customer demand.

The supply chain architect dialed his wife's cell phone about three o'clock. "Hi, it's me. How is your day going so far?"

"Oh, hi. I'm glad you called. This has been the most frustrating day of my life!" she exclaimed.

"What's the matter? Is everything okay?"

"You remember I told you the other night that I had decided to hire another instructor? My business has been growing steadily, and now I'm spending too much of my own time traveling between client sites. After checking around, I decided to hire Suzie Lee. She started work last week."

"Yes, I remember that."

"Suzie came with great credentials. She was an in-house instructor for about seven years at SoftTech on Route 1, and she has taught every module from production scheduling to cost accounting for the same software application I'm currently supporting."

"So, what's the big problem?" the architect asked his wife.

"Suzie started working at my largest, most important client, DataLink, on Monday because I'm behind in class hours for that account. I know she has been on the job only a couple of days, but Fred, their C.E.O, has already called me about instructional quality issues. He said he might have to cancel the contract. That would be a complete disaster! I'm headed over to DataLink right now to talk with Fred."

"Calm down. Fred values your company's services too much to pull the plug. Let's talk this through for a couple of minutes before you run out. It might help put your next conversation with Fred in a better perspective," her husband said. "Has Fred shared any specifics with you?"

"Yes. The class we are currently conducting is for some of Fred's midlevel managers from Atlanta and Dallas. These men are very experienced, and they act tough in the classroom. When Suzie could not answer their questions, she would not admit that she didn't know. They responded by intimidating my new instructor." She continued, "To make matters worse, Suzie is apparently not following my script and used some of her old material from SoftTech. The SoftTech material does not have the instructional design quality of mine. For example, when a PowerPoint figure is missing, Suzie just creates a figure of her own on the whiteboard. Now I'm losing consistency from one class to the next."

"I think you have thee separate problems," said the architect. "The first problem is that you have damage control to do with Fred. The second problem is that you have to restore classroom expectations around mutual respect of diversity. And the third problem, maybe the root cause of the first two, is that you have to figure out how to scale up your training business without losing its quality and consistency."

"Yes, that makes sense. I can get Fred to help me with the classroom discipline. He is the right person to set the upfront expectations with his own managers. But what do you mean about scaling up the business?" she asked.

"As you get more clients, you cannot possibly instruct every classroom hour yourself. You have to analyze what makes the training work when you teach the course. Then you have to create a process that can deliver the training just as effectively when someone else, like Suzie, teaches the course. What do you think are some of the elements that make the classes you personally teach so effective?"

"It begins with the instructional design. I'm using a design consulting company from Chicago," she continued. "Then I put together a powerful PowerPoint slide presentation for use in the classroom that pulls in some multimedia. I link

Internet Web sites, streaming videos, and animated slides together to appeal to a broad range of adult learning. There are many interactive exercises to enhance the learning. Moreover, the classroom physical environment is a big factor. DataLink owns this great learning center with lots of projection equipment, flexible seating, and its own cafeteria."

"Sounds like a supply chain network to me!"

"Yeah. Right. Is that all you ever think about? I have a serious problem here, and I've got to go see Fred this afternoon."

"No. Look, I am serious. In order to get to a process description of your business, you first need to identify the other organizations you depend upon for your service supply chain. If you consider your company with its instructors to be the midstream, it sounds to me like you have a instructional design organization upstream different from the physical classroom environment provided by the customer's organization downstream."

"Oka-a-y," she said. "What is this upstream and downstream stuff? We're not canoeing on a river somewhere."

"Think about your delivery of adult learning as a flow, like a stream. The flow begins far away from your customer with the instructional design consultant; this is called the upstream. The flow then continues through your company, in the midstream, where you develop the multimedia PowerPoint presentations and interactive exercises and train your instructors. The flow ends downstream when it reaches your customer. Downstream is where your instructors deliver the training in the physical classroom using the computers and projectors that a third party provides."

"I get it now!" she responded excitedly.

"Here is one more point. You probably have not had a chance to discuss how this works with Suzie because she is so new. But have you discussed how your company works with the other instructors?"

"Of course not! You just told me this two minutes ago."

"Well, defining the network is key to understanding what makes your particular training company competitive. Once you understand that, you can define a supply chain process that will remain competitive no matter how many instructors you decide to hire. Your service business will become more easily scalable," said the supply chain architect.

"I've got to run. See you tonight."

"Good luck with Fred." As he hung up, he continued to think about all the organizations it took to stretch from the design of courseware to putting a trained instructor in front of students in the classroom.

3 Collaborating Network Relationships

Wednesday, June 26

Joe Triano, the carpenter, was banging away in the kitchen. He was completing the framing work, nailing the new studs to the floor and ceiling joists. Delivery of the Anderson casement window was expected any day. The new bay window would fit snugly into the hole Joe had created in the framing. The supply chain architect and Tom, the building architect, were trying to hold a conversation in the far corner of the room between the blows of Joe's hammer. It was practically impossible.

"You were mentioning that the schedule for the plumber would have to slip a few days," said the supply chain architect.

"Yeah. Tough break. We could really use him tomorrow. Joe will finish the framing work where the plumbing has to go by this afternoon," replied Tom.

"I don't understand why we have to wait now for the plumber. You assured me that your plumber was reliable and did high quality work weeks ago, before I signed the contract. What has changed?"

"It's the old story. I have worked with George, my plumbing contractor, on a lot of jobs. But, I know there will be times when my little jobs will lose priority to someone else's bigger jobs."

"What do you mean?"

"Say, for example, that George agrees to work with me on your kitchen renovation. This is a big deal for you; but frankly, it may be just a schedule-filler for George. Now say George bids on that 100-unit condominium complex going in across town, and he wins the bid. If the condo project needs work done on the same day George was to work here, he will go work on the condos," said Tom.

"Surely you have some leverage with George with all the repeat business you give him!"

"Yes, I have some. But, it really comes down to dollars and cents. The total amount of work George gets from me in a year's time is insignificant compared with his big projects. Not every relationship I have with my subcontractors is created equal."

"Then, how come you are able to get Joe the carpenter to work on my kitchen any time you want?" asked the supply chain architect. Joe stopped hammering for a minute to hear what the two men were saying about him.

"That's a different relationship altogether. Joe and I collaborate. Joe brings me about 20% of my architectural jobs from referrals to people like you who are thinking about renovating their homes. Then, Joe works more than half of his time on jobs where I am the architect of record. It's much more of a win–win relationship where we each respect the other's skills, and we each understand that we could not perform the other's work."

"I still don't get it. You and the plumber respect each other. You and the plumber cannot do each other's work. George the plumber could bring you new customers. Why don't you just collaborate with George, starting with my kitchen?"

"The truth is that George doesn't need me. He has developed his own network of general contractors and other tradesmen who look out for each other. I'm only in his network tangentially. The best I can do is to remind George of the quality of business I do bring his way. George is rarely out of work these days."

After Tom left, the supply chain architect could not help but wonder how many other trade relationships existed where Tom was only loosely connected? Would the electrician, the cabinetmaker, the sheet rocker, or the painter become a problem because Tom had a weak rather than a strong relationship with them? As he battled the rush hour traffic, this troubled him all the way to work.

*****

Arriving at his office, the supply chain architect slid his laptop into its docking station and proceeded to work through the 33 new e-mail messages in his in-basket. Six were spam and could be immediately deleted without being read. Several messages were from his team in Singapore prior to their going home for the evening. One message was an invitation to speak at his local APICS chapter. He had gotten his Certification in Production and Inventory Management (CPIM) through APICS, the Professional Society for Resource Management, long before. Five of the messages were replies and re-replies to an earlier message. He would read the last message thread from bottom to top and delete all the earlier ones as duplicates. Just then, a co-worker walked past his desk and reminded him about the 10:00 a.m. meeting in the conference room. He was glad he did not have to call Germany today because the meeting was scheduled during the prime connect time with Europe.

Hector Morales, V.P. of manufacturing, approached him. "Good morning. Am I glad you could join our discussion again today! We need to move the conversation on to the subject of outsourcing."

"Good morning, Hector. Who else are we waiting for?"

"There will be about eight of us this morning. Dana Hoffmann, C.F.O., has her cost accounting manager, Ray Smith, coming in. Engineering is sending along Nancy Tucker, a hardware section manager, and Dan Cook, our chief engineer. Purchasing is sending an experienced buyer, Carlos Gonzalez. And, Daisy Whitehall, V.P. of quality, is also present."

"Will there be anyone from marketing?"

"No, outsourcing is a manufacturing directive. It doesn't concern marketing. They need to be out finding some new business," said Hector. The sudden loss of the Colonial Distributor account was already being felt.

This was one of a half-dozen meetings to explore how manufacturing could increase product quality and still cut the cost of goods sold to the customer. With the exception of Hector and the architect, however, the players at each meeting had changed. It would be up to him to provide some continuity from meeting to meeting.

Hector began, "Let's get started."

The architect began to summarize, "At our last meeting we looked at some of the quality defect details provided by Adam Stone and the warehouse receiving team at Colonial Distributor. It became obvious that the majority of the defects were related to the manufacture of product options. None of our standard products had any reported quality defects."

"What kind of problems did you see?" asked Nancy.

Daisy jumped in, "We received details on four defective shipments. In two of the cases, the customer ordered an Option 58, but we built and shipped Option 85. In one case, the customer removed the product's cover and discovered that in our rush to ship product at the end of the last quarter, we never finished installing the option. In the last case, the option was out of calibration by the time the customer used the product."

"Sounds like we have an order processing problem, an employee training problem, and possibly a design problem," said Hector.

"Well, maybe," replied Daisy. "In the last case, we shipped the product to the customer back in December, but the customer put the product into use in May. Our calibration spec is good only for 90 days from the date of shipment."

Dan Cook spoke up, "I'm looking at the bills of materials. Options 58 and 85 are identical except for a change in two component part values. It would be very easy to overlook those two parts all the way through final assembly."

"Yes, but why didn't we pick that up in final test?" asked Nancy.

"Final test was never designed to differentiate among options," Dan answered. "We have a ways to go to fail-proof our manufacturing processes."

Dana interrupted them, "We're plowing old ground because some of you were not at our last meeting. We talked at length all last week about the quality issues. I don't mean to be rude, but let's get on with the agenda. How do we intend to take cost out of these products? Ray, please relate to this group the key points we discussed earlier."

"On average the product families that Colonial Distributor bought from us had three hours of labor content and $425 dollars of material content. We believe the competition can build an equivalent product with about two hours of labor and about $345 dollars of material," said Ray.

"The competitor's products are not equivalent. Our products have a much stronger feature set and a broader range of product options!" Nancy interjected.

Ray continued, "One of my accountants is starting to analyze which assemblies take the most labor and which components represent the highest material costs. Maybe manufacturing can come up with some new ways to build the product using less labor. Maybe engineering can come up with a new design that uses less material."

"It's real tough to take costs out of our product designs with all the features our customers say they want," said Dan.

"And we are already buying some cheaper parts from Mexico, but sometimes we have delivery problems crossing the boarder," said Carlos.

"Carlos brings up a good point," said the architect. "There are many other factors that go into landed cost besides the labor and material that Ray is talking about."

"Where are you going with this?" asked Dana.

The architect continued, "I think we have to step back and look at a broader picture than just the labor and material in the product. In fact, there is the whole supply chain network to consider. The bill of materials determines the kind of suppliers we need, but we could buy from anywhere in the world. The upstream supply base becomes a trade-off between a reduction in component cost and the landed cost to bring those parts here, including import duty and inbound freight charges. The bill of labor determines the kind of skilled resources we need, but we could manufacture the product anywhere in the world. The midstream is a trade-off between saving labor and income tax costs by using a different Country Of Origin versus diluting our own value-added manufacturing contribution. Marketing has been effective selling our product into certain market segments worldwide. The downstream supply chain is a trade-off between maintaining higher margins by shipping product directly to our customers versus providing higher service levels by holding inventory in a distribution channel like Colonial Distributor. We have many cost-related trade-offs to consider."

"Well, that's okay for theory, but let's get back to how we can take material cost out of the product," said Hector.

"With all due respect," continued the architect, "The situation we find ourselves in today is not business as usual. We have to be smarter in how we approach a tough competitive situation when our current products are overpriced for the market. Hopefully, the next-generation design that Nancy and Dan are dreaming up in engineering will require significantly fewer labor hours and significantly less material cost. But those designs are more than a year away."

"We seem to be all over the map this morning, although I do agree with some of the points being made. We may need a meeting facilitator to keep us all on track," said Daisy. "What's the next step in this discussion?"

"I'd like to hear more about this supply chain framework that would help us become more competitive," said Dana. They all agreed.

"It seems to me," started the architect, "That we have to decide what piece we do here better than anyone else. Then we can build the right distribution, outsourcing, supply base, or whatever around the core competency that is our competitive edge."

"Yes, it makes sense. But what is it that we do so well?" Ray asked.

The team brainstormed for twenty minutes, and was able to write the following list on the whiteboard:

- We transform customer problem statements into effective product solutions.
- We hold exclusive patent rights on the demodulator assembly.
- We have the most competitive manufacturing cycle times in final assembly (when compared with last year's cross-industry benchmark).
- We have a reputation with our customers for excellent, worldwide service and support (as documented by the last three year's of customer satisfaction surveys).

"Product-development expertise, patent protection for a few more years, time-competitive final assembly, and a solid reputation for service are the capabilities we should build on to win in the marketplace," Hector summarized. "Now, what should we be doing differently to connect with our suppliers and with our customers?"

"To put it in slightly different terms, how many additional organizations should it take to span the gap from selling product to buying materials when we are somewhere in the middle?" asked the supply chain architect.

It should come as no surprise that network relationships are not always equal. This chapter builds on the previous chapter by developing logic for the set of relationships that are essential to form a competitive supply chain network. Chapter 2 located transformation, manufacturing, and fulfillment organizations within network zones. This chapter considers how to complete each network zone with a minimum number of echelons. Different classes of network relationships are defined. Then the required core competency for each organization is mapped to its proper zone and echelon. Comprehensive examples are used throughout this chapter to move from the theory to practice. Finally, the partnership agreement is introduced as a technique for formalizing network relationships and managing relationship risks.

CLASSIFYING NETWORK ORGANIZATIONS

The organizational relationships composing a supply chain network are grouped into four classes. The primary class of network relationships is the trading partner. The second class, nominal trading partner relationships, are the most common. The strategic nominal trading partner is the third class, and the network orchestrator is the fourth class. This is somewhat analogous to a hockey team, with forwards who score, wings and backs who move the puck up the ice to the forwards, and the team captain who has the power to call a change in strategy on the fly.

The Trading Partner

A supply chain network is a mosaic of many buyer–seller relationships. Each relationship has a characteristic intensity and duration. The most intense relationships are in the class of primary relationships, which are focused through a business strategy to deliver value to the customer and the shareholder. The least intense relationships are in the class of secondary relationships, which are necessary to bring the information, physical distribution, and cash to the trading partners. The duration of a relationship depends upon the number of transactions processed through the network. On the one hand, if the sale is a one-time event, the duration of the relationship is only for a single transaction. On the other hand, trading partner relationships may last for hundreds of transactions and dozens of years.

The *APICS Dictionary*, 10th Edition, defines a trading partner as "Any organization external to the firm that plays an integral role within the supply chain community and whose business fortune depends on the success of the supply chain network." A trading partner buys a significant percentage—more than 10%–20% is a good rule of thumb—of its purchases in-network. A trading partner sells a significant percentage—more than 10%–20% is a good rule of thumb—of its sales in-network. To be a trading partner, an organization must simultaneously buy and sell at such significant percentages as to sustain a high level of in-network throughput. A trading partner connects with the network through all three flows: information flow, physical distribution flow, and cash flow. It is both a physical inventory location and a cash-holding location for the order-to-delivery-to-cash cycle within the network. There are relatively few trading partners in a supply chain network because these relationships establish the competitive essence of the business.

The Nominal Trading Partner

The nominal trading partner is the second class of organization found in a supply chain network. The *APICS Dictionary*, 10th Edition, defines a nominal trading partner as "Any organization external to the firm that provides an essential material or service, but whose financial success is largely independent of the financial success of the supply chain network." A nominal trading partner buys an insignificant percentage—less than 1%–2% is a good rule of thumb—of its purchases in-network. A nominal trading partner sells an insignificant percentage—less than 1%–2% is a good rule of thumb—of its sales in-network. Any organization that does not simultaneously buy and sell at significant percentages in-network does not contribute significantly to in-network throughput, and is therefore a nominal trading partner. Nominal trading partners always connect with the information flow and the cash flow of the network, and may connect with the physical distribution flow.

A nominal trading partner is generally easily substitutable. For example, a Less-Than-Truckload (LTL) carrier servicing Philadelphia and New York City may be easily replaced by another competing LTL carrier. There are always a larger number of nominal trading partners than trading partners in a supply chain network. This is because nominal trading partners provide the glue that completes the network flows.

Logistics service providers, information service providers, and financial service providers all fall into the class of nominal trading partners.

Nominal trading partners can play simultaneous roles in multiple supply chain networks. For this reason, the nominal trading partners in your network have a different agenda than the trading partners. You will find it difficult to gain the mindshare of a nominal trading partner. You also will find it difficult to convince a nominal trading partner to invest in a solution to your problem. Where the in-network buying and selling falls between 2% and 10%, the organization's placement and role within the network will decide how that organization should be treated. Network organizations that could be either a trading partner or a nominal trading partner are designated as a *(nominal) trading partners* throughout the remainder of this book. Table 3-1 shows some examples of typical trading partner and nominal trading partner organizations found in each network zone.

The Strategic Nominal Trading Partner

Complex networks for large, multi-echelon supply bases and for international multi-echelon distribution often have a very sparse trading partner population. It is common to have one or more echelons completely populated by nominal trading partners. In some networks, an echelon with trading partners may be separated from another echelon with trading partners by an echelon of nominal trading partners. When this occurs, it may be prudent to develop a near–trading partner relationship with this strategically placed nominal trading partner. The strategic nominal trading partner is a network relationship that spans the gap between trading partners in one echelon and those in another. The strategic nominal trading partner forms a contiguous bridge for the purpose of shared forecasts, collaborative planning, and global performance measures among the trading partner core.

There normally is little economic justification for a nominal trading partner to agree to behave strategically. It is necessary to create some other incentive, such as access to different kinds of information or introductions to senior executives and to new business relationships, to foster cooperation and network loyalty. Maintaining the proper relationship with a strategic nominal trading partner may require a disproportionate amount of communication effort and face-to-face time. Otherwise, a critical network information path may break down.

The Network Orchestrator

The network orchestrator is the fourth class of organization found in a supply chain network. The orchestrator, sometimes called the *channel master*, is the one trading partner who envisions and empowers the network, gathers the trading partners into a network, leads the development of the network business strategy, and maintains alignment during network operations. The network orchestrator is the power broker within a supply chain network. Although the formation of a supply chain network is voluntary, it is important to understand the basis of the network orchestrator's power. This force drives the network's personality and work environment. In addition

TABLE 3-1
Example Network Relationships

Network Zone	Typical Trading Partners	Typical Nominal Trading Partners
Upstream	Tier-One supplier Sole source supplier Other names, depending on the industry 3rd-party logistics that blanket the zone	Single source suppliers Multiple source suppliers Technology suppliers International procurement organizations (IPO) Electronic auction service providers Logistics service providers, including carriers, freight forwarders, customs, and customs brokers Telecom and wireless service providers and internet service providers (ISP) Financial service providers Letter of credit (LOC)–issuing banks and beneficiary banks
Midstream	Original equipment manufacturers (OEM) Manufacturing centers Contract manufacturers Fabricators 3rd-party logistics that blanket the zone	Logistics service providers, including carriers, freight forwarders, customs, and customs brokers Telecom and wireless service providers and internet service providers (ISP) Technology suppliers Financial service providers Letter of credit (LOC)–issuing banks and beneficiary banks Procurement card service providers
Downstream	Large customers Retail and reseller chains Value-added resellers (VAR) Postponement centers Wholesalers Value-added distributors (VAD) Other names, depending on the industry 3rd-party logistics that blanket the zone	Small customers Small retailers and resellers Logistics service providers, including carriers, freight forwarders, customs, and customs brokers Trading companies Telecom and wireless service providers and internet service providers (ISP) Financial service providers Credit card and debit card service providers
Reverse stream	Collection centers Repair depots Remanufacturing centers Recycling centers Separators	Aftermarket customers Spare parts suppliers Smelters Recyclers Landfills Logistics service providers, including carriers, freight forwarders, customs, customs brokers, and HAZMAT transport Telecom and wireless service providers and internet service providers (ISP) Technology suppliers Financial service providers Credit card and debit card services

to holding a strategic vision for the network, the network orchestrator also controls one of the following:

- *Access to a technology*—For example, the network orchestrator owns patent rights to key intellectual property or holds an exclusive license for a technology.
- *Access to a market*—For example, the network orchestrator owns exclusive distribution rights or already controls the dominant share in a particular market.
- *Access to a scarce resource*—For example, the network orchestrator owns property rights to scarce raw materials or already employs the majority of a particular skilled labor force.
- *Access to capital*—For example, the network orchestrator has convinced venture capitalists to invest or already owns the dominant investment position.

The network orchestrator is able to set the information standard for the network and often directs the level of information technology investment needed by each network participant. As time passes, this can become a formidable barrier to the competition, and it reinforces the position of the network orchestrator.

Network Relationship Dynamics among the Trading Partners

The relationship of the trading partners alone sets the network's threshold of competitiveness. Technology and other kinds of investment cannot improve upon this foundational level of competitiveness. For example, technology cannot shorten a network when too many trading partners lengthen it. When the wrong set of trading partners is brought together in a network, technology cannot correct it. When trading partners play in multiple supply chain networks, they can become confused by conflicting sets of business rules. The competitiveness of the network is defined by how well the trading partners move a customer order to a delivery and the delivery to a cash payment. Network dynamics among the trading partners can be categorized as follows:

- *A Static network*—The same set of trading partners complete every order-to-delivery-to-cash cycle. For example, the trading partners enter an exclusive license agreement to conduct business together.
- *A Switched network*—Several trading partners are substituted from time to time to complete the order-to-delivery-to-cash cycle. For example, the product sells with two options. The components for option A are bought from supplier A; the components for option B are bought from supplier B.
- *A Chaotic network*—Different trading partners complete each order-to-delivery-to-cash cycle. For example, components are purchased through a reverse auction involving bids from a dozen suppliers.

Whether the network is static, switched, or chaotic, the network orchestrator is always one of the trading partners.

DESIGNING THE CORE NETWORK

This book is about developing the most competitive supply chain that is possible for your business situation. Borrowing a slogan from the quality gurus, you will achieve a competitive supply chain when you are "doing the right thing" in the design of your network and "doing things right" in the operation of your network. The network design presented in this book is an iterative approach involving four parts. The first part is the architecture of a core network, presented here in Chapter 3. The second part is the completion of a practical network, presented in Chapter 4. The third part is the refinement of a competitive network design using the velocity and variability principles, presented in Chapter 4. The fourth part is the optimization of the network design through a consideration of the touch points with product design and with network operations, presented in Chapters 7 and 8.

Focus on Trading Partners and the Material Flow

Start the core design of your network with a picture of your product in your customer's hands. Limit the core design to considering just the material flow among the trading partners. The network design will be completed in Chapter 4 with the addition of nominal trading partners, information flows, and cash flows. Use these three essential questions in this order to design the core network:

- *Can you reach your downstream target customer?* A company sold its products for years using its technical salespeople to visit customer engineers and capture new orders. Products were built in one location and shipped factory-direct to the end customer. Although the company was profitable, it was never able to achieve much growth in its market. It then decided to invest in the development of a new product line leveraging its technology competency into an adjacent market segment. The target market included decision makers in information systems who were not engineers and who bought through value-added resellers (VARs). The company discovered that it could not reach the new market without collaborating with a VAR channel.
- *Can you make the product midstream?* A company sold a successful line of video amplifiers that were built from fourteen-year-old technology. The solid-state electronic components inside the amplifier were assembled onto a printed circuit board using an older manufacturing technology called *through-hole printed circuit* technology. Demand exceeded the capacity to load through-hole boards, and the market was demanding miniaturization. The company decided to upgrade its design to use newer, smaller electronic components using surface mount (SMT) packaging. None of the company's manufacturing lines were capable of manufacturing SMT assemblies in volume without a significant capital investment. The company discovered that it could not build the new video amplifier design without collaborating with an SMT contract manufacturer.
- *Can you access raw materials upstream?* A company sold a family of ultra-high-precision, direct current power supplies. The precision specification

> was based upon the characteristics of a single component that had the ability to tolerate very high currents while exhibiting an ultra-low-temperature coefficient. The part did not self-heat at high current and drift out of specification. The critical part was made from a special metal alloy composition originally intended for the manufacture of strain gauges. A single ingot of this metal alloy was cast about once every eighteen months at the one foundry that knew its exact formulation. The power supply manufacturer discovered that it could not guarantee access to this critical raw material without collaborating with the foundry.

Place the organizational chart of your company and the bills of materials for your intended products side by side. Identify your target customer, and review the organizational chart to see whether your current sales organization can access this customer and whether your current distribution organization can fulfill this customer? Follow each parallel path through the BOM, and ask whether the required manufacturing processes are currently within your manufacturing organization? Review the raw materials specified in the BOM, and ask whether your organization currently purchases all of these items? If the answer to any of these questions is "no," this is the first indication that other collaborating trading partners will be required to complete the network.

Designing Downstream Fulfillment

The chain of trading partners that defines the core network is a chain of buyer–seller transactions. It is helpful to consider these sales transactions as a process that repeats when moving up or down the supply chain network. Table 3-2 outlines such a sales process. Focus on the physical distribution flow, step 5. Chapter 4 discusses the information flow, cash flow, and reverse logistics suggested by this sales process.

TABLE 3-2
Seven Step Forward Sales Process

Process Step	Description	Flow
1. Aware	The seller makes potential buyers aware of the product.	Information
2. Compare	Potential buyers compare the seller's product with the competitor's product.	Information
3. Decide	The buyer's decision-maker decides to buy.	Information
4. Order	The seller captures the buyer's order.	Information
5. Deliver	The seller delivers the product to the buyer.	Material flow
6. Pay	The seller captures the buyer's payment.	Cash
7. Reassure	The seller reassures buyers of their good decisions.	Information
	Three Step Reverse Sales Process	
8. Inform	The buyer informs the seller of a pending return.	Information
9. Return	The buyer returns the product to the seller.	Material flow
10. Refund	The buyer captures a refund from the seller.	Cash

TABLE 3-3
Order/Payment/Transportation Service Option Combinations

	Transporting Seller Provides Transportation	Transporting Buyer Provides Transportation
Ordering **Seller goes to buyer** **Paying** **Seller goes to buyer**	1. Sales force Sales rep-invoice-LTL	
Ordering **Seller goes to buyer** **Paying** **Buyer goes to seller**	2. Mail order catalog Catalog-credit card-UPS	
Ordering **Buyer goes to seller** **Paying** **Seller goes to buyer**	3. Book club Monthly sample-invoice-UPS	
Ordering **Buyer goes to seller** **Paying** **Buyer goes to seller**	4. Virtual store Self service-credit card-UPS 5. Call center Phone-credit card-UPS	6. Retail store Sales clerk-cash-carry out 7. FAX back Phone-credit card-FAX 8. Software download Self service-credit card-download

There is a continuum of commonly accepted methods for order fulfillment. Product awareness can be built in a market either passively or actively. Common examples include browsing an Internet Web site, shopping at a retail store, shopping by mail-order catalog, and meeting with a salesperson. Any design of downstream order fulfillment must consider how the customer experiences the combination of ordering, payment, and transportation options with order fulfillment. Table 3-3 summaries the eight combinations of the buyer going to the seller (passive approach) or the seller going to the buyer (active approach) for ordering, payment, and transportation. The physical distribution approach must be consistent with the customer's expectations set through the earlier steps of the sales process. For example, if the design objective is total customer convenience, at home, through a 24 hours a day, 7 days a week virtual store with easy credit or debit card payment, then customers would not expect to leave home to take delivery.

Does your current organization have a core competency in fulfillment? Do customer relationships already exist in the market segments where you intend to sell? The network design issue for the downstream zone is the determination of the least number of echelons required to connect from the midstream zone to the end customer. An echelon is created in a supply chain network when an incremental (nominal) trading partner is inserted serially into the end-to-end physical distribution flow. Each downstream echelon must add value because each echelon will take away some margin of profitability. Table 3-4 shows the physical distribution alternatives

TABLE 3-4
Physical Distribution Alternatives for the Downstream Zone Design

Organization	Number of Echelons	Reason for Inclusion
Factory-direct	Midstream-customer	Long order fulfillment cycle. Small total inventory. High margin.
Retail store	Midstream-[1]-customer	Knowledge and reach with local customers. Personalized services.
Value-added reseller	Midstream-[1]-customer	Combines components into systems and bundles services.
Dealer	Midstream-[1]-customer	Product demonstration showroom. Owns factory inventory.
Distribution direct	Midstream-[1]-customer	Shorter order fulfillment cycle. Seasonal inventory. Medium margin. Reach.
Wholesale distributor	Midstream-[2]-[1]-customer	Shorter order fulfillment cycle. Large total inventory. Low margin. Reach.
Postponement center	Midstream-[2]-[1]-customer	Product customization close to the customer.
Factory warehouse	Midstream-[2]-[1]-customer	Shorter order fulfillment cycle. Higher service levels. Seasonal inventory.
Trading company	Midstream-[3]-[2]-[1]-customer	In some countries trading companies control access to distribution.

to the number of echelons required to span from the upstream edge of the downstream zone to the downstream edge of the downstream zone. There should be a competitive reason for each echelon in the downstream zone. This may not always be the case; for example, in some countries, like Japan, a few trading companies have a stranglehold on all imports and control access to internal country distribution. This forces an additional echelon into the network design.

It is sometimes difficult to think about the core trading partner relationships in the downstream zone when the network connects with hundreds of stores and thousands of customers. The problem you are trying to solve is simply whether the downstream zone is one, two, or three echelons in length relative to each channel of distribution. Figure 3-1 shows network diagrams for four alternative physical distribution networks. Alternative A is the factory-direct distribution model. There are no additional echelons of distribution between the factory and the end-customer. Alternative B is the factory-indirect model. Here a store, reseller, or dealer comes between the factory and the end-customer. Alternative C is the multi-echelon single factory indirect model. An additional echelon of distribution or postponement is added between the factory and the end-customer to increase the geographical reach of the supply chain across its target market. Alternative D is the multi-echelon, multiple factory indirect model. This is a commonly used global approach where supply reach is kept within a geographical super-region. For example, one factory supplies the needs of Europe, a second factory supplies the needs of the Americas, and a third factory supplies the needs of Asia and the Pacific. A distribution example

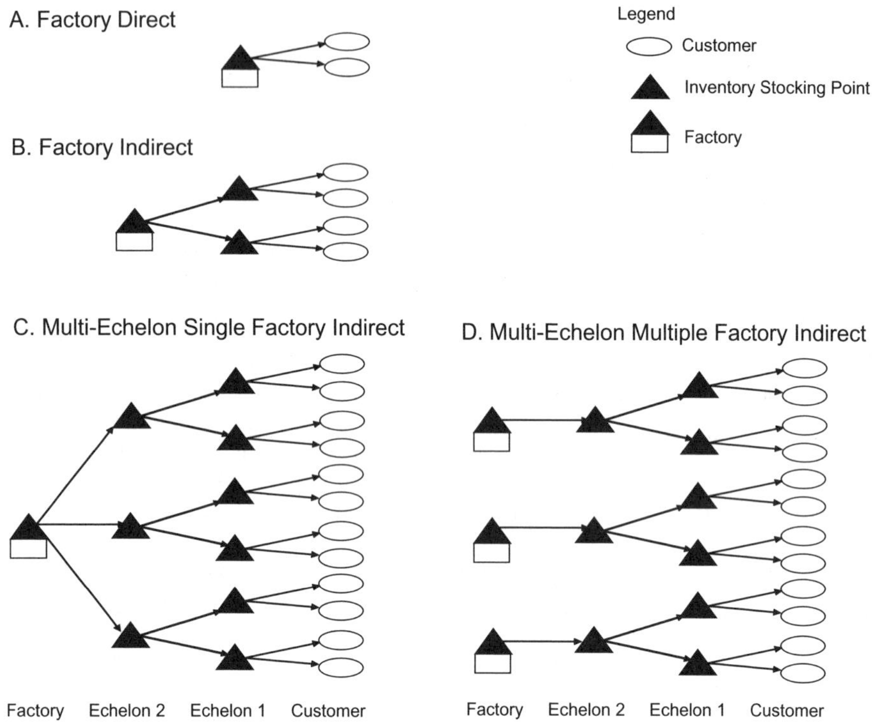

FIGURE 3-1 Distribution network alternatives.

involving a trading company is not shown. Three-echelon distribution should be avoided because it lengthens the supply chain, reducing responsiveness, reducing profitability, and adding inventory.

The customer experiences the design of the downstream zone through trade-offs in product pricing, delivery lead-time, and service levels. The trading partners experience the design of the downstream zone through trade-offs in transportation modes and warehouse locations, total logistics cost, and inventory investment. These trade-offs are complex and depend on situational specifics, such as the number of customers in the service area, the pairing of origins with destinations, the weight and cubic volume of the packaged product, the service level expected by the customer, delivery expectations set by the competition, etc.

Consider the following trade-offs when deciding on a core set of trading partners in the design of the downstream zone. Keep in mind that it may be necessary to use different configurations to reach different market segments.

- *Market segment geography*—Is your target market local or regional, domestic or international?
- *Downstream edge access of the downstream zone*—Can you reach every possible end customer with your physical distribution?

- *Country-specific requirements*—Does the country own or regulate the distribution channel?
- *Product demonstration*—Do you require shelf or floor space to demonstrate the product and brand?
- *Service level*—Can you achieve the desired balance of order-to-delivery time to network inventory?
- *Coordinated delivery*—Are you coordinating a consolidated customer delivery from multiple manufacturing or warehousing locations or coordinating simultaneous deliveries to multiple customer locations?
- *Bundled services*—Are you bundling services such as software, installation, or financing?
- *Warehouse site location*—Is there a strategic supplier or transportation connection that dominates the warehouse site location decision?
- *Public versus private warehousing*—Does your business have exclusive use of the warehouse, or is it shared by other organizations?
- *Special handling requirements*—Are there special handling requirements such as refrigerated transportation or climate-controlled warehousing?
- *Defocusing effect*—Are any of your downstream trading partners also trading partners in larger, independent supply chain networks that work to defocus your network strategy?
- *Comingling of the reverse supply chain*—Are you using a common warehouse or distribution center for fulfillment and returns or recycling?
- *Markup*—Can you afford the markup required by the number of downstream echelons?
- *Upstream edge access of the downstream zone*—Can you gain country access for each preferred distribution channel?
- *Supply chain length*—A shorter supply chain network is generally a more competitive supply chain network. Can you justify the value-adding proposition for each echelon in the downstream network?

Figures 3-2 and 3-3 show the decision logic used to determine the need for zero, one, two, or three echelons of trading partners to support the physical flow in the downstream zone of a supply chain network. The decision trees in these figures read from top to bottom. Each "yes or no" decision should be decided in the order shown on the decision tree. If there is more than one valid reason to add an echelon in the set of decisions between each pair of dashed horizontal lines, then only one new trading partner relationship needs to be added. In some cases, the boxes show how an issue can be remedied without having to add a new relationship. If there are no valid reasons to add an echelon in the set of decisions between each pair of dashed horizontal lines, then skip that echelon. Keep in mind that a legitimate need to add an echelon may insert nominal trading partners in the downstream zone. The design goal is to minimize the total number of downstream echelons and to have every downstream echelon populated by at least one trading partner.

Consider the following practical example: A well-known merchandiser sells men and women's clothing by mail-order catalog. Because many of the items are seasonal, catalogs are printed and mailed once a month. Over the years, this merchandiser has

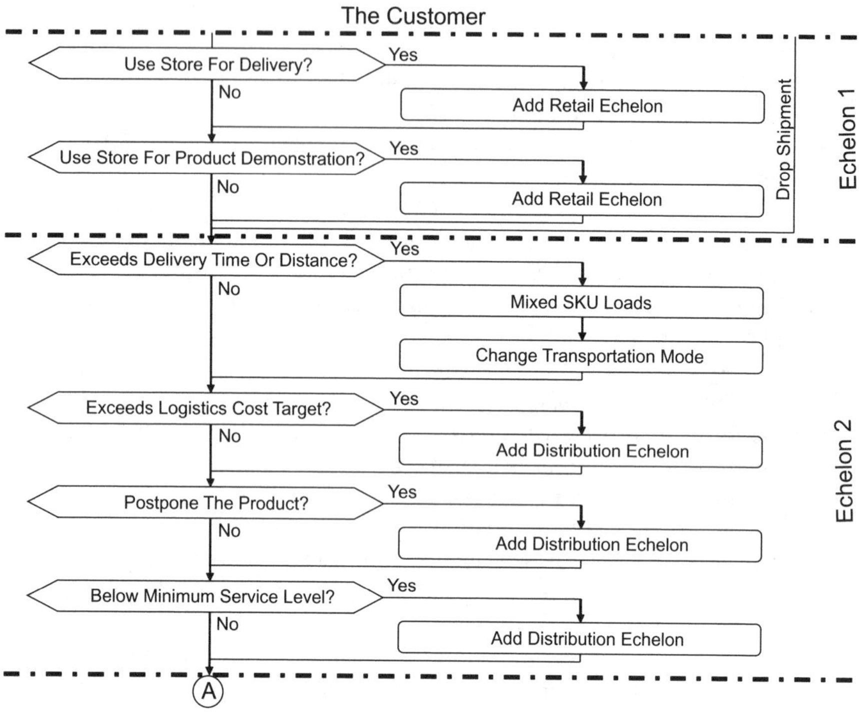

FIGURE 3-2 Downstream decision logic for echelon 1 and echelon 2 trading partners.

honed its process for list management to ensure its expensive, 136-page catalogs go primarily to customers who have made a purchase in the last three years and to new customers selected from qualified, purchased lists. The business is organized around its Midwest distribution center, and customers are given a choice of three-day UPS Ground delivery or UPS Next Day Air delivery for a premium price. The business employs a cadre of experience buyers who purchase finished goods in advance of the season from apparel manufacturers around the world. The Midwest distribution center is the single downstream echelon between the apparel manufacturer and the customer.

This merchandiser offers customized services of their product in the form of monogramming initials on shirts, inseaming pants, and gift wrapping. Each of these is a postponement operation tied to a specific, shippable customer order. Because the monogramming, inseaming, and gift wrapping each are done within the distribution center by the merchandiser's own employees, the postponement does not add an additional echelon.

Historically the mail-order catalog included an order form that would be mailed to the Midwest distribution center along with a personal check. As time went on, customers calling a toll-free 1-800 number and using their credit card to place their orders replaced a majority of the mailed-in orders. Customers appreciated the convenience of the call center being operated 24 hours a day, 7 days a week. Moreover,

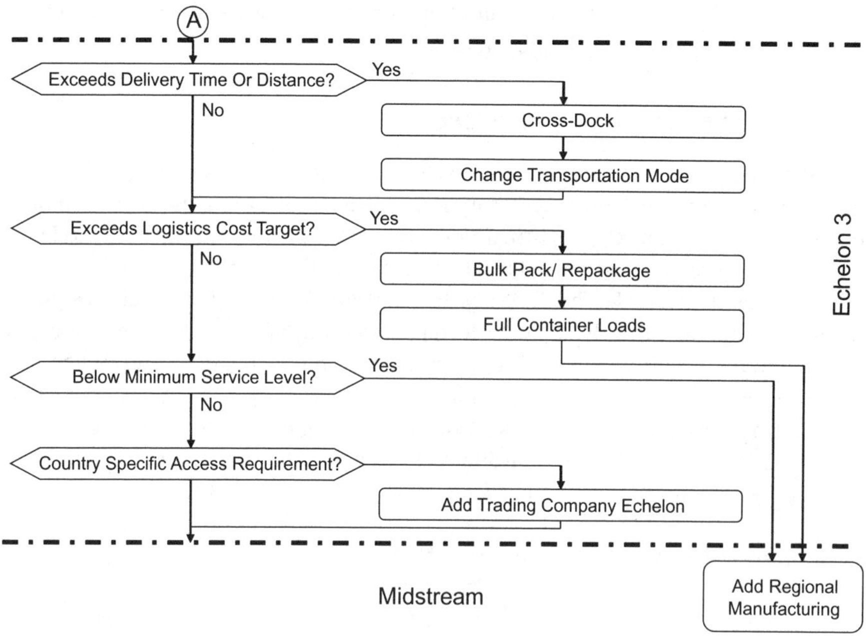

FIGURE 3-3 Downstream decision logic for an echelon 3 trading partner.

customers really appreciated being able to talk with a call center employee to verify they were taking their own measurements the right way to order the correct sizes of apparel. (The information order flow and cash flow are topics discussed in Chapter 4.)

More recently, the merchandiser has expanded its channels of distribution to include a virtual store on the Internet. Customers are now able to shop through an electronic catalog, check that items are in stock, and place their orders electronically using a secure link for credit card information. Customers can even connect and talk with a company employee over the Internet to verify clothing sizes. The virtual store raises two new distribution issues: The first is that the merchandiser must be careful managing the potential for channel conflict between its mail order business and its Internet business. The two channels have different sales strategies and different cost structures that must be kept in balance in order for the company to maintain its profitability. The second is that the virtual store opens the merchandiser up to a customer base that is worldwide rather than domestic. Foreign language translation, foreign currencies, appropriate duties and taxes, extended transit times, and the need to design a logistics infrastructure to reach any customer destination suddenly become relevant issues.

Finally, this merchandiser has always had an easy returns policy. Although the reverse stream zone is discussed in detail later in this chapter, it is important to note here that the business also operates an alternative downstream channel in the form of a small number of outlet stores. These outlet stores are used, in part, to sell inventory overruns and apparel returns at a markdown into a different customer segment. The supply chain network through these outlet stores is two echelons for overruns and three echelons for returns including [1]Midwest distribution center, [0/1]customer return, and [1]outlet store.

Designing Midstream Manufacturing

The next step in defining a core network of trading partners is to determine the minimum number of echelons necessary to implement the physical distribution flow in the midstream zone. The midstream manufacturing process must be able to build a mix of standard and customized products across multiple product lines and in the unit volumes demanded. The BOM is the unifying factor binding the design of the midstream zone. Ideally, a single factory organization can manufacture the full range of BOM's. This would lead to a single echelon midstream design. When this is not the case, the midstream grows in its number of echelons and in its complexity.

Building on the different levels of revenue aggregation described in Table 2-3 in Chapter 2, the set of products available for delivery through a downstream zone can be grouped into the following hierarchy:

- *Business unit*—One or more product lines.
- *Product line*—One or more product families.
- *Product family*—One or more base products with or without product customization.
- *Product customization*—A different configuration of the base product involving a change of features, functions, or packaging.
- *Private label*—A product uniquely labeled and packaged for a specific customer.
- *Stock Keeping Unit (SKU)*—The unique combination of a product, its packaging, and a receiving distribution center. For example, a six pack of 12 oz. bottles of Budweiser beer going to a distribution center in North Carolina is a different SKU than a six pack of 12 oz. bottles of Budweiser beer going to a distribution center in Ohio, which is a different SKU than a twelve pack of 12 oz. bottles going to the same distribution center.
- *Base product*—A complete, standalone product.
- *Product subassembly or module*—A partial assembly of a base product that may be sold separately.
- *Spares*—Components of the complete product that are sold separately for repair and maintenance.
- *Consumables*—Disposable, ancillary items required for the operation of the primary product. Examples include film, paper, toner, ink, oil, etc.

The manufacturing scope of the midstream zone must be established first before determining the core midstream trading partners. In the simplest case every base product, product customization, product family, and product line is manufactured by a single midstream factory. However, this might not be the most competitive arrangement. For example, products with a high level of feature and function customization or with a proliferation of packaging configurations might have the final stages of their manufacture completed through postponement within downstream distribution. This effectively moves a portion of the midstream manufacturing BOM downstream. For example, some electronic instruments look like complete base products but are truly "dumb" instruments until customer-specific firmware is burned into their read-only memories at a distribution postponement center. Some beers brewed in Europe are shipped to the United States in bulk liquid containers for regional bottling.

Manufacturers for low-volume, high-mix businesses sometimes find that their products are not cost competitive at the low end or technologically competitive at the high end of their markets. These manufacturers broaden their product catalogs by licensing complementary products from other supply chain networks. For example, a U. S. manufacturer of 200 watt to 2 kilowatt power supplies licenses a Taiwanese power supply manufacturer to produce product in the range of 10 watts to 100 watts, providing a more complete catalog for one-stop shopping. The U. S. manufacturer is unable to achieve the Taiwanese cost of goods sold at 10 watts, and the Taiwanese manufacturer is unable to achieve the product performance level at 2 kilowatts. The licensing agreement also provides a degree of local content that makes it easier for the U. S. manufacturer to sell into Asian markets. Figure 3-4 shows how a product line with several product families is implemented through a combination of downstream customization and midstream third-party licensing.

Additional trading partner factories might be added within the same midstream echelon to multiply the total capacity to build the product. For example, if demand for a product doubles and then doubles again, a factory running a double shift at full capacity will not be able to keep up. A second factory will have to be brought on-line. In another example, there may be delivery time, local content, or logistics cost reasons to comanufacture the same product at a plant in North America, a second plant in Europe, and a third Asia-Pacific plant.

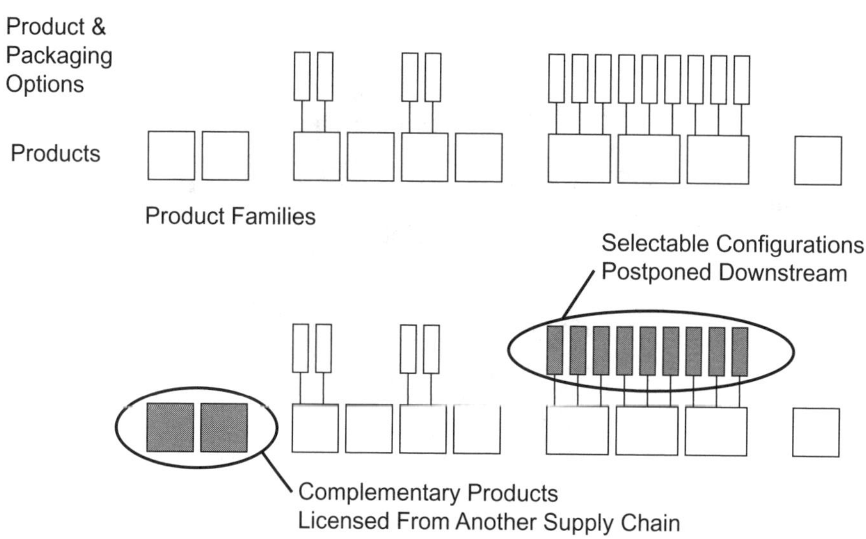

FIGURE 3-4 Midstream manufacturing scope.

Lower level fabrication processes may fall outside of a manufacturer's core competency or lower level labor-intensive assembly may be produced more cost competitively elsewhere. The manufacturer may decide to outsource a portion of the lower level BOM to a contract manufacturer. When the BOM is deep with many lower levels, the manufacturer may choose to partner with an upstream Tier-One supplier who can integrate the lower level complexity into a single line-item purchase for the midstream manufacturer. This effectively moves a portion of the midstream manufacturing BOM upstream. For example, in the automotive industry engines and transmissions are purchased as single components. The midstream car assembly plants look at their Tier-One supplier of engines and their Tier-One supplier of transmissions as though they were purchasing a single component. These upstream Tier-One suppliers manage the hundreds of items and multiple echelons of smaller suppliers necessary to build an engine or a transmission.

Scoping midstream manufacturing is a little like serving a birthday cake. Once the best parts of the icing, the corner slices, and the pieces of the bottom layer are handed out to the guests, there is not as much of the cake left to eat. Once postponement and repackaging is moved downstream, the product line extremes are licensed midstream, and lower level fabrication is outsourced upstream, there is not as much of the product line left to manufacture. Figure 3-5 is a three-dimensional representation, and Figure 3-6 is the corresponding decision logic of how to scope the midstream-manufacturing core.

Once the scope of the midstream manufacturing is decided, the next issue is the number of echelons required to span the midstream. The answer again lies with the bill of materials. A single factory is generally organized around a set of manufacturing processes and core competencies to produce an A-type BOM, an I-type BOM,

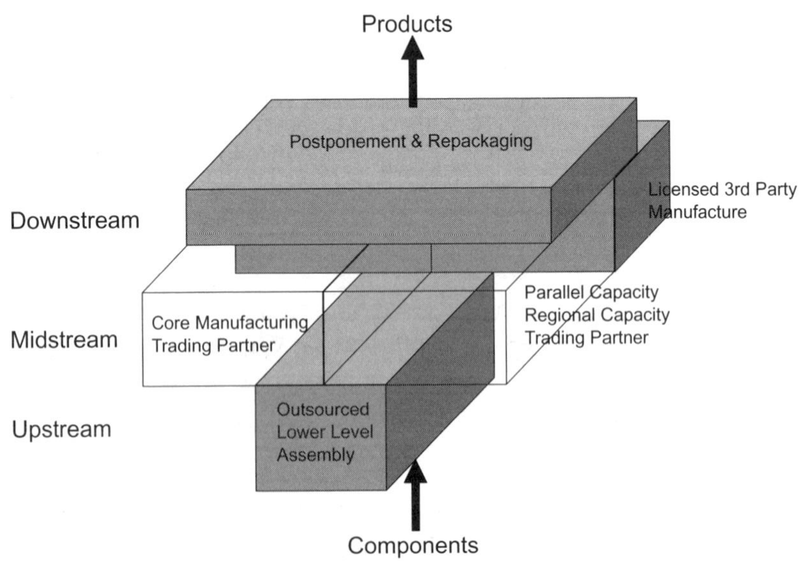

FIGURE 3-5 Scoping the midstream manufacturing core.

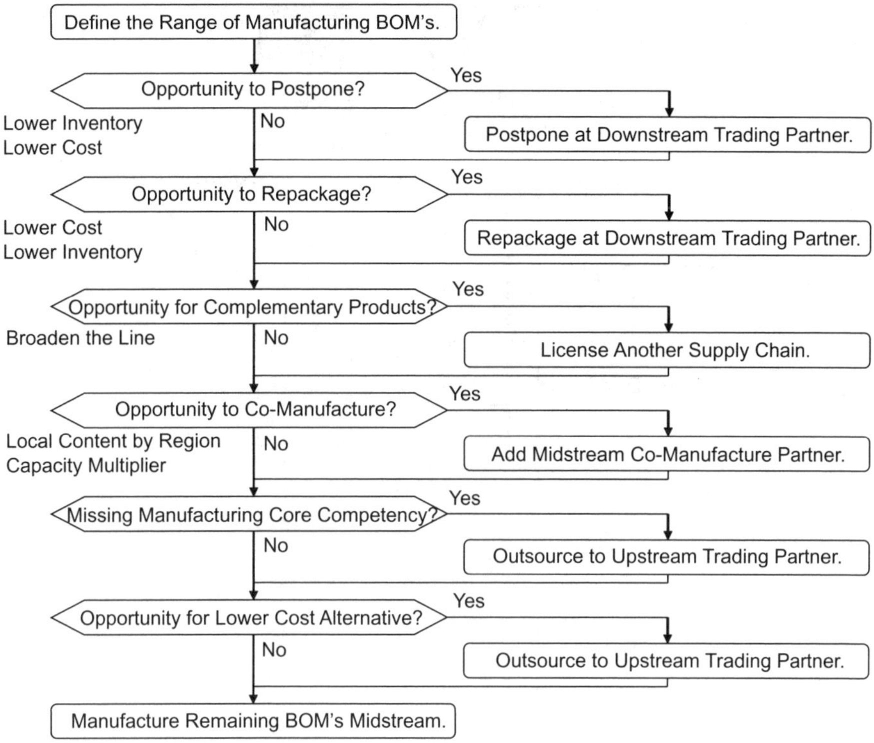

FIGURE 3-6 Midstream trading partner decision logic.

a T-type BOM, or a V-type BOM. When BOM types are mixed within the same factory, the manufacturing production cost and the level of inventory investment increases. This is because the inventory planning and control system and the material handling system are somewhat defocused to handle different situations. At a minimum, each BOM type should be produced in separate production areas that are tailored by type. Products that fall outside the sweet spot of the manufacturing process, because their BOM is radically different, require extra training, extra coordination, and extra handling. There is also a high probability that product quality will suffer because of the additional manufacturing complexity. Figure 3-7 shows the midstream configuration for an A-type, I-type, T-type, and V-type BOM.

The vertical integration of all the BOM levels within a single factory yields a single echelon midstream. This is the simplest midstream configuration and is the starting point for adding complexity. The core manufacturing processes for the single plant need to be well defined. When the product BOM begins to push the envelope of manufacturing competency and production cost, it is time to consider subcontracting and outsourcing alternatives. For example, the product design requires soldering numerous thick-leaded components into a printed circuit board when the standard process is a fixed-speed wave solder machine. With the thicker leads the solder wave does not wick properly, causing the solder joints to be brittle and unreliable. In another example, the final assembly of the product's cabinetry requires welding, but the

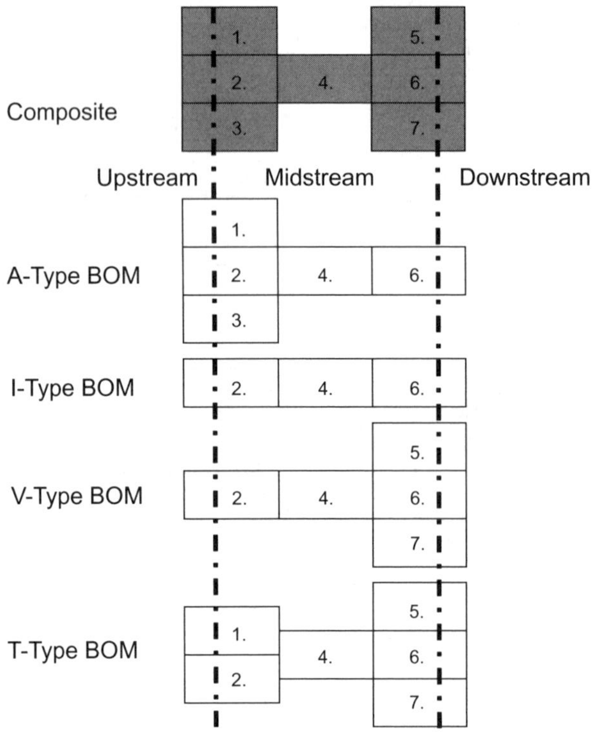

FIGURE 3-7 Manufacturing configurations for the A, I, T, and V-type BOM.

standard manufacturing process was designed to use only hardware fasteners. When the missing core competency adds an organization in series with the main manufacturing process, another echelon of (nominal) trading partner is added to the midstream. When the missing core competency adds another organization in parallel with the main manufacturing process, another (nominal) trading partner is added to the midstream without adding an echelon. Table 3-5 details the number of trading partner additions and echelon additions for each of these configuration changes.

Consider the following trade-offs when deciding on a core set of trading partners in the design of the midstream zone. Chapter 4 covers the income statement implications, and Chapter 7 covers the balance sheet implications when the BOM splits between (nominal) trading partners.

- *Product range*—What is the range of product lines, product customization, product families, and base products that need to be manufactured?
- *A-type, I-type, T-type, or V-type bills of materials*—Which BOM configuration(s) does the midstream manufacturing need to support for each product line?
- *In-sourcing versus outsourcing of core competencies*—Have you identified missing core competencies in the manufacturing organization?

TABLE 3-5
Midstream Manufacturing Configurations

Midstream Design	Adds Echelon Midstream	Adds (Nominal) Trading Partner
Repackage within distribution	No	No—Existing TP
Postpone within distribution	No	No—Existing TP
Missing manufacturing competency added in parallel	No	Yes
License from another supply chain	No	Yes
Comanufacture to multiply capacity	No	Yes
Comanufacture for local content	No	Yes
Missing manufacturing competency added in series	Yes	Yes
Outsource upstream	Yes	Yes
Repartition the lower level BOM to an upstream supplier	No	No—Existing TP

- *Single or parallel manufacturing*—Is there a competitive capacity advantage to comanufacture the same product at more than one location?
- *Centralized versus decentralized manufacturing*—Is there a competitive advantage to centralizing or decentralizing manufacturing support functions in the network?
- *International manufacturing*—Is there a competitive advantage to having local content in a particular region of the world?
- *Country Of Origin (COO)*—Is there a competitive advantage to building the product in some other country?
- *Complementary products*—Are you licensing complementary products from another supply chain network to round out your product offering?
- *Manufacturing site location*—Is there a strategic raw material, supplier, labor pool, or transportation connection that dominates the manufacturing site location decision?
- *Downstream edge of the midstream zone*—Are you postponing or repackaging the product within the downstream distribution channel?
- *Upstream edge of the midstream zone*—Are you purchasing major subassemblies within the upstream supply base, such as using a Tier-One supplier to manufacture lower levels of the BOM?
- *Foldback paths*—Are there wrap-around or foldback paths in the physical distribution flow?
- *Comingling the reverse supply chain*—Do the manufacturing sites also process product returns?
- *Defocusing effect*—Are any of the midstream trading partners also manufacturing for other independent or competing supply chain networks that will work to defocus your network strategy?
- *Supply chain length*—A shorter supply chain network is always a more competitive supply chain network. Can you justify the value-adding proposition for each echelon in the midstream network?

TABLE 3-6
The Product Catalog

Component	Description	Combinatons
Monitors	None, 17 inch, 19 inch, and 21 inch	4
Flat panel displays	None, 15 inch, and 17 inch	3
Mice	Optical and wireless	2
Keyboards	Standard and ergonomic	2
Desktops	2 Speeds of Intel Processors, 2 Sizes of DRAM memory	4
Hard drives	20 gigabyte, 30 gigabyte, and 60 gigabyte	3
CD/DVD drives	CD-read/write and CD-RW/DVD combo	2
Inkjet printers	None, personal, professional, combination print/scan/FAX	4
Laser printers	None, personal, and workgroup	3
Laptops	Screen size, processor speed, hard drive, battery capacity	5
Preloaded software	Microsoft Windows, Microsoft Explorer	1
Application software	Microsoft...Adobe...Norton...etc.	14
Game software	A wide variety	25

The following example puts the theory into practice: A personal computer manufacturer must decide how to organize its manufacturing capacity. The company is positioning itself to be "one-stop shopping" for a full line of computer hardware, software, and peripherals. Marketing has determined from customer surveys that the product catalog should include the items listed in Table 3-6.

The proposed product catalog splits naturally into two product lines: desktop solutions and laptop solutions. Next, engineering and marketing work out the sets of allowable configurations for the desktop computers and for the laptops, see Table 3-7.

The software permutations are handled within the downstream zone on a pick-to-order basis at the store level. The distribution center is responsible for ordering and stocking each of the 39 SKU's directly from one of six software vendors. The SKU's are shipped in cartons of 24. Each software box is display ready for the reseller's shelf. Customers are responsible for installing the software themselves; service support is available should a problem arise. This leaves 13,824 desktop combinations and 960 laptop combinations to be organized. Each hardware component is displayed at the store. But the store has limited storage space and will stock only a small quantity of the fastest-moving SKU's. When a customer places a personal computer order, the hardware is drop-shipped from the distribution center.

The monitors, displays, and printers are bought into downstream distribution as complete components from other independent supply chains. The monitors are the assembly of a power supply, a printed circuit assembly (PCA), a cathode ray tube (CRT), and a plastic housing. The displays are the assembly of a power supply, a PCA, a flat panel, and a plastic case. The monitors and displays are sold with multilingual instruction manuals and cables that plug directly into the desktop or laptop. The inkjet printers are the assembly of a power supply, a PCA, a print mechanism, and

TABLE 3-7
Allowable Product Configurations

Component	Product Line: Desktop Solutions Number of Stock-Keeping Units	Product Line: Laptop Solutions Number of Stock-Keeping Units
Monitors	4	4
Flat panel displays	3	
Mice	2	2
Keyboards	2	
Desktops	4	
Hard drives	3	
CD/DVD drives	2	2
Inkjet printers	4	4
Laser printers	3	3
Laptops		5
Preloaded software	1	1
Hardware SKU combinations	13,824	960
Application software	14	14
Game software	25	25
Software SKU permutations	Too many to think about	

a plastic cover. The inkjet nozzle is an integral part of the replaceable print cartridge. The laser printers are the assembly of a power supply, a PCA, a laser engine, a paper handling mechanism, and a plastic case. The toner cartridge is manufactured separately. After assembly the inkjet and laser printers flow through a postponement center where local language instruction manuals and country-specific line cords are added prior to shipment.

The five models of laptop computer are bought under a licensing agreement with a contract manufacturer (CM) in Malaysia. The CM manufactures the laptops to the company's design and brands the laptops with the company brand. The CD/DVD and hard drives are preselected by laptop model but are customer installable on the desktop models. The CD/DVD drives ship to both the laptop CM and the downstream distribution center whereas the hard drives ship to the laptop CM and the computer manufacturer. Both kinds of drives are assembled from mechanical components and electronic PCA's. The shaded network nodes in Figure 3-8 show how much the overall midstream complexity of the desktop solutions and the laptop solutions product lines has been pared back using independent supply chains and licensing agreements. The downstream distribution center needs to have a core competency in procurement and in high quality pick and pack operations.

The remaining non-shaded nodes reveal two echelons of value-adding trading partners in the midstream. The computer manufacturer assembles the desktop computer; it has also decided to in-source assembly of the optical and wireless mice plus the standard and ergonomic keyboards. The second echelon is a PCA fabricator with

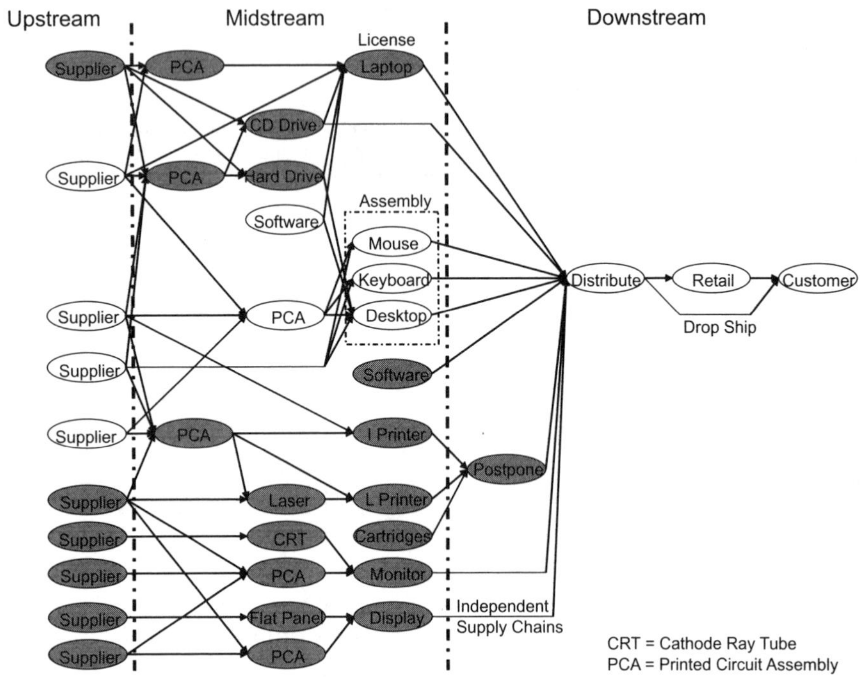

FIGURE 3-8 Supply chain network for a personal computer manufacturer.

the surface mount processing equipment to load the memory chips, memory controller chips, and Intel Pentium processors onto printed circuit boards. The network diagram shows a total of six different PCA fabricators. Here is an opportunity to consolidate the PCA Fabricators. Both the laptop CM and the computer manufacturer buy and load operating system software from Microsoft.

Designing the Upstream Supply Base

Another step in defining a core network of trading partners is to determine the minimum number of echelons necessary to implement the physical distribution flow in the upstream zone. The upstream zone connects with all of the suppliers that are specified in the item master for each product BOM. The design of the upstream supply base is directly tied to the complexity of the number of line items in the item master. There are many paths through a product BOM. Each path terminates upstream. In some cases, more than one component can be purchased from a common supplier or a supplier's distributor. Most of the supply base will turn out to be nominal trading partners. The organizations in the supply base that will be trading partners or strategic nominal trading partners are those suppliers who can provide a number of different components at a consolidated volume and those suppliers who provide a few strategic components that set the price–performance point of the

TABLE 3-8
A Strategy for Segmenting the Item Master

BOM Level	Network Relationships	
Subassembly and assembly	Manufactured midstream, or uses a Tier-One supplier upstream	
	Common to Many Products	**Unique to One Product**
Commodity component	• Consolidate by commodity • Upstream (nominal) trading partner relationships	• Minimize by commodity to reduce issues around mix • Small purchasing power • Nominal trading partner
Strategic component	• Determines the product price–performance point • Probably sole-sourced • Treat as a trading partner	• Work to eliminate from the product BOM • Probably sole-sourced • Strategic nominal trading partner, depending on revenue
Strategic raw material	Develop strategic relationships back into farming or mining, as required.	

product, see Table 3-8. The network relationship for a strategic nominal trading partner must be cultivated as though it were a trading partner. Too much revenue is at stake to do otherwise.

Suppliers sell and distribute to their midstream and reverse stream customers in multiple ways, see Table 3-9. In this table, the type of supplier from the top half of the table is combined with the type of supplier distribution from the bottom half of the table to determine the total number of upstream echelons. For example from the top and bottom of the Table 3-9, a single source supplier who distributes directly to the midstream adds one echelon in the upstream zone, RM-[1]-Midstream. In a second example, a multiple source supplier selling through a distributor adds two echelons in the upstream zone, RM-[1]-[2]-Midstream. Other exceptions that effectively add echelons to the upstream zone include suppliers subcontracting an operation and strategic suppliers dependent upon constrained raw materials that must be mapped back into farming or mining. Two examples of subcontracted operations for a metal fabricator might include subcontracted painting because an inferior in-house process causes flaking and subcontracted plating because an inferior in-house process causes rusting.

It is sometimes difficult to think about the core trading partner relationships in the upstream zone when the item master specifies thousands of components and hundreds of suppliers. The network design problem is simply to minimize the number of upstream echelons. Pay attention to these four different paths through the BOM that have revenue risk and inventory investment implications. Which path supports the highest dollar revenue of end products? Which path contains the highest dollar value component? Which path has the longest cumulative lead-time? Which path is the most strategic in the sense of setting the product's price–performance point in the marketplace? Use the decision logic of Figure 3-9 to analyze the item master for a product line.

TABLE 3-9
Network Design Alternatives in the Upstream Zone

Organization	Number of Echelons	Reason For Inclusion
Farming/mining	Earth-[0]-[1]-	There is some compelling supply reason to include farming or mining processes rather than starting with raw materials.
Sole source	RM-[1]-	Access to the only supplier able to produce the component due to process, material, or patented technology.
Spot source	RM-[1]-	Supply auction or other opportunistic access to a supply of the item.
Lifetime buy	A single purchase covers the entire product life cycle. This should be treated as an existing inventory location and not as an upstream supplier.	
Single source	RM-[1]- RM-[1]-	Access to the preferred of two or more suppliers able to produce the item.
Multiple source	RM-[1]- RM-[1]- RM-[1]-	Access to one of many suppliers capable of producing a commodity item.
Subcontractor	RM-[1]-[2]-	A process step is carried out by another organization in series.
	Combines with...	
Supplier direct	-Midstream -Reverse stream	The supplier connects directly with the midstream or reverse stream.
Supplier warehouse	-[2]-Midstream -[2]-Reverse stream	A supplier owned warehouse separates the seller and buyer.
Supply distributor	-[2]-Midstream -[2]-Reverse stream	A 3rd-party distributor separates the seller and the buyer. The distributor may provide value-added services.
Tier-One supplier	-[2]-I -[2]-I-[3]-Midstream -[2]-I	A key supplier manages a group of lower level suppliers that perform fabrication and assembly.

Consider the following trade-offs when deciding on a core set of trading partners in the design of the upstream zone:

- *Downstream edge of the upstream zone*—Is any of the supply base connected to multiple midstream or reverse stream echelons? Can you identify inventory locations that mark the edge of the zone?
- *Tier-One supplier*—Does any supplier coordinate and manage lower levels of the product BOM?
- *Subcontract operations*—Does any supplier subcontract value-adding process steps to another organization?
- *Cross-channeling*—Is any supplier in an exclusively regional network expected to supply other regions for capacity or continuity of supply reasons?

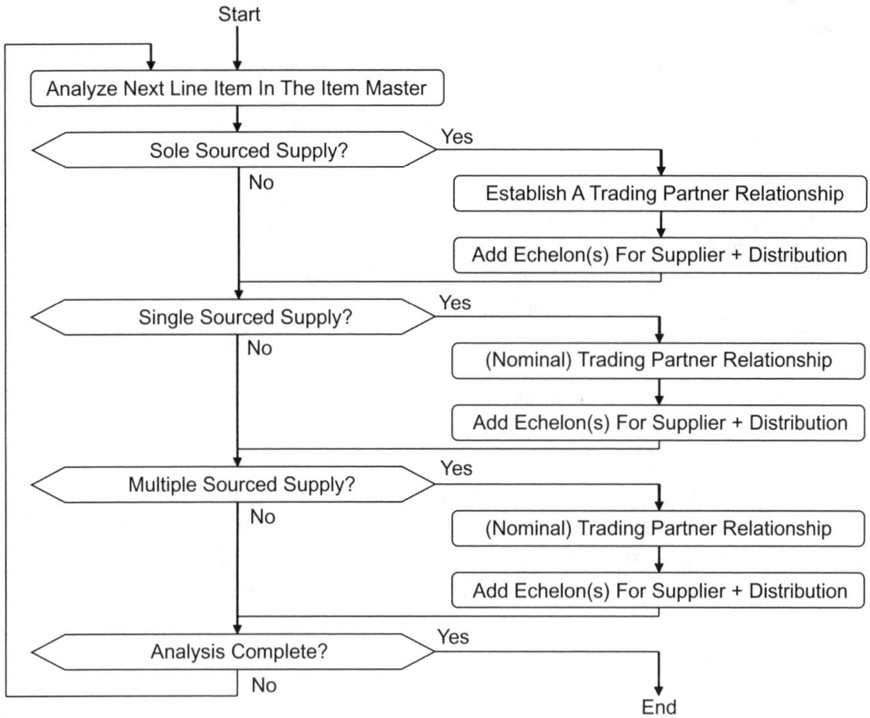

FIGURE 3-9 Upstream trading partner decision logic.

- *Spot auctions*—Is any supplier connected to the network on an opportunistic basis?
- *Source for spare parts*—Is any supplier connected into the reverse stream network?
- *Lifetime buys*—A lifetime buy is a single purchase. Should any supplier be considered as an inventory location rather than as a network connection?
- *Last time buy*—A last time buy is the last purchase. Is any supplier scheduled to be disconnected from the network?
- *Geographical dispersion of the supply base*—How does the network connect with each supplier?
- *Upstream edge of the upstream zone*—What does your industry consider to be "raw materials?" Is there a compelling strategic or constraint reason to include echelons connecting to farming or mining?

The following industrial electronics example puts the theory into practice, see Table 3-10: Each row in this item master represents a unique component required in the BOM. Its item number, component type, description, and cost identify the component. The last three columns on the right document the approved supplier list for this BOM. One, two, or three approved suppliers are listed in these columns,

TABLE 3-10
An Example Industrial Electronics Item Master Listing

Item #	Type	Description	Cost	Preferred	Approved	Approved
160-9203	Capacitor	1600 uF, 2.1A_{rms}	$3.250	UCC		
698-2439	Resistor	1 K ohm, 1%	$0.043	Vishay	KOA speer1	
757-0015	Resistor	1.1 K ohm, 10%	$0.034	KOA Speer	Vishay	
820-1922	Digital IC	Quad Flip-Flop	$0.112	Fairchild	TI	On Semi
820-1925	Digital IC	Hex Nor Gate	$0.085	Fairchild	TI	On Semi
826-0124	Linear IC	Quad Amplifier	$2.335	LTC		Analog Dev

depending on whether the component is multiple sourced. The supplier listed in the left column is the preferred supplier. The United Chemi-Con capacitor supplier is a sole source for a high-volume, expensive part and should be managed as a trading partner. This capacitor has certain characteristics that set the price–performance point of the end product. The digital integrated circuits are multiple sourced. If many other components in the product line are also sourced from Fairchild (alternatively TI or On Semiconductor), then Fairchild may be a trading partner based on its total in-network dollar volume; otherwise it will be a nominal trading partner. The product line uses such a small number of quad amplifiers that even though the component is expensive, LTC (alternatively Analog Devices) is a nominal trading partner. Although Analog Devices also produces the quad amplifier, this component is single sourced to Linear Technologies Corporation for business reasons. Analog Devices is listed in the extreme right column.

These suppliers became approved by being qualified against a set of business, quality, and manufacturing process criteria that satisfy the requirements of the product design. Purchasing is expected to buy from the preferred supplier first and to switch to an approved supplier only when a preferred supplier cannot fulfill the order. Sometimes the BOM tree should be pruned back. The consolidation and elimination of nominal trading partner suppliers is a powerful idea when rationalizing a supply base. For example, take a closer look at the two resistors in Table 3-10. The 1 K ohm resistor from Vishay is about one cent more expensive than the KOA Speer resistor because it has a tighter tolerance. However, if the 1 K ohm 1% resistor can be used to replace the 1.1 K ohm 10% resistor in the product design, then the supply chain network needs to be connected with only one supplier, not two. This eliminates the planning, ordering, logistics, accounts payable, and inventory locations associated with the second supplier. Supply base rationalization should be done concurrently with the upstream network design.

Designing the Reverse Stream

The final step in defining a core network of trading partners is to determine the configuration necessary to implement the physical distribution flow in the reverse stream zone. The reverse stream zone is like a flower with four petals, see Figure 3-10. Working clockwise around the flower's center, the petals represent collections from the

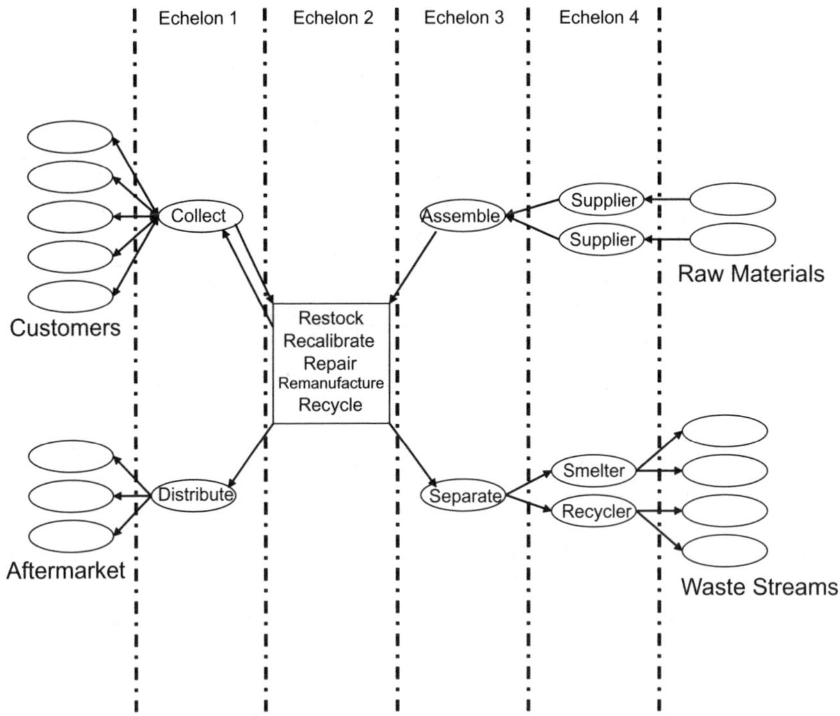

FIGURE 3-10 Reverse stream network echelons.

installed customer base, spare parts supply for repairs, the recycling of waste streams, and distribution into an aftermarket for remanufacturing. The center of the flower is the core process for restocks, recalibration and repair, remanufacture, and recycling. In Figure 3-10 four echelons of (nominal) trading partners connect the installed customer base and aftermarket on the left with raw materials and the waste streams on the right.

The intent of the reverse stream determines which of the petals are implemented see Table 3-11. Three petal network configurations with connections to the installed base, to raw materials, and to waste streams are common. The fourth petal connection to an aftermarket appears in remanufacturing networks and in distribution networks for industries involving large customer returns. For example, magazine and book publishing, greeting cards, catalogue retailers, personal computers, and music CD-ROM's each have return percentages greater than 20%. Product returned from a customer for no apparent reason and within a predetermined period such as 30 days is inspected upon receipt. If the product packaging is unopened and the product shows no sign of tampering, it may be repackaged and put back on the distributor's shelf as a new unit. If the package has been opened and the product is in excellent condition, it may be possible to refurbish the product and resell it at a lower price into a different market. If the package has been opened and the product is damaged, it may be necessary to scrap the product and recycle its raw materials.

TABLE 3-11
Reverse Stream Connections with Downstream Fulfillment

Operation	Connect with Installed Base	Connect with Aftermarket	Connect with Raw Materials	Connect with Waste Streams
Restock	Yes	Yes—used	Yes—packaging	Yes—scrap
Recall	Yes	No	Yes	Yes—scrap
Recalibrate	Yes—loaner	No	Yes—packaging	No
Repair	Yes—loaner	No	Yes—spare parts packaging	Yes—spent parts
Remanufacture	Yes—cores	Yes—rebuilt	Yes—spare parts packaging	Yes—scrap
Recycle	Yes	No	No	Yes
Quality defect reverse stream network connections with midstream manufacture				
Quality defect reverse stream network connections with upstream transformation				

Referring again to Figure 3-10, Echelon 1 includes a trading partner to collect product and loaner returns from the installed customer base and to distribute loaners to the installed customer base. Echelon 1 may also include a trading partner to distribute remanufactured product into an aftermarket. When the installed base of customers is global, additional echelons and (nominal) trading partners may be required to reach the geographical extremes of customer locations. Echelon 2 is the trading partner performing the decisions and processes to restock, recalibrate, repair, remanufacture, or recycle. Echelon 3 includes trading partners performing the assembly of lower level components and spare parts. This connection is often directly coupled with the forward supply chain where production is scheduled to cover both the customer demand plus a forecast of the spare parts demand. Echelon 3 also includes one or more trading partners to disassemble and separate subassemblies, components, and parts made of the same basic raw material, like copper, aluminum, gold, etc. The purpose of the separators is to increase the purity of each waste stream in order to improve the economic value of the reclamation. Echelon 4 includes component suppliers for spare parts and smelters or other recyclers emptying directly into waste streams and landfills. The recycling portion of echelon 4 should be carefully designed and closely managed to ensure environmentally responsible recycling. Figure 3-11 summarizes the decision logic for selecting the reverse stream trading partners.

Consider the following when deciding on a core set of trading partners in the design of the reverse stream zone:

- *Customer edge(s) of the reverse stream*—How does the installed base of customers connect with the reverse stream zone? How does the reverse stream zone connect with the aftermarket?
- *Geography of current and future customers*—Is the geography of the installed base expanding? Will the geographical locations of future customers extend beyond current local or regional markets?

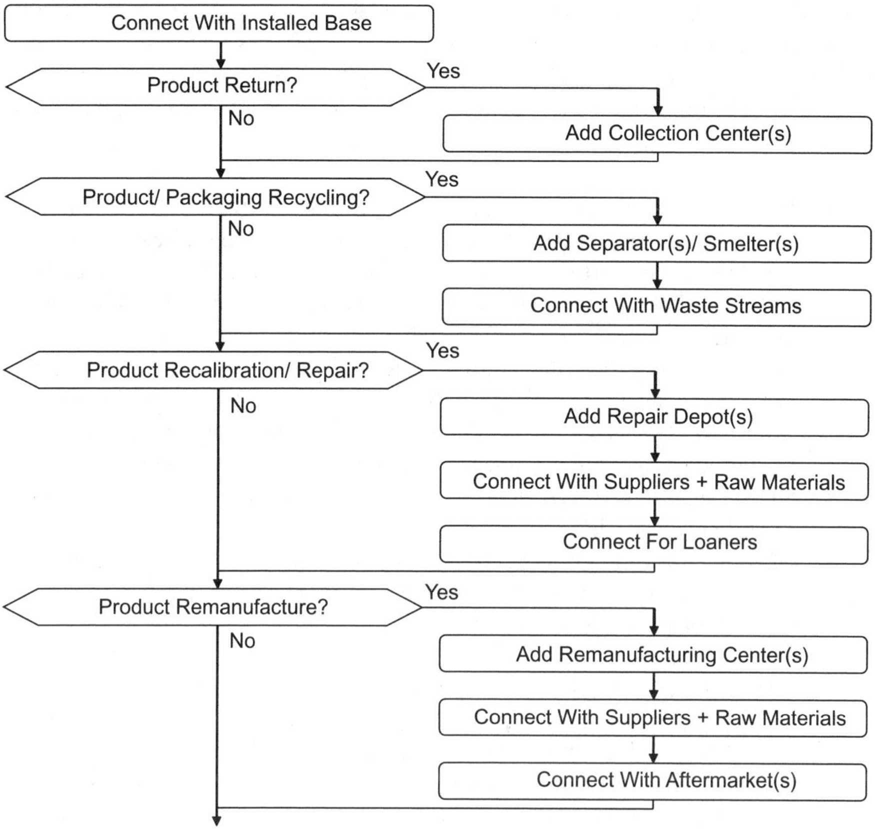

FIGURE 3-11 Reverse stream trading partner decision logic.

- *Collection point/loaner distribution*—Are there convenient, centralized collection points for returns? Do these collection points also track and distribute loaner products?
- *Multifunctional trading partners*—Is it competitive to combine disassembly, repair, reassembly, and remanufacture within a single trading partner?
- *Raw material edge(s) of the reverse stream*—How does the reverse stream zone connect with the geography of spare parts suppliers? How does the reverse stream zone connect with waste streams?
- *Interconnection with the forward supply chain*—Is the reverse stream zone directly connected with suppliers in the upstream zone or with fabricators in the midstream zone?
- *Special handling requirements*—Are there special handling requirements such as hazardous material transportation and warehousing?
- *Environmentally responsible recycling*—Is the separation, transportation, smelting, and injection into the waste stream all done in an environmentally responsible way?

The reverse stream connection with the installed customer base can be complex and is often a key source of customer dissatisfaction. Return situations involve many exceptions to the norm. Return processes are typically low-volume, high-mix sporadic flows. The following issues are unique to the customer interface with the reverse stream:

- *Return authorization*—Is the return customer-initiated, for example because of a product defect, or is it factory-initiated because of a safety recall? Does the customer have to overcome some hurdles to gain a return authorization, a return address, or return packaging materials? Who pays the freight?
- *Return content*—Does the return include product and packaging, packaging alone, or product subassemblies? Is the condition of the returned product new, used, damaged, or a spent core? (A core is that portion or shell of a used product that will become the base for a remanufactured product.)
- *Special handling requirements*—Does the return involve the transport of hazardous materials?
- *Warranty tracking*—Is the returned product under warranty, under extended warranty, or out of warranty? Does the customer expect a loaner for the duration of the recalibration or repair?
- *Loaner tracking*—Is the loaner returned to a different location than the original return? Has the customer returned the loaner? Has the loaner been refurbished? How many times has the loaner gone out to a customer and come back? Is it time to scrap the loaner?
- *Serial number tracking*—Does the customer expect to receive back the same serial number product? This can be a significant issue for calibrated laboratory instruments and government-owned goods.
- *Recall date code and lot code tracking*—Can product be traced and recalled based on date code and lot code? Are date code and lot code records maintained for the period the regulations require?
- *Shipment of recalibrated, repaired, or remanufactured product*—Is the customer expected to pay the freight? Have cartons and shipping labels been designed to fit every product?
- *Returns of packaging materials*—Does the customer expect the distributor or manufacturer to dispose of its packaging materials including wood, cardboard, and plastic?
- *Credits and refunds*—How easy is it for the customer to receive a credit or a refund on a return? Is a full credit or refund tied to the physical return of the loaner?
- *Inventory valuation*—Are the prices of a new unit, a loaner unit, a used unit, and a remanufactured unit differentiated?

The following example concludes this section on selecting trading partners for the reverse stream zone: There is a thriving demand for rebuilt auto parts in the United States to help owners hold down the cost of maintaining automobiles driven more than 75,000 miles. A national auto parts distributor decides to add a line of rebuilt starter engines to its parts catalog. The target aftermarket customer includes the large chain auto repairs shops like Medias, the large auto parts retailers like Pep Boys, and to a limited degree the local service stations who still offer specialized older car repair. The rebuilt starter engines will carry the full reputation and quality standards of this national auto parts distributor backed by a two-year limited warranty on materials and workmanship.

Two factors complicate the profitable addition of a line of starter engines. First, though there has been some standardization of parts among domestic and foreign car manufacturers, there are still a staggering number of automotive makes, models, and model years to be supported. The solution to this problem requires a central warehouse for the remanufactured starter engines. The fast movers will be shipped to a customer's location within 2-3 days, whereas a limited inventory of the slow movers will remain on the shelf in the warehouse. A usage forecast combined with actual customer demand will trigger the replenishment of specific starter engines from the remanufacturing center. The second factor is the ability of the network to obtain enough cores of the correct make, model, and model year to sustain a profitable throughput. The availability of cores will also have to be forecast. Most cores will come from a return of the original equipment taken out of the car when the rebuilt starter engine is installed. The price of the rebuilt starter engine will be discounted for a returned core. Some cores will come from cars scrapped in junkyards.

When a core is recovered from the field, it must be identified and inspected for the internal condition of each of its parts. The remanufacturer must have access to a database with the bills of materials for every type of starter engine. A secondary forecast of internal part yields from the cores will drive the remanufacturer to hold an inventory of the spare and replacement components needed to refurbish a particular core. New stators, rotors, bushings, and other lower level items will be purchased from the same suppliers who are selling these parts to the original equipment manufacturers (OEM). Packaging and labels will have to be designed and purchased for the remanufactured starter engines. Finally, the remanufacturer will have to deal with the cores, internal components, and packaging materials that need to be scrapped. The copper in burned windings, the steel in mangled rotors, and the cardboard used to transport the core are three examples of materials that can be separated, smelted, or recycled into waste streams. The recycling leg can have significant economic value.

The (nominal) trading partners in this example include the following:

- The auto repair shops and auto parts retailers that form the aftermarket and double as the source of cores.
- The remanufacturer and centralized warehouse for the rebuilt starter engines. Note that the remanufacturer is the network orchestrator for this business.
- The supply base for spare parts, which is the same as the supply base for the OEM's.
- The separators, smelters, and recyclers that connect with the relevant waste streams.

MANAGING RISK IN TRADING PARTNER RELATIONSHIPS

The focus of this Chapter is how to flow the physical product through a minimum set of trading partner relationships. Trading partner decision logic is based on building a fulfillment network to reach customers in the downstream zone, on building a manufacturing network that implements the BOM in the midstream zone, and on building a transformation network that connects with each component supplier and raw material in the upstream zone. Where required, the reverse stream zone connects to the installed customer base, to the aftermarket, to raw materials, and to waste streams. When trading partners recognize they are missing certain core competencies to perform the value-adding (value-subtracting) processes within their zone, they will form incremental network relationships to bring the missing competency into the network. The next section clarifies such a trading partner relationship and explains how to manage its inherent risks.

THE RELATIONSHIP LIFE CYCLE

A middle-link trading partner is a network relationship that buys and sells in-network. Trading partner relationships are born, grow, mature, and die just as relationships between people do. They depend on the human chemistry and mutual respect shared between senior executives. Although much can be done to institutionalize these relationships and to form multiple human bonds between the direct report management teams of each participating organization, the divorce or death of the senior executive relationship will certainly cause the business partnership to be terminated. You should expect the bond between each pair of trading partners to have its own life cycle, and you should know the current life cycle phase of that relationship.

In an oversimplification, the upstream zone connects across the supply base, the midstream zone adds value, the downstream zone connects across the customer base, and the reverse stream zone subtracts value. A supply chain network with strong bonds among its trading partners across each of the network zones can withstand changes and substitutions among its more numerous nominal trading partners. Nominal trading partner relationships cannot be managed relationships; there are simply too many nominal trading partners in a typical supply chain network.

Network relationships can be put at risk for a variety of reasons:

- *Personal relationship risk*—The senior manager who first formed the partnership moves on to another organization or retires.
- *Demand risk*—The rate of demand shifts, making the relationship much less significant, or the mix of demand shifts, causing the focus to go elsewhere because the trading partner is simultaneously participating in other competing supply chain networks.
- *Supply risk*—The source of supply dries up or competitive forces make the relationship less than economical.
- *Technology risk*—A patent expires or a technological breakthrough leapfrogs the current technological advantage.

- *Investment risk*—The return on investment is no longer attractive to one of the trading partners.
- *Environmental risk*—A new environmental or regulatory threat looms in the market, causing the relationship to become unattractive.

Each pair of trading partner relationships should be continuously monitored for any change in their risk profile. The network orchestrator, who typically designed the network in the first place, is the logical owner of this risk assessment task.

The Partnership Agreement

One effective way to institutionalize trading partner relationships is the use of a partnership agreement. A partnership agreement is a relationship contract that documents a shared vision of why and how two organizations will work together for their mutual benefit. A partnership agreement is similar to a purchase contract except that it does not document any forecasts, dollars, production volumes, or inventory levels. Its primary purpose is to manage the business risk of the relationship. A middle trading partner would be party to at least two partnership agreements, one as a buyer and one as a seller.

The following articles should be included in such a document:

- *Purpose*—Recognizes that both organizations are trading partners in the network
- *Parties to the Agreement*—Gives the legal names of the two parties to the agreement
- *Basis of the Agreement*—States the shared value proposition
- *Primary Organizational Process Boundaries*—Defines primary areas of process responsibility
- *Interface Response Time*—Sets response expectations across time and geography
- *Decision Escalation*—Documents the hierarchy of titles to resolve an issue
- *Frequency of Face-To-Face Time*—Sets expectations for senior management meetings
- *Performance Measurement*—States a commitment to shared performance measures
- *Intellectual Property*—States each organization's rights to trade secrets, trademarks, copyrights, and patents
- *Investment Decisions and Return On Investment Splits*—Sets expectations for shared investment and shared returns
- *Partnership Agreement Mediation and Conflict Resolution*—Agrees to a mediation process for conflict resolution
- *Non-Exclusive Provision*—Acknowledges each organization's right to participate in multiple, competing networks
- *Evergreen Renewal*—Renews automatically for as long as the agreement makes sense

- *Signatures*—Requires the signature of the senior executive of each organization
- *Appendix*—Defines a set of global performance measures

The text of an example partnership agreement follows in Table 3-12.

TABLE 3-12
A Consumer Packaged Goods Partnership Agreement

1. Purpose:
This Partnership Agreement recognizes that our two organizations are trading partners in a consumer packaged goods supply chain network. The purpose of this Partnership Agreement is to keep our collective resources focused for the benefit of our customers and shareholders. This document is plainly written for both organizations to understand and intentionally written with a minimum of legalese.

2. Parties to the Partnership Agreement:
Company ABC, hereafter called "the Seller," is an independent consumer packaged goods manufacturing organization incorporated under the laws of the State of Illinois. Company XYZ, hereafter called "the Buyer," is an independent consumer packaged goods distribution organization incorporated under the laws of the State of Delaware. This Partnership Agreement is intended to represent the best interests of both the Seller and the Buyer.

3. Basis of the Partnership Agreement:
This Partnership Agreement is a synergistic relationship between the Buyer and the Seller. A synergistic relationship is one that is greater than the sum of its parts. It formally recognizes that the Seller brings value-added manufacturing to the relationship. It formally recognizes that the Buyer brings value-added distribution to the relationship. Table PA1 outlines the elements of value that the Seller gives and gets and the elements of value that the Buyer gives and gets through this Partnership Agreement.

Table PA1: Summary of the Basis of the Partnership

	The Seller	The Buyer
Gives	Seller gives to Buyer • The manufacture of consumer packaged goods products	Buyer gives to Seller • The distribution of consumer packaged goods products • Access to end customers for new product definition
Gets	Seller gets from Buyer • Demand forecasts and point of sale demand information for planning • Cash payment priority	Buyer gets from Seller • Delivery acknowledgements and advanced shipment notices for planning • Manufacturing priority

4. Primary Process Boundaries:
The Seller's process consists primarily of the planning and procurement of materials, the manufacture and bulk packaging of product, and the development of new products. The Seller may from time to time outsource process steps to maintain the highest level of competitiveness. The Buyer's process consists primarily of the postponement, packaging, and distribution of product in North America. The Buyer may from time to time expand into new market segments to maintain the highest level of competitiveness.

TABLE 3-12 (Continued)

5. Interface Response Time:
Table PA2 documents specific employee titles and their backups responsible for maintaining each flow interface. Any flow disruption will be resolved to the best ability of the Seller and the Buyer within the maximum allowable response time.

Table PA2: Responsibility and Response Table

	For the Seller	For the Buyer
Material flow continuity • Primary • Backup • Max response time	 Title, phone, cell, and e-mail Title, phone, cell, and e-mail 12 Hours (Time zone dependent)	 Title, phone, cell, and e-mail Title, phone, cell, and e-mail 12 Hours (Time zone dependent)
Information flow continuity • Primary • Backup • Max respon se time	 Title, phone, cell, and e-mail Title, phone, cell, and e-mail 2 Hours (Time zone dependent)	 Title, phone, cell, and e-mail Title, phone, cell, and e-mail 2 Hours (Time zone dependent)
Cash flow continuity • Primary • Backup • Max response time	 Title, phone, cell, and e-mail Title, phone, cell, and e-mail 24 Hours (Time zone dependent)	 Title, phone, cell, and e-mail Title, phone, cell, and e-mail 24 Hours (Time zone dependent)

6. Decision Escalation:
Should a business issue remain unresolved, each organization will follow this decision escalation process:

- Brought to the Immediate Manager within 2 hours
- Brought to the Functional Manager within 1 day
- Brought to the Senior Executive within 2 days

7. Frequency of Face-to-Face Time:
The Seller's Senior Executive and the Buyer's Senior Executive agree to meet face-to-face a minimum of once per quarter at a mutually agreeable location. The meeting agenda will be published 10 days prior.

8. Performance Measurement:
The Seller and the Buyer agree to operate their mutual business using the set of global performance measures defined in Appendix A.

9. Intellectual Property:
Unless legally agreed upon otherwise, the Seller holds exclusive title and full rights to its own trade secrets, trademarks, copyrights, and patents. Unless legally agreed upon otherwise, the Buyer holds exclusive title and full rights to its own trade secrets, trademarks, copyrights, and patents. Nonpublic

(*Continued*)

TABLE 3-12
(Continued)

demand planning information, inventory levels, customer-requested new product features, cost information, and financial results will be openly shared between the two organizations.

10. Investment Decisions and Return On Investment Splits:
The Seller and the Buyer may from time to time agree to a joint capital investment in inventory, capacity, or capital projects to improve the competitiveness of their supply chain. The Seller and the Buyer agree that the profit (or loss) return resulting from such joint investment will be split in direct proportion to the capital investment made by each organization.

11. Partnership Agreement Mediation and Conflict Resolution:
The Seller and the Buyer agree that irresolvable operational conflict between the two parties will be decided by third-party mediation.

12. Non-Exclusive Provision:
This Partnership Agreement acknowledges the right of the Seller and the Buyer to each participate in multiple, potentially competing networks.

13. Evergreen Renewal:
This Partnership Agreement will remain in effect indefinitely unless modified in writing with 60 days advance notice or terminated in writing with 120 days advance notice.

14. Signatures:
We embrace this Partnership Agreement.

____
Full Name—Senior Executive, Seller Company Date

____
Full Name—Senior Executive, Buyer Company Date

Partnership Agreement Appendix A: Global Performance Measures
This topic is covered in detail in Chapter 6.

IN SUMMARY

This Chapter classifies the network relationships among the organizations found in a supply chain. It presents decision logic with practical examples to minimize the number of echelons required to span each network zone. It introduces the partnership agreement as one way to manage the business risk inherent in a trading partner relationship. This Chapter raises three fundamental questions:

- Who are the trading partners in your network?
- Does your network design minimize the number of echelons required to connect the right core competencies edge-to-edge across the upstream, midstream, downstream, and reverse stream zones?
- Have you formalized each trading partner relationship in order to better manage the relationship risk?

Chapter 4 completes the network design with the addition of the nominal trading partners for connectivity. The principles of velocity and variability define and measure the competitiveness of the information, material, and cash flows throughout the network. Zones, echelons, trading partners, nominal trading partners, and flows—a network structure is taking shape.

He was beat. The week so far had been particularly brutal, including the traffic during his drive home. Maybe this evening he could have a relaxing dinner with his wife without a random phone call from Asia. Germany was fast asleep at this hour, but he just never knew when Singapore might call.

"Hello dear! How was your day?" he called to his wife as he walked in the door.

She was already home fixing a simple dinner of spaghetti and wine. Boiling water for spaghetti was about all she could do on the makeshift stove while the kitchen remained torn up.

"It was okay, but I'll be glad when the range and ovens are installed. We're eating in the living room again tonight."

Halfway through dinner she brought the topic up again, "I've been thinking some more about what you asked the other night concerning my business partners."

"And just when I thought you had stopped listening to what I was saying."

"No, I was listening. You just had me going on about that boat stuff—you know, upstream and downstream. Well, I think I've figured out some of that. For example, the instructional design group in Chicago is my upstream trading partner."

"Yes, I can see that," her husband said.

"And, the DataLink training center with its classrooms, audiovisual equipment, and food service is one of my downstream trading partners. But I'm having trouble understanding the right relationship model for my instructors. Are they midstream, downstream, or something else altogether?"

"That's an interesting question. One answer is that it depends on the legal arrangement. Instructors, such as this new woman, Suzie Lee, that you just hired, are your employees and therefore are part of your own legal organization in the midstream. On the other hand, you may do business, maybe as a limited liability corporation, with some instructors who are self incorporated. These folks may only be nominal trading partners."

"Okay, but what determines whether a self-incorporated instructor is midstream or downstream?" she asked.

"The answer to that question depends on the flow of your process and the bill of materials for your product."

"I don't have a bill of materials for my product."

"Sure you do," said the supply chain architect. "It may not be formally documented, but each course you present requires an instructor's CD-ROM with its media, jewel case, and label; student workbooks with their three ring binders, separator tabs, and printed note pages; and other classroom consumables like flip chart paper, marker pens, and masking tape."

"I never looked at it that way. It's kind of like the recipe for tonight's dinner, isn't it?"

"Yes, that's an excellent analogy. Now if these other instructors are involved in manufacturing the instructor's CD-ROM or the student workbook, then they are part of the midstream zone. If the other instructors are involved only in delivering the instruction, then they are part of the downstream zone.

"Oh…"

"That clears up that mystery," she continued. "Now here's another question that's been bugging me: Is my business better off to continue offering instruction in-house, like I do for Fred at DataLink, or as my business grows, should I lease classroom space and have the students come to me?"

"What do you think you should do?"

They explored both options through the remainder of a bottle of Ravenswood Merlot.

4 Designing a Competitive Network

Friday, June 28

Two days later the supply chain architect was in awe of the copper artwork nested within the framing by George, the plumber. The kitchen had been an empty shell of a room just hours before. Now it sparkled with hand-wiped solder joints where the copper pipes merged and an occasional piece of shiny black plastic PVC piping. The center island would hold the main sink with a garbage disposal unit. A second sink would be in the countertop along the back wall. The dishwasher would be built into the center island, and the refrigerator required a plumbing hookup for its automatic icemaker. The exposed studs showed additional plumbing runs to the upstairs bath and to a powder room adjacent to the kitchen.

"George, how in the world do you keep all those pipes straight in your mind?"

George stopped his work and looked up. "When you have done this as long as I have, it just comes naturally."

"Since you are billing $50 per hour, it's okay to keep working while you talk," he kidded. "But seriously, once this plumbing infrastructure is buried behind sheetrock, isn't it difficult to fix when a hot and cold water connection are mixed up?"

"Not really. It happens more than you know. But you can fix that problem down in the cellar rather than opening up a wall. The key to this 'plumbing infrastructure,' as you call it, is to think in terms of flow."

"What do you mean?"

"The hot water has to originate from the water heater and flow to a destination like the sink. Then the hot water has to have a return flow through the sink's drain back to the sewer. The cold water has to originate from the street, but inside the water meter, and flow to its destination. Likewise, the cold water has to have a return flow back to the sewer. As long as there is a complete closed-loop path for each of these flows, the plumbing works nicely," replied George.

"If it's that simple, why does it take so much copper tubing to plumb my kitchen? Maybe we could redesign the network and save me a bunch of money!" He was starting to get excited about paying George a lot less for the plumbing.

George was patient with his response. "It's also about water velocity. You have to know just where to cut into the cold water and hot water runs to ensure that the water pressure upstairs doesn't suddenly drop when you start the dishwasher downstairs. If a house is plumbed wrong, the system ends up with velocity traps that sap the water pressure."

"Oh, I didn't know that."

"Yep, the pressure off the street, the diameter of the copper pipe, and the length of the run all contribute to what the customer experiences in the upstairs bathroom and the downstairs kitchen. A good plumber also tries to keep the customer experience consistent. That's why you smile after you pay me $50 per hour."

Again the supply chain architect asked, "What do you mean?"

"The worst thing for a customer is to have variability in water pressure during the day. You don't want to be taking a shower when the dishwasher kicks in, only to have your water temperature drop unexpectedly."

The supply chain architect was still thinking about suddenly cold showers as he drove to work.

*****

It was the last order day of the month, but order processing was not busy. The company's revenue picture had continued to erode after the announcement that Colonial Distributor would cancel all its open orders. June was going to be the company's worst order month in five years, coming in at just 43% of the forecast. It cast a pall over the entire operation.

Everything seemed to be working against them. An important large order had not made the month-end cutoff because a routine backup of the order-processing computer had run five hours longer than expected. Another big shipment to Europe was stuck in customs at John F. Kennedy airport because of questions about its export license. Critical parts needed for production on the last day of the month were delayed in transit because of a tractor-trailer accident on Route 95. FedEx would deliver replacement material on Saturday at a cost premium, but the replacements could not be used until Monday, which was the start of July. To make matters worse, they had just received notification from a big account not to expect their payment for another 15 days.

The supply chain architect was working the phones to get the shipment released at JFK. "Look, the Export Control Classification Number is consistent, with no license required, and the destination customer has been checked against the denial list. What's the problem?"

"Damn it!" He slammed the phone down in utter frustration just as Hector Morales, vice president of manufacturing, walked past his desk.

"What's wrong?" asked Hector.

"It's not about the export license at all! You know that Customs changed their requirements and expanded the advance manifest rule to include airfreight. An aircraft cannot be loaded now unless the destination has its freight manifest ready four hours prior to 'wheels-up.' We didn't do anything wrong, but now there's another delay!"

Hector listened, but continued walking down the aisle.

"Hector! Wait a minute. I want to tell you about a conversation this morning with my plumber," he called.

"I don't have time right now to hear any more about your house renovation. We all need to focus on making this business profitable, or we may not have jobs!"

"No. Please listen; this is not about the kitchen. This may be a key part of the answer to the kind of problems we've been experiencing."

Hector paused three desks away. "I'm listening. Make it quick."

He walked over to where Hector was standing so he did not have to shout. "My plumber got me thinking about the velocity and variability of the flows in our supply chain. Look, we take the customer's order, ship a product from stock, and expect to collect a cash payment. That's a complete, closed loop that we do repeatedly for each order. Don't you see?"

"Yes, I can see that."

"Okay. It takes some amount of time to complete that loop. When the computer backup runs five hours late, it takes more time to order. When Customs holds up a shipment, it takes more time to deliver. When a customer delays their payment of our invoice, it takes more time to be paid. When we add these times together, they define a basic order-to-delivery-to-cash cycle time with a pretty low velocity."

"How are you defining velocity?" Hector asked.

"Velocity is the number of days to complete one cycle. If we can turn an order into cash in 35 days, it would be moving at a slower velocity than if we could turn an order into cash in 20 days."

"Though that's interesting, I don't see how it helps us avoid the catastrophes we experienced this month."

"As my plumber explained, that's where variability comes into play," the architect continued. "First we carefully determine a minimum number of process steps for the order-to-delivery-to-cash cycle. For example, who would have guessed our computer backups, done in the middle of the night, are on the critical path for order processing? Then we assign a variability factor to each process step. Some process steps are very short. Other process steps, like logistics and clearing Customs, may be quite long. Third, we ask the question, which process steps are likely to have high variability? Then we must try to either eliminate or fix those steps before bad things happen."

"I think you may be on to something important," Hector replied. "Call a meeting for Tuesday so you can present your ideas to the larger team."

"Another thing my plumber explained was the impact of the diameter of the pipe on the design of the plumbing network in my house. The diameter of the pipe is one of two main factors that determine the water velocity."

"And the other is the water pressure?"

"Exactly. What's relevant to our business situation is the idea that a pipe's diameter can change for a number of reasons. First the plumber, working with the architect, decides what pipe diameter to install. However, when there is a branch or a junction in the plumbing, the pipe's effective diameter is changed.

And you can probably remember in the old days, before we had so much copper plumbing, how a lead pipe could build up sediment, reducing its diameter over time."

"That is like building up cholesterol in your arteries," Hector offered.

"Yes. The point of the changing pipe diameter is that the plumbing network can develop a number of velocity traps that slow down the flow of water. Some of these velocity traps are subtle. They occur in the network where you would least expect them. Or they are the result of some network interaction that appears on the surface to be beneficial. For example, it is beneficial to tap a secondary line into the cold-water plumbing to save the expense of some pipe. But if the tap occurs at the wrong place, both the primary and the secondary cold water runs will suffer from insufficient flow."

"That's interesting."

"There is one more thing—" Just then, Dana Hoffmann, the CFO, joined them in the aisle.

"Dana, we've been discussing a new approach to avoiding the kind of disasters this company has experienced in June. You will be very interested to hear this, but right now I've got a scheduled conference call with our operations manager in Germany," said Hector.

"Oh my! It's good that someone has some new thinking around here. Hector, I wanted to review the agenda for Tuesday's meeting with you. When can you and I get together after your teleconference?" asked Dana. Dana and Hector walked down the aisle toward Hector's office.

The supply chain architect returned to his desk and started to work through a flood of e-mail messages in his inbox.

Larry Holmes, a young logistics analyst in the cubicle across the aisle, came over. "I heard what you were saying to Hector. Where do you come up with all this stuff?"

"If you heard the conversation, then you heard how maximizing velocity and minimizing variability could improve the competitiveness of our business."

"Yeah, it makes a lot of sense. Take the order and ship the product as fast as you can," said Larry. "Once again it's logistics to the rescue!"

"Not so fast! Logistics is certainly a key piece, and you are on your way to becoming a great logistics analyst; but don't overlook the cash flow. The biggest difference between supply chain management and logistics is that logistics traditionally leaves out the cash flow."

"What do you mean?" asked Larry.

"The closed loops that we are talking about involve information-to-physical distribution flows and information-to-cash flows. We don't make any money until our customers pay us. And we don't get any material replenishments until we pay our suppliers. That was the next point to be made with Hector."

"That's true. But it's not my problem."

"Then think about this. You were hired to analyze the transportation and warehouse connections in the current network to see whether there are any opportunities for improvement. When there are many logistics connections to several large distribution centers, there will be a large amount of inventory in the network. It takes cash to buy that inventory. The slower the inventory turns, the longer that cash is tied up. Would you rather that we bought inventory, or would you rather that we paid your salary?"

"Oh. I think I better get back to my analysis," Larry said as he returned to his cubicle.

This Chapter adds the nominal trading partners into the mix to complete the information flows and the cash flows. A discussion of landed costs explores the network's cost tradeoffs when the BOM is partitioned across organizations in different countries. The Chapter focus then turns to optimizing the supply chain by maximizing flow velocity while minimizing flow variability. Comprehensive examples turn the theory into practice.

LINKING THE TRADING PARTNERS

Chapter 3 explains how echelons in the upstream transform raw materials, the midstream manufactures finished products, and the downstream fulfills orders with products and services. A skeletal network of trading partners is determined from the requirements of the material flow. Each trading partner buys from at least one other trading partner and sells to at least one other trading partner. This Chapter completes the network design. The design and optimization techniques described here are applicable not only to forward supply chains delivering products and services, but also to reverse supply chains.

The Basic Building Block of Network Flows

Consider a network in which a single trading partner buys from a single supplier and sells to a single customer, see Figure 4-1. The supplier and the trading partner each have starting inventory positions. They have independent inventories of products or

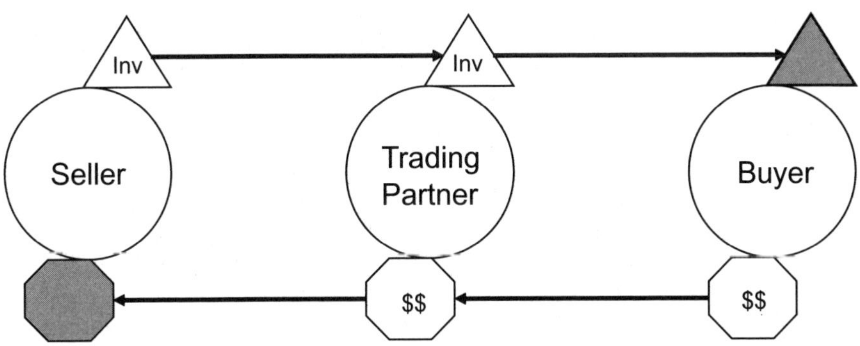

FIGURE 4-1 The basic network building block.

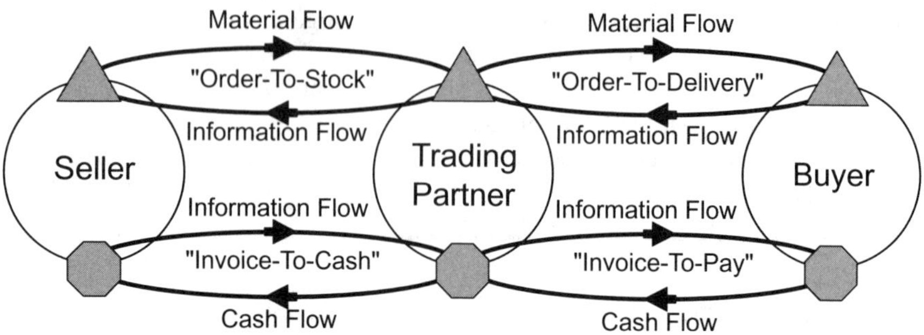

FIGURE 4-2 The four basic subcycles.

components in their respective stocks. The product does not move as long as it remains in stock. The trading partner wants to deliver product to the customer and to replenish components from the supplier.

The customer and the trading partner also each have starting cash positions. They have independent inventories of cash in their respective bank accounts. The cash does not move as long as it remains in the accounts. The trading partner wants to receive a cash payment from the customer for the product and to make a cash payment to the supplier for the components. As the network operates, physical inventory shifts downstream toward the customer and cash shifts upstream toward the supplier.

Inventory is driven downstream and cash is driven upstream in a supply chain network by the order-to-delivery-to-cash cycle. There are order-to-delivery-to-cash cycles connecting each pair of the trading partner's inventory locations and bank accounts. The order-to-delivery-to-cash cycle breaks down into four sub-cycles, as shown in Figure 4-2. The network design must take into account these four subcycles for each of the trading partners. The completion of each subcycle is a requirement for the supply chain network to function properly.

1. *The order-to-delivery subcycle*—The buyer's order (information flow) is paired with the trading partner's delivery (material flow). An order causes product inventory to flow from the trading partner to the buyer.
2. *The order-to-stock subcycle*—The trading partner's order (information flow) is paired with the seller's delivery (material flow). An order causes component inventory to flow from the seller to the trading partner.
3. *The invoice-to-pay subcycle*—The trading partner's invoice (information flow) is paired with the buyer's payment (cash flow). An invoice causes cash to flow from the buyer to the trading partner.
4. *The invoice-to-cash subcycle*—The seller's invoice (information flow) is paired with the trading partner's payment (cash flow). An invoice causes cash to flow from the trading partner to the seller.

The seller and the buyer in Figure 4-2 will be (nominal) trading partners connected to the material flow. In practice, each of the subcycles also has a reverse loop flow:

For the order-to-delivery subcycle:

- The order-to-acknowledgement subcycle is an information-to-information flow pair that informs the buyer that the order was received and booked.
- The order-to-advance shipment notice (ASN) subcycle is an information-to-information flow pair that informs the buyer of the expected delivery date and time from the trading partner.
- Reverse flow: The advise-to-return subcycle is an information-to-material flow pair in which the buyer advises the trading partner of a return of delivered items, and then returns the shipment to the trading partner's shipment.

For the order-to-stock subcycle:

- The order-to-acknowledgement subcycle is an information-to-information flow pair that informs the trading partner that the order was received and booked by the seller.
- The order-to-advance shipment notice (ASN) subcycle is an information-to-information flow pair that informs the trading partner of the expected delivery date and time from the seller.
- Reverse flow: The advise-to-return stock subcycle is an information-to-material flow pair in which the trading partner advises the seller of a return of delivered goods, and then returns the shipment to the seller.

For the invoice-to-pay subcycle:

- The pay-to-acknowledge subcycle is a cash-to-information flow pair that informs the buyer that its payment was received.
- Reverse flow: The return-to-refund subcycle is an information-to-cash flow pair that credits the buyer's account for a return.

For the invoice-to-cash subcycle:

- The cash-to-acknowledge subcycle is a cash-to-information flow pair that informs the trading partner that its payment was received by the seller.
- Reverse flow: The return-to-refund subcycle is an information-to-cash flow pair in which the trading partner's account is credited for a return from the seller.

In addition to the four closed-loop subcycles described above, four unidirectional information flows are required to complete the network design. These additional four flows are used for forecasting and planning purposes. Network operations will stop if a stocking location runs out of inventory or if a bank account runs out of cash. Once the inventory or the cash is replenished, network operations can be resumed.

- The seller plans its inventory position based on its forecast of expected sales.
- The trading partner plans its inventory position based on its forecast expected sales.
- The buyer plans its cash position based on its forecast of expected purchases.
- The trading partner plans its cash position based on its forecast of expected purchases.

Adding Nominal Trading Partners

Suppose a seller, a midstream organization, and a buyer are trading partners. Where do the nominal trading partners come into play? The answer is found by tracing out each information–material flow pair and each information–cash flow pair. Typically, Logistics Service Providers (LSPs) are required to complete the physical distribution flow connection, Information Service Providers (ISPs) are required to complete the information flow connection, and Financial Service Providers (FSPs) are required to complete the cash flow connection, see Figure 4-3. The dashed lines in Figure 4-3 represent cash payments to the information service provider and the logistics service provider for services rendered.

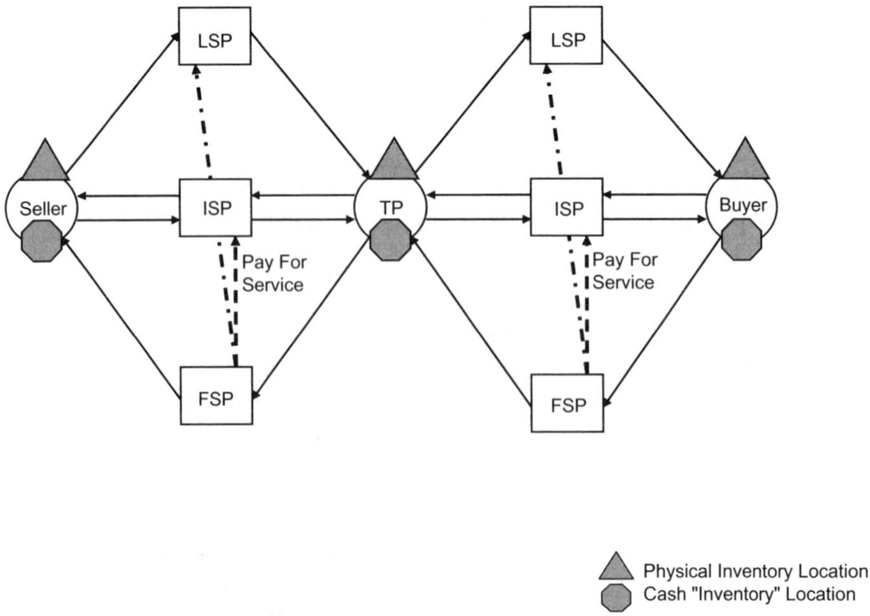

FIGURE 4-3 Nominal trading partners complete the flows for each subcycle.

In general, nominal trading partners enter into the network design for the following reasons:

- *Logistics service provider*—One LSP is required to connect each pair of inventory locations. When returns are involved, the material flow needs to be bidirectional.
- *Information service provider*—ISPs are required to complete the four subcycle flow loops for each of the trading partners. In general, each information flow needs to be bidirectional.
- *Financial Service Provider*—One FSP is required to connect each pair of bank accounts. When refunds are involved, the cash flow needs to be bidirectional.
- *Echelon Partitioning*—Transformation, manufacturing, and fulfillment echelons added to a network for the reasons explained in Chapter 3 will include additional (nominal) trading partners. When the added echelon includes a new trading partner with new inventory locations and bank accounts, new LSP, ISP, and FSP connections are required.
- *Small customer*—Customers with small in-network purchases behave as nominal trading partners.
- *Small supplier*—Suppliers with small in-network sales behave as nominal trading partners.

There are always more nominal trading partners than trading partners in a supply chain network design. It is often possible and highly desirable to use the same service provider in support of several trading partner subcycle loops. For example, large-freight forwarders and third-party logistics service providers (3PL) can provide regional or international coverage across multiple modes of transportation. On the other hand, some logistics companies specialize in handling certain regions (like Latin America) or specialized modes of transportation (like ocean-rail intermodal transport). The more freight that can be consolidated under one LSP, the more nearly that LSP will behave as a trading partner. Consolidated business drives lower costs, increased flexibility, and a greater willingness by the LSP to invest in information system connections and standardized performance measures.

APICS SUPPLY CHAIN MANAGEMENT PRINCIPLES

In 2000, APICS, the professional society for resource management, www.apics.org, introduced its Advanced Supply Chain Management (ASCM) courseware on CD-ROM. APICS is recognized internationally for its education leading to Certification in Production and Inventory Management (CPIM) and Certification in Integrated Resource Management (CIRM). CPIM and CIRM education both address resource management issues inside the four walls of the firm. ASCM education is the first APICS educational program to address resource management issues outside the four walls of the firm.

The ASCM education is built around a common vocabulary and a set of five fundamental business principles. The APICS Supply Chain Management Principles

TABLE 4-1
The APICS Supply Chain Management Principles

	Principle	The APICS Principle Statements©2000 APICS
Network Design	• VELOCITY • VARIABILITY	"Build a Competitive Infrastructure" "Leverage Worldwide Logistics"
Network Operation	• VOCALIZE • VISUALIZE	"Synchronize Supply with Demand" "Measure Performance Globally"
Network Competitiveness	• VALUE	"Supply Chain Creates Net Value"

are positioned at a foundational level, beneath the specifics of any particular vendor's enterprise requirements planning software. The five principles, summarized in Table 4-1, state time-proven business truths that are independent of any particular generation of information technology. This is because a supply chain network has a competitiveness threshold that is determined by the set of relationships, business processes, and operating policies inherent to that network. Education and information technology are the enablers that allow a supply chain network to approach the potential of its competitive threshold. Information technology alone cannot drive the competitiveness of any network beyond its inherent threshold. The design and operation of a supply chain network must be fundamentally competitive before layering on an information technology solution. The design and the operation of a supply chain network also must be fundamentally competitive before people learn how to use the network.

This book reduces the theory and principles into practice. The *velocity* and *variability* principles are discussed together in this Chapter, whereas the *vocalize* and *visualize* principles are discussed together in Chapter 7. The *value* principle, discussed in Chapter 9, integrates network design and network operation into a competitive whole.

EVALUATING A COMPETITIVE NETWORK DESIGN

Before going further, it is necessary to define a way to evaluate the competitive merits of a particular supply chain network design. A portion of the evaluation method is presented here in Chapter 4 as it relates to network design, and a portion of the evaluation method is presented in Chapter 7 as it relates to network operations. The method is used during the successive refinement of a network design to determine the relative competitiveness of each design change. It can also be used to compare the relative competitiveness of your current network design versus a competitor's network design.

The method is a set of relative measurements plotted on a spider diagram. A *spider diagram*, also called a *radar chart* in Microsoft Excel, is a simple graphical device that facilitates the simultaneous consideration of a number of important attributes. Each attribute is plotted on a separate, independent axis that radiates from the central point of the diagram, see Figure 4-4. Normally, a spider diagram is a full

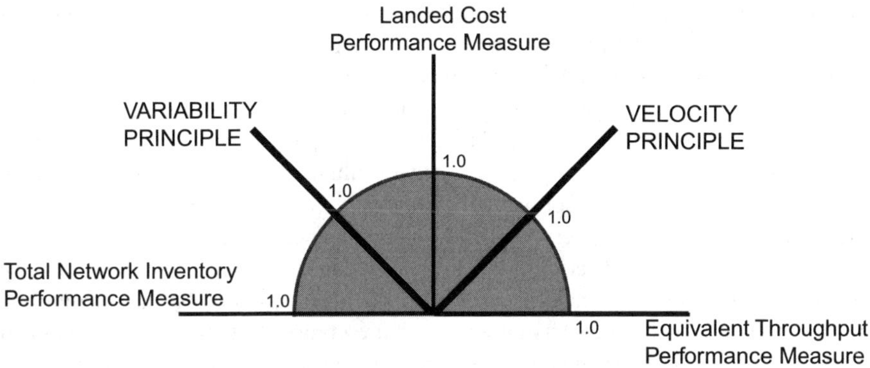

FIGURE 4-4 Measuring network design on the value circle.

circle with each axis radiating away from the center and equidistantly spaced around the circle. Because this Chapter is focused on network design, only the top half of the circle is shown. The sides of the circle are focused on network operations, as discussed in detail in Chapter 7. The bottom of the circle is focused on value, as discussed in Chapter 9. This book calls the entire diagram the *value circle*.

The axes in this evaluation method alternate between network performance measures and the APICS Supply Chain Management Principles as discussed and applied throughout this book, see Table 4-2. Definitions of the measure used for

TABLE 4-2
Network Design Evaluation

Axis	Performance Measure	APICS SCM Principle	Definition
Inventory	X		Common to both network design and network operation. Inventory is added to a network to compensate for increased variability.
Variability		"Leverage Worldwide Logistics"	Reducing variability reduces the need for network inventory and reduces logistics and quality costs.
Landed Cost	X		Partitioning a network geographically to gain a Country Of Origin cost advantage can lengthen a supply chain, slowing velocity, and add transit and customs connections, increasing logistics variability.
Velocity		"Build a Competitive Infrastructure"	Increasing velocity improves throughput and accelerates the order-to-delivery-to-cash cycle.
Throughput	X		Common to both network design and network operation. Increased throughput consumes inventory and generates cash flow.

each axis are presented in sections of Chapters 4, 7, and 9; the Network Blueprint Appendix presents a complete description of all eight measures.

Each axis is marked with the value 1.0 at the midpoint of its respective axis. When a continuous line traces through each of the midpoints, a unit circle is defined around the origin. The unit circle represents a baseline for comparison with either a successive refinement of the network design or a relative evaluation of a competitor's network design. Each axis shows an improvement in competitiveness when moving toward the origin, and each shows a deterioration in competitiveness when moving away from the origin. When a second set of points are plotted on the diagram and connected by a continuous line, the line encloses an area. If the area contained by this second line is smaller than the unit circle, its network is more competitive. If the area contained by the second line is larger than the unit circle, its network is less competitive.

It is common in a design analysis to find that some of the attributes are more competitive, whereas other attributes are less competitive. This evaluation method is used throughout the remainder of this book to assess network improvement relative to some baseline.

NETWORK PARTITIONING TO REDUCE LANDED COST

Network design primarily drives the structure of the income statement, whereas network operations primarily drive the structure of the balance sheet. Together network design and network operations can have a profound impact on both the income statement and the balance sheet of each trading partner. For some reason the term *landed cost* does not seem to be used unless import/export is involved, but the truth is that even domestic products have landed costs. Once the product BOM is partitioned across two or more trading partners, some elements of the product will incur landed costs. There are new incremental costs for freight, information processing, and cash flow processing that did not exist when the single trading partner was vertically integrated.

This section explores the central idea that the drive to reduce direct labor and direct material costs tends to partition the product BOM manufacture across several (nominal) trading partners, whereas the principles of maximizing velocity and minimizing variability tend to consolidate the product BOM manufacture within one trading partner. This is because changing the Country Of Origin can significantly reduce labor cost, material cost, duty expense, and income tax expense. On the other hand, reducing the number of organizations that touch a process, reducing the number of steps in the process, and reducing the variability of the process will accelerate the velocity of the process flow. This is the network design tradeoff between landed cost and velocity-variability, which is plotted on the value circle.

At One Extreme: The Vertically Integrated BOM

Suppose the BOM could be completely manufactured by a single firm that buys all its raw materials from suppliers in the same city and sells all its finished goods to customers in the same city. The supply chain network consists of suppliers, the firm

TABLE 4-3
Income Statement for a Vertically Integrated Firm

Line Item	Volume Dependant	Dollars		Percent Net Revenue	
Gross Revenue			$4,753,125		112.5%
– Volume Discounts	[Variable]	$338,000		8.0%	
– Returns Allowance	[Variable]	$190,125		4.5%	
Net Revenue			$4,225,000		100.0%
Labor	[Fixed + Variable]	$237,638		5.6%	
Material	[Fixed + Variable]	$2,534,800		60.0%	
Overhead	[Fixed + Variable]	$301,057		7.2%	
Cost of Quality	[Fixed]	$95,005		2.2%	
– Cost of Goods Sold		$3,168,500		75.0%	
Gross Margin			$1,056,500		25.0%
– General, Sales, & Admin Expense	[Fixed + Variable]	$460,660		10.9%	
– Depreciation Expense	[Fixed]	$85,000		2.0%	
Operating Profit			$510,840		12.1%
– Interest Expense	[Fixed]	$211,250		5.0%	
Profit Before Tax			$299,590		7.1%
– Income Tax Expense	[Variable]	$134,815		3.2%	
Net Profit			$164,775		3.9%

as the sole trading partner, and customers. The network has no geographical partitioning. Table 4-3 shows an example income statement for this vertically integrated firm.

Net revenue is the gross revenue from the sale of delivered products and services, adjusted down for volume discounts to large customers and for product returns. All of the dollar line items in Table 4-3 are also expressed as a percentage of net revenue. The Cost Of Goods Sold (COGS) is the sum of direct labor, direct material, overhead, and the cost of quality. Gross margin is net revenue minus COGS. Gross margin minus General, Sales, and Administrative (GS&A) expenses and minus depreciation expense for capital assets yields the operating profit. Operating profit minus the interest expense on debt and minus taxes paid yields the firm's net profit.

A portion of the expense structure of this firm is considered fixed relative to the unit volume of product sales. The rest of the expense structure is considered variable relative to the unit volume of product sales. Direct labor and direct material are mostly variable expenses, but they can have a fixed component. Overhead and GS&A are mostly fixed expenses, but they can have a variable component. With such a thin profit margin, it would not take much of a decline in gross sales to drive this firm's profitability to zero because of the fixed portion of its expense structure. With hard work, costs might be trimmed back 3 to 10%. However, a radical restructuring of costs, for example reducing costs by 33 to 50%, can only be accomplished by partitioning the product BOM across lower-cost trading partners.

Table 4-4 details the characteristics of the information flows, material flows, and cash flows for a product BOM built entirely domestically. *Intertrading partner* means

TABLE 4-4
A Product BOM Manufactured Domestically

	Intertrading Partners	Domestic Intratrading Partners
Information Flow	• Same time zone • Same information system • Same business culture • Face-to-face communication • High information velocity	• Similar time zones • Same language • Different business cultures • Voice, e-mail, instant messaging • Velocity delay at the interface
Material Flow	• No packaging • Move by hand carry, hand truck • High logistics velocity • Low logistics variability	• Moderate packaging • Motor, rail, airfreight • Velocity delay to pack and move • Transit time variability
Cash Flow	• No financing • No credit risk • Settlement the same cycle • No duty payments • High cash velocity • Low cash variability	• Same currency • Known credit risk • Settlement the same month • No duty payments • Velocity delay to process • Process time variability

the product manufacture occurs within divisions of the same trading partner. *Domestic intratrading partner* means the product manufacture occurs among two or more trading partners located within the same country.

At The Other Extreme: The Internationally Partitioned BOM

Now suppose the BOM is partitioned across two organizations to leverage the low labor rate, low material costs, and favorable income tax incentives available internationally. In this example 80% of the product BOM is outsourced to a contract manufacturer in a country with 1/25th of the labor costs, one half of the material costs, and one third of the tax expense. The new supply base is in the same city as the contract manufacturer. The customer base does not change. The international movement of subassemblies from the contract manufacturer to the factory requires a significant logistics effort that costs 4% of the value of the subassembly. The network is geographically partitioned, with the contract manufacturer selling an export and the factory buying an import. Because 80% of the value-adding manufacturing takes place at the contract manufacturer, its location determines the Country Of Origin. Table 4-5 is the income statement for the domestic factory at the downstream edge of the midstream zone, and Table 4-6 is the income statement for the international contract manufacturer at the upstream edge of the midstream zone. The factory's net revenue remains the same, for an easy comparison against Table 4-3.

The factory is now highly profitable, with a 13.8% net profit. The landed cost of goods sold at $2,410,019 is 76.1% of the original cost of goods sold at $3,168,500. The percent for COGS has decreased to 57.0% from 75.0%, increasing the factory's

TABLE 4-5
Income Statement for the Domestic Final Assembly Factory

Line Item	Dollars		Percent Net Revenue	
Gross Revenue		$4,753,125		112.5%
– Volume Discounts	$338,000		8.0%	
– Returns Allowance	$190,125		4.5%	
Net Revenue		$4,225,000		100.0%
Labor at 20% Factory Labor	$47,528		1.1%	
Overhead at 20% Factory Overhead	$60,211		1.4%	
Material at 20% Factory Material	$506,960		12.1%	
Subassembly Material	$1,708,000		40.4%	
Import Freight & Duty 4% Subassembly Material	$68,320		1.6%	
Cost of Quality at 20% Factory Quality	$19,000		0.4%	
– Cost of Goods Sold	$2,410,019		57.0%	
Gross Margin		$1,814,981		43.0%
– General, Sales & Admin Expense	$460,660		10.9%	
– Depreciation Expense	$85,000		2.0%	
Operating Profit		$1,269,321		30.1%
– Interest Expense	$211,250		5.0%	
Profit Before Tax		$1,058,071		25.1%
– Income Tax Expense	$476,132		11.3%	
Net Profit		$581,939		13.8%

profitability. Figure 4-5 shows the decrease in landed cost plotted on the value circle. Typically, there will be additional factory overhead to cover the communication and travel expense needed for the factory to manage the contract manufacturer relationship. For simplicity, this example does not include any incremental inbound freight and import duty costs for components purchased outside the contract manufacturer's country, nor does this example include incremental outbound freight and export duty costs on sales outside the factory's country. Product returns, subassembly returns, and the cost of quality due to yield factors in manufacturing represent waste throughout the network. These are hidden opportunities to become even more profitable.

$$\frac{\text{Design Landed Cost}}{\text{Baseline Network}} = \frac{\$2,410,019}{\$3,168,500} = \frac{0.761}{1.000} = 0.76$$

$$\frac{\text{Design Landed Costs}}{\text{Baseline Network}} = \frac{\text{\$ of Cost Of Goods Sold in the new network design}}{\text{\$ of Cost Of Goods Sold in the baseline network}}$$

Where dollar costs are calculated for the same trading partner and include all relevant labor, material, overhead, packaging materials, freight, duty, and cost of quality costs. Landed cost decreases toward the origin of the value circle.

TABLE 4-6
Income Statement for the International Contract Manufacturer

Line Item	Dollars	Percent Net Revenue
Gross Revenue	$1,793,400	105.0%
– Returns at 5% of Gross Sales	$85,400	5.0%
Net Revenue	$1,708,000	100.0%
Labor at 4% of 80% × Factory Labor	$7,604	0.4%
Material at 50% of 80% × Factory Material	$1,013,920	59.4%
Overhead at 200% × Contract Mfg Labor	$15,208	0.9%
Cost of Quality at 5% × Contract Mfg Material	$51,264	3.0%
– Cost of Goods Sold	$1,087,996	63.7%
Gross Margin	$620,004	36.3%
– General, Sales, & Admin Expense	$211,792	12.4%
– Depreciation Expense 400% × Factory Depreciation%	$136,640	8.0%
Operating Profit	$271,572	15.9%
– Interest Expense 200% × Factory Interest%	$170,800	10.0%
Profit Before Tax	$100,772	5.9%
– Income Tax Expense at 33% × Factory Tax Rate	$15,372	0.9%
Net Profit	$85,400	5.0%

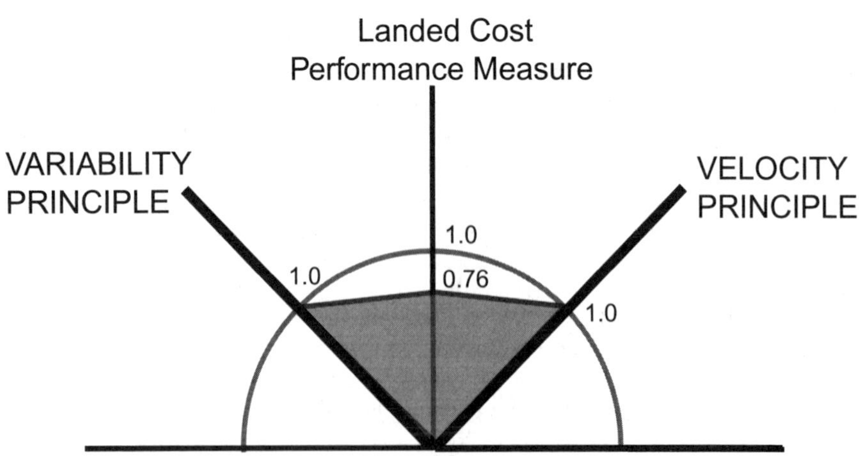

FIGURE 4-5 Landed cost decreases (improves) toward the origin.

TABLE 4-7
Internationally Partitioned Product BOM

	Domestic Intratrading Partner	International Intratrading Partner
Information Flow	• Similar time zones • Same language • Different business cultures • Voice, e-mail, instant messaging • Velocity delay at the interface	• Different time zones • Different languages • Different business cultures • E-mail, instant messaging • Velocity direction dependent
Material Flow	• Moderate packaging • Motor, air, rail freight • Velocity delay to transport • Transit time variability	• Heavy packaging • Air, ocean, rail freight • Velocity delay to transport • Customs time variability
Cash Flow	• Same currency • Known credit risk • Settlement the same month • No duty payments • Velocity delay to process • Settlement time variability	• Different currency • Letters Of Credit • Settlement within a quarter • Import/export duties • Velocity delay to process • Settlement time variability

Table 4-7 details the characteristics of the information flows, physical distribution flows, and cash flows for a product BOM manufacture that is partitioned internationally. Here, *domestic intratrading partner* means that the product manufacture occurs among trading partners located within the same country. *International intratrading partner* means that the product manufacture occurs among trading partners located in different countries.

The Elements of Landed Cost

When a product BOM is partitioned to achieve a lower total landed cost, the supply chain network becomes longer and spreads out geographically. This Chapter considers the impact of this partitioning on the network design and the income statement, while Chapter 7 considers the impact of this partitioning on network operations and the balance sheet. The final selection of trading partners may cause other geographical dependencies. For example, it is common practice to build a base of local suppliers geographically close to a manufacturing center and to locate a distribution center within driving distance of its customer base to save on logistics costs. Table 4-8 summarizes the direct and indirect product cost impact of partitioning the BOM.

An export from the seller becomes an import to the buyer. In the case of a return, an export from the buyer becomes an import to the seller. Import/export boundaries arise in four situations. First, an import/export boundary can occur when downstream order fulfillment in one country exports product to customers in other countries. The outbound freight and duty due, relative to each Country Of Destination, will vary for each product type sold. Second, an import/export boundary will cut through midstream

TABLE 4-8
Landed Cost Elements When the BOM Is Partitioned

Direct Product Costs		
Labor	(—)	Select the Country Of Origin for a significant reduction in labor rate. When the product's design is material intensive, this has a minimal impact.
Material	(-)	Shop the world or select a country where reduced extraction and transformation labor rates favorably impact component material costs. When the product design is labor intensive, this has a minimal impact.
Packaging	(+)	Incremental packaging required to ship partially assembled product around the world.
Quality	(+/-)	The cost of quality can increase or decrease depending on manufacturing competency, process yields, and attention to statistical process controls.
Indirect Product Costs		
Downstream Overhead	(+)	Expect increased levels of spending on information technology, telephone, travel, coordination, and financing.
Upstream Overhead	(—)	Select factories with low levels of automation and low labor rates for management and engineers. Production tooling is less expensive.
Freight	(++)	Airfreight, ocean freight, rail freight, or intermodal freight are added to the cost of domestic motor freight.
Duty	(0/+)	Duty is not a factor in a domestic-only setting. Select countries that operate free trade zones or provide the opportunity for duty-preference.
Returns	(+)	International returns are more expensive because of higher packaging, freight, and warehousing costs.
Income Tax	(—)	Select the Country Of Origin for a significant reduction in income tax. When the product design is not profitable, this has no impact.
Balance Sheet Impact		
Inventory	(++)	There will be more total inventory in the network with longer pipelines.
Cash	(++)	There will be more total cash in the network with longer supply chains.

Note: (+) Some Increase; (++) Significant Increase; (-) Some Decrease; (—) Significant Decrease

manufacturing when a portion of the BOM is outsourced to a different country. Third, an import/export boundary occurs where upstream components are imported from suppliers in other countries. Inbound freight and import duty, relative to the Country Of Origin, will vary for each component commodity purchased. Finally, return paths will often cross an unexpected import/export boundary. The net effect of pluses and minuses in inbound freight, import duty, outbound freight, and export duty must be evaluated whenever a Country Of Origin or Country Of Destination is changed. It is possible that some quirk in the duty schedules and freight tariffs may cause enough of an incremental increase in logistics cost to offset the landed cost advantage expected from changing the Country Of Origin.

Network Length and Width Relationships with the Product BOM

The number of echelons in the midstream zone of a supply chain network is directly related to the number of levels in the BOM. This can be demonstrated as follows. Start with the BOM tree of the product's structure. Circle and label segments of the product structure that are provided by different midstream (nominal) trading partners. Circle and label segments of the product structure that are postponed upstream. Circle and label segments of the product structure that are subassembled or subcontracted upstream. Then turn the listing 90 degrees and count the number of echelons it takes to get from the finished product parent to the lowest level child through each path. A deep BOM with many product structure levels will cause the midstream and upstream zones to have many echelons, whereas a flat BOM with few product structure levels will result in a small number of midstream and upstream echelons. Therefore, the total length of a supply chain network is directly related to the complexity of the product BOM. When outsourcing a portion of the BOM to another Country Of Origin to achieve a lower landed cost, the resulting increase in supply chain length can have a significant negative impact on competitiveness. A longer supply chain is less responsive and requires more total inventory and cash to operate.

The width of the upstream supply chain network is directly related to the total number of suppliers specified in the BOM by the item master. The larger the number of suppliers, the wider the upstream network. The vast majority of these suppliers will be nominal trading partners. One good way to reduce the complexity of a network is to reduce and consolidate the number of different suppliers specified by the BOM.

THE VELOCITY PRINCIPLE

When multiple building blocks are cascaded end-to-end to extend the network from the upstream zone through the midstream zone to the downstream zone, there are many seller–buyer pairs throughout the network. The network is designed around the location of trading partners' physical inventories and cash inventories. The material wants to flow downstream from inventory location to inventory location, to the end-customer. The cash wants to flow upstream from bank account to bank account, to the raw material supplier. This end-to-end exchange of physical goods for cash is governed by interlocking order-to-delivery-to-cash cycles. Increasing the order-to-delivery-to-cash velocity improves the competitiveness of the network design.

The Order-to-Delivery-to-Cash Cycle

Velocity is a measure of the time it takes to go completely through one closed-loop cycle. *A closed-loop cycl*e is defined as a set of process steps that must be completed to connect information flow with material flow and to connect information flow with cash flow. The following two velocity measures are useful in gauging the competitiveness of a network design:

- *Network order-to-delivery-to-cash velocity*—Measures the time per cycle, from the start of an end-customer order until the last payment is made to a raw materials supplier.

- *Trading partner order-to-delivery-to-cash velocity*—Measures the time per cycle from the start of a buyer's order to the trading partner until the last payment to a seller is made by the trading partner. This includes a transfer of product from the seller's inventory to the buyer's inventory and a transfer of cash from the buyer's bank account to the seller's bank account.

The process steps for an order-to-delivery-to-cash cycle can be grouped into process steps for order-to-shipment and process steps for shipment-to-cash. The order-to-shipment group adds value for the end-customer because it moves product and services along to the customer. The shipment-to-cash group adds value for the owner because it moves inventory off the balance sheet and adds profit to the income statement. Figure 4-6 shows a network design where the order-to-delivery and subsequent order-to-stock subcycles occur serially among the trading partners. Chapter 5 explores opportunities to conduct invoice-to-cash subcycles in parallel. Chapter 7 discusses a superior method of broadcasting customer demand that effectively places order-to-delivery and order-to-stock subcycles in parallel.

Process Mapping the Order-to-Delivery-to-Cash Cycle

You are now ready to map the process steps of the order-to-delivery-to-cash cycle for your network. Process mapping is a prerequisite to being able to analyze and optimize loop velocity. Perform the following steps:

- *Step 1*—Assign each trading partner to its respective downstream, midstream, or upstream echelon using the techniques of Chapter 3.

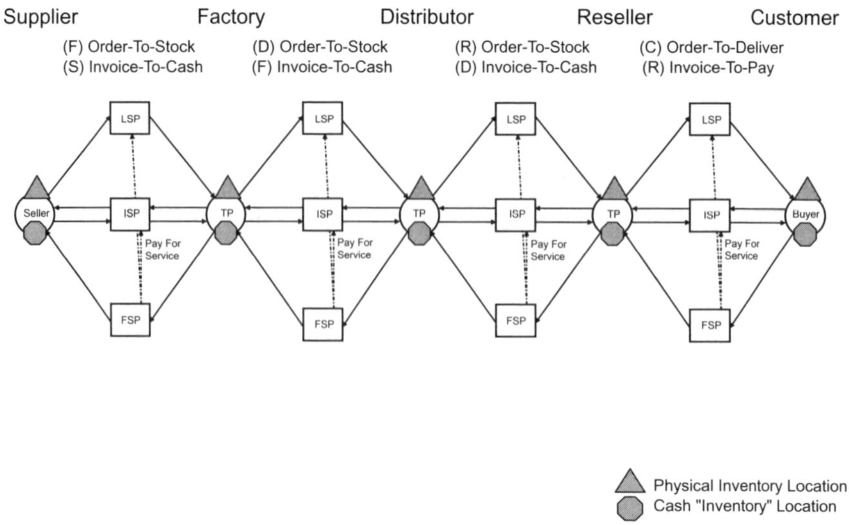

FIGURE 4-6 Subcycles connecting multiple trading partners.

- *Step 2*—Start with the end-customer and most downstream trading partner pair, and then work upstream.
- *Step 3*—Trace the closed-loop path from the end-customer to the downstream trading partner and back for the order-to-delivery (information to material) flow subcycle, as described in this Chapter. Identify any new LSP or ISP nominal trading partner(s) required to complete this subcycle.
- *Step 4*—Trace the closed-loop path from the downstream trading partner to the end-customer and back for the invoice-to-pay (information to cash) flow subcycle, as described in Chapter 4. Identify any new ISP or FSP nominal trading partner(s) required to complete this subcycle.
- *Step 5*—Working only with trading partners, trace the closed-loop path from the first trading partner to the next trading partner and back for the order-to-stock (information to material) flow subcycle, as described in Chapter 4. Identify any new LSP or ISP nominal trading partner(s) required to complete this sub cycle.
- *Step 6*—Working only with trading partners, trace the closed-loop path from each trading partner to the previous trading partner and back for the invoice-to-cash (information to cash) flow subcycle, as described in Chapter 4. Identify any new ISP or FSP nominal trading partner(s) required to complete this subcycle.
- *Step 7*—Repeat Steps 5 and 6 as many times as necessary until four subcycles have been traced out for each trading partner in the network, resulting in loops that connect the end-customer with the upstream raw material.
- *Step 8*—Develop a composite list of nominal trading partners. Consolidate among LSP's, among ISP's, and among FSP's where possible.
- *Step 9*—Working one subcycle at a time, build a table that defines the processing necessary to complete that subcycle. List each process step in a row of the table and leave two additional columns blank.
- *Step 10*—Use Table 4-9 to assign a transaction type and a transaction time frame to each process step. Place the transaction type into column two of the respective process element row of the subcycle table. Place the transaction timeframe into column three of the respective process element row of the subcycle table.
- *Step 11*—Repeat Steps 9 and 10 for each independent order-to-delivery, invoice-to-pay, order-to-stock, and invoice-to-cash subcycle.
- *Step 12*—When the forward supply chain subcycle design is complete, repeat all the steps as needed for the reverse supply chain subcycle design.

For example, a small retail channel consists of twenty retail stores, an independent distribution center, and seven product suppliers. The retail stores each have Internet-based Electronic Data Interchange (EDI) connections with the distribution center for ordering, Advanced Shipment Notification (ASN), and invoicing. The suppliers take their orders by fax and use the postal service to mail invoices and to receive payment checks. The suppliers use a variety of Less-Than-Truckload (LTL) and United Parcel Service (UPS) logistics to move their product, whereas the distribution

TABLE 4-9
Elements of Loop Velocity

For Each Process Step	Transaction Type	Transaction Time Frame
	An **arc** is a process step that defines the flow of material from one (nominal) trading partner to another, or the flow of information from one (nominal) trading partner to another, or the flow of cash from one (nominal) trading partner to another.	• Seconds: Local Area Network (LAN) connection • Seconds/Minutes: Internet connection, e-mail • Seconds/Minutes: Secure Electronic Funds Transfer (EFT) • Minutes: fax, phone, or voice-mail connection • Hours: Motor freight transit time • Days/Hours: Logistics queue time • Days: Clear customs, 24 hour rule—container security • Days: Airfreight, intermodal transit time • Weeks: Ocean freight, intermodal transit time
	A **loop** is a process step that defines value-adding (or value-subtracting) processing of physical goods, or information, or cash completed by a single (nominal) trading partner.	• Seconds: Information system processing • Seconds/Minutes: Internet connection • Minutes: Trained employee processing • Minutes: Manufacturing/distribution cycle time • Hours/Days: Manufacturing/distribution queue time • Hours/Days: Management decision • Weeks: Business policy, e.g. accounts payable
	A **trigger** is a process step that defines a connection between information flow and material flow within a (nominal) trading partner, or a connection between information flow and cash flow within a (nominal) trading partner.	• Seconds: Information system connection • Seconds/Minutes: Internet connection, e-mail • Minutes: Phone or voicemail connection

center uses UPS exclusively. Table 4-10 details the order-to-delivery, invoice-to-pay, order-to-stock, and invoice-to-cash subcycles for the distribution center trading partner. Notice that the timing of certain triggers on the cash payment side aligns with the completion of certain process loops on the physical distribution side. The upstream subcycles are similar to the downstream subcycles except that the upstream velocity is slower. Six additional nominal trading partners are necessary to complete all four of the subcycles.

TABLE 4-10
Subcycles for a Supplier–Distribution Center–Retail Store Network

Order-To-Delivery From: Retail Store To: Distribution Center			Invoice-To-Payment From: Distribution Center To: Retail Store		
Process Element	**Transaction Type**	**Transaction Time**	**Process Element**	**Transaction Type**	**Transaction Time**
Initiate order	R-Loop	Minutes			
Send order	RD-Arc	Minutes			
Process order	D-Loop	Minutes			
Trigger shipment	D-Trigger	Seconds			
Process shipment	D-Loop	Hours			
			Trigger invoice	D-Trigger	Seconds
Deliver product	DR-Arc	Days	Send invoice	DR-Arc	Minutes
Receive product	R-Loop	Hours			
			Trigger a match	R-Trigger	Seconds
			Trigger payment	R-Trigger	Seconds
			Process payment	R-Loop	Weeks
			Send payment	RD-Arc	Minutes
			Apply payment	D-Loop	Hours
			Close order	D-Trigger	Seconds

Order-To-Stock From: Distribution Center To: Supplier			Invoice-To-Cash From: Supplier To: Distribution Center		
Process Element	**Transaction Type**	**Transaction Time**	**Process Element**	**Transaction Type**	**Transaction Time**
Initiate order	D-Loop	Minutes			
Send order	DS-Arc	Hours			
Process order	S-Loop	Hours			
Trigger shipment	S-Trigger	Seconds			
Process shipment	S-Loop	Days			
			Trigger invoice	S-Trigger	Minutes
Deliver product	SD-Arc	Weeks	Send invoice	SD-Arc	Days
Receive product	D-Loop	Hours			
			Trigger a match	D-Trigger	Seconds
			Trigger payment	D-Trigger	Seconds
			Process payment	D-Loop	Weeks
			Send payment	DS-Arc	Days
			Apply payment	S-Loop	Days
			Close order	S-Trigger	Minutes

Nominal Trading Partners Added

Logistics Service Providers	UPS, LTL Carrier
Information Service Providers	Internet Service Provider, Verizon, Postal Service
Financial Service Providers	PNC Bank

Note: (S) Supplier, (D) Distribution Center, (R) Retail Store

In a network with more than one trading partner, you would create a similar table for each of the trading partners. Each trading partner (TP) connects to the network through its four subcycles: buyer order to TP delivery, TP order to seller stock, seller invoice to TP cash, and TP invoice to buyer payment. As each trading partner is woven into the fabric of the network, the order-to-stock subcycle of the last trading partner is merged with the order-to-delivery subcycle of the next trading partner. Likewise the invoice-to-payment subcycle of the next trading partner is merged with the invoice-to-cash subcycle of the last trading partner, see Figure 4-6 again.

Maximizing Velocity

The information from Table 4-10 is rearranged to form the order-to-delivery-to-cash baseline on the left side of Table 4-11. Table 4-11 is stacked vertically in the order of order-to-stock, order-to-delivery, invoice-to-payment, and invoice-to-cash. This is the worst-case scenario in which the product is delivered from the supplier before the distributor can pass it on to the retailer, and the retailer pays the distributor before the distributor pays the supplier. Notice that the process steps to send an invoice run in parallel with and are much shorter than the process steps to deliver the product. Therefore Table 4-11 considers only the longer of these parallel subprocesses and disregards invoicing. A total of 26 process steps on the left side of Table 4-11 define the baseline (retailer's) order—to—delivery—to—(supplier's) cash cycle. The elapsed-time profile for this cycle is plotted as X's down the center columns of the table. Three of the process steps take a week to complete, and four of the process steps take a day to complete.

Order-to-delivery-to-cash velocity is optimized by eliminating process steps and by minimizing elapsed time on the longest process steps. There are several opportunities in this example to improve velocity. These are shown on the right side of Table 4-11. The two steps of receiving the product can be effectively eliminated by identifying the product using bar codes to wand it into stock rather than performing a manual data entry from a paper-based receiver. The bar code scan is nearly instantaneous and highly accurate. The distributor is able to write a software program that matches a payment with a product receipt; this eliminates a third process step.

There are four opportunities to shrink the time required for a given process step. Two opportunities include converting the supplier from fax to EDI for orders and from mail to EDI for payments. The supplier can also elect to pay a higher freight cost and change its transportation mode from LTL motor freight to UPS Third Day airfreight. The retailer can review its accounts-payable policy and elect to pay the distributor in a few days, rather than a few weeks. Now only one process step takes a week, whereas four process steps take a day.

Figure 4-7 shows how this velocity improvement is plotted on a value circle against the baseline network design plotted along the unit circle. Velocity is plotted as the order-to-delivery-to-cash cycle time in days. The number of days of baseline velocity equals one unit on the velocity axis. An improvement in velocity is a ratio less than 1.0, and it is plotted toward the origin of the value circle, causing the area under its curve to shrink in size. In the example, the baseline velocity is 3 weeks + 4 days + 6 hours or 25.2 days, using 7 days per week and 24 hours per day to convert

TABLE 4-11
Order-to-Delivery-to-Cash Velocity Optimization of the Network in Table 4-10

Baseline Timeframe	s	m	h	d	w	Optimization Timeframe	s	m	h	d	w
Supplier delivers product to distributor											
D Initiate D order		X						X			
DS Send D order			X			From fax to EDI		X			
S Process S order No time zone change.			X						X		
S Trigger shipment	X						X				
S Process shipment				X						X	
SD Deliver product No time zone change.					X	Change transportation mode				X	
D Receive product			X			Use bar code to eliminate step					
Distributor delivers product to retailer											
R Initiate R order		X						X			
RD Send R order No time zone change.		X						X			
D Process D order		X						X			
D Trigger shipment	X						X				
D Process shipment			X						X		
DR Deliver product No time zone change.				X						X	
R Receive product			X			Use bar code to eliminate step					
Retailer pays distributor											
R Trigger a match	X						X				
R Trigger payment	X						X				
R Process payment					X	Change payment policy			X		
RD Send payment No time zone change.		X						X			
D Apply payment			X			Automate to eliminate step					
D Close D order	X						X				
Distributor pays supplier											
D Trigger a match	X						X				
D Trigger payment	X						X				
D Process payment					X						X
DS Send payment No time zone change.				X		From Mail to EDI		X			
S Apply payment				X						X	
S Close S order		X						X			
26 Total Steps in 3w + 4d	7	6	6	4	3	23 Total Steps in 1w + 4d	7	8	3	4	1

Column Note: s = Seconds, m = Minutes, h = Hours, d = Days, w = Weeks
Row Note: R = Retailer; D = Distributor; S = Supplier

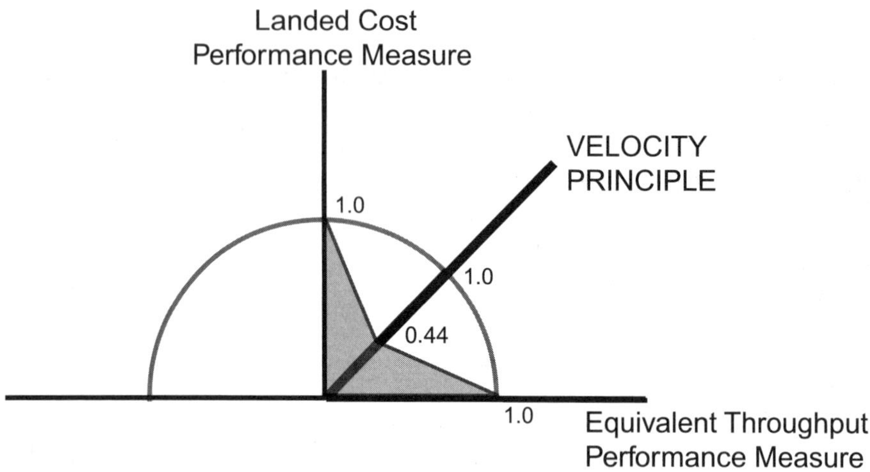

FIGURE 4-7 Velocity increases (improves) toward the origin.

into equivalent days. On the value circle, 1.0 on the velocity axis thus equals 25.2 days of cycle time. The optimized network velocity is 1 week + 4 days + 3 hours or 11.1 days. Velocity increases toward the origin. The optimized network is plotted as 0.44 on the value circle.

$$\frac{\text{Design Velocity}}{\text{Baseline Network}} = \frac{11.1 \text{ Days}}{25.2 \text{ Days}} = 0.440$$

$$\frac{\text{Design Velocity}}{\text{Baseline Network}} = \frac{\#\text{Days to complete one subcycle in the new network}}{\#\text{Days to complete one subcycle in the baseline network}}$$

Where the number of days is the sum of each process step mean. Velocity increases toward the origin of the value circle.

Electronic timestamps on orders, receipts, issues, invoices, and payments can be compared to measure actual network velocity. Consider the following questions when optimizing network velocity:

- Which process steps can be eliminated?
- Which process steps can be done in parallel rather than in series? Which process steps can be synchronized?
- Which process steps can be automated?
- Where in the material flow is drop shipment appropriate? Where can a transportation mode be changed? Where is Vendor-Managed Inventory (VMI) and kanban appropriate?
- Where in the information flow can surface mail and fax become EDI, e-mail, secure Internet, and secure electronic funds transfer? Where can bar code and radio frequency identification tags be used? Where can information flows be routed in parallel rather than in series?

- Where in the cash flow can credit cards and procurement cards be used to speed up the cycle? Where can factoring be useful? Where can cash flows be routed in parallel rather than in series?
- Where can employee education and training speed up a process interface that has changed from manual to automated, or from automated to manual? Where is cross-training imperative?
- Which management policies, for example the accounts payable policy, have become a velocity trap?

THE VARIABILITY PRINCIPLE

Real supply chain networks have high levels of operational *variability.* It takes a different amount of time to complete each subcycle from one pass the next. People vary in how long they take to make decisions and perform their work. Logistics varies in the amount of transit time it takes to move freight and in the time it takes to clear customs. Cash payments vary in how long it takes for them to be processed, and information access time varies in how long it takes to connect to the system to transfer the right information files. It is useful to think of loop velocity in terms of a probability distribution function. The measure of velocity varies a little each time around the loop. Rather than saying the loop velocity will be exactly X, it should be said that the loop velocity will probably fall somewhere between the bounds of Y_1 to Y_2.

The arcs of material flow, information flow, and cash flow that connect the trading partners have an important set of characteristics. Each arc connects a point of origin with a point of destination. Each arc has a cost and a mean time associated with it. Each arc also has a time variability. The threshold of network competitiveness is improved by maximizing velocity while minimizing variability. The days and weeks of queue times, manufacturing and distribution cycle times, logistics transit times, customs clearance times, and time driven by management policy decisions will usually dominate the seconds and minutes of information system transaction times.

Physical Distribution Connections—Transit Time

Many kinds of logistics service providers can connect a point of origin with a point of destination.

Express Small Parcel [Next Day/Days]

Federal Express, United Parcel Service (UPS), DHL, Airborne Express, the U.S. Postal Service, and others offer a variety of express, overnight, two day, multiday ground, and heavy weight freight delivery services. These are hub and spoke arrangements that combine motor freight pickup and delivery with scheduled overnight airfreight connections between hub cities for standard package sizes. Multiday ground options are much less expensive that next-day air options. These services are highly reliable, moving millions of packages per day and offering online Internet package tracking for their customers. These services are available domestically and internationally. Once the customer provides proper declaration of the package contents, the service handles all the customs documentation and clearances.

Motor Freight [Hours/Days/Week]

Motor freight is the most common form of transportation. A motor freight connection to and from an airline is called *cartage;* a motor freight connection to and from an ocean carrier is called *drayage. Rate tariffs* for motor freight are specified in dollars per hundredweight (cwt) based on weight ranges and distance zones. For example, a rate tariff might be quoted as $43.55/cwt coast-to-coast for freight in the range of 150 to 250 pounds. It would then cost $87.10 to transport 200 pounds of cargo from New York, NY to Long Beach, CA. Motor freight rates are quoted as Less-Than-Truckload (LTL) and TruckLoad (TL). A local trucking company can be contracted to make a daily "milk run," stopping at each of several local supplier locations and ending at the factory. Some trucking companies offer higher security by using electronic seals on their trailers and over-the-road cargo tracking with Global Positioning System (GPS) tracking technology. Routing and timing can vary from load to load between the same origin and destination, and is driver dependent. Servicing time at consolidation points, cross-docking facilities, and break-bulk warehouses will vary.

Airfreight [Half Day/Days]

Airfreight is the most expensive mode of transportation. It is priced at dollars per kilogram of freight for an origin–destination pair. Because there are 2.2 pounds per kilogram, a 50-pound package sent by airfreight at a rate of $2.25/kg would cost $51.14 for the shipment. However, a premium is charged once the cubic volume or the weight of the freight exceeds certain thresholds. Although flight time may be only a few hours, many other organizations handle the freight in getting it to and from the aircraft. Cartage companies, freight forwarders, airline agents, ground crews, and customs brokers each contribute to additional hours of elapsed time. Flights may not be scheduled every day. If the cutoff for a particular flight to a remote city is missed, it may be a couple of days until the next flight becomes available. Freight is carried in freighter aircraft and in the bellies of passenger aircraft. There may be uplift capacity constraints, depending on the number of aircraft that service a given city. For example, during the SARS epidemic, Cathay Pacific, Singapore Air, and other airlines cut passenger service to Hong Kong, causing a severe reduction in airfreight capacity out of Hong Kong.

Rail Freight [Days/Week]

Rail freight is a good alternative for high-volume, high-weight cargoes and bulk liquid cargoes. For example, Tropicana ships frozen orange juice concentrate in bulk from Florida to New Jersey on special refrigerated trains. Rate tariffs for rail freight are based on cargo weight and distance traveled for an origin–destination pair. A railcar can be parked on a siding until full and then moved as part of a longer train through a series of destinations to its final destination; this is a low-cost arrangement. A block design is a high-cost arrangement in which certain railcars are blocked out for high-value freight and switched directly from the main train into their destination sidings. Rail freight can be scheduled directly with the railroad, through a freight forwarder, or through an intermodal logistics company. The transit time variability of rail freight is dependent upon the carrier's performance record and the maintenance of the track along the right of way.

Ocean Freight [Days/Weeks]

Ocean freight can be the lowest-cost mode of transportation. It is well suited for high-volume, high-weight containerized cargoes. Ocean freight is priced at a fixed price per container for an origin–destination pair plus terminal handling fees. When more product can be fit into a single container, its rate is effectively cheaper. For example, if a container shipment were priced at $1850 per TEU (Twenty-foot Equivalent Unit) between Singapore and Oakland, CA, plus $150 in terminal fees, then a 40-foot container shipment would cost $3850. If the 40-foot container held 800 cases of molded plastic parts, each case would cost $4.81 to be shipped across the Pacific. If the same container held 64 rolls of building paper, each roll would cost $60.16 to be shipped across the Pacific.

Ocean freight is priced at Less-than-Container-Load (LCL) rates and Container Load (CL) rates. Ocean sailings are often scheduled only once a week, depending on the port. If the cutoff date is missed, the shipment will wait an additional week before being transported. Bad weather also adds to the variability of ocean freight. Ships are scheduled for fixed routes, and containers must be loaded in the reverse order of their offloading. Once a container is lifted aboard, it is committed for the duration of the cruise.

Intermodal

Several forms of intermodal transportation provide interesting tradeoffs of freight cost versus transit time. Several United States trucking companies provide motor-rail intermodal service that puts over-the-road trailers piggybacked on rail cars, cutting a day off the driving time to connect New England with Florida. Product shipped from the Far East into Europe has the option of air-ocean intermodal transport through ports such as Dubai in the United Arab Emirates. The first leg is ocean freight from Hong Kong, Singapore, or Jakarta to Dubai; the second leg is airfreight from Dubai to Frankfurt, Paris, London, or Amsterdam. Logistics carriers like Maersk offer land bridge capability using their ocean–rail intermodal services to move product from the Far East to the East Coast of the United States without passing through the Panama Canal. The first leg is ocean freight into Oakland, CA, and the second leg is rail freight to Newark, NJ, Philadelphia, PA, or Baltimore, MD. Intermodal service combines a transit time that is significantly less than the slower, cheaper mode, with a freight cost that is significantly less than the faster, more expensive mode.

Special Transportation

Refrigerated cargoes and HAZardous MATerial (HAZMAT) cargoes, including corrosive, magnetic, chemical, biological, or radioactive loads, require special transportation arrangements. Such cargoes must be properly declared, labeled, and handled.

Refrigerated and HAZMAT cargoes limit the network design in terms of the available choices of cities for routing and times of day for scheduling. The requirements are much more restrictive. Refrigerated containers come in different temperature ranges, and refrigerated cargoes are subject to spoilage. HAZMAT cargoes are subject to spillage and contamination. The availability of the special trailers and containers needed to move these cargoes and the location of cold-storage warehousing facilities adds additional restrictions to the movement of such freight.

INCOTERMS

The International Chamber of Commerce World Business Organization has established 13 internationally recognized INCOTERMS. These terms define a risk continuum that shifts from the seller bearing all the risk to the buyer bearing all the risk. INCOTERMS are used in purchase agreements, purchase contracts, and shipping papers to standardize the documentation of complicated terms and conditions. Reference materials for INCOTERMS are available through the International Chamber of Commerce World Business Organization and its bookstore, at www.iccwbo.org and www.iccbooks.com respectively. Although some INCOTERMS are transportation mode dependent, they always define the following:

- The responsibility of the buyer or the seller to pay for freight and duty
- The point at which the title to the goods is transferred from the seller to the buyer
- Assignment of risk of loss during transport to the buyer or the seller

Physical Distribution Connections—Customs Clearance Time

In an international network, the total logistics time is the sum of transit time and customs clearance time. Each of these time elements has considerable variability. In some cases the customs clearance time is greater than the transit time, and in many cases the customs clearance time introduces delays and variability greater than the transit time variability. The following sections describe the primary network logistics design issues to consider when *importing* and *exporting* physical goods internationally.

Import Duty Compliance

Import compliance is about paying any necessary duties on foreign imports as a governmental response to protect domestic manufacturers of the same kinds of commodity. Import duties are determined through a number of international treaties. These treaties change often, and the manufacturer must stay up to date with the latest legal requirements. The manufacturer has a responsibility to classify its products for customs, and the importer has the responsibility to comply with all import duty regulations. Every product, product option, product subassembly, product return, and spare part should be classified for import duty. Some services are required to be classified as well. The manufacturer gets to select the import duty classification.

Although it is perfectly legal for the manufacturer to select a duty classification that is duty preferred, the manufacturer must be able to defend its selection against a customs challenge.

Duty classifications and duty rates are documented under the Harmonized Tariff Schedule (HTS), also known as Schedule B. This is a unified worldwide classification scheme from the General Agreement on Tariffs and Trade (GATT), administered by the council for trade in goods under the World Trade Organization (WTO). An HTS code has the format xxxx.yy.zzzz. The first six digits of the code are recognized internationally, whereas the last four digits of the code may have country-specific significance. The HTS code, along with the Country Of Origin, determines the import duty rate to be paid for an item. Import duty is due on the dollar value of the item times its import duty rate when the item is imported. If the import duty is not paid, the item will be held in customs, disrupting the supply chain. Returned items are considered imports and will be charged an appropriate duty.

Import compliance consists of the following steps:

- List every item to be classified—This list should include every product option, product, product subassembly, spare part, and part return. Imported services, such as on-site repair and on-site product training, may require classification.
- Determine the manufacturing Country Of Origin for each item—The Country Of Origin is determined by the rules of origin described below.
- Have the manufacturer classify each of the items using the Harmonized Tariff Schedule—The manufacturer will compare each item to similar items that have been previously classified. Where possible a manufacturer can claim the item under a preferential category with a low or zero duty rate.
- Build a table of import duty rates for every country that will import each of the items—Although the first six digits of the HTS code will be the same for each country of import, the import duty rate can vary widely and may even be duty preferred, depending on the particular international treaty.
- Pay the duty at the time of import—Duty, Value-Added Tax (VAT), and possibly a duty assist are due at the time of import. These increase the landed cost of the item. Some scenarios may be eligible for a duty drawback. Duty drawback is explained later in this Chapter and decreases the landed cost.
- Collect and record statistics about each item—The Commerce Department of the United States requires the importer of record to collect and record vital statistics related to the level of its import activity.

The rules of origin determine the Country Of Origin (COO). These rules are complex. The rules of origin determine the amount of local content that must be present in a partially or fully manufactured product for that product to carry the local Country Of Origin. Sometimes component parts, each with their own individual COO, are combined with enough local value-added labor and local material content for the assembly to take on the local COO. For example, semiconductors and a raw printed circuit board from Malaysia are combined with passive components from Singapore and Japan to create a printed circuit assembly that is "Made in Malaysia." The COO for an automobile might depend upon the relative weights of local content for an engine from Brazil and a transmission from Canada, combined with a car frame, seats, tires, and electronics from the United States. It can be a big cost advantage if the COO is duty preferred when imported. Import duty laws change often; it is good practice to review import duty requirements on a regular basis to avoid this unexpected form of network variability. A *tariff shift* is different from a COO change; a tariff shift occurs when an item is imported under one classification and exported under a different classification with the same COO.

The following are common import duty issues that can delay an item from clearing through customs:

- *The item has never been classified.* The shipment is held in customs until the item is classified. For example, when a new product fails in the field, the manufacturer rushes to disassemble the product and return the defective part to product development for a failure analysis, but because this part is in a lower level of the BOM, it has never been classified for import duty. This unforeseen customs delay may occur at the worst possible time.
- *The HTS codes assigned to the item have changed.* For example, provisions written into the NAFTA treaty caused the reassignment of HTS classification codes over a period of years. Manufacturers had to pay close attention and revise their customs documents when first shipping product each January.
- *The item has not been entered into the customs system for a particular country.* This can occur when a product is unexpectedly cross-channeled. For example, a product manufactured in Latin America is classified and packaged for shipment through United States distribution. Market dynamics shift and suddenly not enough product is available to meet demand in the European Union. A decision is made to divert some of the Latin American product to Europe, but the classification and package labeling is not consistent with the new channel. This may cause a customs delay again at the worst time.
- *There is a discrepancy among the Country Of Origin on the product label, on the packaging label, on the pallet label, and on the manifest.* COO labeling must be consistent from the outside to the inside. When different organizations design the product, the packaging, and the labeling, this requirement can be overlooked.
- *A duty assist has not been paid, and the item is held in customs.* Whenever a domestic manufacturer provides tooling or direct materials to a foreign contract manufacturer, a duty assist is due on the value of the tooling or direct materials. For example, a manufacturer decides to outsource the production of plastic injection molded parts to Taiwan and ships its injection molding die worth $80,000 to the Taiwanese plastics company. If the

plastic parts made from this die have an import duty classification with a 5.0% duty rate, then 5.0% of $80,000, or $4,000, would be due for the duty assist.

Anti-Terrorism Security Measures

Containerized imports have come under a higher level of scrutiny in the war against terrorism. The following are just two examples of policies and procedures that can cause delay and variability in a supply chain network. Under the advance manifest rule, freight forwarders and carriers must provide the United States Customs Service with a detailed description of their containerized cargoes prior to entry into the United States. Notification requirements include a 24-hour advance notice on ocean freight prior to loading at a foreign port, a 4-hour advance notice on airfreight prior to wheels-up, a 2-hour advance notice on rail freight prior to arrival, and a 1-hour advance notice on motor freight prior to arrival. These requirements are subject to change.

The Customs–Trade Partnership Against Terrorism (C-TPAT) is a program whereby importers agree to tighten the physical, procedural, and personnel security of their inbound supply chains through a process of self-audits and customs validation. Customs rewards C-TPAT program compliance by giving the freight clearance of C-TPAT participants priority over nonpartiticipants. Compliance with these important security regulations can become velocity traps when they are not properly managed.

Free Trade Zone/Foreign Trade Zone

A Free Trade Zone (FTZ), known as a foreign trade zone in the United States, is an incentive for foreign manufacturers to employ the local labor of a host country. The host country provides an area, such as an industrial park, with access to its labor pool and logistics infrastructure, duty-free status on imported materials, and sometimes substantial tax advantages. The foreign manufacturer has to employ a certain number of the host country's laborers in order to meet local content requirements on its products and qualify for FTZ benefits.

If any of the products made in the FTZ are sold within the host country, those products do not qualify for the duty-free status on imported materials. The Country Of Destination may still levy a duty on goods exported from a FTZ. This depends on the HTS classification of the exported product. However, it may be possible to use manufacturing within the FTZ to provide a substantial transformation into a lower-duty or no-duty HTS classification.

Export License Compliance

The intent of *export licensing* is to protect the national security and to protect the national economy from adverse effects enabled through the export of a country's own technological, chemical, biological, or nuclear capability. The government expects a manufacturer who exports to know the end-customer and end-usage of its product. This can be a challenge, especially when the product is passed through several tiers of distribution. A manufacturer can be heavily fined if the government discovers that its products have reached the wrong hands. This is true even if the product was first passed through legitimate distribution channels before reaching a fronting organization that forwarded the product into the hands of an enemy. In the United States the Bureau of Export Administration (BXA) in Washington, D.C., administers export controls. Export control regulations change often; it is good practice to review export control requirements on a regular basis to avoid this unexpected form of network variability.

Export compliance consists of the following steps:

- *Classifying the product for export*—The export is assigned an Export Classification Control Number (ECCN) from the Commodity Control List (Ccl). The CCL lists the munitions, drugs and narcotics, nuclear materials, chemical-biological-radiological elements, and restricted technologies under export control. The CCL has fewer classification categories than the HTS.
- *Determining which kind of export license is required*—Licenses are issued in three forms: No License Required (NLR), the Individual Validated License (IVL), and the Special Comprehensive License (SCL). Although every international shipment must be classified for export, many of these shipments will be judged NLR, and will not require a license. The IVL license is the main form of licensing. An IVL license is good for a single shipment to one specific customer. The SCL license applies to qualified distributors or resellers making repeat shipments of the same products to known customers.
- *Consulting the denial list before shipment*—The denial list is a government-generated list of embargoed countries, companies, and individuals. It is unlawful to make a sale or to ship product to anyone on the denial list. The denial list undergoes constant change. The exporter is expected to access the current denial list in real-time prior to shipping its product.
- *Recording vital statistics*—In the United States the Commerce Department requires the exporter of record to collect and record vital statistics related to the level of its export activity.

Information Flow Connections

Many kinds of information service providers connect points of origin with points of destination for the purpose of sending specification drawings, approved vendor lists, BOM listings, product cost rollups, forecasts, orders, order acknowledgements, advance shipping notices, invoices, return notifications, return credit authorizations, etc. Communication channels need to have bidirectional capability. Table 4-12 identifies common types of connection and their respective cycle times. In addition, each type of connection has an associated cost and reliability. For example, the Internet has built-in redundancy because of its packet transmission protocols, but you may never know whether your fax reached the other party. Encryption techniques add a high level of security to electronic forms of information flow.

TABLE 4-12
Information Flow Connection Characteristics

Method	Cycle Time	Handles Text	Handles Graphics
Surface Mail	Days/Week	Yes	Yes
Surface Mail a CD-ROM	Days/Week	Yes	Yes
Voicemail	Hours/Days	Yes	No
Electronic Data Interchange (EDI)	Minutes/Hours	Yes	No
Fax	Minutes	Yes	Yes
e-Mail Attachments	Minutes	Yes	Yes
Modem Internet Connection	Minutes	Yes	Yes
Wireless Telephony	Seconds/Minutes	Yes	Limited
Broadband Internet Connection	Seconds	Yes	Yes

In general, the cycle times for Internet and wireless communications are orders of magnitude faster than other types of flow connections and are not factors in the variability of a network design. On the other hand, if there are chronic issues with difficult connects or unpredictable disconnects, then the cycle times for these information flows can escalate. For example, poor server hardware uptime or a longer-than-expected software backup can become a velocity trap in an information flow connection.

Cash Flow Connections

Many kinds of financial service providers can connect a point of origin with a point of destination.

Letter Of Credit [Days/Weeks/Months]

A Letter Of Credit (LOC) is used for an international cash flow when the buyer and the seller are wary of each other's credit rating. The LOC has an interest charge and a fixed expiration date. The principal tied up in a LOC is subject to currency fluctuation risk. Reference material for letters of credit is available through the International Chamber of Commerce World Business Organization and its bookstore, at www.iccwbo.org and www.iccbooks.com, respectively. These are the steps to execute a letter of credit:

- The buyer arranges the LOC with an *issuing bank* in the buyer's country by depositing the principal amount and by agreeing to pay daily interest through the expiration date of the LOC.
- The buyer notifies the seller that a LOC has been opened.
- When the product has been delivered to the forwarder, the seller provides documentary proof to the *beneficiary bank* in the seller's country and requests the transfer of funds. *Documentary proof* consists of a commercial invoice, a certificate of origin, a bill of lading, and the forwarder's certificate of receipt. These documents must be perfect because the beneficiary

bank will release the funds based only on documentary evidence, without ever seeing the physical product.
- The beneficiary bank notifies the issuing bank that the terms of the LOC have been met. The issuing bank transfers the principal amount to the beneficiary bank, and the beneficiary bank deposits the funds into the seller's account.
- The LOC is closed upon its execution or upon its expiration date, whichever occurs first.

Check Sent by Surface Mail [Days/Week]

This is the most traditional method of cash flow. A check is written against the buyer's commercial bank account and mailed to the seller. The seller deposits the check in its own commercial bank account and waits for the check to clear through the banking system. The buyer can speed the clearing time by sending a certified check. The buyer can insure and register the mail at additional cost.

Check Sent Overnight by the US Postal Service, FedEx or DHL [Day]

This is the traditional method of cash flow wrapped in an express mail envelope. A check is written against the buyer's commercial bank account and sent to the seller through express mail. Depending on whether the destination is domestic or international, the U.S. Postal Service, FedEx, or DHL might provide the express service of choice. Online tracking is provided with the cost of the service. The seller deposits the check in its own commercial bank account and waits for the check to clear through the banking system.

Factoring [Days]

When an invoice is generated for a credit worthy customer, the account receivable may be sold to a *factor*. The factor pays the seller cash for 75–90% of the receivable within 1 or 2 days at a service charge of 2–5%. When the buyer pays the invoice in 30 days, the factor remits the reserve portion of the cash to the seller minus the service charge. The factor takes title on the receivable, and provides all the credit and collection services.

Credit Card/Procurement Card [Minutes]

A credit card is a common form of Business-To-Consumer (B2C) payment, and a procurement card is a common form of Business-To-Business (B2B) payment for purchases. These are the steps to a credit card/procurement card transaction:

- The seller establishes either a Mail Order Telephone Order (MOTO) account or a Card Not Present (CNP) account with a commercial bank, and agrees to pay a service charge for each transaction.
- The buyer is qualified up to a predetermined credit rating at a participating commercial bank, and agrees to a finance charge on the outstanding balance.

- The buyer presents a valid credit card in-person or by FAX or by mail to the seller with the card type, the credit account number and expiration date with a signature. When the information is entered on-line, it is encrypted and sent through Secure Socket Layer (SSL) technology.
- The seller immediately withdrawals the payment minus the service charge from its commercial bank.
- The seller's bank makes settlement with the buyer's bank.
- The buyer's bank invoices the buyer by mail once a month.
- The buyer pays the invoice and finance charge due by the deadline.

Electronic Funds Transfer [Minutes]

An Electronic Fund Transfer (EFT), or wire transfer, is a secure electronic form of cash flow done over a private banking Intranet. The commercial banks around the world are connected together electronically with security provided through encryption of the bank routing numbers, account number and dollar amount information. Wire transfers are used both domestically and internationally.

Methods of Paying Duty

There are three methods commonly used to pay customs duties. If the freight is destined to clear customs for import into a country, the duty is paid at the time the freight clears. The cleared freight is then said to be *liquidated*. If the freight is in transit for reexport to another country, there are two additional payment approaches. Either no duty is paid on entry; the import is held in a customs-bonded warehouse, and the import duty due is paid at the time of the reexport shipment. Or duty is paid upon entry, and an application for duty drawback is made at the time of reexport.

A *duty drawback* is a refund of duty that avoids situations of double taxation. A common example occurs when an import duty is paid on lower-level materials that are manufactured into an assembly for export back to the same country from which the materials were imported. In this case a duty drawback applies only to the value of the lower-level parts. Duty drawback is documentation-intensive in that there must be strict inventory control that proves the exported components are exactly the imported components. There can be no co-mingling with other inventory. Duty drawback can recover 99% of the original value, and may take several months from the time of application to the time of payment. For example, a United States manufacturer exports $5,000 of electronic parts to Mexico. These parts are later assembled into $18,000 of printed circuit assemblies to be sent back to the same US manufacturer. When Mexico exports the completed assemblies, the US manufacturer can apply for a duty drawback, or refund, of $4,950 [0.99 × $5,000].

The Normal Distribution

Although there are many mathematical ways to describe statistical variation, this book will use the *normal distribution*. This is because the normal distribution is better known and less forbidding to most people. The error that is introduced by the use of the normal distribution when another probability distribution function is a

TABLE 4-13
The Normal Distribution Applied to Logistics

For the data points $X_1, X_2, X_3, \ldots, X_n$	For example $X_1 = 4$ days, $X_2 = 3$ days, $X_3 = 3$ days, $X_4 = 5$ days
The mean M of a normal distribution is calculated: The standard deviation SD of a normal distribution is calculated:	$M = \sum_{i=1}^{n} X_i/n$ $\quad M = (4 + 3 + 3 + 5)/4 = 3.75$ days $SD = \frac{\sqrt{(X_1 - M^2) + (X_2 - M^2) + (X_3 - M^2) + \cdots + (X_n - M^2)}}{n}$ $SD = \frac{\sqrt{(4-3.75)^2 + (3-3.75)^2 + (3-3.75)^2 + (5-3.75)^2}}{4}$ $= 0.415$ days
For two or more independent normal distributions in series: M_1, SD_1 M_2, SD_2 M_j, SD_j	$M_s = M_1 + M_2 + \cdots + M_j$ $SD_S = \sqrt{(SD_1)^2 + (SD_2)^2 + \cdots + (SD_j)^2}$ The Root-Mean-Square (RMS) value of the standard deviations. For example: If transit time $M_1 = 3.75$ days and $SD_1 = 0.415$ days and customs clearance $M_2 = 1$ day and $SD_2 = 2.33$ days, then $M_s = 4.75$ days and $SD_s = 2.36$ days
For two or more independent normal distributions in parallel: M_1, SD_1 M_2, SD_2 M_j, SD_j	M_p = Largest of $(M_1, M_2, \ldots, M_j)$ SD_p = Largest of $(SD_1, SD_2, \ldots, SD_j)$ For example: If for a coordinated shipment $M_1 = 1$ day and $SD_1 = 2$ days and $M_2 = 3.75$ days and $SD_2 = 0.415$ days, then $M_p = 3.75$ days and $SD_p = 2$ days
A 95.4% service level equals the mean plus 2 standard deviations:	$M + 2SD = 3.75 + (2)(0.415) = 4.58$ days
A 99.7% service level equals the mean plus 3 standard deviations:	$M + 3SD = 3.75 + (3)(0.415) = 5.99$ days

better fit is a second-order effect compared to the competitive improvements that can realized from following the principles and techniques of this book.

Transit time measurements need to be made for each origin-to-destination pair in the network. It is best to have at least four or five data points for each logistics path. The measurements can be made by comparing system timestamps for shipment triggers and delivery receipts. When a problem connection is identified, that measurement can be refined. A mean and standard deviation that determines a normal distribution can be easily calculated from a small set of data points. The mean and standard deviation can then be used to determine the logistics time necessary to ensure a given service level while considering the impact of additional series and parallel logistics connections. Table 4-13 summaries the key equations to be used with the normal distribution to solve these logistics variability problems.

Minimizing Variability

Optimizing velocity and variability of the four subcycles for each trading partner—order-to-delivery, order-to-stock, invoice-to-pay, and invoice-to-cash—determines the competitiveness of a network design. The cycle time for each process step in a

TABLE 4-14
Network Transit Times

For a Distribution Warehouse located in Joliet, IL

Supplier	Location	Mean	Std Dev
X	St. Louis, MO 300 miles	5.5 hr	1.5 hr
Y	Madison, WI 145 miles	2.6 hr	2.1 hr
Z	Portland, OR 2,238 miles	34.5 hr	6.2 hr
For Transit Times in Parallel		34.5 hr	6.2 hr

Retailer	Location	Mean	Std Dev
A	Columbus, OH 319 miles	6.8 hr	1.5 hr
B	Indianapolis, IN 185 miles	3.4 hr	0.7 hr
C	Peoria, IL 170 miles	3.1 hr	0.7 hr
D	Madison, WI 145 miles	2.6 hr	2.1 hr
E	Milwaukee, WI 92 miles	1.6 hr	1.0 hr
For Transit Times in Parallel		6.8 hr	2.1 hr

subcycle can be described by a mean and a standard deviation. The velocity of a sub-cycle is determined by adding together the mean times for each serial process step. The variability of a subcycle is determined by taking the square root of the sum of the squares, called the Root-Mean-Square (RMS), of the standard deviations of the cycle times for each serial process step. Where the RMS of the standard deviations can be driven lower, loop variability decreases and network competitiveness increases. A fast, predictable subcycle contributes to a competitive network design. A slow, unpredictable subcycle amplifies waste in terms of unnecessary inventory and unnecessary cash buffering throughout the network.

The following detailed example shows how the competitiveness of a network can be improved by minimizing its logistics variability. A distribution warehouse links three suppliers with five retail stores. The distribution warehouse is in Joliet, IL, on Central Standard Time, with one of the suppliers in Portland, OR, on Pacific Standard Time and one of the stores in Columbus, OH, on Eastern Standard Time. Table 4-14 details the logistics connections for each of the suppliers and retail stores. The three parallel inbound transit-time profiles and the five parallel outbound transit times profiles are combined by taking the largest mean and the largest standard deviation. Keep in mind that the elapsed time to move freight cuts across three time zones; adjust departure and arrival times accordingly.

The order-to-delivery subcycle for the distribution warehouse to the five stores is detailed in Table 4-15. The mean time for each process step relates to the subcycle's velocity. The standard deviation time for each process step relates to the subcycle's variability. Once the table is complete, all the times are converted into the same dimensional units (hours). The total order-to-delivery cycle time is profiled as the sum of the means and the root-mean-square of the standard deviations. Minimizing the sum of the means maximizes loop velocity. Minimizing the RMS of the standard deviations minimizes loop variability.

"Capture Order" is the highest-variability process step because it has the highest mean to standard deviation ratio. But in the context of the total subcycle,

TABLE 4-15
Order-To-Delivery Subcycle for the Distribution Warehouse

Process Step	Info/Log Segment	Trading Partner	Nominal Trading Partner	Velocity Mean Time	Variability Std Dev Time
Capture Order	I-Loop	Store(s)		5 minutes 0.1 hours	8 minutes 0.1 hours
Transmit Order	I-Arc		Information Service Providers	25 seconds 0.0 hours	
Process Order	I-Loop	Distributor		10 minutes 0.2 hours	1 minute 0.0 hours
Trigger Shipment	IL-Trigger	Distributor		10 seconds 0.0 hours	
Process Shipment	L-Loop	Distributor		2.2 hours	1.5 hours
Deliver Shipment	L-Arc		Logistics Service Providers	6.8 hours	2.1 hours
Receive Shipment	L-Loop	Store(s)		30 minutes 0.5 hours	45 minutes 0.8 hours
Close Order	LI-Trigger	Store(s)		3 minutes 0.1 hours	1 minute 0.0 hours
For Process Times in Series				9.9 hours	2.7 hours

the order-capture time is insignificant. The logistic process steps "Deliver Shipment" with a standard deviation of 2.1 hours, "Process Shipment" with a standard deviation of 1.5 hours, and "Receive Shipment" with a standard deviation of 0.8 hours are the areas of opportunity to reduce variability.

Once the process step variability has been identified and prioritized, a root-cause analysis can be performed. The root-cause analysis should lead to the minimization or elimination of the cause of the variability. Suppose that by changing the time of day to drive the highways around Chicago, IL, the transit time variability to Madison, WI, can be cut to one hour. "Deliver Shipment" transit time variability is then reduced to 1.5 hours. Suppose that by adding a shipping label printer on the production line and reengineering the workflow the "Process Shipment" cycle time variability can be cut to 0.5 hours. Then the total order-to-deliver subcycle variability is reduced to an RMS value of 1.8 hours. This is 66.7% of the baseline variability. Figure 4-8 shows how a decrease in variability plots toward the origin on the value circle.

$$\frac{\text{Design Variability}}{\text{Baseline Network}} = \frac{1.8\text{ Hours}}{2.7\text{ Hours}} = \frac{0.667}{1.000} = 0.667$$

$$\frac{\text{Design Variability}}{\text{Baseline Network}} = \frac{\#\text{Days of subcycle variability in the new network design}}{\#\text{Days of subcycle variability in the baseline network}}$$

Where the number of days is the RMS value of the standard deviations for each of the process steps. Variability decreases toward the origin on the value circle.

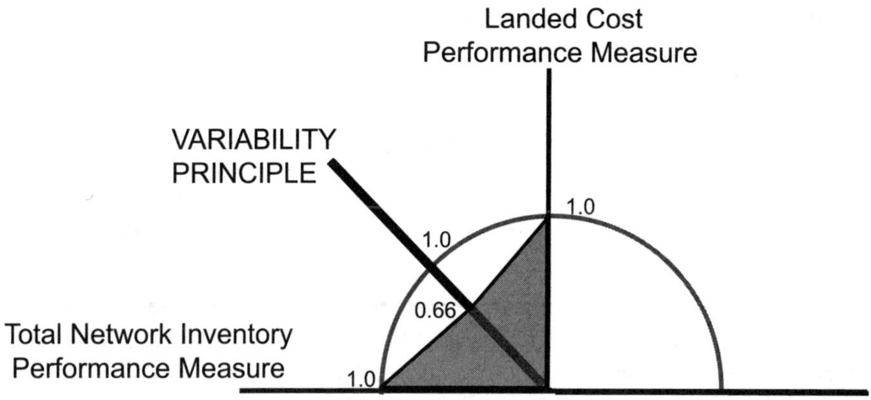

FIGURE 4-8 Variability decreases (improves) toward the origin.

IN SUMMARY

Orders cause material to flow from sellers to buyers, and invoices cause cash to flow from buyers to sellers. The principles and techniques of Chapters 2, 3, and 4 and the parallel loop discussion in Chapter 5 are combined to optimize the network design by maximizing velocity and minimizing variability. The optimization steps, summarized below, apply to both the design of a forward supply chain network and separately to a reverse supply chain network:

1. Each trading partner is rationalized against a focused business strategy.
2. The product BOM is flattened to minimize the number of midstream echelons.
3. The Country Of Origin is chosen as a tradeoff between landed cost and network length.
4. The total number of network echelons is minimized upstream, midstream, and downstream.
5. Nominal trading partners of like kind, i.e., LSPs, ISPs, and FSPs, are consolidated where possible.
6. Where possible, subcycle information flows and cash flows are run in parallel rather than in series.

For each subcycle the optimization continues as follows:

1. The number of process steps in each subcycle is minimized.
2. The velocity for each subcycle is maximized by reducing the mean cycle time for each process step.
3. The variability for each subcycle is minimized by reducing the standard deviation of the cycle time for significant process steps.
4. A measure of the successive network design improvement is plotted on the value circle.

This Chapter has raised two fundamental questions:

- How can you accelerate the order-to-delivery-to-cash cycle and avoid velocity traps?
- How can you take variability out of the order-to-delivery-to-cash cycle?

Chapter 5 refines the basic network design by considering network partitioning, parallel subcycle configurations, and the implications of information technology.

"Why doesn't Fred pay his bill?" the supply chain architect's wife asked. They were waiting for the waiter to bring them chocolate-chocolate cake and espresso at their favorite Italian restaurant. "He was invoiced over six weeks ago."

"Maybe Fred is still upset over your new instructor, Suzie Lee."

"No, that's not it. Suzie is doing a great job, and Fred's managers are coming around to her point of view. It's just hard to understand how Fred can run a large company, yet be so unpredictable in his payments."

Their cake arrived, and the architect knew he would regret having ordered such a rich dish later on. "Tell me about the process you use for getting paid."

"We teach the class, we invoice, and we get paid. There's really not much to tell."

"Okay. Let's start from the top and walk through your order-to-delivery-to-cash cycle."

"What do you mean order-to-delivery-to-cash cycle? It sounds complicated."

"It can be simple. A few questions will help you put it all into a process perspective. First, how does your client, DataLink, order their training classes? Do you have a written agreement to deliver some number of classes or is each class negotiated separately?"

"Fred agreed to a dozen classes taught over a four month period," his wife replied.

"Did you get Fred to put that in writing?"

"Of course. We have a business contract that spells out the number of classes, the maximum number of students per class, and the instructor coverage," she beamed.

"What does the contract say about getting paid?"

"The contract specifies the price of each course. The eight-session courses are more expensive than the six-session courses. Student materials are charged per head and instructors have a per diem travel allowance."

"That all sounds fine for the pricing side of your business, but now we're talking about the billing side of your business," said her husband.

"DataLink is invoiced for each class."

"You are saying that Fred signed a contract for 12 classes. Your instructors teach the classes. Then Fred is invoiced after each class is completed?"

"Yes, that is correct."

"Okay. Now let's look at the velocity and the variability of order-to-delivery-to-cash cycle."

"What in the world are you talking about?" They were interrupted while their waiter served the dessert and again when the waiter brought their espressos.

He resumed, "Think about this. The elapsed time from signing the contract to being paid for the first class is much shorter than the elapsed time from signing the contract to getting paid for the last class. The longer you teach classes using the contract as your single order point, the slower the velocity of getting paid."

"Yes. That's right," she said, mulling it over.

"In addition, there is some variability in each cycle. Some of the classes are eight sessions, whereas others are six sessions. Some of the classes have the maximum of 24 students, whereas other classes are closer to an average of 16 students. Some of your instructors claim the maximum per diem charges, whereas other instructors only claim an average per diem charge. Do you see the variability?"

"Okay. The different velocities and the variability are clear. But although this is an interesting conversation, what does any of this have to do with getting Fred to pay his bill?"

"The most competitive supply chains have learned to maximize their velocity while minimizing their variability. Your business is no different; your business model has some room for improvement. For example, in addition to signing a contract for the 12 classes, you might consider a customer order for each class. The customer order would be due one week before the start of the first class session and would confirm the names and number of your students. You could then invoice twice against this customer order. The first invoice would cover your costs for student materials plus one third of the instructor's fee; the first payment should be payable upon receipt. The second invoice for the remaining two thirds of the instructor fee would be delivered to the customer on the day of the last class; the second invoice should be payable within ten days."

"Why is this extra work necessary?"

"Don't look at this as extra work. The orders define the start of each order-to-delivery-to-cash cycle and keep the velocity for each of your classes about the same. The first invoice covers the variability of the number of students per class, and it greatly improves your cash flow. By hand delivering the second invoice, you eliminate the delay in sending an invoice and the week for the invoice to travel through the mail. You will effectively shorten your time to payment by two to three calendar weeks, said the supply chain architect.

By the way, this chocolate-chocolate cake is good!"

5 Overcoming Information Boundaries

Tuesday, July 9

The supply chain architect could not believe that almost two weeks had passed and still there was no sign of a plumbing inspector. The rough plumbing and electrical work were done. The electrical inspection was done. But the sheetrock work could not begin before the plumbing inspection.

He decided to call Tom, the house architect, on the phone.

"I'm sorry; I'm unavailable to answer your call right now. If you would like to leave a message, please dial 'one' at the tone."

He identified himself and left a voicemail, "Good afternoon, Tom. Listen, you said it would only take a couple of days to get the plumbing approved. It's been nearly two weeks! Isn't there some way to move this along?"

Tom returned his call two hours later. "Yes, it has got to be frustrating for you. The plumbing inspection is scheduled for Thursday morning between 8:00 a.m. and noon. Will someone be home to let the inspector into the kitchen?"

"The electrical inspection was so fast and painless. Why can't one inspector do all the inspections? Why is this so complicated?"

"The different trades need different kinds of information. Inspectors are licensed under different jurisdictions. And there are different levels of regret factors if we continue with the work."

"What do you mean?" asked the supply chain architect.

"The risk of the plumber having a bad solder joint on a copper pipe is that the pipe will spring a leak and ruin the sheetrock. But the regret factor of an electrician miswiring a connection behind the wall is the potential to create enough heat to cause a fire or to cause a life-threatening shock hazard."

"You didn't even mention adherence to the building codes?"

"That's right, but that's my job. That's why you are paying an architect to make sure the design is in compliance with all of the relevant building codes. We must pay attention to all the different kinds of code and regulation information that each of the building trades requires. Each municipality and state is a little different with its codes and zoning ordinances; very little of this is unified."

"How do you deal with such partitioned information?"

"It can be difficult. Over time, you learn how to prioritize different sets of information and how to determine the least common denominator among conflicting data. Fortunately municipal information systems make it easy to look up the different building codes, and the Internet makes it easy to look up different component specifications. But you do have to be smart enough to know which databases have the necessary information," said Tom.

"What happens if you can't find a specification you need for the design?"

"In that case you would call the component manufacturer directly. You would be amazed at how much information can be gotten in just a few minutes in my profession."

*****

They were enmeshed in an information systems consolidation with their sister division in Singapore. In a ploy to cut operating expense, certain product lines were being transferred to Singapore to take advantage of the lower landed cost. Each of the manufacturing systems in support of these product lines was being consolidated under Asia-Pac.

Hector had asked the supply chain architect to represent manufacturing on the consolidation team, along with all his other responsibilities. It was 10:00 p.m. and time for the conference call with B.T. Lam, the Asia-Pac I.T. Director, and his information technology team. This meeting was to problem solve the mapping of data structures for the product line being transferred. C.B. Ng, senior I.T. engineer, and Esther Lam, a database programmer, were expected on the call. The Singaporean Chinese used initials and anglicized their first names to make communications with the Americans easier.

"Good morning. Is everyone there so we can get started?"

"Good evening. Yes, we are here. We have already mapped 65% of the necessary data fields to the Asia-Pac database schema," began B.T. "It shouldn't be a problem to migrate the rest of your data."

"This is good news!" replied the architect. "We wanted to let your team know how we have been handling the customer option BOM for these products."

"This is C.B. Can you say that again, please?"

"Yes. We wanted to let your team know how we have been handling the customer option BOM for these products. First, can you tell us if the remote terminal driver software is working for the Asia-Pac database?"

"Could you repeat that please?"

"Yes, is the remote terminal driver software working for the Asia-Pac database?"

"It shouldn't be a problem," said C.B.

"Okay. We can use the remote terminal capability on our next call to demonstrate the customer option BOM structure. The customer can choose the product with or without polarity reversal relays."

"Yes."

"The customer can also choose the product for 120Vac line voltage operation or 220–240Vac line voltage operation. This must be specified on the customer's order. So, there are a total of four options."

"Yes."

"Do you have any questions?" asked the architect.

"Go ahead. Wait, Esther just joined us. Okay, go ahead."

"Can you dedicate a data element for the relay option and a second data element for the line voltage option?"

"It is not a problem," said B.T.

"Which data element will you dedicate for the relay option and which data element will you dedicate for the line voltage option?"

"We already have line voltage on the Asia-Pac manufacturing database schema," replied B.T. "We can map the relay option to the Asia-Pac order processing database."

"Can the manufacturing database access data elements from the order processing database? Where is the order-processing database server located, anyway?"

"This is Esther. The order processing database server is located in Hong Kong. It should be no problem."

"Do you agree B.T?"

"This is Esther. B.T. had to go to another meeting."

The teleconference continued for another hour at the same frustrating pace. The architect hung up from the call with more questions than answers. It was sultry as he drove home, and the car's air conditioner was working hard to cool off the car. As he drove, he realized that the interaction between the Singapore and Hong Kong databases used by Asia-Pac was still a mystery. He continued to worry that C.B. and Esther probably misunderstood the combinations of customer product options.

The next morning Hector Morales asked, "How did your conference call go last night with Singapore?"

"You know, talking half way around the world with people of another culture is always a challenge. It's like we don't even work for the same company."

"What do you mean?" asked Hector.

"There are so many real and self-imposed boundaries that partition our supply chain network—like time zones, distance, language, Chinese culture, and company culture, to name a few—that it is really difficult to get both sides on the same page."

"That is why information technology is the glue that makes such a network possible. Can you imagine running a global network without the benefit of computers?" asked Hector.

"But it's much more than just interconnecting computers around the world. There was a lot of face-saving going on last night. That really gets in the way of asking some direct questions. You have to learn to ask all your questions in a nonthreatening way, and then guess at the answer. It really takes a lot of time and is very frustrating."

"What do you suggest?"

"The only way we will be able to overcome this fragmentation and keep the program on track is to spend some face-to-face time with B.T. and his team. Flying to Singapore is expensive, but many more weeks of these kinds of calls will be even more expensive," replied the supply chain architect.

"I agree," said Hector. "In my experience relationships are everything. It is clear that there is not much of one yet with our sister division in Singapore. Let me know when your travel plans are firm with Singapore."

Information technology is the glue that makes a distributed supply chain network possible. The number of ways a network design is partitioned in practice is mind-boggling. Time zone boundaries, cultural boundaries, import/export boundaries, legal boundaries, intellectual property boundaries, data access boundaries, etc., slice and dice real networks with unexpected ramifications to network operations. This Chapter completes the design of a competitive network and begins the transition to competitive network operations. Chapter 2 provided a high-level network framework in terms of the business strategy, core competencies, and network zones. Chapter 3 grouped trading partners and nominal trading partners for transformation, manufacturing, and fulfillment by echelon in their respective zones. Chapter 4 defined a competitive network design as maximizing order-to-delivery-to-cash cycle velocity while minimizing its subcycle variability. This Chapter explores the competitive benefits of moving information in parallel rather than serial flows and expands on the relationship of the network with the product BOM. By the end of this Chapter, you will be better able to assess the requirements and the business risks of your information technology infrastructure.

SCOPING THE INFORMATION SYSTEM DISCUSSION

Anyone who has dealt with information system architecture in a large company environment knows that it is an expensive proposition, and it consumes scarce company resources. It only gets worse in a network environment. It doesn't matter whether you are talking about buying an enterprise resource planning system, installing radio frequency identification tag technology for the warehouse, or writing your own eXtensible Markup Language (XML) module to interface trading partners over the Internet. The scope of a discussion on information systems could include any of the following topics, but this book will stay focused on understanding what the information system is really doing. There are plenty of experts and lots of literature on all of these topics, but what is missing is a balanced presentation of the integrated capability and business risk that the network information system provides. Software applications have become so complex that most users have lost their perspective on what they accomplish and the risks they involve. This complexity is fueled by the twin dynamics of new technologies rendering older information system platforms obsolete and the seemingly continuous integration and disintegration of legacy information systems driven by business reorganization.

The following topics are beyond the scope of this book:

- *Mapping the set of business requirements to a system specification*—All the business processes required to run the network are documented into one massive specification.
- *Selecting the best information system alternative*—An attempt is made to match different commercially available alternatives to the system specification. One strategy is to cover as many process requirements as possible with a single, multi-module application and then to fill in the gaps with a number of smaller, highly specialized applications from other software vendors.
- *Presenting a compelling return on investment argument*—These systems are a huge expense for installation and maintenance. The return comes from the one-time reduction in inventory assets and from growth in market share due to sustained higher operational levels of customer service.
- *Deciding who pays for the information system*—This becomes a dilemma as the original set of assumptions changes and as the original trading partners are substituted in the network.
- *Programming the business process algorithms*—This is a deep dive that maps the business process design into Internet connectivity, database design, and software programming using the latest generation of programming languages.
- *Managing the program for an information system installation*—The techniques of good program management are applied to the staffing, implementation, testing, and training for the new system.
- *Operating the information system to its full potential*—Learning to use the full functionality of the software application. Tuning the hardware to achieve the highest bandwidth and deepest memory.
- *Maintaining the information system*—License agreements, user assignments and privileges, security audits, hardware and software upgrades, etc.

ASSESSING THE INFORMATION SYSTEM AS AN ASSET OR A LIABILITY

A supply chain network cannot function today without an information technology infrastructure, but many supply chain networks today cannot function with the information systems they have. Is it better to run your business with a five million dollar ERP system or with five hundred Excel spreadsheets? The place to start is with an assessment of what you currently have in terms of data versus information, process requirements, risk exposure, and maintenance costs.

Provides Information versus Data

Although you are probably awash in data, do you have the necessary information to run the business? This question becomes all the more relevant when the business extends across other trading partners, each of whom is a separate legal entity with independent information systems. It is both painful and expensive to cobble together information systems that were never intended for information sharing. As a first step in the assessment, the following basic data attributes must be present in an information system infrastructure:

- *Data accuracy*—The definitions in the data dictionary and the data in the database must be accurate. Periodically sampling data elements and reconciling the root cause of data errors, like cycle counting for inventory accuracy, can be used to sample data accuracy.
- *Data memory*—A data element has no memory of its previous values. It is what it is.
- *Data duplication*—In sophisticated information systems each data element resides in a single database. But in most legacy information systems and when information systems are merged through process reengineering and business acquisition, the same data element may be repeated in multiple databases. When this is true, the same data element may hold different values at the same time.
- *Data refresh timing*—Consider a single database containing many data elements. In *batch mode* all the data elements are updated at a time that is unrelated to any network transaction. In *real-time, asynchronous mode*, some of the data elements are updated at slightly different times soon after the occurrence of a network transaction. In *real-time, synchronous mode*, the relevant data elements are updated at a time concurrent with a network transaction.
- *Data availability*—Sometimes a critical data element does not exist anywhere in any database. This can happen when new information system applications are built on top of sparse legacy systems.
- *Data owner*—One person in the organization is responsible for the data accuracy of a subset of the database. For example, a buyer is responsible for part of the purchasing database accuracy.
- *Data integrity*—The data element remains accurate over time. A known good database is not corrupted during the normal operation of an information system.
- *Data cleansing*—When two or more databases are merged during an information system consolidation, new data integrity issues can arise. It may be necessary to perform a manual sampling and data cleansing to ensure a one-time accuracy of the combined data. But when the database is very large, it becomes impractical to cleanse 100% of the data.

Relational databases and data warehouses are techniques invented to convert data into information. A *relational database* is a software program that links two or more databases together to relate a particular data element content to an information context. For example, an accountant asking for the cost rollup on a product BOM, a logistics Analyst checking the freight payment for an import, and a buyer working the details of a contract negotiation each need to access the data element that holds the item standard cost. Here the item standard cost is the data content. The accountant would query the cost accounting module, the logistics analyst would query the freight payment module, and the buyer would query the contracts module. The standard cost data resides in just one place, but is related to three kinds of information. These are the information contexts. If the accountant, the logistics analyst, and the buyer had pulled the "same" data from three different sources or sources that were updated at three different times, then the three information contexts could not be reconciled.

A *data warehouse* pulls from multiple databases to support decision making. Data warehouses are useful for bridging data across different software applications for the same trading partner and for bridging data across the same software application from different trading partners. Data warehouses can be used to capture and assign time frames and geographical contexts to historical data. For example, suppose a data warehouse is built to capture customer order statistics for the eastern, southern, and western regions in January, February, March, and April. It would then be easy for a salesperson to query for information about how much product their largest customer ordered in February and March from the western and southern regions. The process of studying data to search for new relationships is called *data mining*.

Meets All Process Coverage Requirements

The second step in the assessment is to perform a gap analysis of the process coverage of the information systems infrastructure. In spite of the claims made by some ERP solution providers, it takes more than one database and often more than a dozen independent software applications to run a global business enterprise. Unexpected gaps can occur within large, single-vendor software applications and between applications created by different software vendors. This is because different definitions and assumptions were used as the starting point for each application. Sometimes, software developers are not exposed to the practitioner's view of the world, and they force a process definition into the business application that is foreign to the way such business is conducted. For example, the business wants to push information to its trading partner, but the software design forces the trading partner to pull information from the business. Such a simple change can cause chaos in a business relationship without a disciplined reengineering of the process and extensive retraining of employees on both sides of the relationship. Other coverage gaps include:

- *Scalability*—The system will easily adjust up or down to fit the volume of business transactions in terms of number of customers, number of products, number of suppliers, number of orders, number of invoices, etc. There are no noticeable system performance breakpoints as the number of transactions escalates.
- *Missing functionality*—A business-critical capability is missing. For example, in a business where the average BOM has eight levels, the application supports the download of a single-level BOM, but cannot download a multi-level BOM.
- *Excessive functionality*—Every conceivable capability has been built into the application making it difficult and expensive to learn.
- *Shared employee access*—The number of personal computers or the number of software licenses is restricted such that several employees must time-share system access to perform their jobs.

- *Nominal trading partner connection gaps*—One or more nominal trading partners obtain operating information from outside the formal information system. This issue can be common to small customers and small suppliers around the network fringe.
- *Hardware least common denominator*—One or more of the trading partners is unwilling or unable to make the investment in the required minimum hardware configuration. This might be for wide area network (WAN) access, for the required number of application servers, for local area network (LAN) bandwidth, for personal computer memory depth, or for wireless access. The hardware least common denominator becomes a constraint that limits full information systems performance among the other trading partners.
- *Software least common denominator*—One or more of the trading partners is unwilling or unable to make the investment in the required minimum software configuration and training. This might be for the latest version of operating system or the latest version of Internet browser or the latest version of software encryption and digital signatures, for EDI protocols, for software licenses, for installation of missing modules, etc. The software least common denominator becomes a constraint that limits full information systems functionality among the other trading partners.
- *Unidirectional interfaces*—Sometimes a customized, process-critical module from a legacy system is kept and interfaced with a new, enterprise-wide software application. If the interface was designed to be unidirectional to save development costs, then the legacy module will only upload or download. The legacy module cannot benefit from data flow in the opposite direction.
- *Exception reporting and alarming*—The system reports every number every time and prints reams of paper. This is inferior to programmable exception reporting and alarming.
- *Limited management reporting*—Management reporting is limited to a few preprogrammed reports. The information system should have a powerful, easy-to-use report generator for one-time and customized management reports. The report generator should include graphics capability.
- *Missing "what-if analysis" capability*—The information system cannot be used to predict or forecast future scenarios. For example, if a potential customer asks about the delivery of a big order, it is impossible to identify committed inventory or predict relevant capacity constraints.
- *Missing maintenance resources*—Human resources for hardware upgrades, software version control, software license maintenance, help desks, and application training have not been provided.

Information system gaps often occur around the edges of a business. For example, the processes that support import/export are mostly manual and lack critical customs information from certain countries. In another example, a distribution channel shipped most of its product by FedEx and UPS but had no automated way to accumulate daily revenue across FedEx and UPS plus DHL, Airborne, and each of a dozen other carriers. A separate software program was dedicated to this one small task. Some information systems lack currency conversion routines or the capability to convert weights and measures into both English and metric systems.

Minimizes Risk Exposure

A third step in the assessment is to evaluate the potential for business risk caused by the information systems. The business risks being considered here are the subtle lapses in the information system that can cause a business loss. These risks go beyond the process gaps previously described. Other kinds of business risk, including customer credit risk, continuity of supply risk, and excess inventory risk, are operational in nature. The network design should test for and eliminate the following kinds of business risk:

- *A nonstandard information system*—The design does not follow open industry standards for software and hardware. There is significant software customization implemented through closed interfaces using previous generation programming languages and significant reliability issues tied to now obsolete hardware components.
- *Only a few people understand the whole system*—This is particularly problematic if those few people are consultants and not your employees. This risk often comes into play in a feature-rich application environment. For example, a new business need requires the first time use of a feature, but no one really understands all the interactions and ramifications throughout the network.
- *Missing or nonexistent documentation*—Missing database schema, load sequences, system flag setting, system customization settings, or software feature functionality documentation prevent an accurate recovery to the present state or the proper enabling of new functionality. Nonstandard source code and software enhancements are not fully documented. For example, a disaster recovery requires restarting the entire system on different computer hardware at an offsite location.
- *Information system fails to protect intellectual property*—The system allows unauthorized access to intellectual property by persons inside and outside the network. For example, an unauthorized supplier gains access to specification drawings for an unreleased new product design.
- *Information system fails to support internal controls*—Business processes require internal controls and audit capability for Sarbanes-Oxley compliance. For example, the information system does not block purchases that exceed an authorized limit nor set an alarm when quantities and dollars do not reconcile within a tolerance. The information system should thwart fraud.
- *Flawed configuration control logic*—The information system does not accurately pair the correct revisions of child files with the correct revision of parent files in a multi-level BOM.
- *Lost inventory and inventory spoilage*—Inventory write-offs caused by information system error and data corruption result in lost inventory locations and spoilage from exceeding shelf life.

- *Unspecified dependencies*—An upstream or downstream process attaches critical meaning to an unspecified attribute. For example, an upstream fabricator depends on a manufacturer's file naming convention to determine how to open and read secondary files for numerically controlled tooling. When the files are merged in another system, the naming convention is lost and the tooling is at risk.
- *Data theft*—Online, sensitive information or a money transfer is not properly encrypted, such as with Secure Socket Layer (SSL) technology, and results in a theft. Off-line the lack of physical security for server hardware and backup media storage fails to prevent unauthorized persons from stealing information.
- *Data corruption from external sources*—Systems lack the proper firewalls with virus scanning and protection that blocks hackers and computer viruses from destroying network data. Data was never backed-up.
- *Missing system roadmap, change management plan, and communications plan*—A large system implementation lacks proper planning for phase two and follow-on phases. The information technology conversion is driven part way between the old legacy system and the promised new system only to stall.

Everyone has a favorite information technology disaster story. For example, it was time for a pilot run after nearly two years of an expensive new product development effort that promised to radically change the business from build-to-stock to assemble-to-order. Product marketing had sold management on an aggressive plan that called for an early manufacturing release with advertising that emphasized easy product customization. The schedule provided limited time for a thorough pilot run evaluation. So much attention was focused on managing the risks of what might go wrong with the product design that no one thought about a well-known, but forgotten information technology risk. It seems that the code for the Master Production Schedule (MPS) had been written some twenty years earlier in a programming language called RPG-II, and that source code was now lost. The assemble-to-order product line required a fresh approach to master scheduling and a revision of the MPS code to modify its available-to-promise algorithm. Other commercially available master scheduling modules required either a full ERP implementation project to convert from the legacy systems or customized software interfaces to marry a new MPS module with older legacy applications. The oversight was discovered two months before the scheduled start of pilot run. The actual product introduction was delayed by four months until a workaround could be devised.

Costs Minimized for Information Systems Maintenance

The last step is to assess the costs of ongoing information system maintenance. This is the operational extension of many of the issues addressed in the first three steps, such as hardware and software standards, data integrity, software license renewals, system backups, configuration control, forced password revisions, system audits, and scheduled employee training. Each of these will degenerate over time unless proper maintenance resources are built into the network design. Because it is difficult to determine the return on investment for these human resources, they are among the first to go when profitability slips.

There are two additional practical considerations. First is the fact that most trading partners participate in multiple supply chain networks that use different information technology designs. Employees quickly learn that user interfaces, process steps, and procedures vary from network to network. It is painful to interface with SAP in one network and Oracle in another. This is an area where employee education and information technology standards are helpful. The trading partner's internal business processes should remain common across all network relationships.

The second issue relates to integrating two IT systems into one during a merger or splitting one IT system into two during a divestiture. At issue is the gain of new, unnecessary functionality and the loss of old, necessary functionality. Turning off a long-established legacy application can cause operational hardship. The supply chain network in general and each trading partner in particular need an information technology roadmap that they can follow. Trading partners need to control their own information technology decisions rather than just allow the yin and yang of business to set their course.

BASIC DATA STRUCTURES

As trading partners embrace the massive software applications programs used to run business today, it is easy to lose the network design perspective. Today's applications are so complex that they begin to exceed the limits of any one person's comprehension. Consequently, the current application training becomes modularized to such a degree that it emphasizes operations within functional silos rather than operations integrated across the entire network. The current generation of ERP programs has been built with a bewildering breadth of functionality. For example, you want to place an order for a new item, but setting up the item on the item master requires the assignment of nearly 70 attributes. You want to place an order for a new item having set up the item on the item master, but the software forces you to choose among ten different lot-sizing algorithms. You want to place an order for a new item having set up the item on the item master and having selected a lot-sizing algorithm, but your supplier has not completed the 20 hours of training required to interface with your system. One simple business requirement has suddenly become a project of its own.

SUBCYCLE DATA STRUCTURES

The architecture of a new network begins with the basics of the information sets required for the subcycles from Chapter 4 that integrate the trading partners with the network. Going back to basics provides an unparalleled opportunity to invent new ways to use information technology to overcome the practical difficulties that arise when a network is artificially partitioned. Figure 5-1 is typical of just one layer of network partitioning. A seller, a trading partner, and a buyer are connected to form a network. Although all are part of the same legal entity, the seller has different

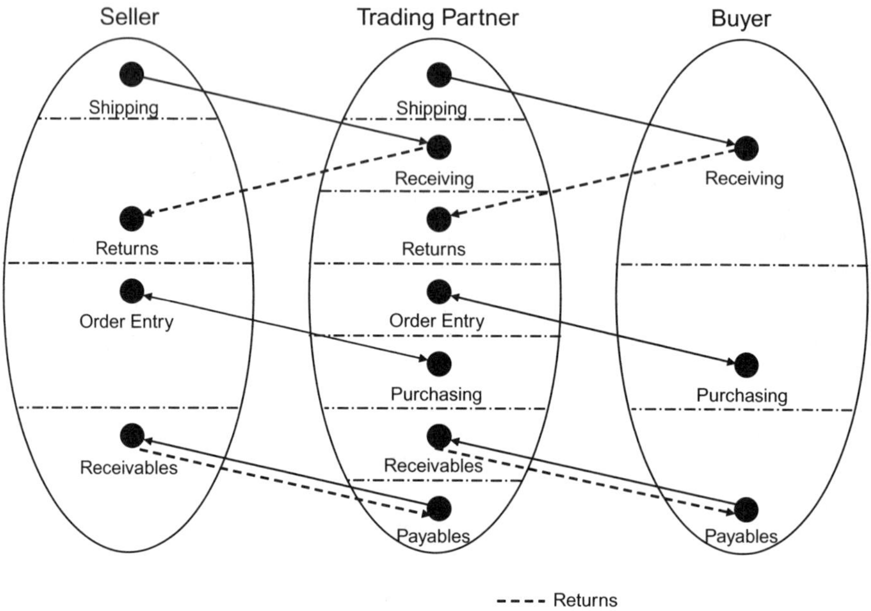

FIGURE 5-1 A basic network partitioned into multiple points of contact.

employees and different geographical locations responsible for shipping, returns, order entry, and accounts receivable. The trading partner, though legally independent of the seller and the buyer, has different employees and different geographical locations responsible for shipping, receiving, returns, order entry, purchasing, receivables, and payables. The buyer, a third legal entity altogether, is different yet in its employees and geographical locations responsible for receiving, purchasing, and payables. The information systems must somehow sort out the data elements needed to complete the order information to the material flows and other data elements needed to complete the invoice information to the cash flows.

Table 5-1 details the data elements required for the order-to-delivery subcycle and Table 5-2 details the data elements required for the invoice-to-pay subcycle that connect the trading partner with the buyer. Some of the data elements, like the contact information, are common to both tables. The key to understanding these tables is to simply ask what is the set of questions whose answers complete the subcycle in a reliable way? And, what is the set of data elements whose combined information complete the subcycle in a reliable way?

- Who is the seller, and who is the buyer?
- What products and services are being bought?
- How can the seller plan for the purchase?
- When is delivery promised, and where is the point of delivery?
- How is the seller doing against this delivery promise?
- How will the buyer acknowledge delivery?

TABLE 5-1
Data Elements Required for the Order-to-Delivery Subcycle

	Trading Partner = Seller	Customer = Buyer
Planning Information	• Supply Forecast	• Demand Forecast
The Two Parties	• Company Name of Seller • Company Address • Sales Agent's Name • Sales Agent's Phone Number • Sales Agent's e-mail Address	• Name of Buyer • Address of Buyer • Buyer's Phone Number • Buyer's e-mail Address
Product Configuration	• For Each Line Item: SKU #, Description, Quantity, Price • Purchase Order Terms and Conditions • Purchase Order Form • Service Contract Terms and Conditions • Serial Number and Warranty	• Customer Specific Configuration
Delivery Information	• Weight and Cube • Freight Method and Payment • Delivery Promise Date, Time • Order Acknowledgement • Advance Shipping Notice • Installation Services	• Ship-to Address • Ship-to Phone Number
Returns Information	• Return-to Address • Return-to Contact • Return-to Phone Number • Returns Packaging and Labeling Requirements • Removal Services	• Advise To Return • For Each Line Item: SKU #, Description, Quantity • Returns Timing • Under Warranty • Weight and Cube • Freight and Method Payment

EDI is Electronic Data Interchange.

- What is the agreed upon price, including other terms and conditions?
- How can the buyer plan for the purchase?
- When and where will payment be made?
- What form of payment will the buyer use?
- How will the seller acknowledge payment?
- If there is a return, where and how is the return delivered to the seller?
- If there is a return, where and how is cash refunded to the buyer?

Table 5-3 details the data elements required for the order-to-stock subcycle, and Table 5-4 details the data elements required for the invoice-to-cash subcycle that connect the trading partner with the seller. As before, some of the data elements are common to both tables, and returns add a level of complexity. The description and packaging of the physical item will change dramatically from transformation through manufacture to fulfillment.

TABLE 5-2
Data Elements Required for the Invoice-to-Pay Subcycle

	Trading Partner = Seller	Customer = Buyer
Planning Information	• Cash Supply Forecast	• Cash Demand Forecast
The Two Parties	• Company Name of Seller • Company-Unique Identifier*	• Name of Buyer • Company-Unique Identifier
Product Configuration	• For Each Line Item: SKU #, Description, Quantity, Price • Purchase Order Terms and Conditions • Service Contract Terms and Conditions • Serial Number and Warranty	
Payment Information	• Pay-to Address • Pay-to Phone Number • Invoice Form • Discount Structure • Freight Method and Payment • Buyer's Credit Rating	• Bill-to Address • Bill-to Phone Number • Bill-to e-Mail • Buyer's Bank Information
Returns Credit	• Warranty Period • Condition of Return • Returns Refund Structure	• Advise to Return • For Each Line Item: Item #, Description,Quantity, Serial # • Weight and Cube • Freight and Method Payment

*A Company-unique identifier such as a DUNS Number issued through Dunn and Bradstreet.

BOM Data Structures

The BOM is organized into two parts: an item master and a product structure. The item master holds the attributes that describe the item, including its identification number, description, revision, price, Unit Of Measure, yield factor, approved vendor(s), documentation file number(s), documentation revision number(s), and more. The Approved Vendor List (AVL) for a product is derived from its item master. The product structure describes the parent-child linkages for each level of the BOM beginning with Level 0, which is the complete product. Each line item in a product structure includes the BOM level, the parent's identification number, the child's identification number, and the quantity per. A brief example of a typical indented product structure listing would look like the following and continues on the next page:

- **Product Derivative**, Revision, Documentation Number(s), Documentation Revision(s)
- ...(Means a continuation of more line items)
- **Product Accessory**, Revision, Documentation Number(s), Documentation Revision(s)
- ...

TABLE 5-3
Data Elements Required for the Order-to-Stock Subcycle

	Supplier = Seller	Trading Partner = Buyer
Planning information	• Supply Forecast	• Demand Forecast
The Two Parties	• Company Listed on the Approved Supplier's List • Company Address of Seller • Sales Agent' Name • Sales Agent's Phone Number • Sales Agent's e-mail Address	• Company Name of Buyer • Company Address • Purchasing Agent's Name • Purchasing Agent's Phone • Purchasing Agent's e-mail
Bill of Materials	• For Each Line Item: Item #, Description, Quantity, Price • Purchase Order Terms & Conditions • Purchase Order Form • Warranty for Materials and Workmanship • Lot Number, Date Code	• Approved Vendor List
Delivery Information	• Weight and Cube • Freight Method and Payment • Delivery Promise Date, Time • HAZMAT Labeling • Order Acknowledgement • Advance Shipping Notice	• Ship-to Address • Ship-to Phone Number
Returns Information	• Return Authorization • Return-to Address • Return-to Contact • Return-to Phone Number • Returns Packaging and Labeling Requirements • HAZMAT Labeling	• Advise to Return • For Each Line Item: Item #, Description, Quantity • Under Warranty • Weight and Cube • Freight and Method Payment • Returns Timing

- **Product** (Level 0.), Revision, Documentation Number(s), Documentation Revision(s)
  - **Assembly** (Level 1.), Revision, Doc Num, Doc Rev
  - **Assembly** (Level 1.), Revision, Doc Num, Doc Rev
  - …
  - **Item** (Level 1.), Revision, Doc Num, Doc Rev
  - **Item** (Level 1.), Revision, Doc Num, Doc Rev
  - …
    - **Subassembly** (Level 2.), Rev, Doc Num, Doc Rev
    - **Subassembly** (Level 2.), Rev, Doc Num, Doc Rev
    - …
    - **Item** (Level 2.), Rev, Doc Num, Doc Rev
    - **Item** (Level 2.), Rev, Doc Num, Doc Rev
    - … (Means a continuation of more line items)

TABLE 5-4
Data Elements Required for the Invoice-To-Cash Subcycle

	Supplier = Seller	Trading Partner = Buyer
Planning information	• Cash Supply Forecast	• Cash Demand Forecast
The Two Parties	• Company Name of Seller • Company Unique Identifier	• Company Name of Buyer • Company Unique Identifier
Product Configuration	• For Each Line Item: SKU #, Description, Quantity, Price • Purchase Order Terms and Condition • Lot Number, Date Code	
Payment Information	• Pay-to Address • Pay-to Phone Number • Invoice Form • Discount Structure • Freight Method and Payment • Buyer's Credit Rating	• Bill-to Address • Bill-to Phone Number • Bill-to e-mail • Buyer's Bank Information
Returns Credit	• Warranty Period • Condition of Return • Returns Refund Structure	• Advise to Return • For Each Line Item: Item #, Description, Quantity, Serial # • Weight and Cube • Freight Method and Payment

In some information system implementations, the BOM is built across three software applications that are managed from three different functional areas. This causes information partitioning as follows:

- *Configurator*—The set of rules that determine which product derivatives are valid and which product accessories are necessary. For example, for a mainframe product with plug-in modules the configurator would specify the maximum number of each model of plug-in that will work within a single mainframe. In another example, the configurator would specify the need for an Australian line cord and English language manual for a product shipped to an Australian Country Of Destination. Marketing owns the configurator.
- *Manufacturing BOM*—The engine that generates a complete product BOM for either a demand forecast or an actual customer order. The BOM engine is computational and memory intensive. For these reasons, some information systems create an instance of a specific BOM only as required. These information systems do not store every BOM permutation. The implementation and time sequencing of Engineering Change Orders (ECO) are driven from the manufacturing BOM and actual inventory balances. Manufacturing BOM product structures are updated continuously by the engineering BOM. Manufacturing owns the manufacturing BOM.
- *Engineering BOM*—The engine used to introduce new products and to manage the obsolescence and discontinuance of old products. The engineering

> BOM is used to maintain strict configuration control over the parent item, the parent's revision, the parent's documentation file set, and each of the parent's documentation revisions with a child item, the child's revision, the child's documentation file set, and each of the child's documentation revisions. Documentation file sets typically contain data sheets, specification control drawings, assembly drawings, and Computer Aided Design (CAD) files. Configuration control over nested levels of parent-child relationships is a nightmarish problem. Engineering Change Requests (ECR) are synchronized to particular revisions of the engineering BOM. Engineering owns the engineering BOM.

Unexpected results can happen when two or more databases are combined. The schema of old data elements from each of the old databases must be mapped to a schema of new data elements for the new database. Once the mapping is complete, the data is loaded by a sequence of overlays. This means one of the original databases must be chosen for the first load. Then the second of the original databases is overlaid on the populated new database. Then the third of the original database is overlaid, etc. The mapping and the first loading define each data element in the new database. Something as simple as Unit Of Measure (UOM) can become a huge issue during the overlay process. For example, suppose three legacy databases are to be combined, and each contains the same part number for a product label. In the first database the UOM is "each." In the second database the UOM is a "sheet" of 20 labels. In the third database the UOM is a "roll" of 1000 labels. If the second database is used to define the schema, the new UOM will be sheets. One of the overlays will have to multiply the quantity per for this label by 0.05, whereas the other overlay will have to divide the quantity per for this label by 50. Data mapping is tedious.

Physical Inventory and Cash Inventory Data Structures

Most trading partners are comfortable working with data that cuts vertically through their own organization. However, the data flows that define network inventory and network cash are horizontal data flows. A trading partner looking downstream wants to know what configuration the buyer is buying. Some examples of configuration data include price, quantity, packaging, labeling, serial numbers, coordinated accessories, software, firmware, complementary products, color, fashion, and returns. A trading partner looking upstream wants to know what portion of the product structure the seller is selling. Some examples of product structure data include cost, quantity, description, integrated lower-level subassembly, completed secondary operations, lot number, date code and returns.

The information associated with the material flow changes dramatically as raw materials are transformed into components, components are manufactured into products, and products are fulfilled together with services into solutions, see Table 5-5. Again, the combination of a product, its packaging, and its distribution warehouse is called a stock keeping unit. SKUs are different than product numbers, item numbers, and manufacturer's part numbers. One easy way to visualize how the physical distribution changes across a network is to think in pictures of the inventory

TABLE 5-5
Typical Information Associated with Physical Inventory

	Upstream	Midstream	Downstream	Reverse Stream
Item Identification	• Manufacturer's Part Number	• Item Number or Part Number	• SKU • Product Option	• SKU • Item Number • Part Number • Manufacturer's Part Number
Description	• BOM • Material List	• BOM • Return	• Configuration • BOM • Service Support • Return	• Core • Reverse BOM • Where Used • Service Contract
Quantity (English & Metric)	• Each • Weight • Cubic Volume	• Package • Weight • Cubic Volume	• Package • Weight • Cubic Volume	• Each • Weight • Cubic Volume
Lot Identification	• Melt • Lot Code • Shelf Life	• Batch • Lot Code • Date Code • Serial Number • Shelf Life	• Lot Code • Date Code • Serial Number • Shelf Life	• Lot Code • Date Code • Serial Number • Shelf Life
Labeling (Multilingual)	• Raw Material • Drum • Component • Bar Code • RFID Tag • COO • HAZMAT	• Product • Assembly • Drum • Bar Code • RFID Tag • COO • HAZMAT	• Carton • Pallet • Drum • Container • Bar Code • RFID Tag • COO • HAZMAT	• Packaging • Pallet • Drum • Container • Bar Code • RFID Tag • COO • HAZMAT
Packaging	• Rolls • Sheets • Cartons • Drums • Other	• Rolls • Sheets • Cartons • Drums • Other	• Rolls • Sheets • Cartons • Drums • Other	• Rolls • Sheets • Cartons • Drums • Other

as it flows across the network. The inventory might be a long rod of raw materials on the back of a truck, a carton of subassemblies shipped as LTL motor freight, a pallet of finished goods shipping in the belly of an airliner, or an oceangoing container holding bulk packaged products bound for a distant warehouse. Information derived from the data structures must be able to fully describe each scenario. One picture is worth a thousand data elements.

In a similar manner, the information associated with cash flow is horizontal in its nature. The downstream trading partner must assess the customer's credit risk and wants to know how the customer intends to pay. Will the customer be offered a dynamic price against an expiration date, a fixed price, a discounted price, or a contract price? What will be the currency of the transaction if the sale is an international one? Will the customer pay in cash or by credit card, by mail, in person,

TABLE 5-6
Typical Information Associated with Cash "Inventory"

	Upstream	Midstream	Downstream	Reverse Stream
Price	• Reverse Auction Price • Spot Price • Contract Price	• Fixed Price • Discount • Contract Price	• Factory Price • Discount • Dynamic Price • Contract Price	• Loaner Price • Core Allowance • Aftermarket Price
Cost	• Variable Cost • Fixed Cost • Yield • Cost of Goods	• Variable Cost • Fixed Cost • Yield • Cost of Goods	• Variable Cost • Fixed Cost • Spoilage • Cost of Goods	• Repair Cost • Recycle Cost • Remanufacture Cost
Returns	• Credit Refund	• Credit Refund	• Credit Refund	• Credit Refund
Financing	• LOC Interest • Procurement Card Charges	• LOC Interest • Procurement Card Charges • Factor Fees	• Credit Card Charges • Credit Rating • Factor Fees	• Credit Card Refunds
Currency	• Currency • Exchange Rate	• Currency • Exchange Rate	• Currency • Exchange Rate	• Currency • Exchange Rate

or over the Internet? The upstream supplier must assess the trading partner's credit risk and wants to know how the trading partner intends to pay. Will the price be fixed or by a Request For Quote (RFQ) with an invitation to a reverse auction? What will be the currency of the transaction if the sale is an international one? Will the trading partner pay by check, by letter of credit, or by procurement card, by mail or by a wire transfer? If products or components are returned, how is the cash refunded to the buyer? Table 5-6 describes some typical information associated with cash as it flows across the network.

Public, Private, and Trade Secret Information

At some point, an arrangement of data yields information. This information will contain certain intellectual property that must be protected. Information systems are designed to discriminate their context access through user names and user passwords. However, information content discrimination is more difficult. The information system doesn't understand how data elements merge into information or what transforms particular information into intellectual property. It is best to classify data elements for three levels of confidentiality: public information, private information, and trade secret information. Then the information system can restrict each level of confidentially to mutually exclusive information "containers" as follows:

- *Public information*—Available to anyone inside or outside the supply chain network. Examples include product catalogs, product price lists, and product availability.
- *Private information*—Shared only with the network trading partners. May be shared with the strategic nominal trading partners on a need-to-know

basis. Examples include product cost information, dollar volume statistics, and top customer lists. This category may include information related to supply and demand for a new product introduction.
- *Trade secret information*—Must not be shared beyond the most trusted employees of a single trading partner. This is typically the technology, material, or process-related intellectual property that defines this trading partner's competitive edge.

Intellectual property and trade secrets can be protected through a variety of legal arrangements. Trademarks can be registered. Copyrights and patents can be registered for royalty income producing properties. Trading partners typically use a NonDisclosure Agreement (NDA) as legal protection against the theft of ideas and information during the exploration and due-diligence of potential new business partnerships. The NDA specifies the two parties involved, the information content, and a fixed time frame. For example, two parties (an instrument manufacturer and an integrated circuit supplier) might sign a NDA valid for a three-year period covering a specific technology (amplifier bandwidth enhancement). The NDA is binding on information sharing by any employee of either party for the duration of the agreement. Should the manufacturer decide not to do business with the supplier, under the NDA the manufacturer has agreed not to share what was learned until three years have passed. This protects the technology investment made by the manufacturer.

PARTITIONED NETWORKS

The architecture of a competitive network, as detailed in this book, is derived from the velocity, variability, vocalize, visualize, and value principles. In an ideal network design, information is available for each subcycle to flow with maximum velocity and with minimum variability. In an ideal network operation, information is available for every trading partner to vocalize demand and to visualize the supply of network inventory and throughput in real-time. In an ideal network information is available to every trading partner that relates value to customers and to owners. However, what happens in practice when the partitioning of the information technology infrastructure cannot be avoided?

NONUBIQUITOUS INFORMATION

Network information is not *ubiquitous*. It is not everywhere at exactly the same time. The information will not reach every person in every organizational fringe of the network in exactly the same way. There are many reasons why every network is partitioned in some way. Some of the more common reasons include:

- *Legal entities*—Each (nominal) trading partner in a network is its own legal entity. The same (nominal) trading partner parent may be multiple legal entities across different countries.
- *Geographical locations*—Different functional areas reside in different buildings, different cities and states, and different countries even when they belong to the same legal entity.

- *Horizontal versus vertical organizations*—Some organizations are horizontal with blended functional boundaries and few information handoffs, whereas other organizations are vertical with rigid functional boundaries and many information handoffs.
- *Manufacturing versus service organizations*—Service organizations have minimal physical distribution.
- *Single versus multiple points of contact*—The interface of some relationships depends upon all the information flowing through a single person, whereas the interface of other relationships compartmentalizes information flow through multiple functionalized relationships.
- *Cultural diversity*—In some cultures the boss makes all the decisions, whereas in other cultures it is more of a team effort. In some cultures every worker has access to a personal computer, whereas in other cultures the workers time-share a few personal computers.
- *Network substitutions*—Whenever an organization is substituted within the network, there is a transition period for the information flow to adjust.
- *Time zones*—One or more of the (nominal) trading partners operate in a different time zone. It can make a big difference whether information flows east to west versus west to east for timely decisions.
- *Import/export boundaries*—When (nominal) trading partners are located in different countries, some will be exporting, whereas others will be importing. Customs regulations vary by country, for example the legality of encrypting private information.
- *Language differences*—Subtle difference in language change the meaning of information in unexpected ways, for example in the ways dates and large numbers are expressed.
- *Legacy systems and legacy databases*—Earlier generations of information systems were organized around smaller, more restrictive databases for applications with limited functional scope. When these legacy systems were integrated, they shared data elements from multiple databases.
- *Product BOM*—The BOM may be partitioned among a configurator, the manufacturing BOM, and the engineering BOM as explained earlier in this Chapter.
- *Batch cutoffs*—Any process that involves batching will have a cutoff date and time to end one batch and start the next. This is an artificial boundary. For example, for a 24/7 operation information cutoffs driven by the timing of system backups will inconvenience someone somewhere in the world.
- *Acquisitions and divestitures*—As businesses merge together and spin apart, information systems from different software vendors are blended, integrated, and segmented.
- *WAN connection*—Different Wide Area Network (WAN) technologies are used to transmit the information. Satellite, fiber optic cable, microwave, wireless, Internet, FAX, courier, and surface mail each have different characteristics, timeframes, and costs for getting the message through.
- *Forward supply chain and reverse supply chain*—The information system designed for a forward supply chain network does not run in reverse. The

TABLE 5-7
Subcycle Design Checklist for Partitioned Networks

Network Context Issues to Compensate Learn to compensate around these issues	**Information Content Issues to Eliminate** These issues must be driven out of the design
[ ] Split legal entities	[ ] Missing data elements
[ ] Geographical location, time zone, local language, local currency	[ ] Duplicated data elements
[ ] Import/export boundaries	[ ] Inaccurate data
[ ] Business culture, organizational design	[ ] Random mixing of batch and real-time data causing data corruption
[ ] Legacy system boundaries	[ ] Different definitions for the same data caused by mixing local languages or software vendors
[ ] Multi-vendor software solutions	[ ] Faulty decision logic
[ ] WAN connections	[ ] Faulty BOM version control
	[ ] Mixing factory, channel, and return cost factors
	[ ] Losing tracking integrity for lots, date codes, serial numbers and shelf life
	[ ] Cash to inventory reconciliation not closed
	[ ] Private and trade secret information leaks
	[ ] Missing internal controls

information system designed for a reverse supply chain network does not run in forward.

Auditing the Network Design

Network partitioning cannot be avoided. It is important to separate the partitioning issues related to network context from those related to information content. For example, differences in the relative date and time that the responsible person at each trading partner location receives the same information are a network context issue. Operating from the wrong version of a lower-level bill of materials for a partitioned product, BOM is an information content issue. Information content issues must be eliminated from the network while network context issues should be identified and a compensation strategy applied. You cannot operate with inaccurate information, but you can learn to operate with small differences in the timing of information. Each (nominal) trading partner should have a primary and a backup person responsible for key information, and all network players should understand the window of time when the information is valid. The checklists in Table 5-7 can be used to audit the information technology infrastructure supporting each order-to-delivery, order-to-stock, invoice-to-pay, and invoice-to-cash subcycle design.

A Virtual Enterprise Example

A network orchestrator located in Rockaway, NJ, implemented and provided oversight for a global supply chain that included a contract manufacturer in Kuantan, Malaysia, and a European distribution center in Amersfoort, Netherlands. European

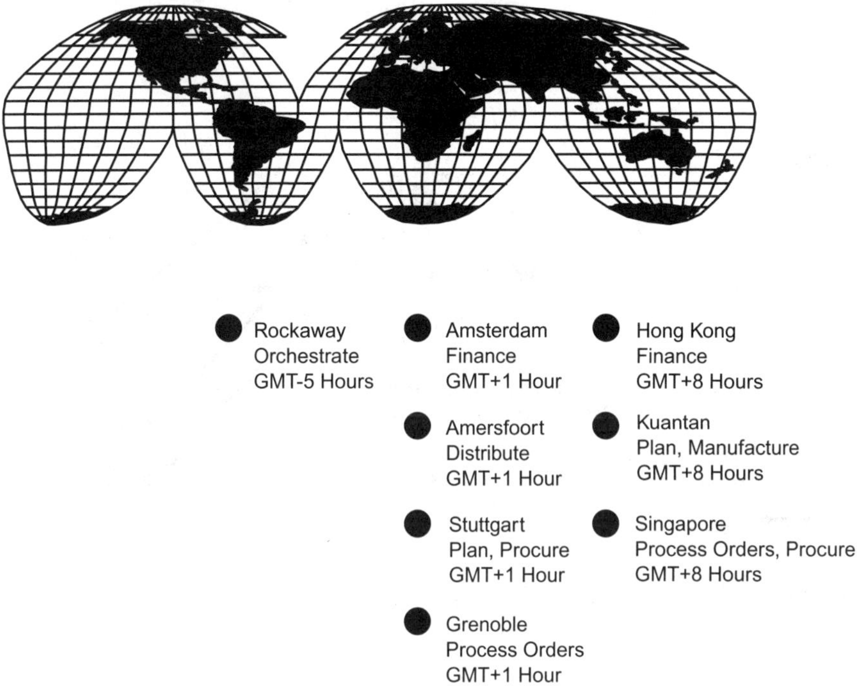

FIGURE 5-2 Trading partners partitioned by geography.

customer orders were received through the company's customer service center in Grenoble, France, for centralized order processing. Grenoble triggered a centralized planning and procurement group in Stuttgart, Germany, for distribution inventory replenishment. The inventory was financed through letters of credit handled by the company's financial service center in Amsterdam, Netherlands. The contract manufacturer maintained its order processing and parts procurement in Singapore with all financial arrangements made through its corporate offices in Hong Kong. Finished goods were planned, manufactured, and exported from Kuantan, Malaysia, through Singapore by a Malaysian motor freight company, then re-exported into Amsterdam by airfreight arranged through the logistic service provider Kuehne & Nagel working with the airline Lufthansa. Once the finished goods cleared customs in Amsterdam, they were moved by motor freight to the distribution center in Amersfoort.

Figure 5-2 shows the geographical partitioning of the European distribution center and the Asian contract manufacturer along with the network orchestrator in New Jersey. The city, function, and time zone relative to Greenwich Mean Time (GMT) for each are noted in Figure 5-2. Hong Kong, Malaysia, and Singapore are in the same time zone. They share British English as the language of business, and they each have a strong Chinese culture. Amsterdam, Amersfoort, Stuttgart, and Grenoble are in the same time zone. Though the Netherlands, Germany, and France are all members of the European Union, they are each proud of their native culture and language. This caused some unexpected nuances in the flow of information.

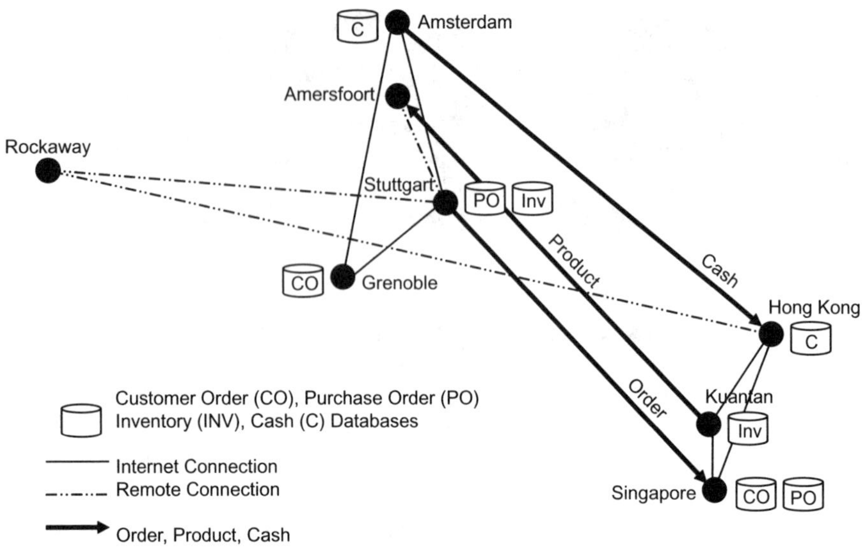

FIGURE 5-3 Trading partners partitioned by databases.

The patchwork of legacy information systems used to implement this supply chain network resulted in a further partitioning of information databases as shown in Figure 5-3. Each of the sites maintained the data elements that were relevant to their business function, such as order processing, inventory planning and control, and procurement. Surprisingly, the distribution center operation in Amersfoort was implemented as a remote link to a centralized European inventory management database on a server located in Stuttgart. The network orchestrator was given full access into the distributor's systems through Stuttgart and limited access into the contract manufacturer's systems through Hong Kong.

The order-to-delivery subcycle for the contract manufacturer was the same as the order-to-stock subcycle for the distribution center. The invoice-to-pay subcycle for the contract manufacturer was the same as the invoice-to-cash subcycle for the distribution center, as shown in Figure 5-4. The material flow was dependent upon seven logistics service providers who were all nominal trading partners: the Malaysian motor freight carrier, Malaysian Customs, Singapore Customs, logistics company Kuehne & Nagel, the airline Lufthansa, Netherlands Customs, and the Netherlands motor freight carrier. The information flow was dependent upon the global and in-country Internet infrastructure used to interconnect Hong Kong, Malaysia, Singapore, New Jersey, the Netherlands, Germany, and France. The cash flow was dependent upon a number of financial service providers who were all nominal trading partners: the letter of credit issuing bank in Amsterdam, the LOC beneficiary bank in Hong Kong, and the interconnecting electronic funds transfer network. Simply connecting a contract manufacturer in Malaysia with a distribution center in the Netherlands turned out to be quite complex.

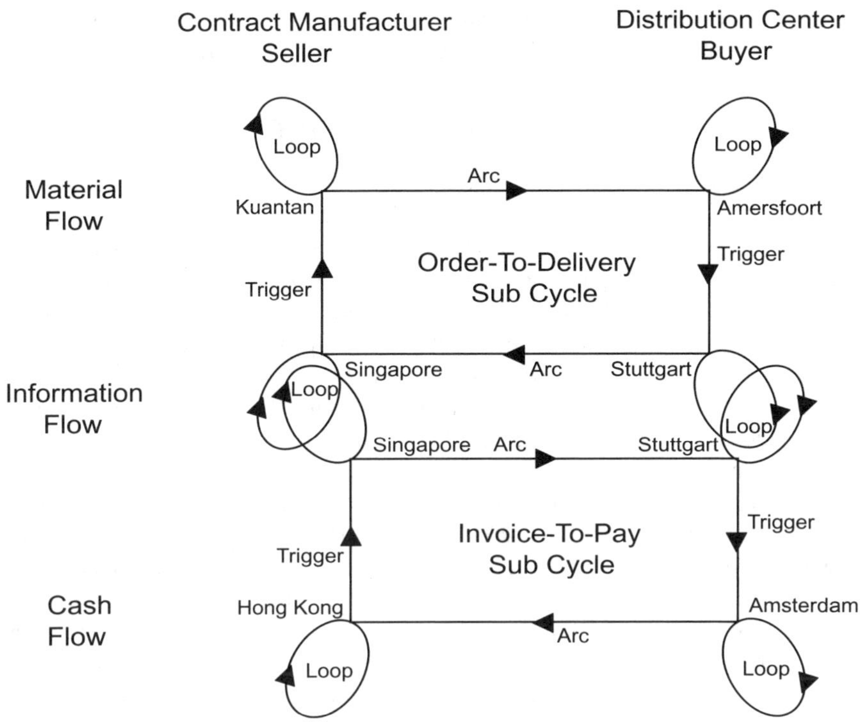

FIGURE 5-4 Subcycles mapped to the trading partners.

The large number of databases and information handoffs caused an unexpected data integrity problem. The product the contract manufacturer produced included a rechargeable battery. The battery technology specified a maximum number of charge-discharge cycles and a maximum shelf-life period at full discharge before the battery had to be replaced. The contract manufacturer performed a charge-discharge-charge sequence during final assembly and test. A "birthdate" of the battery was then associated with the product's serial number. The inventory management system used by the distribution center had no provision for a birthdate record for its finished goods inventory. Consequently, the decision was made to change the meaning of an unused field in the database and to programmatically set the birthdate equal to the inventory receipt date. It was later discovered that the finished goods inventory holding time in Kuantan plus the month of ocean freight transit time plus the holding time in Amersfoort could exceed the battery life specification. Upon auditing the distribution center's physical inventory, it was further discovered that the integrity of the first-in, first-out inventory management data had been corrupted by an untrained employee. The distribution center was not able to tell from its computer system how long a particular serial-numbered product had been stored in the warehouse. The resolution of this problem was painful. It included a 100% physical inventory where the product was unboxed so the birthdate could be verified from the product's firmware. The real birthdate of each product was manually keyed into the inventory management system. In the end 22% of the finished goods inventory had to be written off, and a senior distribution manager was fired.

TRACKING AND TRACING

An important function of the information system is its ability to provide tracking and tracing across network boundaries. Physical material is tracked working downstream through value-added transformation, manufacturing, and fulfillment. Physical material is traced working upstream through fulfillment, manufacture, and transformation to the source of its raw materials. Tracking downstream is the opposite of tracing upstream from an information perspective. Identity loss, caused by organizational and information system boundaries, is the central issue in tracking and tracing. For example, if a lot code is carried forward through the manufacturing process and then dropped within distribution, the identity thread of the physical material is broken.

The information density now supported by database technologies and tracking technologies has made end-to-end tracking and tracing practical across a supply chain network. A SKU can accumulate a considerable information pedigree from the time its raw materials are transformed into components, its components manufactured into products, and its products fulfilled into SKUs. Although it has often been impractical to record the lot code, date code, Country Of Origin, serial number, and expiration date in bar code small enough to be printed on most physical material, it is quite possible to encode this level of information into a Radio Frequency IDentification (RFID) tag attached to the physical material. Although it has been impractical to store and sort this density of information through multiple small databases, it is now quite practical to manage such information on a large relational database.

In addition to technology, tracking and tracing requires great organizational discipline. A well-designed information system is like a closed box. Whenever something penetrates the box, complete information about the event must be captured. Typical events include receiving a raw material or component or product into the network, receiving an empty pallet into the network, receiving an empty container into the network, issuing an SKU from the network, issuing an empty pallet from the network, issuing an empty container from the network, and receiving an SKU or product or component return into the network. The breakdown in discipline that allows any of these events to penetrate the box without getting a lot code and/or a date stamp and/or a serial number will result in the premature termination of an identity thread used for tracking and tracing.

TRADING INFORMATION FOR INVENTORY

If the trading partners have reliable, accurate information about the quantity and location of every raw material and return, every component and return, every product and return, and every SKU and return in real-time, then the network can operate with less inventory. The trading partners do not need to invest in just-in-case inventory because the actual inventory profile is known with certainty throughout the network. This is called "trading information for inventory." Each

TABLE 5-8
Tracking the Physical Distribution Flow

Raw Material							
	Carton, Pallet, or Container						
Raw Material Return		Component					
			Carton, Pallet, or Container				
		Component Return		Product			
					Carton, Pallet, or Container		
				Product Return		SKU	
							Carton, Pallet, or Container
						SKU Return	
← Lot Code →							
← Date Code →							
← Country Of Origin →							
← Serial Number →							
← Expiration Date →							

raw material, component, product, and SKU is identified at the time they are born in the network. Each physical material is tracked until it is associated with a carton, pallet, or container. Multiple cartons can be associated with a single pallet, and multiple pallets can be associated with a single container. Then each carton, pallet, or container is tracked until the specific physical material is disassociated from its container or pallet or carton. Returns are tracked in the same manner. Table 5-8 shows the progression.

Technology enables network-wide tracking. RFID tags identify each physical material and are effective in tracking stationary cartons, pallets, and containers within a warehouse or out in the yard. Once the pallet or container is loaded onto a truck, railcar, aircraft, or ship, Global Positioning System (GPS) technology provides the tracking information while the packaged physical material is on the move. A large relational database is used to store and sort the tracking information. The association and disassociation of the physical material with its container or pallet can be traced through Supply Chain Event Management (SCEM) technology. SCEM extends the monitoring of these kinds of events beyond the boundaries of typical ERP Systems.

The following three examples highlight how trading information for inventory can be used effectively to lower costs and to improve competitiveness:

- *Cross-docking*—Truck Load (TL) transportation is less expensive than LTL transportation. TL transportation routed between primary cities will overshoot the desired secondary destinations; the customer then has to pay for incremental LTL transport back to the secondary destination. Cross-docking is the solution to maximizing TL shipments for a wider variety of destination cities. For example, a TL shipment of SKU A can be driven part way to a cross-docking facility where part of the load is combined with a partial load of SKU B to become a TL shipment the remainder of the way to the secondary destination. This is an information-intensive solution because the departing truck now carries a number of pallets of SKU A and a number of pallets of SKU B. The combined weight and cube of SKU A plus SKU B must safely fit the trailer while qualifying as a TL shipment.
- *Mixed SKU pallets*—A fully cubed unit load, i.e., a full pallet load, is less expensive to transport than a partially cubed unit load. However, once past the factory and the first echelon of distribution, deliveries to retail stores tend to be small quantities of multiple SKUs. When the information system is capable of tracking a mixed SKU pallet, the factory and the distribution center can customize unit loads for specific end-customers. Mixed SKU pallets combined with cross-docking can be very cost-effective transportation. However, the information system must be up to the task of tracking the association and disassociation of individual cartons across pallets and containers.
- *Merge in-transit*—Systems of products often require the coordinated arrival of subsystem components built at different factories in different geographical locations, each with a different lead time. The traditional solution for this problem has been to ship each of the subsystem components to an integration center, where the system is integrated for delivery to the end-customer. This is an expensive proposition because the customer has a wait equal to the longest lead-time component, and the integration center carries the inventory value of a nearly complete system. A superior but information-intensive solution is to merge in-transit. In this scheme the start of manufacturing of the shorter lead-time components are triggered after the longer lead-time components are in-transit. Arrival of each component is coordinated through a logistics service provider, and the system is integrated on-site at the customer, by the service provider.

Subtlety in Tracing

Although an information breakdown may preclude a better return on investment through tracking physical material across a boundary, an information breakdown in the tracing of physical material across a boundary can raise operational risk to unacceptable levels. For example, a U.S. Customs Officer notes that the Country Of Origin on the bill of lading reads, "A Product of Taiwan." However upon closer inspection, the pallet label reads, "Made In China;" the carton label reads, "A Product of Hong Kong;" and the physical product is marked as, "Made In Malaysia." This critical parts shipment will be held at customs indefinitely until its Country Of Origin can be substantiated and the appropriate duty, and perhaps fines, paid.

Another good example is the return of serialized product. A customer may return a scientific instrument to the factory for its annual calibration, and expects the same serialized product back once the calibration is completed. The factory must be able to trace from the serial number whether the product is still under warranty or an extended service agreement that covers the cost of calibration. If the factory returns product with a different serial number or double charges the customer for a covered calibration fee, the customer will switch its business to a competitor.

Operational risk and liability escalate when product is stored beyond its specified shelf life or product is distributed beyond its expiration date because of an information breakdown. Before a distributor, factory, or supplier can properly recall defective product from the field and purge all defective product within the network, it must be able to reliably trace lot codes and date codes back to the source of the defect. If the chain of traceability is broken, it becomes impossible for the network to complete a purge and recall. Information systems applied to supply chain networks in the pharmaceutical industry and the food industry must adhere to Food and Drug Administration (FDA) regulations for strict traceability.

COMPETING WITH PARALLEL INFORMATION FLOWS

There are four fundamental ways to speed-up a process. First is to eliminate some process steps, thereby reducing the total number of steps. Second is to minimize the cycle times of the longest process steps. Third is to overlap process steps by taking a serial sequence and converting it into a parallel sequence. Fourth is to synchronize process steps. The idea of converting serial flow into parallel flows applies to the network information flow and may apply to the network cash flow. Converting to a parallel flow generally does not apply to the material flow because the product structure of the BOM dictates a manufacturing sequence. This section explores how to parallel the subcycles of multiple trading partners in a complex network.

Subcycles in Serial Networks

Imagine each of the trading partners as individual pots of flowers ready to be planted in a garden. The flowerpots have been bought from several different sources, and as yet the flowers have no relationship with one another. As the root system from each flower is removed from its pot and transplanted to its prescribed place in the garden, the roots will begin to intersect in the soil, forming a root network. Some will grow down vertically while others will grow out horizontally. Each of the flowers will thrive given the right chemical balance in the soil, enough water, and some sunlight. Likewise, as each trading partner is added into the network mix, its material, information, and cash roots must be properly connected to the network soil for the trading partner to flourish.

The physical inventory sites and the cash "inventory" sites become the linchpins of a supply chain network. Each physical inventory site connects to the next as prescribed by the product structure in the BOM. The product structure dictates where the value-adding network may be parallel and where it must be serial. In the most general sense, in this tree-like structure, upstream roots are mostly parallel, midstream trunks are mostly serial, and downstream branches are mostly parallel. Likewise, upstream transformation is largely parallel, midstream manufacturing is largely serial, and downstream fulfillment is largely parallel. Some product processing loops are wholly contained inside a single trading partner; they combine product processing with information flow. The material flow arc connections are made through one or more logistics service providers who are nominal trading partners. Figure 5-5 shows how the material flows from the bottom level to the top level of the BOM product structure tree.

The trading partners extract their revenues and margins, in turn, from each dollar paid by the end-customer while traversing the BOM tree structure from downstream

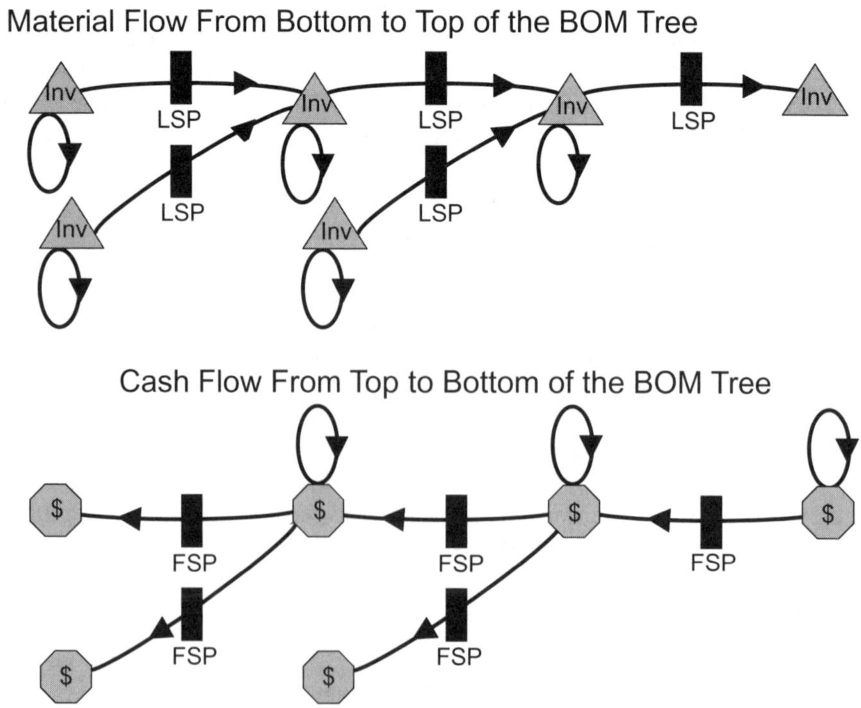

FIGURE 5-5 Material flow and cash flow traverse the BOM tree.

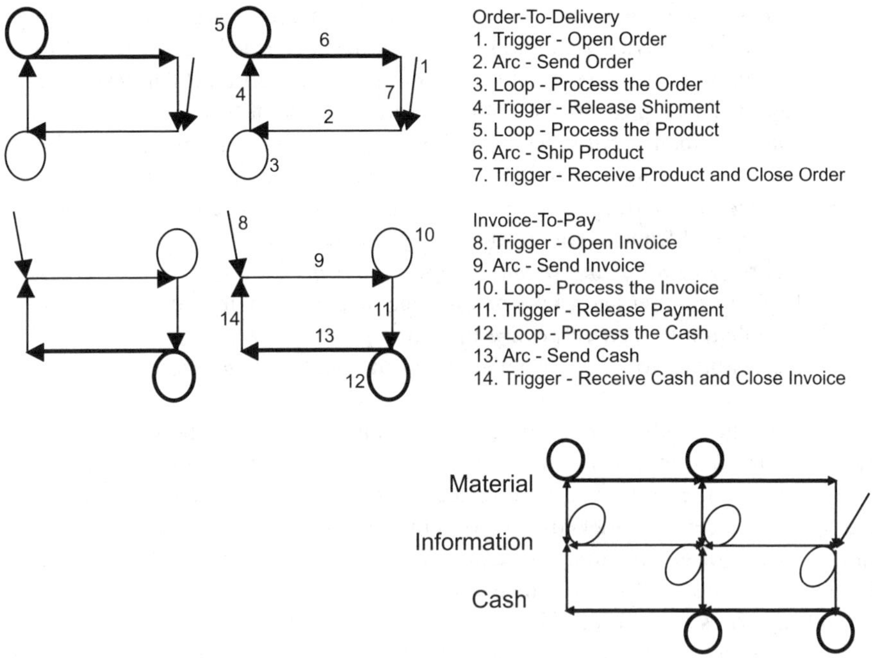

FIGURE 5-6 Information flows in serial networks.

to upstream. Some cash processing loops are wholly contained inside a single trading partner; they combine cash processing with information flow. The cash flow arc connections are made through commercial banks and other financial service providers who are nominal trading partners. Cash often flows as a specialized form of encrypted information flow. Figure 5-5 shows how the cash flows from the top level to the bottom level of the BOM product structure tree. In a serial network design, the invoice-to-pay subcycle is triggered by a shipment in the order-to-delivery subcycle.

When subcycles are interconnected in serial networks, the information flow for orders must follow a completed closed loop and the information flow for invoices must follow another complete closed loop. Each closed loop is composed of a combination of information triggers, loops, and arcs. Figure 5-6 shows how the information subcycles merge when trading partners are brought together within a serial network. The information flow design for reliable serial subcycles involves managing the individual life cycle for each order and each invoice:

- *Closed loop for orders*—Once an order from a buying (nominal) trading partner to a selling (nominal) trading partner is opened, its related information must circulate around a complete, closed path until that order is closed. This represents the birth-to-death life cycle of that order.
- *Unique, simultaneous orders*—Each order needs a unique identifier because there will be multiple orders open in the loop at any time.

- *Closed loop for invoices*—Once an invoice from a selling (nominal) trading partner to a buying (nominal) trading partner is opened, its related information must circulate around a complete, closed path until that invoice is closed. This represents the birth-to-death life cycle of that invoice.
- *Unique, simultaneous invoices*—Each invoice needs a unique identifier because there will be multiple invoices open in the loop at any time.
- *Invoice-to-pay trigger*—In a serial network the invoice-to-pay subcycle is triggered from the order-to-delivery subcycle.
- *Inserting/withdrawing (nominal) trading partners in a serial network*—Each open order and each open invoice must be individually managed to completion in their respective operating subcycles when these subcycles are disrupted to insert or withdraw a (nominal) trading partner.

The information triggers are like traffic lights conditioning the progress of the material flows and the cash flows. Triggers can be arranged to process information in a serial batch mode or in a serial nearly real-time, asynchronous mode. For example, consider an order-to-delivery subcycle containing nine open orders at various stages of completion. These open orders could be processed through their life cycle as three batches of three orders each. Alternatively, each of the nine individual orders could proceed to its next trigger, as required. This is the nearly real-time, asynchronous case. The order does not wait for its batch to complete. It is event driven in the sense that the completion of each phase in the order's life cycle progression is an event. This event interrupts the normal scheme of things to trigger the order's continuation within the subcycle.

Paralleling Subcycles to Overlap Orders

A parallel subcycle can be defined as a real-time, synchronous mode of operation. Rather than being event driven, these designs are time driven. A system clock drives a periodical sampling of the state of the network. The completion of each phase of each subcycle for an order is locked to the synch pulse from the system clock. Phase transitions are allowed to occur only in synchronization with the beat of the system clock. As long as the system clock runs at a faster pace than the shortest timing of any process phasing, phase transitions will occur in nearly real time, locked to the system clock.

A parallel network runs faster and is more competitive than a serial network. It has already been shown that the product BOM limits the material flow progression to a serial network configuration. The next two sections will discuss how improvements can be made toward a parallel network configuration by overlapping order information subcycles and by eliminating cash invoice subcycles.

Figure 5-7 and Table 5-9 describe a scheme to overlap multiple order-to-delivery and reorder-to-replenish subcycles in an otherwise serial network. This is called a *broadcast demand*. The customer order is broadcast simultaneously to each trading partner in the network. Chapter 7 explains how this is implemented and how this works to defeat the bullwhip effect. As the broadcast moves farther upstream, the respective trading partner uses the BOM to translate a product quantity into an

TABLE 5-9
Overlapping Order-to-Delivery and Reorder-to-Replenishment Subcycles

Serial Subcycle Sequence Every Trading Partner Holds Starting Inventory	**Parallel Subcycle Sequence** Every Trading Partner Holds Starting Inventory
1. Order Product—Information Flow #1	1. Order Product and Reorder Assembly and Reorder Component—Information Broadcast
2. Deliver Product—Physical Flow #1	2. Deliver Product—Physical Flow #1
3. Reorder Assembly—Information Flow #2	3. Replenish Assembly—Physical Flow #2
4. Replenish Assembly—Physical Flow #2	4. Replenish Component—Physical Flow #3
5. Reorder Component—Information Flow #3	Time Savings
6. Replenish Component—Physical Flow #3	

assembly quantity or into a component quantity. Table 5-9 demonstrates how the information cycle times for all but the original customer order are eliminated, making this a higher velocity network design. The overlapping of orders does not impact the serial manufacturing cycle times or the serial logistics transit times. Notice that the customer's order cannot be closed on the system until each of the parallel subcycle paths has been completed.

The broadcast demand becomes the order. The information system should be used to automate the translation of raw customer data into quantities and timeframes that are appropriate for each trading partner. Figure 5-8 shows a multi-level product structure diagrammed over the seven weeks of purchasing lead-time and manufacturing cycle time that it takes to build the product. In this figure, the product structure has been repeated for each of three successive weeks to show the relative interaction of the broadcast demand with the weekly build cycle. The point of sale demand flows to the starting point for Parts C, D, and E, for Assembly B and for End Product A. The following considerations are important when working with a broadcast demand:

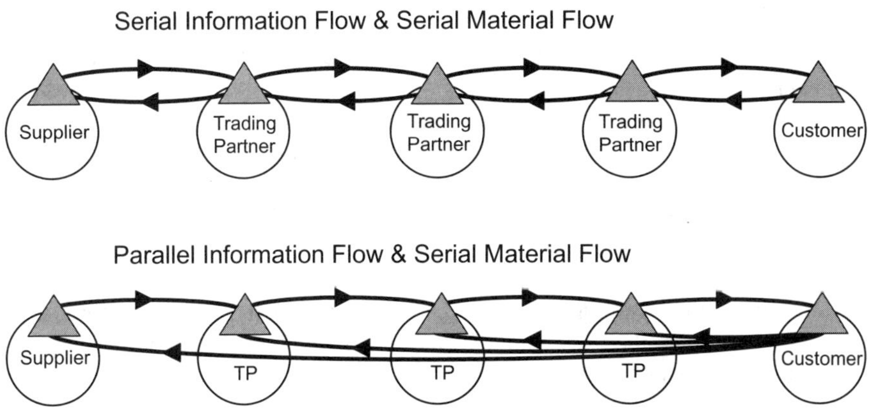

FIGURE 5-7 Broadcast demand.

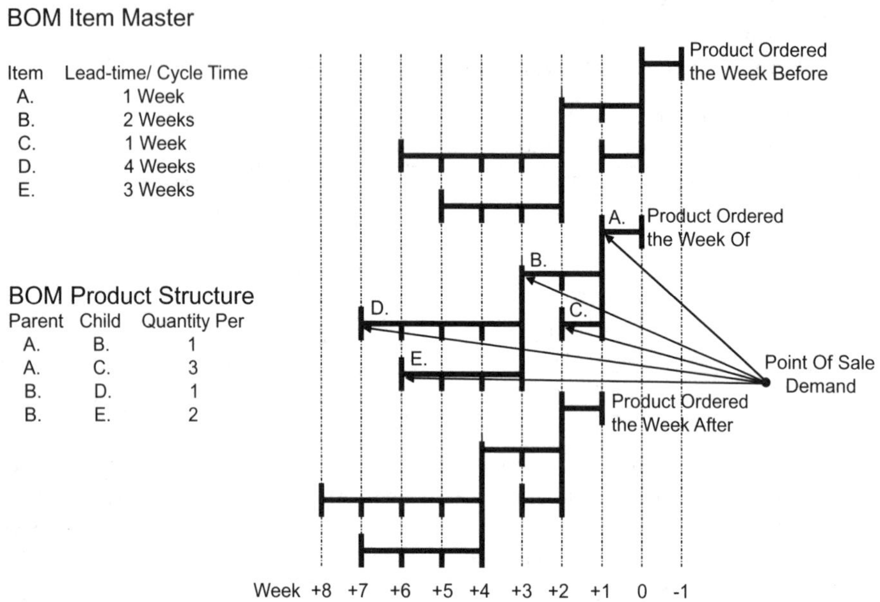

FIGURE 5-8 Using the BOM to translate point of sale demand.

- *Trading partner trust in sharing point of sale data*—Sometimes distributors feel that a large part of their value-added is their intimate knowledge of the customer. They feel that when this kind of information is shared, it may be easier to disintermediate them out of the network. Downstream trust can be built into network relationships by communicating and understanding the core competencies each trading partner provides.
- *Communicate unit quantities, not sales dollars*—The information communicated must be an accurate reflection of demand useful for planning. Trading partners are likely to have different discount schedules and may have dynamic pricing.
- *Differentiate rate from mix*—Split the Point Of Sale (POS) demand during each reporting period into a rate of total product units ordered and the mix of individual product units ordered.
- *Translate demand quantity*—Use the BOM product structure parent-child relationships and quantity per to translate the POS demand in units into the unit demand for downstream product, for midstream assemblies, and for upstream components.
- *Translate demand timing*—Use the BOM item master manufacturing cycle time or purchasing lead time plus the transit time and customs clearance time to offset the POS demand data for the trading partners at each level in the product structure.

Table 5-10 is an example of using the BOM to interpret point of sale daily demand information for a family of five products. The five products are designated

TABLE 5-10
An Example of Translating POS Demand

POS Rate All Product Colors				
POS Mix—Red BOM Changes Part C Quantity = 1 Part E Quantity = 1	**POS Mix—Green** BOM Changes Part C Quantity = 2 Part E Quantity = 2	**POS Mix—Blue** BOM Changes Part C Quantity = 1 Part E Quantity = 2	**POS Mix—Orange** BOM Changes Part C Quantity = 2 Part E Quantity = 3	**POS Mix—Brown** BOM Changes Part C Quantity = 1 Part E Quantity = 3
Monday Products 37 Total				
5	17	0	3	12
Tuesday Products 41 Total				
7	19	2	0	13
Wednesday Products 22 Total				
0	14	0	5	3
Thursday Products 29 Total				
4	18	1	4	2
Friday Products 55 Total				
8	25	3	4	15
Monday	**Tuesday**	**Wednesday**	**Thursday**	**Friday**
Assembly B—No Cycle-Time Offset				
37	41	22	29	55
Part C—No Lead-Time Offset				
57	60	41	51	84
Part D—No Lead-Time Offset				
37	41	22	29	55
Part E—No Lead-Time Offset				
84	88	52	60	121

by the names of colors: Red Product, Green Product, Blue Product, Orange Product, and Brown Product. The five products share the common product structure shown in Figure 5-8, except the quantity per of part C and part E varies by product model. The total daily product demand in units by model at the top of the table is exploded without lead-time offset to the lowest levels of the BOM at the bottom of the table. For example, the total demand for all products on Monday is 37; this includes 5 Red, 17 Green, 3 Orange, and 12 Brown products in the mix. From this Monday's demand for part C is 57 and for part E is 84.

Paralleling Subcycles to Eliminate Invoicing

If an upstream supplier can get a buyer's order and a buyer's payment at the same time, there is no need for an invoice. This is an extremely powerful business model

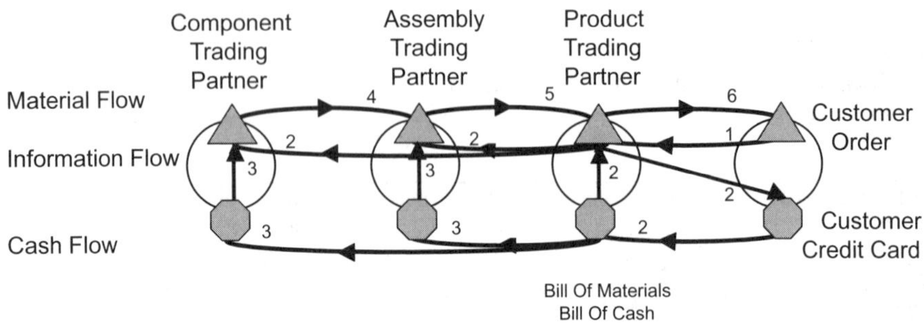

FIGURE 5-9 Accessing the customer's payment before building the customer's product.

because it uses the end-customer's cash to pay the upstream supplier directly rather than the traditional approach where the manufacturer has to put up its own cash to pay its suppliers. Dell Computer implemented this kind of a network design by combining virtual retailing over the Internet, immediate access to its customer's credit card cash flow, and trading partner information interconnectivity over the Internet with a build-to-order strategy to deliver customized products. Dell's trading partners hold inventory positions measured in hours. Material flows only after the customer order has been booked and the cash flow from the customer authorized credit card transaction has been accessed. Dell's customers are willing to wait a few days while their personal computers are built, customized, tested, and shipped directly to their location.

Figure 5-9 and Table 5-11 describe the essence of such a network design. Everything keys off the order-to-delivery cycle for the end-customer. When the network orchestrator books the customer order, it triggers a demand broadcast to each of the other trading partners. At the same time, a cash withdrawal is triggered from the customer's credit card account. The cash withdrawal flows immediately to the network orchestrator. The network orchestrator then uses a Bill Of Cash (BOC) to match parallel payments to each trading partner according to the product BOM. The BOC represents the total dollars paid to each trading partner for their slice of the total sales revenue. The network orchestrator pays based on the BOC prior to receiving the physical goods from upstream. The trading partners now have their order and their payment; there are no invoices with this arrangement. Such a parallel network design is predicated on trust by the network orchestrator that it will receive a perfect component or assembly or product as has been ordered and paid. This design works best in a build-to-order environment where the lower-level order-to-delivery cycle times are kept short.

Notice how the customer order is broken down into many parallel branches that match a lower-level order generated from the BOM and a lower-level payment generated from the BOC. The network design is information system intensive and depends on reliable Internet-based connectivity. The customer order cannot be closed on the system until each of its parallel branches has been completed. And, then each open branch must be individually managed to completion whenever the network is disrupted to insert or withdraw a (nominal) trading partner.

TABLE 5-11
Simultaneous Ordering and Cash Payment Eliminates the Need to Invoice

Serial Subcycle Sequence Every Trading Partner Holds Starting Inventory		Parallel Sequence No Invoicing, No Starting Inventory	
Order-to-Delivery	**Invoice-to-Cash**	**Order-to-Delivery**	**Bill of Cash**
1. Order Product		1. Order Product	
2. Ship Product, Reorder Assembly	2. Trigger Invoice, Invoice Product	2. Broadcast Order for Assembly + Component	2. Trigger Credit Card, Pay for Product
3. Deliver Product			3. Pay for Assembly, Pay for Component
	4. Pay for Product	4. Deliver Component	
5. Ship Assembly, Reorder Component	5. Trigger Invoice, Invoice Assembly	5. Deliver Assembly	
6. Deliver Assembly		6. Deliver Product	
	7. Pay for Assembly	Time Savings	
8. Ship Component	8. Trigger Invoice, Invoice Component		
9. Deliver Component			
	10. Pay for Component		

For example, a network sells customized instrumentation systems that consist of a mainframe and different models of electronic instruments including voltmeters, frequency counters, signal generators, and power supplies that are plug-in modules. Each mainframe holds up to eight modules. The customer orders a customized configuration over the Internet. The network orchestrator assembles modules to the customer order and performs verification testing on the assembled system. The mainframe is purchased from a contract assembler. The mainframe's packaging carton is designed to be reused as the shipping carton for the customized system. The voltmeter, frequency counter and signal generator modules are purchased from stock under a private label arrangement with an instrument manufacturer. The power supply modules are purchased off the shelf from a distributor and repackaged as modules by the network orchestrator. Table 5-12 shows the bill of cash for a single customer order. The BOC totals the dollars due to each of the trading partners for their slice of the revenue. The BOC total equals the sales price total paid by the customer.

INDUSTRY STANDARDS AND BEST PRACTICES

The design and operation of a competitive supply chain network would be remiss without the consideration of industry standards and best practices. The intent of this section is only to point toward some example organizations that provide such standards and best practices. A thorough discussion of the standards, and their respective regulatory bodies, is outside the scope of this book. Because many standards organizations are funded through annual membership fees, access to their complete

TABLE 5-12
An Example Bill of Cash

Customer Order	Bill Of Materials	Trading Partner	Bill Of Cash
1-Mainframe 1-Frequency Counter 2-Voltmeters 2-Power Supplies Total Price $3,750.00		Network Orchestrator	$770.00
	1-Mainframe Lower-Level BOM	Contract Assembler	$762.00
	1-Shipping Carton Lower-Level BOM	Packaging Supplier	$48.00
	1-Frequency Counter Module Lower-Level BOM 2-Voltmeter Modules Lower-Level BOM	Instrument Manufacturer	$1,720.00
	2-Power Supply Modules Lower-Level BOM	Distributor	$450.00
			Total $3,750.00

information requires membership. Additional information can be found through the Web sites listed in the Bibliography.

Standards and best practices are bounded in different ways. In order to understand their intent, it is necessary first to understand their context. Some, like the Internet XML protocol, are information technology standards, whereas others are business process standards. Some are industry-specific, whereas others, like the SCOR model, strive to relate across industries. Some are country-specific, whereas others, like INCOTERMS, are international in their scope. Some exist for the benefit of a few, whereas others, like VICS, have evolved through voluntary consensus. Some, like C-TPAT, the Customs and Trade Partnership Against Terrorism, are guidelines, whereas others become legal requirements. The following two organizations are representative of interindustry best practices and standards.

The Supply-Chain Council Interindustry Best Practices

The Supply-Chain Council, www.supply-chain.org, was formed to advance interindustry best practices and to benchmark common performance measures. This organization of member companies levels the playing field through their SCOR model. SCOR stands for Supply-Chain Operations Reference-model. SCOR defines a small number of standard process elements grouped under "Plan," "Source," "Make," "Deliver," and "Return" to model complex supply chain networks. The purpose of the SCOR model is to use industry-standard language to communicate among network organizations, to share best practices, and to benchmark common performance measures. It serves as an excellent, normalized basis of comparison between trading partners within the same industry and across different industries. Because every network is described using the same standard, it becomes possible to identify best practices in one industry that can benefit other industries. It becomes practical to collect metrics from member companies in a standardized way to build a benchmarking database.

When a supply chain network is mapped using SCOR, specific Plan, Source, Make, Deliver, and Return process elements are combined to represent network functionality in the upstream, midstream, downstream, and reverse stream zones. The SCOR model drills down through a hierarchy of increasing levels of detail. The three top-level process descriptions in the model are generic while the fourth level process description is company-specific. The detail at level 4 is proprietary in nature, and is generally not disclosed. Best practice comparisons and performance benchmarking are built around the top three levels of the model.

The VICS Interindustry Standards

The Voluntary Interindustry Commerce Standards Association (VICS), www.vics.org, identifies, develops, and implements volunteer standards, protocols, and guidelines across the supply chain that benefit the retail customer. VICS maintains a portfolio of approved and in-draft standards and guidelines. Some of the VICS approved standards include the Bill Of Lading Standard, the Direct To Consumer Standard, and the CPFR® Standard. Voluntary Guidelines for Floor Ready Merchandise, Synchronized Movement, and Logistics Modeling are examples of other initiatives within the VICS Committees.

Collaborative Planning, Forecasting, and Replenishment (CPFR®) strives to increase sales with higher inventory turns, improved wholesale and retail service levels, and decreased logistics costs. The application of CPFR® has brought the apparel industry, among other industries, huge savings. CPFR® is a nine-step business process framework that starts with a collaborative arrangement and a joint business plan. The core of this framework is focused on creating a sales forecast, resolving exceptions to the sales forecast, creating an order forecast, and resolving exceptions to the order forecast. Once these demand and supply forecasts have been wrung out, there can be a smooth order generation for the replenishment inventory. The CPFR® standard spells out the behavior required by each of the network trading partners.

IN SUMMARY

This Chapter has raised and answered the following fundamental questions:

- How can you assess risk in an information system?
- How can you deal effectively with partitioning in the real world?
- How can the bill of materials be used to accelerate the flow of ordering information?
- How can a bill of cash be used to eliminate the need for invoicing?

Chapter 6 transitions from competitive network design to competitive network operations beginning with the consideration of key change management issues.

He had forgotten how hot it could get on the East Coast in July. He walked quickly from the office through the parking lot to his car. The closed car was an oven, but at least he didn't have to raise the windshield wipers off the windshield during the day to prevent them from melting like they did in Singapore.

Racing from his air conditioned car to his air conditioned home he plopped down on the sofa, "Whew, a person could wilt out there in this heat!"

His wife joined him on the sofa halfway through a tall gin and tonic. "Yes, and we did today."

"I'll bet you did," said the supply chain architect.

"No, it gets a lot better than that. The air conditioning unit failed this morning in our classroom at DataLink. We had to scramble, but we were able to move the class temporarily by renting a classroom at the local community college."

"That was a fortunate that a classroom was available."

"Yes, but that created a whole new set of problems to be solved."

"What do you mean?"

"As luck would have it, Suzie Lee was the instructor. It took a couple of hours to get the class moved. Suzie squeezed the remaining material into the afternoon session and got the class back on track. But, now Fred's managers are telling Fred that we need to reschedule the class and run it again. The cost of repeating a class is not in my contract. The community college room rental and an additional day of Suzie's time come right out of my profits."

"Do you know exactly what Suzie was able to teach? Or, did she partition the instruction in some new way to fit the time frame?" her husband asked.

"The information is all there for the student. They can read everything we teach from the Student Guides. Suzie probably shuffled some of the content around and maybe dropped some of the interactive exercises. After all, she is a professional instructor."

"You need to differentiate between the information context and content. The context may change, but the content must be accurate. On the one hand, if Fred's managers are saying that the instruction they received was inaccurate because the class was partitioned between two locations and between unrelated instructional methods, then you should reschedule the original class. On the other hand, if you are sure that everything Suzie presented was accurate and only the presentation style changed, then you satisfied the intent of your contract."

"Hum...flexible context, but accurate content," she mused.

6 Leading Change in Performance Measurement

Thursday, July 11

It had rained early that morning, and everything still felt damp. The plumbing inspector had shown up yesterday about 11:00 a.m. He was gone within 15 minutes. Tom, the house architect, and the supply chain architect were standing in the kitchen, each holding a cup of Starbucks coffee.

"This is going to be an exciting day for you. It's a good thing your wife is able to stay home to direct all the traffic," said Tom.

"Yeah. She was able to juggle her class schedule to stay home today. I'm going to be leaving soon because there is an important meeting this afternoon at my office. What happens in the kitchen today?"

"First the sheet rockers will come in and finish the ceiling and the walls. They are amazing to watch as they work the room on their stilts. While the sheet rockers are taping and spackling, the cabinet maker will be here to take a final set of measurements. Then the refrigerator is being delivered late this afternoon."

"That is exciting! How did you get all that to come together so fast when it took days just to get the plumbing inspector?"

"It took quite a few phone calls last night to get it all coordinated. On a small job, like this one, the architect ends up becoming the project manager and general contractor all rolled into one. At this point in a project, it often seems to be a continuous negotiation, communication, and coordination effort."

"That is interesting because that is exactly my job at this phase of an implementation project. It seems like there is an educational piece, too, especially when new technology is involved. You have to explain what can be done, get agreement that it will be done, and then let everyone else know how it is being done. Our jobs seem to have a lot in common."

"Now that you mention it, you may be right. There is an educational piece in home architecture as well. My clients don't understand building codes and what can be accomplished with the range of today's building materials."

"You mean like being able to span the width of the kitchen ceiling with a laminated beam without a floor-to-beam pillar?"

"Yes, that's a good example of having to reacquaint myself with the local building code and the laminate beam strengths now available. Then you and your wife had to be educated about this alternative. Something is always changing in this business."

"What do you mean?"

"You know, it's funny to me. My clients will readily accept a new material or a different appliance in a home renovation, but they often resist changing very far from what they have. Some jobs are just not worth doing because there is not enough change to warrant my fees. Now, your kitchen design, on the other hand, is a significant departure from where you started."

"My wife pushed the envelope partially because she works in this kitchen every day and felt constrained. She had a compelling reason to change. My compelling reason was to keep her happy."

"You are a very wise man," said Tom.

*****

A question had come up during the data mapping with Singapore about what data would be required to drive the performance measures. Representatives from every functional area were now assembled in the conference room to formulate their answer for Singapore. In addition to the supply chain architect, the people in the room included operations manager Roberta Perez, sales manager Bob Donovan, purchasing manager William Smith, chief engineer Dan Cook, vice president of quality Daisy Whitehall, Mary Chen with general accounting and Ray Smith from cost accounting, human resources manager Alice Way, Mohamed Hashim from information systems, engineering section manager Nancy Tucker, and Hector Morales, vice president of manufacturing. This was going to be a very expensive meeting.

Dan was explaining, "Engineering doesn't care what other metrics you people decide to use as long as you keep the Break-Even Time metric. That's the one measure that really makes sense for our long-term projects. Don't screw around with my BET numbers."

"You only care about BET because your bonus is tied to it," said Daisy. "What would you say if there was some better measure, say of conformance to customer need, which drove shorter projects with better returns? Would you still want to hang on to BET?"

"Thanks Dan. We have heard a lot from Engineering. What about hearing from some of the other functional areas?" Hector said ignoring Daisy's question.

"We need to be able to value inventory for our financial statements," said Mary. "And we currently measure inventory turns, but maybe we could use something else."

"Purchasing gets graded on purchased price variance as much as anything," said William.

"Our college hiring is a priority for human resources. We get graded on that," said Alice.

"Wait a minute! There is an important pattern here. It is clear that each functional area has at least one performance measure that it gets graded on—BET, inventory turns, purchased price variance, the number of college new hires, etc. But notice that none of these performance measures align with each other, and not one is directed at the end-customer," said the supply chain architect.

"That's an important observation. We need to stay focused on our customers," said Bob.

"It is an important observation," agreed Hector. "And we are making our answer to Singapore too hard. It would seem that there are really two issues on the table. The first is the data-mapping question asking what information we need to run the business? The second is a performance measurement question asking what performance measures do we need to stay focused on the customer and to stay aligned with the other trading partners on our business strategy?"

"Hector, after all this time, you really have been thinking about the supply chain! Right on!" said the architect.

Mohamed spoke thoughtfully, "So what exactly is information systems supposed to be doing?"

"Maybe there is a way to simplify what we are trying to do. Maybe we need two groups or even have the wrong people trying to answer the question. Maybe we don't even know the question," said Daisy.

"It would seem that some of the measures that have been brought up, specifically BET and the number of college hires, are pretty far removed from our day-to-day operations of delivering product to customers competitively. We need to stop thinking functional departments and start thinking about those processes that are directly involved in moving product to the customer, processes that touch sales, order processing, planning, purchasing, manufacturing, logistics, and accounting," continued the architect.

"So, you are saying that engineering is not important!?" challenged Nancy.

"Not at all. Engineering and new products are the lifeblood of our growth. However, the 'supply chain' for new product design and development is a largely independent network until pilot run. Likewise, the 'supply chain' for new hires, including college graduates, is a largely independent network until a key position gets filled."

"What you're saying is that by pairing back these ancillary 'supply chains' from the end-to-end network we can simplify this discussion?" clarified Roberta.

"Exactly."

"What do you expect of information systems?" asked Mohamed again.

After a long pause in the conversation the architect offered, "Our current performance measures fall into three categories. There are some good metrics that have a functional focus that we should keep. There are some historical metrics that frankly cause misalignment and drive the wrong behavior. Those we should drop. And there are some new performance metrics necessary to keep the supply chain network aligned and competitive that we should adopt."

"Yes, that makes sense," said Hector. "How would you recommend that we proceed?"

"A good way to proceed would be to redefine our working teams. The teams can be a lot smaller, maybe five to seven members, which report to this larger group. We should invite a representative of our upstream and downstream trading partners to join the team working on new global performance measures. Mohamed and the information system group can be a resource for each team to let us know what is possible from an information technology perspective."

"That sounds good," said Hector. "It's important that we set a direction that makes sense for the business and for our customers, rather than being pushed in a direction we don't want to go because of the Singapore connection."

"It's still confusing to me," said Alice. "Are you saying that we're going to stop measuring the number of new college hires?"

Hector replied, "We're saying that it is important to differentiate a set of performance measures that move our operational alignment to be horizontal with our other trading partners. And we're saying that some functional areas, human resources and engineering to mention two, have other metrics that we will continue to use independently."

"What about measures required for legal reporting, like inventory valuation?" asked Mary.

"Clearly if there is a legal or audit requirement, we must continue to have that process."

"What about Purchased Price Variance (PPV) as a measure?" asked William.

"PPV is an interesting measure. On the one hand, in a cost driven world, it is a key performance measure. It aligns well with the effectiveness of the purchasing department. On the other hand, in a throughput-driven world, it causes misalignment. This is because PPV tells us not to make certain purchases and to slow the rate of purchase. A two-cent PPV on a five-cent part would tell us not to buy that inventory even though 20% of our revenue might be contingent on having the part in stock. The role of a performance measure like PPV needs to be carefully reviewed. For example, we might keep it as a secondary indicator but drop it as a primary measure," said the supply chain architect.

"Oh, sorry I asked," replied William. "Purchasing never liked getting beat up over it anyway."

Hector stepped in again, "These are all good questions. However, this is an expensive crowd, and we run the risk of spinning our wheels in such a large meeting. Roberta, please work with us to pick a small team to look at supply chain performance measures. Alice and Nancy, please work with us to pick a team to look at functional performance measures. Daisy, please work with us to pick a team to review the current metrics that we should consider discontinuing. Mohamed, please let Singapore know that it will be a few more days until we get back to them with a better defined process to answer their question. Thanks everyone. That's all."

The concepts in this book require supply chain organizations to change their perspective of the world and to adopt a different set of rules to play the network game competitively. This is the soft side of supply chain management. Few people want to discuss change management, and most people say that they are not resistant to change. Yet, we live in a time of accelerating change where people's actions belie their claims of an ability to cope. Sometimes change takes the form of having to learn a new information system to do your job differently. You feel out of control, and many things are out of your control. In addition, when there are many people in a trading partner's organization and several trading partners in a network, there are political situations. The politics of change can be overcome only through excellent communications and consensus building.

This Chapter discusses how to lead change in the context of a supply chain network. This change is the move from a functional cost-driven view of the supply chain to a network throughput–driven view of the supply chain. This Chapter applies some key concepts from the work of Kevin McCormack and William Johnson on Business Process Orientation (BPO) and a key thinking process from Eli Goldratt's Theory Of Constraints (TOC). It focuses on defining a new global performance measure, equivalent throughput, which facilitates the right behavioral change.

MOVING FROM A COST VIEW TO A THROUGHPUT VIEW

The Queen Elizabeth 2 (QE2) is a magnificent ship. It is fast, and it can cross the Atlantic Ocean from Southampton, England, to New York City in 4.5 days. It is flexible, being short enough at 963 feet to just fit the 1000-foot locks of the Panama Canal. Nevertheless, like any huge ship of its tonnage, the QE2 does not turn on a dime. The turn begins with an imperceptible sideward motion that slowly leads to the new heading directed from the bridge. The captain knows the ship's position by reading the Global Positioning System (GPS) receiver and the LORAN navigation readout. The pilot knows when the turn is complete by reading the gyro compass heading. When docking, the QE2 can accelerate faster in reverse than while moving forward.

Although the current state may be uncomfortable, such as when a company is losing market share, it is still the current state. Everyone knows the rules of the road. You have the experience to know whom you can trust and whom you cannot. The organizational politic is stable. There is a balance to how things work. Change in an organization is like turning the QE2. Organizations begin to turn with an imperceptible motion, but they sometimes never make the heading directed by senior management. Many organizations start the turn failing to have put into place the measurements to gauge their heading. In addition, all organizations accelerate faster in reverse than while moving forward.

STATE A CLEAR OBJECTIVE

When the captain orders a heading for latitude 40° 44′ N and longitude 74° 2′ W to make port by Tuesday at 1100 hours, it is clear that the objective is to dock at the Port of New York by 11:00 a.m. on Tuesday. In too many business situations, the objective is murky or has incompatible, competing elements. For example, a clear objective to move all production from the company's manufacturing facility in New Jersey to the company's manufacturing facility in Penang, Malaysia, within the next ten months could be clouded by a subobjective to redesign certain products during the move.

The objective in this book is to move from the current state of making business decisions based on an internal view focused on cost to a future state of making business decisions based on an external view focused on network throughput. Chapter 9 explains how a throughput focus creates value for all the stakeholders while a cost focus creates value for only one trading partner. Your first questions should be: Why would you want to do this, and how would you know where you are and when you are done? The question of "why" is answered by communicating a vision with all its rewards and risks. The questions of "where and when" are answered by a set of performance measures.

Speak to a Compelling Vision

A supply chain network achieves competitiveness when it delivers great products and services to its customers and great value to its stakeholders. When you are convinced that an external view focused on network throughput can achieve and sustain higher value than an internal view focused on cost, the vision becomes compelling. Reducing cost implies less with less. Your eye is off the customer and glued to the bottom line. Less material purchases and fewer inventories are better because they cost less. Fewer employees are better because it reduces cost. Less overhead such as spending for tooling, training, and travel is better because it costs less. The bottom line improves, but the customer moves on to your competitor. Network throughput implies that information, material, and cash are all constantly in motion. Moving information leads to new business opportunity and growth in market share. Moving product leads to customer satisfaction and improving asset turns. Moving cash leads to growth in earnings and return on investments.

This is not to suggest that you can forget about cost. However, a cost-reduction focus is suboptimal when it is internally focused and driven from a silo mentality. For example, a purchasing department with four employees and three inventory turns per year is given the order to cut inventory by 20% and to reduce departmental expense by 25%. The only course of action is to cancel all open purchase orders, stop all buying for 3.5 weeks (52 weeks divided by three turns times 20%) and layoff one buyer (four employees times 25%). The purchasing manager achieves the departmental goal, but how does this make any sense for the network? Throughput and revenue decrease because the mix of components left in inventory is short critical material to complete any production run. Information flow with suppliers and planners is disrupted because one of four knowledge workers has left the network, and the remaining three do not have the time or the commodity knowledge to answer questions. Cash flow is disrupted because of cancelled orders and delayed new purchases. When purchase orders are turned back on, suppliers will have found new business with other customers.

Or take the example where a company is operating at a loss and hemorrhaging money. The senior management team decides to take a ratio approach to lower the breakeven point and regain profitability. Discretionary funds, including all advertising, all capital tooling, all travel, and all training, are cancelled until further notice. All overtime is cancelled. A freeze is placed on hiring and any outstanding job offers are retracted. Every department is told to cut 7% now and to give the boss a plan for an additional 5% in later cuts. Now what happens when the sole direct labor operator at the throughput constraint is not allowed to work overtime and a backup cannot be cross-trained? What happens when the technical information services department, a group of four employees with critical and unique skills to manage product BOMs, must lay off one or two employees? What happens when the most talented engineer decides to go to work for the competition? What happens when sales stops making contact with new customers? Cutting costs to a ratio formula is not a compelling vision. Throughput and revenue slows because flexibility has been taken out of the network. Information slows or is disrupted because key knowledge workers are displaced from the network. Cash flow slows because the order-to-delivery-to-cash cycle has been delayed.

A compelling vision is one that speaks of a flexible, responsive supply chain network that delivers products of exceptional value and quality at a competitive price, with reliable and predictable delivery and with a set of unexpectedly delightful services. The compelling vision is one of growth in throughput with sustained profitability for every trading partner in the network. Everybody in the network wins rather than a few winners and many losers. Cost reduction in the compelling vision is rifle shot cost reduction rather than shotgun cost reduction. It is the trading partners working together to eliminate certain costs from the network once and for all for the benefit of the end-customer.

Fully Disclose the Rewards and the Risks

An organization must have a compelling vision, full disclosure of the rewards and risks, and the right performance measures to achieve its goals. The rewards and risks related to a supply chain adopting the goal of becoming externally focused on network throughput include:

- *Reward: Higher value to the customer*—The supply chain network is more responsive to customer delivery at a competitive price through trading partner collaboration.
- *Reward*: *Profitability*—The long-term survival of each trading partner for the benefit of the owners depends upon sustaining its profitability through trading partner collaboration.
- *Reward*: *Growth and enhanced revenue opportunity*—A network delivering products and services through trading partner collaboration offers the opportunity for continuity and growth in demand for trading partners and suppliers.
- *Reward*: *Reduced network working capital*—A competitive network learns how to operate with less inventory asset and lower accounts payable and accounts receivable to benefit the owners through trading partner collaboration.

- *Reward*: *Reduced network cost*—A competitive network learns how to minimize cost to benefit the customer and the owners by end-to-end process re-engineering through trading partner collaboration.
- *Reward*: *WIIFM*—Sustainable employment opportunity is "What's in it for me" for employees.
- *Risk*: *Resistance to change*—The organization does not want to change or is incapable of changing.
- *Risk*: *Wrong performance measures*—Performance measures that drive individual bonuses and local or silo optimization drive counterproductive behavior. For example, a bonus tied to the number of units produced per quarter rewards growth in inventory rather than growth in throughput.
- *Risk*: *Re-skill the workforce*—New skills are required for the workforce. Some people will join, some people will retrain, and some people will leave. A network in transition will be less than competitive during the timeframe to re-skill its workforce.
- *Risk*: *Technology leapfrog*—Investment in a current technology becomes obsolete with the announcement of an unexpected new technology, or if the competition is quicker to adapt.
- *Risk*: *Structural change in market demand*—Market demand in an industry shifts in some unanticipated, permanent way. The network of trading partners becomes less relevant.

Define the Right Global Performance Measures

You get what you measure. If you want to steer the ship in a new direction, then you must be able to measure the rate of change, the completion of the turn, and your ability to stay on the new course. When trading partners are joined into a network for the first time, their performance measurement systems often do not mesh. Some of these trading partners will be further disadvantaged by owning a performance measurement system focused on the wrong measures. For example, in one company research and development is measured on time-to-market, marketing is measured on net revenue versus last quarter, order fulfillment is measured on on-time shipments and months of inventory, purchasing is measured on purchased price variance, finance is measured on asset turns and net profit, human resources is measured on the number of college hires, and the general manager receives an annual stock option based on the percentage improvement to contribution margin. This is a dysfunctional set of performance measures. Each one is specifically targeted to optimize performance within a functional silo. Taken together they elicit a confusing set of directives for change. Not one of these measures is focused on the end-customer!

When the performance measure is correct, the trading partner's internal functional areas can align themselves with a winning business strategy. When the performance measure is embraced among all the trading partners, each network organization can mesh more easily and at a lower cost. When the performance measure is end-to-end, the focus of every trading partner is customer centric. It takes setting expectations in a network context, negotiating, communicating, and educating to accept global performance measures.

BUSINESS PROCESS ORIENTATION

The first step toward the right global performance measures is to achieve consensus around the network's business processes. It is essential that each of the trading partners agree to a common process description; it is even better to get buy-in from the strategic nominal trading partners. The business processes of interest in this book are defined by combining the order-to-delivery subcycles from each trading partner until they stretch end-to-end from raw materials to the end-customer and by combining the invoice-to-cash subcycles from each trading partner until they stretch end-to-end from the end-customer to raw materials. Such an orientation toward business processes will lead to the right organizational structure, process ownership, and global performance measures.

The BPO Components of Supply Chain Management

Business Process Orientation (BPO), as developed by Kevin P. McCormack and William C. Johnson, kmccormack@drkresearch.org, extends earlier work done by Michael Hammer, Rummler and Brache, Thomas Davenport, and others. BPO is a methodology that formally recognizes that business results are accomplished horizontally through processes rather than vertically through organizational structures. McCormack and Johnson first focused on cross-functional relationships within the four walls of the single firm. They used the components of process view, process values and beliefs, process structure, process job, and process measures to define standard processes and common performance measures across functional boundaries. They defined the net impact of the maturity of an organization's business process components in terms of its correlation with improved business performance. Their research showed that *conflict*, defined as the tensions among organizations arising from the incompatibility of actual or desired responses, decreased. *Connectedness*, defined as the degree of formal and informal direct contact among organizations, increased. Moreover, *esprit de corps*, defined as the feeling by an organization of belonging and its strong identification with the business goals and purpose, increased with the application maturity of the BPO components. [1]

Later work focused on intercompany relationships across a supply chain network. Again, McCormack and Johnson used the components of process view, process values and beliefs, process structure, process job, process measures, and process technology support to define standard processes and common performance measures that extended outside the four walls of the single firm and crossed trading partner boundaries:

- *Process view*—Trading partner interfaces are an extension of standard, horizontal processes. This is achieved by sharing a common vocabulary and by agreeing to a standard representation to define process flows. Processes are defined and documented through process mapping.
- *Process values and beliefs*—In a supply chain network, each trading partner shares in a common view of the end-customer and believes that all the network trading partners are customer focused.

- *Process structure*—Each network trading partner understands the framework that defines the network team and the shared responsibility used to implement the order-to-delivery-to-cash cycles.
- *Process job*—Each network trading partner recognizes and respects the person responsible for owning the end-to-end process. This person may be an employee of the network orchestrator and must be effective working with the other (nominal) trading partners.
- *Process measure*—Interfaces among trading partners align with a common set of global performance measures that reflect end-to-end performance against the business strategy.
- *Process technology support*—The network trading partners invest in information technologies that enable and enhance process connectivity.

Levels of BPO Maturity Drive Competitive Results

McCormack and Johnson used five levels of BPO Maturity, see Table 6-1, to gauge the effectiveness of business process orientation within a supply chain network.[2] They recognized that network relationships, like personal relationships, have natural life cycles. The level of BPO maturity is generally not homogeneous across a network. This is because the individual trading partner relationships are born, mature, and die at different times over the network's life cycle.

Competitive improvement is driven in two dimensions: First, the lowest level of network BPO maturity can be raised from the ad hoc level toward the extended level. Second, an effort can be made to narrow the spread of different BPO maturity

TABLE 6-1
Business Process Orientation Maturity Levels for a Supply Chain Network

BPO Maturity Level	Processes	Targets and Measures	Relationships
Low BPO Maturity			
Ad Hoc	Ill-defined and undocumented	Missed target and unpredictable results	Trading partners act independently
Defined	Defined within each trading partner	Targets defined and inconsistent results	Functional coordination within a trading partner
Linked	Horizontal processes linked externally	Team targets and predictable results	Cooperation between trading partners
Integrated	Network processes define structures and jobs	Targets achieved with reliable results	Collaboration with customers and suppliers
Extended	Multi-firm teams; joint investments	Continuous network improvement	Competes as a supply chain network
High BPO Maturity			

levels across the network. For example, suppose there are four trading partners in a network. Moving from 1.Defined–2.Linked–3.Ad Hoc–4.Integrated to 1.Defined–2.Linked–3.Defined–4.Integrated would raise the lowest common denominator of BPO maturity across the entire network from the ad hoc level to the defined level. Then, moving from 1.Defined–2.Linked–3.Defined–4.Integrated to 1.Linked–2.Linked–3.Linked– 4.Integrated would result in a more nearly homogeneous level of BPO maturity. The message of Business Process Orientation is that the highest level of competitive performance requires a process focus. However, a network cannot gain this focus without the right global performance measures.

DEFINING A GLOBAL PERFORMANCE MEASURE

Performance measures, also called *metrics*, *Key Performance Indicators* (*KPI*), or *business analytics*, are used to manage network operations. Performance measures can be ineffective in a network context for a variety of reasons. Financially oriented measures are too aggregated and reported too late to make a difference in daily operating decisions. Measures used to optimize functional silos do not align with the business strategy and usually lack a customer focus. Measures used to drive employee or management bonuses can be manipulated for the advantage of the employee or the manager. Measures of static versus real-time data measure that "the horse has left the stable after the gate was left open." The definition of a network performance measure should provide a cause-and-effect linkage between operational decisions and the creation of value for customers and stakeholders.

THE EQUIVALENT THROUGHPUT GLOBAL PERFORMANCE MEASURE

The performance measures that are the most useful for managing a competitive supply chain network operation are end-to-end or global performance measures. This means that the performance measures are defined in a horizontal, process sense rather than in a vertical, functional sense. A handful of such measures keep every trading partner in alignment with the business strategy to create maximum value for the customer and for all the stakeholders. This Chapter describes how to define, set expectations around, negotiate, communicate, educate, and collaborate with other trading partners using a global performance measure called equivalent throughput. Table 6-2 lists the attributes that are to be documented for an effective performance measure definition.

The equivalent throughput performance measure was first defined in the context of a synchronized supply chain. It was later found to have general applicability across the entire supply chain network. The general idea is that when the physical distribution flow is well balanced, the throughput measured across each network echelon should be equal in terms of its BOM equivalency. For example, one automobile sold at a dealership equals one auto on a car train, which equals one auto shipboard, which equals one auto rolling off the production line, which equals four tires, which equals four doors, which equals two bucket seats and one bench seat, which equals one engine and transmission, which equals one body, etc moving sequentially upstream through the BOM.

TABLE 6-2
Global Performance Measure Attributes

Attribute	Consideration	Explanation
Description	• Purpose • Definition	Provides a unique description for the performance measure.
Inputs	• Defined inputs • Timing	Identifies the transactional or real-time data elements from specific databases or data warehouses.
Formulation	• Aggregation level • Calculation	Defines the formula and the dimensional units used to calculate the performance measure.
Network Connection	• Scalability • Cause and effect linkage	Defines the impact on the performance measure definition with trading partner changes to the network.
Outputs	• Defined outputs • Review period • Management dashboard	Defines the presentation and timing of the output. Identifies when the output is valid.
Value	• Actual value • Target value • Exception limits • Gold standard	Plots the actual value versus a target value between upper and lower control limit values. The gold standard is the best value in the industry.
Responsibility	• Single owner • Accountability • Network trust	Uses the concepts of BPO to identify a single owner responsible for the performance measure. Builds network trust around the owner.

Equivalent Throughput is a trading partner's in-network material flow in units per day relative to daily end-customer demand, offset by the number of separating network echelons, and with a child–parent unit equivalency based on the BOM, where:

- Equivalent throughput is measured in units, not dollars, entering the outbound pipeline.
- Within a network, the dimension of units (each) may change to an equivalent dimension of weight (pounds or kilograms) or to an equivalent liquid dimension (gallons or liters), depending on the nature of the product.
- Equivalent throughput is the net of units returned.
- Equivalent throughput measures only in-network units and does not include out-of-network units.
- The bill of materials defines the numerical equivalency of children to their parents, see Figure 6-1.

In general, equivalent throughput is offset by the amount of cycle time and transit time in days required to transverse the number of network echelons separating the trading partner from the end-customer. Figure 6-2 shows the three distinct cases:

- *Replenish backward (build-to-stock)*—The end-customer's order causes product to ship immediately from finished goods inventory. Then sequential

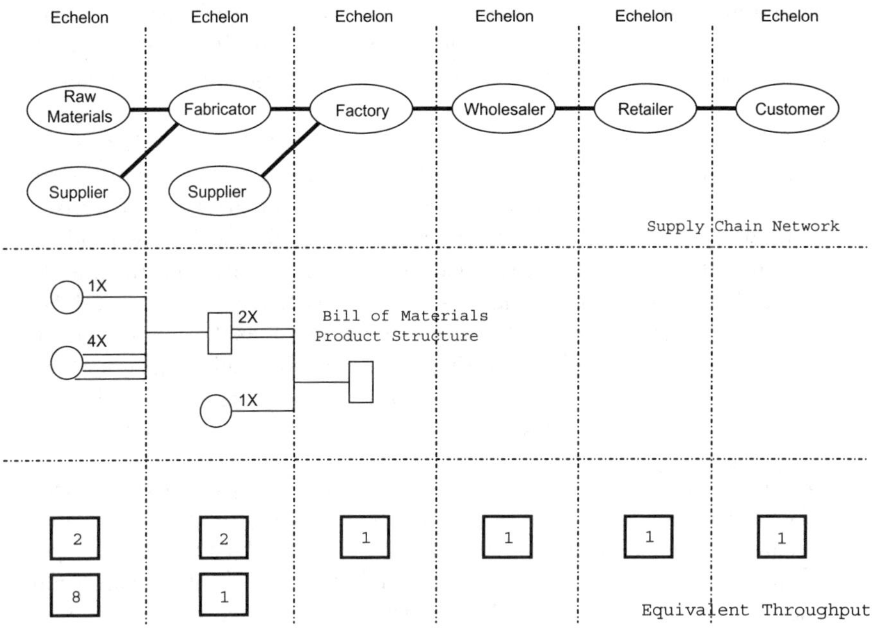

FIGURE 6-1 The BOM defines numerical equivalency of children to their parents.

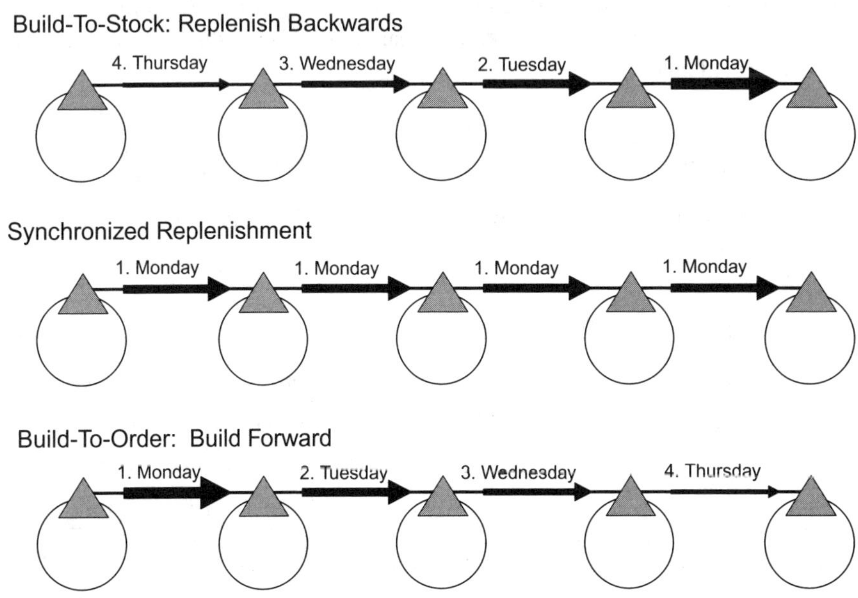

FIGURE 6-2 Three cases for equivalent throughput offset.

inventory replenishment orders work their way upstream. The equivalent throughput for each trading partner is offset from the end-customer demand by the successive cycle times plus transit times per echelon moving upstream.

- *Synchronized replenishment*—The end-customer's order is broadcast to all the trading partners, causing product, assemblies, and components to ship simultaneously. The equivalent throughput for every trading partner is offset from the end-customer demand by a single cycle time and is independent of transit time. A supply chain network may be partially synchronized.
- *Build forward (build-to-order)*—The end-customer's order causes the product's lowest BOM level to ship immediately. Then the product is built in sequential stages as it progresses downstream. The equivalent throughput for each trading partner is offset from the end-customer demand by the successive cycle time plus transit time per echelon moving downstream.

In networks with complex, multi-echelon distribution (such as consumer package goods) or with complex, multi-echelon supply bases (such as electronics), additional conversion considerations come into play. Equivalent throughput measures the physical distribution in-network. When distribution splits the flow into many parallel branches to reach every customer, the product flow in each echelon is aggregated, or added together, across all the parallel branches within that echelon. When a supplier delivers the same raw material or the same component to several customers, only the in-network portion of the physical distribution is counted. Table 6-3 summarizes all the equivalent throughput conversion factors.

Equivalent throughput is a performance measurement axis on the value circle. This axis is used to show the change in throughput relative to a network improvement or relative to a competitor's network. The change is plotted as a ratio of a baseline value of throughput as follows:

$$\frac{\text{operating throughput}}{\text{baseline throughput}} = \frac{\text{Units of operating equivalent throughput}}{\text{Units of baseline equivalent throughput}}$$

Where throughput increases toward the origin of the value circle.

TABLE 6-3
Equivalent Throughput Conversion Factors

	Upstream	Midstream	Downstream
Measurement point	Into outbound pipeline Net of returns	Into outbound pipeline Net of returns	Into outbound pipeline Net of returns
Quantity adjustment	Aggregate parallel paths Only count in-network	Only count in-network	Aggregate parallel paths Only count in-network
BOM equivalency	BOM children	Parent-child relations	BOM parent
Timing offset	1. Replenish backwards 2. Synchronized 3. Build forward	1. Replenish backwards 2. Synchronized 3. Build forward	1. Replenish backwards 2. Synchronized 3. Build forward

INTEGRATING THE PERFORMANCE MEASURE INTO A NETWORK DASHBOARD

The real value of a global performance measure is the visibility it brings to network operations. A detailed discussion of the visualize principle is presented in Chapter 7. The network view is enhanced by grouping a small number of performance measures into a network dashboard. This dashboard is like the dashboard on a car. You can see whether you are driving at the speed limit, whether you have gas, and whether the car's engine is functioning properly with a quick glance at the car's dashboard. Likewise, you can see whether the network operation is driving to customer demand, whether the network has inventory, and whether the network operation is functioning properly with a quick glance at the network dashboard.

The network dashboard includes several carefully selected global performance measures including equivalent throughput and total network inventory $-days, discussed in Chapter 7. Other measures should capture performance as viewed by the end-customer and additional aspects of the business to present a balanced scorecard. The emphasis in this book is to present enough information to be able to implement equivalent throughput and total network inventory $-days as two key network operational measures included in a balanced scorecard. Figure 6-3 shows the equivalent throughput dashboard for the food industry example described in detail below. A simple gauge represents each echelon of the supply chain network. Each gauge measures the equivalent throughput quantity that is in-network and net of returns. Each gauge has a tolerance band of expected throughput and a pointer of actual throughput. When the pointer is within the tolerance band, the network throughput is okay. When the pointer is either above or below the tolerance band, the network throughput needs management attention. Each trading partner has a complete network dashboard.

- *Gauge*—Each gauge is defined for a specific network echelon and range of SKU's.
- *Tolerance band*—The demand throughput calculated from actual end-customer demand.

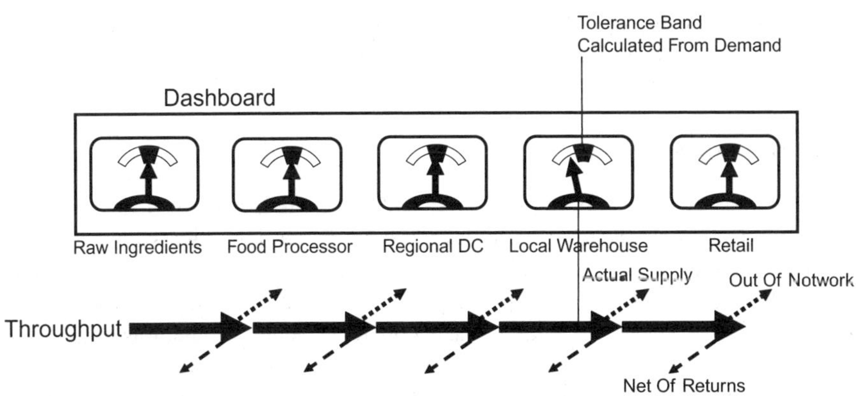

FIGURE 6-3 A performance measurement dashboard.

TABLE 6-4
An Example of Data Driving One Gauge of the Equivalent Throughput Dashboard

For echelon ____ For SKU range____	Day 1	Day 2	Day 3	Day 4	Day 5
End customer demand (units)	10,200	8,400	7,600	12,100	9,200
Offset adjustment (days)	−2	−2	−2	−2	−2
BOM equivalency (units/units)	24/1	24/1	24/1	24/1	24/1
Calculated demand throughput (units)	450	396	425	350	317
+/−2% tolerance (units)	+/−9	+/−8	+/−9	+/−7	+/−6
Count of actual units entering the pipeline	632	610	652	493	483
Returns adjustment (units)	5	0	0	17	0
Other customer out-of-network (units)	200	195	227	155	183
Actual supply throughput (units)	437	415	425	355	300
Difference in demand—supply (units)	+13	−19	0	−5	+17
Accumulated difference (units)	+13	−6	−6	−11	+6
Dashboard interpretation	Take action	Okay	Okay	Take action	Okay

- *Pointer*—The actual supply throughput measured by counting the number of units entering the outbound pipeline adjusted for returns and units going to out-of-network customers.
- *Delta*—The difference between the demand throughput units calculated minus the supply throughput units counted.
- *Accumulated difference*—This is a running summation of the plus and minus deltas.

When the set of equivalent throughput gauges are arranged to mirror the supply chain network, it is easy to monitor operations. The dashboard triggers the need for any operational adjustment in real-time. This is accomplished by continuously comparing a calculation of the demand throughput with the actual supply throughput and accumulating any deviation in performance. Table 6-4 is a detailed example of the data feeding one such gauge during a five-day period.

A Food Industry Example

The following example shows how the equivalent throughput performance measure is used. A food manufacturer processes a recipe of raw ingredients plus vitamins and minerals into breakfast cereal. The raw ingredients include rice, wheat gluten, sugar, wheat germ, salt, corn syrup, whey, malt flavoring, and calcium. The cereal's BOM includes ten different vitamins and minerals, including vitamins B_1, B_2, B_6, C, and E. The ingredients are mixed and toasted into flakes later to be stored in temporary storage hoppers. The storage hoppers are used to gravity feed a number of fill lines where the cereal is vacuum packed in different sized liner pouches to fit

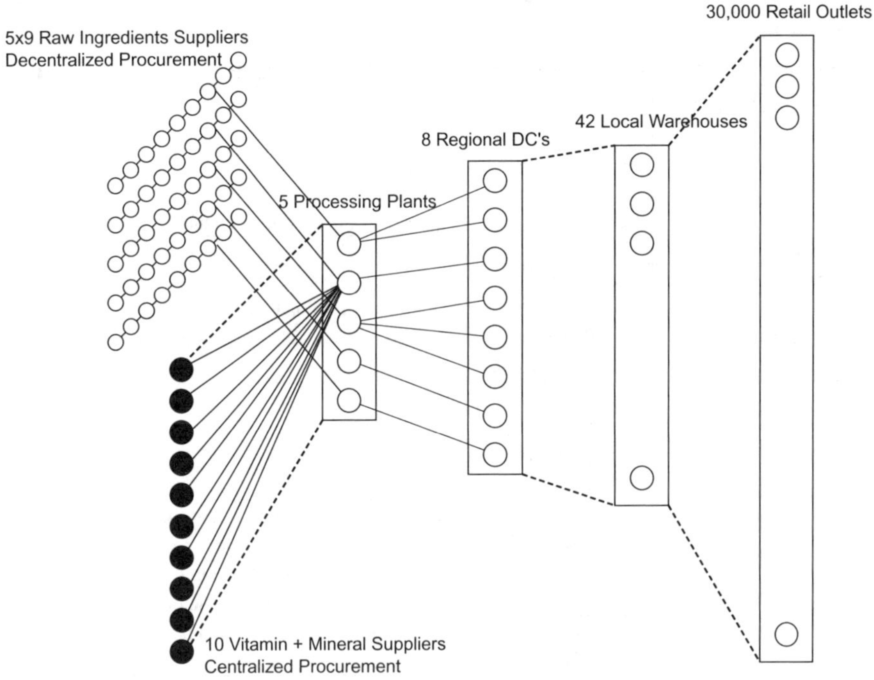

FIGURE 6-4 A supply chain network in the food industry.

a variety of consumer packaging found on the grocer's shelf and in restaurants under a private label. The food manufacturer operates five processing plants feeding eight regional distribution centers and 42 local warehouses that service 30,000 retail stores. Each processing plant purchases its own supply of raw ingredients. The vitamins and minerals are purchased centrally. The cereal is bought in a number of different package configurations. The supply chain network, as described, involves one echelon of supply (5 times 9 raw ingredient suppliers plus 10 vitamins and minerals suppliers), one echelon of manufacturing (five cereal processing plants), and three echelons of distribution (eight regional distribution centers, 42 local warehouses, and 30,000 retail stores and restaurants), see Figure 6-4.

The supply chain network involves different trading partners for retail, local warehousing, processing and regional distribution, and the raw ingredients including vitamins and minerals. Prior to the practice of using a common definition for equivalent throughput, each of the trading partners had their own favorite key performance indicators. When the network was first formed, these KPI's did not align with meeting customer demand. Once the trading partner's management were educated about the new performance measure and the details were negotiated by the processing plant, the network orchestrator, communication and training of the employees at each trading partner was completed. Table 6-5 shows the attributes for equivalent throughput that were mutually agreed upon for this network.

TABLE 6-5
Specific Performance Measurement Attributes for Equivalent Throughput

Attribute	Explanation
Purpose	Measures end-to-end throughput from the purchase of raw ingredients to delivery of packaged cereal to consumers. Ensures that every echelon of the network stays in alignment with customer demand.
Definition	See the previous equivalent throughput discussion.
Defined inputs	See the previous equivalent throughput discussion.
Timing	Each supply chain echelon inputs data daily at 4:00 p.m..
Aggregation level	The products and packaging for all the SKU's included in this measure are related to a single cereal brand.
Calculation	See the previous equivalent throughput discussion.
Scalability	(Nominal) trading partners added to or deleted from an echelon will be aggregated or disaggregated from the equivalent throughput calculation for that echelon.
Cause and effect	Increasing equivalent throughput is directly related to increasing revenue.
Defined outputs	See the previous equivalent throughput discussion.
Review period	Once a day at the 8 a.m. production planning meeting.
Management dashboard	Equivalent throughput gauges representing each echelon in the network.
Actual value	Product counted or weighed going into the outbound pipeline adjusted for returns and out-of-network shipments.
Target value	1. Targets derived from the sales and operation plan. 2. BOM equivalency calculated by echelon from the actual daily point of sales demand offset for cycle time and transit time.
Exception limits	+/–2%
Gold standard	Best-in-class throughput achieved by a comparable operation in the industry.
Single owner	The processing plant supply chain director owns the equivalent throughput performance measure.
Accountability	Each trading partner is accountable to the processing plant supply chain director for local data accuracy and for taking the necessary steps in daily operations to regain alignment with customer demand within two business days.
Network trust	The trading partners agree to run the business from equivalent throughput information.

Negotiate—COMMUNICATE—EDUCATE

Once you have a vision of where the business is headed and have defined a set of performance measures to drive new behavior, it is time to implement change by negotiating, communicating, and educating. This section explores some of the concerns that other trading partners will express when challenging equivalent throughput as a performance measure. Later sections address how to communicate the use of the new performance measure throughout the organization, how to educate others in its use, and finally, some project management pointers on the implementation of the new performance measure. Remember that the right set of performance measures is a critical success factor to achieve and sustain behavioral change.

There are three groups of relationships that can either encourage or discourage a change. The first group represents the horizontal relationships among the most senior people at each trading partner in the network. This group gets first consideration. At the end of the day, this group must be signed on to support an implementation. The second group represents the vertical, functional relationships of the teams within each of the trading partners. These are the people who run the operations and either conform to the intended change or resist its implementation. The third group represents the nominal trading partners and all other employees who are tangential to network operations. These are people who would like to know and understand what is going on, but who do not really have a stake in making the change successful. One common scenario begins with the network orchestrator educating and negotiating with the first group followed by the first group communicating with and educating groups two and three. The scenario ends with the change institutionalized across all network organizations.

The negotiation begins with a reminder of the compelling reason for change. Old performance measures are driving old behaviors. New behavior is essential to regain a competitive edge. New performance measures are essential to motivate new behaviors. Perhaps the old performance measures reward meeting a monthly production target regardless of whether the finished goods are shipped or accumulated in inventory. The old measure is a vertical, functional measure that does not align well with the network business strategy. The new measure is a horizontal, global performance measure. It aligns perfectly with the network strategy. The definition of equivalent throughput encapsulates product flowing end-to-end to meet customer demand. The negotiation then moves into education and buy-in of the features, advantages, and benefits of adopting the new performance measure. Table 6-6 summarizes four features of the new measure with their advantages and benefits to the other trading partners.

TABLE 6-6
Features, Advantages, and Benefits of Using Equivalent Throughput

Feature	Advantage	Benefit
Global performance measure	Measures horizontally across the process.	Aligns operations with the business strategy.
Applicable at every echelon	Easy to translate customer delivery quantity and timing to a specific echelon.	Easy to visualize each echelon in terms of the end-customer.
Scalable	Easy to add/subtract echelons; easy to add/subtract (nominal) trading partners.	The performance measure remains valid with the inevitable changes to a network.
Daily reporting	**Real-time operational reporting rather than delayed financial reporting.**	**Provides operations management with a tool to identify problems quickly and act.**

TABLE 6-7
Countering Objections to the Equivalent Throughput Performance Measure

Objection	Counter Argument
"Now is not a good time to change; maybe later."	Remind the other trading partners of the compelling reasons for this behavioral change.
"Never heard of this metric. Who else is using it? What are their results?"	Think of equivalent throughput as a measure of product line revenue expressed in a special kind of unit that is applicable to everyone in the network.
"The quantity conversions and time offsets are too complex. We need simple measures."	Leave the details to the operations people. Let the computer do the conversion arithmetic and offsets.
"The dimensions of the measure call for units, but we measure by weight or by volume."	Continue to measure children by weight or by volume. The parent is expressed in units using conversion factors from the BOM.
"We don't collect data in this format. It would be too expensive to change right now."	Yes, part of the investment is in data formatting. The other part is education and training.
"What happens to the measure if operations change from build-to-stock to build-to-order?"	A simple adjustment to the timing offsets for the echelons impacted will accommodate this.
"The organization already has too many measures. Why do we need another one?"	The current measures are vertical, functional measures that do not align across the network.
"Who is going to pay for the implementation?"	This is a political issue. State the cost in terms of the one-time incremental throughput that will cover it.
"What is the return for making this investment? How long will it take?"	Calculate how long it will take to produce enough incremental throughput to cover the investment.
"The level of detail reveals confidential information."	Sign a non-disclosure agreement or aggregate the data in a way that masks the information.
"This company is a player in many supply chains. Each network wants a different set of measures."	This is a difficult and real issue. One solution is to negotiate the use of equivalent throughput as a performance measure in the other networks.

At first, the management of the other trading partners will object to the use of the equivalent throughput performance measure. These senior people will cite a variety of issues and tell stories of their own experiences to explain why this may not be a good idea. Listen carefully during the negotiation, and use the counter arguments from Table 6-7 to move toward a win–win conclusion.

It is common for a negotiation to deteriorate into a conflict. One party feels they must win at the expense of the other party losing. The outcome is always a win–win solution in a successful negotiation. Getting there is hard work, and it takes a different set of skills and techniques than the ones used to bully an opponent into your point of view. Eli Goldratt, famous for his book *The Goal* and the founder of the Theory Of Constraints (TOC), teaches a thinking process that can lead to a win–win solution. Goldratt teaches the need for a logical cause-and-effect approach to negotiation because compromise leads to a win–lose outcome.

TABLE 6-8
A Structured Approach to Resolving Conflict

Party 'A' in the conflict: The distribution center		**Party 'B' in the conflict:** The processing center	
	Their common objective: To operate a competitive supply chain.		
Party 'A' assumptions: 1. Competing on price and delivery.		**Party 'B' assumptions:** 1. Competing on price. 2. Has to get its house in order first.	
	Party 'A' requirement A network focus on throughput.	**Party 'B' requirement** An organizational focus on cost reduction.	
More Party 'A' assumptions: 1. Believes small wins for the network are more powerful than big wins for the distribution center.		**More Party 'B' assumptions:** 1. Material cost out of control because of yield issues. 2. Senior management bonus tied to yield improvement. **Injection:** Higher throughput relates to better yields.	
	Party 'A' prerequisite Optimize using global performance measures like equivalent throughput.	**Party 'B' prerequisite** Optimize using local performance measures like process yield.	
	The conflict Opposite perspectives for defining measures.		

The "evaporating cloud" is a part of Eli Goldratt's thinking process.[3] The evaporating cloud is a structured way to dissect the root cause of a seemingly intractable issue, to place its underlying assumptions into a new context, and to make the issue go away, or evaporate. It is best explained through an example, see Table 6-8. It takes two parties to have a conflict. Yet these two parties often share a common objective. In order to meet the objective, Party A feels it needs certain requirements and prerequisites. In order to meet the same objective, Party B feels it needs different requirements and different prerequisites. However, the prerequisite of Party A is in direct conflict with the prerequisite of Party B. Neither side is willing to give an inch. Must there be a winner and a loser? The next and hardest step is to expose underlying assumptions for each party. Once the underlying assumptions surface, it becomes possible to suggest an injection that will radically change the context of at least one assumption to make the cloud evaporate. If the two parties can then agree to implement the injection, it is possible for them to achieve a win–win solution.

- *Participants*—The two parties in conflict.
- *The objective*—Both parties agree to a common goal.
- *Requirements*—In order to have the objective you must have this requirement.

- *Prerequisites*—In order to have the requirement you must have this prerequisite.
- *The conflict*—The two prerequisites are stated in a way that opposes the other.
- *Underlying assumptions*—Each party reveals their deepest underlying assumptions.
- *The injection*—Radically change the context of an assumption to make the cloud evaporate.

In Table 6-8, the conflict is between a distribution center and a processing center. Both parties are in agreement over the objective of operating a competitive supply chain. Party A, the distribution center and network orchestrator, says, "In order to have a competitive supply chain there must be a network focus on throughput." Party A also says, "In order to have a network focus on throughput we must optimize using a global performance measure like equivalent throughput." Party B, the processing center, says, "In order to have a competitive supply chain we must have an organizational focus on cost reduction." Party B also says, "In order to have an organizational focus on cost reduction we must optimize using local performance measures like process yield." Clearly, global or horizontal performance measurement definitions are in direct conflict with local or vertical performance measurement definitions. There seems to be an impasse in the negotiation.

Now comes the hard part. In order to evaporate the cloud, both parties must be willing to reveal their most deeply held underlying assumptions. This takes some trust in the relationship. It does not matter where an assumption is broken; it only matters that one of the underlying assumptions can be broken. The distribution center assumes that it is competing on both price and delivery and that small wins in network optimization are more powerful than big wins at the distribution center. The processing center assumes that it is competing on price and that it must get its own house in order before it can contribute to network optimization. A breakthrough comes when the two parties realize that network throughput and local cost are not completely independent. The processing center has had an historical issue with material cost driven by inconsistent process yield. Its senior management has part of its bonus currently tied to a cost reduction target. The processing center needs to continue to measure and control process yield. However, it agrees that a higher network throughput means a higher, more consistent process yield and therefore a lower material cost. The processing center agrees that moving from a local cost view to a global throughput view is compatible with higher yields. They agree to pilot the equivalent throughput performance measure. The injection leading to this win–win solution relates throughput with process yield.

The following trading partner conflicts come up frequently in negotiations. The issues involved in these conflicts often appear to be intractable. Goldratt's evaporating cloud technique of surfacing deeply held underlying assumptions to inject a win–win solution is an appropriate way to resolve such conflict.

1. The conflict over which trading partner is the network orchestrator.
   - A assumes it is the network orchestrator because it defined the network relationships.

- B assumes it is the network orchestrator because it has access to markets, or technology, or financing.

2. The conflict over the definition of a global performance measure.
   - A assumes its definition for a performance measure best serves its business.
   - B assumes its definition for a performance measure is an industry standard.
3. The conflict over who pays for information technology infrastructure in a network.
   - A assumes the other trading partners will contribute funding to buy the system.
   - B assumes the investment is A's decision and therefore A's expense.
4. The conflict over splitting the gain, or the loss, from the investment in a network project.
   - A assumes receiving all of the gain for taking all of the risk.
   - B assumes receiving a large gain for taking a large risk.
5. The conflict over the protection of intellectual property.
   - A assumes collaboration will expose trade secrets.
   - B assumes collaboration does not involve trade secrets.
6. Conflicting operating rules when a trading partner plays simultaneously in different networks.
   - A assumes the rules must be the same for all networks.
   - B assumes the rules can be different for each network.

NEGOTIATE—*Communicate*—EDUCATE

Once the trading partners are signed up for a collaborative project, it is important to communicate about the project with all the employees at each trading partner's location. But why is it so difficult to spread the message you want to spread and so easy to spread a message you do not want spread? Maybe this is because, on the one hand, many network messages go out unplanned, whereas on the other hand, there is always someone around the network who wants to put their own spin on your message. This section looks at three questions that are central to effective trading partner communications.

WHAT IS THE MESSAGE?

It is important to separate the message content from the message context. The *message content* is the answer to the question of what do you want to say. The *message context* is the answer to the questions of media, timing, sequence, and intended audience. A message calling for change should be simple yet compelling. Although it might start by acknowledging people's comfort zone, it should build to a vision of the future. The message content should clearly articulate the purpose of the change, the rewards of success, and the risks of failure. The message should be engaging and genuine.

A message may contain ancillary parts. For example, prior to sending a formal message on organizational change, you may want to document likely questions and answers and make this information available to the managers at each of your trading partner organizations. There may be implementation instructions or handouts of the slides used during the communications meeting. There may be message feedback forms to gather quickly inputs from the intended audience about what they heard and saw.

How Is It Communicated?

Once the content of the message is decided, the context of the communication should be determined. Communication context includes the media used to send the message, the timing or sequencing of the message, and the intended audience(s) for the message. Internet and CD-ROM technologies provide a wealth of media alternatives, see Table 6-9, which can overcome geographical distance and span each time zone without requiring all of the trading partner employees to be in one room at the same time. Because people respond differently to messaging, it is a good idea to project the same clear message through the spoken word and through printed text and graphics. Remember that nonverbal body language may be conveying a very different message than the one intended. The message should be repeated, perhaps seven times, before everyone "gets it." You will want to sample the intended audience to have them feed the message back to you to ensure message congruence. Did they hear and read the same message you sent, or did it develop some unintended spin along the way?

In these times of electronic messaging, it is important to realize that every message has its own life cycle. Any message generated within an electronic format can be time-stamped, encrypted, edited, copied and pasted, forwarded, deleted, and archived. This can work to your advantage for economical message dissemination and to your disadvantage when misinformation is used to prevent a change. When a message is confidential, think about the steps you will have to take to maintain its confidentiality.

When Is It Communicated?

Another aspect of the communication context is the timing and sequencing of the message to its intended audience. Some messages require sequencing. An example sequence might include an e-mail to announce an upcoming meeting, phone calls to key managers to take action, department meetings with impacted employees to preview the change, a web cast from the general manager and CEO to present the change, follow-up small group meetings to answer questions, and periodic follow-ups using newsletters and an electronic bulletin board to collect employee feedback.

Network communications occurs through both formal and informal paths. Be aware that nominal trading partners are often the backbone for informal communications. Network communications build along political lines. Network politics reflect the trust factor in relationships. Organizations that are both for and against change can be efficient transmitters of the message, but their spin can be quite different. Controversial ideas need to be nurtured first among like-minded trading partners

TABLE 6-9
Communication Media Alternatives

Media	Advantage	Disadvantage
Letter	• Formal notification. • Permanent record of communications.	• Uncertainty of delivery timing. • Lack of control over who sees and reads the letter.
Phone	• Point-to-point. • Private and confidential.	• Unable to see body language. • Presently, unable to display graphics. • If the same phone call is repeated, the message will be different.
Voicemail	• Use of distribution lists for broad domestic and international dissemination. • Effective for announcing the main meeting time and place.	• Message becomes very long when relayed through layers of managers and organizations. • Lack of control over who forwards the message and with what spin.
Instant messaging	• Good for scheduling meetings in real-time. • A direct connection to the people involved.	• Disruptive to other activities.
e-Mail	• Use of distribution lists for broad domestic and international dissemination. • Effective for announcing the main meeting time and place.	• People miss the meeting because their in-baskets are full. • Lack of control over who forwards the message and how it might have been edited.
Department meeting	• Everyone hears the same message. • Visible body language. • Recommended way to communicate change to the people immediately effected before going to a mass meeting. • Good for question and answer.	• Can become confrontational. • Have to repeat the message at another time to people who are out of the office.
Face-to-face assembly	• Everyone sees and hears the same message. • Can put senior people in front of an audience. • Visible body language. • Opportunity for limited question and answer.	• Requires good audiovisual equipment for everyone in a large audience to hear and see. • Tends to be one-way communication. • Need to sign for the hearing impaired.
Web-cast	• Everyone sees and hears the same message with graphics. • Can put a senior person in front of an audience. • Broad dissemination. • Opportunity for limited question and answer. • Record and replay for secondary audiences.	• Unable to see body language. • Receiving sites require technology hookups. • International audiences must deal with time zone change. • Misinterpretation due to issues of language. • Largely voice over graphics.

(*Continued*)

TABLE 6-9 (Contiuned)

Media	Advantage	Disadvantage
CD-ROM	• Everyone sees and hears the same message with graphics. • Can put an expert in front of an audience. • Broad dissemination. • Can be interactive. • Read-only CD's give excellent control against tampering with the intended message.	• One-way communication. • Uncertainty of delivery timing. • Misinterpretation due to language. • Lack of control over who views the CD.
Poster	• Good for reinforcement of a message sent by other media.	• Easily outdated.
Newsletter	• Good for periodic reinforcement of a message. • Good for explaining and interpreting the message. • Good for testimonials and evidence of group buy-in.	• One-way communication. • Uncertainty of delivery timing. • Lack of control over who views the newsletter. • Communicates mostly old news.
Electronic bulletin board	• Good for raising awareness. • Good for announcing meetings. • Good for reporting on meetings.	• Engages a limited percentage of the intended audience. • Difficult to control the message.

before being negotiated with opposite-minded trading partners. Coalitions can be built when there is trust and a shared vision.

Scenario planning is a useful technique to decide the context of an import message for change. Scenario planning takes into account the political alignment of the trading partners and the nature of their internal organizations in determining an optimal sequence for rolling out a message of change. Who needs to know? Where are they located in geography and time? Of the people who need to know, who is likely to support and who is likely to resist the change? Who is needed to convince those who will resist taking a risk? What is the organizational level of the people who need to know? How many layers of managers must be contacted to reach this level? What is the optimal timing sequence to communicate the change? After having worked through the answers to each of these questions, the sequence of communication in Scenario A might be this, this, and this. The sequence of communication in Scenario B might be this, this, and that. What if a key person is on vacation? What if a nominal trading partner leaks the message prematurely? The communications plan should be robust enough to deal with such likely scenarios.

An Example Communications Plan

A supply chain architect is meeting with all the trading partners to lay out a communication plan for the new equivalent throughput performance measure. They are meeting on the second level of the Chicago O'Hare Hilton in Board Room 2025.

The meeting includes Matt representing the retail grocers, Ben representing the local warehouses, Jill representing regional distribution, Oscar representing the five processing plants, Frank one of the rice growers, and Amir representing the vitamin suppliers. Megan, Oscar's communication specialist, has been asked to join the meeting for her technical expertise.

"The e-mail announcing next Wednesday's meeting will go out tomorrow," Megan began. "This will signal the kickoff of our two month equivalent throughput performance measure project."

"We need to think of a jazzy project name for this," said Jill.

"Oh, here we go. Form before substance," quipped Frank.

"Look, Frank, it would be better if we worked together as a team on this," said Jill. "Equivalent throughput is more for your benefit as a supplier because your rice is just one ingredient in the BOM. My distribution centers handle all the products."

The supply chain architect weighed in. "We all agreed to respect each other's perspective, and we know Frank and Jill are just kidding. But, a teaching moment has come upon us. Equivalent throughput also benefits distribution because of the way we package our product. We have different SKU's for exactly the same cereal packaged many different ways. Equivalent throughput aggregates all those SKU's into a single measure for Jill's benefit."

"Maybe we could get back to the communications plan?" asked Matt. "How are we going to time the message to reach my 30,000 retail grocers spread across three time zones?"

"That would have been impossible before the Internet," replied Megan. "The grocers will see the least amount of change because the new performance measure keys off of their Point Of Sale uploads. These stores are already very comfortable uploading daily POS data. The main purpose of communicating with the grocers is to include everyone in this major change taking place across the rest of the network. Now to answer your question, Matt, we will deliver the same Web-cast twice: once at 7 a.m. eastern time on Wednesday before the East Coast stores open, and again at 7 a.m. pacific time before the West Coast stores open."

"Why only twice? My Midwest stores will have opened before the Web-cast begins."

"That's a good point. We can hold the Web-cast three times if that will help. We were reacting to the fact that 80% of the grocers are on the East and West Coasts, where the population centers tend to be clustered," continued Megan.

"What about a store that forgets to tune in?" asked Jill.

"The Web-cast will be recorded and stored on a Web site for future viewing. We can also burn a few CD-ROMs of the Web-cast that the management team can take on the road with them," replied Megan.

"Megan, please explain the rollout sequence we have planned for the distribution centers, processing plants, and the growers," said Oscar.

"Sure, I'd be happy to explain the plan. This audience is smaller, but it needs a deeper level of communications. We have decided to take a tiered approach, at least across the processing centers, distributors, and local warehouses. The first tier will be a 30-minute Web-cast on the objective, the return and the risks made to all the trading partner senior managers at the same time. The second tier will be scheduled two-hour classes for about 300 key people directly involved in day-to-day operations at each of the trading partner locations. The third tier will be a 10-minute video shown to all employees and immediately followed by departmental question and answer sessions. Finally, the next three monthly issues of our network newsletter will contain feature articles on project progress."

"Isn't a video an expensive way to communicate?" asked Ben.

"We have budgeted a $1,000 per minute. The full ten minutes will cost about $10,000. However, every audience sees and hears exactly the same message. The professional quality of a video and the sense of urgency it can deliver to an audience tell our employees that this is a really important project. We can also share this with some of our nominal trading partners," replied Megan.

"Thank you, Megan. It sounds like you have put a lot of good thought into our communications plan. Now we'd like to dry-run some of the more critical slides that we'll show during the Web-cast. Let's flip through these right now, and you can give us your feedback," finished the supply chain architect.

Feedback and Damage Control

Effective communication is never one way. You need to know whether anyone was listening. You need to know whether they heard your message accurately. Because many of the media alternatives used to send your message involve one-way communication technologies, you need a way the close the loop with some feedback. The best feedback paths are short, real-time, and continuous. Sometimes there is noise in a feedback path, and the message you get back is highly garbled. You have to define the path, provide a non-threatening environment, and demonstrate that bad news and negative feedback are welcome and will be received without reprisal.

However, it is sometimes quite appropriate to practice damage control. Again, you will not know that you need damage control unless you have implemented appropriate feedback mechanisms. Damage control is necessary when a competitor or those resisting change have turned your message around and are attacking you with your own message. A politicized project management debate is a good example. Damage control is also necessary when the stakes are high and the timing of an inaccurate message is perilously close to tripping some irreversible action—for example, the loss of a major customer contract or the default on a critical loan. In the damage control message it is a good idea to acknowledge the events that have led to your predicament, to take responsibility for your actions (whether or not it is your fault), and to restate the positive, correct message. Repetition of the new message is essential if you are to have any hope of being heard.

NEGOTIATE—COMMUNICATE—*Educate*

Negotiation, communication, and education occur simultaneously. People must be educated to work together effectively as a team in any competitive situation. Peter Senge, in his 1990 book *The Fifth Discipline,* makes the point that business people rarely allow themselves time to practice learning. Professional sports teams, the performing arts, and military organizations all survive through continuous learning and practice, but such discipline is unfamiliar in most business relationships. Senge develops the case for building a "learning organization" that survives by being able to adapt through learning how to change behavior.

A competency in learning may be the most sustainable competitive advantage that a supply chain network can have. The following four elements are essential to transform a supply chain network into a learning organization. The most effective education plan schedules a mix of each of these elements and rewards individuals and teams who achieve competency in learning. These elements are often ignored because each one has a cost. Education is generally not given its proper investment priority because it is difficult to measure the return on investment.

- *Common vocabulary*—Each employee at every trading partner should be taught a common, industry-standard vocabulary for doing business together in a supply chain network. The APICS *Dictionary* and other industry-specific standards should be the source of this vocabulary rather than the non-standard language of some software vendors. Everyone should be encouraged in the proper use of vocabulary to reinforce the learning.
- *Principles-based education*—Each employee at every trading partner should be provided some education in supply chain management based on the five APICS SCM Principles that are the foundation of this book. The number of hours of education per employee can be tailored according to their position and job function within the network. An annual refresher and regular new employee education should be scheduled.
- *Application-specific training*—Each employee at every trading partner should be trained on the particulars of the information systems application software used in getting their job done. This training typically originates with the respective software vendor(s). It is very specific, work-task oriented, and often functionally focused. Some employees learn better being shown or tutored by another person, whereas other employees can be self-taught. If the training is self paced either on-line or with a CD-ROM, then the employee learning should be tested. Retraining should be scheduled when current employees change jobs and when new employees are hired.
- *Simulation games and practice*—The management and operations teams from every trading partner should practice together using team simulators. The teams should be intercompany teams. The purpose of the simulation is to learn the supply chain network response in different business scenarios without putting real customers or real investments at risk. These practices should be scheduled periodically. A business cannot afford the

loss of a customer because it is trying to learn how to operate a new information system feature at the customer's expense.

Sharing the responsibility for education is a great way to begin or to strengthen collaborative relationships among trading partners. You should invite strategic nominal trading partners to participate as well. When employees from multiple companies come together for learning, this has a normalization effect on the proper use of vocabulary. People share stories and are respectfully challenged to consider different points of view. It is refreshing to learn that other people from other companies often have the same problems as you. In the process of learning and practicing together, lasting personal relationships are formed between people who do business together. Personal relationships forged in the classroom engender much greater trust around business decisions. You will find yourself saying, "I met Bill when he taught the Principles of Supply Chain Management class. He knows what he's doing, and you can trust him."

Consider how this four-step education plan applies to the rollout of the equivalent throughput performance measure. All of the (nominal) trading partners must agree to use the standard definition for equivalent throughput. Principles-based education provides a means for people to learn the "what" and the "why" of equivalent throughput as a performance measure. Application-specific training teaches people the "how" and the "when" of applying equivalent throughput to their portion of the network. The operations teams from each of the trading partners should practice using equivalent throughput as one of several dashboard performance measures in a simulated operation of the supply chain. They should learn how to work with any nuances in this performance measure before going live with real customers. Refresher learning should be scheduled periodically and whenever key employees change roles.

PROJECT MANAGEMENT FOR PERFORMANCE MEASURES

A strong resistance to change can derail the implementation of any new measure. After all, these measures are being put into place to drive an intended behavioral change. What better way to stop the change than to kill the performance measures before they have had a chance to take root? It is for this reason that new global performance measures should be defined, collaborated, and implemented within the context of a project plan led by a strong project manager. This kind of a project may not be viewed as a particularly exciting project. However, without strong project management, it is easy for even a well-intended organization to slip its priorities only to watch this project become another "fad of the month."

SET THE PROJECT SCOPE AND ORGANIZE THE TEAM FOR SUCCESS

Setting project scope correctly is a critical success factor. The failure of many a project has been determined at the time the project scope was defined. "Scope creep" during an implementation consumes resources, bloats expenses, and chews up time. A project to implement a new performance measure is not rocket science! It has been done before. Its challenges are threefold: First is the people-related challenge of working successfully across legally independent trading partner organizations. Second is a measurement-related challenge of properly describing the interaction of the information for the intended result. Third is the technology-related challenge of gaining access to the proper data to generate the information. You will find the following checklist helpful:

- *Put it in writing*—The project scope, investment in time and money, full time plus part time staffing, and expected return should all be in writing.
- *Collaborate with every trading partner sponsor*—The scope of the project should be understood by, negotiated with, and agreed upon by a sponsor from each trading partner.
- *Commit to an investment from every trading partner*—Investments can be in the form of committing an employee to the development team or contributing funding, as each trading partner is able. Every trading partner needs some "skin in the game."
- *Set a single, clear objective*—Specify the list of performance measures and the list of connected trading partners that define the scope of the project. Avoid adding non-related tasks, such as fixing an old measurement problem or cleaning up an existing database.
- *Set an aggressive timeframe*—The project team should feel their schedule is very aggressive but not impossible. A tight schedule results in creative solutions and crisp decisions.
- *Staff with the right skill mix*—If the project is information technology intensive, assign a full time IT person to the team. If the project requires a thorough understanding of logistics, assign a full time logistics person to the team. Staff it for success, whatever skills are required.
- *Separate what is inside of team control from what is outside of team control*—Specify an escalation path for things that are outside the project team's control.
- *Leave open one degree of freedom*—Make sure that among time, cost, and resources, at least one of these is left open in the scoping document. When the project team runs into unanticipated challenges, they will need to be able to exercise that remaining degree of freedom.
- *Document the expected return*—The performance measure is expected to drive behavioral change to reduce inventory 'w' amount, increase revenue 'x' amount, accelerate order-to-cash velocity 'y' amount, or improve return on invested capital 'z' amount. Document a range for 'w,' 'x,' 'y,' and 'z.'
- *Establish periodic review meetings with all the trading partners*—The project team should meet face-to-face at the beginning of the project and in-person or by teleconference once a week. The trading partner sponsors should conduct formal project reviews every one-to-two months.
- *Reward and recognize success*—Celebrate early successes and reward the results appropriately in terms of the team's commitment and the impact to the business. Learn how to reward team members across legal company boundaries.

The Red Dot/Green Dot Project Management and Communication Tool

Although detailed PERT charts, such as those produced using Microsoft Project, are necessary for the effective planning of a complex project, a chart with hundreds of task interactions is not an effective communications tool during a project team meeting. Microsoft Project is a planning tool that can capture exhaustive detail about project implementation. A green dot/red dot chart can be done in Microsoft Excel, and it facilitates management by exception. Its information detail should be grounded in Microsoft Project. Table 6-10 is an example of a green dot/red dot chart for a project implementing the equivalent throughput performance measure.

- *Left side of a row*—Names the one person on the project team responsible for the row deliverable.
- *Right side of a row*—Describes the deliverable when all the tasks in that row are complete.
- *The columns*—Documents the Friday dates of each calendar week over the duration of the project.
- *The cells*—Each cell represents one or two key tasks due to be completed that week. For complex projects, the key weekly tasks map back into the detailed PERT chart.
- *Current date*—This bar indicates the current week of the review.

TABLE 6-10
Green Dot/Red Dot Project Management Chart

Person Responsible	Week Ending 8/20	Week Ending 8/27	Week Ending 9/3	Week Ending 9/10	Deliverable
Current Date	******************				
Robert	POS feed	Echelon 2	Echelon 4		Input: multi-echelon data
	Echelon 1	Echelon 3	Echelon 5		
Sanjay	Calculate expected	Format actual 1,2,3	Format actual 4,5		Calculations and tolerance band
Danny		1st gauge	All gauges		Output: 5 gauge dashboard
Joyce	Senior management	Functional staffs	Brief all employees		Employee communication
Helen		1 hr—educate managers	2 hr—train operations		Educate and train team
Thomas				Trial run	Validate Measure
				Fix issues	

Red—task incomplete   Green—task complete

On Monday morning, the previous week's tasks are reviewed by the entire project team by either a face-to-face meeting or by sharing desktop information using a remote teleconferencing technology, such as WebEx or NetMeeting. Each of the previous week tasks must have either a green dot or a red dot. Responsible team members can e-mail their weekly updates to the project manager prior to the weekly meeting, or the project manager can call around to each team member for their update. A green dot indicates that the task is complete. A red dot indicates that the task is incomplete. There is no allowance for some other color or partially completed task. The chart is powerful because peers typically do not want to admit that they are the exception and have let the team down. Teams have been known to work weekends to move a red dot into green dot status between Friday afternoon and Monday morning; other team members off the critical path often jump in to help.

Only the red dot exceptions are discussed; the green dots are not discussed. The discussion should not be accusatory, but rather should focus on the implications that the incomplete task has on the work to be done in the current week. Clearly, a red dot on the critical path is much more serious than a red dot on a slack path of the PERT chart. The Monday morning meeting is used to shift resources to bring the plan back in line or to adjust the plan if the full team is in consensus. Of course, any modification of the plan needs to be reflected in the underlying PERT chart, documented, and approved by management. The green dot/red dot chart is a good graphical representation of team progress, focuses resources in real-time, and accelerates the pace of team meetings. A team meeting that follows this technique should never run more than one hour.

"Good morning team. Hope all of you had a good weekend," said a supply chain architect in the role of project manager. "Let's begin our review of last week, the week ending August 27, on our green dot/red dot chart. We are less than two weeks away from our first trial run of the new equivalent throughput performance measure. Robert and Sanjay, please give us an update."

"Good morning, all," said Robert. "I'm calling today from our local warehouse in Kansas City where we seem to have a problem uploading data. This is the reason for my red dot. Of the 42 local warehouses in the second echelon of the network, 38 are feeding data okay, one is not recognized on the network, and three are sending unstable data. Their data is not repeatable."

"That shows real initiative that you traveled to Kansas City. Who is working with you on the problem?"

"The warehouse manager here has assigned his best person, Larry, to work with me. You may know him. He seems very knowledgeable about how the data should interface."

"That is good to hear. Sounds like you are close to a solution. How long will it take you to resolve all four data feeds?"

"Give us two more days until Wednesday at noon. If we solve the problems any sooner, we will contact Sanjay directly."

"Thanks," said Sanjay. "Actually, the formatting work for Echelon 2 is complete except for the last four local warehouses. Integrating that data will just take a few hours. After all, we expect to have to add or subtract local warehouses over the life of this performance measure. We need to keep the procedure simple and clean."

"That's great! Thank you Robert and Sanjay. Now, looking ahead to this week, the week ending September 3, does anyone have any new risks to completion caused by this small delay?"

"Good morning, this is Danny. We need to have all the echelon data in-place to guarantee the five gauges will be up and running properly. We need as much time as possible this week with the gauges running to work through a reality check of the throughput numbers."

"Hi! This is Thomas. Hey, Danny, don't forget that the first two days of data are a simulated test suite of point-of-sale orders and pipeline counts. This will make your life easier because you will know ahead of time what the tolerance bands and the pointers on the gauges should be."

"Okay, this is great teamwork. Robert, please call me if you run into anything that you didn't expect. All other tasks on the chart are green. Joyce and Helen, we will plan to hear from you next time how communications and education are progressing. Are there any other critical issues before we get back to work? No? Okay then, until next time."

Risk Management: Scenario Planning, Contingencies and Triggers

All investments have some degree of risk. Your plan to invest in new global performance measures, such as equivalent throughput and a total network inventory $-days, is no different. The risk is that your investment in data retrieval, information formatting, performance dashboards, and employee training will not result in higher value returns. Though you may have had a compelling set of business reasons to change, you still have to implement your plan flawlessly to bring home the return. A seasoned project team will think through the set of likely scenarios, plan for contingencies, and set triggers.

A *scenario* is a documented sequence of events related to the plan. The scenario that comes to mind first is that the implementation proceeds exactly as planned, on time and on budget. Two other scenarios might be that the implementation is completed one month early or one quarter late. A fourth scenario might be that, after everyone else has made significant investments, one of the trading partners reneges on their agreement and withdraws from the project. It is a good idea to dream up one really out-of-the-box scenario that pushes the project team to understand its true boundary conditions. For example, what if a key portion of the product has no bill of materials to establish equivalency? Scenario planning helps you to separate out what you and your trading partners control versus what is out of your control. For example, in the pharmaceutical industry if a new Food and Drug Administration regulation suddenly dictates a change in the way you must account for inventory, then that might knock out the particular way you anticipated being able to measure product flow. Some troublesome scenarios that might be considered include:

- *A trading partner divorce*—The underlying operational assumptions are no longer valid because a trading partner relationship is disintegrating.
- *A new competitive threat*—A new competitor or an old competitor with a new technology discovers how to leapfrog your approach and threatens to be many times faster or cheaper.
- *A new regulatory or environmental consideration*—An unexpected government regulation or environmental threat becomes a barrier to a current, preferred process.

A *contingency* is a detailed secondary plan complete with deliverables and assigned responsibilities that can move the project team beyond an impasse. Each scenario should have its own contingency plan. The trick is to keep only a limited number of scenarios alive at any one time and to leverage the core plan into each contingency plan. This means that contingency plan A might look exactly like the 25 steps of the core plan except for steps 7 through 12, and contingency plan B might look like the 25 steps of the core plan except for steps 19, 20, and 22. There is always a tradeoff between how much time you invest in contingency planning and the speed at which you can switch between plans.

Project planning has three degrees of freedom: time, cost, and human resources. A flexible plan is fixed in one degree of freedom and has some flexibility over the other two. For example, if a project has a hard time deadline, then the project team may be authorized to spend more money to outsource some tasks and they may be authorized to bring additional people onto the team. A less flexible plan has two degrees of freedom fixed and only one degree of freedom as a safety valve. For example, if a project has a hard time deadline and a fixed headcount, the project team may be authorized to spend its way out of a problem. A project plan where all three degrees of freedom are fixed is an inflexible plan that will lead to failure.

A *trigger* is used to determine when you should modify your approach and switch to a contingency plan. The purpose of a trigger is to cut your losses. Ideally a trigger is knife edged, either on or off, either yes or no. You need to consider how long the trigger criteria must be true before you take action. Will you take action at the first instance a trigger criterion is met, or will you wait until the trigger criterion is sustained for some period of time? In practice, some triggers have mushy definitions and many a management team agonizes over whether to pull the trigger. For example, you need to invest in inventory to guarantee the delivery date for an anticipated order in a competitive market. Sales has every indication that the customer will place an order for your product soon. As the fixed trigger date comes and goes with no customer order, you wonder if you should act. A trigger can be fixed in time, or it can slide ahead depending its definition. Some common rule based triggers include the following:

- *Days off plan*—Actual delivery performance is ‘x’ days behind or ahead of the schedule.
- *Dollars off plan*—Actual demand is ‘y’ dollars over or under the forecast.

- *Missing critical resource*—A key employee leaves, a scarce material goes into allocation, or an unproven technology fails to meet expectations.
- *Changing priorities*—A critical resource that was promised for the project implementation is withdrawn because of changing business priorities.
- *Out of scope*—Part way through the implementation a task outside the scope of the project is thrust upon the project team. For example, a project team implementing a new performance measure is suddenly tasked to perform data cleansing on a related, legacy database.

Project Tracking with Contingency Triggers

It is easy to combine the tracking of project implementation time and project implementation cost with contingency planning and triggers. Any plan to implement a new set of performance measures and integrate them into a management dashboard should have a *project time schedule* and a *project cost budget*. Once the project plan has been approved, the trading partners will want to know how the actual implementation is progressing against the plan. If the schedule starts to slip or if the project goes into a cost overrun, this should trigger some kind of action by the project manager.

Project planning is normally broken down into different phases in a life cycle approach. For example, the *life cycle* for a performance measurement project might include phase names like 'Investigation and Definition,' 'Design,' 'Implementation,' 'Validation and Release,' 'Operation and Maintenance,' and 'Discontinuance.' The project schedule and the project budget are then broken down by project phase. A major project deliverable marks the end of each phase. For example, the investigation phase ends with every trading partner signing off on the project concept and the definition of the global performance measure. The design phase deliverable is a data map for the trading partners. The implementation phase delivers data feeds via the Internet and a working dashboard. The validation phase delivers repeatable, accurate measurements from test suites developed collaboratively by the trading partners. At the end of the validation phase, the new performance measure is brought on-line.

Smaller task deliverables that are due within a phase are captured on the green dot/red dot chart. A project should not be allowed to go more than two to three weeks without at least one deliverable being due. Too many things can go wrong if the length of time between deliverables is excessive. A project should not be allowed to enter its next phase unless a representative from every trading partner has signed-off on the phase completion.

Figure 6-5 shows a one-page summary-tracking chart. The x-axis is used to track project time whereas the y-axis is used to track project cost. Each project phase is delineated on the chart along the light diagonal line with the diamond shaped symbols that represents the project plan. The actual project time and cost is plotted on the chart along the heavy zigzag line with the octagon shaped symbols. The shaded areas prior to each project phase deadline are the trigger zones. When the actual line intersects trigger zone A1 (B1, C1, and so on), this signifies that the project is nearing a phase completion potentially over budget, but ahead of schedule. When the actual line intersects trigger zone A2 (B2, C2, and so on), this signifies that the project is

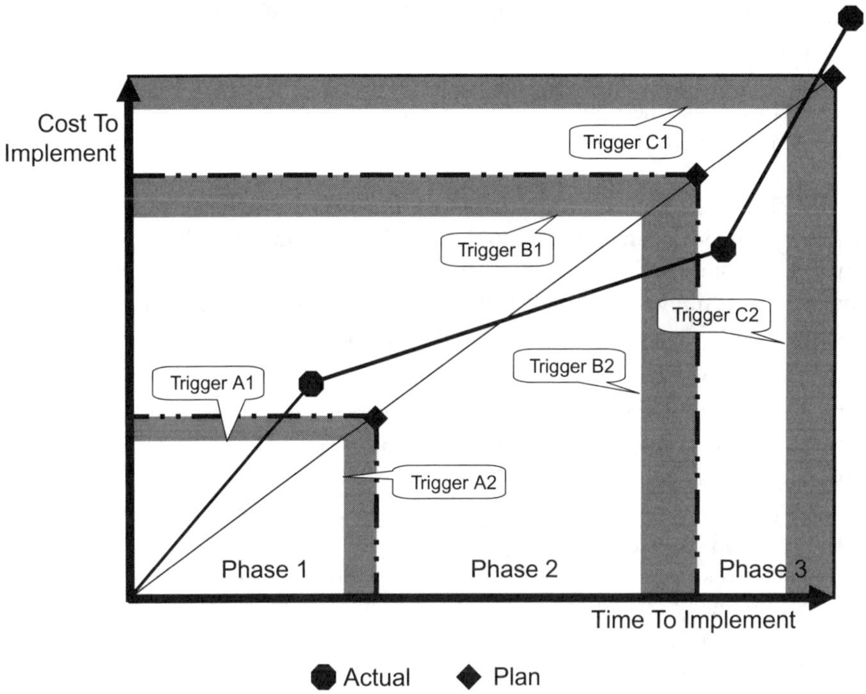

FIGURE 6-5 Tracking actual versus plan with contingency triggers.

nearing a phase completion potentially under budget, but behind schedule. The trigger zones are set as a percentage of the expected cost and expected time, and they provide some early warning that the project is off plan. When the actual project line tracks the planned project line, the team is both on schedule and on budget.

Each pair of phase triggers, A1 and A2, B1and B2, C1 and C2, describe a pair of contingencies that will be used to get the project back on-track. These contingencies should be expressed in terms of degrees of freedom. For example, if the project is running late, more cost might be traded for a shorter time or some remaining tasks might be outsourced to another resource. If the project is running over budget, a resource might be taken off the project to reduce the rate of spending understanding that time to completion will be extended. If the actual project is exceeding both its schedule and its budget, then the trigger might call for re-scoping the project to something less ambitious.

IN SUMMARY

This Chapter has explored a number of soft skills practices to drive permanent change across the trading partners within a supply chain network. A thorough definition of the global performance measure, equivalent throughput, was presented in detail. This chapter has raised and answered the following fundamental questions:

- How to implement change through effective negotiation, communication, and education?
- How to organize and manage a global performance measurement project?
- How to use the right performance measures to change people's behavior in a network context?

In Chapter 7, the vocalize principle and the visualize principle are used to optimize network operations and to defeat the bullwhip effect. The placement of network inventory and the management of trading partner capacity contribute to the competitive flexibility and responsiveness of the entire supply chain. The value circle is completed to measure the relative competitiveness of the network operation.

"You're good at this stuff. Maybe you can help me with a work problem," his wife said as they sat down to eat.

"What's the problem?" asked the supply chain architect, pouring some Ravenswood Merlot.

"After taking your advice to heart, we have been trying to take some steps to become more competitive. But my instructors seem to be showing a lot of resistance to change."

"Tell me about it. By the way this, parmigiana dish is delicious!"

"My instructors don't come right out and tell me they will not change, but they continue to do business the old way. For example, we all agreed to copy our presentations to our main business computer. That way there is a backup for our slides. If any instructor is out sick, one of the others can download a copy of their master file and act as a substitute. Well, the other day we ran an inventory of the presentations on the main computer. Only 65% of our current classroom slides had been uploaded."

"Um—"

"Are you listening?" she asked.

"Yes, only 65% of the class material had been uploaded. That is rather odd, especially when you had a verbal agreement. How do you measure your instructors?" her husband asked.

"They get measured based on the course evaluation forms we get back at the end of each class."

"When you changed the process, did you change your measures?"

"What do you mean?" she asked.

"Uploading class materials to the computer is not a requirement for an instructor to be successful under the old performance measures. But now you expect a change in the behavior of your instructor. If you don't put some different measures in place, you will continue to get the old behavior. There is no penalty not to comply, and it is more comfortable not to change."

"You're right. Never thought about it quite that way," she said. "You deserve a nice big slice of pie for that advice! Would you like it a la mode?"

REFERENCES

1. McCormack, K.P. and Johnson, W.C., *Business Process Orientation: Gaining the E-Business Competitive Advantage*, St. Lucie Press, Boca Raton, FL, 2001, 48–49.
2. McCormack, K.P. and Johnson, W.C. with Walker, W.T., *Supply Chain Networks and Business Process Orientation: Advanced Strategies and Best Practices*, St. Lucie Press, Boca Raton, FL, 2003, 49.
3. Noreen, E., Smith, D., and Mackey, J.T., *The Theory Of Constraints and Its Implications For Management Accounting*, North River Press, Great Barrington, MA, 1995, 165.

7 Operating a Competitive Network

Thursday, July 18

By all outward appearances the kitchen renovation was nearly complete. The old, dysfunctional cabinetry had been demolished and the room had been gutted down to the wall studs. The new kitchen design created a workspace and an eating space separated by an island countertop near the center of the room. The plumbing, air conditioning, and electrical infrastructure lay invisible behind new sheetrock. Spacious new cabinets lined the walls of the workspace, and the eating space had a view through a bay window of rose gardens in the back yard. The microwave, hung beneath one of the cabinets, had a built-in AM/FM radio console. A hooded range, stainless steel sink, and KitchenAid dishwasher graced the center island. A side-by-side refrigerator and freezer combination stood next to the Chambers double oven along the back wall. The design was done except for some painting and wallpaper to edge the ceiling.

The supply chain architect stood admiring the design while holding a cup of instant coffee with boiling water just poured from the Instant Hot tap.

"This is really great!"

"We're not done yet," said his wife, joining him for coffee. "The design may be complete, but now the operating kinks have to be worked out."

"What are you talking about—operating kinks?"

"We will have to establish all new routines for putting groceries away, preparing food, and serving up meals. The operation of my new kitchen is fundamentally different than the operation of my old kitchen."

"Oh."

Tom, the house architect, having been outside inspecting the flashing around the bay window, let himself in through the back door, "It's a bright, beautiful day outside."

"My wife was just explaining how we're not done until the operational flow is worked out."

"She is correct. This kitchen will run differently, depending upon whether one of you is having orange juice and toast for breakfast, the kids are joining you for sandwiches at lunch, or you decide to throw a dinner party for 20. The large countertop space and expanded kitchen seating will come in handy for that dinner party."

"That's interesting. In my line of work, I would have expressed what you just said in this way: First, we manufacture a range of products that have very different bills of materials. Some BOMs are flat, with just a couple of layers and a short material list, whereas other BOMs are deep, with many layers and a very long material list. The menu for breakfast involves different food groups than the menu for lunch, and the menu for lunch involves a shorter recipe than the menu for dinner. Second, the demand for our products is highly uncertain. Some days we might ship only 5 boxes, whereas other days we might ship 105 boxes. This is just what you said about breakfast for one or dinner for 20. The quantity of food to be prepared for any given meal is highly uncertain."

"That's one way of looking at it, I suppose," said Tom. "Actually, you got me thinking about how different the menu and the food preparation is in the kitchen of a private home like yours versus a professional kitchen for fast food. Your wife wants to cook everything from apples to ziti, but in a fast food establishment the menu is fixed and the kitchen flow is built around the menu."

"Oh. Now you're talking about the difference between a job shop environment and a process flow environment."

"I'm certainly going to remember all I have learned about supply chain management from working on this job," Tom said.

"What really interests me in this analogy is where the constraint will be in our new kitchen," the supply chain architect continued.

His wife had an answer. "It depends," she said. "For one person at breakfast or even four people at lunch, there is no constraint. When we start to have company and throw a large dinner party, it will depend on the size of my cooking pots, or the constraint may move out of the kitchen altogether and become the number of chairs we have to comfortably seat our guests in the rest of the house. The constraint moves depending on the menu and the number of guests."

"We put all that money into the double oven, and now you say it comes down to the size of your pots and pans?" he asked incredulously.

"Again, it all depends. The double oven is an excellent investment; it really expands what I can bake and broil. For example, I can do a pot roast in the top oven at the same time that I'm baking a cake in the bottom oven. Besides you told me all about investing hundreds of thousands of dollars in a piece of machinery that isn't even your manufacturing constraint."

"Yes, but we're not talking about flexible machining centers right now."

"Okay. Now about the pots and pans—When I cook spaghetti for the two of us, I use one burner on the range and one pot to boil the water. When I cook spaghetti for twenty people, I still use only one burner, but the pot of boiling water must be much larger. Otherwise we end up eating in shifts."

"I understand. The room infrastructure design is complete. Now, the throughput we can achieve in terms of the number of guests happy with their tummies full depends upon optimizing the operations to prepare, cook, and serve a quantity of food. Our kitchen is constrained in different ways depending on both the menu and the number of servings."

Tom interjected, "Not to change the subject, but I must leave for another appointment. We still have some finish work to schedule."

They talked a few minutes longer and set a tentative date for the installation of the tile backsplash along the counter.

*****

The supply chain architect sensed that very little forward progress was being made. They were in the midst of endless meetings at the plant and teleconferences with team members around the world, including the information technology group in Singapore. Each of the performance measurement task groups had recruited members and had held their first meetings. Much of the conversation to this point seemed like a giant debate, except for the fact that they had lost Colonial Distributor as their third largest customer. At least they were starting to see some activity with a few new customers. Something radical needed to happen, and fast.

Larry Holmes, the logistics analyst, approached walking at a quick gait.

"They're calling an all-hands meeting in the cafeteria in 15 minutes. I'll go tell the others."

"Wait! What's the meeting about? I don't remember an all-hands meeting being scheduled."

"Rumor has it we have been sold! You better come to the meeting," Larry rushed off.

The crowd was sullen as employees filed down the stairwell and into the cafeteria. A podium and projector had been hastily erected. People were grabbing chairs from a stack and pushing them along to where they would listen to the presentation.

Dana Hoffman, CFO, took the podium. She was flanked by Roberta Perez, the operations manager, and Alice Way from human resources. Dana began, "Thank you for joining us today and taking time from your busy schedules. We know that many rumors are flying about, and we want to tell you what we know and what we don't know."

"Oh brother, this is going to be real bad news, scripted straight from the Human Resources Handbook," someone whispered to his neighbor.

"When this plant is doing well, corporate pretty much leaves us alone. We all can be very proud that over the years this location has been a major contributor to corporate growth and profitability. It is not a surprise that times have changed. The plant is not doing as well, and frankly the management team is getting a bit more help from corporate than we need."

Dana paused, but the audience was resigned, waiting for the other shoe to drop. "Corporate has helped us to see that there is a lower-cost, more competitive way to manufacture our products. We will be splitting this plant into two operations. Final assembly will remain here, for now. Shortly, preassembly and subassembly will be moved to Singapore. Hector Morales, our VP of manufacturing, will oversee the transition and will relocate immediately to Singapore. Roberta will take over here from Hector. We are going to need each of you to stay focused on meeting customer expectations while we implement the transition. We will do our best to keep as many of you employed as we can. That's all we know right now. Alice is ready to answer a couple of questions; frankly there are many details still to work out."

Employees filed silently out of the cafeteria.

Walking back upstairs, the architect was reeling with feelings of compassion for Hector, anxiety over continued employment, and questions too numerous to recall about how the business could remain competitive for its customers when cost seemed to be the only thing that mattered.

Larry wandered over dazed. "That's it. I'm out of here. They'll cut my job in no time," he grieved.

"Not so fast, Larry. Logistics is even more important with the supply chain stretched between here and Singapore."

Hector began making the rounds, checking in with each of his direct reports and staff. He approached them with a positive attitude.

"How's it going, Hector? Sorry to hear you have been reassigned. We are going to miss you," Larry said. "Don't these MBA types at corporate get it? It's the economy, stupid."

"Actually, this strategy makes a lot of sense," Hector replied. "First, many of our customers have moved to Asia, and they expect our products to have significant Asian content. Second, our product is material intensive. If we can buy raw materials cheaper in Asia and make a smaller number of part shipments here, we will save material and logistics costs. And third, as you know, Singapore is a country with a highly educated, English-speaking workforce, where it will be easier to transfer this work."

The supply chain architect spoke, "That's all well and good, Hector. I respect the fact that you seem to be motivated to make a go of this. But what happens to all the employees on this site who lose their jobs? How do they pay their mortgages, send their children to school, and continue to have medical insurance coverage? Dana did not comment on any of that today. And what happens to our domestic customers who value the way we do business?"

"It is too early to tell what kind of severance package corporate will offer our employees, but what specifically do you mean with your second question?"

"Most of our product is build-to-order. Customers tell us what they need, and we manufacture it quickly for them. We can generally beat the competition because we are able to vocalize real customer orders to our local parts distributor and our local sheet metal fabricator. We are able to visualize where the capacity constraint resides as our product mix changes. We are able to visualize where all our inventories are located because all the trading partners are tied into the same inventory control system. How will we make that work halfway around the world in Singapore when it has taken weeks just to unravel a simple data migration issue?

"These are all good questions that must be answered over time," said Hector. Then, he walked away.

Operations within the four walls of the single firm were directed through familiar capacity and inventory planning and control methods. However, when multiple echelons of trading partners are networked, coupling their physical inventories and their checkbooks, each of the trading partners must work from a different set of capacity and inventory planning and control principles. The APICS SCM *vocalize* and *visualize* principles are the foundation for a competitive network operation. This Chapter focuses on inventory, capacity, and cash control, whereas Chapter 8 focuses on inventory, capacity, and cash planning. The end-customer benefits from a competitive operation in terms of responsive, reliable delivery. The owners benefits from a competitive operation in terms of larger revenues built on a smaller base of inventory and cash assets.

AN INTRODUCTION TO NETWORK OPERATIONS

The focus of this Chapter returns to the trading partner portion of the network. The trading partner order-to-delivery and order-to-stock subcycles described in Chapter 4 are linked through inventories of physical materials. The trading partner invoice-to-pay and invoice-to-cash subcycles described in Chapter 4 are linked through inventories of cash. Network operations architecture involves determining the optimal structure and placement of the physical and cash inventories throughout the system. It also involves the optimal capacity management of the material flows, the information flows, and the cash flows to operate competitive order-to-delivery-to-cash cycles. This Chapter explores the optimization of network operations from the perspective of integrating the product BOM within the network. Chapter 8 describes the planning aspects of network operations from the perspective of matching the patterns of supply and demand. The right network operations architecture will result in the right income statement versus balance sheet tradeoffs.

THE COMPOSITE BOM

A forward supply chain builds the BOM from bottom to top. Upstream raw materials and component items are combined to form midstream assembly items that become downstream product SKUs. Often the network is expanded downstream to distribute products combined with services to the end-customer. This is the value-adding network typically found, for example, in durable goods and consumer packaged goods supply chains.

A reverse supply chain transverses the BOM from top to bottom. Upstream, product SKUs are disassembled into subassembly items. Midstream, the subassemblies are separated into waste streams according to their dominant raw materials. Downstream, each waste stream is reduced to its base elements. This is the value-subtracting network typically found, for example, in remanufacturing and recycling supply chains.

It is a common practice to deliver a wide variety of products and services through the same network architecture. The wisdom of this practice lies in the range of BOM types in the product mix. A-type BOMs, I-type BOMs, T-type BOMs, and V-type BOMs are explained in Chapters 2 and 3. Although some combinations can be made to work together, the most competitive network will be focused on a single BOM type. Combined A-type and T-type product BOMs can be made to work with a common supply base. T-type and V-type BOMs can be made to work with a common distribution channel. However, an attempt to mix a process flow I-type BOM with

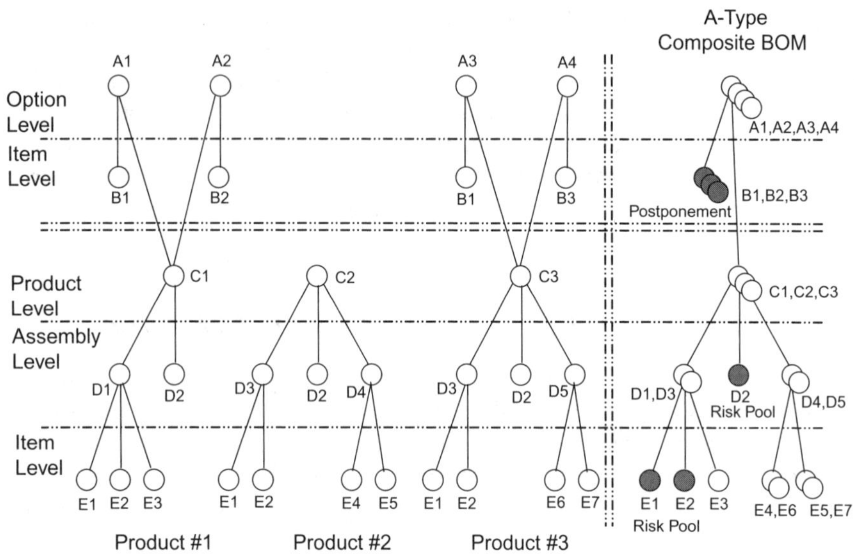

FIGURE 7-1 The composite bill of materials.

a batch flow A-type BOM will reduce overall network competitiveness because the operations become defocused.

A useful supply chain management technique is to merge each of the individual product BOMs into a single composite BOM, see Figure 7-1. The composite BOM can then be identified as a pure A-type, I-type, T-type, or V-type BOM, or as some combination of these types. The composite BOM presents an opportunity to isolate those products that are fundamentally different from everything else delivered through the supply chain network. Forming the composite BOM facilitates identifying opportunities to consolidate items and suppliers across the network and to simplify product distribution. A composite BOM is extracted from the set of individual BOMs using the following simple steps:

- *Step 1*—Align each BOM so that Level 0, Level 1, Level 2, etc. of Product A corresponds to Level 0, Level 1, Level 2, etc. of Product B and corresponds to Level 0, Level 1, Level 2, etc. of Product C, and so on.
- *Step 2*—Pick two products to start.
- *Step 3*—Work from the highest-level parent to the lowest-level child.
- *Step 4*—For each product structure level, combine all the items at that level for both products. List only new, unique items. If an item is already listed once for that level, then skip over it.
- *Step 5*—Continue working down the product structure tree until the last levels of every branch of both products are exhausted.
- *Step 6*—Combine the next product with the earlier combination by repeating steps 3 to 5. Stop the process when every applicable level of every product has been combined into one composite BOM.

Two operationally useful item groupings can be easily identified through a composite BOM. The first is a high level grouping of unique items. Here the products are identical except each product has a small number of unique items at the highest level. This suggests that the lower-level manufacturing operation can be organized in a generic way for every product, whereas the last stage of manufacture can be a postponement operation. Postponement means that a small, inexpensive inventory of each unique item is kept on hand for final assembly, and a particular assembly is not finalized to make an end product until a customer order is in hand. Product completion is postponed until the last possible moment. This avoids having to carry expensive finished goods inventory with the wrong mix.

Second, a low-level grouping of common parts can be used for inventory risk pooling. Suppose there are three products each with independent demands that each use the same lower-level material. Three separate safety stocks of this common material could be kept in support of each of the three independent end products. However, if a common safety stock was properly placed within the network such that each of the end products could pull from this one inventory as required, then the total inventory investment for the common material could be significantly reduced. The safety stock is present in the network to reduce the demand risk of not being able to deliver product. With proper inventory placement the risk for all three products can be shared, or pooled, with a single safety stock. The mathematical reason behind risk pooling is as follows. The demand risk is the standard deviation of the product's demand. When the demand for multiple products is independent, the standard deviation of their demand risks combine as the root mean squared (RMS) value of the individual standard deviations. The RMS standard deviation is significantly less than the sum of the individual standard deviations. The probability is that though some of the products have a higher demand, other products will have a lower demand, resulting in a net pull on safety stock that is statistically smaller. Use a composite BOM to identify opportunities for both postponement and risk pooling.

The Push/Pull Boundary

The discussion of the equivalent throughput performance measure in Chapter 6 alluded to the fact that there are fundamentally different ways to operate a supply chain network. Competitive, practical networks are a combination of push and pull operations.

- *Push*—Inventory and cash flows are pushed through the network, driven by a forecast of demand.
- *Pull*—Inventory and cash flows are pulled through the network, driven by actual customer demand.

When both push and pull operations exist in the same supply chain network, there will be a push/pull boundary somewhere in the network. This push/pull boundary is the set of inventory and cash buffer locations that cut across the entire width of the network, separating it into two distinctly different zones for capacity and inventory planning and control. The push/pull boundary acts as a shock absorber between the steady production planned to a forecast and the flexible production triggered by actual customer orders.

EVALUATING A COMPETITIVE NETWORK OPERATION

Just as Chapter 4 describes a method for evaluating the relative competitiveness of a network design, this Chapter describes a method for evaluating the relative competitiveness of network operations. The method can be used to evaluate the merits of a new or changed operation during the successive refinement of the network. It can also be used to compare the relative competitiveness of your network operation versus a competitor's network operation.

The measures of relative competitiveness are plotted on the value circle. The sides of the value circle are focused on network operations and are discussed in the following sections of this Chapter. The top of the value circle is focused on network design as discussed in Chapter 4. The bottom of the value circle is focused on value as discussed in Chapter 9. The axes alternate between global performance measures and simple measures related to the APICS SCM Principles, see Table 7-1. The definitions of the measures used for each axis related to competitive network operations are described in this Chapter and are summarized in the Network Blueprint Appendix.

TABLE 7-1
Network Operation Evaluation

Axis	Performance Measure	APICS SCM Principle	Definition
Variability		"Leverage Worldwide Logistics"	Reducing variability reduces the need for physical inventory and cash within the network.
Network Inventory	X		Common to both network design and network operation. Inventory is added to a network to compensate for supply and demand uncertainty.
Vocalize		"Synchronize Supply with Demand"	Increasing the ability of the trading partners to vocalize demand reduces the need for physical inventory and cash.
Velocity		"Build a Competitive Infrastructure"	Eliminating velocity traps improves throughput.
Equivalent Throughput	X		Common to both network design and network operation. Increased throughput requires increased order-to-delivery-to-cash velocity.
Visualize		"Measure Performance Globally"	Increasing the ability of the trading partners to visualize network capacity and inventory improves throughput.

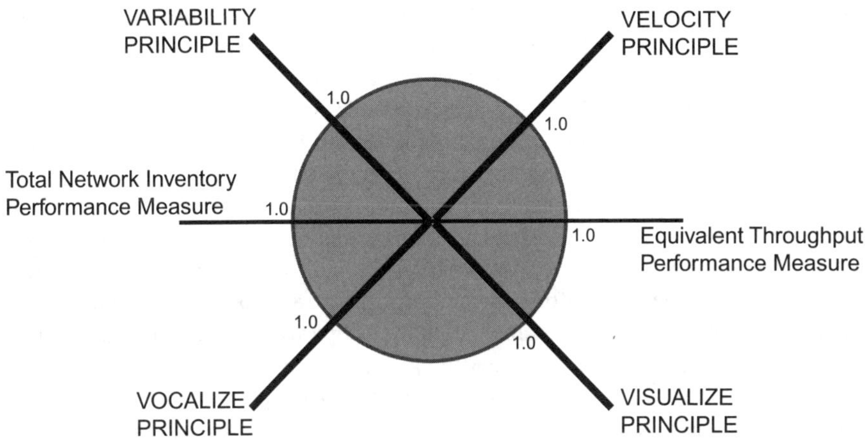

FIGURE 7-2 Measuring network operations on the value circle.

Referring to Figure 7-2, network inventory is positioned between the variability axis and the vocalize axis on the value circle. This is not a random axis assignment. Reducing network variability and improving demand vocalization among the trading partners are drivers to reduce network inventory. Network throughput is positioned between the velocity axis and the visualize axis; again, this is not a random axis assignment. Increasing network velocity and improving capacity and inventory visualization among the trading partners are drivers to increase network throughput.

THE IMPACT OF NETWORK PARTITIONING ON WORKING CAPITAL

Network operations primarily drive the structure of the balance sheet, whereas network design primarily drives the structure of the income statement. Together network operations and network design have a profound impact on the balance sheet, statement of working capital, and the income statement for each trading partner. Each trading partner needs a certain amount of working capital to operate its portion of the supply chain network. Working capital is inventory plus Accounts Receivable (A/R) minus Accounts Payable (A/P). These are balance sheet line items. When working capital is positive, the trading partner's inventory assets plus its A/R from sales exceed its A/P from purchases. When working capital is negative, the trading partner's A/P from purchases exceeds its inventory assets plus its A/R from sales.

Accounts receivable are the cash payments a (nominal) trading partner has not yet collected and is owed by its downstream customers for products and services delivered. Accounts payable are the cash payments a (nominal) trading partner has not yet paid and owes to its upstream suppliers for the raw materials, components, and assemblies it has received. Income statement items for staffing including wages, salary, benefits, and employment taxes can become payables on the balance sheet whenever they are accrued for some period. Inventory is the dollar value of the raw materials, components, and products a trading partner holds that have not yet been transformed or manufactured or fulfilled. A trading partner must manage its operations such that the cash flow from its sales and receivables covers its purchases of inventory, the payables it owes, and its other expenses. Inventory, accounts receivable, and accounts payable are current asset and current liability line items on the balance sheet. They exhibit a high turnover lasting only months, weeks, or days before being replenished.

In addition to inventory, each trading partner needs transformation, manufacturing, or fulfillment capacity to conduct its operations. Capacity assets can take the form of investments and long-term debt on real estate, plant, equipment, and tooling. The income statement item for depreciation expense can become an asset on the balance sheet whenever it is accumulated for some period. Real estate, plant, equipment, and tooling are fixed assets and long-term liability elements of the balance sheet. They exhibit a low turnover sometimes lasting for years before being replenished. Part of the motivation for a trading partner to outsource its operations is to redistribute network capacity and network inventory such that its own income statement, balance sheet, and working capital position looks better to its owners. Whether the supply chain network has become more competitive with this maneuver remains a key question? The answer is that it all depends.

Outsourcing Implications on the Balance Sheet

Chapter 4 looked at the improvement made to the income statement of a vertically integrated firm when its BOM was partitioned and partially manufactured offshore. In the example, the decreased costs for labor, material, and income tax more than offset the increased costs for packaging materials, freight, and duty. This section looks at the same scenario from the perspective of the balance sheet. If the product BOM from the same vertically integrated firm is partitioned to minimize cost, what are the implications both good and bad to the balance sheet and to working capital?

Table 7-2 is the balance sheet of the vertically integrated firm from Chapter 4. This firm sells all the product, purchases all the inventory, and owns all the manufacturing capacity for the product line in question. Current assets include the accounts receivable in support of the total throughput and on-hand inventory in support of the entire BOM. Current liabilities include the accounts payable in support of new inventory purchases. This balance sheet is the basis of comparison for the partitioned approach that follows.

Pre-tax Return On Assets (ROA) is defined as the ratio of operating profit before interest and income tax to total assets × 100%. ROA for the vertically integrated firm in this example is ($510,840/$4,344,900) × 100% or 11.76%. The working capital again is inventory plus A/R minus A/P ($1,267,400 + $487,500 – $243,730) or $1,511,170. ROA can be improved one of two ways: by increasing operating profit, and by decreasing total assets. Chapter 4 showed that when the vertically integrated firm is split in two, such as with a domestic final assembly factory and an international subassembly contractor, operating profit improves and ROA improves. Now if the domestic final assembly factory can also shed some of its inventory and capacity assets associated with the portion of the BOM shifted to the international contract manufacturer, then its total asset base will decrease and its

TABLE 7-2
Balance Sheet for a Vertically Integrated Firm

Assets		Liabilities + Net Worth	
Cash	$210,000	Accrued Expenses	$135,000
Accounts Receivable	$487,500	Accounts Payable	$243,730
Inventory	$1,267,400	Income Tax Payable	$27,000
Current Assets	$1,964,900	Current Liabilities	$405,730
Fixed Assets	$3,400,000	Long Term Debt	$1,000,000
– Accumulated Depreciation	$1,020,000	Total Liabilities	$1,000,000
Asset Book Value	$2,380,000		
		Paid-In Capital	$1,200,000
		Retained Earnings	$1,739,170
		Net Worth	$2,939,170
Total Assets	$4,344,900	Total Liabilities + Net Worth	$4,344,900

ROA will become further improved. The BOM can be manipulated in a variety of ways to accomplish such an asset split:

- *Shop the world*—If the product is material intensive, then it makes sense to shop the world for the best material pricing and pay any incremental freight and duty charges. This is not a balance sheet partitioning strategy, but it can reduce both the inventory asset and the accounts payable liability.
- *Outsource upstream*—If the product is labor intensive, then subassemblies, assemblies, or the entire product can be outsourced to a fabricator or contract manufacturer as a contract, box build, or turnkey operation in a Country Of Origin with a lower labor rate. This can reduce both the inventory asset and the accounts payable liability.
- *Change the tax rate*—If the product is profitable, then the manufacture of some or the entire product can be moved to a Country Of Origin offering income-tax incentives. This can reduce the inventory asset plus the accounts payable and the income tax payable liabilities.
- *Postpone downstream*—If the product is option intensive, then the final stage of postponement can be moved downstream into distribution. The value of the product and its net revenue will decrease a small amount for the manufacturer, whereas accounts receivable, inventory, and accounts payable will each see some reduction.

Tables 7-3 and 7-4 show the balance sheets for a domestic final assembly factory and international subassembly contractor after the example product BOM has been split 20% domestic and 80% international. In general, the expected asset changes would include:

- *Cash*—Either favorable or unfavorable for the trading partner; a net increase of cash in the network.

TABLE 7-3
Balance Sheet for a Domestic Final Assembly Factory

Assets		Liabilities + Net Worth	
Cash	$210,000	Accrued Expenses	$135,000
Accounts Receivable	$487,500	Accounts Payable	$328,460
Inventory	$253,480	Income Tax Payable	$95,220
Current Assets	$950,980	Current Liabilities	$558,680
Fixed Assets	$2,550,000	Long Term Debt	$750,000
– Accumulated Depreciation	$765,000	Total Liabilities	$750,000
Asset Book Value	$1,785,000		
		Paid-In Capital	$1,200,000
		Retained Earnings	$227,300
		Net Worth	$1,427,300
Total Assets	$2,735,980	Total Liabilities + Net Worth	$2,735,980

- *Accounts receivable*—No change when the BOM is outsourced upstream; some reduction when the BOM is postponed downstream.
- *Inventory*—A favorable reduction for the trading partner; a net increase of inventory in the network.
- *Accounts payable*—Although that portion of accounts payable tied to inventory purchases for the factory decreases, a new element of accounts payable tied to the purchase of the contract manufactured goods increases.
- *Income tax payable*—The income tax payable liability is reduced when less income tax is owed.

TABLE 7-4
Balance Sheet for an International Subassembly Contractor

Assets		Liabilities + Net Worth	
Cash	$55,000	Accrued Expenses	$42,600
Accounts Receivable	$197,080	Accounts Payable	$145,000
Inventory	$1,045,000	Income Tax Payable	$3,100
Current Assets	$1,297,080	Current Liabilities	$190,700
Fixed Assets	$850,000	Long Term Debt	$525,000
– Accumulated Depreciation	$396,700	Total Liabilities	$525,000
Asset Book Value	$453,300		
		Paid-In Capital	$300,000
		Retained Earnings	$734,680
		Net Worth	$1,034,680
Total Assets	$1,750,380	Total Liabilities + Net Worth	$1,750,380

- *Fixed assets, depreciation, and associated long-term debt*—When a portion of manufacturing is outsourced, machinery and tooling dedicated to the outsourced product may be sold to the contract manufacturer, sold at auction, or scrapped. Unfortunately, it is often difficult to realize any gain from the sale of an empty plant or its real estate unless there is a willing buyer. A big chunk of underutilized fixed assets, depreciation, and associated long-term debt remain on the balance sheet.
- *Net worth*—Assets and liabilities are rebalanced through the adjustment seen in net worth.

After outsourcing, ROA for the domestic final assembly factory increases to ($1,269,321/$2,735,980) × 100% or 46.39%. Working capital decreases to ($253,480 + $487,500 – $328,460) or $412,520. Total assets for the domestic final assembly factory shrink 37.0%.

The Downside of Outsourcing

Distributing the BOM across several trading partners can improve the balance sheet ratios and reduce the working capital requirements for a single trading partner. What is the downside of outsourcing? If one trading partner wins, is it a win for the network or are there losers? The following factors represent the downside of outsourcing. Unfortunately many of these aspects are subtle, longer-term and not easily quantifiable; they do not pack as much punch in the decision to outsource as do some financial ratios. However, each of these factors is real, and they contribute to the loss of network competitiveness.

- *Reduced network velocity*—Outsourcing adds an echelon to the network, increasing the length of the supply chain. The order-to-delivery cycle time experienced by the customer becomes less responsive. The order-to-delivery-to-cash cycle time experienced by the trading partners becomes slower.
- *Increased network variability*—Although the inventory and working capital position of one trading partner seems to improve, the increased variability of a longer supply chain amplifies a higher level of just-in-case network inventory and just-in-case network cash.
- *Idle assets*—No return is generated on the past investments of plant, machinery, and real estate assets that stand idle after manufacturing is transferred. However, debt service, security, utility expense and real estate taxes associated with these idle assets continue to drag on the profitability of the firm.
- *Hollowing out of core competency*—The unintended transfer of intellectual property to a nominal trading partner and the permanent loss of the learning of highly experienced employees and craftspeople does irreparable damage to the sending firm/country's core competency. Again, this reduces the wealth creation capability of the sending firm/country.
- *Loss of jobs and domestic wealth*—Outsourcing contributes to local unemployment. Unemployment consumes available personal wealth. The transfer

of inventory and machinery assets to a receiving firm/country reduces the wealth-creation capability of the sending firm/country.

- *International currency fluctuation risk*—Assets and investments denominated in other world currencies run the risk of becoming devalued due to world currency fluctuation.
- *Network disruption due to international conflict*—Terrorism, violence, and open hostilities internationally can disrupt network operations for indeterminable periods. New trade barriers and quotas may exist.
- *Reduced network vocalization*—A longer supply chain network increases the risk of schedule nervousness and the reoccurrence of the bullwhip effect. This can result in unnatural oscillatory swings in inventory position and capacity requirements.
- *Reduced network visualization*—A longer supply chain network increases the risk that some of the trading partners are separated from the global performance measures that provide visibility for the correct inventory and capacity to support throughput and maintain the desired customer service level.
- *One-time project management costs*—Retained earnings and dividends are diverted from investments to pay the significant one-time project management costs to outsource manufacturing.
- *One-time asset management costs*—Some assets are sold at a loss or written off the books at their scrap cost. Retained earnings and dividends are diverted from investments to pay the costs of refinancing debt and real estate brokerage fees. This shrinkage in the absolute value of assets diminishes wealth.
- *Forced reverse stream network redesign*—The reverse stream network must react to changes in the sourcing of repair parts and to shifts in the country of origin's manufacturing and repair facilities.

THE VOCALIZE PRINCIPLE

Throughput depends upon knowing the customer's demand, buying the right inventory buffers in advance of the demand, and having unconstrained capacity in the timeframe to meet the demand. Sufficient cash flow must be available to make the necessary inventory and capacity purchases. The trading partners in a competitive network learn how to vocalize the end-customer's demand, how to synchronize supply and demand, and how to vocalize the need for cash.

A Continuum of Network Operating Modes

The lead time until a product becomes ready for shipment is a major component of the order-to-delivery cycle time. In Chapter 4 lead time is in the context of the loop transaction for a given trading partner. What the end-customer sees as lead time availability is the combination of procurement lead time plus transit time plus customs clearance time plus queue time plus manufacturing cycle time plus distribution cycle

TABLE 7-5
Customer Availability Versus Network Operating Mode

Operating Mode		Customer Availability	BOM Type	Manufacturing Control
Continuous Flow	CF	Flowing or empty process and deliver	I-type BOM	Flow
Build-to-Stock	BTS	Deliver from finished goods inventory	A-type BOM	Lot Push
Assemble-to-Order Pick-to-Order	ATO	Build, pick from partial assemblies, and deliver	T-type BOM	Kanban or Repetitive
Build-to-Order Mix-to-Order	BTO	Build, mix from raw materials, and deliver	V-type BOM	Lot Pull
Engineer-to-Order	ETO	Order and wait for material, build entirely, and deliver	Any type	Project Management

time that depends on the network's operating mode. There is an inverse relationship between lead time and capacity. When one goes up, the other goes down. Some industries, such as grocery and consumer packaged goods, are inventory intensive. These industries run their business with a fixed lead time by allowing capacity to vary according to demand. Other industries, such as semiconductors and automotive, are capital intensive. These industries run their business with a fixed capacity by allowing lead time to vary according to demand.

The product structure of the BOM sets practical limits on the product availability seen by the end-customer versus favorable economics for the trading partners, as shown in Table 7-5. Liquefied products are manufactured and distributed in a continuous flow mode until their sourcing container runs dry. For example, the cubic volume of flow is based on processing a railcar's cubic volume of base liquid. Electronic instrumentation with a deep BOM driving hundreds of suppliers are built-to-stock, providing customers off-the-shelf availability. Small truck manufacture is customized with a body style, engine size, transmission type, tire capacity, and cab seating assembled-to-order from a limited set of standard designs. Customers wait a short while for final assembly and delivery of their vehicle. Replacement windows for older homes are built-to-order when the window sash dimensions are not a standard size. Windows are built from a few raw materials including glass, wood, and latching hardware, but the range of possible combinations makes it uneconomical to stock finished windows. The customer must wait a few weeks for the window to be manufactured and delivered. Finally, when a product is engineered-to-order, the customer must wait the procurement lead time to purchase any outstanding raw materials plus the full manufacturing cycle time plus the delivery transit time. ETO is typically managed as a project.

Figure 7-3 represents all the trading partners in an end-to-end network split between push and pull zones. The upstream push zone is driven from a forecast, whereas the downstream pull zone is driven from actual customer demand. When the network

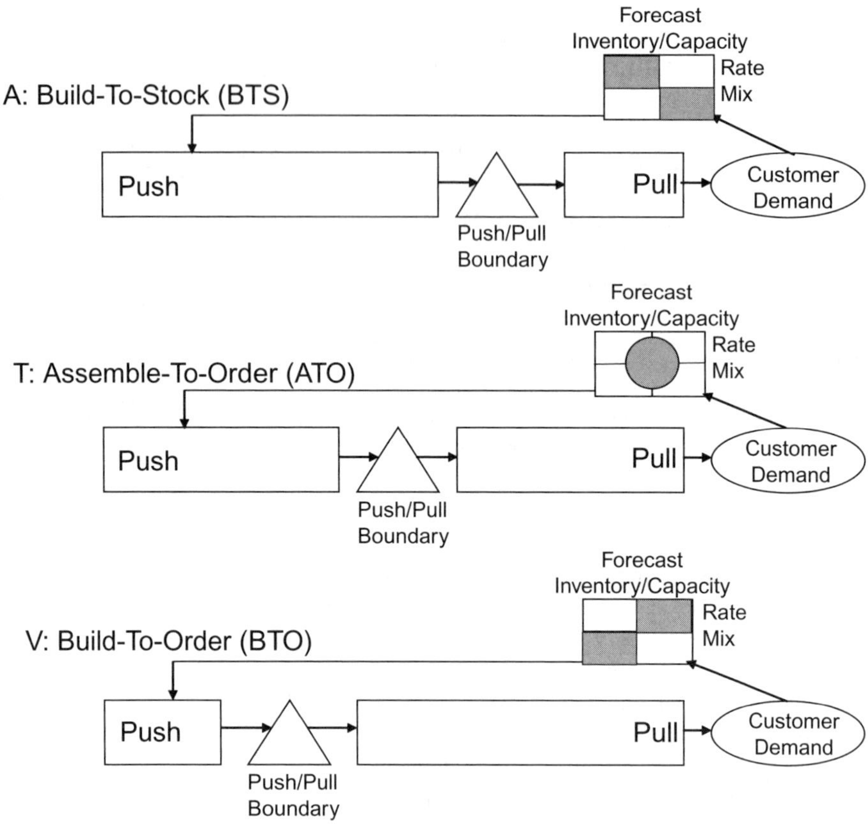

FIGURE 7-3 Network operating modes.

operates in a BTS mode, production and inventory planning and control is organized as push for most of the network length. The push/pull boundary is typically downstream depending on the product. Only the most downstream portion of the network, such as a postponement operation for local country/local language options, may be organized as pull. Under BTS the planning focus should be on forecasting the rate of upstream inventory buffering and the capacity mix at the constraint.

When the network operates in an ATO mode, production and inventory planning and control is organized as push for part of the network length and as pull for the remainder. The push/pull boundary is typically midstream depending on the product. This is the most difficult network configuration to forecast as inventory rate, inventory mix, capacity rate, and capacity mix must each be forecast. When the network operates in a BTO mode, production and inventory planning and control is organized as pull for most of the network length. The push/pull boundary is typically upstream depending on the product. Pull production assumes reliable, high-yielding processes. This is important because only one product is started for each customer order; if that product is lost within the manufacturing process, that customer order goes unfulfilled. Under BTO the planning focus should be on forecasting the mix of upstream inventory buffering and the rate of capacity at the constraint.

Production and Inventory Control Inside the Four Walls

The lead time availability promised to the customer is determined by where the single factory's implementation of the product BOM falls along the CF-BTS-ATO-BTO-ETO continuum. The factory has the ability to produce a number of different products, and each product has its own unique BOM. The factory produces these products from a set of work centers organized into a static, switched, or chaotic flow. Static flow is called a *process flow* shop. Switched flow is called an *alternative routing*. Chaotic flow is called a *job shop*.

One of the factory's work centers is the capacity constraint that determines the maximum throughput rate. This capacity constraint may be common to every product, or other work centers in the factory may become the capacity constraint under a different product mix. Inventory buffers the capacity constraint and acts as safety stock to buffer changes in both the production rate and the production mix. The following operational questions are traditional inside the four walls of a manufacturer:

- What lead time availability does the customer see?
- What constrains capacity and sets the throughput rate?
- Does the capacity constraint move when the product mix shifts?
- How much long lead time inventory is necessary to sustain the throughput rate?
- What level of safety stock inventory is required to maintain production flexibility?

Production and Inventory Control in Distributed Networks

The lead time availability promised to the end-customer is determined by where the supply chain network's implementation of the product BOM falls along the CF-BTS-ATO-BTO-ETO continuum. The network has the ability to produce a number of different product SKUs and each SKU has its own unique BOM and packaging. The network produces these SKUs from a set of trading partners organized into a static, switched, or chaotic flow. The network nodes are interconnected by pipelines for material flow, information flow, and cash flow. Both nodes and pipelines can be capacity constrained.

One of the trading partner nodes is the network capacity constraint that determines the maximum throughput rate for all the trading partners. This network capacity constraint may be common to every SKU produced. However when the mix of market demand shifts, the network constraint may shift from one trading partner to a different trading partner. Because the network capacity constraint needs to consume raw material quicker than the lead time necessary to procure the material, there needs to be an inventory buffer just ahead of the network capacity constraint. Otherwise throughput becomes material constrained rather than capacity constrained. This time buffer is sized to support the maximum throughput rate. When the product

TABLE 7-6
Network Operational Control

Zone Type	Operational Control	Demand Trigger	Forecast
Push	MRP II	Reorder point tied to a level of safety stock	Inventory mix and rate Capacity rate and mix
Push	Vendor Managed Inventory	Push to replenish stock driven from the supply side	Gross rate or mix changes
Pull	Kanban	Serial pull to replenish stock driven from the demand side	Gross rate or mix changes
Pull	Synchronized	Parallel pull tied to an actual customer order	Preload inventory Maximum capacity

SKU mix shifts, other materials may be in shorter supply and begin to constrain the throughput. Consequently, additional buffer stocks of unique materials need to be placed at their respective points of consumption to support swings in SKU mix.

Network Operational Control

When the product BOM and competitive environment allows the push/pull boundary to be all the way upstream, the network operates as a single pull zone. When the product BOM and competitive environment forces the push/pull boundary to be all the way downstream, the network operates as a single push zone. In most cases the product BOM and competitive environment collide, causing the network architecture to be split into multiple operational controls to take advantage of operating with some knowledge of actual demand over operating only from a forecast. Table 7-6 lists four different types of operational controls that may be combined within a network. Chapter 8 describes the network planning aspects for each type of zone.

Manufacturing Resource Planning

Manufacturing Resources Planning (MRP II) applies to the push zone beginning at the supply end of the supply chain and extending to the push/pull boundary. In some businesses the entire network is pushed from a forecast. MRP II is a more mature generation of materials requirements planning, and it was originally invented for capacity and inventory planning and control inside the four walls of the firm. MRP II logic is also at the core of some enterprise resource planning systems. MRP II recognizes that though independently demanded products must be forecast, dependently demanded lower-level items should be calculated with lead time offsetting over the planning horizon using the following toolset:

- *Demand Forecast (DF)*—The expected rate of demanded items in aggregated dollars by period over a planning horizon.
- *Supply Forecast (SF)*—The expected rate and mix of supplied items in aggregated units and dollars by period over a planning horizon.

- *Sales and Operations Plan (S&OP)*—Matches the expected demand with the expected rate and mix of supply in both dollars and units at an aggregated level. The plan is reviewed monthly.
- *Distribution Requirements Planning (DRP)*—Time phased, netting logic that combines the requirements for the same SKU in the same time frame from each of the different distribution centers as input into the master production schedule at the factory producing that SKU.
- *Master Production Schedule (MPS)* — A time-phased plan developed from the supply forecast and order backlog for every SKU in units, dollars, and weeks. The MPS drives MRP and CRP. The MPS is completely revised monthly, but reviewed and adjusted weekly. If the MPS is not valid because MRP predicts a material shortage and/or CRP predicts a capacity shortage, then the MPS must be revised.
- *Bill Of Materials (BOM)*—Contains the item master and the product structures for all products.
- *Materials Requirements Planning (MRP)*—Time-phased, netting logic that takes the consumption of material predicted by the master production schedule, the on-hand inventory balance of lower level materials, the lead time offset of procured materials, and the product structure of the bill of materials to calculate replenishment plans for all lower-level inventory. MRP assumes infinite capacity.
- *Capacity Requirements Planning (CRP)*—Time-phased, netting logic that takes the consumption of capacity predicted by the master production schedule, the availability of capacity, the lead time offset of the scheduled production, and the product structure of the bill of materials to calculate capacity plans for each manufacturing work center. CRP assumes infinite material availability.
- *The Dispatch List*—Establishes the relative priority of work released to the shop floor.
- *Input/Output Control*—Used to monitor the actual versus planned hours of work scheduled to start and the actual versus planned hours of work completed for the capacity assigned to each work center. I/O control is a key indication that priorities are being followed and that the MPS remains valid.
- *Enterprise Resource Planning (ERP)*—Combines the functionality and logic of all of the above components, and more, into one integrated software application supported by a single relational database. ERP integrates some, but not all, of the trading partner's planning into one central system.

MRP II uses a serial form of vocalization. For example, the DRP output of the distribution center feeds into the MPS input of the factory. The MRP output of the factory feeds into the MPS input of the fabricator. The MRP output of the fabricator feeds into the MPS input of the supplier. Under MRP II the supplier, the fabricator, the factory, and the distribution center each run independent planning systems. The information is propagated sequentially over successive planning cycles. Also, though the general ledger and other financial elements are modules with these systems, MRP II typically does not integrate cash flow into its planning logic.

Vendor Managed Inventory

Vendor Managed Inventory (VMI) control applies from an upstream or midstream internal network inventory location to the push/pull boundary. VMI is a low-cost push method of controlling inventory replenishment. It is not a planning system. VMI is subordinated to MRP II; one configuration is upstream MRP II coupled with multiple, parallel, and/or paralleled-series VMI in the midstream reaching to the push/pull boundary. VMI pushes replenishment inventory in a manner that is managed from the supply side.

Under a VMI agreement, a buyer and a seller come to an agreement that the seller will be given access to the buyer's inventory balances and will be given the responsibility to maintain the buyer's inventory balances within predefined limits. A VMI agreement is built on trust. The seller may come on-site to count stock or may access inventory balances electronically. Minimum/maximum inventory limits are established by SKU from a gross forecast of the business level. When the seller observes that the current inventory balance has dropped below the reorder point, the seller is authorized to replenish stock up to the maximum level. The VMI process is conducted without purchase orders. Under VMI, the buyer holds the seller's inventory on consignment, whereas the seller retains title to the inventory until it is consumed. The seller typically invoices the buyer once a month with a single invoice that summarizes all the stock transactions from the past month. VMI localizes the vocalization of demand between (nominal) trading partners. VMI reduces processing cost and accelerates the order-to-delivery velocity, but has little impact on cash-to-cash velocity shorter than the monthly processing cycle. Finally, VMI should not be used when there is a high risk of design changes that will render the consigned inventory obsolete.

Kanban

Kanban control applies from the push/pull boundary to an internal midstream or downstream network inventory location. One configuration is a synchronized downstream coupled with multiple, parallel, or paralleled-series kanbans in the midstream reaching to the push/pull boundary. Kanban is a low-cost pull method of controlling inventory replenishment; it is not a planning system. Kanban pulls replenishment inventory in a manner that is managed from the demand side. The idea of kanban originated from the Toyota production system, and there are now several common implementation methods, including 2-card physical systems, 3-card physical systems, and electronic kanbans.

Kanbans are used both internal to a (nominal) trading partner and between (nominal) trading partners. Under a kanban arrangement, a buyer and a seller come to an agreement that when the buyer observes that a stocking point has fallen below its reorder point, the buyer will send a kanban, such as a container, card, or electronic signal, to the seller. This kanban specifies the item being replenished and the fixed lot size of the replenishment. No purchase order is involved, as the kanban is the authorization to the seller to produce and ship the next lot of that item. The number of kanbans per item in the system is monitored against a gross forecast of the business level. The number of kanbans is periodically adjusted to maintain a service level with minimum inventory. The seller typically invoices the buyer once a month with a single invoice that summarizes all the kanban transactions for the past month. Like VMI, kanban localizes the vocalization of demand within and between (nominal) trading partners. Kanban reduces processing cost, reduces inventory, and accelerates the order-to-delivery velocity, but has little impact on cash-to-cash velocity shorter than the monthly processing cycle.

Synchronization

Synchronized control applies from the customer or demand end of the supply chain to the push/pull boundary. In some businesses, the entire network can be synchronized. Under synchronization every trading partner is triggered into action by actual customer demand. Raw material is pulled to suppliers, supplier parts are pulled to fabricators, fabricated items are pulled to the factory, finished goods are pulled to the distributor, distributed SKUs are pulled to the retailer, and retail goods are pulled to the customer all at the same time, all driven by a customer order. This degree of synchronization is found, for example, in some repetitive grocery and consumer packaged goods networks. Vocalization among the trading partners is complete. The cash-to-cash cycles among the trading partners are accelerated by being synchronized.

Synchronized control is best understood from the concept of Drum-Buffer-Rope (DBR) created by Eli Goldratt in the Theory Of Constraints (TOC).[1] Although DBR was originally applied inside the four walls of a single factory, it is now understood that DBR is directly applicable to the trading partners across a complex supply chain network.

- *Drum*—The rate of manufacture (or transformation or fulfillment) set by the network constraint. System resources are synchronized to the rate of the drum.
- *Buffer*—Time protection against uncertainty so that the network can maximize throughput. TOC buffers are maintained at the constraint, at assembly points for constrained parts, and at shipping points in a network.
- *Rope*—The communication process from the network constraint to the gating operations that limits material flow released into the network. The rope avoids the over activation and misallocation of nonconstraint resources.

Network Routing of the Demand Signal in a Synchronized Operation

Chapter 4 discussed the improvement in the order-to-delivery-to-cash velocity through the design of parallel rather than serial subcycles. How exactly should a parallel demand signal be routed? Figure 7-4 shows a complex network with six echelons of (nominal) trading partners. Product is delivered to customers through the retail stores in Echelon 5. The factory in Echelon 3 is the network constraint. Two separate demand signals link each of the (nominal) trading partners. The first is the *actual demand*. It originates from the point of sale with the end-customer and runs in parallel directly to each of the other network echelons and nodes that supply it as a destination. Although every node can connect to the actual demand signal,

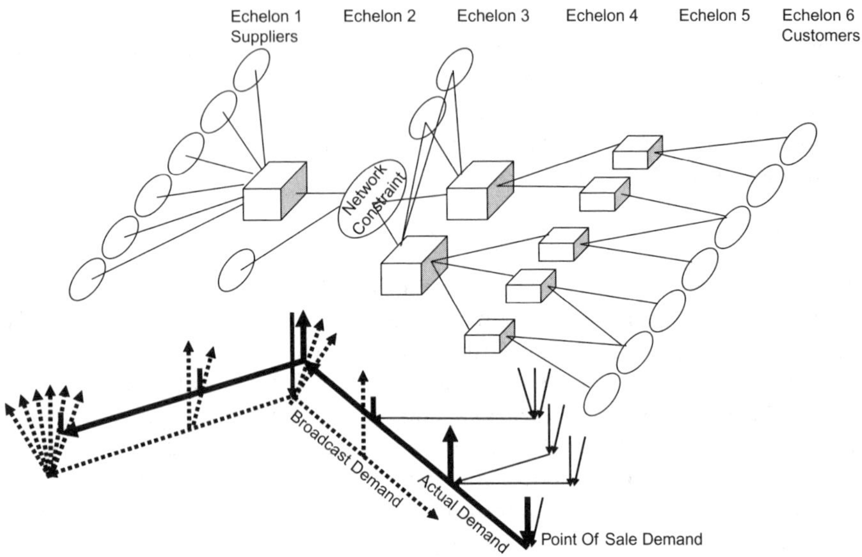

FIGURE 7-4 Broadcasting demand from the network constraint.

the two nodes that must connect are the customer-facing retail store in Echelon 5 and the network constraint in Echelon 3.

The second demand signal is the *broadcast demand.* It originates with the network constraint and runs in parallel directly to each of the other network echelons and nodes. In Figure 7-4, it is the broadcast demand signal that carries the demand information into Echelons 1, 2, and 4. Both signals must be made available to every network node because as the product mix of the customer demand shifts, the trading partner that is the system constraint may also shift. If for some reason a trading partner falls momentarily behind, then that trading partner will manage its own backlog for a day until it is caught up. If a trading partner falls steadily behind for a predetermined period, like five working days, then that trading partner becomes the new network constraint. Having both demand lines live at all times facilitates the smooth and orderly transfer of control over the network constraint from one trading partner to another.

These are the daily operating rules for vocalizing demand for each SKU in a synchronized operation:

- *Rule 1*—The customer-facing end of the supply chain delivers the ordered rate and mix from its shipping buffer.
- *Rule 2A*—If the network constraint has the daily capacity to meet the rate and mix of the actual demand, then the rate and mix in the broadcast demand is identical to the actual demand.
- *Rule 2B*—If the network constraint does not have the daily capacity to meet the rate and mix of the actual demand, then the broadcast demand signal contains a constrained rate or mix. The network constraint manages the order backlog for the entire network until it is caught up.

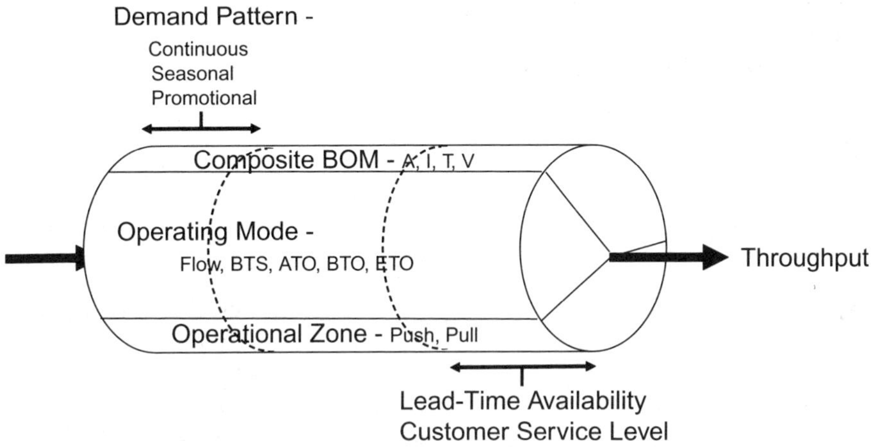

FIGURE 7-5 The network throughput engine.

- *Rule 3*—All other nodes produce an equivalent throughput of products, assemblies, or components that will satisfy the rate and mix of the broadcast demand signal.
- *Rule 4*—The supplier end of the network orders raw materials to match the cumulative daily rate of the actual demand.

Optimizing the Network Throughput Engine

The composite BOM, the operating mode, and the operational zones combine to form the network's throughput engine, see Figure 7-5. This engine takes both actual and forecast demand in a continuous, seasonal, or promotional demand pattern and converts it into throughput with a sustained lead time and availability of supply. This is analogous to optimizing the match-up of a car's engine, its transmission, and its tire selection to convert gallons of fuel into a driving distance and a maximum speed. When the engine, transmission, and tires are properly matched, the car can be driven a great distance with competitive speed and acceleration. When the BOM, operating mode, and operational zones are properly matched, the network can be driven at great throughput with competitive lead time and availability. On the other hand when the BOM, operating mode, and operational zones are mismatched, the network will produce some throughput. However, the network lead time and availability will fluctuate.

Use the following steps, summarized in Table 7-7, to optimize the network throughput engine:

- *Step 1*—Combine the individual product BOMs into a composite BOM to determine the predominate BOM-type as A, I, T, or V.
- *Step 2*—Match the composite BOM-type with the corresponding operating mode. The operating mode should only allow the product to be built

TABLE 7-7
Throughput Engine Combination Criteria

	List of Alternatives	Criteria
Composite BOM & Operating Mode	[I]-[CF] [A]-[BTS] [T]-[ATO] [V]-[BTO] [All]-[ETO]	Steps 1. and 2. Match the predominate BOM-type with the corresponding operating mode. Build only as far as the end product is customer defined.
Push/pull Boundary		Step 3. Locate the echelon with the push/pull boundary based on a competitive lead-time. (See criteria below.)
Operational Zones	[Pull-Synchronized] [Pull-Kanban]	Step 4. Define the operational control methods from the customer to the push/pull boundary.
	[Push-VMI] [Push-MRP II]	Step 5. Define the operational control methods from the push/pull boundary to raw materials.

to the extent to which it is customer defined. Building finished goods inventory for speculation is not an objective. In general, [I-type BOM] goes with [CF], [A-type BOM] goes with [BTS], [T-type BOM] goes with [ATO], and [V-type BOM] goes with [BTO]. [ETO] can be used with [all BOM-types].

- *Step 3*—Locate the push/pull boundary echelon using the criteria described below. Start with the end-customer and work upstream until the ordering time from the customer plus the remaining network manufacturing and distribution time plus the outbound logistics time to the customer exceeds the competitor's lead-time. The push/pull boundary is a physical inventory and cash inventory location.
- *Step 4*—Define the operational control methods from the customer to the push/pull boundary.
  - Use pull-synchronize when all trading partners can act in parallel to pull to actual customer orders.
  - Use pull-kanban when a demand side (nominal) trading partner controls the pull to a stocking level.
- *Step 5*—Define the operational control methods from the push/pull boundary to raw materials.
  - Use push-MRP II when the push is forecast from a stocking date or from a stocking level.
  - Use push-VMI when a supply side (nominal) trading partner controls the push to replenish.

Figure 7-6 is another way to look at the same optimization problem. A network diagram of the complete network shown in the top third of the figure is echelon-aligned with the composite BOM product structure shown in the center third of the figure. Note that more than one level of the BOM can be completed within a single echelon.

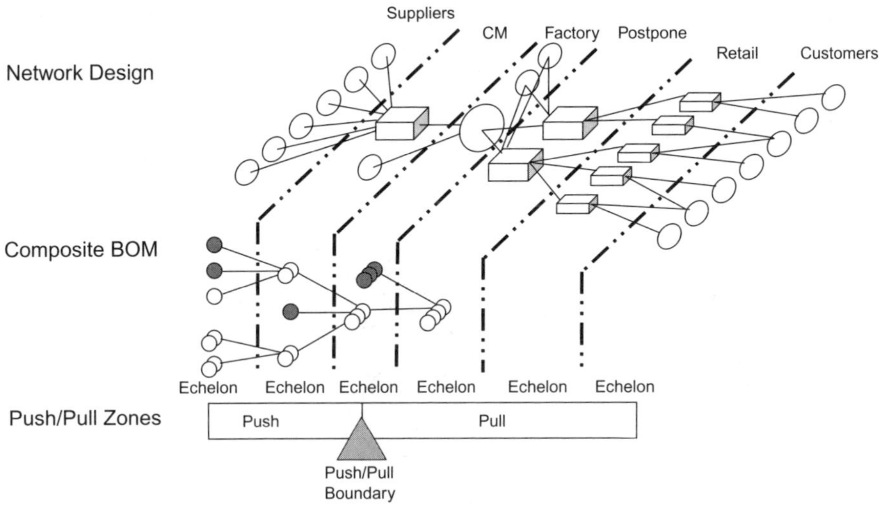

FIGURE 7-6 Relation of the network design, the composite BOM, and the push/pull zones.

The push/pull boundary inventory location is located in its proper echelon as shown in the bottom third of the figure. Push zone(s) extend to the left of the boundary and pull zone(s) extend to the right of the boundary. Different combinations of synchronized control and kanban control may be used to reach from the end-customer to the push/pull boundary, see Figure 7-7. Different combinations of VMI control and MRP II control may be used to reach from the push/pull boundary to raw materials.

Locating the Network Push/Pull Boundary

Because defining each network zone depends on first properly locating the push/pull boundary, it is important to understand the following criteria. To locate the push/pull boundary, start with the end-customer and work upstream until either one or more of the following three rules fail:

- *Rule 1*—The network location of the push/pull boundary must satisfy the following equation:

Order processing cycle time + Manufacturing and distribution cycle time
+ Outbound logistics time
≤ Customer's expectation for availability
≤ Competition's order-to-delivery cycle time

- *Rule 2*—Some complex products have a "head and shoulders" look to their BOM. A pull operation is practical in the head portion of the BOM product structure where the number of communication linkages, particularly with nominal trading partners, is manageable. The pull operation becomes

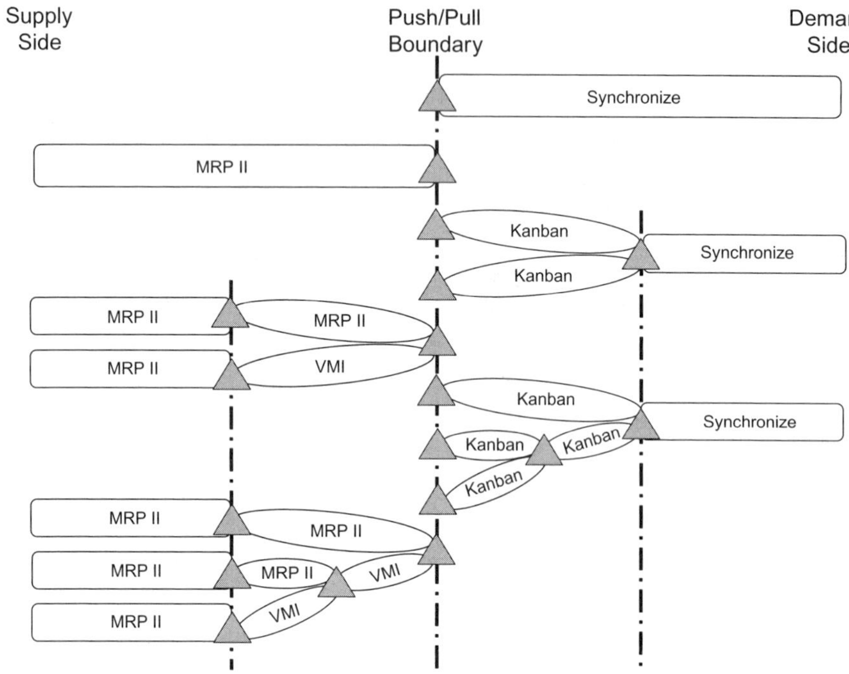

FIGURE 7-7 Network operational control combinations.

impractical in the shoulders portion of the BOM product structure where the number of communications with nominal trading partners is so large that it becomes unmanageable.

- *Rule 3*—The push/pull boundary line cuts completely across the network width. Depending on the composite BOM product structure, the push/pull boundary may consist of a set of inventory locations and cash "inventory" locations corresponding to a number of parallel legs within that echelon.

Table 7-8 shows an example of how to locate a push/pull boundary. The first criterion sets the boundary starting from the customer and working upstream. With the boundary located between the wholesaler and the factory, 1.5 days is less than the competition's 3.0 days. The second criterion locates the boundary where the number of communication paths is manageable. The third criterion says that the set of connection(s) between the factory and the wholesaler(s) is part of this push/pull boundary.

Percent of the Network Vocalized

Adoption of the vocalize principle can be simply measured as the percentage of relevant network nodes actually connected to the broadcast demand signal. In a well-designed network, the network constraint will be a trading partner. However, many of the network nodes essential to the physical distribution of the product are nominal

TABLE 7-8
A Network Example of Locating the Push/Pull Boundary

Echelon	Communication Paths	Order Time	Cycle Time	Transit Time	Cumulative Time
The customer is willing to wait 3 days because the competition can deliver in 3 days.					
Customer					
	1	0.1 day		0.2 day	0.3 days
Retail			0.1 day		0.4 days
	1	0.5 day		0.3 day	1.2 days
Wholesale			0.3 day		1.5 days
					Push/Pull Boundary
	1	0.5 day		2 days	4.0 days
Factory			8 days		12 days
	87	1.0 days		6 days	19 days
Supplier			45 days		64 days

trading partners; strategic nominal trading partners need to be connected to the broadcast demand.

$$\frac{\%\text{ of Network Vocalizing}}{\text{Baseline Network}} = \frac{\text{Actual number of nodes connected to the broadcast demand}}{\text{Total number of relevant nodes}} \times 100\%$$

Where the term relevant node includes all trading partners plus strategic nominal trading partners essential to the network's material flow.
Vocalization improves toward the origin of the value circle.

Table 7-9 uses the network from Figure 7-4 as an example of the improvement in the vocalize principle. This network has a total of 18 nodes associated with physical distribution; the 18 nodes include all the nodes shown in Echelon 1 through Echelon 5, but do not include end-customers. Six of the nodes are known to be

TABLE 7-9
Competitive Improvement under the Vocalize Principle

	Trading Partner Nodes	Nominal Trading Partner Nodes	Total Relevant Network	Percent Vocalized
Relevant Nodes	6 TP/3 echelons	12 NTP	18 nodes/5 echelons	
Before Vocalize Optimization				
Actual Demand	2 TP/2 echelons	5 NTP	7 nodes/2 echelons	
Broadcast Demand	3 TP/3 echelons	0 NTP	3 nodes/3 echelons	3/18 = 16.7%
After Vocalize Optimization				
Actual Demand	3 TP/3 echelons	5 NTP	8 nodes/3 echelons	
Broadcast Demand	6 TP/3 echelons	9 NTP	15 nodes/5 echelons	15/18 = 83.3%

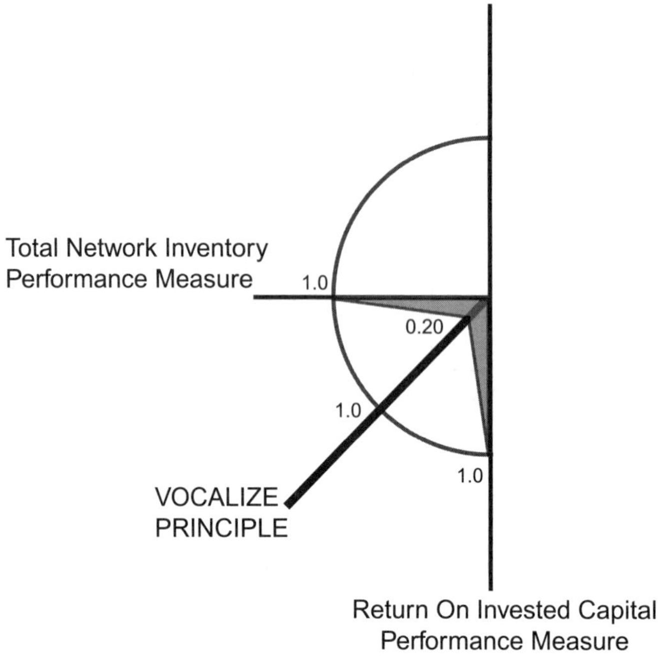

FIGURE 7-8 The percent vocalized improves toward the origin.

trading partners, whereas the remaining 12 are nominal trading partners. Notice that many other nominal trading partners, including the logistics service providers, information service providers, and financial service providers, are not shown and are not included in the total node count for this measure. Before optimization only 3 nodes, or 16.7%, are connected to the broadcast demand.

Figure 7-8 shows how a competitive improvement plots on the value circle. In this example, a baseline of $(3/18) \times 100\% = 16.7\%$ of the relevant nodes are connected leaving $(100\% - 16.7\%) = 83.3\%$ disconnected. Therefore, 1.0 on the vocalize axis equates to 83.3% disconnected from vocalizing. After optimization an additional 12 nodes, including all the trading partners, are connected to the broadcast demand. This raises the percent of the network vocalizing to $((3 + 12)/18) \times 100\% = 83.3\%$ leaving $(100\% - 83.3\%) = 16.7\%$ of the relevant nodes disconnected. The improvement is plotted on the vocalize axis as the ratio $(0.167/0.833) = 0.20$, near the value circle's origin.

THE VISUALIZE PRINCIPLE

It has been said many times that you are what you measure. If a network trading partner is expected to look beyond the four walls of its immediate organization and to contribute to the end-to-end optimization of the network, then the right global performance measures must be in place. The visualize principle is about ensuring that all of the trading partners agree to and comply with a set of measures that drive performance end-to-end. When each trading partner is able to visualize network capacity and network inventory in real-time, it becomes empowered to make the right operational decisions. Chapter 6 presents a thorough discussion of how to define and implement a global performance measure and introduces equivalent throughput as one of the preferred global performance measures. This section introduces another preferred global performance measure: total network inventory. Once again, the value circle is used to monitor competitive improvement in terms of the percentage of the network aligning operations using global performance measures.

The Capable Network

A network node is capable when it has the ability to transform, to manufacture, or to fulfill the customer's demand without becoming constrained. In any complex network, there will be at least one network constraint. This constraint may be fixed at a single node, or it may move about the network as product mix shifts with customer demand. The network constraint may fall within one of the nominal trading partners; this should be avoided because the network orchestrator will lose control of the network's throughput when the nominal trading partner has some other priority.

Figure 7-9 shows the same network as Figure 7-4, this time from a network constraint perspective. Echelons 1 to 5 are shown with the end-customer echelon having been dropped. Multiple paths interconnect the network nodes. Each path represents the demand driven by a different SKU with the number of parallel paths determined by the BOM corresponding to each SKU. Notice that not every SKU is in demand at every retail outlet, nor does every supplier source items for every BOM. The heights of the normal distribution curves shown for the fabricator, the factory, and the two distributors indicate that though the fabricator and both distributors are capable of meeting daily demand, the factory is the network constraint. The factory is the least capable relative to the other network trading partners.

The Network Constraint

It is natural to think of a constraint only as a scarcity of capacity, but networks can also be constrained by inventory, information, cash, and scarcity caused by poor management policy. A list of the types of constraints commonly found in network operations follows.

- *Skilled labor constraint*—This capacity constraint could be either direct labor working to transform, manufacture, or fulfill the product, or indirect labor such as engineering working to resolve a product or process problem. Although the proper headcount may be available, the specific people lack the training and experience to get the job done when it is needed most.
- *Machine constraint*—Machine capacity is constrained by the number of hours available, the number of hours required for setup, the immediate availability of tooling, the immediate availability of trained operators, scheduled preventative maintenance, and unscheduled downtime.
- *Logistics constraint*—The uplift capacity of airlines, the availability of railcars, the availability of ocean-going containers, the cutoff time of

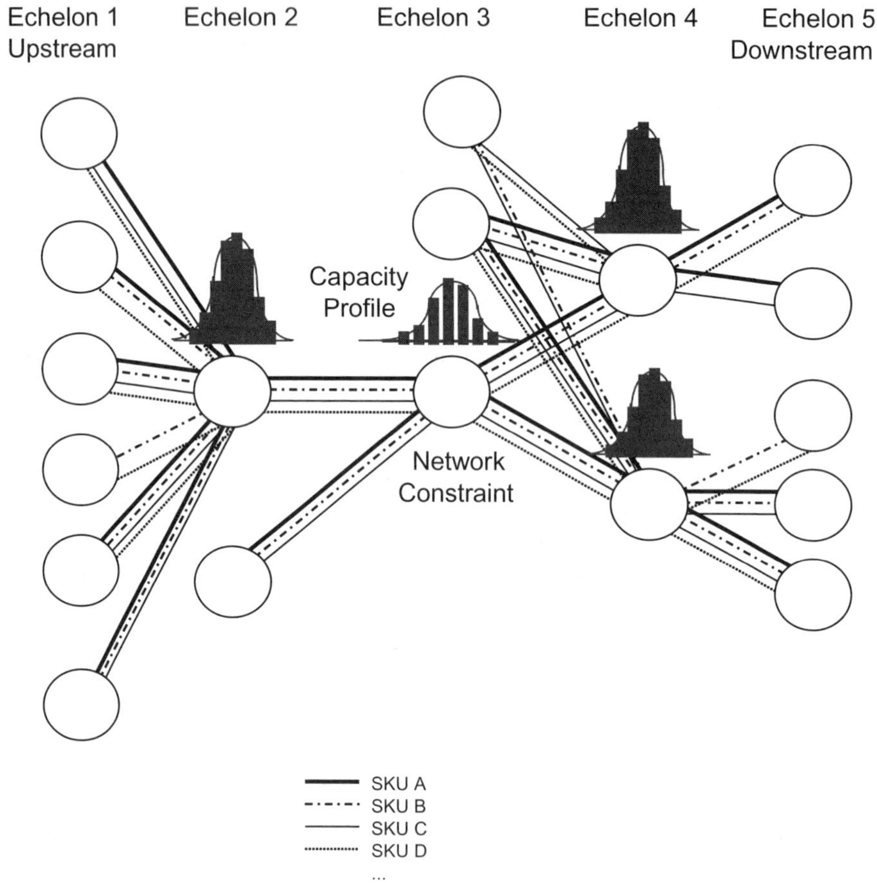

FIGURE 7-9 The capable network.

freight forwarders, the departure schedule of transportation, and the available cubic storage of warehousing all work to constrain transportation.

- *Customs constraint*—This capacity constraint results from a processing overload or the intensive security inspection of freight at a customs point.
- *Material constraint*—Throughput becomes constrained when a person, machine, or transport waits to receive operating inventory.
- *Cash constraint*—Throughput becomes constrained when a process waits to receive operating cash.
- *Information constraint*—Throughput becomes constrained when a process must wait to receive needed information, for example, delay caused by a virus attack on the Internet.
- *Management policy constraint*—Throughput becomes constrained when a process is delayed by a management policy. For example, a management policy decision is constraining the process when ERP has eliminated paper

purchase orders and invoicing is done electronically, but the accounts payable department stills waits 31 days to pay a supplier.

The network constraint determines the maximum throughput of the network. If the actual throughput is less than the desired throughput, one of two courses of action may be followed. The first course of action is to elevate the constraint. To be elevated means that the last ounce of capacity is wrung out of the constraint. Eli Goldratt's Theory Of Constraints is helpful in identifying and elevating any kind of constraint. When the constraint involves machine capacity, Single Minute Exchange of Die (SMED) is another helpful technique to elevate a machine constraint. SMED separates setup work into that which can be done while the machine is running from that which can only be done while the machine is stopped. For example, heavy dies located in the tool crib are moved to the machine bed and pre-positioned for a quick exchange while a 40-ton punch press is operating. The machine stroke must be halted for the old die to be extracted and a new die inserted. If such a die exchange can be completed in one minute using leverage and positioning pins, versus 20 minutes the old way with the machine stopped, then this punch press just gained 19 minutes of "new" capacity very inexpensively.

The second course of action is to make a permanent adjustment by buying additional capacity or selling excess capacity. It is important to remember that there is lead time to buy or sell capacity. This lead time expands as the capacity increment expands. For example, working overtime might add 5%–10% to current capacity; the overtime might begin tomorrow afternoon. Adding a second shift might add 25%–33% to current capacity; a supervisor might be moved to the second shift and employees hired in the next six weeks. Purchasing a second 40-ton punch press might double capacity; a used machine might be located in the next 4–6 months, but the lead time to buy a new machine might be 40 weeks. Shedding capacity is similar. It can take weeks or months to plan and implement the termination of employees. It takes time to find a buyer willing to pay more than the scrap value of a machine and to move the machine off the premises. It can take years to find a qualified buyer for an empty factory on a piece of real estate.

Determining the Required Network Constraint Capacity

The question becomes how much capacity is required for the network constraint? The answer comes from a demand analysis such as the one shown in Table 7-10. A domestic supply chain network provides six SKUs to its industrial customers. The six SKUs are similar in design, but have independent demands. Demand for SKU A and C is volatile, whereas the demand for SKU B, D, E, and F is more stable, see Table 7-10. Demand volatility appears in the table as the ratio of the mean to the standard deviation for each SKU. In order to achieve a 99.7% service level, the network must have daily capacity to sustain the total mean demand plus three standard deviations of the RMS demand uncertainty. The total mean demand is the sum of the individual SKU means, or 214 units per day. The market demand for each SKU is statistically independent of the demand for any other SKU; the standard deviations are combined into a RMS value of 113.6 units per day. The network constraint should be capable of (214 + (3)(113.6)) = 555 units/day.

TABLE 7-10
Market Demand in Units/Day

SKU	Percentage Mix	Daily Demand—Mean From Past 6 Months Data	Daily Demand—Standard Deviation From Past 6 Months Data	Demand Volatility
A	37.9%	81	102	1.26
B	31.3%	67	19	0.28
C	15.4%	33	45	1.36
D	10.2%	22	10	0.45
E	3.3%	7	2	0.29
F	1.9%	4	3	0.75
	100.0%	214 Total Mean Demand	113.6 Root Mean Squared Uncertainty	
		Mean + 3 Standard Deviations = 555 Units/Day		

The following three rules, appearing here and following, establish the criteria for a network to be capable in terms of its capacity and inventory.

- *Capable Network Criterion 1*—To achieve a 99.7% service level, the network constraint should have the daily capacity to process [the sum of the means plus three times the RMS value of the standard deviations of] the equivalent throughputs of each independent demand. Two times the RMS value of the standard deviations drops the service level down to 95.4%. All nonconstraint capacities are larger by definition.

Classifying Network Inventory

The distribution of inventory across a network is different from the distribution of inventory within the four walls of a single trading partner. In order for every trading partner to gain visibility of the network inventory, there must be some understanding of how to properly position of inventory in a network to be competitive. The following list classifies acceptable use of inventory in network operations; all other inventory should be eliminated.

- *Shipping buffer (downstream)*—Finished goods inventory held at a customer-facing node, such as a retail store, is the first product delivered to fulfill the customer's order. This inventory provides an immediate response; it is the most competitive delivery in terms of response time. When the demand quantity exceeds the shipping buffer, additional product is drop shipped from a distributor or the remaining shipments are spread out over time as the store can be replenished. The shipping buffer is sized to protect against variability in the fulfillment cycle times and transit times between the network constraint and the shipping buffer.
- *Postponement inventory (downstream)*—Nearly finished product is completed to the customer's selection from a predefined set of options. Postponement is not customization. This inventory holds a safety stock of the

unique items necessary to complete each option BOM. For example local language instruction manuals and country-specific power cords are dropped into the shipping carton after the Country Of Destination is known. Postponement inventory can double as the shipping buffer.

- *Preload inventory (typically downstream)*—This inventory is stocked at each node in a synchronized supply chain before synchronized operations can begin. Preload inventory establishes the maximum rate of throughput ramp-up that can be achieved during one synchronization cycle.
- *Constraint buffer (any zone)*—The constraint buffer is a time buffer used to resolve upstream problems before the network constraint is stopped, causing the unrecoverable loss of throughput. The constraint buffer is sized to protect against variability in the manufacturing cycle times and inbound transit times between the source of raw materials and the network constraint. Inventory should only be allowed to enter the constraint buffer if it is tied to a shippable order. Inventory should not be allowed to enter the constraint buffer with missing components or with a known quality defect.
- *Assembly buffer (any zone)*—An assembly point occurs where the flows of constrained material and nonconstrained material converge and diverge. An assembly point can occur either upstream or downstream from the network constraint. The assembly buffer is sized to protect against variability in the cycle times and transit times between the source of constrained materials and the assembly buffer.
- *Push/pull boundary (any zone)*—This inventory location acts as the shock absorber between the relatively smooth, forecast-driven operations and the relatively erratic, order-driven operations. Sometimes the push/pull boundary doubles as the constraint buffer and/or as risk pooled safety stock.
- *Risk pooling inventory (upstream)*—This safety stock inventory location is far enough upstream that it can pool the risks of parallel, statistically independent flows. Risk pooling inventory is typically used to protect service level performance against unexpected swings in product mix. This safety stock is sized to cover the RMS value of the standard deviation component of each independent demand.

Determining the Required Inventory Buffer Size

Inventory buffers are sized one of two ways. When the buffer is a time buffer, the buffer contents are representative of some equivalent number of days of value-added cycle time plus transit time. When the buffer is a quantity buffer, the buffer contents are calculated from the BOM equivalency of the independent demand driving the product. The requirements for inventory buffers are time-phased backwards from forecast and actual end-customer demand.

- *Capable network criterion 2A*—To achieve a 99.7% service level, a time buffer should have an inventory level equal to three times the RMS value of the standard deviations of the relevant value-added cycle times plus transit times. Two times the RMS value of the standard deviations drops the service level down to 95.4%.

- *Capable network criterion 2B*—To achieve a 99.7% service level, a quantity buffer should have a safety stock level equal to three times the RMS value of the standard deviations of the BOM equivalent of each independent demand. Two times the RMS value of the standard deviations drops the service level down to 95.4%.

For example, independent demand for SKU X has a mean of 100 units/day and a standard deviation of 25 units/day, independent demand for SKU Y has a mean of 75 units/day and a standard deviation of 125 units/day, and independent demand for SKU Z has a mean of 10 units/day and a standard deviation of 2 units/day. Under Rule 2B the safety stock level for risk pooling inventory for a common part used 2 per SKU should be set at (2)(3)(127.5 units) = 765 units of safety stock. The RMS value of the 25, 125, and 2 units of the independent demand standard deviations is 127.5. In the same network, the raw materials are two echelons, A and B, upstream from the constraint buffer. Cycle Time A has a mean of 0.2 days and a standard deviation of 0.5 days. Cycle Time B has a mean of 0.1 days and a standard deviation of 1 day. Each of the three logistic legs has a mean transit time of 3 days and a standard deviation of 0.3 days. Under Rule 2A the constraint buffer should be set at (3)(1.23 days) = 3.7 days of inventory. The RMS value of 0.3, 0.5, 0.3, 1.0, and 0.3 days of transit + cycle + transit + cycle + transit time standard deviations is 1.23 days.

Finally, in order to achieve a capable network there must be criteria for the level of safety cash maintained at each cash buffer. Like inventory, the requirements for cash buffers are time-phased from forecast and actual end-customer demand.

- *Capable network criterion 3*—To achieve a 99.7% service level, a cash buffer should have a safety cash level equal to three times the RMS value of the standard deviations of the mean accounts payable computed from the bill of cash and the equivalent throughput in that echelon. Two times the RMS value of the standard deviations drops the service level down to 95.4%.

The Total Network Inventory Performance Measure

A shoebox has the dimensions of height and width and length. Rotate the shoebox with the short side facing out. Define the height of the shoebox as the demand rate in dollars and the width of the shoebox as a dimensionless demand mix. Now, rotate the shoebox with the long side facing out. Define the length of the shoebox as the total cycle time plus transit time in days. Taking the lid off the box reveals a cubic volume of space enclosed by the box. With the lid off, sweep your hand inside from one short end to the other. This sweep, enclosed by the dimensions of the shoebox, represents a cubic volume with the dimensions of $-Days.

When customer demand is applied throughout the entire supply chain network, it takes some number of days to sweep the value of upstream raw materials through the value-adding midstream and downstream fulfillment portions of the network. As forecasts push material through the inbound pipelines into network nodes and as demand pulls material out of network nodes through the outbound pipelines, a "cubic volume" of inventory $-Days is swept end-to-end throughout the network. The network nodes contain $-Days of moving, in-process inventory, and $-Days of stopped,

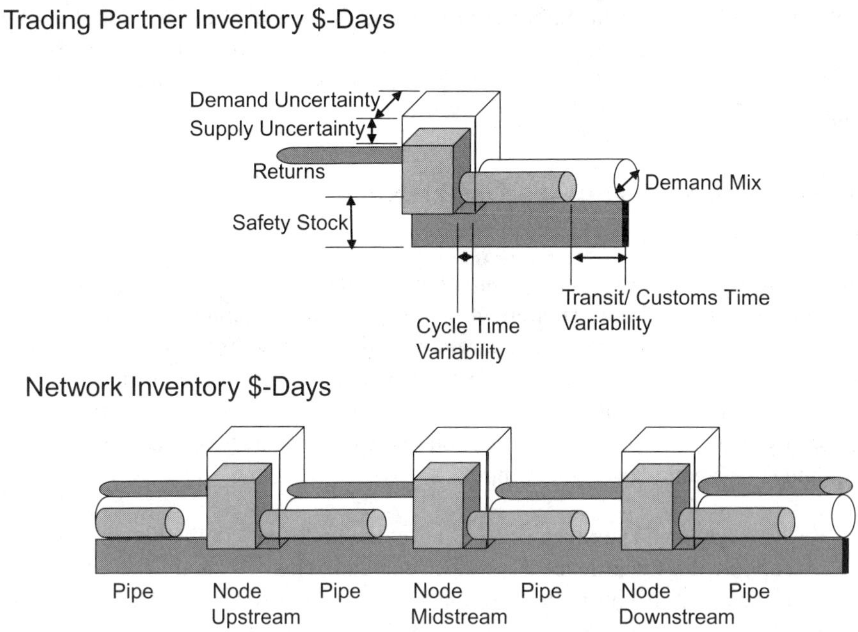

FIGURE 7-10 Inventory $-days model.

in-buffer inventory. The pipelines contain $-Days of moving, in-transit inventory and $-Days of stopped, in-warehouse and in-customs inventory.

Figure 7-10 is a model of the inventory $-Days being swept through the network. Ideally, rectangular-shaped volumes represent the network nodes while pipe-shaped volumes represent the network logistics. Practically, the picture is much more complex. The node volumes are a little higher and a little wider due to supply and demand uncertainty. The node volumes are also a little longer due to cycle time variability. The pipelines are a little longer due to transit time and customs clearance time variability. The pipelines are also a little fatter due to supply and demand uncertainty. Inventory returns flow through additional smaller pipelines extended from the inbound side of each node. Finally, the whole network rides on top of a fin of safety stock inventory.

$-Days of Total Network Inventory =
The sum of the $-Days of moving in-process node inventory +
The sum of the $-Days of stopped in-buffer node inventory +
The sum of the $-Days of moving in-transit pipeline inventory +
The sum of the $-Days of stopped in-warehouse and in-customs pipeline inventory

The $-Days can be summed over just one product or over all products. When the supply chain network is static, the $-Days of inventory are computed in a consistent fashion for all customer orders. When the supply chain network is switched, the $-Days of inventory are related to the specific network configuration for groups of customer orders. When the supply chain network is chaotic, the $-Days of inventory are related to the different specific network configuration for each customer order.

The Impact of Variability and Uncertainty on Total Network Inventory

The inventory $-Days in a network are always higher than that necessary to support the demanded throughput. This effect on total network inventory is caused by the five primary drivers and three secondary drivers listed below. Total network inventory is best managed by having the visibility to allocate actual network inventory between demand-based throughput and these other factors. The smaller the uncertainty and variability in a network, the closer the total network inventory approaches only that required for demand-based throughput.

- *Throughput*—The inventory $-Days at the nodes and in the pipelines that support the mean level of product demand. This is exactly the quantity of physical inventory delivered as product to customers.
- *Demand uncertainty*—The inventory $-Days in the network driven by the uncertainty in quantity, mix, and timing of the individual product demands.
- *Transit time variability*—The inventory $-Days in the network driven by variability in warehousing, transportation, and customs clearance times within the logistics connections.
- *Cycle time variability*—The inventory $-Days in the network driven by the variability in queuing times, manufacturing cycle times, and distribution cycle times within the network nodes.
- *Supply uncertainty*—The inventory $-Days in the network as a hedge against the lead time or yield uncertainty of suppliers.
- *Secondary factors that expand inventory*—Upstream minimum buy policies and midstream lifetime buy situations artificially expand inventory $-Days.
- *Secondary factors that distort inventory*—Manufacturer price increases, distributor price protection policies, and retail price markdowns distort inventory $-Days.
- *Secondary factors that contract inventory*—Downstream "inventory rot" including shelf life and product lifetime issues plus midstream inventory obsolescence contract inventory $-Days.

Returning to the network description and demand analysis of the six SKUs in Table 7-10, the following example summarizes the practical application of using the composite BOM and inventory $-Days as a performance measure to gain visibility over the total network inventory. Table 7-11 shows the results of combining the individual BOMs of the six products from Table 7-10 into a composite BOM. Ninety supply nodes provide 264 lower-level items that are combined to form the six product SKUs. The 21 unique items at Level 1 are potential candidates for a postponement

TABLE 7-11
The Composite BOM (For the Products in Table 7-10)

BOM Level	Common Items	Unique Items	# Supply Nodes	Manufacturing Cycle Time-Days	Purchasing Lead Time-Days
0.		6-Products	1	3	
1.	9	21	15	6 –> 7	20
2.	36	3	22	5	35 –> 40
3.	176	5	49	8 –> 11	45 –> 60
4.	14-Raw Materials		3		5
	264 Total Lower Level Items		90 Supply Nodes	3 + 7 + 5 + 11 + 60 = 86 Cumulative Days Worst Case	

operation. The 176 common items at Level 3 are candidates for the risk pooling of network safety stock. The longest cumulative BOM path of 86 days is longer than any customer is willing to wait. There is cycle time variability and supply uncertainty.

Table 7-12 is a tabular form of the supply chain network diagram shown in Figure 7-11. Each echelon of the network from the raw material suppliers in Echelon 1

TABLE 7-12
The Supply Chain Network in Tabular Form Showing the Logistics Connections

Supply Chain Echelon	Upstream Suppliers	Midstream Value-Add	Downstream Customers	$ Value of One Unit of Product	# Logistics Connections	Transit Time-Days
E6.-End			325-Customer			
				$220	325	2
E5.			4-Distributor	$220		
				$200	4	3 –> 5
E4.-Constraint		1-BOM L0 + 1-BOM L1		$200 $169	1-Internal	0
				$136+ $18+ $15	3 19 14	5 10 6
E3.	14-Suppliers 19-Suppliers	3-BOM L2		$136		
				$58+ $68	2 47	5 18 –> 25
E2.-Imports	2-BOM L3+ 47-Suppliers			$58		
				$50	3	3
E1.-End	0-BOM L4 + 3-Raw Mat'l					
			Total Logistics Connections		417	

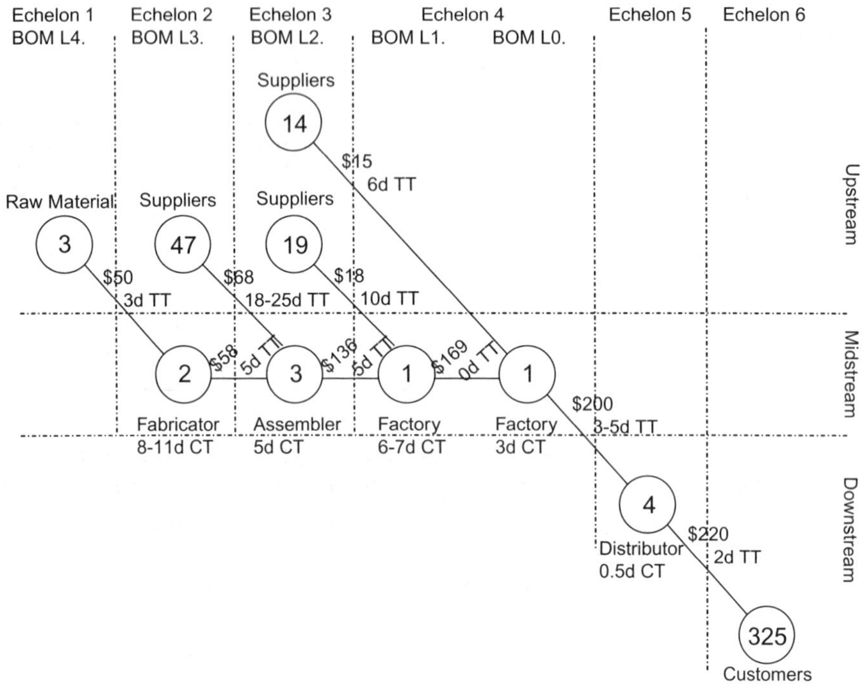

FIGURE 7-11 Supply chain network diagram.

to the end-customers in Echelon 6 is a row in the table. Notice that BOM Level 0 is combined in the same echelon with BOM Level 1 because both levels are built at the same factory; no transit time is assigned to this connection. The rows alternating between the echelon rows detail the number of logistic connections and the transit times plus customs clearance times in days. A total of 417 logistic connections are in this network. The 325 industrial customers in Echelon 6 get their orders filled by the 4 master distributors in Echelon 5. The factory in Echelon 4 is the system constraint. Imported items consumed in Echelon 3 pass through U.S. Customs on their way from Echelon 2 Asian suppliers. There are three raw material suppliers in Echelon 1. The dollar value of the product builds from a raw material value of $50 in the upstream pipeline between Echelon 1 and Echelon 2 to a product value of $220 in the downstream pipeline between the Echelon 5 master distributor and the Echelon 6 end-customer. Items cycling through a node are valued at their exit value going into the outbound pipeline to simplify the analysis.

The mean annual revenue of this network is (214 mean units/day)(250 working days/year)($220 cost of goods sold to the customer)(1.667 for a 60% cost of goods sold) = 19.6M$. A mean total of 53,500 units across the 6 SKUs will be built in a year's time. Table 7-13 details the 6,522 $-Days of inventory sweep for one unit of the composite BOM to move end-to-end through the Figure 7-11 network. Inventory $-Days are the greatest for items with long cycle times or long transit times and for

TABLE 7-13
Inventory $-Days to Sweep One Unit of the Composite BOM Through the Network

Supply Chain Echelon	Node Buffer	Node In-Process	Pipeline In-Transit	Pipeline Buffer	Throughput Mean $-Days
E6.-Customer					
			2 days × $220		440 $-Days
E5.-Distributor		0.5 days × $220			110 $-Days
			3 days × $200		600 $-Days
E4.-BOM L0		3 days × $200			600 $-Days
BOM L1		6 days × $169			1,014 $-Days
			5 days × $136		680 $-Days
			10 days × $18		180 $-Days
			6 days × $15		90 $-Days
E3.-BOM L2		5 days × $136			680 $-Days
			5 days × $58		290 $-Days
			18 days × $68		1,224 $-Days
E2.-BOM L3		8 days × $58			464 $-Days
			3 days × $50		150 $-Days
E1.-BOM L4 Raw Mat'l					
				Total Sweep	6,522 $-Days

items of high value. This suggests managing the combination of a long cycle time or long transit time with a high value item.

The competition takes 12 days to deliver a similar product. If customer orders can be placed and processed in 0.1 days and if the distributor can receive, stock, and ship SKUs in 0.5 days, then the push/pull boundary is between BOM Level 0 and BOM level 1 within Echelon 4. Order time (0.1 day) plus cycle time completion (0.5 days distribute + 3 days manufacture) plus transit time (2 days + 5 days) equals 10.6 days, which is less than the competitive delivery of 12 days. Notice that the 10.6-day order-to-delivery cycle time is much less than the 86-day cumulative lead-time.

The customer-facing distributor maintains a 6-day shipping buffer. The BOM Level 0 factory is the network constraint; therefore, the push/pull boundary doubles as the constraint buffer. The uncertainty of international supply due to 15 days of purchasing lead-time variability and 7 days of transit time and customs clearance time variability is buffered with safety stock held in Echelon 3. Table 7-14 details the extra inventory $-Days caused by demand and supply uncertainty plus cycle time and transit time variability in this network.

Using Network Visibility to Reduce Total Network Inventory

Table 7-15 shows how the total network inventory of 22,893 $-Days splits between inventory held to support throughput at the mean and extra inventory held to protect

TABLE 7-14
Extra Network Inventory for a 99.7% Service Level of One Unit of the Composite BOM

Supply Chain Echelon	Node Buffer	Node In-Process	Pipeline In-Transit	Pipeline Buffer	$-Days
E6.-Customer	Demand Uncertainty—full sweeps for equivalent number of units (6,522 $-Days)(3 std dev)(113.6 units RMS)/(214 units mean)				10,386 $-Days
E5.-Distributor				(3) 2d × $220 Shipping Buffer	1,320 $-Days In the Warehouse
			(3) 2d × $200 TT Variability		1,200 $-Days In the Pipeline
E4.-BOM L0 BOM L1	(3) 6 days × $169 Constraint Buffer Push/Pull Boundary	(3) 1 day × $169 CT Variability			3,042 $-Days At the Node 507 $-Days At the Node
E3.-BOM L2	(3) 22 days × $68 Uncertain Supply Risk Pooling				4,488 $-Days In the Stockroom
			(3) 7 days × $68 TT Variability		1,428 $-Days In the Pipeline
E2.-BOM L3		(3) 3 days × $58 CT Variability			522 $-Days At the Node
E1.-BOM L4 Raw Mat'l					
				Total Extra	22,893 $-Days

against various uncertainties and variabilities. Shipping buffer $-Days are included in demand uncertainty $-Days. Push/pull boundary $-Days are included in supply uncertainty $-Days. Opportunities for network inventory reduction can be prioritized by studying the location of inventory from Table 7-14 and the Pareto order of excess inventory shown in Table 7-15.

TABLE 7-15
Total Network Inventory Drivers and Opportunitie 7s

Network Inventory Driver	Inventory $-Days		Greatest Opportunity for Network Inventory Reduction
Throughput at the Mean	6,522	22.2%	
Demand Uncertainty	11,706	39.8%	SKU-C and SKU-A
Supply Uncertainty	7,530	25.6%	Echelon 2 Suppliers
Transit Time Variability	2,628	8.9%	BOM Level 3 Purchased Internationally
Cycle Time Variability	1,029	3.5%	Echelon 2 Fabricator
	29,415	100.0%	Total Network Inventory

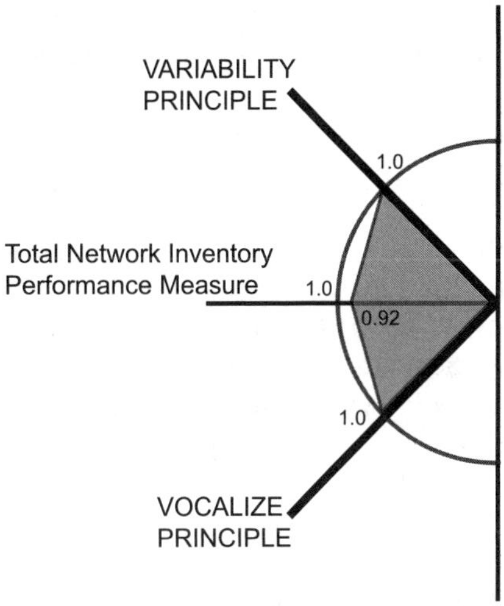

FIGURE 7-12 Total network inventory reduction.

The ratio of $-Days actually in the network to the $-Days required to sustain the mean throughput of the composite BOM is a key performance indicator.

$$\frac{\text{Operating Total Network Inventory}}{\text{Baseline Network}} = \frac{\text{Actual Inventory \$-Days}}{\text{Throughput Inventory \$-Days}}$$

For the inventory $-Days to sweep one unit of the composite BOM end-to-end through the network plus the incremental inventory $-Days driven by network uncertainty and variability. Total network inventory decreases toward the origin of the value circle.

Competitive improvement in total network inventory is plotted on the value circle. In this example, 1.0 on the total network inventory axis equates to a (29,415/6,522) = 4.51 operating to throughput ratio. Suppose 2,400 $-Days can be taken out of the 10,386 $-Days of demand uncertainty shown in Table 7-14 through regular communications with the top customers for SKU C. The total network inventory decreases to (29,415 – 2,400) = 27,015 $-Days with a (27,015/6,522) = 4.14 operating to throughput ratio. This improvement plots on the value circle as (4.14/4.51) = 0.92, as shown in Figure 7-12.

Driving Inventory Out of a Network

Inventory reduction is driven through the reduction of demand and supply uncertainty and the reduction of cycle time, transit time, and customs clearance time variability. Consider each of the following before starting an inventory reduction program:

- *Shorten the supply chain network*—Shorten the network by flattening the BOM and rationalizing the distribution channels to minimize the total number of end-to-end echelons. Shrink the network width by consolidating the total number of unique suppliers and consolidating distribution warehouses.

- *Properly locate the push/pull boundary*—Undercut the competition's order-to-delivery cycle time. Strive for reliable and predictable delivery every time. Strive for the perfect order, with the right product delivered complete and to the right place at the right time with the right invoice with no returns and with no hassle for the end-customer.
- *Reengineering the BOM to optimize risk pooling*—Pull common lower-level materials to the same BOM level across SKUs. Locate safety stock strategically upstream to risk pool across individual products.
- *Reengineer the BOM to optimize postponement*—Pull unique upper-level materials to the same BOM level across end products. Use postponement to complete SKUs to customer demand.
- *Establish $-Day performance measures for each node and pipeline in the network*—Agree to consistent definitions and measurement intervals among trading partners. Make one person responsible for the total network inventory performance measure. Give full visibility to each trading partner.
- *Establish the right customer service level*—A service level of 99.7% requires three standard deviations of coverage; a service level of 95.4% requires two standard deviations of coverage.
- *Identify and eliminate demand and supply uncertainty*—Measure the mean and the standard deviation of product demand and purchasing lead times. Determine uncertainty, prioritize the opportunity, and identify the root cause.
- *Identify and eliminate transit time, customs clearance time, and cycle time variability*—Measure the mean and the standard deviation of logistic transit times, customs clearance times, and manufacturing cycle times. Determine variability, prioritize the opportunity, and identify the root cause.
- *Trade information for inventory*—Get close to the actual order before committing to any inventory. Use technologies, like bar coding, Radio Frequency IDentification (RFID) and Supply Chain Event Management (SCEM), to enable postponement, merge-in-transit, and cross docking strategies.
- *Identify and eliminate stopped information flow that amplifies inventory*—Follow a complete, closed path to look for any unnecessary amplification of inventory caused by information delay. Optimize each interface where a material flow or an information flow crosses a trading partner boundary.
- *Identify and eliminate stopped information flow that amplifies cash*—Follow a complete, closed path to look for any unnecessary amplification of cash caused by information delay. Optimize each interface where a cash flow or an information flow crosses a trading partner boundary.
- *Prioritize opportunities to improve forecasting*—Improvement in forecast error can reduce demand uncertainty. Go after the biggest opportunity. Segment products into stable products and volatile products based on the ratio of standard deviation divided by mean demand.

Percent of the Network Visualized

Like the vocalize principle, adoption of the visualize principle begins with the trading partners and should include strategic nominal trading partners. This is because it takes an investment to participate in defining and implementing a set of global performance measures like equivalent throughput and total network inventory. Having visibility of the network constraint and the network inventory buffers is extremely useful as individual trading partners adjust their operations to optimize for end-to-end throughput. You are what you measure. If the new behavior is to maximize throughput to meet actual customer demand, then each of the trading partners needs to have visibility through the right set of global performance measures to behave appropriately.

Adoption of the visualize principle can be simply measured as the percentage of the trading partner nodes collaborating in the full set of global performance measures. In a competitively operated network, 100% of the trading partners will be managing their operations using equivalent throughput as a measure of capacity and \$-Days of inventory as a measure of total network inventory. However, in practice, for a variety of reasons, some of the trading partners and most of the nominal trading partners may not have such visibility. The percent visualized measure is:

$$\frac{\text{\% of Network Visualizing}}{\text{Baseline Network}} = \frac{\begin{array}{c}\text{Actual number of nodes}\\ \text{connected to global performance measures}\end{array}}{\text{Total number of relevant nodes}} \times 100\%$$

Where the term relevant node includes all trading partners plus strategic nominal trading partners essential to the network's material flow.
Visualization improves toward the origin of the value circle.

Table 7-16 uses the network from Figure 7-11 as an example of the improvement in network visualization. The network consists of 94 nodes spread over 5 echelons

TABLE 7-16
Competitive Improvement under the Visualize Principle

	Trading Partner Nodes	Nominal Trading Partner Nodes	Total Relevant Network	Percent Visualized
Relevant Nodes	16 TP/4 echelons	78 NTP	94 nodes/5 echelons	
Before Visualize Optimization				
Equivalent Throughput	6 TP/2 echelons	0 NTP	6 nodes/2 echelons	
Total Network Inventory	6 TP/2 echelons	0 NTP	6 nodes/2 echelons	
Management Dashboard	6 Yes/10-No			6/16 = 37.5%
After Visualize Optimization				
Equivalent Throughput	14 TP/4 echelons	7 NTP	21 nodes/5 echelons	
Total Network Inventory	14 TP/4 echelons	3 NTP	17 nodes/5 echelons	
Management Dashboard	14 Yes/2-No			14/16 = 87.5%

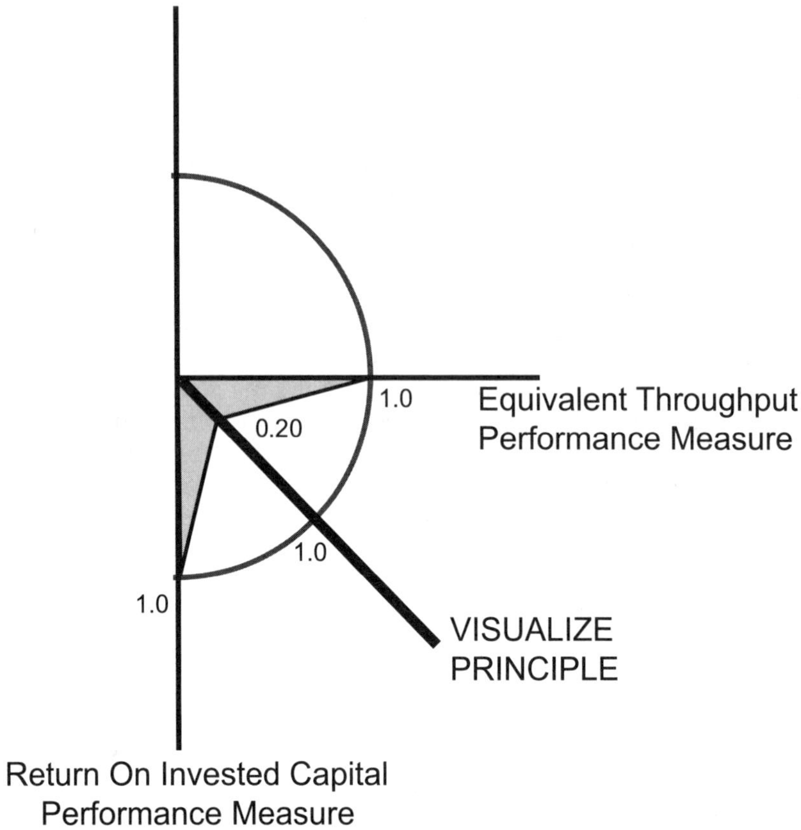

FIGURE 7-13 The percent visualized improves toward the origin.

not counting customer nodes. There are 16 trading partners and 78 nominal trading partners; these are mostly suppliers of lower-level materials. Once again, logistics service providers, information service providers, and financial service providers are not included as nominal trading partners in the total node count. Before the operating optimization only 6 trading partners, or 37.5%, had network capacity and inventory visibility using equivalent throughput and total network inventory as global performance measures.

Figure 7-13 shows how this competitive improvement plots on the value circle. In this example, a baseline of $(6/16) \times 100\% = 37.5\%$ of the relevant nodes are connected leaving $(100\% - 37.5\%) = 62.5$ disconnected, Therefore, 1.0 on the vocalize axis equates to 62.5% disconnected from visualizing. After optimization 14 trading partners are connected to the equivalent throughput and total network inventory performance measures. This raises the percent of the network visualizing to $(14/16) \times 100\% = 8.75\%$ leaving $(100\% - 87.5\%) = 12.5\%$ of the revelant nodes disconnected. The improvement is plotted on the visualize axis as the ratio $(0.125/0.625) = 0.20$, near the value circle's origin.

IN SUMMARY

This Chapter focuses on vocalizing demand among the trading partners and using global performance measures to visualize network capacity and network inventory. The composite BOM, BTS-ATO-BTO modes, push and pull operational zones, the push/pull boundary, synchronization, broadcast demand, the network constraint, and inventory $-Days are all techniques that optimize network operations. The sides are added to the value circle picking up the vocalize principle, the visualize principle, total network inventory, and equivalent throughput. This results in competitive product lead time and availability using less inventory and cash assets. The placement of network inventory and the management of trading partner capacity contribute to the competitiveness of the entire supply chain.

This Chapter raises and answers these fundamental questions:

- How does the BOM product structure integrate with the network operations?
- What determines product lead-time for customers?
- When is a supply chain network capable?
- What constrains the network throughput?
- How is demand communicated upstream?
- What is the optimal placement of inventory in a network?

Chapter 8 moves the discussion of network operations architecture from control to planning. Material inventories and cash "inventories" must be forecast and planned. There are system interactions between velocity and schedule nervousness. There are system interactions between variability and the amplification of network inventory and network cash. Scenarios, risk management, and contingencies surround big deals and volatile products. Network design and the network operations have an intimate influence on each other.

They parked near Saks Fifth Avenue and decided to walk the length of the mall before going to lunch at Legal Seafood. As they window shopped along a string of outrageously expensive boutiques, she said, "That reminds me. There's something I've been meaning to ask you."

The supply chain architect gave his wife a noncommittal glance.

"What? We were going to go eat."

He was preoccupied with when he would tell his wife about his company's announcement.

"It's not about going in that store. I have been wrestling with a new problem at work, and I know you can help me with it."

"Oh, you had me worried. I thought you were going to buy something that we couldn't afford!"

"There's suddenly a lot of new training business out there, but I don't think I'm operating the right way to go after it. Several of my previous clients have called this past week to inquire about training schedules and pricing. Two of them specifically requested customization that would amount to a total revamping of my Basics course. When I asked them what was behind their request, they replied they were anticipating some new government regulation that would require their employees to become certified."

"It is nice to have some satisfied customers and repeat business."

"Yes, that part is great. But what is keeping me awake at night is the sudden realization that my company has neither the capacity to deliver such a new course nor the content inventory from which to customize this course. Why didn't I see this coming?"

"Capacity, inventory—now you're speaking my lingo, kid!"

She continued, "What I need to know from you is whether there is a different operational approach that could make a difference?"

"Why don't you back up and explain to me what you consider to be capacity and inventory in your service business."

"The capacity part is easy. It is just the number of instructors that currently work for me. There are three. Now the inventory part is a little more difficult."

"Hold on a minute. We are not finished talking about capacity. Do all three instructors work a full week? Would any of them work overtime? Do all three instructors work at the same site? Would any of them be willing to drive to a different site in the afternoon? Is there anyone who used to work for you that you could rehire? How long would it take to train the new person? What other kind of capacity is important to your business besides instructional capacity? What about your capacity to develop and test new courseware?"

"Stop! I get it! Capacity is not a simple issue. You're giving me a headache with all those questions."

They paused near the second entrance to Macy's. She gazed beyond the security sensors, past the racks of clothing, toward the men's department. "You need to buy a new tie for your suit."

"Not now. We were having this great conversation about your work."

She sighed, and they walked on down the mall. "Okay, I think I have three kinds of capacity that constrain the amount of business my service company can do. One is instructional capacity. One is courseware development capacity. And one is marketing capacity."

"That's very good. You seem to be successful outsourcing courseware development?"

"Yes, that is true to a degree. However, in the end I'm just leveraging what only I can do. This is a key competitive core competency for my business. You know, come to think of it, I think the real constraint is my capacity to develop new courses. I'm comfortable with other people marketing and teaching my courses."

"Okay, what are your thoughts about defining inventory?" her husband asked.

"We are almost to the restaurant. Let's go in and order, then we can tackle the inventory piece."

They were seated in midst of a noisy crowd. Their center table held a view of both the mirrored back wall and the tinted glass leading into the mall's cavernous interior. She ordered shrimp over linguini with a glass of Mondavi Chardonnay; he ordered Boston scrod and a Pinot Grigio.

"So, here is what I think about my company's inventory," she said finally. "A service company doesn't manufacture a product per se. If we forget about student guides for a minute, there is no material inventory in my business. I used to think, maybe there's no inventory at all. But now I think my inventory is the intellectual property delivered through the content of each instructor slide and the associated pages in the student guide."

He looked at her for a long time. Then he said, "That's really a marvelous model. I would not have thought of it that way. And I think you are right."

"Yes, that is my inventory."

"Let's talk about the fact that there are a couple of different ways you can deliver this inventory to your customer." He had to speak loudly to be heard over the lively conversations at the surrounding tables. "When you build-to-stock, your customer gets a canned product and your instructors can deliver the training immediately. However, when your customer demands in-house customization or a whole new subject matter, you are building-to-order and the customer must wait the lead-time for that courseware to be developed."

"Are those the only two ways to operate—build-to-stock or build-to-order?" she asked.

"No. There is an interesting third way called assemble-to-order that applies here. Under an assemble-to-order scenario, you could take everything you have created so far and group the instructor slides and the corresponding student guide pages by topic on your computer. Then you could quickly customize the sequencing of topics and add some company-specific material when you got a firm customer order to teach. Of course, any totally new material would have to be developed as its own topic segment."

"That's a really interesting suggestion. You're saying that I could outline a new course at any time by mixing and matching pieces of my existing courses. Then it would be a simple matter to pull the slides and pages together from a library with a little new development thrown in for good measure. I like that!"

"The advantage of the assemble-to-order scenario is that the courseware is customized, yet the customer does not have to wait nearly as long as with the build-to-order scenario. Do you want any dessert or should I just get the check?" the supply chain architect asked.

"Of course I want dessert. They have chocolate on the menu!"

He would wait until they were back in the car to tell her about Hector and the move to Singapore.

REFERENCE

1. Noreen, E., D. Smith, and J.T. Mackey (1995), *The Theory Of Constraints and Its Implications For Management Accounting,* Great Barrington, MA: North River Press, 30–31.

8 Planning for Network Operations

Saturday, August 10

It was dark and raining at 5:30 a.m. on Saturday morning. The supply chain architect was driving to work because everyone had been called in for a transition-planning meeting. "Why can't they fit this into our normal work week?" he thought. "This is a real pain!"

As he drove northwest in light traffic, he remembered that his last big conversation a week ago with Tom, the house architect, was also about planning—planning for the first big dinner party they were going to throw now that the kitchen renovation was complete. The party was coming up fast; it was tomorrow night, Sunday. He hoped his wife had remembered to send Tom an invitation. What was it they had been debating so excitedly? Oh yeah…

"It all comes together right here on this very counter top—the yin and the yang, the push and the pull," his wife had said.

"Although that is very poetic, I have no clue what you are talking about."

"Oh, you know. The push is the planning for our open house dinner party, and the pull is the rush for beverage and food once everyone arrives. We are inviting 24 of our closest friends. Tom, you must come!"

"I don't know; even with this spectacular kitchen, 24 sounds like a lot of people?" said the supply chain architect.

"Trust me. It's not a problem. We own place settings and glassware for 24, and we can borrow a couple of folding chairs to be able to seat 24 guests. I'll cook up a storm."

"Just how are you going to plan the food?" He had no idea how this meal would be prepared.

"Let me break it down for you by food group. Tom, see what you think. The salad will be self-served here at the counter. We'll offer both lettuce and spinach salads with lots of different kinds of dressing. People can help themselves and see the new kitchen at the same time. I'll make three different entrees. You can take orders from everyone during cocktails, and I'll cook the entrees to order. My special dessert will be prepared in advance and kept refrigerated until needed."

"That sounds good. I'll handle the beverages. We should offer both wine and beer, with some soft drinks thrown in for good measure. I can buy a couple of cases of beer and some six packs. We can chill one whole case in the refrigerator, and then as the beer is consumed, rotate the chilled bottles to the front and replenish with six packs of warm bottles in the back but what if you buy all this food, and some of our guests can't make the party? Shouldn't we try to forecast who on the list would probably attend? Alice and Jay always say they are going to come, but they rarely attend. And Jim is in the habit of just showing up; it would be like him to show up uninvited."

"Yes, we should do that. The food is really not a problem. Most of what I need to buy at the store will keep for a while. Fresh salad is probably our biggest area of risk, but it is not expensive. As for all the rest, you and I might eat very well for a couple of nights." She started to write a shopping list.

Tom interjected, "Don't forget that you're replenishing the cupboards from scratch. You will also need sundries and spices and cleaning supplies and—"

"Okay! We're all set! This is exciting; I love to plan parties!"

"Wait a minute. Are you sure we have enough cash on hand to buy all this stuff?"

*****

"You shouldn't have to work on a Saturday," thought the supply chain architect as he trudged toward the conference room at the end of the hall. "We just left here a few hours ago."

Roberta Perez, the acting V.P. of manufacturing, wanting to get a jump on Hector Morales' team, had ordered her team back to work for six hours on Saturday.

Hector, already established in Singapore, was filling everyone's e-mail inboxes with requests for information and other work. It seemed as though the guy never slept. Fortunately, it was now Saturday evening in Singapore, and Hector would not be sending any new e-mail for a few hours.

The conference room had been outfitted with white boards and corkboards on opposite sides of the room. The team had painstakingly documented their current U.S.-based supply chain on the left wall, and were in the process of modeling their future U.S.–Singapore supply chain on the right wall. This side-by-side comparison had already proven useful.

The network redesign would not change the way the finished product was distributed to the end-customer. The U.S. manufacturing center had been split into two parts: final assembly done in the U.S. and subassembly done in Singapore. Parts shipments from each sole sourced supplier would be rerouted to Singapore. Hector's team would identify potential local suppliers for the bulk of the material, and purchasing in Singapore would validate these new suppliers. Halfway around the world, Roberta's purchasing team would notify the current supply base that their business was to be terminated. Orders would have to be placed for last time buys.

Roberta entered the room, "Good morning team. You all saw Hector's last message. We both agree that this team's next task is to figure out the changes that are necessary for our operations planning."

"Why can't we just treat Singapore like another supplier in our ERP system?" asked William Smith, the purchasing manager.

"It's a little more complicated than that," replied the architect.

"What do you mean? Oh, you mean because we have a new set of local suppliers in Singapore?"

"It's even more complicated than that. Look, we have to ask whether the new network is capable. Where do we place the inventory buffers? Where do we place the cash buffers? How does the demand seen by our factory and by Singapore differ? Our customers must continue to see the same responsiveness and service level they expected from the old network."

"You said a mouth full," chimed in Daisy Whitehall, sitting down with a simmering cup of coffee. "By the way, the coffee is ready. .It's the least I could do!"

"Let's break this down, starting with the forecast of demand," said Roberta.

The architect interrupted, "Actually, we need to talk about how the BOM splits across the network first. If we keep all the product option manufacture and postponement here, then Singapore only sees dependent demand."

"That might cause us to have two suppliers for the same item: a local supplier for subassembly manufacture in Singapore and a second supplier for postponement inventory in the U.S.," said William.

"Maybe not if we are willing to carry a slightly larger safety stock for some inexpensive postponed materials. Okay, so with the forecast and actual demand still coming to planning and order processing here, and Singapore seeing only dependent demand, the issue becomes how do we communicate this demand with Singapore without introducing serial delay in the planning cycle? We must avoid introducing the bullwhip effect into our network."

"Also, how will the new, local suppliers in Singapore get forecast and demand information?" William wanted to know.

"When the manufacture of the entire product was vertically integrated at our factory, the push/pull boundary was between level 3 and level 4 of the BOM. In the future, with level 3 and level 4 being built in Singapore and a long transit time between the two sites, this site can continue as a pull operation, but Singapore becomes a push operation," offered Larry Holmes, their logistics analyst.

"That's good—and also bad. It's a really important observation that we should capture on the whiteboard. But it's a problem because it means more total inventory in the network and a less responsive supply chain overall," said the architect.

"What if we run all of our requirements and all of Singapore's requirements together on one ERP system?" asked William. "If we worked with the information technology folks to give both sites access to the same system, there would only be the twelve hours of worldwide time difference between the planning teams and not the delay of a complete planning cycle."

"That idea seems to have a lot of merit," said Roberta. "I'll work with Hector to see whether we can get some IT resources assigned. Our team is making good progress this morning. Maybe we should have more Saturday morning meetings when we are not so distracted?"

"Yeah, whatever. The next issue is the question of whether the future network is still capable. Several important new constraints have entered the network, such as Singapore subassembly manufacture, new local Singapore suppliers, and the logistics connections back to the United States. We need to identify and possibly elevate the network constraint," said the supply chain architect. "We will need to collect some information from Hector's team, and Larry will prepare a trade-off analysis of airfreight versus ocean freight out of Singapore."

"I've already started collecting uplift capacity, container cost, and transit time information from our two largest freight forwarders," said Larry.

"You may want to request information from some other global 3PL's who run significant volumes between Singapore and the West Coast. Don't forget we will need a small reverse logistics capability," said Roberta.

"Last for this morning, we need to update our planning tools and spreadsheets with the new inventory buffer locations and the new cash buffer locations. Dana Hoffmann, our CFO, and Ray Smith, from Cost Accounting, should be present for this part of the discussion. We need to be intentional about placing and managing a few critical inventory buffers while forcing any other inventory buffers to zero. That will be hard to influence half a world away with our cultural differences."

"It's coming up on noon," said Roberta. "How about if I have some pizza delivered while you finish documenting all that we have covered this morning? I'd like to fill Hector's inbox for once!"

Chapter 4 detailed the order-to-delivery, order-to-stock, invoice-to-pay, and invoice-to-cash subcycles that connect the trading partners. This Chapter explains the role of planning in the competitive operation of a supply chain network. Although much is written about forecasting and planning for inventory, this book advances the need to forecast and plan both inventory and cash. Running out of either can slow network throughput. Much is also written about machine and transport capacity constraints for the material flow. This book promotes the idea that each subcycle has a material flow constraint, an information flow constraint, or a cash flow constraint. One of these constraints for one of the trading partner subcycles will be so severe as to become the overall network constraint. Chapter 7 describes network operations from the perspective of integrating the BOM with the network; this Chapter describes network operations from the perspective of matching the patterns of supply and demand.

SETTING A NETWORK CONTEXT FOR PLANNING

It is easy to work out the operations of a static network running repetitive order-to-delivery-to-cash cycles. The trading partners never change, and there is a constant rhythm of business. When orders are taken out of such a system, the repetition rate of the operation slows down until there is a significant time gap between consecutive orders. Under this scenario, the completion of each order appears to be an independent event with its own lifecycle. Going one step further, consider the scenario where each of these independent orders is processed through a chaotic network where the set of trading partners changes for every order. Now the execution of the processes that complete the order-to-delivery-to-cash cycle must be perfect. Waste and imperfection can no longer be hidden when a chaotic, nonrepetitive network is unable to complete a single customer order. The operation of a value-adding, competitive network is focused on achieving the highest velocity, lowest variability order-to-delivery-to-cash cycle completion while maximizing the vocalizing and visualizing among its trading partners to match supply and demand. This is true whether orders are continuous, seasonal, or one-time demand and whether the network configuration is static, switched, or chaotic.

Basic Network Operations

Consider a supply chain network that is operating in the midst of a repetitive order-to-delivery-to-cash cycle. At the start of each cycle, when the next new order is received, all but the customer-facing trading partners are holding inventory, and all but the supplier-facing trading partners are holding cash. Time T1 in Figure 8-1 shows the initial state of inventory and cash in a three-echelon network. In order to complete the order-to-delivery-to-cash cycle, inventory must flow downstream to the end-customer with transformation, manufacture, and fulfillment occurring along the way. At the same time, cash must flow upstream to the raw material supplier in exchange for each value-adding operation. Time T4 in Figure 8-1 shows the final

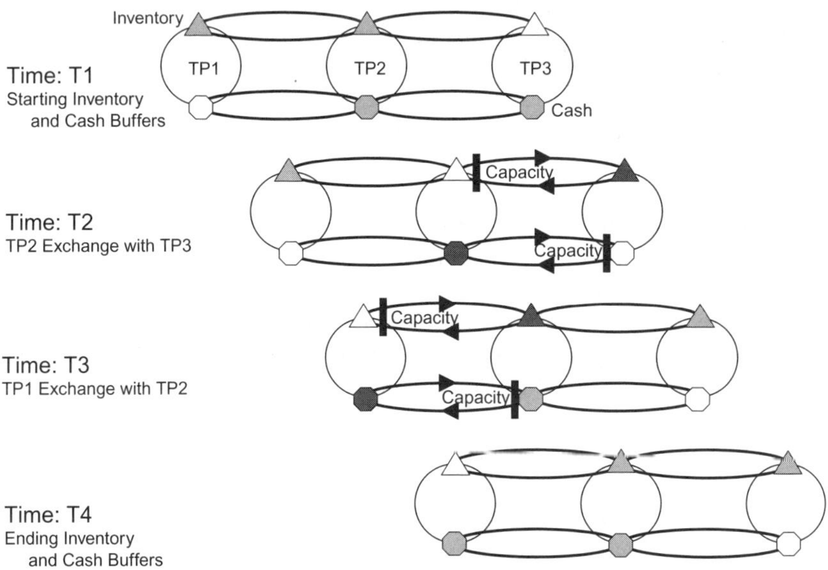

FIGURE 8-1 The network exchange of inventory for cash.

state of the network. The trading partner's physical inventory balances and cash balances are the linchpins that keep a supply chain network operational.

There are two kinds of operational events that can prevent the end-to-end exchange of inventory for cash. The first is that one of the trading partners exhausts either its inventory buffer or its cash buffer. This would cause a serious disconnect in one of the subcycles, halting its flow and disrupting operations. The planning methods described in this Chapter are to ensure that network inventory buffers and cash buffers are never completely exhausted. The second is that the flows through each of the subcycles are constrained and that one of these constrained flows is the network constraint. It is important to understand that the subcycle constraint is not limited to a material flow constraint, but may also be an information flow constraint or a cash flow constraint. The planning methods described in this Chapter ensure that the network constraint is a material flow constraint.

Matching the Pattern of Demand and Supply

Product demand drives the operation of any supply chain network. This demand has many attributes including its rate, mix, and the timing of its life cycle. With multiple SKUs flowing through a supply chain, the demand rate is the total or aggregated demand across all the SKUs and the demand mix is the percentage split of each SKU to the total. For example, with a daily demand of 25 units/day of SKU-A, 16 units/day of SKU-B, and 31 units/day of SKU-C, the demand rate is 72 units/day and the demand mix is 34.7% for SKU-A, 22.2% for SKU-B, and 43.1% for SKU-C. When there are thousands of SKUs in a network, the demand mix can be put into descending order from the largest unit demand to the smallest unit demand (C-A-B in the example) to determine which material flows are the most significant.

It is natural to think about customer demand in deterministic terms, that is, exactly 25 cases of beer. However, market demand is best described as a probability, that is, a mean of 24 cases of beer with a standard deviation of 3 cases. It is always best to describe demand as a range of customer orders. This is particularly important when supplying product for seasonal and promotional demand patterns. The following are basic patterns of demand:

- *Continuous demand*—A number of customers order a similar mix of products all the time. For example, food staples like bread, cereal, and orange juice sell year round.
- *Seasonal demand*—The rate of customers ordering specific products varies significantly depending on the calendar. For example, women's and men's fashions by color and fabric are highly seasonal.
- *Promotional demand*—The rate of customer orders is artificially inflated by using advertising, coupons, or rebates to increase demand for a particular product. For example, car dealerships heavily promote end-of-the-year sales to clear last year's car models out of inventory.
- *One-time demand*—A single customer places a single order. This is the predominant demand pattern in an engineer-to-order (ETO) business, and requires a project planning approach.

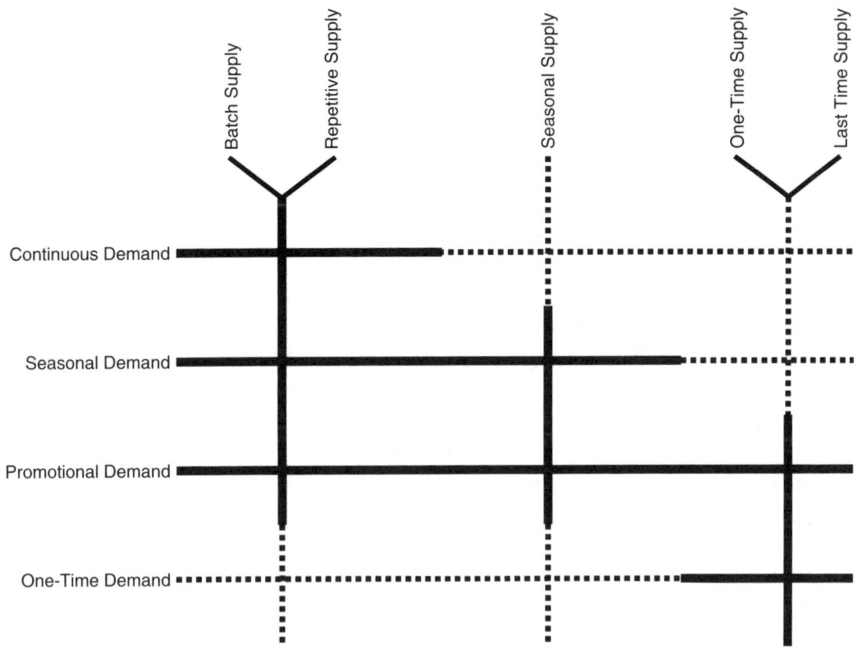

FIGURE 8-2 Matching supply and demand.

If your network cannot deliver, then a competitor's can. Customer expectations run high especially when the competition is responsive. For example, a business was wrestling with the implementation of a distribution network design that could deliver product to customers in the London suburbs within a period of three days. The development team was completely demoralized when they learned that a competitor routinely put product into a London taxi and had it delivered to the customer inside of three hours! The first cut at achieving customer satisfaction is to match the pattern of demand with the pattern of supply, see Figure 8-2. Clearly, it would be inappropriate to try to meet continuous customer demand with a one-time supply. It would also be inappropriate to try to meet a seasonal demand with a repetitive supply. The following are basic patterns of supply:

- *Flow supply*—Supply flows continuously until all the raw materials are consumed. For example, a rail car of liquid chemical is continuously processed until the tank is empty.
- *Batch supply*—Supply is continuous until the batch is consumed. For example, a hardware manufacturer sets up and runs its screw machine until the batch of bar stock is consumed.
- *Repetitive supply*—The supply follows an unbroken rhythm or repetition. For example, a fill line injects powder into a container once every four seconds.
- *Seasonal supply*—The timing of supply is tied to a season. For example, rice is harvested three times per year in China. Christmas trees are cut and transported once a year from Canada.

- *One-time supply*—The supply is available once. For example, a purchase for an engineer-to-order project must be large enough to supply the entire life cycle of product demand plus spares.
- *Last time supply*—The supply is available one last time. For example, a semiconductor wafer fabricator produces one last batch of a microprocessor chip before the process is dismantled.

Demand Distortion and the Bullwhip Effect

Demand distortion is a fundamental issue in the operation of a supply chain. The symptoms of demand distortion are most easily seen midstream and upstream by observing that individual trading partners struggle with either a glut of inventory or a work stoppage caused by a lack of orders in their echelon. These trading partners assume that end-customers have radically changed their demand patterns, but this is not always the case. In the 1960s Jay Forrester developed the discipline of System Dynamics at the Massachusetts Institute of Technology. His early work led to a popular simulation called the Beer Game. In the Beer Game, a retailer, a wholesaler, and a brewery form a supply-chain network to deliver a single product: beer. Peter Senge, in his book *The Fifth Discipline: The Art & Practice of The Learning Organization* (1990), describes how the game is played with the retailer withholding customer demand information from the wholesaler and the wholesaler withholding retailer demand information from the brewery. Interpreted demand is relayed serially upstream while there are fixed logistic delays as the beer is transported downstream. Regardless of how smart the players may be, the network exhibits both excess inventories and unexpected shortages after a short period of play. This network behavior later became known as the *bullwhip effect* from the work of Hau Lee and others at Stanford University.

Closing the loop around a multiechelon network causes that network to oscillate. This is because the demand is communicated serially while moving upstream, and the logistic delays accumulate while moving downstream, resulting in enough phase shift for positive feedback. A small change in end user demand is amplified out of proportion until the supply oscillates at one of the upstream nodes between excess inventory and out of stock conditions. Under the bullwhip effect, this trading partner is never able to reach supply equilibrium. The bullwhip effect is defeated by broadcasting demand information in parallel and by synchronizing network operations to end the accumulation of logistics delays.

Exchange Curves

Although demand is mostly about price and delivery, supply is all about inventory and service levels. The service level for product pulled from stock is expressed as a percentage of the number of times the product is found in stock versus the number of attempts. For example, if product is found in stock 93 times out of 100 attempts, the service level is 93%. The service level for product yet to be built is expressed as a percentage of the number of times the first delivery date is met versus the number of attempts. For example, if product is delivered on the first delivery date 93 times out of 100, the service level is 93%.

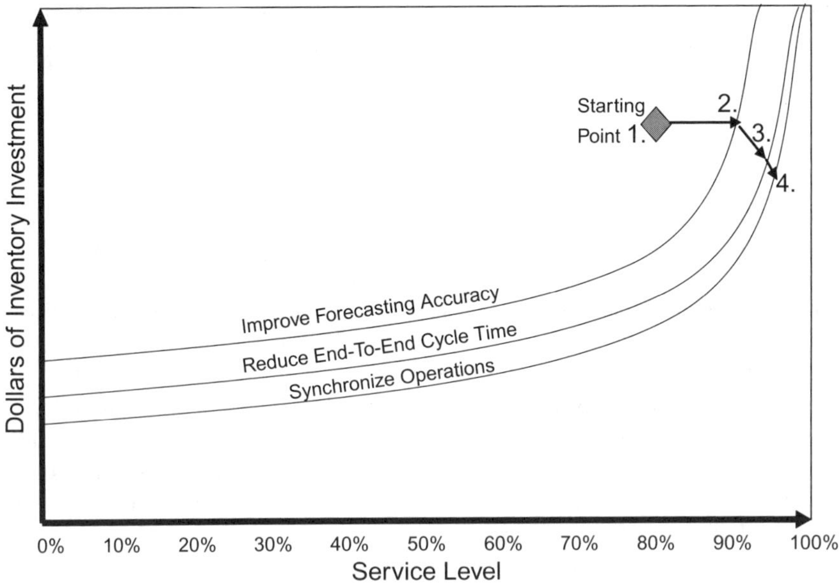

FIGURE 8-3 The exchange curve relates inventory investment to service level.

An exchange curve is used to show the relationship between inventory investment and the service level, see Figure 8-3. The dollars of inventory investment are shown on the y-axis and the percent service level is shown on the x-axis. Exchange curves are asymptotic in shape, meaning that the inventory investment goes to infinity before the service level reaches 100%. Even with a staggering level of inventory investment, the service level will not be perfect. There is often more than enough total inventory in the network, but this inventory is either of the wrong mix or in the wrong location.

It is difficult to plot an actual exchange curve because the equation that generates the curve requires knowing a precise value for inventory holding cost. The truth is that inventory holding cost is dynamic. The methods to improve an exchange curve in a relative sense are more relevant. Start by measuring the current dollars of inventory investment and the current percentage service level, shown as Point 1 on Figure 8-3. This starting point, more often than not, lies above the exchange curve line.

Two types of actions can improve the situation. First, the current operating point can be brought onto the exchange curve. Second, the entire exchange curve can be shifted down and to the right to achieve a better service level with less inventory investment. Improving forecast accuracy moves the current operating point closer to the current exchange curve, shown as Point 2 on Figure 8-3. Reducing network cycle time, Point 3, and going to a synchronized operation, Point 4, both shift the entire exchange curve down and to the right. The service level goes up while the inventory investment goes down because of essentially trading better, more timely demand information for inventory. Measure the change in dollars of inventory investment and the change in percentage service level after each successive improvement in forecast accuracy, cycle time reduction, and synchronized operations. A smaller inventory also means a smaller accounts payable that in turn strengthens the working capital position.

NETWORK OPERATIONS COMPLEXITY

This section is a buildup of the layers of complexity that lie just below the surface of most network operational planning. The starting point is the network in a continuously repetitive state. Demand and supply are level, forecast error is low, the network is capable, there is data accuracy throughout the network, the bullwhip effect is under control, and inventory and cash buffers are each replenished in a timely manner. Complexity is introduced in the form of mix changes and product life cycles such as ramp-ups for new product introductions or promotions and ramp-downs for product obsolescence or discontinuance. Next is the issue that some trading partners are simultaneously operating in multiple competing supply chain networks that confuse the planning rules. Likewise, a preponderance of nominal trading partners can dilute the network orchestrator's centralized planning. Finally, this section considers the added network complexity for acquisitions, insourcing, outsourcing, transfers, and divestitures. Here, demand and supply have no relationship; forecast error is high, with organizations forecasting the wrong things; some data inaccuracies exist in the network; the network is no longer capable; and the bullwhip effect is rampant, with inventory and cash buffers out of stock and out of cash.

Constant, Repetitive Demand as the Planning Baseline

The objective of planning is to fill and/or replenish the inventory buffers and the cash buffers in a network while maximizing the order-to-delivery-to-cash velocity. When the network operates in a BTS mode, the inventory and cash buffers are replenished in time to maintain competitive availability for the customer. However, this is not just a question of overstocking every buffer with lots of inventory and cash. Networks have limited resources and must be capable and profitable at the same time. When the network operates in a BTO mode, the inventory and cash buffers are filled just in time to achieve a competitive availability for the customer.

The filling and replenishing of the buffers is deceptively simple. For each inventory buffer:

Ending inventory = starting inventory + inventory receipts − inventory issues

In units or in dollars, where the level of inventory cannot be zero at the time of an issue.

And, for each cash buffer:

Ending cash = starting cash + cash receipt − cash payment

In dollars, where the level of cash must never be allowed to fall to zero.

TABLE 8-1
Linked Network Inventories

	Supplier	Upstream Trade Partner$_1$	Midstream Trade Partner$_2$	Downstream Trade Partner$_3$	Customer
Starting Inventory		Starting Inventory$_1$	Starting Inventory$_2$	Starting Inventory$_3$	
+Receipts		#Units = A	#Units = B	#Units = C	#Units = D
–Issues	#Units = A	#Units = B	#Units = C	#Units = D	
Ending Inventory		Ending Inventory$_1$	Ending Inventory$_2$	Ending Inventory$_3$	
Starting Cash		Starting Cash$_1$	Starting Cash$_2$	Starting Cash$_3$	
+Receipts	#Dollars = Z	#Dollars = Y	#Dollars = X	#Dollars = W	
–Payments		#Dollars = Z	#Dollars = Y	#Dollars = X	#Dollars = W
Ending Cash > 0		Ending Cash$_1$ > 0	Ending Cash$_2$ > 0	Ending Cash$_3$ > 0	

When these buffers are linked from end-to-end across a supply chain network, the issue out of one buffer becomes the receipt into the adjacent buffer, see Table 8-1. For the material flow, the supplier's issue A flows to become the customer's receipt D. The actual number of units that flow through linkages A, B, C, and D are related through the BOM equivalency. The starting and ending inventory balances for one trading partner are independent of the starting and ending inventory balances for any other trading partner. These inventory balances can float high or low, but they must cover their respective issues in the timeframe that propagates the material flow. For the cash flow, the customer's payment W flows to become the supplier's receipt Z. The actual number of dollars flowing through linkages W, X, Y, and Z are related through the bill of cash for each trading partner. The starting and ending cash balances for one trading partner are independent of the starting and ending cash balances for any other trading partner. Cash balances can float high or low, but they must never be zero.

Plan inventory in units and only convert to dollars for managerial and legal reporting. When inventory levels are planned in dollars, the planner will experience some nasty surprises while trying to reconcile cost, price, and quantity numbers, for example:

- *Volume discounts in purchased inventory*—The standard cost for inventory is based on a unit volume assumption. When the number of units purchased is less, the actual purchase cost is higher. When the number of units purchased is more, the actual purchase cost is lower.
- *Cost accounting for manufacturing inventory*—Starting inventory at standard cost plus receipts at material cost minus issues at material, labor, and overhead cost equal ending inventory at standard.

- *Price change in distributed inventory*—Organizations periodically reprice their finished goods inventory. The number of units in inventory immediately before and immediately after a price increase is the same, but the dollar value of the inventory suddenly has a step discontinuity that ripples through all the planning tables.
- *Price protection in distribution inventory*—Old finished goods inventory is retained in stock for 30 days or 60 days valued at the old price, whereas new finished goods inventory of the same SKU is held in stock valued at the new price.

When demand is constant and repetitive, it is easy to plan. Next week is the same as this week. The capacity for a capable network is set equal to the mean of the demand; the standard deviation of demand is nearly zero. The inventory buffers and cash buffers are lowered to levels just above that required for constant flow. Notice that the planning process for a network determines how fragile the network operation will be. If a required inventory issue were to exceed its inventory buffer level, if a required cash payment were to exceed its cash buffer level, or if the required throughput were to exceed the capacity of the network, then actual network operations will deviate from the plan. In the extreme case, network operations are disrupted, whereas in the more general case product delivery will be late, causing a reduction in the expected customer service level.

Operating under Dynamic Demand Patterns

Table 8-2 shows that the next degree of planning complexity is operating under a dynamic demand pattern. As the demand pattern becomes more irregular and less repetitive, the network capacity and the buffer levels must be increased to accommodate this dynamic. Sometimes the demand dynamic originates with the buyer, such as a subtle change in product mix or a seasonality in buying. Other times the demand dynamic originates with the seller, such as an undiscovered bias in forecasting or a product promotion.

As the rate and mix of customer demand varies from period to period, the standard deviation about the mean grows from near zero to some significance. Once the ratio of the mean to the standard deviation exceeds one, the demand pattern is quite volatile and hard to predict. Operations planning for peak inventory and peak cash in the buffers now has to account not only for the mean but also for the multiplier of the RMS standard deviation that equates to the desired customer service level.

The effect of seasonal demand drives the mean demand up and down from season to season. The variation in the highs and lows of the mean demand and the variations of the starting and ending times for each season add a second order component to the standard deviation about the mean. Forecasting the seasonal demand for items such as snow blowers or Christmas trees is extremely risky. A single order is planned months in advance, whereas other extenuating circumstances such as the weather, freshness, and competitive pricing influence any buying decision. In the textile/apparel industry there may be six to eight fashion seasons a year with each one based on a risky assessment of fashion trends and people's desire to change their dress with the season.

TABLE 8-2
Degrees of Planning Complexity

Degree of Complexity	Planning Dynamic	Central Planning Issue
1	Continuously repetitive demand	The planning baseline
2	Demand mix change Demand seasonality Forecast bias Marketing promotions Product life cycle inflection points	Operating under dynamic demand patterns
3	Simultaneous operation in competing networks Preponderance of nominal trading partners	Operating with different sets of planning rules causes a lack of focus.
4	Switched networks Chaotic networks	Operating with discontinuities in the network configuration
5	Acquisition, insourcing Outsourcing, disintermediation, divestiture New product introduction	Operating while integrating and disintegrating different product lines and different information systems

Product promotions are a way of creating artificial demand and often of creating havoc on the supply side. Specific SKUs are marked down on the rack or given a price discount at the cash register when the customer presents a coupon. The reality is that these SKUs are often excess inventory or inventory that needs to be cleared to make rack space and shelf space for the next season or for a new product introduction. Promotions cause havoc when they are conducted by the marketing and sales organization without collaboration with each trading partner's planning organization. Upstream planners see a significantly changing demand pattern, and they make every effort to replenish the exact items the store is trying to eliminate! Adding insult to injury, this unwanted replenishment inventory is usually manufactured at a cost premium and transported using premium logistics. The standard deviation about the mean for promotional SKUs is volatile in a way that is unrelated to real customer demand behavior.

Each SKU has a unique life cycle from introduction to maturity to obsolescence. When the individual demands for all the SKUs in a network are aggregated, the growth and decline of the demand rate is tied to the relative life cycle position of each individual SKU. The inflection points along a product's life cycle cause yet a different dynamic to the demand pattern. One inflection point occurs when the steep ramp of new product demand flattens out into the more constant rate of mature demand. A second inflection point occurs when mature demand starts to decline toward obsolescence and ultimate discontinuance. The standard deviation about the mean grows significantly higher near the timeframe of each inflection point. When the ramp-up of a new product aligns in its timing with the decline of an existing product,

TABLE 8-3
Flat Aggregate Demand Masks Significant Change in Individual SKU Demand

In Units	Period 1	Period 2	Period 3	Period 4	Period 5	Period 6
SKU A	100	100	100	100	100	100
SKU B	0	25	50	75	100	100
SKU C	100	75	50	25	0	0
Aggregate	200	200	200	200	200	200

the total demand picture may look flat. However, the aggregate is masking a significant change in demand happening just beneath the surface.

For example, Table 8-3 shows a constant aggregate demand of 200 units per period. However, in just four periods demand for SKU C falls to zero and is replaced by demand for SKU B. When the demand for a mature SKU, which has been responsible for a majority of sales, declines more rapidly toward obsolescence than a recently introduced SKUs demand can grow toward maturity, the aggregate demand rate for the business will decline.

Operating with Different Sets of Planning Rules

One of the most frustrating experiences for a trading partner is to be held accountable to different sets of conflicting planning rules. This comes about in practice for two reasons: First, a middle node may be simultaneously participating as a (nominal) trading partner in a static, switched, or chaotic supply chain network configuration in multiple or even competing supply chain networks. For example, a components supplier might simultaneously sell directly to its largest customer, sell significantly through a distributor network, and sell opportunistically through a reverse auction. In this example, the components supplier is simultaneously a trading partner in a static network, a (nominal) trading partner in a switched network, and a nominal trading partner in a chaotic network.

Second, the preponderance of nominal trading partners in a supply chain network can defocus the planning rules set by the network orchestrator and its trading partners. This is particularly true when nominal trading partners, with other customer priorities, occupy strategic positions in the network or command entire echelons of the network. Suppose a contract manufacturer is a nominal trading partner and the only node in the network echelon between a factory trading partner and a supplier trading partner. This contract manufacturer can cause a discontinuous gap to the demand communication, performance measures, and planning rules set by the network orchestrator. In this example the contract manufacturer relationship should be developed as a strategic nominal trading partner.

The planner must always consider the full context of the product SKU being planned:

- In which echelon is the planner situated within the network?
- How much of the demand is in-network versus out-of-network?
- How much of the supply is in-network versus out-of-network?
- How do the out-of-network planning rules differ from the in-network planning rules?
- Are there any echelon breaks in the way the network vocalizes demand or visualizes throughput?

Operating with Discontinuities in the Supply Chain Network

In a *switched network*, one or more of the trading partners differs depending on the SKU. For example, the lowest price version of a digital voltmeter is designed with a Light Emitting Diode (LED) display, the middle price version has a Liquid Crystal Display (LCD), and the highest price version has a Vacuum Fluorescent (VF) display. Each display comes from a different component supplier. The display portion of the BOM and its associated network are switched depending on the relative demand mix for low price, medium price, and high price digital voltmeters, whereas the rest of the BOM and the network remain static.

In a *chaotic network*, each order-to-delivery-to-cash cycle involves a different set of (nominal) trading partners. This is perhaps most evident when the supply chain network involves a supplier auction. Procurement strategy, driven by intense competitive pressures to remain profitable, has shifted from concentrating purchasing volume with a few preferred suppliers to spot price auctions among many competing suppliers. The sourcing cycle of Request For Information (RFI), Request For Quote (RFQ), reverse auction, bid analysis, and business award is all done electronically. The procurement staff no longer travels to the supplier to interview their management team or to perform an assessment of the quality of their manufacturing process. The procurement relationships are managed through third party appraisals and by controlling the information access of the supply base to the auction. The *reverse auction* of one buyer and many sellers is conducted as a *Dutch auction* where price-bidding decreases to the lowest winning price within a predetermined window of time. The supplier who wins the auction is briefly coupled into the supply chain network to fulfill the purchase.

Many reverse auction implementations place the burden of difficult logistic connections and inventory financing on the supplier. The primary auction is not complete without the logistic and financial component. The real issue is one of creating the right environment to solve these problems from a secondary set of preferred logistic service providers and financial service providers. One solution is to structure a second tier of service provider auctions for logistics and financial services that is triggered from the primary spot price auction. The same software technology and the same process steps of RFI, RFQ, reverse auction, bid analysis, and business award can be used for these secondary auctions. Once a set of preferred logistic service providers and financial service providers are selected to participate, the same set is included in every secondary auction to preserve some control over network integrity with different sets of primary auction trading partners.

Operating While Integrating or Disintegrating the Network

Acquisitions and insourcing drive the integration of new customers, new products, and different information systems into the operations planning equation. Outsourcing, disintermediation, and divestitures drive the disintegration of old customers, established products, and legacy information systems out of the operations planning equation. Acquisitions and divestitures are opposites; a new business is bought and integrated with an acquisition, whereas an old business is sold and spun-off with a divestiture. Insourcing and outsourcing are opposites; external processes are bought and integrated with insourcing, whereas internal processes are sold and extracted with outsourcing. *Disintermediation* means that the supply chain network is reconfigured to operate without one or more of its echelons; total supply chain length becomes shorter. It may also be necessary to reconfigure a supply chain network whenever a new product family is introduced. This is because the product introduction may require an entirely different channel of distribution and/or an entirely different supply base.

Each of these network reconfigurations should be organized and managed as a project that will permanently transform the boundary conditions of the operations plan. Such projects are destabilizing one-time events, and their duration may be measured in months and years. It is also possible that before one project can be completed another project is being initiated. For example, in the timeframe of 1998 through 2003, Agilent Technologies was spun off from Hewlett-Packard, completed the Y2K conversion of its information systems, divested its Medical Systems Group to Phillips, redistributed its manufacturing globally, replaced its legacy systems with Oracle, and introduced a record number of new products. This caused extreme destabilization of the operations planning organization.

Ensure that the project plan for any such event includes transition planning for each of the following:

- *Network inventory levels*—Starting inventory, build-ahead inventory, ending inventory, and contingency inventory.
- *Timing of inventory placement*—When will the old inventory buffers be terminated by geographic location versus when will the new inventory buffers be initiated by geographic location?
- *Network cash levels*—Starting cash, transition financing, ending cash, and contingency financing.
- *Timing of cash placement*—When will the old cash buffers be terminated by geographic location versus when will the new cash buffers be initiated by geographic location?
- *Network capability*—The transfer and sale of one-of-a-kind manufacturing equipment and tooling, the duplication of unique manufacturing equipment and tooling, the hiring and training, the transfer and reassignment, or the layoff and outplacement of skilled employees.
- *Timing of capacity placement*—When will the old network configuration stop being capable? Is there a different interim network constraint? When will the new network configuration be capable? Where is the new network constraint?

FORECASTING

Every business operation depends on some kind of forecast. To the degree that the trading partners in a supply chain network operate in a pull, Build-To-Order manner, the business becomes less dependent on the forecast. To the degree that the trading partners in a supply chain network operate in a push, Build-To-Stock manner, the business becomes more dependent on the forecast. When the forecast is wrong, as it always will be, it is a mistake to think that a more complex forecasting method will solve the problem. The central issues are knowing what to forecast and understanding how to manage the risk inherent in the forecast error.

FORECASTING THE RIGHT THINGS

Business is planned from two kinds of forecasts: one for demand and a second for supply. Sometimes the supply forecast is implicit and equivalent to the demand forecast; but in the better-planned business, it is explicit. Forecasting the right things on the demand side depends on a clear understanding of the market, the customer, and the network echelon position of the forecaster within the network. Forecasting the right things on the supply side depends on a clear understanding of the relationship of the product BOM to the network and the network echelon position of the forecaster within the network.

Forecasting Demand

Consider the following when deciding which demand to forecast:

- *Independent versus dependent demand*—The demand for independent end products is forecast, whereas the demand for lower level dependent items is calculated. This rule is sometimes forgotten across organizational boundaries. For example, an AM/FM radio manufacturer is an original equipment manufacturer (OEM) to the big three auto companies in Detroit. The demand for these radios is a dependent demand that should be calculated from the number of automobiles produced.
- *Adjust for returns*—Subtract the historical rate of returns when forecasting new demand.
- *Forecast in both dollars and units*—Work the demand side forecast in dollars and units because revenue planning requires dollars, while operations planning requires units. Beware that an aggregate dollar forecast can be disaggregated an infinite number of ways where the total forecast in dollars equals the sum of [each unit volume forecast times each product price]. Reconcile the difference to be within an acceptable tolerance band.
- *Separate volatile versus nonvolatile demand*—Divide the standard deviation by the mean for each product SKU forecast. Separate the list of product SKUs into volatile products where the standard deviation exceeds the mean and nonvolatile products where the mean exceeds the standard deviation.

- *Rate versus mix*—In a forecast of aggregate demand, the percentage mix may hold constant while the aggregate rate varies or the aggregate rate may hold constant while the percentage mix varies. It is important to focus on forecasting the right attribute, rate or mix.
- *Customer support requirements*—Adjust the number of units in the demand forecast to include any customer support requirements.
- *Forecast error*—Demand forecast error should be statistically random and should not show a mathematical bias. Otherwise, adjust the demand forecast by the [+/–] mean of the forecast error.

Forecasting Supply

Consider the following when deciding which supply to forecast:

- *Forecast in units*—Work the supply side forecast in units, and dollarize the unit forecast as required. Beware that an aggregate dollar forecast can be disaggregated an infinite number of ways where the total forecast in dollars equals the sum of [each unit volume forecast times each product price]. Reconcile the difference to be within an acceptable tolerance band.
- *Forecast both inventory and cash balances*—Both inventory and cash need to be forecast so that neither one constrains throughput.
- *Inventory rate, inventory mix, capacity rate, and capacity mix*—Forecast inventory rate and capacity mix for a Build-To-Stock business. Forecast inventory rate, inventory mix, capacity rate, and capacity mix for an Assemble-To-Order business. Forecast inventory mix and capacity rate for a Build-To-Order business. Forecast capacity rate and capacity mix for an Engineer-To-Order business.
- *Quality yields*—Adjust the number of units started in the supply forecast to compensate for any known process yields.
- *Forecast error*—Supply forecast error should be statistically random and not show a mathematical bias. Otherwise, adjust the supply forecast by the [+/–] mean of the forecast error.

Forecasting Supply for Remanufacturing

Two additional kinds of forecasts are required for planning remanufacturing:

- *Forecast the supply of cores*—The throughput of a remanufacturing business depends, in part, on the supply of cores returned from the field. A *core* is the used, disposed product or assembly that will be remanufactured. Core returns may show some seasonality depending on the type of product.
- *Forecast the reusability of component parts within the core*—When a core has a lower level BOM, not every lower level part from every returned core will be reusable. It is necessary to explode the core's BOM and then to forecast a reusability rate for each component. For example, suppose customers return the high voltage doubler assembly (core) for a particular model of television because it is burned out. If the core is burned out,

then it is unreasonable to expect that all four diodes in the lower level BOM for this assembly can be reused. For example, there is a diode forecast based on an historical replacement rate of 1.85 new diodes per remanufactured assembly.

Forecasting Things Right

All forecasting methods require some amount of historical data. When the historical data covers too short a period, expect the forecast error to be large because very little is really known about demand. When the historical data covers too long a period and is averaged, key inflection points in the demand pattern can be masked unintentionally. The new forecast fails to take into account a change in trend or the start of seasonality in the demand. About six points of demand history are good as a starting place to make a forecast. For example, the following data set could be used to begin a forecast: April, 217 units; May, 176 units; June, 189 units; July, 103 units; August, 208 units; September, 192 units. This data set has a mean of 180.8 units, a standard deviation of 91.2 units, and a low volatility (standard deviation/mean = 91.2/180.8 = 0.504).

A new product introduction may be heavily promoted to build demand. The problem with a new product is that there is no demand history. This is true except when the new product is a replacement or an upgrade of an existing product, and it is expected to offset some significant percentage of the existing product's demand. When the new product is a module of a larger system, the new product's demand can sometimes be calculated as a fixed percentage of the system's forecasted demand. When key customers are willing to underwrite the initial offering of a new product, the forecast demand will equal the key customer's demand in both quantity and timing.

There are many mathematical forecasting methods, each with an increasing degree of sophistication. Avoid being caught up in the trap that if a forecasting method is more sophisticated, then it must be good. In fact, the opposite is true. If a forecasting method is simple, then it must be good. Level forecasting models, trend forecasting models, seasonality forecasting models, and econometric forecasting models are rungs up the ladder of mathematical complexity. Start forecasting from the lowest rung, and only move up to the next complexity level when the forecast error shows a consistent statistical bias, see Figure 8-4. Simplicity in forecasting and paying close attention to the statistical parameters of forecast error are much more important to successful forecasting than using fancy mathematics. The following are representative simple forecasting methods that can be used to forecast aggregated or individual demand or supply, units or dollars, inventory or cash, or capacity. There are many other methods that are just as good and are beyond the scope of this book.

The Level Forecast

Use a level forecasting method when the forecast is thought to be the same, or level, for each future period. Simple exponential smoothing is one well-known method for level forecasting. Simple exponential smoothing utilizes a weighing factor, alpha (α),

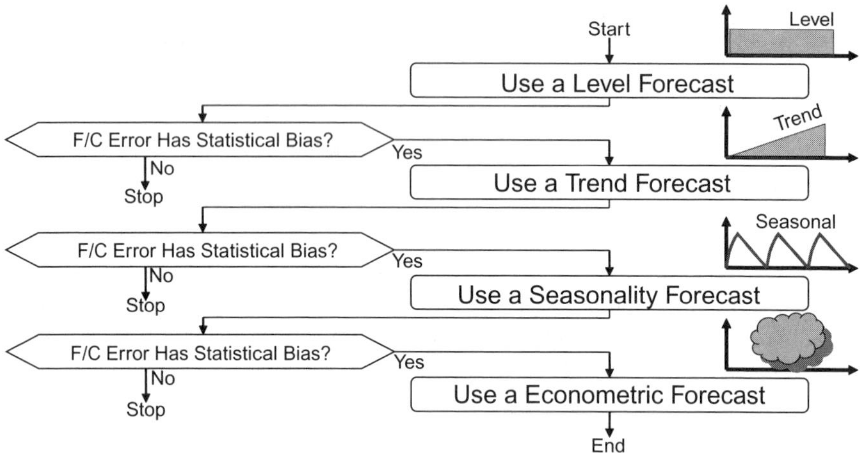

FIGURE 8-4 Use forecast error statistical bias as the signal to move up in forecast complexity.

to weight the present or the past more heavily in the new forecast. An alpha close to zero favors the past, whereas an alpha close to one favors the present. The equation for simple exponential smoothing says that the new forecast equals the old forecast plus alpha times the difference between actual demand and the old forecast. This second term can be plus or minus. Forecasts using this method always lag behind the actual.

$$F_{new} = F_{old} + \alpha\,(D_{actual} - F_{old})$$

For $0 < \alpha < 1.0$

Where α can be determined from a Least Sum of the Squares error analysis over ten periods, and $\alpha = 0.2$ is a good starting value. $\alpha = 0.2$ adds or subtracts 20% of the difference between forecast and actual.

For example, when actual demand is higher than forecast, the new level forecast is:

$F_{new} = 35 + 0.2\,(41 - 35)$

$F_{new} = 35 + 1.2$

$F_{new} = 36.2$ . . . rounded to 36 units

And, when actual demand is lower than forecast, the new level forecast is:

$F_{new} = 35 + 0.2\,(27 - 35)$

$F_{new} = 35 - 1.6$

$F_{new} = 33.4$ . . . rounded to 33 units

TABLE 8-4
Data Pairs for the Linear Regression Example

Data Set n	Period	X Historical	Y Historical	XY Calculated	X^2 Calculated
1	January	10	24	240	100
2	February	20	23	460	400
3	March	30	31	930	900
4	April	40	34	1360	1600
5	May	50	45	2250	2500
	Sum	150	157	5240	5500

The Trend Forecast

Use a trend forecasting method when the forecast is thought to be continuously increasing, or continuously decreasing, for each future period. Linear regression is one well-known method for trend forecasting. Most scientific calculators have special function keys to calculate a linear regression. Linear regression is a best straight-line fit through a set of X, Y data pairs. The equation for a straight line says that Y equals X times the slope (m) plus the Y-intercept (b):

$$Y = m X + b$$

Linear regression calculates a best-fit slope and Y-intercept from the following two relationships. The example data set in Table 8-4 is used to show one example calculation for m and b. Notice that the monthly periods January, February, March, and so on are assigned equal X-axis increments as 10, 20, 30, and so on.

$$m = \frac{n\,\Sigma(XY) - \Sigma(X)\,\Sigma(X)}{n\,\Sigma(X^2) - (\Sigma(X))^2} = \frac{(5)(5240) - (150)(157)}{(5)(5500) - (150)(150)} = 0.530 \text{ Slope}$$

$$b = \frac{\Sigma(Y)\,\Sigma(X^2) - \Sigma(X)\,\Sigma(XY)}{n\,\Sigma(X^2) - (\Sigma(X))^2} = \frac{(157)(5500) - (150)(5240)}{(5)(5500) - (150)(150)} = 15.5 \text{ Y-Intercept}$$

The trend forecasts for July, August, and September are calculated as follows:

$$Y_{Jun} = m X + b = (0.530)(60) + 15.5 = 47.3 \text{ units}$$

$$Y_{Jul} = m X + b = (0.530)(70) + 15.5 = 52.6 \text{ units}$$

$$Y_{Aug} = m X + b = (0.530)(80) + 15.5 = 57.9 \text{ units}$$

The Seasonal Forecast

Use a seasonality forecasting method when the forecast is thought to have a repeating seasonality. The Winter's Model is one well-known method for seasonality forecasting. The Winter's Model uses the history of two complete seasons to calculate the percentage of the total, called a seasonality index, to be assigned to each period of

TABLE 8-5
Period Data for a Winter's Model Example

Period	Last Season (A)	This Season (B)	Sum of Two Seasons (A) + (B)	Historical Seasonality Index	New Forecast for a Seasonal Demand
1	47	60	107	107/600 = 0.178	(425) (0.178) = 75.7 units
2	53	64	117	117/600 = 0.195	(425) (0.195) = 82.9 units
3	65	80	145	145/600 = 0.242	(425) (0.242) = 102.8 units
4	100	131	231	231/600 = 0.385	(425) (0.385) = 163.6 units
Totals	265	335	600	1.000	425.0 units

the future forecast. An example is shown in Table 8-5. In this example, 17.8% of the demand is forecast for period 1, 19.5% of the demand is forecast for period 2, 24.2% of the demand is forecast for period 3, and 38.5% of the demand is forecast for period 4. A trend model is used to forecast the total aggregate demand for a third season at 425 from 265 total for the first season and 335 total for the second season. The 425 total for the third season is proportioned into four periods using the seasonality index. Winter's Model can be used for any number of periods, but it requires the averaging of at least two complete seasons.

The Econometric Forecast

A season is over and done in a shorter timeframe than a cycle. Some cycles take years to complete and appear as subtle changes to a demand or supply pattern. Econometric models are sets of simultaneous differential equations that attempt to model the complexity of long cycles. They are beyond the scope of this book.

Calculating Forecast Error

The period forecasting errors from a good forecasting method will pass the test for randomness. In the best case, the [actual – forecast] error term will flip-flop randomly between a positive and negative sign showing no mathematic bias. The set of [actual – forecast] error terms can be described statistically by a mean and a standard deviation. A positive mean should be added to each forecast to improve its accuracy, whereas a negative mean should be subtracted from each forecast to improve its accuracy. The adjusted forecast is only accurate within the band defined as:

Actual Value = Forecast Value +/– Mean of Forecast Error
+/– (n) Standard Deviations of Forecast Error

Where the Forecast Error = [Actual – Forecast] for each period, and
where n = 1, 2, or 3

Table 8-6 shows an example of how to compare the best forecasting method for use on a particular set of demand data. The upper left portion of the table shows

TABLE 8-6
Comparing the Error of a Level Forecast versus a Trend Forecast

67	Sep							-1 Level Forecast with α = 0.33				
	75	Oct			Forecast->			-2 Trend Forecast				
		71	Nov		Jan-1	Jan-2	Feb-1	Feb-2	Mar-1	Mar-2	Apr-1	Apr-2
	<-History		79	Dec	76.3		76.3		76.3		76.3	
						81.0		84.2		87.4		90.6
				Jan	86.0	Actual	79.5		79.5		79.5	
					9.7	5.0		88.0		92.1		96.2
					Actual-F/C							
				Feb			92.0	Actual	83.6		93.6	
							12.5	4.0		99.5		106.5
				Mar					83.0	Actual	83.4	
									−0.6	−16.5		89.5
				Apr							100.0	Actual
											16.6	10.5
										Mean	9.55	3.00
									Std Deviation		12.71	21.01

four months of history with 67 units in September, 75 units in October, 71 units in November, and 79 units in December. This historical information is needed for a linear regression of the trend. The last level forecast for December, not shown in the table, was 75.0 units. The right part of the table shows forecasts made once a month using two different methods. For example, in December simple exponential smoothing with $\alpha = 0.33$ was used to forecast 76.3 for January, 76.3 for February, 76.3 for March, and 76.3 for April. At the same time in December, linear regression was used to forecast 81.0 for January, 84.2 for February, 87.4 for March, and 90.6 for April. Each vertical column shows the sequence of forecasts made for a future month consistently using the same method. For example, the column Mar-2 indicates that linear regression was used to forecast 87.4 for March in December, 92.1 for March in January, and 99.5 for March in February, whereas the March actual was 83.0.

The [actual – forecast] error terms are calculated along the lower right diagonal. These error terms are calculated from the last forecast in the month prior to each actual. Notice that the algebraic sign of the error term changes from [+] to [–] to [+] indicating some degree of randomness for both forecasting methods. If the error term from one method had kept a consistent algebraic sign, either [+] or [–], then the forecast bias would indicate that a more complex forecasting method might give better results. However, in this example when the means and standard deviations are computed for the respective sets of error terms from January through April, each forecasting method shows its own issues. The simple exponential smoothing, or level, forecast lags the actual demand each period by a mean of 9.5 units with a standard deviation of 12.71 units. The linear regression, or trend forecast, lags the actual demand each period by a mean of only 3.0 units but with a standard deviation nearly twice as large as that of the level forecast model at 21.01 units. Simple exponential smoothing is the better choice for this data set.

PRACTICAL PUSH PLANNING TECHNIQUES

Inventory and cash locations define the boundaries of each of the supply chain network operational zones. In order to promise and deliver product and services to the end-customer, sufficient inventory and cash must be available in the customer's required timeframe and the network must be capable. Only then can the network quote Available-To-Promise (ATP) and Capable-To-Promise (CTP) numbers realistically. ATP is the uncommitted portion of inventory and planned production maintained in a trading partner's master production schedule. CTP commits orders against available capacity and inventory taking into account the entire network. The following sections describe some practical techniques that can be used to plan push network operations.

THE BIG PICTURE

It should be clear at this point that network operations are planned in the context of the customer's requirement, the competition's response and the fit of the composite BOM with the network architecture. The push/pull boundary splits the network operation into two zones that are quite different. Pull operations are driven by customer demand with a collaborative pull plan focused on keeping the zone capable. Push operations are driven by a supply forecast with a hierarchical push plan focused on keeping the zone stocked with inventory. One overall objective of supply chain architecture is to optimally locate the push/pull boundary in order to diminish operational dependence on a forecast. The farther upstream the push/pull boundary can be located, the less the business is at risk with forecast error. The inventory and cash locations representing the push/pull boundary are also boundary conditions for the operations plan, see Figure 8-5. Here the term boundary condition means that the ending inventory position and the ending cash position for the push zone are equal by definition to the starting inventory position and the starting cash position for the pull zone.

Forecasting is about being able to anticipate how much inventory and how much cash will be needed to cover customer ordering in the future. The future might be the next hour, the next weeks and months, or the next year. The question becomes how far must the future be planned? The answer defines the *planning horizon* for the business. In a traditional push environment, the Sales and Operations Plan (S&OP), Distribution Requirements Planning (DRP) and the Master Production Schedule (MPS), Materials Requirements Planning (MRP) and Capacity Requirements Planning (CRP) each have their own planning horizons. Some distribution will include planning for *wave picking*, where the sequencing of picking minimizes the wait time for product delivered by the same carrier or to the same destination.

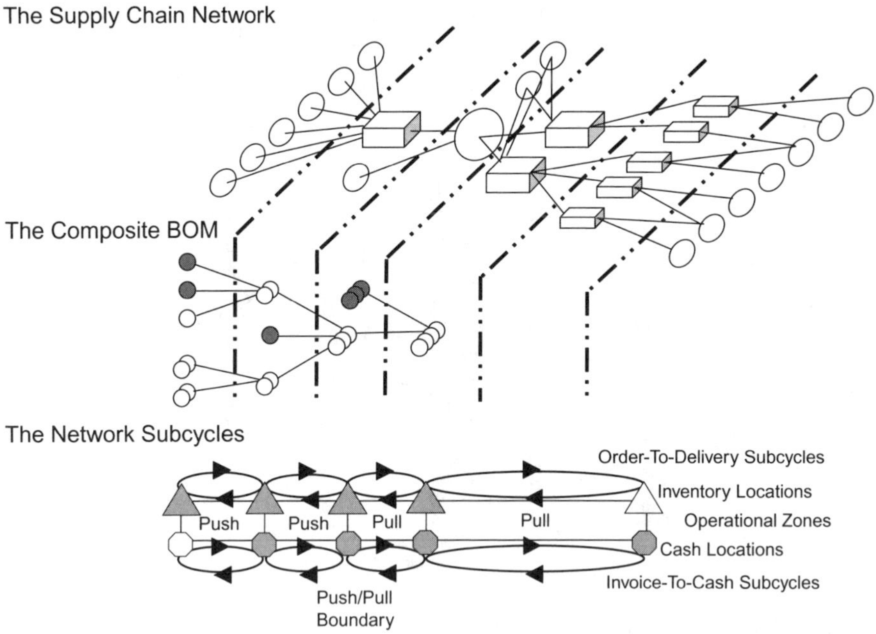

FIGURE 8-5 Relating inventory and cash locations with the operational zones.

Some manufacturing will include a Final Assembly Schedule (FAS) or a fill schedule where product is packaged in a multitude of shipping containers and/or private labels, each becoming a unique SKU. The timeframe covered by the forecast and the set of planning horizons must be consistent such that the demand is driven all the way down through the cumulative transit times, cycle times, and lead times to the lowest levels of the BOM. One common mistake is to shortchange one of the planning horizons only to discover, after it is too late, that some lower-level item was never planned because it was decoupled from its demand forecast. When the planning system is Enterprise Resource Planning (ERP), the equivalent of S&OP, DRP, MPS, MRP, and CRP are integrated within the system software of the ERP application.

The planning system extends the entire length of the supply chain network and interacts with each operational zone separately, see Figure 8-6. The following sections detail the differences in the planning logic used for a push zone versus a pull zone. Particular attention is paid to the inventory and cash boundary conditions at the interfaces between the zones. The purpose of a planning system is to answer all of the following questions:

Over the planning horizon…

- What is the capacity of the network during each time period, and where is the constraint?
- How much inventory is needed in the network during each period, and where should it be positioned?

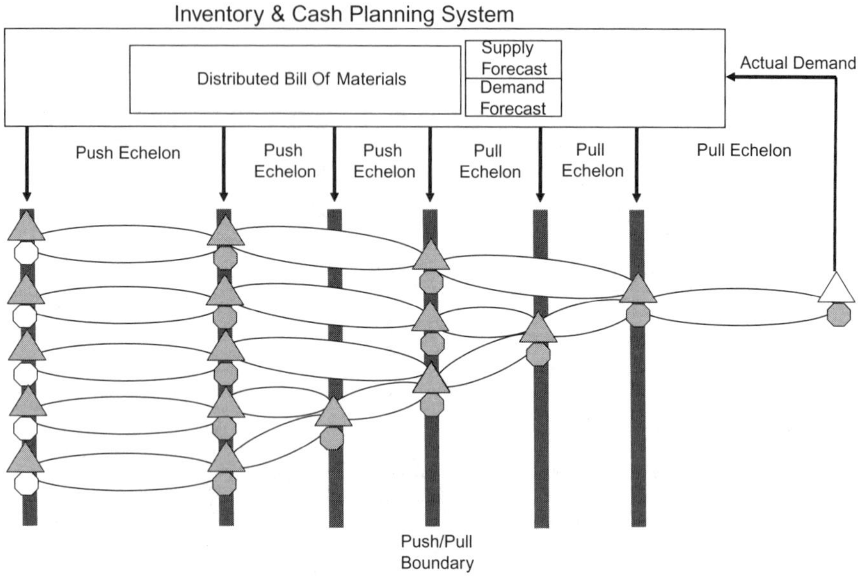

FIGURE 8-6 Interfacing the inventory and cash planning system with the network.

- How much cash is needed in the network during each period, and where should it be positioned?
- What is the accuracy of the ATP and CTP estimates?

Under a push scenario, inventory is replenished to a forecast or replenished to a level. It is often helpful to differentiate between a rate forecast and a mix forecast. A *rate forecast* is used to predict material usage per unit of time for the longest lead time materials, for example kilograms per week or linear feet per day. A rate forecast must be able to support the total number of products, no matter what the mix. A *mix forecast* is used to predict subtle changes in material usage across families of products, as the demanded quantity of individual product models or packaging shifts with customer demand. The mix forecast must be able to support the range of shifting demand for unique materials, at a sustained production rate, necessary to complete finished goods inventory. The portion of the composite BOM associated with upstream risk pooling is likely to fall in the push zone.

Push Planning Examples

When the push planning process is put into a network context, its boundary conditions are cast in a new light. This is because the pull planning process exists between the end-customer and the push planning process. The push planning process sees the demand generated at the push/pull boundary, which may be many echelons removed from the end-customer demand. The push process may be used to replenish the entire BOM or only a partial BOM depending on how the product BOM is distributed

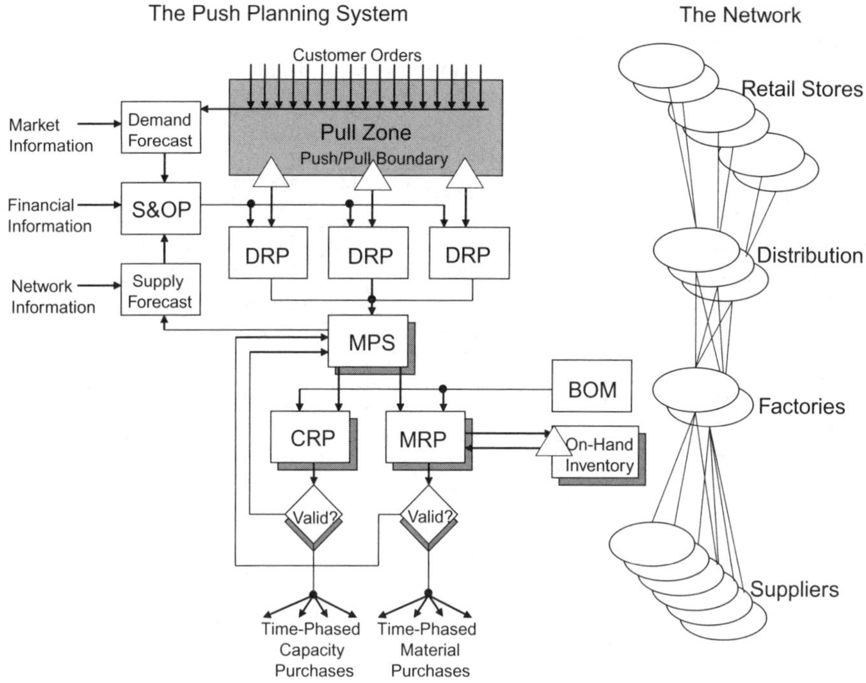

FIGURE 8-7 Push planning for multiple distribution centers and parallel factories (See Table 8-7.)

through the network. The following examples show two very different implementations of a push planning process. In the first example, Figure 8-7 with Table 8-7, multiple distribution centers order sets of products manufactured at multiple, parallel factories, and the entire product BOM is encapsulated within the push zone. This is typical of a network operated in a build-to-stock mode with a small downstream pull zone of perhaps only one echelon. This planning table is incomplete in the sense that many additional SKUs are aggregated to form the product line and many additional items are combined into the product's BOM.

In the second example, Figure 8-8 with Table 8-8, there are no distribution centers in the push zone and a partial BOM is distributed across two factories arranged in series. This is typical of a network operated in a build-to-order mode with a large downstream pull zone extended across several echelons that include the final assembly and/or postponement. Notice however, that although the customer receives the benefits of a BTO operation, the upstream push zone replenishes the push/pull buffer as a BTS operation. This planning table is incomplete in the sense that many additional SKUs are aggregated to form the product line and many additional items are combined into the product BOM.

In Table 8-8 the output of MRP_1 from the first factory feeds the input of MPS_2 for the second factory. It takes two planning cycles to propagate any changes in demand. The inventory position in the second factory gets amplified by the lot sizing

TABLE 8-7
Push Planning for Multiple Distribution Centers and Parallel Factories (See Figure 8-7.)

S&OP	"A" Product Line; FGI_{Start} = 650; $Backlog_{Start}$ = 0								
Month	Jan	Feb	Mar	Apr	May	Jun	Jul	Aug	
Demand (Sales) Plan	325	110	145	185	220	235	290	315	Σ1,825
Supply (Production) Plan	225	215	225	220	225	220	220	225	Σ1,775
Inventory (Financial) Plan	550	655	735	770	775	760	690	600	

DRP	SKU 101; Transit Time = 1 Week; Lot Size = 24 (2 pallets); Safety Stock = 12										
	Week	1/7	1/14	1/21	1/28	2/4	2/11	2/18	2/25	3/4	3/11
1st Echelon Forecast		7	7	7	7	7	7	7	7	7	7
2nd Echelon Demand Backlog		3		5	2		1				
Gross Requirements		10	7	12	9	7	8	7	7	7	7
Scheduled Receipts				24							
Net Requirements On-Hand	32	22	15	27	18	35	27	20	13	30	23
Planned Factory Order					24				24		

MPS	SKU 101; Cycle Time Offset = 0; Lot Size = 30; Safety Stock = 5										
	Week	1/7	1/14	1/21	1/28	2/4	2/11	2/18	2/25	3/4	3/11
Forecast			24		24				24		
Demand Backlog			31								
Dependent Demand				1				1			
Consumption Rule		0	31	1	24	0	0	1	24	0	0
Projected Available Balance/Start FGI	11	11	10	9	15	15	15	14	20	20	20
Master Schedule			30		30				30		
Available-To-Promise			10		40				70		

MRP	Item B632; Quantity per = 3; Lead Time =3 Weeks; Lot Size = 200; Safety Stock = 55										
	Week	1/7	1/14	1/21	1/28	2/4	2/11	2/18	2/25	3/4	3/11
Gross Requirements			90		90				90		
Scheduled Receipts			200								
Net Requirements On-Hand	112	112	222	222	132	132	132	132	242	242	242
Planned Order Release						200					

and network variability of the first factory. When both factories can be planned from a single ERP system, these issues are eliminated.

The push planning process begins with the sales and operations plan. The S&OP balances the demand forecast (the sales plan) with the supply forecast (the production plan) and with an inventory projection (the financial plan). The S&OP is updated once a month by cross-functional representation of the trading partners impacted by the plan. In the S&OP, the supply forecast equals the demand forecast with planned adjustments to the level of finished goods inventory (FGI) or order backlog or both. An *order backlog* includes orders accepted from customers that have not yet shipped. The traditional supply plan will attempt to smooth production, taking into account

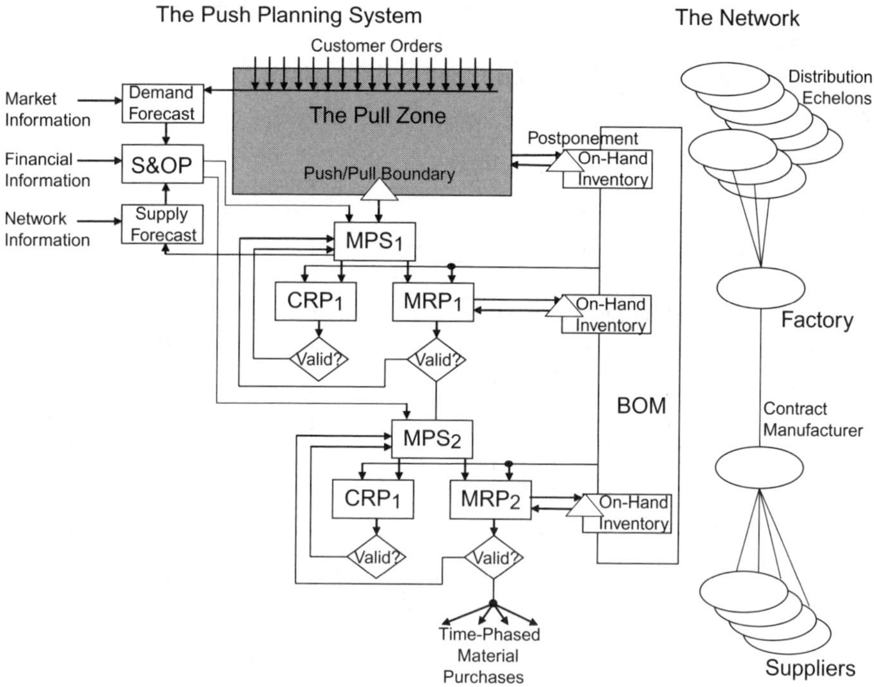

FIGURE 8-8 Push planning with a distributed BOM and serial MRP's (See Table 8-8.)

the number of days per month, to meet anticipated demand. The S&OP is the place where new product introduction and old product obsolescence are ramped into and out of the supply forecast. It is best to plan in units and then dollarize for financial reporting. There should be only one collaborated sales and operations plan for the end-to-end network.

To level the supply forecast start by adding the demand forecast over three consecutive months and divide by 65 working days (13 weeks × 5 working days/week). The total supply forecast can then be segmented into months according to the ratio of the number of working days per month. The supply forecast is adjusted up or down for the desired change in ending backlog and/or ending finished goods inventory. If the plan is to build inventory, then the cumulative supply forecast will exceed the cumulative demand forecast. If the plan is to build backlog, then the cumulative demand forecast will exceed the cumulative supply forecast. The following relationship holds over the entire planning horizon:

$$\text{Supply Forecast} = (\text{Backlog}_{\text{Start}} - \text{FGI}_{\text{Start}}) + \text{Demand Forecast} - (\text{Backlog}_{\text{End}} - \text{FGI}_{\text{End}})$$

Where FGI will be near zero for a BTO operation, and backlog will be near zero for a BTS operation.

Ending Inventory = Starting Inventory + Supply Forecast − Demand Forecast
For each period.

TABLE 8-8
Push Planning with a Distributed BOM and Serial MRPs
(See Figure 8-8.)

S&OP	"B" Product Line; FGI_{Start} = 174; $Backlog_{Start}$ = 0								
Month	Jan	Feb	Mar	Apr	May	Jun	Jul	Aug	
Demand (Sales) Plan	100	98	105	110	108	116	121	118	Σ876
Supply (Production) Plan	110	108	111	110	108	111	110	108	Σ876
Inventory (Financial) Plan	184	194	200	200	200	195	184	174	

MPS1	SKU 3095; Cycle Time Offset = 0; Lot Size = 12; Safety Stock = 12										
	Week	1/7	1/14	1/21	1/28	2/4	2/11	2/18	2/25	3/4	3/11
Forecast		4	4	4	4	3	4	4	4	4	5
Demand Backlog		2		6	1						
Dependent Demand											
Consumption Rule		6	4	10	5	3	4	4	4	4	5
Projected Available Balance/Start FGI	15	9	5	7	2	11	7	3	11	7	2
Master Schedule				12		12			12		
Available-to-Promise				18		30			42		

MRP1	Item M68; Quantity per = 2; Lead Time = 2 Weeks; Lot Size = 50; Safety Stock = 0										
	Week	1/7	1/14	1/21	1/28	2/4	2/11	2/18	2/25	3/4	3/11
Gross Requirements				24		24			24		
Scheduled Receipts											
Net Requirements On-Hand	27	27	27	3	3	29	29	29	5	5	5
Planned Order Release				50							

MPS2	Item M68; Cycle Time Offset = 0; Lot Size = 48; Safety Stock = 0										
	Week	1/7	1/14	1/21	1/28	2/4	2/11	2/18	2/25	3/4	3/11
Forecast				50							
Demand Backlog											
Dependent Demand-Service							2				
Consumption Rule		0	0	50	0	0	2	0	0	0	0
Projected Available Balance/On-Hand	7	7	7	5	5	5	3	3	3	3	3
Master Schedule				48							
Available-to-Promise				55							

MRP2	Component DD451; Quantity per = 2; Lead Time = 3 Weeks; Lot Size = 200; Safety Stock = 35										
	Week	1/7	1/14	1/21	1/28	2/4	2/11	2/18	2/25	3/4	3/11
Goss Requirements				96							
Scheduled Receipts											
Net Requirements On-Hand	53	53	53	157	157	157	157	157	157	157	157
Planned Order Release		200									

Time-Phased Offsets and Net Requirements Logic

In networks where distribution centers fall within the push zone, distribution requirements planning aggregates the demand for each SKU across all distributors and steers the total demand to the factory responsible for manufacturing that SKU. DRP adds any firm orders already in backlog with the time-phased supply forecast from the S&OP. The aggregate monthly quantity of S&OP is split into weekly quantities by individual SKU for DRP. Net requirements are calculated from left to right until the net falls below the desired level of safety stock or goes negative. A planned factory order is placed one lead time in front of that point, and the calculation continues moving to the right. DRP takes into account the transit time offset to move product to the warehouse and the lot sizing driven from bulk quantities being packed as cartons, pallets, containers, and/or truckloads. The output of DRP becomes the input to the factory's MPS. A single DRP should be used to plan the entire network. Planning can become very convoluted when, for example, an SKU shortage forces an allocation, and someone decides to "cross-channel" or divert inventory from another SKU as a substitution for this SKU.

Gross Requirements = 1st Echelon Forecast + 2nd Echelon Demand Backlog

Net Requirements = FGI_{Start} + Scheduled Receipt – Gross Requirements

> Where net requirements falling below the safety stock level or going negative trigger a planned factory order. the release of the planned factory order is offset by the transit time.

Independently demanded SKUs are replenished on the MPS through reorder point logic. When distribution planning falls within the push zone, this independent demand is derived from the S&OP supply forecast, time-phased and accumulated through DRP. There is a one-to-one SKU and timeframe relationship between the output of DRP and the input of the MPS. It is possible to have a firm order backlog for SKU, independent of the demand forecast, which might come from an extended delivery agreement or a contractual purchasing agreement with a downstream trading partner. The MPS can also be driven by dependent demand, for example by demand to fill the service pipeline for loaner or replacement products. The MPS is calculated using a consumption rule of how the MPS consumes the forecast. The following two consumption rules are common:

- The period demand is the larger of the backlog or the forecast.
- The period demand is the sum of the backlog plus the forecast.

In Table 8-7 the reorder point logic is calculated using the fixed order quantity, continuous review method. The same quantity is master scheduled once demand drives the Projected Available Balance (PAB) below the reorder point. PAB is a netting logic that is calculated from left to right until the net falls below the desired reorder point. A master scheduled lot is started one cycle time in front of that point, and the calculation continues moving to the right. The MPS takes into account the cycle time offset to manufacture the product and the lot sizing used to optimize machine, final assembly, and fill line setups while considering product packaging.

$$PAB_{End} = PAB_{Start} + MPS_{Period} - \text{Demand Consumption}_{Period}$$

Where the reorder point is the safety stock level as a positive PAB number for a BTS scenario, or the desired order backlog as a negative PAB number for a BTO scenario.

Available-To-Promise (ATP) is calculated from the MPS at the product level. When ATP is calculated by a midstream trading partner in a network, it is less reliable than using a Capable-To-Promise (CTP) number collaborated through the downstream trading partners in the network. The ATP calculation for the first period is different than the ATP calculation for the later periods. Suppose the MPS runs from week 1 through week N, with product master scheduled in weeks 1,… M,…, N – 2, N – 1, and N. Then:

- For the timeframe from the start of the schedule through the week of the first master scheduled lot:

$$ATP_1 = FGI_{Start} + MPS_1 - \sum_{i=1}^{M-1} (\text{Demand Backlog}_i)$$

Where the next master scheduled product lot is scheduled for week M.

- For the timeframe starting immediately after the week of a master scheduled lot through the week of the next master scheduled lot:

$$ATP_M = ATP_{M-1} + MPS_M - \sum_{i=M}^{N-1} (\text{Demand Backlog}_i)$$

Where the next master scheduled product lot is scheduled for week N.

The net requirements logic for MRP is third in line after the net requirements logic of DRP and the projected available balance logic of the MPS. MRP time phases the dependent demand for each child component, based on lead times and the BOM product structure, required to manufacture a parent item. MRP takes into account the lead time offset to procure raw materials and the lot sizing that is driven by factory setup tradeoffs and the minimum order quantity policies of suppliers. Although there is a one-to-one quantity relationship between the output of DRP and the input of the MPS, the BOM determines how the parent item in MPS relates to quantity per of the child item in MRP. Net requirements are calculated from left to right until the net falls below the desired level of safety stock or goes negative. The planned order release is placed one lead time in front of that point, and the calculation continues moving to the right. Net requirements are calculated as supply minus demand in MRP:

$$\text{Net Requirements} = \text{On-Hand Inventory} + \text{Scheduled Receipts} - \text{Gross Requirements}$$

The Impact of Lot Sizing

Most manufacturing and distribution is not continuously divisible. Fractions of a product or item called out in planning are often not physically possible. Fractions of a month, day, or hour that might smooth the planning of a schedule are often not realizable. Information systems sometimes force unnatural boundary conditions in their division of quantities and timeframes. The bottom line about lot sizing is that it causes unnecessary network inventory and cash to be present, as follows:

- *Number of days per month in S&OP and DRP*—Some information systems force the same number of days per month, whereas actual months run 28, 29, 30, or 31 days. The planned month and the actual month may not align across a calendar-reporting boundary.
- *Transportation lot sizing in DRP*—Lot sizing is driven to less frequent, full truckload quantities to save transportation costs. For example, an SKU quantity of 150 that would be delivered as less-than-truck-load freight is changed to a SKU quantity of 2000 and delivered as truckload freight.
- *Number of days per week in MPS*—Some information systems force the same number of days per week, whereas actual weeks include one or two holidays or periods of shutdown. The planned week and the actual week may not align across a calendar-reporting boundary.
- *Packaging lot sizing in MPS*—Lot sizing is driven to the integral number of units that fit a carton or a pallet to save handling and packaging costs. For example, the master schedule specifies product in multiples of 24 to fit a standard shipping carton. When 26 products are required, 2 cartons or 48 products are scheduled.
- *Manufacturing batch lot sizing in MPS*—Lot sizing is driven to maximize throughput and to minimize setup time at a factory constraint. For example, the master schedule lot size for a temperature-calibrated probe is 19 because the calibration oven in final assembly holds exactly 19 probes. A customer order for 21 probes would require the master scheduling of 2 lots, or 38 probes.
- *Number of hours/day in MRP and CRP*—Some information systems force the same number of hours per day, whereas actual days can have different work shifts. The planned day and the actual day may not align across a calendar-reporting boundary.
- *Manufacturing batch lot sizing in MRP*—Lot sizing is driven to minimize material scrap and machine run time to minimize cost. For example, the planned order release for a metal part punched from an aluminum sheet is in multiples of 17 because exactly 17 parts fit on one sheet. When 35 parts are required, 3 sheets or 51 parts are fabricated.
- *Procurement lot sizing in MRP*—Suppliers specify minimum purchase quantities to offset setup costs. For example, a requirement for 45 surface-mounted capacitors results in the purchase of a reel of 5,000 surface-mounted capacitors.

Purchase Orders versus Vendor Managed Inventory

Under a MRP II push planning process, the control or implementation phase splits between manufactured and purchased items. Manufactured items are controlled on the shop floor through the dispatch list and input/output control. The dispatch list prioritizes the sequence of job starts. Input/output control is a real-time comparison of actual versus plan of job releases to critical work centers against the actual versus plan of job completions at that same work center. Input/output control is effective at identifying and correcting capacity related problems as they occur in real-time on the shop floor. Items purchased from upstream (nominal) trading partners are handled differently under MRP II. A planned order release in the buyer's MRP causes a purchase order to be generated and pushed to the supplier (seller) far enough in advance to allow adequate lead time plus transit time. When the supplier ships the item, the supplier pushes an invoice to the buyer.

Vendor managed inventory (VMI) changes the sense of which party pushes the inventory replenishment. VMI is a lower-cost implementation of purchasing control. Under VMI the supplier (seller) pushes the inventory replenishment, rather than the buyer, by continuously monitoring buffer inventory levels for a minimum quantity. When the inventory level falls below the agreed upon minimum level, the seller is authorized to replenish the inventory level up to an agreed upon maximum level. A summary purchase order is prepared, after the fact, at month end by the supplier, and a single invoice is pushed to the buyer. VMI is planned from the MRP II push planning system. The planned order release information is sent upstream as a forecast for the supplier to plan its raw materials and capacity requirements. Inventory receipts and issues at the buyer's location are entered into the buyer's inventory control system ensuring that the planning boundary conditions remain accurate. VMI is effectively subordinated to the MRP II push planning system for midstream and upstream inventory replenishment between trusted (nominal) trading partners. VMI is an execution technique and not a planning system; Table 8-9 compares VMI with traditional purchase orders.

TABLE 8-9
Procurement under VMI versus MRP II

Attribute	Vendor Managed Inventory	MRP II Purchase Order
Push Operation	Seller pushes inventory.	Buyer pushes inventory.
Advantage	Lower cost, lower inventory levels.	General purpose.
Disadvantage	Requires trust among Buyer and Seller; VMI is not a planning system.	Susceptible to lead time variability and inventory balance inaccuracies.
Planning	From the MRP push planning system.	From the MRP push planning system.
Ordering	Seller monitors inventory level; summary of purchases at month end.	Suggested order release generates a purchase order.
Lot Sizing	Order up to maximum quantity.	Usually a fixed reorder quantity.
Payment	Summary invoice at month end.	Invoice matched with purchase order.

PRACTICAL PULL PLANNING TECHNIQUES

Pull planning is altogether different than push planning. Pull operations are driven from customer orders, and pull planning is focused on keeping the network zone capable while optimizing the inventory and cash buffer levels. Pull planning leads the push planning. The degree to which the product BOM is embedded within the pull zone depends upon the configuration of the fulfillment channel and the echelon location of the push/pull boundary. That portion of the composite BOM associated with downstream postponement will fall within the pull zone.

Chapter 7 described a pull operation by relating network throughput to the elements of Drum, Buffer, Rope (DBR) from the Theory Of Constraints. The *drum* is the network constraint that determines when the supply chain network is capable of meeting the demand. The *buffer*, in the form of a shipping buffer, a constraint buffer, and an assembly buffer, provides safety time to deal with network variability. The *rope* is the broadcast communication that signals the actual demand to each of the trading partners in parallel. This section revisits DBR from a planning perspective. From time to time, the drum capacity, the inventory buffers, and the cash buffers must be recentered within the dynamic range of current demand.

PLANNING THE DYNAMIC RANGE OF A CAPABLE NETWORK

Push planning gives the illusion of being deterministic. Forecasts, reorder points, lot sizes, and lead times are all entered into the net requirements logic as though they are known precisely. This is not really the case even though the methods are deterministic. Pull planning, on the other hand, is an approach based on probability. Pull planning is about ensuring the network can maintain a desired service level across a probable range of demands. A pull operation delivers consistently high service levels for an intentional investment in capacity, inventory, and cash. The following network attributes are key when planning for a pull operation:

- *Desired service level*—Determines the multiple of RMS standard deviations, for a normal distribution, that must be added to the mean daily throughput to define a capable network. For example, a 99.7% service level requires a capability of the [mean + 3 standard deviations].
- *Downstream process yield*—Determines the amount of product lost to the process. Pull operations start one product to complete one order. If there are process yield issues, there is a probability that starting one product will complete zero orders. There may not be enough resources left to recover.
- *Safety stock backing up the changes in mix*—The mix of inventory is critical in a pull operation because the daily demand can see radical swings from one SKU mix to another. Consider the placement of the right inventory far enough upstream in the network to facilitate risk pooling or far enough downstream in the network to facilitate postponement.
- *Available cash position*—Just as inventory must be available to support a step change in throughput, cash must available to replenish the inventory

used to support this step change in throughput. If the network is capable and the inventory is in place but the cash buffers are empty, then the network will lose its synchronization.

- *Lead time to change capability up/down*—Over time, the demand range will trend up or down. Network resources of capacity, inventory buffers, and cash buffers will need to be periodically readjusted. It will take some significant amount of time to buy or sell capacity, to buy or sell inventory, and to finance or liquidate a cash position.
- *The willingness to invest*—Pull operations require deliberate investments in capacity, inventory, and cash. Pull operations will feel like idle resources and excess investment for someone coming from a push mentality. The tendency will be to run the network near full capacity all of the time and to build ahead when customer ordering is light. Such actions will destroy the pull capability of the network. For example, a synchronous operation working a 20-day month with a 95% service level should expect one day/month with no throughput and one day/month with an order backlog.

Subordinating Information and Cash Constraints to Physical Distribution Constraints

Chapter 7 describes how to determine the required capacity, from an analysis of the mean and standard deviation of demand, and the desired service level to make the network capable. Although the idea of a capable network is discussed in the context of material flow capacity, a network must also be capable in terms of its information flow and its cash flow. A network architecture with a higher order-to-delivery-to-cash velocity than the competition will beat the competition. Chapter 4 explains how the operation of a supply chain network is defined by a set of interlocking order-to-delivery-to-cash subcycles. Each subcycle must have a complete, closed loop path and each subcycle has at least one constraint, or velocity trap, in its information flow, material flow, and cash flow.

Because planning for the pull zone covers a very wide dynamic range, it is possible for the single network constraint to move about the set of physical distribution constraints, information constraints, and cash constraints depending on the particular level of throughput. The role of pull planning is to subordinate any possible information flow constraint or cash flow constraint to the network's material flow constraint. If it is found that the flow of information or the flow of cash is the network constraint, then an investment should first be made to increase the subcycle's information or cash capacity. The pull zone constraint should be a capacity constraint in the material flow that is known and well behaved. The hit rate of a punch press, the fill rate of a packaging line, the cycle time of an automated test station, the cubic volume of a holding tank, and the cubic volume of a transportation container are some typical examples.

Suppose a distributor's order-to-delivery-to-cash cycle is comprised of four subcycles: order-to-delivery, order-to-stock, invoice-to-pay, and invoice-to-cash. This distributor has been unable to sustain its required daily throughput in spite of having adequate staffing, docking, warehouse space, and forklift capacity. Upon inspection it is found that the distributor's aged accounts receivable are running 31% due in 30 days,

14% due in 60 days, and 55% due in 90 days, whereas the distributor's aged accounts payable are running 84% due in 30 days and 16% due in 60 days. It turns out that because a major customer is in bankruptcy proceedings, the distributor's limited cash flow in its invoice-to-pay subcycle has unexpectedly become the network bottleneck. A remedy for this situation must be worked out before realistic pull planning can resume. The remedy could be that the distributor establishes a new line of revolving credit with its bank or factors the accounts receivable of its remaining credit worthy customers.

Operating Rules at the Push/Pull Boundary

The push/pull boundary is the set of inventory buffer locations and cash buffer locations that separate the push zone from the pull zone. The push/pull boundary cuts across the entire width of the supply chain network. The push/pull boundary inventory buffer sometimes doubles as the constraint buffer and/or generally includes some amount of risk pooling inventory. The following planning conditions must be true at the push/pull boundary:

- Any partial BOM embedded in the push zone is independent of any partial BOM embedded in the pull zone. Each BOM structure is either in the push zone or in the pull zone, but cannot overlap into both.
- For each item or SKU, the push plan inventory level equals the pull plan inventory level at the push/pull boundary.
- For each cash buffer, the push plan cash level equals the pull plan cash level at the push/pull boundary.
- The demand output from the pull zone, by definition, is a forecast input into the push zone.

Preload Inventory for Synchronous Operation

Chapter 7 describes how to determine the required level of buffer inventory from an analysis of the mean and RMS standard deviation of variability and the desired service level. In a synchronous operation, there is one additional class of inventory buffers to plan called the *preload inventory*, see Figure 8-9. Preload inventory must

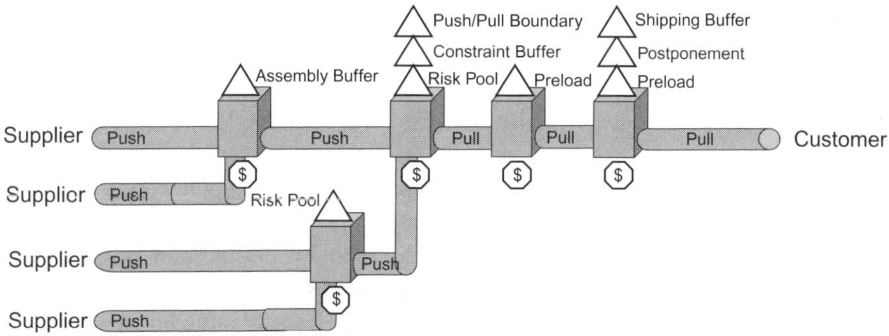

FIGURE 8-9 The positioning of network inventory.

TABLE 8-10
Preload Inventory at $Node_1$ and $Node_2$ for Synchronous Operation

Synchronous Network: Echelon$_2$ Echelon$_1$ Upstream Supplier –> Node$_2$ –> Pipeline$_2$ –> Node$_1$ –> Pipeline$_1$ –> Downstream Customer	
For cycle time$_2$ > cycle time$_1$ For transit time$_1$ > transit time$_2$	For Echelon$_1$ $PL_1 = TP_{Max} (t_{cycle2}/t_{cycle1})$ Where TP_{Max} is maximum throughput.
For cycle time$_2$ > cycle time$_1$ For transit time$_2$ > transit time$_1$	For Echelon$_1$ $PL_1 = TP_{Max} (t_{cycle2}/t_{cycle1} + t_{transit2}/t_{transit1} - 1)$
For cycle time$_1$ > cycle time$_2$ For transit time$_2$ > transit time$_1$	For Echelon$_1$ $PL_1 = TP_{Max} (t_{transit2}/t_{transit1})$
Preload Inventory for Echelon$_2$	$PL_2 = TP_{Max}$

be placed in each echelon of the synchronized portion of the supply chain before synchronization can begin. In a synchronous operation, each echelon matches supply with demand in one operating cycle, typically one day. The purpose of preload inventory is to allow the network to step from minimal throughput to maximum throughput in one operating cycle. The preload inventory gets replenished in each echelon during each cycle. Without preload inventory, it would take several operating cycles for the network to fully respond. This would cause undesirable backlog to develop, and the network to fall out of synchronization.

The preload inventory for echelon$_1$ depends on the relative ratios of the cycle times in echelons 1 and 2 and the relative ratios of the transit times in Pipelines 1 and 2, see Table 8-10. The preload inventory for echelon$_2$ is determined from the maximum throughput planned for the network.

A Detailed Pull Example

A supply chain network manufactures and distributes small forged hand tools for a regional market. The market area is small, occupying 2,500 square miles, and can be traversed by truck in a few hours. The push/pull boundary for the network is located at the interface between the tool factory and the distribution warehouse. The distribution warehouse and the set of regional hardware stores form two network echelons between the factory and the end-customer. The entire BOM for each tool occurs upstream from the push/pull boundary. The push/pull boundary is stocked with FGI, and the two echelons of distribution are planned and operated as a synchronous supply chain. Actual demand seen at the push/pull boundary is the accumulation of the daily point of sale demand from each store; this is used to develop a forecast for the upstream push zone. Planning for the pull zone involves determining that the network is capable based on a statistical analysis of demand and the desired service level, calculating the right level of preload inventory for synchronous operations, and monitoring that these network resources remain centered relative to actual demand. Table 8-11 highlights each of these points.

TABLE 8-11
A Synchronized Network Planning Example

Monthly Order Statistics in Units			Daily Pull Plan in Units		Centering Adjustment	
July to December Historical						
SKU	Mean	Std Dev				
A	26	8	January Pull Plan (22 days)			
B	7	11	Service Level	95%		
C	182	112	Max Throughput	24		
D	61	45	Mean Throughput	12.6		
Total Mean = 276		RMS = 121	Preload $Echelon_1$	36		
			Preload $Echelon_2$	24	Delta Constraint	0
August to January Historical					Delta $Preload_1$	0
SKU	Mean	Std Dev			Delta $Preload_2$	0
A	35	10	February Pull Plan (20 Days)		+/–25% Threshold = 3	
B	6	12	Service Level	95%	No Change	
C	155	93	Max Throughput	24		
D	54	47	Mean Throughput	13.0		
Total Mean = 260		RMS = 105	Preload $Echelon_1$	36		
			Preload $Echelon_2$	24	Delta Constraint	+9
September to February Historical					Delta $Preload_1$	+14
SKU	Mean	Std Dev			Delta $Preload_2$	+9
A	44	17	March Pull Plan (21 Days)		+/–25% Threshold = 3	
B	10	15	Service Level	95%	Adjust	
C	227	148	Max Throughput	33		
D	83	66	Mean Throughput	17.3		
Total Mean = 364		RMS = 164	Preload $Echelon_1$	50		
			Preload $Echelon_2$	33	Delta Constraint	–4
October to March Historical					Delta $Preload_1$	–7
SKU	Mean	Std Dev			Delta $Preload_2$	–4
A	41	15	April Pull Plan (22 Days)		+/–25% Threshold = 4	
B	8	12	Service Level	95%	No Change	
C	209	134	Max Throughput	29		
D	78	58	Mean Throughput	15.3		
Total Mean = 336		RMS = 147	Preload $Echelon_1$	43		
			Preload $Echelon_2$	29		

The tool factory manufactures four SKUs: A, B, C, and D. A rolling six months of historical demand data is used to calculate the mean and standard deviation for each SKU. This data is combined into a total mean and RMS value of the standard deviations. The network maintains a 95% service level, which requires a 2x multiplier of the RMS standard deviation. Monthly statistical demand quantities are converted into daily throughput requirements by dividing by the number of working days per month. The network is capable when it can support the total mean plus twice the RMS standard deviation on a daily basis. The inventory level at the distribution warehouse and the total inventory distributed across the set of stores are calculated from the equations for preload inventory in $echelon_2$ and preload inventory in $echelon_1$ respectively.

Once a month the daily pull plan is checked for any centering adjustment. First, the rolling six month historical demand is updated for each product SKU by dropping the oldest month's data and adding the latest month's data. Next, the updated demand is used to recalculate the maximum daily throughput and the preload inventory levels. These new values are compared with those of the previous month. Finally, if the difference, either up or down, exceeds a threshold, then the network capacity, inventory buffers, and cash buffers are adjusted to be centered on the new demand. In this example, +/–25% of the daily pull plan is used as the threshold. The +/–25% is a tradeoff between the pull plan becoming too nervous versus a change in capacity or inventory that is too large to be implemented within one month. Because the preload inventory is FGI, the inventory centering adjustment is made by adding or subtracting demand at the front-end of the factory's master production schedule. It then takes the manufacturing cycle time plus the transit time to implement the delta changes in buffer levels.

Synchronizing the Cash Flow

In a synchronous operation, there is a simultaneous physical flow of material out of each seller's inventory buffer into each buyer's inventory buffer. The distributor flows product to the store at the same time the store flows product to the customer. The same needs to happen with the cash flow. With only the order-to-delivery and order-to-stock subcycles synchronized, just half of that trading partner's order-to-delivery-to-cash cycle is synchronized. In a synchronous operation, there should be a simultaneous flow of cash out of each buyer's cash buffer and into each seller's cash buffer. The customer flows a cash payment to the store at the same time the store flows a cash payment to the distributor.

When the seller's finance organization has a policy of batching invoices and payments to save administrative costs, it precludes the possibility of synchronizing the cash flow. Sometimes organizations embrace a progression of process solutions while making the transition from paper orders, paper invoices, and net 30 days terms to paperless orders, paperless invoices, and synchronous cash payments. Although the seller's invoicing may be implemented by Electronic Data Interchange (EDI) or web-based EDI, and although the buyer's funds may be transferred electronically through Electronic Funds Transfer (EFT) services, the subcycle will not be synchronous if the buyer's cash management policy keeps A/P terms at net 30 days.

Synchronized versus Kanban Pull Operations

Under a synchronized operation, material flow is pulled to fulfill a customer order. Under a kanban operation, material flow is pulled to replenish an inventory location that has been consumed to fill a customer order. The echelons of a synchronized operation flow simultaneously, whereas the echelons of a kanban operation ripple serially. Kanban results in lower levels of inventory than with a push process because small quantities of inventory arrive where needed, just in time. Kanban results in a lower cost operation because the kanban itself replaces traditional purchase orders. A kanban operation is a better choice than a synchronous operation where the BOM

TABLE 8-12
Kanban Operations versus Synchronous Operations

Attribute	Kanban	Synchronous
Pull Operation	Serial ripple pull to replenish inventory consumed to fill a customer order.	Simultaneous pull to fulfill a customer order.
Advantage	Low cost; small inventory; just-in-time philosophy; visual management.	Only build what can be shipped; not dependent upon a forecast.
Disadvantage	MRP is a better choice for long lead time items; it is not a planning system.	Requires an investment in capacity and preload inventory; requires discipline.
Planning	Requires initial inventory fill from MRP push plans; self replenishing for short lead times.	From the pull planning system; preload and push/pull boundary inventories are planned from MRP push plans.
Ordering	Kanban cards or bins or signals.	Broadcast demand signal.
Lot Sizing	Fixed lot size; total number of kanbans in the system adjusted periodically.	Lot size of one or variable lot size determined by actual customer order.
Payment	Summary invoice at month end.	Synchronized cash flow.

begins to broaden and where strict synchronous control becomes too expensive or too difficult because of the number of nominal trading partners in that part of the network.

Kanban is an execution technique and not a planning system. Once the initial, and subsequent, kanbans are filled from upstream inventory, it is a self-replenishing technique that works best for short lead time items. Planning for the upstream inventory ultimately comes from MRP II push planning. The number of kanbans active within the pull operating zone at any one time is readjusted as the mean demand shifts up or down. The number of active kanbans is reduced as the manufacturing and distribution process yield improves. The calculation of the kanban quantity is outside the scope of this book. John Gross and Kenneth McInnis in their book, *Kanban Made Simple: Demystifying and Applying Toyota's Legendary Manufacturing Process*, ISBN 0-8144-0763-3, offer a methodology for calculating kanban quantities. Table 8-12 compares a kanban operation with a synchronous operation.

CLOSING THE NETWORK PLANNING LOOP

When all the pieces of network planning are finally put together and the planning loop is closed, there are subtle differences between replanning, undesirable network effects, and risk management in network operations. Push operations require continuous replanning because the push planning process attempts to fit a deterministic model to a set of forecasts, lead times, lot sizes, and inventory balances that have statistical fluctuation. Pull operations require periodic replanning to center the mean demand within the capacity, inventory buffer, and cash buffer capabilities of the network. At times, it is possible for network planning to get stuck in some very undesirable operating modes. Finally, some customer and supplier situations are so risky that they require an additional disciplined risk management approach.

Operations Replanning

Whenever a buffer is too empty or too full at a time that is too early or too late, the planning system will replan. The root cause for the inventory buffer or cash buffer being different from expected is usually the result of an inaccuracy or some variability for push planning, see Table 8-13. Employee education and training, inventory cycle counting, and systematic audits of the product BOM are the remedies to accuracy issues. The identification, root cause analysis, and elimination of lead time, cycle time, and transit time variability is the preferred remedy to variability issues. When variability cannot be eliminated, the value of the lead time, cycle time, or transit time should at least be extended past its mean to include a multiple of its standard deviation for planning. On the pull planning side, replanning is most often driven by the need to recenter the network's capability to meet the mean demand.

At least three different undesirable effects can occur when planning across an entire supply chain network. First, the bullwhip effect, mentioned earlier, is the network oscillating as a closed loop feedback system. This oscillation is caused by the serial communication of demand moving upstream coupled with cumulative

TABLE 8-13
Root Causes Behind Replanning

	For Push Planning
Inaccuracy	• Inventory balance inaccuracy • Cash balance inaccuracy • BOM inaccuracy
Variability	• Purchasing lead time • Manufacturing cycle time • Logistics transit time and customs clearance time
Quantization Effects	• Disaggregation • DRP transportation lot sizing • MPS packaging lot sizing • MRP procurement lot sizing and minimum buys • Dollars to units reconciliation
Uncertainty	• Forecast error and demand uncertainty • Process yield and supply uncertainty • Safety stock lost to shelf life or obsolescence
	For Pull Planning
	• Recentering a capable network relative to the mean demand • Cash flow or information flow as the network constraint
	Undesirable Network Effects
	• The network response oscillates due to the bullwhip effect • Accelerating network velocity causes schedule nervousness • Amplification of network variability inflates inventory and cash buffers

logistics delays moving downstream. Second, as the order-to-delivery-cash velocity of a network is accelerated and the overall responsiveness of a network increases, it is possible for operations planning to become too nervous. A *nervous plan* ratchets up or down toward an ever more optimum solution continuously overshooting or undershooting a realistic, stable plan. Any efficiencies in the plan are lost to the cost of having to constantly replan. When a plan is nervous, a minor change to the MPS causes significant change to the timing and quantities of lower-level items. A third undesirable network interaction occurs when the variability of logistics transit times and/or purchasing lead times and/or manufacturing and distribution cycle times stack up and become amplified, causing excessive amounts of network inventory and network cash. An example of such buffer inflation is described below.

A Network Example of Buffer Inflation

A supply chain network has five echelons between its customers and its raw material suppliers. Echelon 1 is customer facing, whereas Echelon 5 is raw materials facing. Echelons 1 and 2 are the in the pull zone and are synchronized to customer demand. Echelons 3, 4, and 5 are in the push zone and are pushed through a supply forecast using MRP II. In this example, for simplicity, the demand forecast and the supply forecast are identical. Echelon 2 is the network constraint. The $preload_2$ inventory buffer in Echelon 2 is the push/pull boundary and also the constraint buffer. MRP II also plans the product inventory used to adjust both preload inventories. This is done by prioritizing any preload inventory adjustments to the start of the supply forecast. A secondary calculation driven from MRP II is used to determine the level of safety stock for the risk pooling inventory buffers. Figure 8-10 shows the multiplication

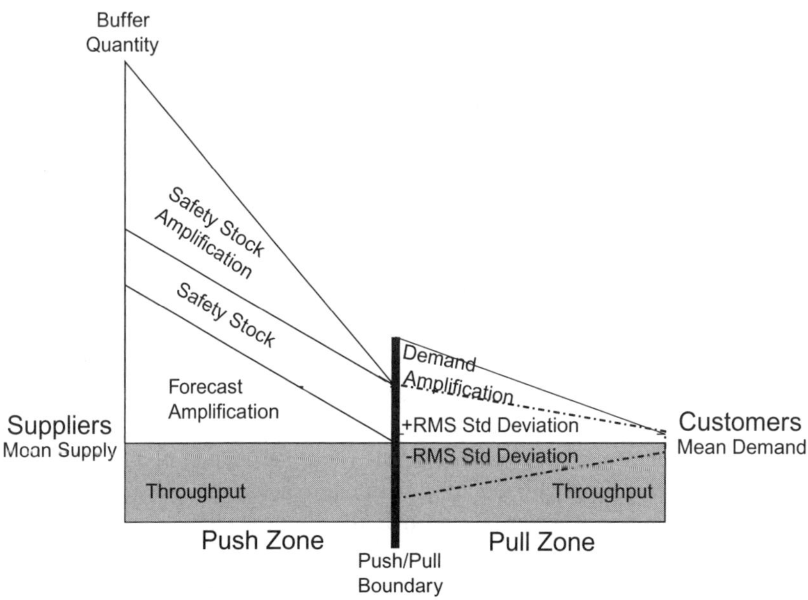

FIGURE 8-10 Pull zone and push zone multiplication and amplification of the buffers.

and amplification in the pull and push zones that tend to inflate the inventory and cash buffers in this network.

Table 8-14 details the inventory and cash buffers for the two-echelon, synchronous pull zone. The daily mean demand drives the table starting from the left center above the center line; demand uncertainty and network variability drive the table starting from the left center below the center line. The mean customer demand is 100 units and the RMS standard deviation of demand is 75 units. The pull plan is set to achieve a 99.7 service level for the customer. In this example the operating cash buffers are used to purchase preload inventory; there would be additional financial investment to buy network capacity. The mean throughput, the multiplier of the RMS standard deviation of throughput, and the amplification of cycle time and transit time variability each drive the need for inventory and cash in the customer facing $echelon_1$ buffers. Variability amplification is not a factor for the inventory and cash buffers in $echelon_2$. The dollar value of each cash buffer is the multiplier times the dollar value ($$) of one unit of FGI.

Table 8-15 details the impact on inventory and cash buffers for the three-echelon push zone. The supply forecast mirrors the mean and safety stock required to achieve the desired service level in the pull zone. The forecast error is an additional term that drives an unnecessary amplification of the inventory and cash buffers. Planning for lot sizing and lead time variability at each echelon also amplifies the inventory and cash buffers. A complete analysis of the push zones requires capturing every line item on the product BOM. The cash buffers shown in Table 8-15 are representative, but incomplete. $\$\$_3$, $\$\$_4$, and $\$\$_5$ refer to the cash buffers within their respective (nominal) trading partner echelons.

Risk Management

During the normal course of business, a few customer deals will be seen possibly as high return but definitely as very high in business risk. It is important to be able to spot these situations as planning patterns that are exceptions to the norm. As such, it is prudent to backstop the normal planning process with a formal risk management process including *scenario planning* with *predefined triggers* and *contingencies*. Some typical examples include:

- *Buying ahead*—The close of a big deal hinges on the guarantee of a better-than-competitive lead time. The network makes a significant investment to buy ahead on long lead time inventory that is unique to this customer. If the deal is not closed, the inventory will remain on the network's books with a very low probability of ever being consumed.
- *Unplanned product promotions*—Sales and distribution create a product promotion without collaborating with manufacturing. The extra demand catches supply by surprise, and manufacturing scrambles to adjust network capability. Overtime, premium logistics, and unfavorable material purchase price variances are thrown at the problem, eliminating the possibility of marginal profit.

TABLE 8-14
Pull Zone Inventory and Cash Buffers for the Example Network

Daily Demand	Daily Throughput	Capability	Preload$_1$ Inventory	Preload$_2$ Inventory	Partial Network Cash
			Cash Buffer$_1$ Mean 400 × $$	Cash Buffer$_2$ Mean 100 × $$	Mean 500 × $$
			$t_{cycle2}/t_{c1} = 3$ $t_{transit2}/t_{t1} = 2$		
Mean 100	Mean 100	Mean 100	Echelon$_1$ 400	Echelon$_2$ 100	
RMS S.D. 75	RMS S.D. 75	3 × S.D. 225	900	225	
		Service Level 99.7%	Cash Buffer$_1$ 3 × S.D. 900 × $$	Cash Buffer$_2$ 3 × S.D. 225 × $$	3 × S.D. 1125 × $$
			Variability $\Delta t_{cycle2}/t_{c1} = 0.50$ $\Delta t_{transit2}/t_{t1} = 0.33$		
			Amplification 270		
			Cash Buffer$_1$ Amplify 270 × $$		Amplify 270 × $$
					Network Cash Sum 1895 × $$

TABLE 8-15
Push Zone Inventory and Cash Buffers for the Example Network

Forecast (per month)	S&OP/MPS (per week)	MRP for Echelon$_3$	MRP for Echelon$_4$	MRP for Echelon$_5$	Partial Network Cash
Supply F/C = Demand F/C	ΔFGI = 0 ΔBacklog = 0				
20 days/month	4.33 wks/month	Quantity 1 per	Quantity 2 per	Quantity 2 per	
Mean 20 × 100 = 2000	Mean 2000/4.33 = 462				
	Lot Size = 500 MPS = 500 Δ = +38	500			Cash Buffer 500 × $$$_3$
		Lot Size = 500 MRP = 500 Lead Time = 2 wk	1000		Cash Buffer 1000 × $$$_4$
Safety Stock 20 ×225 = 4500	Safety Stock 4500/4.33 = 1039		Lot Size = 1250 MRP = 1250 Δ = +250 Lead Time = 8 wk	2500	Cash Buffer 2500 × $$$_5$
	Lot Size = 500 MPS = 1000 Δ = −39	1000			Cash Buffer 1000 × $$$_3$
		Lot Size = 500 MRP = 1000 Lead Time = 2 wk	2000		Cash Buffer 2000 × $$$_4$
Forecast Error 20 ×50 = 1000	Forecast Amplification 1000/4.33 = 231		Lot Size = 1250 MRP = 2500 Δ = +500 Lead Time = 8 wk	5000	Cash Buffer 5000 × $$$_5$

TABLE 8-15 (Continued)
Push Zone Inventory and Cash Buffers for the Example Network

Forecast (per month)	S&OP/MPS (per week)	MRP for $Echelon_3$	MRP for $Echelon_4$	MRP for $Echelon_5$	Partial Network Cash
	Lot Size = 500 MPS = 500 $\Delta = \pm 269$	500			Cash Buffer $500 \times \$\$_3$
		Lot Size = 500 MRP = 500 $\Delta = 0$ Lead Time = 2 wk	1000		Cash Buffer $1000 \times \$\$_4$
			Lot Size = 1250 MRP = 1250 $\Delta = \pm 250$ Lead Time = 8 wk	2500	Cash Buffer $2500 \times \$\$_5$
		Lead Time Variability $\Delta t_{Lead} = 1$ wk	Lead Time Variability $\Delta t_{Lead} = 3$wk		
			Amplification 1 wk/2 wks × 4000 = 2000	Amplification 3wks/8wks × 10,000 = 3750	Cash Buffer $2000 \times \$\$_4 +$ $3750 \times \$\$_5$

- *Material or capacity allocations*—A critical lower-level item goes on allocation from its supplier due to either a shortage of raw material, severely constrained production capacity, or the supplier's temporary loss of the formula. This allocation constrains the network throughput.
- *Foreign currency fluctuation*—Inventory is purchased in a non–U.S. dollar denominated currency and held through a significant foreign currency fluctuation. The financial techniques to hedge this investment are beyond the scope of this book, see *Global Supply Management: A Guide to International Purchasing* by Dick Locke, ISBN 0-7863-0797-8.
- *Moving to a Country Of Origin with a lower labor rate*—Product manufacture is outsourced to a multinational contract manufacturer with plant locations throughout the world who chases the lowest labor rates. Trading partner relationships and collaborative planning never quite gel because they are in a constant state of flux.

IN SUMMARY

This Chapter focuses on planning the network capacity constraint, inventory buffers, and cash buffers to be capable relative to customer demand. Push planning and pull planning techniques are described in some detail. Practical issues that get in the way of trading partner collaboration are identified, and where possible, remedies are suggested. Undesirable network effects including the bullwhip effect and variability amplification are discussed with possible remedies. A competitive supply chain network operates from a single, collaborative operations plan that answers these fundamental questions:

- What should be forecast?
- How much capacity, inventory, and cash does it take to make the network capable?
- How does push planning differ from pull planning?

Chapter 9 details the cause and effect relationships between competitive network design and operation with the creation of value for customers and stakeholders. A competitive supply chain network favorably impacts the income statement, the balance sheet, and the cash flow statement. Chapter 9 completes the journey from an internally focused, cost-based perspective to a network focused, throughput-based perspective.

They needed to unwind from the long workweek. The weather was fine, and they decided to go for a walk around Briant's Pond. The Canadian geese were a big problem at the pond, leaving their mark on the pathway. The supply chain architect had to pay close attention to where they walked as he listened to what his wife was saying.

"I can't believe I just spent Saturday morning working on a plan for my business! What was I thinking? I should be tending my rose garden, baking in my new kitchen, or shopping."

"Well, at least you didn't have to drive into work for another brutal day at the office. What's the big plan you are working so hard on?"

"My cash flow is very tight again. My instructors keep wanting to be paid all the time. I need to do a better job of predicting my income and expense levels over the next six months. You already know how I feel about forecasting. No one can tell the future; it feels sometimes like it is just a waste of time to plan too far ahead."

They were approaching the northern edge of the path as it narrowed to squeeze between the entrance road into a new tract of condominiums and the retaining wall for the pond's spillway. "We have had this conversation before. Planning is not a waste of time as long as you forecast the right things."

"What do you mean?"

"In my business there is often confusion about whether to forecast inventory or to forecast capacity. The push zone is driven from a supply forecast for inventory, whereas the pull zone is driven from actual orders with a capacity forecast to keep the network capable."

"My problem is different, I think," she said. "I have more control over the number of classes offered than the number of students attending any one class. My pricing is structured to take advantage of that by charging a fixed price per class for up to ten students with a per student adder for class sizes above ten. I'm able to forecast the class base revenue pretty well, but the additive revenue is all over the map."

"Um—"

They were now walking through a wooded area where the temperature was a little cooler and the gnats a little more annoying.

She continued, "There's another problem with my planning. The demand for my basics classes seems to have peaked. Fortunately, we started offering intermediate level classes last spring. But now I have to forecast both the decline of the basics level classes plus the growth of the intermediate level classes."

"Yes, it is always difficult to predict how a new product will do and whether its revenue stream will totally replace the revenue stream from the old product. The only advice I can offer you is to compare the startup of the intermediate level product with your demand history from the basics level product. Plan for the new product demand as a range of demand rather than an exact demand. For example, plan what it would take to offer two to three intermediate level classes during September and October rather than two classes the third week of October."

"That is interesting advice, but it puts my business right back in a cash flow jam." They were near the end of their walk and could see the car again.

"Maybe you have to plan a couple of things simultaneously. Not only do you have to plan for the instructor capacity your business has to deliver on-demand training to your customers, you also must plan your cash position differently. Your cash flow may have a seasonality pattern that requires a seasonal cash buffer, such as a revolving line of credit, for the business to pay its instructors until the revenue stream picks up again. The seasonality of your classes will be tied to your client's spending patterns and their fiscal years."

"I think you are right," she said as they got back in the car. "I haven't been planning my cash flow for an entire year, and I need to do that. All this thinking about planning makes my head hurt. Do you want to buy me some ice cream?"

9 Generating Top Line Growth and Bottom Line Profit

Sunday, September 1

It was Sunday morning. Tomorrow the supply chain architect would return to the never-ending routine of work, but for now, he could savor this quiet moment alone in the house drinking coffee and enjoying *The New York Times*. It was funny that with all the Internet news services there was still something to be said for reading the newspaper.

The front page of the real estate section caught his eye. He stared at a stunning interior photo of a kitchen that might as well be his. The article beneath described the complete property including the kitchen, breakfast nook, and bay window. It was not far away in a neighboring town. The article concluded on page seven that the property was a steal for $695,000. "I know right where that property is located. They must be joking," he thought.

Just then, his wife came home. "Hi, anybody here?" she called out.

"Yes, I'm here in the kitchen," he replied. "You would not believe how much they want for this house advertised in *The Times!* And, it has *our* kitchen!"

She stood behind him and looked over his shoulder at the newspaper. "Guess the renovation added a lot of value to our house. I wonder what we could get for this place now?"

"I'm not moving."

"We're not talking about moving; we're talking about the value of our home. When we decided to renovate the kitchen, we increased the value of the house both for us as the current owners and for someone else as future owners when we sell."

"I'm not selling the house either."

Ignoring his last statement she continued, "You have to look at the value of a house from two points of view. The current owner gains the immediate benefit of improved kitchen convenience while a future owner gains the benefit of a modernized property that continues to appreciate with the market."

"I see value differently," he said finally.

"Oh?"

"I see value inherent in the 'process.' When we decided to renovate the kitchen, we began a process that balanced our personal values of quality versus cost versus time to completion. Take the selection of material for the countertop as just one small example. We had choices of, say, marble, Corian, or laminate. The process we used to choose Corian reflected our value of wanting high quality at a reasonable price available in the right timeframe."

"That's interesting. I see the value of the end product from the eyes of an owner or buyer while you see value in the process of decisions bounded by our balance of quality, cost, and time."

"Maybe we are both right," said the supply chain architect.

"Yes, but some of our decisions might have been made differently if we had designed the kitchen for a future owner," she replied. "Maybe that person would want to entertain larger parties. Or maybe that person would want to bake more, or microwave more, or—"

"At least we can agree that value begins with a clear understanding of the owner's needs."

"Yes."

"Good! As one of the owners, I'm hungry and could use a sandwich for lunch. Shall I fix one for you, too?"

*****

The supply chain architect snoozed on the sofa after lunch, his thoughts drifting in lazy circles as he reawakened. He looked at his watch to see the time; their symphony tickets were for a 3 p.m. performance.

With the twelve-hour difference in time zones, it was already Monday morning, September 2, in Singapore. They had been making steady progress with Hector and the operations team in Singapore. Their immediate goal was to keep the outsourcing transition transparent to the end-customer while they worked feverishly to reestablish a reliable supply chain. However, the real issue was how to use this new supply chain to both increase revenues and reduce costs. He lay on the sofa reflecting on their latest debate.

"If we make the supply chain any longer, it will take forever to get product to our customers! Our availability dates keep moving out! Stone & Jenkins is about ready to place a $1.8 million order, but are we ready to commit for one of our very best customers?" ranted Bob Donovan, the sales manager.

"If you want to talk about a real nightmare, talk about this. Our stock price has fallen five months straight. We need to expand our borrowing, and our bank will no longer offer us preferred client rates," moaned Dana Hoffmann, CFO.

"Not to mention that we lost some of our best employees with the decision to outsource to Singapore," said Alice Way from human resources.

"Being the acting VP of manufacturing hasn't been a picnic either," said Roberta Perez. "Let's stop the 'pity party' and get back to running the business. You are all well aware that we made the decision to move subassembly operations to Singapore in order to reengineer our cost structures and become more competitive."

"Roberta, a competitive network can provide value in more than one dimension to more than one stakeholder," said the architect. "Cost reduction is certainly very important, especially when it improves profitability and earnings for our owners. But it doesn't help our customers unless we choose to drop product pricing. When the cost reduction is accomplished by lengthening the supply chain, it can actually hurt delivery performance to our customers."

"So, you are questioning management's decision?" replied Roberta.

"Not at all. I'm working towards making the point that there are other important value dimensions we haven't yet addressed. A second value dimension is to use the supply chain network to grow revenue. If we drop product prices, our revenue base shrinks. If we can gain entry into new market segments or introduce significant new products, our revenue base grows. We have not talked about what it would take to convince Stone & Jenkins to buy more. Are we their preferred supplier in Paris? Are we their preferred supplier in Tokyo?"

"The local competition has a significant advantage in France and Japan. We can't compete against their in-country distribution," said Bob.

"I'm sure there are many reasons why this is very difficult. However, we have no choice but to make our new supply chain work. The third value dimension is to grow returns by shrinking our asset base. How can we operate through Singapore with less total network inventory and less total network cash? With higher profits from reduced costs and higher returns from reduced inventory and cash assets, our stock price will appreciate in value for our owners."

"That would be very good. How much could we reduce inventory?" Dana wanted to know.

"The point is that a competitive supply chain network creates value in three ways through improved profits, through growth in revenue, and through improvement in return on assets. We have been intensely focused on only one dimension."

"It sounds like a good theory, but how can it be put into practice?" asked Dana.

"There are direct cause and effect linkages between the design and operation of a competitive supply chain network and the creation of value. Here, let me show them to you," replied the supply chain architect.

The *competitive threshold* of a supply chain network is determined from the principles of supply chain management and the relationships of the trading partners. It is the application of the velocity, variability, visualize and vocalize principles, explained in Chapters 2 through 8, that determine the degree to which the supply chain network can win relative to its competition. This Chapter is about generating both top line growth and bottom line profit through the fifth APICS SCM Principle: "A supply chain creates net value."

THE VALUE PRINCIPLE

Earlier Chapters present network design, the composite BOM, and network operations. These three essential building blocks combine into a competitive supply chain architecture under the value principle. There are many tradeoffs to make, such as optimizing the income statement relative to the balance sheet. There are many misconceptions to overcome, including thinking that top line growth and bottom line profit are either/or rather than both. In the end, all the pieces must fit together perfectly.

VALUE IN THE EYE OF THE BEHOLDER

Shifting your point of view from an internally focused cost perspective to a network focused throughput perspective requires a cultural change in your thinking. This change moves the competitive threshold from investment and operational decisions that optimize locally to investment and operational decisions that optimize globally. A natural place to start is with the fact that any organization can be viewed one of three ways:

- *As an independent firm*—It is a myth to believe that a single, vertically integrated firm can conduct business in complete isolation from all other firms. However, income statements and balance sheets are constructed for legal entities as though this were true.
- *As a trading partner within a single network*—One main point of this book is that business organizations exist as trading partners in the context of a competitive network. However, being a trading partner operating within a single network is a pure play rarely found in business.
- *As a (nominal) trading partner in multiple networks*—A business organization is typically both a trading partner and a nominal trading partner while simultaneously operating in multiple, and sometimes competing, networks. The firm's income statement and balance sheet aggregate and hide the various network pieces in which the firm is a participant.

There are four classes of stakeholders in any supply chain network:

- End-customers
- Raw material suppliers
- Each trading partner's owners
- Each trading partner's employees

Each class of stakeholder is looking to win from the competitive business situation in a different way. Table 9-1 shows the fundamental value that each stakeholder expects from the network. Sometimes value to one class of stakeholder comes at the expense of another class of stakeholder. For example, when a business decides to outsource manufacturing to a lower cost Country Of Origin in order to improve owner returns, the employees of the former trading partner lose their employment. Every investment and operational decision in a system environment cause favorable and unfavorable effects to ripple through the network.

TABLE 9-1
Fundamental Benefits to Stakeholders

Stakeholder Class	End-Customers	TP's Owners	TP's Employees	Raw Mat'l Suppliers
Fundamental Benefit	The perfect order	Return on investment	Employment stability	Sustained business

VALUE CAUSE AND EFFECT

The cause-and-effect relationships within a supply chain network are one of the least understood aspects of supply chain management. Supply chain networks are complex feedback systems that often respond in a non-linear manner. It is a common practice to gauge the success of a public business by analyzing the financial performance (the income statement and the balance sheet) of its parent organization. Over time the value of these financials are reflected in the share price of the parent organization's common stock traded in the financial markets. A company's stock price certainly seems disconnected in time and place from the day-to-day operations of the business.

Compounding this issue is the tendency to separate the individual trading partner's performance from the network's performance. Common stock shares are not sold for supply chain networks, nor does anyone bother to review the income statement and balance sheet financial performance of the network as a whole. Yet the operational and financial performance of the globally optimized network is perhaps more important than the operational and financial performance of the locally optimized single firm. This is because when one of the trading partners is optimized at the expense of the network, it commands a higher stock price—for a while.

There are three ways that competitive supply chain architecture can benefit a trading partner:

- Trading partner revenue increases when the supply chain network is able to penetrate new market segments and sustain increased levels of throughput. A network has an advantage over an individual trading partner because the network can more easily bundle customized products and services to attract new customer segments.
- Trading partner profitability is improved in the face of fierce competition when the supply chain network collaborates to reduce its cost structure. A network has an advantage over an individual trading partner because the network has more resources and opportunities to apply to cost reduction.
- Trading partner inventory and cash assets are minimized while the supply chain network delivers at the same level of customer service. Inventory and cash can be better planned, more optimally placed, and synchronized through network collaboration. This sustains a positive cash flow and provides a higher return on investment.

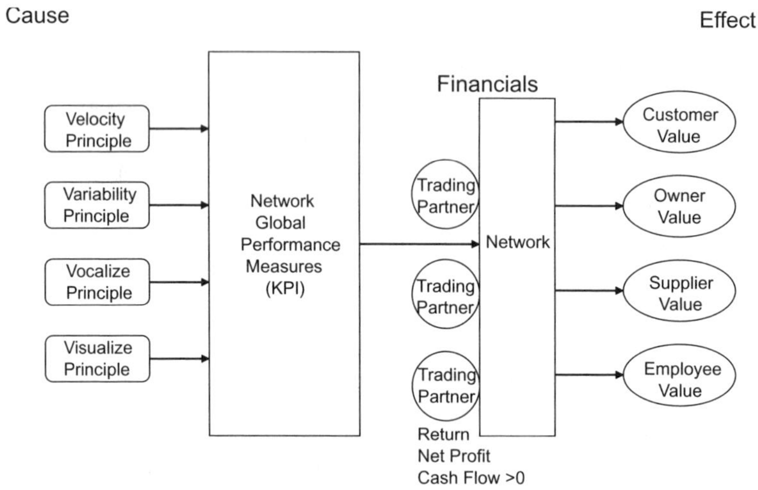

FIGURE 9-1 Value cause and effect in supply chain networks.

Positive cash flow, net profitability, and a competitive return on investment are all essential to the financial health of the individual trading partner. Each of these can flourish in the context of the right network architecture, yet somehow it is difficult to see a clear cause and effect. Figure 9-1 diagrams this cause and effect at a high level; more detail is provided in the following sections of this Chapter. Working from left to right, the application of the velocity, variability, vocalize and visualize principles cause a change in the network. This change is reflected first through the global performance measures of the network operations, and second through the financial performance of the individual trading partners. The ultimate effect is the flow of value to each class of stakeholder including an appreciation of stock price.

The Value Circle

This Chapter completes the value circle by adding an eighth axis, Return On Invested Capital (ROIC), to the diagram introduced for network design in Chapter 4 and extended to network operations in Chapter 7. Figure 9-2 shows the complete value circle. The smaller the area enclosed by a continuous line plotted on the value circle, higher the network's value to its customers and to its other stakeholders.

The axes of the value circle alternate between the APICS SCM Principles and the set of global performance measures. The order of these axes is not random. Improvement through the application of each pair of principles causes a measurable effect in the corresponding performance measure. Table 9-2 puts it all together.

- The vocalize and variability principles drive the total network inventory performance measure.
- The variability and velocity principles drive the landed cost performance measure.

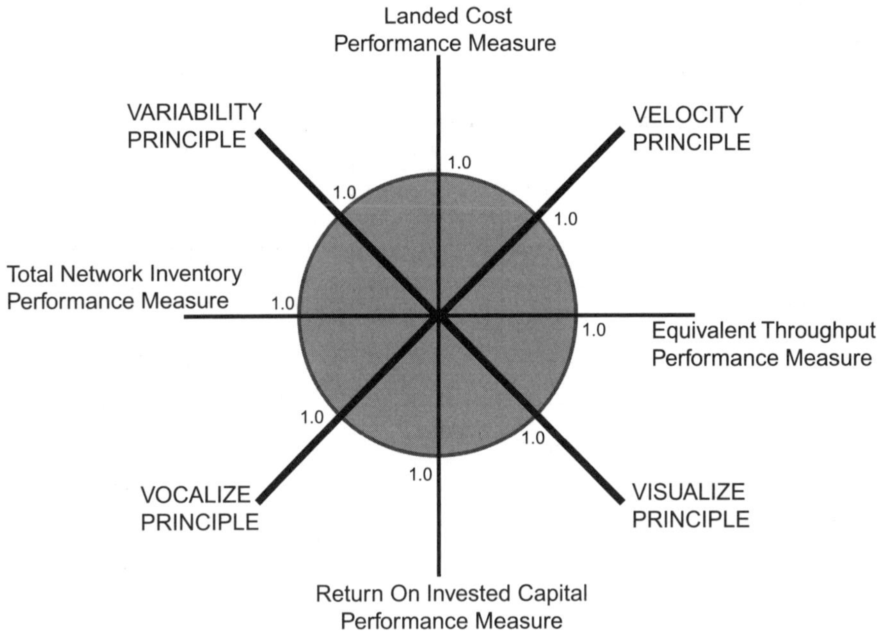

FIGURE 9-2 The value circle.

- The velocity and visualize principles drive the equivalent throughput performance measure.
- The visualize and vocalize principles drive the return on invested capital performance measure.

Return on Invested Capital

The ROIC axis is opposite the landed cost axis, and it lies between the visualize and vocalize axis on the value circle. In general, return on asset ratios are very important because they integrate a measure of the strength of the trading partner's income statement with a measure of the strength of its balance sheet. ROIC is a particularly valuable financial ratio because it shows a strong correlation, over time, with the trend of a company's stock price. When ROIC increases as a percentage, the market price of the common stock usually increases.

Moreover, ROIC can be calculated based on a network income statement and a network balance sheet. This makes ROIC a valuable network performance measure because it can be used to analyze the impact of outsourcing and insourcing decisions. For example, a decision to outsource might improve the after tax profitability and reduce the asset base of a manufacturing trading partner resulting in a better ROIC for the manufacturer; see Table 9-3. However, this same decision might result in lower total after tax profitability and higher total assets for the network resulting in a poorer ROIC for the network as a whole. This would suggest that the decision to

TABLE 9-2
Value Cause and Effect

Value Circle Axis	SCM Principle (Cause)	Performance (Effect)	Explanation
Vocalize	"Synchronize supply with demand"		Competitiveness is achieved by synchronizing capacity, inventory, and cash relative to the product BOM with demand.
Total Network Inventory		X	Measures the minimization of network assets in \$-Days. Lower network inventory can result in a higher return on investment.
Variability	"Leverage worldwide logistics"		Competitiveness is achieved by eliminating variability from the network making product delivery and quality more predictable.
Landed Cost		X	Measures the optimization of the network cost structure relative to the product BOM. Lower landed cost can result in higher bottom line profitability.
Velocity	"Build a competitive infrastructure"		Competitiveness is achieved by accelerating the order-to-delivery-to-cash cycle raising the level of end-customer satisfaction.
Equivalent Throughput		X	Measures the matching of supply and demand. Higher throughput can result in higher top line revenue for all the trading partners.
Visualize	"Measure performance globally"		Competitiveness is achieved by keeping the network aligned with the business strategy through the use of global performance measures.
Return On Invested Capital		X	Measures the optimization of the income statement with the balance sheet. A higher ROIC can result in a higher stock price.

outsource benefits one trading partner at the expense of the network and at the expense of other owners.

ROIC is calculated and plotted as:

$$\begin{aligned} \text{ROIC} &= [\text{Net Profit After Tax}/[\text{Fixed Assets} + \text{Inventory} + \text{Receivables} \\ &\quad - \text{Payables}]] \times 100\% \\ &= [\text{Net Profit After Tax}/[\text{Capacity Assets} + \text{Working Capital}]] \times 100\% \end{aligned}$$

TABLE 9-3
An Example ROIC Calculation

	The Vertically Integrated Firm	The Firm After Outsourcing
From the income statement: • Profit after tax	Chapter 4, Table 4-3 $164,775	Chapter 4, Table 4-5 $581,939
From the balance sheet: • Fixed assets (book value) • Inventory • Accounts receivable • Accounts payable	Chapter 7, Table 7-2 $2,380,000 $1,267,400 $487,500 $243,730	Chapter 7, Table 7-3 $1,785,000 $253,480 $487,500 $328,460
Return on invested capital	$\frac{164.8\text{K} \times 100\%}{2{,}380\text{K} + 1{,}267\text{K} + 487.5\text{K} - 243.7\text{K}}$ ROIC = 4.2%	$\frac{581.9\text{K} \times 100\%}{1{,}785\text{K} + 253.5\text{K} + 487.5\text{K} - 328.5\text{K}}$ ROIC = 26.5%

$$\frac{\text{Operating ROIC}}{\text{Baseline ROIC}} =$$

$$\frac{\text{Operating [Profit After Tax / [Capacity + Inventory + Receivables − Payables]]} \times 100\%}{\text{Baseline [Profit After Tax / [Capacity + Inventory + Receivables − Payables]]} \times 100\%}$$

Where ROIC improves toward the origin of the value circle.

OPTIMIZING THE NETWORK

In this Chapter, the building blocks of network design, the composite BOM, and network operations are combined into a value delivery system. The value delivery system is multi-dimensional and often non-linear. It exists within either a friendly or a hostile environment defined by the business strategy, the competitive context, and an information technology backdrop. Its stability depends upon intentional change management and feedback control mechanisms. The value delivery system is optimized for demand responsiveness, kept flexible to competitive thrusts, and made adaptable to external threats.

NETWORKING THE FLOW OF MATERIAL, INFORMATION, AND CASH

The subtitle of this book is "*A Blueprint for Networking the Flow of Material, Information, and Cash.*" Figure 9-3 is the cover graphic, depicting a trading partner enmeshed within a network. The inventory buffer of the trading partner connects the downstream order-to-delivery subcycle with the upstream order-to-stock subcycle. This material flow is limited by a network constraint that appears to be the capacity of the outbound logistics pipeline. The cash buffer of the trading partner connects the upstream invoice-to-cash subcycle with the downstream invoice-to-pay subcycle. The cash flow is international, with euros converting to dollars and dollars converting to yen.

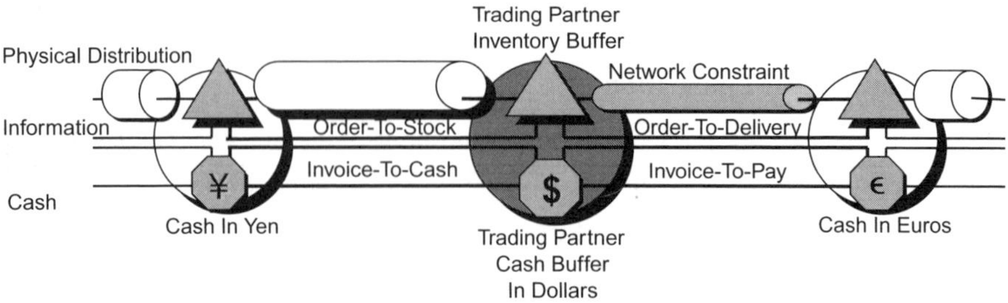

FIGURE 9-3 Networking the flow of material, information, and cash.

Stakeholder value is created when the supply chain network delivers throughput. The network's *threshold of competitiveness* is defined through the selection of trading partners, the business relationships established among these trading partners, the business processes that link these trading partners, and the performance measures that keep these trading partners in alignment with the business strategy. *The higher the network velocity, the lower the network variability, and the higher the network vocalization and visualization are, the greater the network's competitiveness.*

AN EXCEL SPREADSHEET ANALOGY

What form does the value-delivery system take? Do the pieces combine into the network as a linear chain, or is the network more like a web, with every piece touching every other piece? Are the connections one-to-one, one-to-many, many-to-one, or many-to-many? Where is there feedback? How are responsiveness, flexibility, and adaptability implemented? Suddenly, the task of optimizing a supply chain network becomes very complex and difficult to conceptualize.

Creating an Excel spreadsheet is a powerful analogy for optimizing a supply chain network. A new spreadsheet is begun by placing something into one cell. It does not matter which cell is chosen first because rows and columns can be inserted or deleted, above and below, to the left or to the right of the first cell. The work progresses with more things entered into adjacent cells either down a column or across a row. The copy and paste function makes it easy to replicate something from one cell into many other new cells. After a while, a contiguous core of cells has been entered into the spreadsheet. Some optimization takes place using the cut and paste function to rearrange the cell core. Next, some logical and mathematical relationships are defined among the cells in the cell core. Occasionally upon entry, Excel will remind the user that a syntax rule has been violated, and an error has to be fixed.

Some later time, after the cell core has been defined and its logical and mathematical relationships programmed and debugged, it becomes desirable to insert, rearrange, or delete a column or row that intersects the cell core. Rearrangement is the most difficult. It is done by first inserting a blank column or row to expand the cell core, second cutting and pasting the specific column or row, and third deleting the old column or row to close the gap in the cell core. When an entire column or row is manipulated, it is often the case that the logical and mathematic relationships with the cell core become broken. These breaks must be fixed in order for the spreadsheet to function properly. The spreadsheet is optimized when the geometry of cells is minimal, the logical and mathematical relationships among the cells are all functional, and the page settings produce the proper printed format.

- *Copy and paste*—A cell is replicated and the relationships to the cell are replicated.
- *Cut and paste*—A cell is moved and the relationships to the cell are kept intact.
- *Insert [cell/row/column]*—A new cell, row, or column placement is established without any relationships to other cells.
- *Delete [cell/row/column]*—Eliminates existing cell, row, or column placements and relationships.

It is easy to relate this Excel spreadsheet analogy to a supply chain network. Cells are the placement of core trading partner nodes, including a capacity capability, an inventory buffer location, and a cash buffer location per trading partner. The columns of the spreadsheet represent the echelons of the network. The rows of the spreadsheet represent the width of the network. A network design is begun by placing a midstream trading partner into a cell. Echelons of downstream (nominal) trading partner cells are added to reach the end-customer. A check of market reach versus a competitive order-to-delivery cycle time determines the downstream network length. A check of market reach versus the desired channel segmentation and geography determines the downstream network width. Echelons of upstream (nominal) trading partners are added to reach each raw material. The composite BOM is checked for fit against the core network with the necessary adjustment made to the number of echelons in the midstream. A check of the suppliers needed to support each BOM level and their geography determines the upstream network width. The copy and paste function is used to extend the network width for additional suppliers, channels of distribution, and customers along the network edge. At this point, all the core (nominal) trading partners are identified on the grid. All the customers in each target market can be reached, the composite BOM product structure is fully connected, and each raw material is accessed.

The first level of network optimization occurs, before considering anything about the subcycle connections, through a reduction in the cell footprint of the core network. When the footprint reduction involves the manipulation of an entire column or row, the new column or row must be created before cutting and pasting an existing column or row. Then, the remaining column or row gap is closed. An analogous set of commands to build the core network footprint would include:

- Insert a core trading partner into a cell
- Copy and paste (cell) at the network edge to add a supplier or to add a customer
- Copy and paste (cell) within the core to add a (nominal) trading partner
- Delete a core trading partner from a cell
- Insert an internal network echelon (column) to add (nominal) trading partners

- Cut and paste a network echelon (column) to rearrange (nominal) trading partners
- Delete an internal network echelon (column)
- Insert an internal network width (row) to add (nominal) trading partners
- Cut and paste network width (row) to rearrange (nominal) trading partners
- Delete an internal network width (row)

The second level of network optimization occurs in the individual subcycle connections after the core network footprint has been set. Upstream portions of the network retain some linear relationships that reflect the structure of the bill of materials. Each of the core trading partners is connected to demand signals, planning forecasts, and global performance measures. The node connections are optimized through simplification, reduction, parallel processing, and synchronization.

A third level of network optimization occurs in the closed loop performance of the core network. Is the network responsive to changes in demand, or does it oscillate under the bullwhip effect? Is the network kept flexible, matching supply and demand in its competitive environment, or is the network out of sync? Is the network adaptable to unexpected external threats, or would the business fold up? The following sections discuss each level of network optimization.

FIRST LEVEL NETWORK OPTIMIZATION

When a supply chain network is successful in making the change from being internally focused and cost driven to being network focused and throughput driven, the change in perspective optimizes the relationships among the core trading partners. The core network footprint has a length, a width, and a shape. Although some would argue that the shape of the core network footprint is ultimately a web, with every trading partner touching every other trading partner, the reality is that a supply chain network must preserve the linear integrity of its bills of materials. Therefore, a supply chain network has a distinctive upstream, midstream, downstream, and reverse stream pattern. The notion of a web-like structure comes from the idea that most trading partner nodes and all of the nominal trading partner nodes operate simultaneously within multiple supply chain networks.

RATIONALIZING THE CORE NETWORK FOOTPRINT

The first level of network optimization is in the rationalization of the material flow among the core network of (nominal) trading partners. The core network footprint, by itself, can shift the network's competitive threshold as plotted on the value circle, see Figure 9-4. In this figure, when the network length is shortened at the same level of throughput, the results is a tradeoff of a higher landed cost for a lower network inventory and a higher network ROIC.

Rationalize the core network footprint by working through the following checklist. The first level of optimization has a direct positive impact on throughput, landed cost, network inventory, and return on invested capital on the value circle.

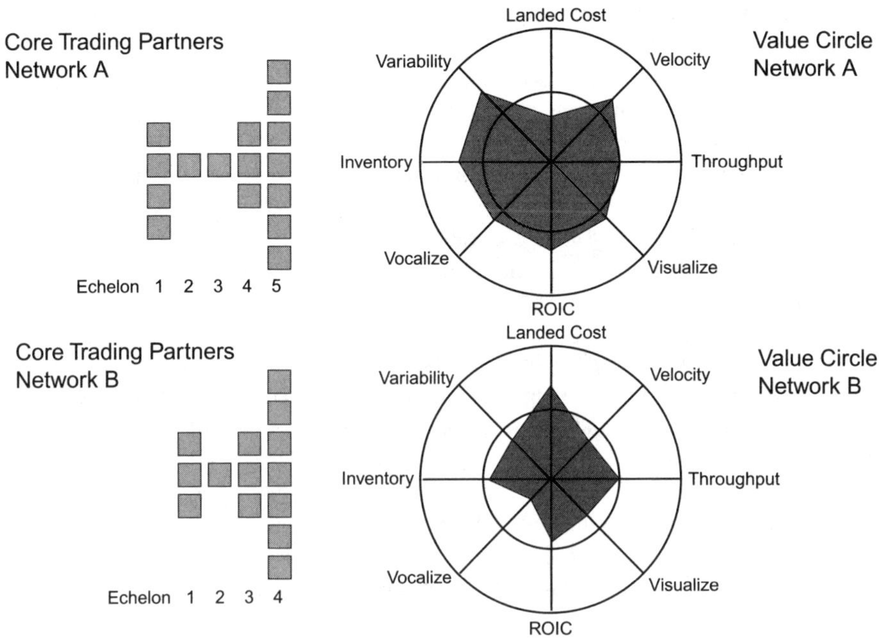

FIGURE 9-4 Optimizing the core network to improve the value circle.

- ☑ What is the value-adding reason for each network echelon that contributes to the total network length?
- ☑ The upstream [width × length] of the network is a function of how the composite BOM fits with the network. Can the number of suppliers be consolidated to reduce network width? Can the BOM be flattened to reduce network length? At this level, the rationalization of the supply base is limited to the physical distribution of raw materials and component parts. Material cost, logistics costs, and profit margins are all factors in such rationalization.
- ☑ Is the network path a contiguous connection of trading partners? Strive to have at least one trading partner or strategic nominal trading partner in every echelon.
- ☑ Does the midstream [width × length] of the network properly reflect the static, switched, or chaotic nature of the core (nominal) trading partner relationships? Is there some manufacturing echelon that should be insourced or outsourced? Will some other Country Of Origin provide a cost advantage without compromising the value circle?
- ☑ The downstream [width × length] of the network is a function of the market and channel reach. Can the market be more focused on a smaller number of larger customers? Is there an additional distribution echelon that should be inserted or one to be removed? At this level, the rational-ization of (nominal) trading partner connections is limited to the physical

distribution of the product. Pricing policy, logistics costs, and profit margins are all factors.

☑ Avoid channel conflict where the same SKU is offered in competition with itself. Eliminate alternative network paths that place trading partners simultaneously in multiple echelons.

☑ Understand that the transformation, manufacture, and fulfillment across the network echelons results in income statement versus balance sheet tradeoffs for each of the core trading partners.

☑ Plot each improvement in throughput, landed cost, network inventory, and ROIC on the value circle.

The core network footprint for a reverse supply chain network is optimized by breaking the reverse supply chain into one or more of the following unidirectional subnetworks. Rationalize and optimize each reverse subnetwork like a small forward network.

- Recover -> Disassemble -> Recycle
- Recover -> Replace/Repair/Recalibrate -> Return
- Recover -> Remanufacture -> Distribute

An Example of Rationalizing the Core Network Footprint

An established, old-line drywall business in a highly competitive domestic market is struggling to retain its profitability. Over the years, the business has experienced a commingling of its commercial and retail market segments and a growing demand for smaller volume, mixed SKU purchases from its dealers and distributors. Market fragmentation has resulted in additional echelons of distribution being inserted between the drywall plant and some of its end-customers. These trends have driven higher logistics costs and lower margins. The business has decided that it is time to rationalize its core network footprint to regain its competitiveness.

The current network competes by meeting customer needs in four market segments:

- 15% of demand from owner/developers of commercial property needing lowest price, high volume, full offerings of 5/8 inch product, lead time in days, and deliver and scatter with technical support services.
- 60% of demand from production home builders needing lowest price, high volume, full offering of 1/2-inch product, lead time in days, and deliver and scatter with technical support services.
- 20% of demand from homeowners needing medium price, low volume, 1/2-inch product, one-week lead time, preferred offerings, delivery or pickup, and no technical support services.
- 5% of demand from do-it-yourself retail customers needing medium to high price, low volume, 1/2-inch product, limited offerings, in-stock, customer pickup, and no technical support services.

TABLE 9-4
Network Nodes in the Drywall Supply Chain

Zone	Node	Value-Added
Upstream	Quarry	Mines gypsum rock.
Upstream	Paper mill	Produces paperboard.
Midstream	Drywall plant	Gypsum is crushed, dried, ground and calcined. Calcined gypsum is sandwiched between paperboard for continuous processing into drywall.
Downstream retail	Central distributor	The wholly owned distribution network of a super store.
Downstream retail	Super store "big box" retailer	Sells a broad range of retail merchandise, including a limited selection of construction materials, to both commercial and retail customers. Examples include Lowes and Home Depot.
Downstream commercial	Building materials wholesaler	Sells a full range of construction materials wholesale to commercial customers.
Downstream commercial	Buying group	A virtual organization of distributors and contractors that consolidate their purchasing power when ordering drywall.
Downstream commercial	Drywall specialty dealer or "master distributor"	A distributor that specializes in drywall, ceiling tile systems, and insulation materials for commercial customers.
Downstream commercial	Subdistributor	A smaller distributor with a limited selection of building materials for commercial and retail customers such as a "mom and pop" lumber yard.
Downstream commercial	Contractor	A contractor with a large building capacity primarily for commercial customers.
Downstream commercial	Owner—developer	A builder of commercial real estate such as office space or strip malls using drywall construction.
Downstream commercial	Production home builder	A builder of private homes using drywall construction.
Downstream commercial	Small contractor	A smaller contractor with a limited building capacity for commercial and retail customers that use drywall.

Drywall is an example of a V-Type BOM where a single gypsum raw material becomes many different sheet sizes and shapes. Table 9-4 identifies the current network nodes shown in Figure 9-5. The quarry, the drywall plant, the drywall specialty dealer, and the largest contractors are the trading partners.

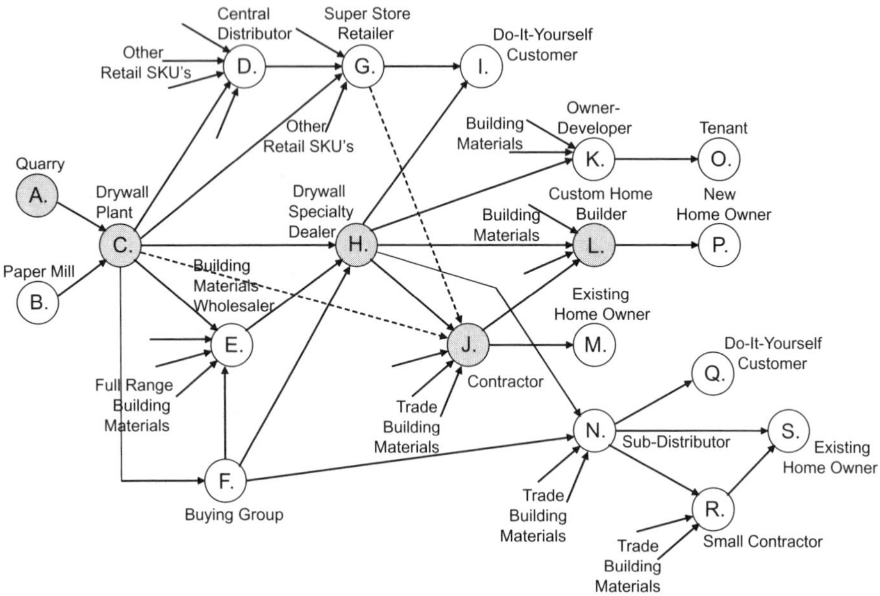

FIGURE 9-5 A supply chain network from the drywall industry.

Referring again to Figure 9-5, the material flow is connected from raw materials to each of the end-customer segments. The specialty dealers and building materials wholesalers allow for a percentage of edge damage and sheet warp from forklift handling. Returns to the drywall plant are not allowed; therefore no provision has been made for a reverse supply chain network. In Table 9-5, percentages of in-network

TABLE 9-5
Testing Nodes to Identify Trading Partners

Node	In-Network Purchases	In-Network Sales	Node Classification
Quarry	Significant	Significant	Trading partner
Paper Mill	Insignificant	Insignificant	Nominal TP
Drywall plant	100%	100%	Trading partner and network orchestrator
Central distributor	Insignificant	Insignificant	Nominal TP
Super store retailer	Insignificant	Insignificant	Nominal TP
Builder's wholesaler	Significant	Insignificant	Nominal TP
Specialty dealer	Significant	Significant	Trading partner
Subdistributor	Insignificant	Significant	Nominal TP
Contractor	Significant or Insignificant	Significant or Insignificant	(Nominal) trading partner
Owner developer	Insignificant	Insignificant	Nominal TP
Home builder	Significant	Significant	Trading partner
Small contractor	Insignificant	Insignificant	Nominal TP

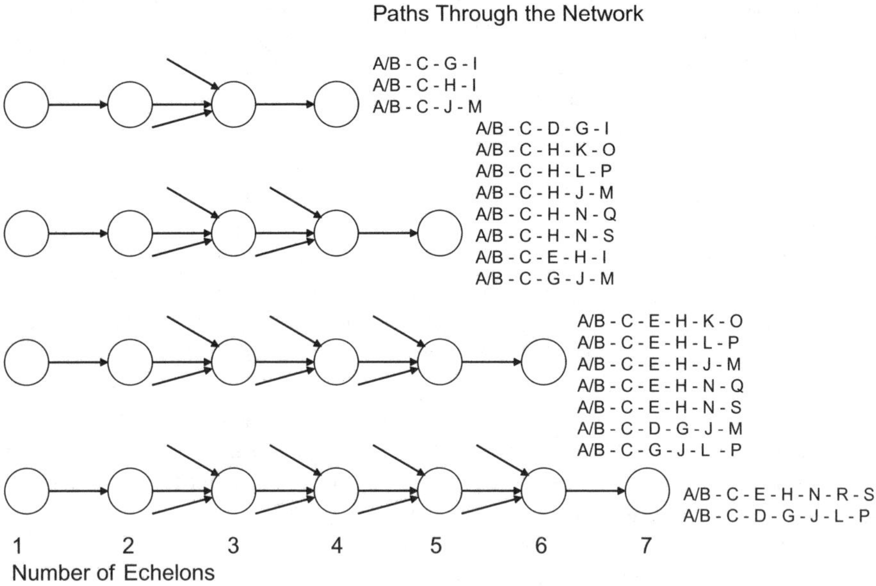

FIGURE 9-6 Rationalizing the paths through the drywall network.

purchases and in-network sales are used to differentiate the trading partners from the nominal trading partners. A node is a trading partner when the in-network throughput from purchase to sale is relatively significant.

Figure 9-6 shows the many multi-echelon paths through the original network:

- *Four-echelon paths*—Favors the do-it-yourself customer buying through a super store.
- *Five-echelon paths*—Capable of reaching all four market segments. These are the highest concentration of trading partners and highest throughput paths through the network. There is channel conflict for the end-customer between retail and commercial subpaths. The drywall plant is burdened with service and logistics requirements from too many nodes in the network. The do-it-yourself customer segment should be eliminated from these network paths through dealer pricing.
- *Six-echelon paths*—Capable of reaching lower-volume demand from all market segments. These network paths have a higher logistics cost than the five-echelon paths and a lower concentration of trading partners. Again, there is channel conflict for the end-customer between retail and commercial subpaths.
- *Seven-echelon paths*—Lowest volume, highest cost paths through the network resulting in minimal total throughput.

Network rationalization results in a minimization of network echelons, a minimization of the total number of network nodes, a maximization of the ratio of trading partner to nominal trading partner nodes, and a minimization of network connections.

In this drywall industry example, the multi-echelon nature of downstream distribution causes network inefficiencies. This is because many of the nodes have the unusual circumstance of trying to operate in up to three different echelons simultaneously. Channel conflicts and extraneous logistics handling can be minimized by careful elimination of certain network connections and by subtle changes to pricing policy. The total number of network nodes will not change unless specific contractors or builders decide to change from drywall construction to some other kind of construction, or leave the industry.

Network connection G-J in Figure 9-5 is the main cause of channel conflict between retail and commercial channels. A reworking of the pricing policy for drywall sold to super stores versus drywall sold to specialty dealers can effectively eliminate connection G-J. Second, contractors can order directly from the drywall plant, using connection C-J, bypassing the drywall specialty dealer. This results in higher than necessary logistics costs for LTL deliveries to the contractor and extensive traffic management by the drywall plant. A change to a full truckload policy at the drywall plant and more attractive pricing of delivered product from the drywall specialty dealer will effectively eliminate connection C-J.

In Figure 9-7, the network path combinations enumerated in Figure 9-6 are used to plot each of the operating echelons for each of the network nodes. A given trading partner may simultaneously span one, two, or three echelons depending on the end-customer segment being served. Although delivery velocity is very competitive, the

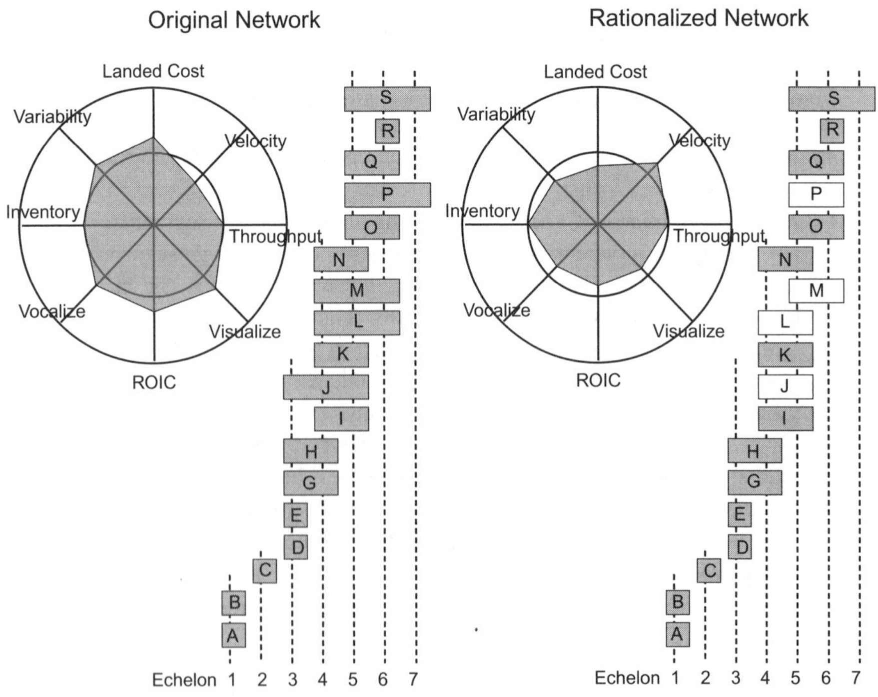

FIGURE 9-7 The value circle before and after network rationalization.

value circle indicates that the original network configuration has high variability due to scheduling conflicts plus low vocalization and visualization due to the intentional separation of the retail and commercial channels. The right half of the figure shows the network rationalized with connections C-J and G-J eliminated. Now the velocity for some customer segments is a little slower, but the value circle encompasses a smaller area indicating a more competitive network overall.

SECOND LEVEL NETWORK OPTIMIZATION

Though the first level network optimization focuses on the core network footprint and its physical distribution relationships, the second level network optimization focuses on the subcycle connections and network operations. In the analogy, the logical and mathematical relationships that are programmed among the cells in an Excel spreadsheet represent the subcycles, BOM logic, demand signals, planning connections, and performance measures that define the material flow, the information flow, and the cash flow among the core trading partners. Just as an Excel spreadsheet provides logical and mathematical operators and standardized rules of syntax, the subcycles among the core trading partners should be connected using widely accepted logic and standardized processes across each interface. Just as in an Excel spreadsheet when a column or row of trading partners is cut and pasted into a different column or row, the old subcycle may be interrupted and will need to be reconnected. Ideally, it would be possible to easily "plug and play" or "unplug" a trading partner from the core network. However, the combination of information technology protocols, database schemas, process standards, and non-standard performance measure definitions currently make this impossible.

THE ESSENTIAL NODE CONNECTIONS

Table 9-6 lists the set of essential connections that interconnect the core trading partners. These connections facilitate the planning, operation, and measurement of the material flow, the information flow, and the cash flow throughout the supply chain network. On the one hand, if any of these connections is severed, network

TABLE 9-6
Node Connections

Plan	Operate	Measure
• Inventory planning • Inventory accuracy	• Order-to-delivery subcycle • Order-to-stock subcycle • Bill of material relationships	• Capable-to-promise • Equivalent throughput • Total network inventory • Order-to-delivery cycle time • The perfect order
• Cash planning • Cash accuracy	• Invoice-to-pay subcycle • Invoice-to-cash subcycle • Bill of cash relationships	• Cash-to-cash cycle time

operations are interrupted. On the other hand, there is more than one way to make each connection, and therefore room to optimize the subcycles. The subcycle for a reverse supply chain network is optimized, as explained earlier in this chapter, by breaking the network into one or more subnetworks using the same criteria as for a forward network.

Rationalizing the Core (Nominal) Trading Partner Subcycles

The allowable node interconnections are where network architecture gets messy. Is the network a linear chain or a circular web? Are the trading partners static, switched, or chaotic for different "plug and play" situations? Is the number of echelons dynamic over time? Do the BOM types vary from SKU to SKU? The infrastructure of subcycles, the BOM connections, the planning, supply and demand signals, and the performance measures must accommodate each of these network scenarios.

Rationalize each core (nominal) trading partner subcycle with a four-step approach:

1. Simplify
2. Reduce
3. Parallel
4. Synchronize

This second level of optimization is driven from the velocity, variability, vocalize, and visualize principles along the value circle. Use the following checklist:

- ☑ Optimize operations around the highest revenue generating, highest gross margin bearing SKUs. Build around the majority rather than around the exception.
- ☑ Understand that the order-to-delivery and order-to-stock subcycles of the network must reflect the bill of materials. A linear BOM product structure is not consistent with an upstream circular web network.
- ☑ Use cycle counting or RFID technology to ensure inventory accuracy.
- ☑ Eliminate or simplify the number of process steps in each order-to-delivery, order-to-stock, invoice-to-pay, and invoice-to-cash subcycle to increase subcycle velocity.
- ☑ Compress cycle time, transit time, and customs clearance time relentlessly to increase subcycle velocity.
- ☑ Parallel the information flow from the source to the destination in the ordering and invoicing legs of the subcycles, where possible, to increase subcycle velocity.
- ☑ Use a bill of cash derived from the bill of materials to eliminate invoicing, parallel the cash flow subcycles, and increase velocity.
- ☑ Eliminate or reduce variability in material flow, information flow, and cash flow.
- ☑ Synchronize the cash flow within the pull zone.
- ☑ Make all the information flow connections to plan each inventory buffer and each cash buffer. Ensure that there is only one plan for the pull zone and only one plan for the push zone.

☑ Make all the information flow connections for the set of global performance measures including capable-to-promise, equivalent throughput, total network inventory, order-to-delivery cycle time, the perfect order, and the cash-to-cash cycle time.

☑ Plot each improvement in velocity, throughput, visualization, ROIC, vocalization, network inventory, variability, and landed cost on the value circle.

An Example of Rationalizing the Subcycles

A supply chain network delivers 1,450 different SKUs through 30,000 retail stores. The distribution warehouses have learned to carry 90 days of supply of inventory to ensure a competitive service level to the retail stores. Even with this entire inventory the factories and suppliers face constant material shortage problems and depleted cash buffers. Revenue and profitability has fallen in recent months. The network orchestrator, the factory, is unsure where to begin to solve these problems when the complexity of the network is so overwhelming.

Upon analysis, the 1,450 SKUs can be grouped into 82 product families with many of the SKUs being custom packaging options and private labeling of similar products. Additional analysis shows that the composite BOMs for the base products fall into one of three configurations as shown in Figure 9-8. Composite BOM_1 configuration is implemented across five echelons, ending at the distribution warehouse echelon. It is a variation of an A-type BOM with some part value changes at BOM level 2 and BOM level 3. Composite BOM_2 configuration is implemented

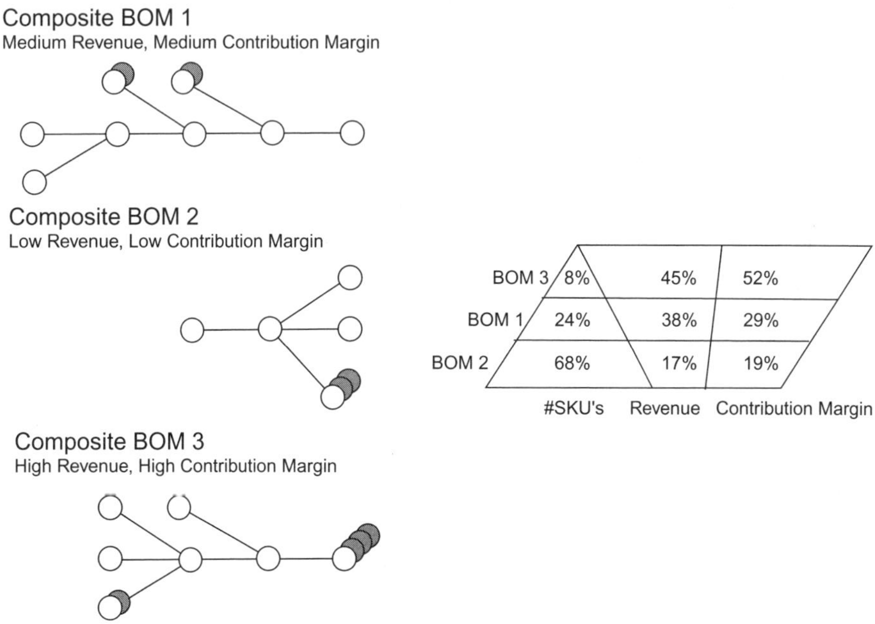

FIGURE 9-8 Grouping SKUs by revenue and contribution margin.

across three echelons, including the distribution warehouse echelon. It is a high-mix product with a V-type BOM; the distribution warehouse normally stocks every variation. The composite BOM_3 configuration is implemented across four echelons, ending at the distribution warehouse echelon. It is a high-volume, low-mix product with an A-type BOM and some postponement done in distribution.

When the 82 product families are listed in pareto order first by the throughput revenue each generates, second by relative contribution margin, and third by composite BOM type, a clearer picture of the situation begins to emerge. Referring again to Figure 9-8, though the BOM_3 products account for only 8% of the total SKU numbers, they account for 45% of the total throughput revenue and 52% of the contribution margin. On the other hand, though BOM_2 products account for 68% of the total SKU numbers, they account for only 17% of the total throughput revenue and 19% of the contribution margin. It is also apparent that BOM_1 is similar to BOM_3. It is now clear that the network subcycles should be optimized for the BOM_3 products, even if it is a little less efficient to manufacture the BOM_2 products.

Figure 9-9 shows the optimized subcycle connections for the midstream and upstream portions of the network. In this supply chain network the push/pull boundary is at the distribution warehouse with some postponement for BOM level 0 also performed there. The remaining BOM levels fall within the push zone. The factory is the network constraint; the network constraint does not move with changes to the product mix. In the push zone, the demand signal is threaded from the distribution warehouse to the network constraint, the factory. From there the demand signal is broadcast in parallel to all the other (nominal) trading partners; however, the push zone is not synchronized. In the push zone a bill of cash replaces invoices. The distribution warehouse is triggered to make payment to the factory each time it

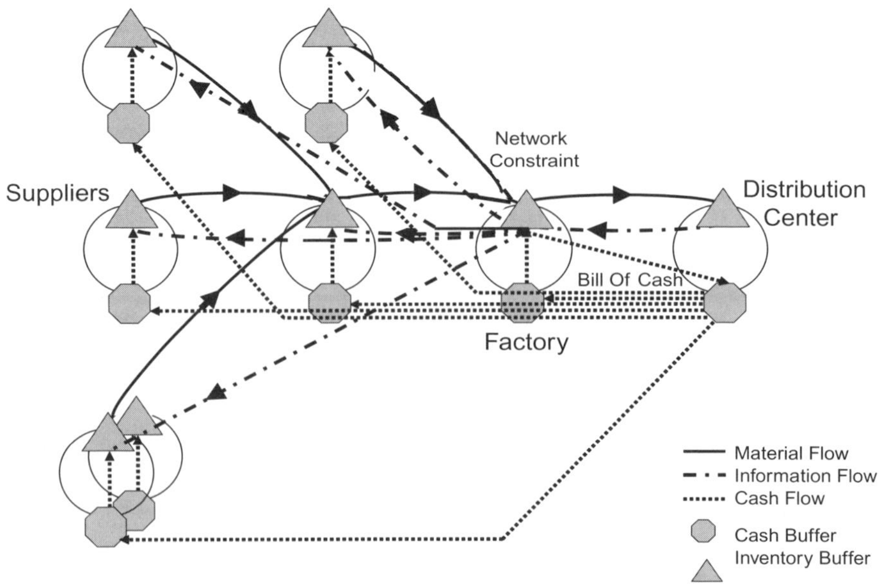

FIGURE 9-9 Optimizing the network subcycles for BOM_3.

receives a product shipment and to pay each of the upstream (nominal) trading partners in parallel. In this way the cash flow is accelerated but not synchronized within the push zone. Subcycle velocity is increased by the parallel nature of the information flows. Subcycle variability is reduced because the network has been focused on the highest volume, highest margin SKUs. Network vocalization is maximized by the parallel nature of the demand broadcast and by the use of a BOC.

With the core trading partner subcycles tailored for the dominant BOM configuration, the network is optimized to plan, operate, and measure for the highest revenue, highest contribution margin SKUs. The measurement piece requires that all of the (nominal) trading partners contribute information for a common set of global performance measures, and align their operations using a standardized dashboard. Specifically, these nodes are connected into the equivalent throughput and total network inventory performance measurement logic. The number of units flowing into the outbound pipeline and the number of units remaining at the node by item number and by time increment provides this information. Technology, such as radio frequency identification, makes it practical to count inventory at the node and in the pipeline on a continuous basis. Network visualization is maximized when all of the core trading partners agree to manage operations using one set of performance measurement definitions.

THIRD LEVEL NETWORK OPTIMIZATION

The third level of network optimization is both the most difficult and the most subtle. This optimization determines the degree to which a fully functional network is responsive, flexible, and adaptive. For example, upon checking into your hotel you are impressed with the efficiency of the desk clerk as she locates your registration record, swipes your credit card, and programs your door key. As you leave the counter to go to your room, a busload of guests line up at registration. Upon entering your room, you remember that you must call some colleagues to have them join you for dinner; however, you do not know their room numbers. When you call down to the front desk, the harried clerk says that she is taking guest registrations and cannot place the calls for you right now. You are left with no way of contacting your colleagues because the network has just broken down. In this example, the level one footprint of core trading partners, the hotel and the guest, is minimized. The level two process subcycles, the well-trained and efficient clerk operating a simple process of data entry, credit cards, and programmable room keys, is optimized. Unfortunately when the loop is closed and a guest interacts with the hotel in a different way, the network fails to deliver level three responsiveness.

Level three optimization is about the closed loop nature of the network. Some information from within the network is fed back upon itself, and the result may be both unexpected and startling. In the spreadsheet analogy, Excel will occasionally display an error message stating that a mathematical or logical expression in a cell is attempting an illegal, circular definition or that perhaps the equation solver cannot converge. Sometimes when feedback is put into place, the Excel spreadsheet program stops working altogether. At other times, the Excel spreadsheet seems to function properly. What is going on?

Responsiveness, Flexibility, and Adaptability

Feedback is built into a network in order for the network to operate more predictably and consistently in spite of the natural performance spread of the network's components. For example without feedback, a supplier can order too much or too little raw material based on an erroneous forecast. With feedback, the supplier is able to significantly reduce the forecast error and perceive actual customer demand patterns resulting in a smarter investment for raw material. Without feedback, a factory can produce more or less than expected. With feedback in the form of performance measurement and review, the factory can hold to the planned throughput. Without feedback, a distributor can carry too light or too heavy a mix of finished goods. With feedback, the distributor is able to achieve a higher service level with a smaller total inventory investment. Without feedback, the supply response to demand stimulus for a supply chain network will be unpredictable and inconsistent. With feedback, the supply response to demand stimulus for a supply chain network will be both predictable and consistent.

When information from the output of a network is fed back to the input of a network, the network becomes a closed loop feedback system. There are two primary forms of feedback in a supply chain network. The planning process closes one feedback loop, and the performance measurement system closes a second feedback loop, see Figure 9-10. A closed loop feedback system responds differently to a stimulus depending on whether the feedback is negative or positive. Negative feedback

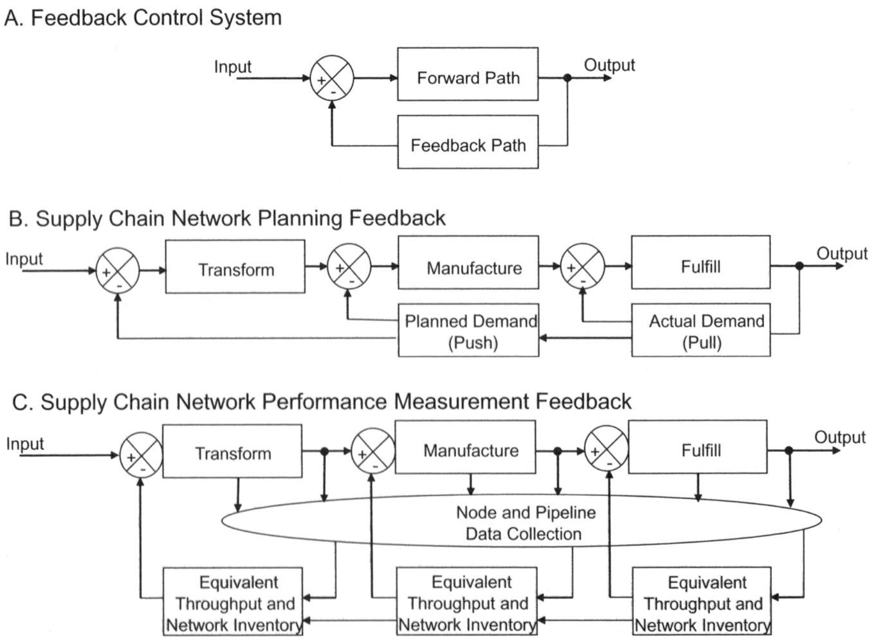

FIGURE 9-10 The supply chain network as a closed loop feedback system.

TABLE 9-7
Static versus Dynamic Optimization

Level	Optimization	Static	Dynamic		
			Responsive	Flexible	Adaptive
1	Minimize the core network footprint.	X			
2	Optimize the network subcycles to plan, operate, and measure.	X	X		
3	Stabilize the feedback loops.		X	X	
	"Harden" the network.				X

is good because the stimulus/response dynamic is well behaved; negative feedback can improve the network's responsiveness to give consistent results. Positive feedback is bad because the stimulus/response dynamic is unpredictable; positive feedback leads to network oscillatation.

Optimization of the core network footprint and the network subcycles mostly affects the static conditions of the network. On the other hand, the dynamic characteristics of a network's responsiveness, flexibility, and adaptability are affected both by the stability of the network feedback loops and by the inherent network architecture, see Table 9-7. Four dynamic characteristics of a network can be classified relative to their respective stimulus and response as follows:

- *Responsive*—The *stimulus* is customer initiated. The *response* is to accommodate the customer's need through operations planning and scheduling with no change to the network configuration. Some examples include customer requests for product mix change, delivery quantity change, delivery timing change, delivery location change, and product returns.
- *Supply flexible*—The *stimulus* is initiated from within the network. The *response* is to match supply with demand through supply management. This can require changes to product and network configurations. Some examples include asset investment, alternative routings, inventory substitution, outsourcing and insourcing, and network substitution, plus organizational centralizing and decentralizing.
- *Demand flexible*—The *stimulus* is initiated from within the network. The *response* is to match demand with supply through demand management. This can require a change to the product pricing. Some examples include revenue management, dynamic pricing, product promotions, reverse auctions, and excess inventory auctions.
- *Adaptable*—The *stimulus* is environment initiated. The *response* is to radically change the network configuration. If the external event is too extreme, the network will break, and the business will fail. Some examples include leapfrogging product technology, market restructuring, regulatory

change, political unrest, financial stress, exchange rate excursions, trade quotas, security breaches, terrorist's threats, and environmental restrictions.

Closing the Feedback Loop for Planning

When downstream planning information is fed back to the upstream trading partners, a feedback loop is closed. The upstream trading partners will attempt to change their operations based on this planning feedback. As can be seen in Figure 9-10, there are three planning feedback loops at the network level. The inner loop is the "pull" loop, primarily driven by actual demand. The middle loop and the outer loop are "push" loops, primarily driven by planned demand. Table 9-8 defines the characteristics of these network level feedback loops. The planning feedback loop may respond in an underdamped, overdamped, or oscillatory manner. Level three optimization should include a check that none of these loops oscillates under the bullwhip effect.

Various loop compensation techniques can be used to optimize the network response without becoming oscillatory. This is an area where the trading partners

TABLE 9-8
Characteristics of Planning Feedback

Inner Loop Definition The "Pull" Loop	Input = Forecast × Transform × Manufacture	Forward Path = Fulfill Feedback Path = Actual Demand	Output = Throughput Mix and Rate
Middle Loop Definition The "Push_1" Loop	Input = Forecast × Transform	Forward Path = Manufacture × Fulfill Feedback Path = Actual Demand + Planned Demand	Output = Throughput Mix and Rate
Outer Loop Definition The "Push_2" Loop	Input = Forecast	Forward Path = Transform × Manufacture × Fulfill Feedback Path = Actual Demand + Planned Demand	Output = Throughput Mix and Rate
Overdamped	Delayed or late in making capacity, inventory, and cash adjustments.		
Underdamped	Nervous response with excessive capacity, inventory, and cash readjustments.		
Oscillatory	A bullwhip effect response with instability of capacity, inventory, and cash.		
Loop Compensation Techniques	☑ Proper positioning of the push/pull boundary. ☑ Network constraint matched to market demand. ☑ Broadcast demand in parallel rather than in series. ☑ Synchronized logistics delays. ☑ Forecast error minimized by BOM flattening and cycle time reduction. ☑ Min/max thresholds set before capacity, inventory, or cash is adjusted. ☑ One overarching planning system used by all the trading partners with a planning horizon that covers the network.		

can collaborate to optimize network level performance. The longer the supply chain, the more likely it is that the network can easily oscillate. The Theory Of Constraints and synchronization methods explained in Chapter 7 can be used as powerful loop compensation techniques. It may also be possible to develop a computer simulation to model the planning feedback loop and to use such a simulator to predict network oscillation.

Capable-To-Promise (*CTP*) is a network-wide delivery estimate. Although available-to-promise is a delivery estimate for the end-customer made from the master production schedule of a single trading partner, capable-to-promise is a delivery estimate made for the end-customer from the network-wide planning system. It is a forecast of the network's throughput ability taking into account the capacity, inventory buffer, and cash buffer positions of all the core trading partners.

The perfect order is the end-customer's performance measure of network quality. The perfect order is the right product(s), to the right customer, in the right location(s), at the right time(s), for the right price(s), with a perfect invoice, no return(s), and no hassle(s). It is stated as a percentage of the number of line item orders completed as perfect orders versus the total number of line item orders completed for that customer. It must be measured at the external customer end and cannot be approximated by an internal customer facing trading partner. Each major account should track its own perfect order metric. The perfect order measures how well the supply chain network lives up to its delivery promises. Strive for consistent network quality across all customers serviced by the network.

$$\text{The Perfect Order}_{\text{(Customer A)}} = \frac{\text{Number of Line Item Orders Delivered Perfectly}_{\text{(Customer A)}} \times 100\%}{\text{Total Number of Line Item Orders Delivered}_{\text{(Customer A)}}}$$

Where the perfect order is measured by each end-customer.

Closing the Feedback Loop for Performance Measures

When global performance measurement information is fed back to a trading partner, a second feedback loop is closed. The network trading partners will attempt to change their behaviors based on this performance measurement feedback. You can see in Figure 9-10, that there are three performance measurement feedback loops at the network level. The first loop is the fulfillment loop, primarily driven by downstream operations. The second loop is the manufacture loop, primarily driven by midstream operations. The third loop is the transformation loop, primarily driven by upstream operations. Table 9 9 defines the characteristics of these three network level feedback loops. The measurement feedback loop may respond in an underdamped, overdamped, or oscillatory manner. Level three optimization should include a check to verify that each of these loops is stable.

Various loop compensation techniques can be used to optimize the network response without becoming oscillatory. The sampling rate of the performance measure and any differential in timing or definition across the network can aggravate

TABLE 9-9
Characteristics of Performance Measurement Feedback

First Loop Definition The Fulfill Loop	Input = Forecast ×Transform ×Manufacture	Forward Path = Fulfill Feedback Path = Fulfill Performance Measures	Output = Throughput Mix and Rate
Second Loop Definition The Manufacture Loop	Input = Forecast ×Transform	Forward Path = Manufacture ×Fulfill Feedback Path = Manufacture Perform Measures + Fulfill Performance Measures	Output = Throughput Mix and Rate
Third Loop Definition The Transform Loop	Input = Forecast	Forward Path = Transform × Manufacture ×Fulfill Feedback Path = Transform Perform Measures + Manufacture Perform Measures + Fulfill Performance Measures	Output = Throughput Mix and Rate
Overdamped	Late in adjusting to a performance measurement.		
Underdamped	Excessive number of readjustments to a performance measurement.		
Oscillatory	Performance measurement loop instability.		
Loop Compensation Techniques	☑ Continuous information accuracy. ☑ The same performance measure definitions for equivalent throughput and total network inventory are used consistently by each trading partner. ☑ Synchronized data collection methods and measurement periods. ☑ A common dashboard is used consistently by each trading partner to stay focused on the business strategy.		

an oscillation. This is an area where the trading partners can collaborate to optimize network level performance. It may also be possible to develop a computer simulation to model the performance measure feedback loop and to use such a simulator to predict network oscillation.

An Example of Optimizing Responsiveness

A retail store in the consumer packaged goods industry carries a large number of SKUs. Many of the SKUs are alternative package styles of the same basic product. A few customers have complained at the cash register that their desired product is out of stock and that the store's level of service has fallen. These customers say that

TABLE 9-10
Historical Demand Detail for a Retail Store

SKU	Wk14	Wk15	Wk16	Wk17	Wk18	Wk19	Wk20	Wk21	Wk22	Wk23	Wk24
1129	725	698	713	722	709	695	711	714	697	692	715
1130	112	110	115	127	176	224	439	337	156	129	115
1131	0	0	0	0	0	0	37	58	63	225	237
1132	227	119	0	0	172	269	271	87	0	156	243
1133	36	36	38	37	36	38	37	35	38	36	38

the store is not responsive to their needs. They say that if were not for the price discounts they receive from their preferred shopper cards, they would have switched to a competitor long ago. The store manager knows the level of inventory kept in the store and in the warehouse for every item. The supply network is efficient, having been built around a small number of suppliers, factories, and warehouses. The processes for reordering and cash management are clean, and the inventory counts are accurate. The store manager does not understand how customers could feel that the store is unresponsive. Table 9-10 shows the latest quarter of historical demand data available to the store manager.

Consolidated inventory planning for this retail store is the responsibility of the distribution warehouse. This was implemented some time ago to minimize the outbound logistics costs of moving product to a number of stores. Three different demand patterns are jumbled together in this spreadsheet. SKU #1129 and SKU #1133 are examples of continuous demand items, each with low demand volatility. These are the easiest to plan, and they should never be out of stock. The safety stock level per SKU is based on periodically recalculating the standard deviation of demand and using a multiplier based on the percent service level desired.

SKU #1130 is an example of a SKU having a significant seasonal demand. Seasonality is difficult to forecast both in its timing and in its magnitude. Seasonality can introduce nervousness into planning. A better approach is to identify the set of SKUs having seasonality and work to minimize the manufacturing cycle time and logistics transit time for those products. One-time orders are highly risky. Minimize the risk by reducing the dependence on forecasting. If the replenishment cycle can be made short enough, it may be possible to deliver on reorders for fast moving product early in the season. Explore the possibility of being able to substitute with another product late in the season.

SKU #1131 is a new product offering that was put on the shelf for the first time in week 20 and was heavily promoted in week 23. Product promotions can be made low risk when the trading partners in a supply chain network communicate with each other. Sometimes this is not the case. In fact, sometimes the marketing/sales and manufacturing offices within the same company do not talk with each other. There are many stories about manufacturing and logistics doing whatever was necessary to replenish an out-of-stock condition when sales had merely been promoting an undesirable item to clear it out of inventory. Any savings that sales managed to eek out of the promotion were more than offset by purchased price variances, overtime, LTL freight premiums, etc. Whether a new product is simply an old product being repackaged or a revolutionary new product being launched, there must be solid vocalization and visualization of the product introduction throughout the network.

The store manager finally realizes that the problem lies with a bullwhip effect on SKU #1132.

MATCHING DEMAND WITH SUPPLY

Matching demand with supply is fundamentally different from matching supply with demand. In some business situations, large capital investments are made on capacity and inventory assets before making the first customer sale. This capacity and inventory is perishable if it cannot be sold by its expiration date. Such businesses understand that the fixed costs incurred with such an investment are sunk costs. They build demand through pricing changes to match supply and to recover their marginal variable costs.

There are many examples of perishable capacity in service related industries. For example, the airline industry has perfected revenue management by charging a variety of different prices for the same commodity, an airline seat. A flight's pricing structure and the class allotment, such as the number of seats assigned to economy, business and first class, is determined months in advance based on fuel costs, usage forecasts and the competitive environment. The fight revenue is then segmented by the type of customer, such as tourist, business, or Saturday night stay over, and segmented temporally. Temporal, or time-based, segmentation adjust pricing 21 days in advance, 14 days in advance, 7 days in advance, and for walk-ups. The airline reservation systems are carefully designed to keep from booking a lower revenue coach class customer to a seat while there is still a possibility that a higher revenue business class customer will buy that seat. Once a day all the firm reservations are checked against the revenue segmentation; prices then are published on the airline's Web sites and on the travel Web sites such as www.expedia.com and www.travelocity.com. What appears to the consumer to be significant, random price changes are really the once-a-day remapping of reservation bookings against the revenue segmentation model. The published pricing is automatically readjusted when a seat class fills or when a temporal segment expires. As the departure date gets closer, the airline may make small boundary adjustments to the number of seats assigned within a class, and may make blocks of seats available through nontraditional sales channels such as www.priceline.com. Once a flight departs the gate, every unoccupied seat on that aircraft represents perishable capacity that cannot generate revenue.

Examples of perishable inventory are common in manufacturing-related industries. For example, in order to offer a competitive lead time to a Japanese battery manufacturer, a battery forming equipment OEM decides to invest in an inventory of printed circuit boards. The cumulative lead time to manufacture and transport the battery forming equipment is 26 weeks while the competition offers its stock product in 8 weeks. If the OEM does not buy ahead, the customer in Japan will order its battery forming equipment from the competitor. However, the customer operates in a highly competitive and secretive high technology market. The customer is spending more than a year and more than 80 billion yen to build a one-of-a-kind automated battery manufacturing center. The battery-forming equipment the customer will order is highly customized. If the customer does not buy from the OEM, the printed circuit board inventory is perishable because it will have been customized. In this scenario, the OEM manages its inventory risk through the dynamic pricing of its battery forming equipment. If the sale cannot be made, the OEM can only recover the scrap value of the inventory.

The Pricing Interface

Drawing a circle around any network trading partner reveals relationships with other upstream, midstream, downstream, or reverse-stream (nominal) trading partners. Each relationship pair represents a pricing interface, see Figure 9-11. The price and the pricing method of what is bought and sold at each interface need not be the same.

Demand is matched with supply by optimizing the pricing interface for each network relationship pair. Some pricing methods are appropriate when buying from a more upstream relationship, whereas other pricing methods are appropriate when selling to a more downstream relationship. Common methods for buying and selling unique and commodity items follow:

- *Static pricing*—Product pricing is fixed and only occasionally updated. Typical examples include price lists that change once a quarter and mail order catalogs that are printed periodically. Coupons and discounts may be combined with static pricing to promote sales within certain market segments.

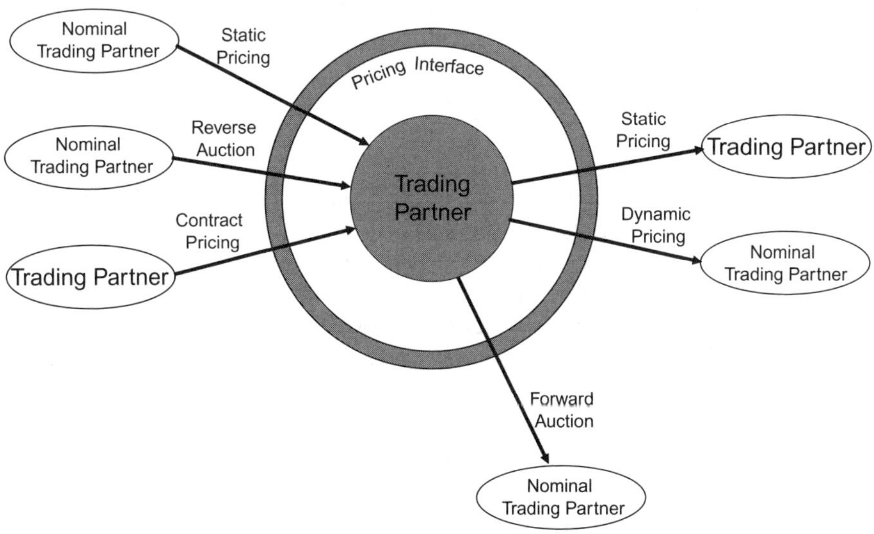

FIGURE 9-11 A trading partner's pricing interfaces.

- *Contract pricing*—Product pricing is fixed by a contract between two trading partners. Contract pricing is tied to an expected unit volume of consumption, and usually offers favorable pricing because of the preferred nature of the buyer-seller relationship. Contract prices may be fixed for a period of time, such as one year, or may be shown in a pricing schedule accompanying a multi-year agreement. A single contract may cover the pricing for a limited range of SKUs or a whole product line. Pricing contracts always have escape mechanisms should the unit volume assumption prove to be more than X% below or Y% above forecast. Contract pricing is appropriate for buying and selling unique or customized materials or for services provided under a long-term agreement.
- *Dynamic pricing*—The seller uses a pricing model that recalculates price based on preserving the contribution margin across its remaining perishable capacity. The price increases as the last of the capacity is purchased close to its expiration date. Dynamic pricing is appropriate when the seller has many potential buyers for the seller's commodity-like material or services.
- *Reverse auction*—One buyer benefits from a price auction among many sellers. The buyer provides a specification and requests an initial quote from each participating seller. The auction is conducted as a dutch auction, where bid prices decrease from the starting asked price that is usually the lowest of the initial quotes. The auction is conducted on-line for a period of time against a fixed deadline. Reverse auctions are commonly used to buy commodity materials for manufacturing.
- *Forward auction*—One seller benefits from a price auction among many buyers. The seller provides a description and a minimum asking price for the item being sold. The auction is conducted as an English, auction where bid prices increase from the starting asked price. The auction is conducted in person or on-line for a period of time against a fixed deadline. A forward auction is appropriate to sell unique or excess inventory and production machinery.

DYNAMIC PRICING

Given the right price elasticity in the market and numbers of willing buyers in the segment, dynamic pricing can successfully create incremental demand. When a supply chain network is matching supply with demand, one trading partner's capacity is the network constraint and all other (nominal) trading partner capacity runs slack. The network constraint appears as a large revenue generator in series with the network. Network throughput is increased by increasing the capacity of the network constraint. When a supply chain network is matching demand with supply, the network capacity appears as a number of small revenue generators in parallel with the network. Network throughput is increased by engaging all of the revenue generators. Dynamic pricing is a method that strives to engage as many of the parallel revenue generators as possible by segmenting the market and offering different, attractive pricing alternatives to each segment thereby driving incremental demand to the supply.

Dynamic pricing is implemented as follows:

1. Segment the market by customer type and by temporal boundaries. Price each segment separately.
2. Identify the segment-related fixed costs from an analysis of the balance sheet and the income statement. A service business will have perishable capacity assets while a manufacturer will have perishable inventory assets.
3. Identify the segment-related variable costs from an analysis of the income statement.
4. Calculate the breakeven price based on the fixed costs and the variable costs. Ensure a consistent timeframe is used between the fixed and variable costs for this calculation. Check that the equation is dimensionally correct.

$$\text{Breakeven Price/Unit} = \frac{\text{Fixed Cost} + [\text{Variable Cost/Unit} \times \text{Breakeven Volume}]}{\text{Breakeven Volume}}$$

5. Calculate the contribution margin based on the breakeven price and the variable costs.

$$\$\ \text{Contribution Margin} = \$\ \text{Price} - \$\ \text{Variable Cost}$$

6. Periodically recalculate the breakeven price change necessary to marginally cover the variable costs. Check that the equation is dimensionally correct. Add the breakeven price change to the breakeven price/unit to determine the new breakeven $ price/unit for the perishable asset. Note that this pricing adjustment only applies to this particular segment.

$$\$\ \text{Breakeven Price Change} = \$\ \text{Contribution Margin} \times \frac{[\text{Remaining Capacity/Total Capacity}]}{1 - [\text{Remaining Capacity/Total Capacity}]}$$

$$\text{New Breakeven \$ Price/unit} = \$\ \text{Breakeven Price/unit} + \$\ \text{Breakeven Price Change}$$

For example, a transportation company decides to develop a new market segment for its service business by equipping its fleet of trucks with new equipment to move oversized loads. Customers needing to move oversized loads do not have many options; they have to pay as the service is priced. The transportation company invests in three customized 20-ton tractors with lowboy trailers to complement their fleet. Each rig costs $140,000 and is depreciated over a five-year life. Part of the total investment—$120,000—is paid in cash, and the remaining $300,000 of the investment is financed through a 15-year loan at 6.5% interest. Annualized payments for principal and interest equal $31,360. Customer pricing is based on a usage assumption that each rig will be scheduled a minimum of 150 days/year and driven a maximum of 7,500 miles/year. Fuel costs are $0.35/mile, and driver costs are $300/day. Table 9-11 shows the incremental entries to the balance sheet and the income statement for the first year of operation.

TABLE 9-11
An Incremental Balance Sheet and Income Statement

Balance Sheet Assets At Year Start		Income Statement Annualized		Balance Sheet Assets At Year End	
• Cash	$120,000			• Cash	$0
• Accounts Receivable				• Accounts Receivable	
• Inventory				• Inventory	
Current Assets		Gross Revenue		Current Assets	
• Fixed Assets	$0	– Discounts			
– Depreciation		Net Revenue		• Fixed Assets	$420,000
Book Value		Fuel	$7,875	– Depreciation	–$84,000
Total Assets		Labor & Overhead	$135,000	Book Value	$336,000
• Accrued Expense		– Cost Of Services Sold		Total Assets	
• Accounts Payable		Gross Profit		• Accrued Expense	
• Income Tax Payable		– Sell & Admin Expense		• Accounts Payable	
• Short Term Debt		– Depreciation Expense	$84,000	• Income Tax Payable	
Current Liabilities		Operating Profit		• Short Term Debt	
• Long Term Debt	$0	– Financing Expense	$31,360	Current Liabilities	
– Principal Paid		Pretax Profit		• Long Term Debt	$300,000
Total Liabilities		– Income Tax		– Principal Paid	– $20,000
• Paid-In Capital		Net Profit		Total Liabilities	$280,000
• Retained Earnings				• Paid-In Capital	
Net Worth				• Retained Earnings	
Total Liabilities and Net Worth				Net Worth	
				Total Liabilities and Net Worth	

In this example, the fixed costs equal $120,000 in cash plus $470,400 in principal and interest, for a total fixed cost of $590,400. Over the five years of useful life, this equates to an annualized fixed cost of $118,080. The variable costs include $135,000 in annualized driver expense plus $7,875 in annualized fuel expense, for a total annualized variable cost of $142,875. Three rigs used 150 days/ year/rig gives a variable cost/day equal to $317.50/day.

$$\text{Breakeven Price/Unit} = \frac{\$118{,}080 + [\$317.50/\text{day} \times 3 \times 150 \text{ days}]}{3 \times 150 \text{ days}}$$

$$= \frac{260{,}955}{450} = \$580/\text{day}$$

A rig and driver priced at $580/day will just break even, with no net profit, when each rig is employed at least 150 days/year and driven no more than 7,500 miles/year. The contribution margin is calculated as:

$ Contribution Margin = $580 – $317.50 = $262.50

As the year progresses and the lowboys are not used to capacity, the breakeven pricing is adjusted to marginally cover the variable costs. For example, suppose the pricing is recalculated each month. At the end of the first month the lowboys have been used the equivalent of 8 days. The contribution margin of the planned for 4.5 days that were not used needs to be spread over the rest of the year.

$$\text{\$ Breakeven Price Change} = \$262.50 \times \frac{[4.5 \text{ days}/137.5 \text{ days}]}{1 - 4.5 \text{ days}/137.5 \text{ days}}$$

$$= \$262.50 \times \frac{0.033}{0.967} = \$8.96$$

New Breakeven \$ Price/Unit = \$580.00/day + \$8.96 = \$589/day

The contribution margin lost over the first month equals the incremental contribution margin gained over the next eleven month. This dynamic pricing model means that the monthly per day price quoted for the usage of a low boy and driver will vary depending on how demand has met supply through the earlier part of the year.

THE TOP AND BOTTOM LINE

Network optimization can have a profound impact on the financial performance of the single trading partner. But it is often hard to see the direct cause and effect. This is because operational decisions are made in nearly real-time, whereas financial reporting occurs after the fact, often with four to six weeks of delay. Operation decisions involve capacity, inventory, and cash, whereas financial decisions involve income statements, balance sheets, and working capital. Operational reporting details the unit volumes of specific SKUs, whereas financial reporting aggregates dollar volumes across SKUs.

Although financial reporting requirements are determined by legal boundaries, and though stock price fluctuations are associated with the single trading partner, it is useful to consider the idea of a network income statement and a network balance sheet. Most optimization decisions can be evaluated from both an individual trading partner perspective and a network perspective. For example, under an outsourcing scenario assets and liabilities taken off one trading partner's balance sheet end up on another trading partner's balance sheet. Although the one trading partner now has stronger financial ratios, the other trading partner's financial ratios are weakened. Total network assets may have increase, and the network may be less competitive than before.

NETWORK OPTIMIZATION (CAUSE) AND THE INCOME STATEMENT (EFFECT)

The velocity principle has a primary impact on the revenue line of the income statement. As the order-to-delivery-to-cash velocity accelerates, each trading partner gets paid faster for its value-added contribution. This adds revenue to the top line. Velocity also has a secondary impact on the balance sheet when the cash-to-cash cycle is accelerated. The variability principle has a primary impact on the Cost Of

Goods Sold (COGS) and on income taxes. This is because labor, overhead, material costs, and income taxes vary greatly with the Country Of Origin, whereas freight and duty costs depend upon both the Country Of Origin and the Country Of Destination. Variability has a secondary impact on the balance sheet because safety stock inventory levels can be reduced when the logistics variability is eliminated from the network. Figure 9-12 is a cause and effect diagram that shows how an operational strategy of *maximizing velocity while minimizing variability* causes a direct increase in profits after taxes across the network.

It is important to keep the context of the income statement clear. Each trading partner's legal entity has an income statement. However, conceptually, there is also a network income statement, as shown in Table 9-12. The network income statement in the table is the serial consolidation of three separate income statements. The network income statement is read from the right to the left, from downstream to upstream. The product "material" portion of the fulfillment trading partner's Cost Of Goods Sold explodes into the complete income statement shown in the center for the manufacture trading partner. Likewise, the component "material" portion of the manufacture trading partner's COGS explodes into the complete income statement shown to the left for the transform trading partner. Each additional network echelon adds costs and takes away a slice of the profits. The network income statement is a useful tool for a network operations council to analyze network cost reduction opportunities and equitable gain sharing potentials.

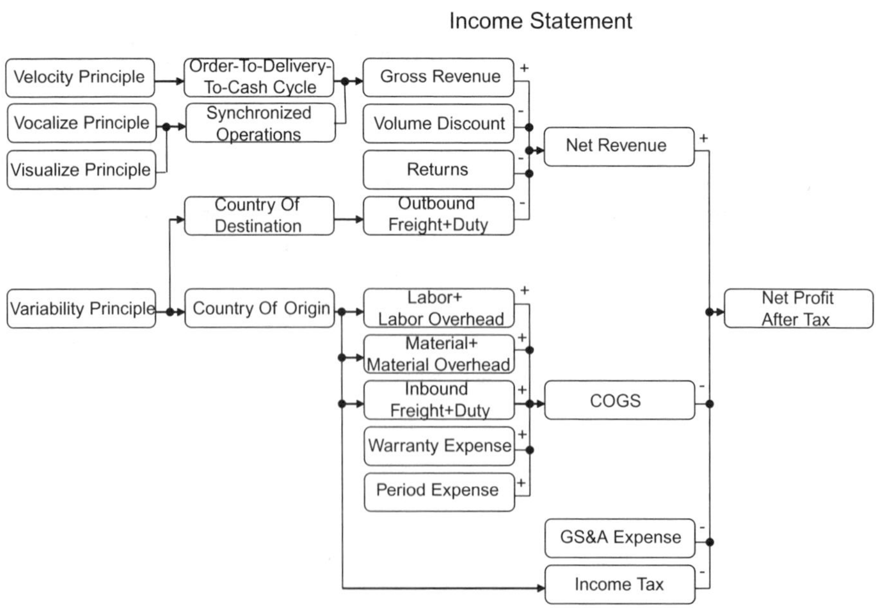

FIGURE 9-12 Velocity and variability principles drive improvements in after tax profits.

TABLE 9-12
The Network Income Statement

Transform Trading Partner	**Manufacture Trading Partner**	**Fulfillment Trading Partner**
Gross Revenue...............	Gross revenue..................	Gross Revenue
• Discounts and Returns	• Discounts and returns	• Discounts and Returns
Net Revenue	Net Revenue	Net Revenue
Cost Of Goods Sold	Cost Of Goods Sold	Cost Of Goods Sold
• Labor + Overhead	• Labor + Overhead	• Labor + Overhead
• Raw Material	• Raw Material	
	• Component "Material"	**• Product "Material"**
• Freight & Duty	• Freight & Duty	• Freight & Duty
• Cost Of Quality	• Cost Of Quality	• Cost Of Quality
Contribution Margin	Contribution Margin	Contribution Margin
Expenses	Expenses	Expenses
• GS&A	• GS&A	• GS&A
• Interest Expense	• Interest Expense	• Interest Expense
Profit Before Taxes	Profit Before Taxes	Profit Before Taxes
Income Taxes	Income Taxes	Income Taxes
Net Profit	Net Profit	Net Profit

Use the following checklist to improve top line revenue through competitive network design and operation:

☑ Restructure discounts.
☑ Offer services that differentiate the products in the marketplace.
☑ Increase the hours of call center coverage to 24/7 for excellent customer service.
☑ Provide automated information retrieval services for customers and sales people.
☑ Accelerate order-to-delivery-to-cash velocity to compress lead time.
☑ Offer a broader range of product customization and product packaging.
☑ Build delivery infrastructure to reach new market segments.
☑ Develop a virtual store channel on the Internet for convenient 24/7 order fulfillment.
☑ Utilize B2C connectivity downstream to accelerate ordering and payment functions.
☑ Decide on the appropriate pricing method (static pricing, contract pricing, or dynamic pricing) when selling to other (nominal) trading partners.
☑ Broaden the range of payment options to include procurement cards and debit cards.
☑ Allow payments to be made in a variety of foreign currencies.
☑ License complementary products to broaden catalog of offerings.
☑ Move up the value chain by insourcing a portion of the customer's process.
☑ Reduce or eliminate returns.
☑ Develop a revenue stream from recycling, repair, or remanufacturing.

Use the following checklist to improve bottom line profitability through competitive network design:

☑ Reduce or eliminate the cost of quality by improving manufacturing yields.
☑ Subcontract low quality process steps.
☑ Change the ratio of full time employees to temporary employees.
☑ Outsource noncompetitive operations.
☑ Outsource noncompetitive overhead.
☑ Consolidate the number of financial service providers.
☑ If the product is labor intensive, change the Country Of Origin to reduce labor costs.
☑ License the design to a lower cost producer.
☑ Consolidate the design around fewer different materials and fewer different suppliers.
☑ If the product is material intensive, shop the world.
☑ If the product is material intensive, change to a Country Of Origin closer to the raw materials.
☑ If the product is material intensive, shop for materials through reverse auctions.
☑ Consolidate the number of logistics service providers.
☑ Consider reusable packaging materials.

- ☑ Reduce or eliminate logistics variability in transit time and customs clearance time.
- ☑ Use free trade zones to minimize or eliminate import duty.
- ☑ Identify opportunities for duty drawback.
- ☑ If the product is profitable, change the Country Of Origin to reduce income tax.
- ☑ Shorten the financing period for international letters of credit.
- ☑ Sell unproductive and unused capital assets to reduce depreciation expenses.
- ☑ Leverage the reduction in logistics variability to reduce inventory and cash financing.
- ☑ Refinance loans for lower interest rates.

Network Optimization (Cause) and the Balance Sheet (Effect)

The vocalize principle has a primary impact on the inventory and cash current assets and the capacity related fixed assets on the balance sheet. As supply is synchronized to demand, capacity, inventory and cash are optimized for each of the trading partners. The vocalize principle has a secondary impact on the income statement because synchronized operations increase throughput and, therefore, revenue. The visualize principle has a primary impact on working capital. This is because trading partner accounts payable and accounts receivable are optimized to cover just the right amount of balance sheet capacity, inventory, and cash across the network. The visualize principle has a secondary impact on the income statement because global performance measures focus and increase throughput for higher revenue. Figure 9-13 is a cause

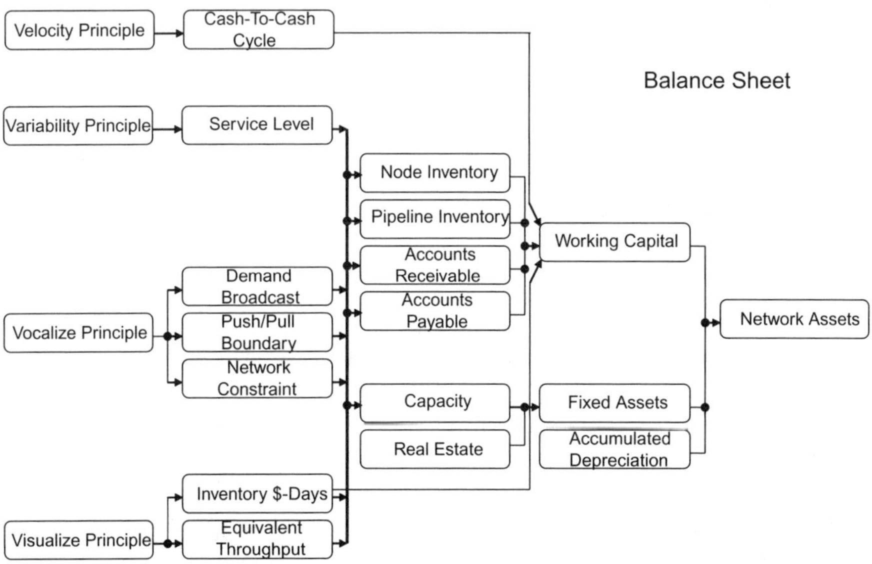

FIGURE 9-13 Vocalize, visualize, and variability principles drive asset reduction.

and effect diagram that shows how an operational strategy of *maximizing core trading partner vocalization and visualization* causes a direct reduction in network assets necessary to sustain a given level of service.

It is important to keep the context of the balance sheet clear. Each trading partner's legal entity has a balance sheet. Conceptually, however, there is also a network balance sheet, as shown in Table 9-13. The network balance sheet in the table is the parallel consolidation of three separate balance sheets. Current and fixed assets of the transform, manufacture, and fulfillment trading partners are grouped together on the left side. Current liabilities, long-term debt, and net worth of the transform, manufacture, and fulfillment trading partners are grouped together on the right side. Total network assets are in balance with total network liabilities and net worth. Internal to the network, the accounts payable of one trading partner become the accounts receivable of another. Total inventory includes inventory at every level of the BOM. The network balance sheet is a useful tool for a network operations council to analyze the minimization of total network inventory and the opportunities to reduce working capital while sharing risk.

TABLE 9-13
The Network Balance Sheet

Network Assets	Network Liabilities + Net Worth
Cash (T)	Accrued Expenses (T)
Cash (M)	Accrued Expenses (M)
Cash (F)	Accrued Expenses (F)
Accounts Receivable (T)	Accounts Payable (T)
Accounts Receivable (M)	Accounts Payable (M)
Accounts Receivable (F)	Accounts Payable (F)
Inventory (T)	Income Tax Payable (T)
Inventory (M)	Income Tax Payable (M)
Inventory (F)	Income Tax Payable (F)
Total Network Current Assets $$$	**Total Network Current Liabilities $$**
Fixed Assets (T)	Long Term Debt (T)
- Accumulated Depreciation (T)	Long Term Debt (M)
Fixed Assets (M)	Long Term Debt (F)
- Accumulated Depreciation (M)	**Total Network Long Term Liabilities $$**
Fixed Assets (F)	
- Accumulated Depreciation (F)	Paid-In Capital (T)
Total Network Asset Book Value $$	Retained Earnings (T)
	Paid-In Capital (M)
	Retained Earnings (M)
	Paid-In Capital (F)
	Retained Earnings (F)
	Total Network Net Worth $
Network Total Assets $$$$$	**Network Total Liabilities + Net Worth $$$$$**

(T) = Transform, (M) = Manufacture, (F) = Fulfillment

Use the following checklist to reduce network assets through collaborative network operations:

- ☑ Flatten the BOM to shorten the network length and the amount of pipeline inventory.
- ☑ Risk pool inventory upstream to service changes in product mix with less total inventory.
- ☑ Properly locate the push/pull boundary.
- ☑ Postpone inventory downstream to service changes in product mix with less total inventory.
- ☑ Eliminate an echelon to cause a one-time reduction in network assets.
- ☑ Reduce manufacturing and purchasing lot sizes.
- ☑ Sell excess inventory through a forward auction or an exchange.
- ☑ Accelerate the cash-to-cash cycle time.
- ☑ Convert to electronic funds transfer payment.
- ☑ Change the cash payment policy for a shorter payment cycle.
- ☑ Move to credit card and procurement card forms for immediate payment from customers.
- ☑ Drive the pull zone and the push zone from one overarching plan.
- ☑ Institute network-wide cash planning.
- ☑ Sell unused and obsolete capacity through a forward auction.

The Cash-To-Cash Cycle

As a supply chain network advances from one product sale to the next, each incremental sale needs a little up-front investment. In a successful business, the last sale is quickly converted into cash to pay for the materials, capacity, and other expenses to make the next sale. Hopefully, each trading partner is able to maintain a strong working capital position with a positive cash flow. Otherwise, revolving lines of credit and other forms of debt borrowing against assets are required to carry the business through from the time it must pay until the time it receives payment. The efficiency of working capital replenished by the cash-to-cash cycle is fundamental to running a business. Cash-to-cash cycle time should be computed for each trading partner in the network. Figure 9-14 shows two very different scenarios including one with a negative cash-to-cash cycle and one with a positive cash-to-cash cycle.

Scenario A, at the top, is all too common where a trading partner is invoiced for lower level materials that were purchased against a forecast before the product has been built and sold. The trading partner will need to pay the invoice before any cash payment is received from the product sale. In general, a buyer receives the invoice (2), makes note of the remaining time to the payment deadline (1), processes the invoice according to its payment policy (3), and sends payment either by check or electronically back to the seller (4). Some indeterminate amount of time later the same trading partner makes a product sale and immediately invoices its customer. The customer receives the invoice, processes the invoice according to its payment policy and eventually forwards a payment back to the trading partner. This is a negative

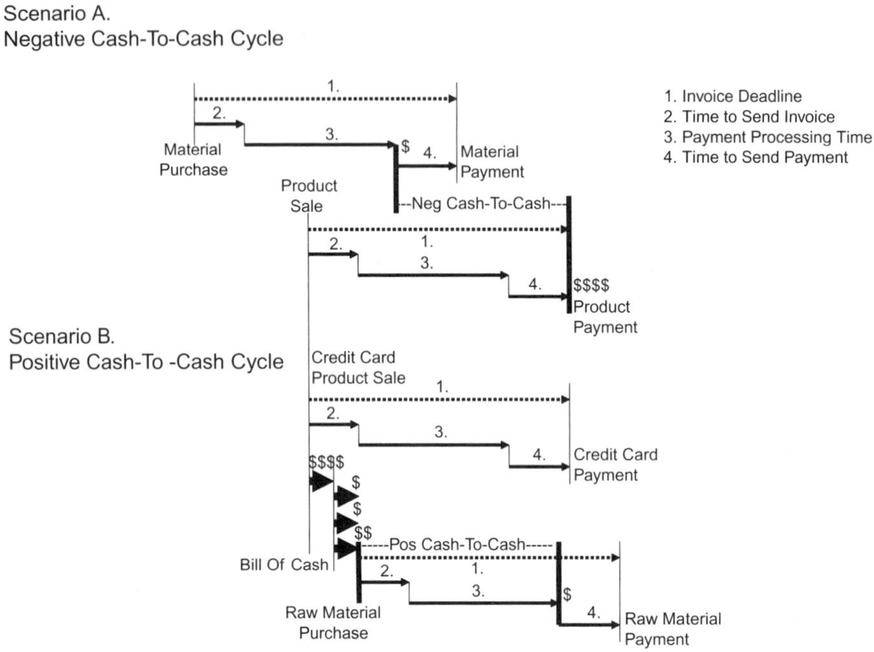

FIGURE 9-14 Cash-to-cash cycle time.

cash-to-cash cycle because the trading partner must front the cash to pay for the lower level materials. The trading partner is using its own cash to make the purchase.

Scenario B, at the bottom, is an example of the more desirable positive cash-to-cash cycle. Here the customer uses a credit card or a procurement card to buy the product. Although the buyer experiences a traditional payment cycle of being invoiced, deciding when to pay, and making a payment, the seller immediately receives a full payment for the product from the buyer's credit card bank. In turn, the trading partner uses a bill of cash to make nearly immediate payments to the next BOM level of suppliers. At some point upstream, the network must operate from a forecast, and at least one echelon of trading partner will have the traditional invoice and payment relationship with its raw material supplier. The middle trading partners experience positive cash-to-cash cycles because they are able to use the end-customer's cash to make their own purchases.

Network Risk Management Related to Financial Performance

It is prudent and necessary to develop and maintain excellence in business governance, internal control, and information disclosure practices to preserve shareholder value. In the United States, compliance with the Sarbanes-Oxley Act requires an annual audit of the effectiveness of internal controls over financial reporting. Such control is much more difficult across a supply chain network that extends into other legal entities, other business cultures, and other accounting and legal standards.

There must not be any potential for fraudulent activity associated with the balance sheet and the income statement of any trading partner, especially when outsourcing. Revenue, profit, and inventory must be properly stated.

The optimization of network design, the optimization of the product BOM fit with the network, and the optimization of network operations each contribute to enhanced financial performance. At the same time, it is prudent to manage the network risks that can affect a trading partner's financial performance. No trading partner wants to see the fruits of a sale lost through the irresponsible handling of capacity, inventory, or cash within the network. Manage the risk of network capacity, inventory, and cash by monitoring and controlling the following basics:

- *Constrained capacity*—It is possible to squander a network's constrained capacity through poor planning and control. Once time passes at the network constraint, it can never be regained. Manage network constraint risk by avoiding both schedule nervousness and the processing of defective materials.
- *Inventory buffer in units*—Inventory count accuracy is of paramount importance across a supply chain network. When inventory is missing, customer service levels fall and revenue expectations cannot be met. When inventory positions are excessive, balance sheets swell and investment returns are diminished. Manage inventory buffer risk through inventory count accuracy, avoiding schedule nervousness, physical security against theft, physical rotation to prevent spoilage, and planned consumption to avoid obsolescence.
- *Inventory buffer in dollars*—There is another set of inventory risks to consider when inventory is dollarized. Even though the inventory count accuracy is perfect, the dollar valuation of inventory on the books can be at risk. Foreign currency exchange rate fluctuation can deflate or inflate inventory purchased in non–U.S. dollar denominated currencies. For example, the currency conversion rates for Euro dollars and for Japanese yen are not pegged to the U.S. dollar. These currencies fluctuate relative to the US dollar. In addition, artificial price supports or price erosion on product held too long in the pipeline can affect the dollar value of inventory, as can aggregation errors in the unit to dollar reconciliation.
- *Cash buffer*—Cash balance accuracy is also of paramount importance across a supply chain network. When cash is missing, it becomes possible to default on scheduled payments. Planned inventory and capacity purchases are delayed, or worse. When there is an excessive level of cash in the cash buffer, balance sheets swell and investment returns are diminished. Manage cash buffer risk through cash balance accuracy, physical and electronic security against theft, attention to cash leakages for service and interest charges, careful management of letter of credit expiration dates, and through hedging strategies to offset foreign currency exchange fluctuation.

IN SUMMARY

The architecture of a supply chain network uses the velocity, variability, vocalize, and visualize principles to establish the network's competitiveness threshold and to optimize the network's value circle. As a result, each core trading partner benefits from reinvestment opportunities made possible through increased top line revenue, increased bottom line profitability, and the reduction of working capital and inventory for operations. Figure 9-15 shows the cause and effect relationships between the direct benefits to network stakeholders achieved through supply chain management.

A trading partner can use its incremental revenue to improve its competitive position one of four ways:

1. It can keep its experienced workforce intact while raising salaries and wages.
2. It can spend significant amounts of "discretionary" dollars on employee training, travel to build trading partner relationships, advertising to generate demand, and consulting to tune processes.

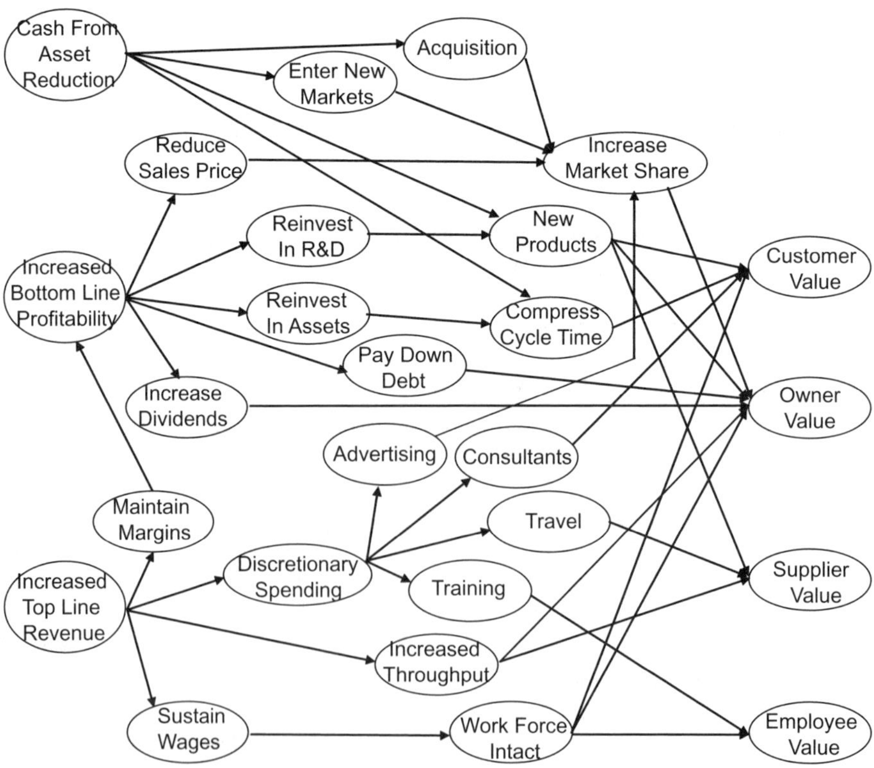

FIGURE 9-15 Stakeholder benefits from top line revenue, bottom line profits, and reduced assets.

TABLE 9-14
The Reality of Supply Chain Management

The Myth	The Reality
The full benefit of supply chain management comes from the installation of ERP software.	The competitiveness threshold for a network is established through relationships and business processes rather than from software technology.
The investment for ERP is too large and the return too low. Too many ERP implementation projects have failed.	The decision to invest in any kind of information technology, ERP or otherwise, should be made after the principles and techniques of *Supply Chain Architecture* are applied to the network.
The information technology that large companies can afford is a barrier for smaller companies.	This can be a real issue that can be addressed through a shared investment approach.
SCM is only for large companies. SCM cannot work for small companies because of conflicting agendas, conflicting priorities, and multiple network operating rules.	Most companies, large or small, operate in multiple networks simultaneously. The principles and techniques of *Supply Chain Architecture* explain how to separate and deal effectively with each.
A network is too complex to understand. A company controls only what is inside its own four walls.	The principles and techniques of *Supply Chain Architecture* clarify and demystify typical network complexity.
Companies have to clean their own house before joining a network.	A serial approach is never complete. The principles and techniques of *Supply Chain Architecture* should be applied in parallel.
Networks fail because of greed by one of the trading partners.	This is a real issue that can be addressed through the institution of global performance measures.
Networks fail because of a lack of trust among the trading partners.	This is a real issue that can be addressed through relationship management.
Networks fail because people at all levels resist change.	Change is manageable and requires agreement on the right objectives and measures.
Every network member organization has to be an equal for the network to work.	Network member organizations are not equals. They include the network orchestrator, trading partners, strategic nominal trading partners, and nominal trading partners.

3. It can leverage its increasing market share to discourage new competition.
4. It can maintain its profit margins.

A trading partner can use its incremental profit to improve its competitive position one of five ways:

1. It can reduce the sales price of its products to improve its market share.
2. It can reinvest its profits in new product development to beat the competition.
3. It can reinvest its profits in new plant, equipment, or information systems to compress cycle time.

4. It can declare a dividend for its shareholders.
5. It can pay down long-term debt.

A trading partner can use cash from reduced assets to improve its competitive position one of five ways:

1. It can reinvest its one-time profits in new product development to beat the competition.
2. It can reinvest its one-time profits in equipment or information systems to compress cycle time.
3. It can pay down long-term debt.
4. It can reinvest its one-time profits to fund the inventory and accounts receivables to expand a market.
5. It can buy a related business.

Chapter 1 of this book began with ten myths of supply chain management that have largely kept the promise from becoming reality. Table 9-14 summarizes the reality brought forward in *Supply Chain Architecture*. In the next and last Chapter, the business storyline is concluded. This time the firm bases its decisions on the principles and techniques of *Supply Chain Architecture,* and it quickly benefits from a much stronger competitiveness threshold.

They were driving along Route 78 on their way to the symphony on a fine Sunday afternoon. The program included Tchaikovsky's Serenade in C Major for Strings Op. 48 and Sir James Galway featured in Mozart's Flute Concerto No. 2.

As they drove past the exit for the Garden State Parkway, she talked about how the changes she had made to the way she forecast the capacity for course offerings and planned her cash flow were paying off.

"You know what Fred, the CEO at DataLink, told me on Friday?" she asked.

"I have no idea," said the supply chain architect.

"He said that DataLink really valued the responsiveness of my little company," she replied proudly.

"You and your employees have worked very hard and deserve that kind of recognition."

"You don't know the number of times we had to accommodate DataLink changing schedules, reassigning meeting spaces, and reprioritizing which of their employees could attend."

"It's not everybody that can consistently deliver in the face of dynamic changes in customer demand."

"Yes, I think our responsiveness is even starting to win some training business from the competition."

"So what's the next big challenge?" her husband asked. A confusing set of road signs marked a split in the road ahead with one turnoff leading to the airport and the other turnoff leading to the turnpike. They stayed on the airport ramp, taking the first exit and crossing back over the way they had just come.

"I just hope we can learn some different ways to be flexible for Fred and our other customers. First, DataLink will be asking us to develop a new kind of courseware with subject matter content that my present group of instructors cannot deliver. Second, my pricing structure is still 4–5% higher than the market. And third, we have to complete the project to modularize and catalog our existing courseware."

"Build new relationships, restructure costs, and modularize content," he repeated. "That is a lot of hard work, but it will pay off in greater future flexibility. It will continue to build the value of your company as seen by your clients. What do you think is the difference between responsiveness and flexibility?"

"I think they are related."

"They are related. The way I see it, a competitive supply chain network is responsive to customer demands and flexible in the methods used to match supply and demand. Responsiveness is required when the customer changes the delivery date, quantity, or location. Flexibility is required when management seeks a lower cost structure, a faster process, or a different relationship to win in spite of competitive pressures. Does that make any sense?"

She paused to consider what he had just said. "Yes. You are saying that though my business has been recognized for its responsiveness, I need to work on its flexibility."

They headed down the ramp and into the underground parking for the Performing Arts Center.

Getting out of their car, the supply chain architect summarized, "Being responsive keeps your supply chain competitive today. Being flexible can keep your supply chain competitive tomorrow."

10 A New Start

The principles of supply chain management—velocity, variability, vocalize, visualize and value—are worthless unless their application results in significant competitive improvement in a network context. We expect these principles to simultaneously drive revenue growth, increased profitability, improved return on invested capital, and share price appreciation. The storyline, in this book, is about the journey of an internally focused, cost-driven organization striving to become an externally focused, throughput-driven network trading partner. We have not seen much improvement so far. Something else must be going on within this organization.

SYMPTOMS OF A DEEPER PROBLEM

The core of each Chapter vignette is reproduced here sequentially. The story unfolds with an organization in shock. This shock is the unexpected loss of significant revenue and the stark realization that their value proposition is no longer working. The organization naturally turns inward, looking to save itself through consolidation and cost cutting. The organization wastes months of calendar time trying to get a grip. By now, it is apparent that key information has been left out of the description of this supply chain. This was done intentionally throughout the earlier Chapters to introduce each topic in a way that allows us to best identify our own business experience with the storyline. But in order to proceed to a conclusion, it is now necessary to describe the business in more detail. For example, we have insufficient information to answer the question: Does the loss of Colonial Distributor affect all or only some of the product lines?

The storyline is broken into three sections in this final Chapter, see Table 10-1. The first section, June 10 through July 9, announces the crisis; gives a feel for the organization, its personalities, and its culture; and highlights a number of symptoms that point to more fundamental competitiveness issues. The second section, July 11 through July 18, solidifies an understanding that improvement is doomed because of a lack of proper organization and project management. In the third section, August 10 through September 1, the organization drifts with little or no real improvement in its business situation. This last Chapter adds detail to the first section, adds an organization for success to the second section, and adds a different, results-oriented ending to the third section. We can use the blueprint in this book to change the ending of our own story.

The storyline, as told, lacks a network context. We need to understand something of the business, its customers, its products, its suppliers, and its set of core trading partners. We need to understand the echelon location of the organization.

TABLE 10-1
Symptoms of a Deeper Problem

Monday, June 10	
"Joining us this morning on the speakerphone is Adam Stone, President and CEO of Colonial Distributor, our third-largest customer."	
Adam started, "What I'm about to say will not be pleasant for you to hear. I had wanted to attend your meeting to be able to deliver this message face-to-face, but the scheduling was just not possible. Anyway, my company has decided to pull its account and to go with one of your competitors." "Your product quality has been steadily slipping. Your order processing has been making an excessive number of entry mistakes, and our product returns to your company now exceed 14%," Adam continued. "We provided defect details to your sales people, and asked your company in April and again in May to clean up your act. Then you really pushed us over the edge when you announced, last week, your across-the-board price increase of 6%. Colonial Distributor has worked at being a good customer, but this is unacceptable."	***Shocking the Network:*** The organization is shocked by the loss of revenue from its third largest customer. In addition, the organization's value proposition is challenged.
"I've thought about your situation for some time. Based on my experience, I have come to the following conclusions. First, your organization appears, to me, to be too internally focused instead of being focused on your customer. It is no longer fun to do business with your company. Second, there is too much friction in the flow of orders, products, and cash between us. You seem to have lost much of your earlier competitiveness," Adam concluded. Someone summarized on the flipchart: • Quality defects unresolved over 2 months • Repeated ordering errors • Customer returns 14% of product shipments • Customer balks at 6% price increase • #1 Too internally focused • #2 Too much friction to do business	***Direct Customer Feedback:*** The organization has been operating in isolation. Product and process quality defects have gone unaddressed while the organization raises prices to cover its internal costs. The organization seems unconcerned about other competitors in the market.
Wednesday, June 26	**The Current State**
This was one of a half-dozen meetings to explore how manufacturing could cut the cost of goods sold and increase product quality to the customer. The supply chain architect began to summarize, "The majority of the defects were related to the manufacture of product options. None of our standard product had any reported quality defects." Daisy jumped in, "We received details on four defective shipments. In two of the cases, the customer ordered an Option 58, but we built and shipped Option 85. In one case, the customer removed the product's cover and discovered that in our rush to ship product at the end of the last quarter, we never finished installing the option."	

(*Continued*)

**TABLE 10-1
(Continued)**

"Sounds like we have an order processing problem, an employee training problem, and possibly a design problem," said Hector. Dan Cook spoke up, "I'm looking at the bill of materials. Option 58 and Option 85 are identical except for a change in two component part values. It would be very easy to overlook those two parts all the way through final assembly."	
Dana interrupted them, "How do we intend to take cost out of these products?" "On average the product families that Colonial Distributor bought from us had three hours of labor content and $425 dollars of material content. We believe the competition can build an equivalent product with about two hours of labor and about $345 dollars of material," said Ray. "It's real tough to take costs out of our product designs with all the features our customers say they want," said Dan.	***Symptom:*** The organization cannot prioritize among quality, cost, and product feature issues. The organization has difficulty stating its core competency.
"And we are already buying some cheaper parts from Mexico, but sometimes we have delivery problems crossing the border," said Carlos. "Carlos brings up a good point," said the architect. "There are many other factors that go into landed cost besides the labor and material that Ray is talking about." "We have to decide what piece we do here better than anyone else. Then we can build the right distribution, outsourcing, supply base, or whatever around the core competency that is our competitive edge." The team brainstormed this: • We transform customer problem statements into effective product solutions. • We hold exclusive patent rights on the demodulator assembly. • We have competitive manufacturing cycle times in final assembly. • We have a reputation with our customers for excellent, worldwide service support.	***Symptom:*** The effort seems poorly organized. It does not have the feel of a project with a clear objective and deadline. The debate is missing the right set of participants. Although the organization seems to understand data-based decision making for quality related issues, its view of customers and competition is more anecdotal. The cost analysis of competitive products is new.
"Product development expertise, patent protection for a few more years, time-competitive final assembly, and a solid reputation for service support are the capabilities we should build on to win in the marketplace."	***Symptom:*** It is important to use facts rather than anecdotal reasoning to define a core competency. For example, the reputation for excellent customer service should be traceable back to end-customer surveys. Factual information takes the emotion out of the debate and moves the team along to quicker issue resolution.

(Continued)

TABLE 10-1 (Continued)

Friday, June 28	
Everything seemed to be working against them. An important large order had not made the month-end cutoff because a routine backup of the order processing computer had run five hours longer than expected. Another big shipment to Europe was stuck in Customs at JFK because of questions about its export license. Critical parts needed for production the last day of the month were delayed in-transit because of a tractor-trailer accident on Route 95. "It's not about export licensing at all! Customs has changed their requirements and expanded the 24 Hour Rule to include airfreight. An aircraft cannot be loaded now unless the destination has its freight manifest four hours prior to 'wheels-up.' We didn't do anything wrong, but now there's another delay!" said the architect. "This got me thinking about the velocity and variability of the flows in our supply chain. Look, we take the customer's order, ship a product from stock, and expect to collect a cash payment. That's a complete closed-loop that we do repeatedly for each order.".	***Symptom:*** The organization has a poor understanding of its current process. The disastrous month-end closing is a graphic symptom of this.
"Okay. It takes some amount of time to complete the loop. When the computer backup runs five hours late, it takes more time to order. When customs holds up a shipment, it takes more time to deliver. When a customer pushes out their payment of our invoice, it takes more time to be paid. When we add these times together, they define a basic order-to-delivery-to-cash cycle time with a pretty low velocity." "Then variability comes into play," the architect continued. "First, we carefully define a minimum number of process steps in the order-to-delivery-to-cash cycle. For example, who would have guessed our computer backups done in the middle of the night are on the critical path for order processing? Then, we ask which process steps are likely to have high variability? We try to either eliminate or fix those steps before bad things happen." "The network can develop a number of velocity traps that slow down the flow. Some of these velocity traps are subtle. They occur in the network where you would least expect them."	***Symptom:*** The concept of being embedded within a network is new to this organization. People are not used to thinking about how their piece of the operation is interconnected with other pieces and with other organizations.
Tuesday, July 9	
They were enmeshed in an information systems consolidation with their sister division in Singapore. In a ploy to cut operating expense, certain product lines were being transferred to Singapore to take advantage of the lower landed cost. Each of the manufacturing systems in support of these product lines was being consolidated under Asia-Pac. It was 10:00 p.m. and time for the conference call with B.T. Lam, the Asia-Pac IT Director, and his information technology team. This	***Symptom:*** One natural way to cut expense levels is to look for opportunities to reorganize. Here the corporate organization has decided to move ahead with an IT consolidation. It is unclear whether a new architecture has

(Continued)

TABLE 10-1
(Continued)

meeting was to problem-solve the mapping of data structures for the product line being transferred. C.B. Ng, Senior IT Engineer, and Esther Lam, Database Programmer, were expected on the call. "We have already mapped 65% of the necessary data fields to the Asia-Pac database schema," began B.T. "It shouldn't be a problem to migrate the rest of your data." "This is good news!" replied the architect. "We wanted to let your team know how we have been handling the customer option BOM for these products."	been established for the entire network or whether this is an incremental change to optimize locally. Whatever the plan, it has been communicated in a limited fashion.
"This is C.B. Can you say that again, please?" "Yes. We wanted to let your team know how we have been handling the customer option BOM for these products. First, can you tell us whether the remote terminal driver software is working for the Asia-Pac database?" "Could you repeat that please?" "Yes, is the remote terminal driver software working for the Asia-Pac database?" "It shouldn't be a problem," said C.B. "Okay. We can use the remote terminal capability on our next call to demonstrate the customer option BOM structure. The customer can choose the product with or without polarity reversal relays." "Yes." "The customer can also choose the product for 120VAC line voltage operation or 220–240VAC line voltage operation. This must be specified on the customer's order. So, there are a total of four options." "Can you dedicate a data element for the relay option and a second data element for the line voltage option?" "It is not a problem," said B.T. "Which data element will you dedicate for the relay option and which data element will you dedicate for the line voltage option?" "We already have line voltage on the Asia-Pac manufacturing database schema," replied B.T. "We can map the relay option to the Asia-Pac order processing database." The teleconference continued for another hour at the same frustrating pace. The architect realized that the interaction between the Singapore and Hong Kong databases used by Asia-Pac was still a mystery. He continued to worry that C.B. and Esther probably misunderstood the combinations of customer product options. "There are so many real and self-imposed boundaries that partition our supply chain network—like time zones, distance, language, Chinese culture, and company culture, to name a few—that it is really difficult to get both sides on the same page."	***Symptom:*** There are geographical, time zone, and cultural barriers stressing this relationship. The manufacturer thinks it is in charge. The participants have never had an opportunity to meet face-to-face. There are issues of trust between the two parties.

What Is the Business, and What Markets Are Served by This Organization?

The organization is a manufacturer in the business of designing and manufacturing electronic instrumentation sold to customers in the aerospace industry, in oil and gas services, and in high-end automotive markets. Their niche is instrumentation that requires some form of transducer to measure a physical property, like strain or flow or temperature, and converts the measurement into a digital electronic signal for transmission, display, and analysis. Their product is considered to be technically sophisticated and at the high end of the market. Over the years, this organization has developed a full line catalog of standard and custom transducers that are sold through a field sales force of engineers trained to provide applications engineering services for customers. At one time, this organization held the dominant market share in flow transducers. More recently, competition attracted by the higher margin business has made significant inroads into this market. Table 10-2 shows the revenue, profit, and return breakdown by market segment as reported in the organization's latest annual report.

What Is the Product Delivered by This Organization?

The strain gauges are primarily sold to research and development laboratories in the aerospace industry. The volume of strain gauge sales are directly dependent on the number of program contracts won by their aerospace customers. The strain gauge transducers have T-type composite BOM supply streams, see Figure 10-1. The base assembly, base electronics, and cabling are generic, along with a few common raw materials that are made into a broad range of transducer elements, each with specific characteristics. The flow gauges are primarily sold to the building and construction services of gasoline refineries and retail filling stations in the oil

TABLE 10-2
The Organization's Annual Report

Market Segment	Net Revenue (1,000's)		Net Profit (1,000's)		Return On Assets
Aerospace	$21,575	25.3%	$1,834	8.5%	11.3%
Oil and Gas*	$35,625	41.7%	$1,782	5.0%	8.4%
Automotive	$28,050	33.0%	$870	3.1%	7.9%
	Total $85,250	100.0%	Total mix $4,486	5.3%	Total mix 9.0%

*Net Sales by Oil and Gas Customer (1,000's)

1. Petroleum Outfitters	$6,127
2. Texas Oil and Gas	$4,872
3. Colonial Distributor	$4,033
4. Continental Pipelines	$3,552
5. Star Petroleum	$3,286

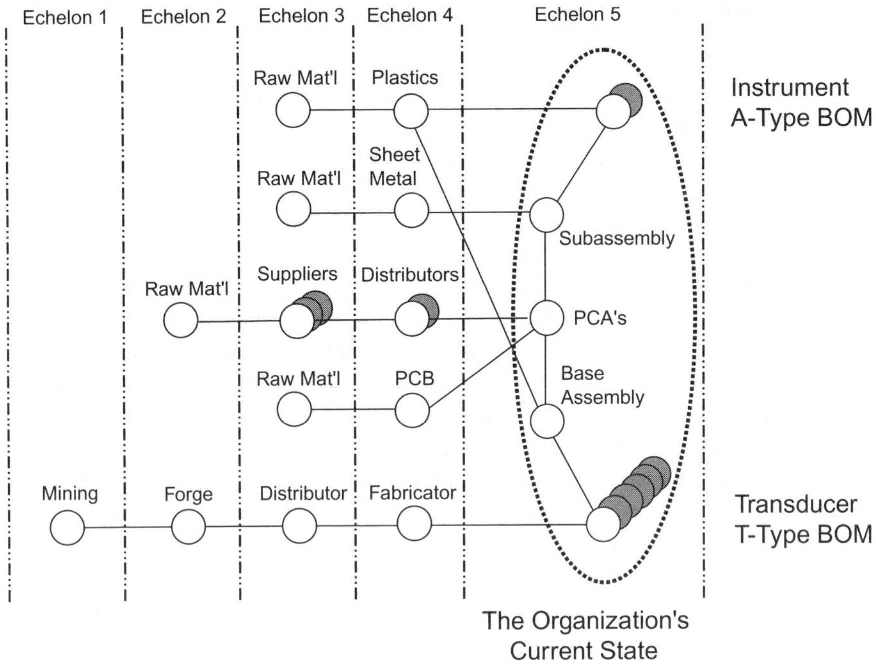

FIGURE 10-1 Using the composite BOM to map the supply streams.

and gas industry. The volume of flow gauge sales is seasonal, and it depends on statewide programs to upgrade filling station equipment. The temperature gauges are primarily sold into the luxury automotive market. The high volume of temperature gauges is driven by specific model production schedules for Mercedes-Benz and other high-end automobiles. The same family of universal display and analysis instruments can be used to read a strain gauge, a flow gauge, or a temperature gauge. These instruments have A-type composite BOM supply streams, see figure 10-1. A large number of electronic components from dozens of suppliers are loaded onto Printed Circuit Boards (PCB) to become Printed Circuit Assemblies (PCA). The instrument is housed in a sheet metal cabinet with some plastic extruded parts used in the front panel display.

What Are the Main Commodities Supplied to This Organization?

A large supply base provides a variety of active and passive electronic components both directly and through distribution. The supply base requires international logistics. Copper-clad raw printed circuit boards, aluminum sheet for chassis stampings, and plastic pellets to make extruded plastic parts are essential raw materials. The transducer elements are fabricated from exotic metal alloys procured under very long lead times. The upstream supply base is both wide and deep.

Who Are the Other Trading Partners in the Current Network?

The manufacturer is positioned in the midstream of a long, complex supply chain. The manufacturer connects a number of demand streams with a number of supply streams. It takes two to three upstream echelons to connect the factory with raw materials, depending on the lower-level path taken through the BOM. Figure 10-1 shows how the width of the upstream network splits among the various commodity supply chains: plastics, sheet metal, printed circuit assemblies, and the transducer element. It takes an additional two to three echelons downstream to connect the factory with the end-customer. Figure 10-2 shows how the width of the downstream network splits by industrial market segment among three demand streams: aerospace, oil and gas, and automotive. The network footprint of upstream commodities by echelon and downstream market segments by echelon still does not identify the trading partners. Each node in the footprint that has a majority of both its buying and selling in-network is a trading partner to the manufacturer. In the more distant echelons, all the organizations in that echelon are likely to be nominal trading partners. Here the manufacturer is dependent upon maintaining strategic relationships.

In fact, this manufacturer simultaneously participates in three distinct networks. One network is the supply of strain gauges to meet the demands of the aerospace industry, a second network is the supply of flow gauges to meet the demands of the oil and gas services industry, and the third network is the supply of temperature gauges to meet the demands of the automotive industry. The manufacture of the analysis and display instrumentation is common to all three supply chains. The loss

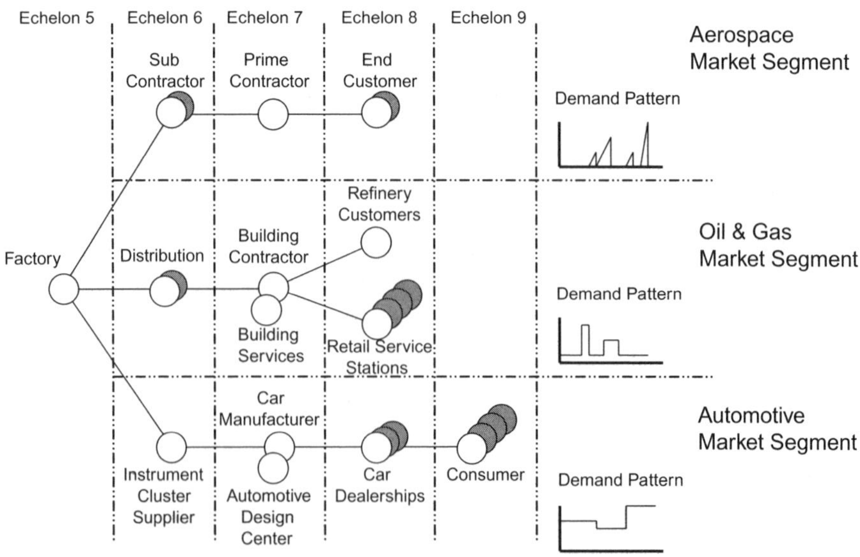

FIGURE 10-2 Using market segmentation to map the demand streams.

of Colonial Distributor, their third largest customer, is limited to the oil and gas market segment.

The total number of suppliers, the different commodity supply streams, the total number of product SKUs, the different BOM types, the total number of customers, and the different industry demand streams determine supply chain network complexity. It is not too early to ask, "How can the network be simplified?" Eliminate products that do not fit the A-type instrument BOM or the T-type transducer BOM. Eliminate products at the end of their product life cycle. The marginal revenue that is lost from these outliers can be made up with the refocusing of the main product offering. Eliminate nonrepeating customers whose purchases fall below a predetermined threshold. Flatten the BOM and collapse the number of midstream echelons. Eliminate second- and third-source suppliers, where the commodity is readily available through distribution. But protect the relationships with each sole source supplier.

PREPARE FOR SUCCESS

This second section of the storyline, as shown in Table 10-3, solidifies an understanding that improvement is doomed because of a lack of proper organization and project management.

The symptoms make it apparent that this manufacturer is not properly organized to successfully transition from an "independent," internally focused, cost-driven organization to an externally focused, throughput-driven network trading partner. The issues are clear, and each needs to be addressed.

1. The transition goal and its timeframe are unstated.
2. There is no coordinated program management structure.
3. Other trading partners are missing from the conversation.
4. Performance measures are functional and internally focused.
5. There is little responsibility and no accountability for making necessary changes.

Where Does This Organization Fit into the Current Supply Chain Network?

The organization is a midstream manufacturer simultaneously operating in three different markets. The organization has been in business a long time and is well respected by the industries it serves. Though its downstream fulfillment channels are very different, its upstream supply base is largely the same for all three markets. The organization has been acting all along as though it were the network orchestrator, except that it never before considered its actions in the context of a network. This may sound odd. However, when an organization views itself as fully independent of all other organizations and able to control its own destiny, it loses sight of the fact that being successful within a network context requires a different behavior. Probably none of the other suppliers or distributors see this manufacturer as their network orchestrator.

TABLE 10-3
Prepare for Success

Thursday, July 11	Issues to be Addressed
A question had come up during the data mapping with Singapore about what data would be required to drive the performance measures. Representatives from every functional area assembled in the conference room to answer the question.	
Dan was explaining, "Engineering doesn't care what other metrics you people decide to use as long as you keep the break-even time metric. That's the one measure that really makes sense for our long-term projects. Don't mess with my BET numbers." "We need to be able to value inventory for our financial statements," said Mary. "And we currently measure inventory turns." "Purchasing gets graded on purchase price variance as much as anything," said William. "Our college hiring is a priority for human resources. HR gets graded on that," said Alice.	***Issue:*** Performance measures are internally focused. Functional areas are unwilling to compromise on new metrics.
"Wait a minute! There is an important pattern here. It is clear that each functional area has at least one performance measure that it gets graded on—BET, inventory turns, purchased price variance, or the number of college new hires. But notice that none of these performance measures align with each other, and not one is directed at the end-customer," said the architect. "We are making our response to Singapore too hard," said Hector. It would seem that there are really two issues on the table. First is a data-mapping question asking what information we need to run the business. Second is a performance measurement question asking what performance measures we need to stay focused on the customer and to stay aligned with the other trading partners on our business strategy. It's important that we set a direction that makes sense for the business and for our customers, rather than being pushed in a direction we don't want to go because of the Singapore connection." "We're saying that it is important to define a set of network performance measures that will ensure our operational alignment with the other trading partners. And we're saying that in some functional areas, human resources and engineering to mention two, there are other metrics that we will continue to use independently." "What about measures required for legal reporting, like inventory valuation?" asked Mary. "Clearly if there is a legal or an audit requirement, we must continue to have that process." "What about purchased price variance as a measure?" asked William. "PPV is an interesting measure," replied the architect. "On the one hand, in a cost-driven world, it is a key performance measure.	***Issue:*** There is little responsibility and no accountability for making an overall change. Each manager is driven by different criteria. The tie back to an overarching business strategy is minimal.

(*Continued*)

TABLE 10-3 (Continued)

On the other hand, in a throughput-driven world, it causes misalignment. The role of a performance measure like PPV needs to be carefully reviewed. For example, we might keep it as a secondary indicator, but drop it as a primary measure."	
Thursday, July 18	
It felt to the architect that not much forward progress was being made. They were in the midst of endless meetings at the plant and teleconferences with teams around the world, including the information technology group in Singapore. "They're calling an all-hands meeting in the cafeteria in 15 minutes. I'll go tell the others," Larry called out. Dana Hoffman, CFO took the podium. She was flanked by Roberta Perez, the Operations Manager and Alice Way from human resources. Dana began, "Thank you for joining us today and taking time from your busy schedules. We know that many rumors are flying about, and we want to tell you what we know and what we don't know." "When this plant is doing well, corporate pretty much leaves us alone. We all can be very proud that over the years this plant has been a major contributor to the company's growth and profitability. But times have changed. The plant is not doing as well, and frankly the management team is getting a bit more 'help' from corporate than we need."	***Issue:*** The transition goal and its timeframe are unstated. In spite of "communications meetings" the overall plan has not been communicated.
"Corporate has helped us to see that there is a lower cost, more competitive way to manufacture our products. We will be splitting this plant into two operations. Final assembly will remain here, for now. Shortly, preassembly and subassembly will be moved to Singapore. Hector Morales, our VP of Manufacturing, will oversee the transition and will relocate immediately to Singapore. Roberta will take over here from Hector. We are going to need each of you to stay focused on meeting customer expectations while we implement the transition. We will do our best to keep as many of you employed as we can. That's all we know right now. There are many details still to work out." "Actually, this strategy makes a lot of sense," said Hector. "First, many of our customers have moved to Asia, and they expect our products to have significant Asian content. Second, our product is material intensive. If we can buy raw materials cheaper in Asia and make a smaller number of part shipments here, we will save material and logistics costs. And third, as you know, Singapore is a country with a highly educated, English-speaking workforce where it will be easier to transfer this work."	***Issue:*** There is no coordinated program management structure. Just as someone higher up made the decision to consolidate information systems, someone higher up has decided to split manufacturing into two locations. Perhaps this is a well-considered decision for shareholders. We just do not know.

(Continued)

TABLE 10-3
(Continued)

The architect spoke, "That's all well and good Hector. I respect the fact that you seem to be motivated to make a go of this. But what happens to all the employees on this site who lose their jobs? How do they pay their mortgages, send their children to school, and continue to have medical insurance coverage? Dana did not comment on any of that today. And what happens to our domestic customers who value the way we do business?"	
"Much of our product is build-to-order. Customers tell us what they need, and we manufacture it quickly for them. We can generally beat the competition because we are able to vocalize real customer orders to our local parts distributor and our local sheet metal fabricator. We are able to vocalize where the capacity constraint resides as our product mix changes. We are able to visualize where all our inventories are located because all the trading partners are tied into the same inventory control system. How will we make that work halfway around the world with Singapore when it has taken weeks just to unravel a simple data migration issue?"	***Issue:*** The other trading partners are missing from this conversation. The manufacturer is making unilateral decisions that impact the entire supply chain.

What Is the Business Strategy?

The organization is at a big disadvantage until it decides and communicates a coherent business strategy. This will focus the organization's energy and keep it from drifting aimlessly. The organization must decide on a value growth strategy, a revenue growth strategy, or a profitability growth strategy as outlined in Chapter 2. Revenue growth is the immediate issue for this organization with the loss of demand from Colonial Distributor. Revenue growth is also the longer-term issue because sales and marketing predict flat sales in aerospace over the next seven years, a slowing of new service station construction over the next three years, and intense, new foreign competition for automotive electronics over the next five years. Table 10-4 documents the reasoning behind the manufacturer's choice of a revenue growth strategy. Supply chain management lies at the core of both the short term and the longer-term solutions.

Who Should Be Part of the Solution?

Table 10-5 shows who is currently active in the conversation. Unfortunately, the team most responsible for change is internally focused and vertical with almost no horizontal representation. No one has been designated as program manager. It is unclear who the functional counterparts may be for information systems and for operations. The voice of the customer is really only the voice of the distributor, and the voice of the supplier is nonexistent.

Figure 10-3 connects the upstream supply with the downstream demand. The breadth of both the supplier base and the distribution channels result in only a few real trading partners in the network core. The sheet metal fabricator, a few commodity

TABLE 10-4
Deciding the Business Strategy

Strategic Alternative	Short Term Business Issue	Longer-Term Business Issue
As-Is State	Revenue shortfall of $4 million in oil and gas is 11.3% of oil and gas revenue and 4.7% of total revenue.	Business Forecast: Aerospace: 1% growth over 7 years Oil and Gas: –3% decline over 3 years Automotive: 0% flat auto sales with intense new competition for automotive electronics over 5 years
☐ Profitability Growth	Current cost structure exceeds the revenue shortfall. Would require deep cuts and layoffs to rebalance.	Declining revenue would force additional restructuring and organizational shrinkage, resulting in a general loss of competitiveness.
☑ Revenue Growth is the best strategic alternative for this manufacturer.	• Form a Network Operations Council that extends two echelons upstream and two echelons downstream. • Focus externally by focusing on throughput with the right set of global performance measures. • Eliminate velocity traps in the order-to-delivery-to-cash cycle. • Implement a dynamic pricing system to match supply. • Resolve open product and process quality issues. • Accelerate new product development for heavy oils and natural gas flow transducers. • Close pending aerospace and automotive deals to offset lost revenue in oil and gas.	Growing revenue solves the profitability issue and is consistent with positioning as a growth investment for shareholders. Strain Gauge Segment: rebalance sales among commercial, military, and space vehicle offerings. Flow Gauge Segment: Invest in new product development to expand flow gauge sales in bunker oil and natural gas applications. Temperature Gauge Segment: Develop lower cost temperature sensors for the midrange auto market.
☐ Value Growth	Shareholders are not yet aware that the organization is in trouble.	Would require repositioning as a value investment for shareholders.

suppliers, the raw printed circuit board fabricator, the aerospace subcontractor, and the automotive instrument cluster supplier are trading partners; all the rest are nominal trading partners. If the manufacturer is to act as the network orchestrator, then the manufacturer should form a Network Operations Council with representation from each trading partner plus other strategic nominal trading partners. The transducer fabricator and the oil and gas distributor are obvious chokes for strategic nominal trading partners. It is in the best interests of the other trading partners to ensure the continued competitiveness of the manufacturer's organization.

TABLE 10-5
As-Is Participants In Change

The effort is internally focused and vertical.	
Downstream Distribution	• President and CEO of Colonial Distributor: Adam Stone • Large aerospace customer: Stone & Jenkins
Senior Management	• Chief Financial Officer: Dana Hoffmann • Vice President Manufacturing: Hector Morales • Vice President Quality: Daisy Whitehall
Middle Management	• Sales Manager: Bob Donovan • Operations Manager: Roberta Perez • Cost Accounting Manager: Ray Smith • Purchasing Manager: William Smith
Functional Experts	• General Accounting: Mary Chen • Chief Engineer: Dan Cook • Purchasing: Carlos Gonzalez • Logistics Analyst: Larry Holmes • Human Resources: Alice Way
Upstream Subassembly	• AsiaPac Information Technology Director: B.T. Lam • Singapore Information Technology Engineer: C.B. Ng • Singapore Database Programmer: Esther Lam

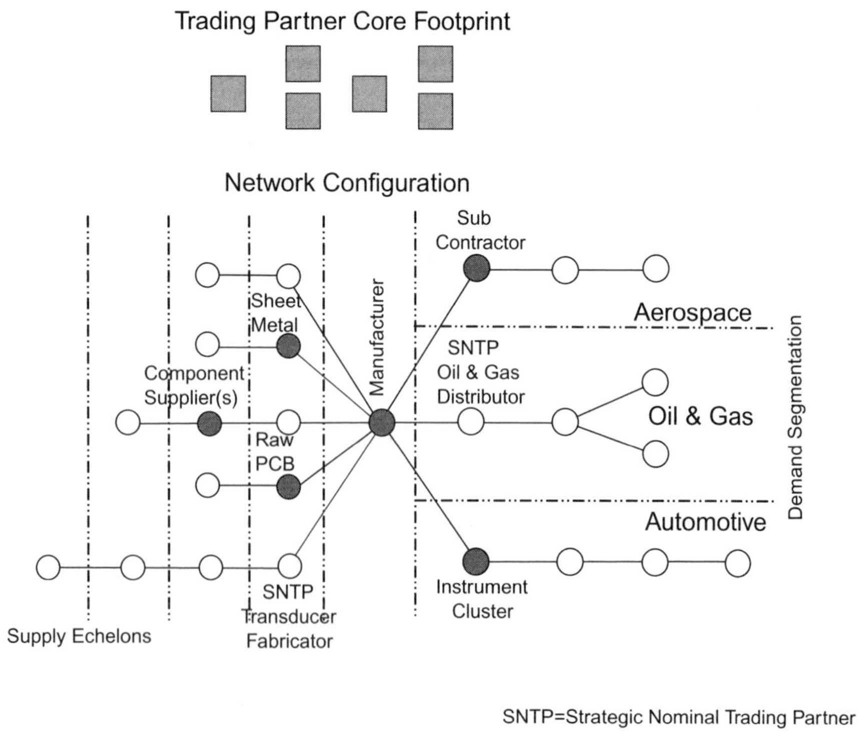

FIGURE 10-3 The network core footprint.

TABLE 10-6
Should-Be Participants In Change

An externally focused program team led by a program manager with an executive level steering committee and a Network Operations Council advisory having representation at least two echelons above and below the manufacturer.	
Upstream trading partners	Voice of the Supplier • Sheet metal fabricator representative • Raw printed circuit board fabricator representative • Commodity supplier(s) representative
Upstream strategic TP	• Transducer fabricator representative
Manufacturer	Trading partner change management team • Three-person executive-level steering committee • Program team – Supply chain architect and program manager – Team leader for planning/operations – Team leader for purchasing – Team leader for finance – Team leader for information Technology – Team leader for marketing/Sales – Team leader for product development – Team leader for quality – Performance measurement specialist
Downstream Trading Partners	Voice of the customer • Aerospace subcontractor representative • Automotive instrument cluster supplier representative
Downstream Strategic TP	• Oil and gas distributor representative

Table 10-6 outlines a successful organization structure. It has four key elements.

1. The program manager is responsible for a successful transition. The program manager is an employee of the network orchestrator and a member of the network operations council.
2. The program team is kept small and agile; it includes the program manager, a number of team leaders, and a performance measurement specialist. The team leaders are full-time people who do some implementation work themselves and have others to help with implementation tasks.
3. The executive level steering committee is accountable for a successful transition. The steering committee decides the scope of the program, allocates critical and scare resources to the program team, and holds regular progress review sessions with the program team.
4. A Network Operations Council extends the reach of the program team multiple echelons upstream and downstream, grounding the program team in a network perspective.

TABLE 10-7
The Current State Value Circle

Axis	As-Is
Velocity	Estimated order-to-delivery-to-cash cycle time is 6–9 weeks. The competition delivers product in 3 weeks.
Throughput	$35.6 million in oil and gas revenue is used as the 1.0 reference point. The loss of Colonial Distributor puts revenue at $29.6 million and outside the unit circle.
Visualize	Internally focused, functional measures. Few measures align with the business strategy or with the needs of the end-customer.
ROIC	9.0% return on assets (ROA) published in the annual report to shareholders. Note that ROA is a different measure than ROIC.
Vocalize	Only the manufacturer and the sheet metal fabricator share planning data.
Network Inventory	Not currently measured.
Variability	Not currently measured.
Landed Cost	A highly developed direct labor and direct material internal accounting system. Overhead allocated over units produced. Set to 1.0 as the starting reference point.

Where Is the Organization Competitively?

Table 10-7, plotted in Figure 10-4, shows the organization's current state value circle. Because the organization is unaccustomed to measuring competitive value in this manner, there are significant measurement gaps along some of the axis. Completing the As-Is column helps to sharpen and prioritize the program team's objective.

How Does This Organization Currently Measure Its Performance?

The manufacturer behaves as a loose collection of functional areas, each with their own performance metrics. For example, research and development measures break-even time, finance measures inventory turns, purchasing measures purchase price variance, and human resources measures the number of college hires. None of these measures aligns very well with the business strategy or the needs of the end-customer.

How Should the Organization Be Measured?

Organizations cannot be expected to change unless and until the right performance measures are implemented. These performance measures should be global, externally focused, and in alignment with the business strategy. The manufacturer should implement the perfect order, order-to-delivery-to-cash cycle time, equivalent throughput, and total network inventory measures described in this book. Figure 10-5 shows how

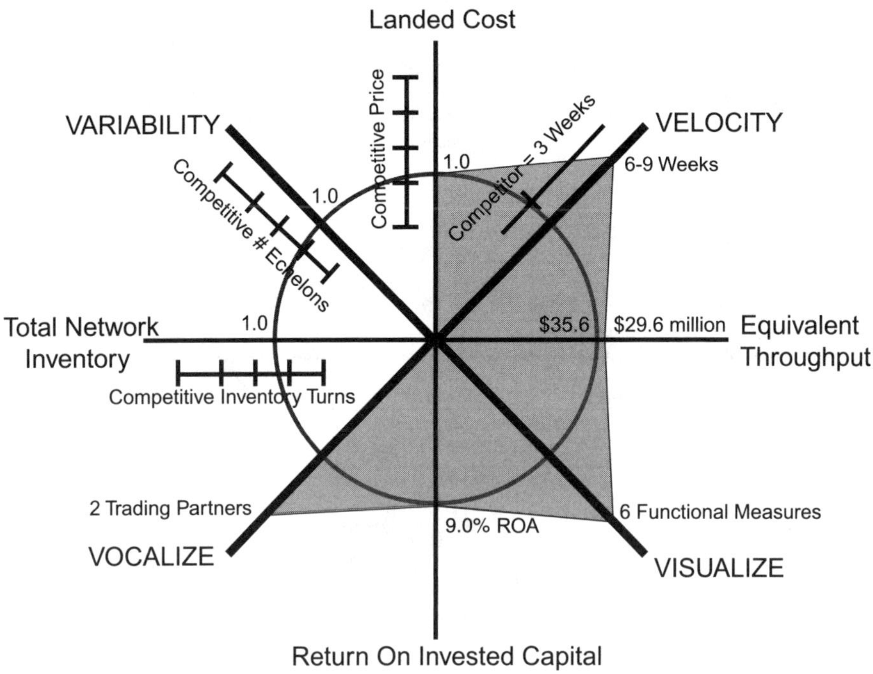

FIGURE 10-4 The current state value circle.

this small set of measures can be the operations portion of a balanced scorecard dashboard used to run the business.

What Is the Program Objective and Deadline for Change?

The objective should be focused and the deadline aggressive. Once a program manager is selected and the program team chartered, the program objective and deadline are set. In phase one, the program team is chartered to drive the order-to-delivery-to-cash cycle time from its estimated current range of 6–9 weeks to a consistent period of less than 10 days. The competition can deliver product in 3 weeks. The program team is given 90 days, from calendar day 1 through calendar day 90, to make this improvement. Next, the senior executive agrees to get involved establishing a Network Operations Council, with the program manager invited to be a member. In phase two, the program team is chartered to work with the Network Operations Council to implement the perfect order, equivalent throughput, and total system inventory performance measures across three echelons of the supply chain. The program team is given 200 days, from calendar day 91 through calendar day 290 to integrate these measures into the management dashboard. The longer timeframe is a reflection of having to learn to work through other trading partners. Table 10-8, plotted in Figure 10-6, integrates the program team's phase one charter with the future state value circle.

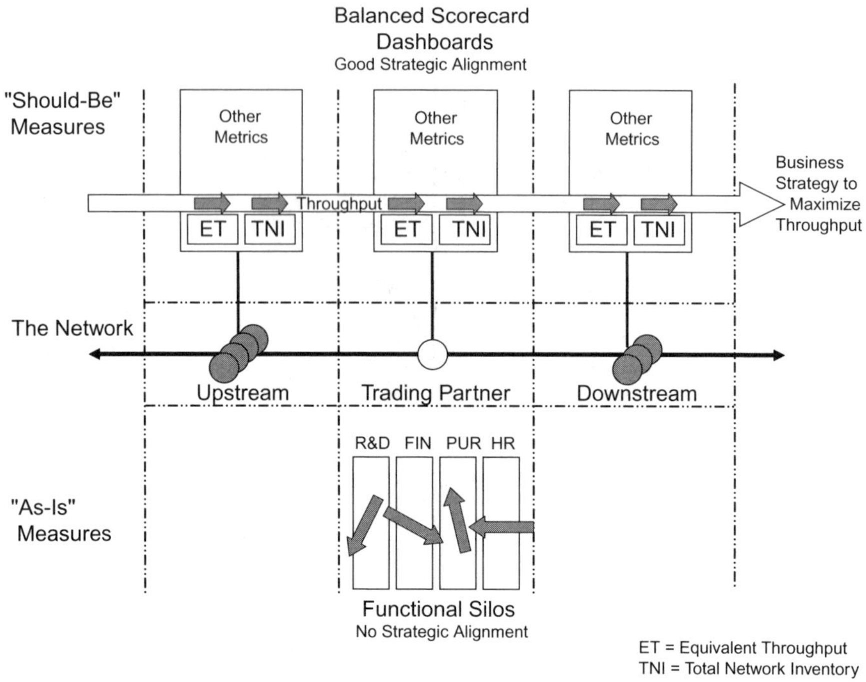

FIGURE 10-5 Global performance measures keep alignment with the business strategy.

TABLE 10-8
The Future State Value Circle

Axis	Should-Be
Velocity	Goal of 10 days order-to-delivery-to-cash cycle Time. Set competitor's 21 days as the 1.0 reference point. See Figure 10-6.
Throughput	Recover to $35.6 million in oil and gas revenue as the 1.0 reference point. See Figure 10-6.
Visualize	Implement order-to-delivery-to-cash cycle time, the perfect order, equivalent throughput, and total network inventory. Align with the revenue growth strategy.
ROIC	Calculate ROIC for the oil and gas segment.
Vocalize	Establish a multi-echelon Network Operations Council. Share planning and demand information with all the trading partners and strategic nominal trading partners.
Network Inventory	Analyze competitor's inventory turns. Reset inventory levels to be consistent with the 10 day order-to-delivery-to-cash cycle time goal.
Variability	Analyze the number of echelons in competitor's networks. Set variability goals as part of the 10 day order-to-delivery-to-cash cycle time project.
Landed Cost	Analyze competitor's price points. Focus on throughput rather than cost.

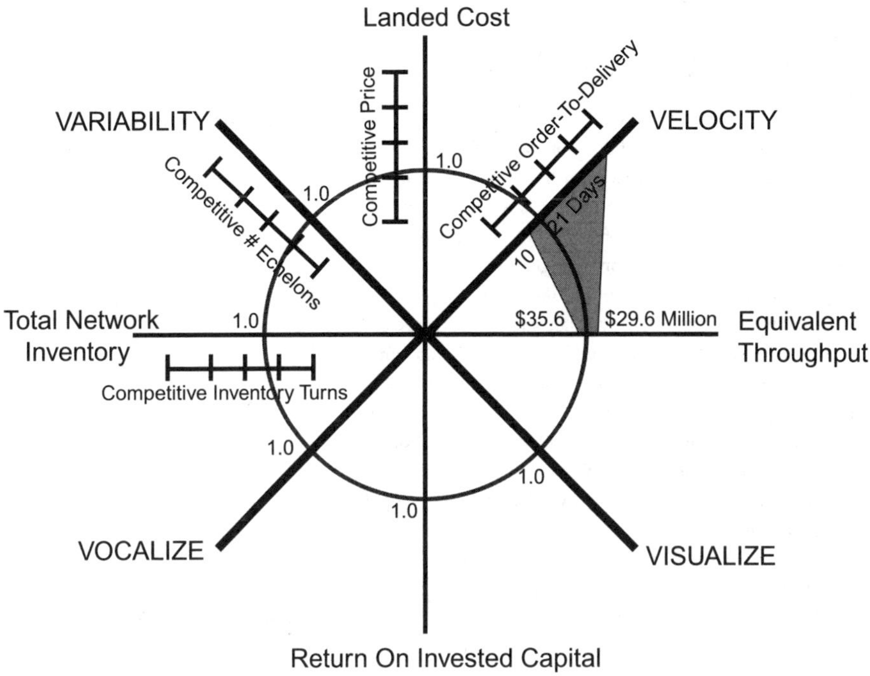

FIGURE 10-6 The future state value circle for phase one.

Why Will Focusing on Supply Chain Management Make a Difference when the Issue Is a Revenue Shortfall? Why not Just Increase the Sales Effort?

It would seem to some that accelerating velocity and realigning performance measures is a long way from recovering $4 million dollars in lost revenue. This scenario is typical of organizations isolated within complex networks. *The root problem is not a sales problem; it is a network problem. The solution is not a sales solution; it is a network solution.* The competitiveness threshold of this network must be fundamentally altered in order to win a higher level of business from its customers. The customer base for such specialized products is limited. The network will have to find ways of taking business away from other competitors. Consistent product availability, a frictionless customer interface, and the fastest delivery time in the industry can all contribute to winning orders. The solution will not be easy.

NAVIGATING AN AGGRESSIVE COURSE

In the third section, August 10 through September 1, the organization drifts with little or no real improvement in its business situation, see Table10-9. We need a different, results-oriented ending in the third section. We can use the blueprint in this book to change the ending of our own story.

TABLE 10-9
Navigating an Aggressive Course

Saturday, August 10	Additional Signs of Dysfunction
The conference room had been outfitted with white boards and corkboards on opposite sides of the room. The team had painstakingly documented their current U.S.-based supply chain on the left wall and were in the process of modeling their future U.S.–Singapore supply chain on the right wall. This side-by-side comparison had already proven useful. The network design would not change the way finished product was distributed to the end-customer. The U.S. manufacturing center had been split into final assembly done in the U.S. and subassembly done in Singapore. Parts shipments from each sole-sourced supplier would be rerouted to Singapore. Hector's team would identify potential local suppliers for the bulk of the material, and purchasing in Singapore would validate these new suppliers. Halfway around the world, Roberta's purchasing team would notify the current supply base that their business was to be terminated. Orders would have to be placed for last time buys.	
"We both agree that this team's next task is to figure out the changes that are necessary for our operations planning." "Why can't we just treat Singapore like another supplier in our ERP system?" asked William Smith, the purchasing manager. "We have to ask if the new network is capable? Where do we place the inventory buffers? Where do we place the cash buffers? How does the demand seen by our factory and by Singapore differ? Our customers must continue to see the same responsiveness and service level they are used to from the current network." "Let's break this down starting with the forecast of demand," said Roberta. The architect interrupted, "Actually, we need to talk about how the BOM splits across the network first. If we keep all the product option manufacture and postponement here, then Singapore sees only dependent demand." "Okay, so with the forecast and actual demand still coming to planning and order processing here, and Singapore only seeing dependent demand, the issue becomes how do we communicate this demand with Singapore without introducing serial delay in the planning cycle? We must avoid introducing the bullwhip effect into our network." "Also, how will the new, local suppliers in Singapore get forecast and demand information?" William wanted to know. "When the manufacture of the entire product was vertically integrated at our factory, the push/pull boundary was between level 3 and level 4 of the BOM. In the future state with level	***Signs of Dysfunction:*** There is little sense of urgency. Though Roberta and Hector both agree what work comes next, the work assignment is not given context. Roberta and Hector do not set a deadline nor push the team to accelerate their progress.

(Continued)

TABLE 10-9 (Continued)

3 and level 4 being built in Singapore and a long transit time between the two sites, the factory can continue as a pull operation, but Singapore becomes a push operation," offered Larry. "That's good, and also bad. It's a real important observation that we should capture on the whiteboard. But it's a problem because it means more total inventory in the network and a less responsive supply chain overall," said the architect.	
"The next issue is the question of whether the future network is still capable? Several important new constraints have entered the network, such as Singapore subassembly manufacture, new local Singapore suppliers, and the logistics connection back to the United States. We need to identify and possibly elevate the network constraint," said the architect. "Last for this morning, we need to update our planning tools and spreadsheets to account for each new inventory buffer location and each new cash buffer location. Dana Hoffmann, our CFO and Ray Smith, from cost accounting, should be present for this part of the discussion. We need to be intentional about placing and managing a few critical inventory buffers while forcing any other buffer remaining from the old configuration to be zero. That will be hard to influence a half a world away with our cultural differences."	***Signs of Dysfunction:*** The organization's progress is not aggressive. New issues are opened before old ones are closed. There is no tracking of when issues are closed.
Sunday, September 1	
With Hector and the operations team in Singapore, their immediate goal was to keep the outsourcing transition transparent to the end-customer while they worked feverishly to reestablish a reliable supply chain. However, the real issue was how to use this new supply chain to both increase revenues and reduce costs. "If we make the supply chain any longer, it will take forever to get product to our customers! Our availability dates keep moving out! Stone & Jenkins is about ready to place a $1.8 million order, but are we ready to commit for one of our very best customers?" ranted Bob Donovan, the Sales Manager.	
"If you want to talk about a nightmare, talk about this: Our stock price has fallen five months straight. We need to expand our borrowing, and our bank will no longer offer us preferred client rates," moaned Dana Hoffmann, the CFO. "Not to mention that we lost some of our best employees with the decision to outsource to Singapore," said Alice Way from human resources. "Being the acting VP of Manufacturing hasn't been a picnic either," said Roberta Perez. "You are all well aware that we made the decision to move subassembly operations to Singapore in order to reengineer our cost structures and become more competitive."	***Signs of Dysfunction:*** The organization is not moving forward. Team members, including the CFO, keep bringing up the past with no clear vision of the future.

(Continued)

TABLE 10-9
(Continued)

"Roberta, a competitive network can provide value in more than one dimension to more than one stakeholder," said the architect. "Cost reduction is certainly very important especially when it improves profitability and earnings for our owners. But it doesn't help our customers unless we choose to drop product pricing. When the cost reduction is accomplished by lengthening the supply chain, it can actually hurt delivery performance to our customers." "So you are questioning management's decision?" replied Roberta. "No. Not at all. I'm working toward making the point that there are other important value dimensions we haven't yet addressed. A second value dimension is to use the supply chain network to grow revenue. If we drop product prices, our revenue base shrinks. If we can gain entry into new market segments or introduce significant new products, our revenue base grows. We have not talked about what it would take to convince Stone & Jenkins to buy more. Are we their preferred supplier in Paris? Are we their preferred supplier in Tokyo?" "The local competition has a significant advantage in France and Japan. We can't compete against their in-country distribution," said Bob. "I'm sure there are many reasons why this is very difficult. However, we have no choice but to make it our new supply chain work. The third value dimension is to grow returns by shrinking our asset base. How can we operate through Singapore with less total network inventory and less total network cash? With higher profits from reduced costs and higher returns from reduced inventory and cash assets our stock price will appreciate in value for our owners." "The point is that a competitive supply chain network creates value in three ways through improved profits, through growth in revenue, and through improvement in return on assets. We have been intensely focused on only one dimension."	

A NEW START

Without proper organization, objectives, and a timeframe, the manufacturer continues to drift with little or no improvement to its competitiveness threshold. There are additional signs of dysfunction:

1. There is little sense of urgency.
2. The organization is not moving forward.
3. Their progress is not aggressive.

Because this is a story, knowing what we now know, we have the luxury of resetting to an earlier time and restarting the dialogue. We can make a new start, see Table 10-10. There is new clarity around the orwith the introduction of a program

TABLE 10-10
Take Two

<table>
<tr><th></th><th>Wednesday, August 14</th></tr>
<tr><td rowspan="2">This Is What You Must Do!
• Have an organization, a plan, and a focused goal.
• Follow the network blueprint.
• Think in three integrated flows.
• Lead with the velocity, variability, vocalize, visualize, and value principles.
• Hold people accountable for measured results.</td><td>The supply chain architect had been named program manager over the program team. The project team leaders included Mary Chen from general accounting, Mohamed Hashim from information systems, Bob Donovan from sales, Nancy Tucker from product development, Gus Lopez from planning, Hank Johnson from quality, and Larry Holmes from logistics. Ray Smith from cost accounting, known for his excellent grasp of both information systems and metrics, became the team's performance measurement specialist. The team makeup was a combination of experienced managers and practitioners, each with a demonstrated record of accomplishment.
The newly formed network council had already met a couple of times. The council was still working on getting Jim Stone, a partner from the Stone & Jenkins aerospace sub contractor, to join. Roberta Perez, the manufacturer's operations manager, was voted chairwoman of the council. The other members included:
• Barry Taylor, the automotive instrument cluster supplier representative, trading partner
• Joe Darby, the oil and gas distributor representative, strategic nominal trading partner
• Jose Esposito, President of Allied Sheet Metal, trading partner
• Ted Keating, VP Sales for High Tech PC Boards, trading partner
• Joanne Donnelly, a commodity supplier representative, trading partner
• Brenda Romano executive VP for Omega Transducers, strategic nominal trading partner
• The supply chain architect, program manager.</td></tr>
<tr><td>Hector Morales had left in July to take a lucrative position in the pharmaceutical industry. When the revenue growth business strategy and program charter were firmly in place, the cost-cutting tactic of outsourcing subassembly to Singapore was put on hold. Reengineering the network cost structure would become a priority at some point in the future, but for now it was counterproductive to the program goal.
Joe was saying, "Look, I know I'm new to the council, but it seems to me that when a shipment is held up waiting for the matching transducer, that delay can lose the order. It happened again just last week. By the time Roberta was able to acknowledge the transducer ship date, my customer had gone to a competitor. If you want to follow a revenue growth strategy, fix the transducer coordination problem."
"Why is the transducer shipment late?" asked Barry.
"It's not really late," replied Brenda. "There are so many different types of transducers that in order to save the costs of carrying inventory, Omega waits to confirm what the customer needs."</td></tr>
</table>

(Continued)

TABLE 10-10 (Continued)

	"Why are the transducers different?" asked Barry. "For my part the transducers are not really different," said Ted. High Tech produces only four kinds of printed circuit boards for more than a hundred different transducers. We could reduce that to just two PCB's with a little engineering support from Roberta." "Why are there more than a hundred different transducers?" asked Barry. "Well, obviously, there are different sensor materials for strain gauges, flow gauges, and temperature sensing," replied Brenda, getting a little defensive.
This is what you must do! • Have an organization, a plan and a focused goal. • **Follow the network blueprint.** • **Think in three integrated flows.** • Lead with the velocity, variability, vocalize, visualize, and value principles. • Hold people responsible for measured results.	Roberta jumped in, "I think this line of questioning is good. Let's remember that we are addressing a business issue and not attacking each other." "Why are there more than a hundred different transducers?" asked Barry again. "If you were to group all the transducers into strain gauge, flow gauge, and temperature sensing application, is the 100 number split evenly?" Roberta answered that question, "No. Actually, the strain gauges have the most variety because they are built from the most exotic alloys. Our highest volume business, particularly in oil and gas, comes from a much smaller number of transducers." "Aren't the sheet metal housings and the printed circuit board assemblies pretty much the same across the board?" asked Jose. "Yes, that is correct," replied Roberta. "So, we have some serial processing going on that if we could turn it into a parallel process, it would take a bunch of time out of the order-to-delivery cycle," said Barry. "What is keeping the transducer fabrication from being organized as a parallel process?" "To be very frank, the history has been that Omega just doesn't get paid promptly," replied Brenda. "And we have a lot of other customers with many other requirements." "What percentage of your business does Roberta represent? asked Ted. "Well, um, about 38%," said Brenda quietly. Ted continued, "That's a huge percentage of your total revenue. It would easily justify doing something special for Roberta." "Our accounts payable to Omega are slow because our accounts receivable from distributors, like Joe, are slow," said Roberta. "Ouch," said Joe. "Sounds like we have a bit of a trust issue here," mused Barry. "Let me summarize our conversation so far," offered the architect. "As you all know, my program team's goal, with your help, is to drive the order-to-delivery-to-cash cycle time from between 40–60 days down to 10 days. I am personally responsible for achieving this goal by October 30th."

(Continued)

TABLE 10-10 (Continued)

This is what you must do! • Have an organization, a plan and a focused goal. • Follow the network blueprint. • Think in three integrated flows. • **Lead with the velocity, variability, vocalize, visualize, and value principles.** • **Hold people responsible for measured results.**	"Let's stay focused on velocity. So far, in this meeting we have learned that Roberta's shipments depend on a coordinated, serial shipment of transducers from Brenda because of cost, that the transducer base components from Ted and Jose's are largely the same, and that slow payments from Joe to Roberta translate into slow payments from Roberta to Brenda because of trust." They all agreed, nodding their heads. "Okay. Let's see whether we can brainstorm some ways to parallel the production of transducer sensors with instrument final assembly and to parallel the flow of cash from Ted to Roberta with that from Roberta to Brenda." Joe began, "How do you receive your transducer requirements, Brenda?" "We get our transducer requirements once a week after Roberta has processed her orders. If there is a rush order, we may get a fax from Roberta at any time." Joe continued, "And how long does it take you to process my order and send it on to Omega, Roberta?" "It can take up to two days to enter your order, Joe, if a change order is involved. Then we process the order through our weekly planning cycle and send the order to Omega electronically." "What if I could send my orders simultaneously to Roberta and Brenda? Would that help you at all, Brenda?" asked Joe. "Yes, that could take nearly eight days out of my order entry process, and it would lead to better capacity planning at Omega." "What if Roberta agreed to pay for the transducers immediately at the time I paid for the order? This should be a low risk scenario for Roberta because every instrument order goes out with a transducer, and there are very few returns. Would that help you at all, Brenda?" asked Joe. "Yes, that would take more than 30 days out of the payment cycle." "This is very encouraging, Brenda. Joe and I each have some work to convince our senior executives that these are good return versus risk decisions," replied Roberta. "I'm thinking there are some more opportunities we have overlooked," said Barry. "There is a predictable base of transducer business and a more volatile level of business driven by seasonality, the model year, special end-customer needs, etc. The planning system could segment demand to be pushed by predictable demand and to be pulled by unpredictable demand. Roberta would need to invest in a small inventory of high volume transducers while tuning her process capacity for high mix transducers." "You have just identified 38 of the 50 days that the program team needs to eliminate. This is what we must do to be competitive," concluded the supply chain architect.

team and a Network Operations Council. The program team is chartered to focus on the velocity of the order-to-delivery-to-cash cycle and to reengineer new global performance measures that align with a clearly stated revenue growth strategy. Getting it right moves the storyline from the left column to the right column for emphasis. Now we can complete our transition, in Table 10-10, from being internally focused and cost-driven to being externally focused and throughput-driven.

Have an organization, a plan, and a focused goal. Follow the network blueprint. Think in three integrated flows. Lead with the velocity, variability, vocalize, visualize, and value principles. Hold people responsible to measured results. *This is what you must do.*

EPILOGUE

It had been quite a night in early October! His presentation on *Supply Chain Network Turnarounds* had just won the "Best Technical Session Award" during the annual awards banquet at the APICS International Conference and Exhibition. The supply chain architect and his wife were toasted and congratulated by friends and colleagues alike.

The paper he had submitted to APICS for the April deadline had told only half the story. It was heavy on theory and light on the practical application. Then the loss of Colonial Distributors precipitated the real turnaround story! The best part was when the new Network Operations Council threw their full support behind accelerating network velocity. The order-to-delivery-to-cash cycle time had plummeted down from 60 days to 52 days to 51 days to 26 days to 24 days during the weeks of September. September actual orders were a full 24% ahead of the August actual orders. Their customers were taking notice, and they were increasing their orders.

The architect had cleverly worked some details of these business results into his talk. Then at an opportune time, he had asked Brenda Romano and Joe Darby, who were in the audience, to come on-stage and talk about the turnaround. Brenda and Joe spoke eloquently about how the manufacturer collaborated in its role as the network orchestrator for a highly competitive network. They explained to the audience how much easier it was for the distributorship to make a sale with the accelerated velocity. The audience responded enthusiastically and asked many questions.

Exhausted by the day, the supply chain architect and his wife retired to their hotel room. As they prepared for bed, his wife turned to him and said, "Honey, I've been thinking. After all this excitement is over let's redo the bathrooms."

Appendix A: The Network Blueprint

An architect's blueprint package consists of a set of drawings and a book of specifications constructed in such a manner that someone skilled in the art 10,000 miles away can build to the design and operate within the space. This appendix is a complete blueprint package to build a competitive supply chain network from a design and to operate that network competitively within its space. The network blueprint is applied successively to the forward supply chain, the consumables supply chain, and the reverse supply chain. The network blueprint applies both to manufacturing and to its related services.

Each process step is referenced to one of three "architectural sheets" in the network blueprint, see Figure A-1, and to the relevant Chapters in this book. Each sheet begins with a specification table followed by the process steps. Each process step in bold, with supporting statements or questions as bullets, and with possible alternatives denoted as: (...)(...)(...). Follow the process steps in order within each sheet, and then optimize through iteration.

FIRST STEPS AND THE ENVIRONMENTAL CONTEXT

It is first necessary to have a clear understanding of the business strategy, markets and customer requirements, and competitive landscape that form the context for a supply chain network.

Step 1: State the Network Objective in the Context of the Business Strategy (Chapter 2)

- To design and operate a new network. The network for a (manufacturing) (service) business will include (a forward supply chain for (manufactured products) (services)), (a forward supply chain for consumable products), (a reverse supply chain for (returns) (repairs) (recycling)), or (a reverse supply chain for remanufactured products).
- To rationalize and optimize an existing network.
- To analyze the competitive advantage of a competitor's network.
- Under a (value growth) (revenue growth) (profitability growth) strategy.

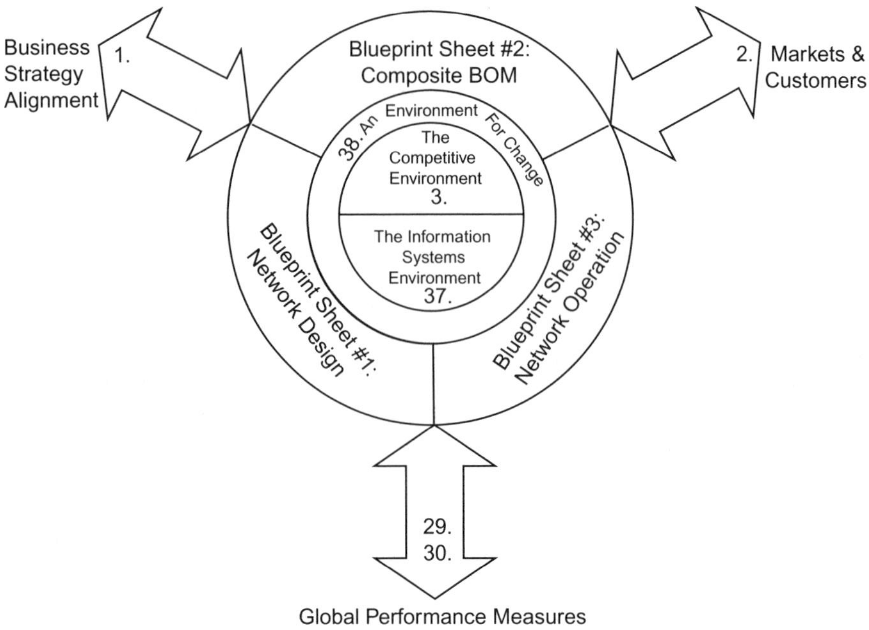

FIGURE A-1 The network blueprint.

Step 2: Identify Customer Requirements in the Context of the Competitive Environment (Chapter 2)

- Segment the market (by Geography) (by Customer need) (by Temporal segmentation) and understand product and service pricing elasticity by segment.
- Where is the market? (Local) (Regional) (National) (International) (Global)
- How is the product or service delivered? (Network delivers to customer) (Customer pickup from the network) (Coordinated product delivery) (Range of services offered) (Competitive availability)
- How is the product or service priced? (Market based) (Cost plus) (Contract pricing) (Dynamic pricing) (Auction)
- What services does the customer expect? (Sales support) (Application engineering) (Financial services) (Installation services) (Return services) (Repair services) (Calibration services) (Recycling) (Other)

Step 3: Benchmark the Competition (Chapter 2)

- Who are the competitors? (Largest) (Fastest growing) (Newest)
- What is the competitive advantage of their network? (Cost) (Responsiveness) (Quality) (Service)
- Plot the competitive order-to-delivery cycle time along the velocity axis of the value circle.

- Plot the competitive delivered pricing along the landed cost axis of the value circle.
- Plot the number of competitive network echelons along the variability axis of the value circle.
- Plot the competitive inventory turns along the network inventory axis of the value circle.

NETWORK BLUEPRINT SHEET #1: NETWORK DESIGN

Sheet #1 of the network blueprint is the plan for designing a competitive network, see Figure A-2. It defines a set of core value-adding relationships among a small number of trading partners and draws boundaries around other necessary nominal trading partners. The network cost structure, its velocity threshold, and its susceptibility to logistics variability are all determined by decisions made from sheet #1.

THE NETWORK DESIGN SPECIFICATION

The network design specification in Table A-1 documents key aspects of a network design. The specification table helps to differentiate this particular network design from competing network designs and modifications. The network design specification should be updated each time the network design is iterated.

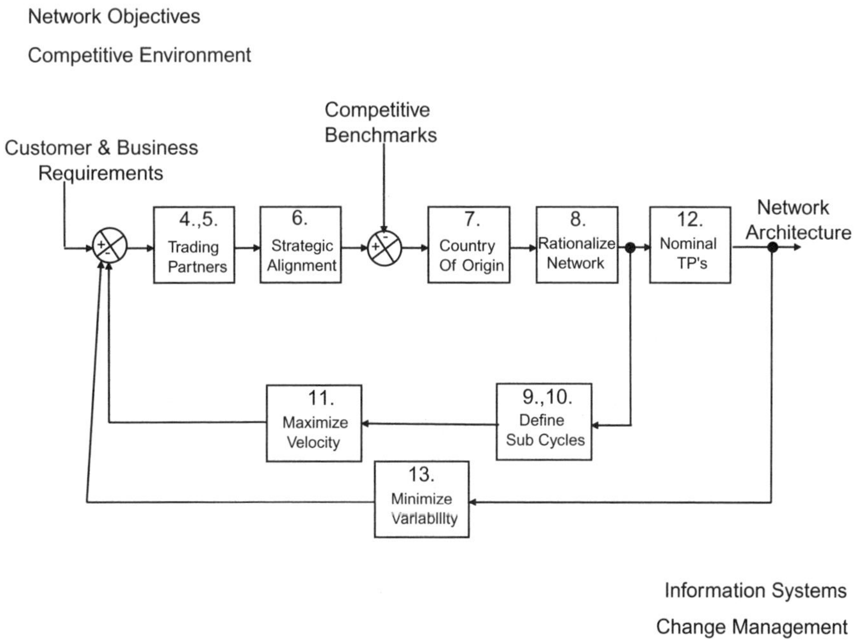

FIGURE A-2 Network blueprint sheet #1: network design.

TABLE A-1
The Network Design Specification

Specification	Qualifier—Circle one qualifier per row
Document the Business Strategy and Objectives	
Business strategy	[Product leader] [Broad line] [Move up the value chain] [Lowest cost provider] [Recovery and remanufacture]
Market breadth	[Local] [Regional] [National] [International] [Global]
Competitive situation	[Price] [Delivery] [Service] [Product Features]
Rough Cut the Network	
Rationalize the upstream zone	[Value-added transformation] [Echelons populated by nominal TP]
Rationalize the midstream zone	[Value-added manufacturing] [Echelons populated by nominal TP]
Rationalize the downstream zone	[Value-added fulfillment] [Echelons populated by nominal TP]
Network orchestrator	[Technology access] [Market access] [Financing access] [Other]
Forward supply chain delivery	[Products] [Services] [Consumables]
Reverse supply chain delivery	[Returns] [Repairs] [Recycling] [Loaners] [Remanufactured Products] [Services]
Rationalize reverse stream zone	[Value-subtracting transformation] [Value-adding remanufacture]
Maximize Subcycle Velocity	
Infrastructure	[Order-to-deliver] [Order-to-stock] [Invoice-to-pay] [Invoice-to-cash] Subcycle mean
Minimize Subcycle Variability	
Infrastructure	[Order-to-deliver] [Order-to-stock] [Invoice-to-pay] [Invoice-to-cash] Subcycle standard deviation

Step 4: Assemble a Set of Value-Adding Trading Partners to Transverse the Network (Chapter 3)

- How are raw materials transformed into components upstream?
- How many echelons (1) (2) (3) are required to reach to the raw materials?
- How are components manufactured into products midstream?
- How many echelons (1) (2) (3) are required to implement the BOM?
- How are products and services fulfilled downstream?
- How many echelons (1) (2) (3) are required to reach the end-customer?
- What are the network reverse stream requirements? (Return) (Repair) (Remanufacture) (Recycle)
- How many echelons are required in the reverse stream?

Step 5: Test that the Organizations in the Core Network are All Trading Partners (Chapter 3)

- Are both the majority of node purchases and the majority of node sales in-network? (Trading partner) (Nominal trading partner)

- Has a partnership agreement been negotiated with each trading partner? (Yes) (No)
- If an essential node is a nominal trading partner, can its value-added function be consolidated with an adjacent trading partner? (Yes) (No)
- Are the network echelons populated by trading partners contiguous? (Yes) (No)
- Is there a need to develop strategic nominal trading partners? (Yes) (No)

Step 6: Ensure That the Core Network Aligns with the Business Strategy (Chapter 2)

- If the business strategy is to be the lowest cost producer in the market, then the network architecture requires a supply chain length that is shorter than that of the competition.
- If the business strategy is to be a leader in product technology, then the upstream network architecture requires including the technology supplier and the technology supplier's raw material supply base.
- If the business strategy is to be the broadest line supplier for "one stop shopping," then the midstream network architecture requires the inclusion of products licensed from other supply chains.
- If the business strategy is to move up the value chain by in-sourcing customer processes, then the downstream network architecture requires including trading partners to deliver value-added services.
- If the business strategy is to recover and remanufacture for an aftermarket, then the reverse stream network architecture requires collection points, remanufacturing, parts supply, and recycling.

Step 7: Optimize the Product Cost Structure within the Core Network (Chapters 4, 9)

- Establish a baseline by costing out a complete BOM for the highest throughput product, assuming the core network, typical logistics costs, and typical pricing from network nodes yet to be identified.
- Identify each pricing interface and determine the appropriate pricing model based on buying or selling a unique or commodity material. (Static pricing) (Contract pricing) (Dynamic pricing) (Reverse auction)
- How can the cost structure of the network be reduced? (Shop the world) (Outsource at the component level) (Outsource at the product level) (License) (Disintermediate) (Consolidate) (In-source)
- Identify all import/export partitions in the network.
- Use landed cost to compare Country Of Origin alternatives. What is included in landed cost? (Labor) (Overhead) (Material) (Packaging material) (Outsourced material) (Freight) (Duty) (Cost of quality)

- Compare the cost plus price markup for total product landed cost against the competitive range of market pricing for each Country Of Destination.
- Though some countries may offer significantly reduced or near-zero income taxes, incremental profits sometimes can not be repatriated back to the home country manufacturer. (VAT) (Income tax)

Step 8: Rationalize the Length and Width of the Core Network (Chapter 3)

- Minimize the total number of network echelons. Eliminate any echelon that is not essential for adding value to upstream transformation, midstream manufacture, downstream fulfillment, or reverse stream remanufacturing.
- Review the network length tradeoffs for outsourcing. (Increased profitability from a particular Country Of Origin) (Lower network responsiveness due to increased network length) (Lower returns from increased network asset investments in inventory and cash buffers)
- Are there opportunities to shorten the network by flattening the product structure of the BOM? (Yes to all products) (Yes to some products) (No)
- Determine the width of the downstream network. Will there be parallel network structures for reasons of competitive delivery time or reach across geography? Optimize the location of distribution centers and warehouses.
- Determine the width of the midstream network. Will there be parallel network structures for reasons of dissimilar product BOM types, manufacturing capacity, or breadth of product line?
- Determine the width of the upstream network. Will there be parallel network structures for reasons of product cost or continuity of supply? Optimize the total number of suppliers.

Step 9: Define the Set of Information-to-Material Subcycles (Chapter 4)

- Start with the end-customer and work upstream, coupling each trading partner's inventory buffer to the next and defining complete subcycles of ordering information to material flow.
- Map each order-to-deliver and order-to-stock subcycle by combining relevant arcs, loops, and triggers, see Table A-2. Assign a single process owner for each subcycle.
- Does the seller deliver the product to the buyer or does the buyer pickup the product from the seller?
- Any import/export partition cuts an information-to-material loop in two places.
- Add the necessary information service providers and logistics service providers as nominal trading partners to complete the network.
- Consider the implications of the subcycle loop design on network security.

TABLE A-2
Mapping Network Processes

Process Element	Definition	Process Velocity	Process Variability
Arc	A set of process steps that defines the flow of material, the flow of information, or the flow of cash from one trading partner to another.	Mean	Standard deviation
Loop	A set of process steps that defines the value-added processing of material, or information, or cash done by one trading partner.	Mean	Standard deviation
Trigger	A set of process steps that defines a connection between information flow and material flow at one trading partner, or a connection between information flow and cash flow at one trading partner.	Mean	Standard deviation

Step 10: Define the Set of Information-to-Cash Subcycles (Chapter 4)

- Start with the raw material suppliers and work downstream, coupling each trading partner's cash buffer to the next and defining complete subcycles of invoicing information to cash flow.
- Map each invoice-to-pay and invoice-to-cash subcycle by combining relevant arcs, loops, and triggers, see Table A-2. Assign a single process owner for each subcycle.
- Does the buyer pay before delivery, or does the buyer pay after the delivery of a product?
- Any import/export partition cuts an information-to-cash loop in two places.
- Add the necessary information service providers and financial service providers as nominal trading partners to complete the network.
- Consider the implications of the subcycle loop design on network security.

Step 11: Maximize the Order-to-Delivery-to-Cash Velocity Among Trading Partners (Chapters 4, 5)

- Assign a mean time to each process step paying attention to management policy, transit time, customs time, security clearance time, manufacturing

cycle time, distribution cycle time, queue time, information transmission time, and information systems time.
- Import/export partitions add incremental process steps and cycle time.
- Required security processing adds incremental process steps and cycle time.
- Use the sum of the means as the velocity measure for the combined serial process steps.
- Maximize velocity by reducing the total number of process steps, by reducing the times of individual process steps, and by converting serial process flows into parallel process flows.
- Rank order the mean process step times, and maximize velocity by shortening the mean process step time for the longest steps.
- Compare the resulting order-to-delivery velocity to the end-customer with that of the competition.

Iterate the integration of the core network trading partners back to Step 4 (as required).

Step 12: Extend the Core Network to Reach Every Customer, to Complete the Composite BOM, and to Access Every Supplier (Chapter 4)

- Large customers may be trading partners, whereas small customers are nominal trading partners.
- Add additional downstream nominal trading partners to reach all customers. Notice that this will widen the downstream and may add new echelons to the downstream.
- Large suppliers or distributors may be trading partners, whereas small suppliers are nominal trading partners.
- Add additional upstream and midstream nominal trading partners to complete the BOM for every product. Notice that this will broaden the upstream and may add new echelons to the upstream and midstream.

Step 13: Minimize Network Order-to-Delivery-to-Cash Variability (Chapters 4, 5)

- Assign a standard deviation of processing time to each process step, paying attention to management policy, transit time, customs time, security clearance time, manufacturing cycle time, distribution cycle time, queue time, information transmission time, and information systems time.
- Import/export partitions can add significant incremental variability.
- Required security processing can add significant incremental variability.
- Use the root mean square of the combined serial process step standard deviations as the variability measure for each subcycle, see Table A-3.

TABLE A-3
The Normal Distribution

For the data points $X_1, X_2, X_3, \ldots X_n$	
The mean M of a normal distribution is calculated:	$M = \sum_{i=1}^{n} X_i/n$
The standard deviation SD of a normal distribution is calculated:	$SD = \frac{\sqrt{(X_1 - M)^2 + (X_2 - M)^2 + (X_3 - M)^2 + \cdots + (X_n - M)^2}}{n}$
For two or more independent normal distributions in series: M_1, SD_1 M_2, SD_2 M_j, SD_j	$M_s = M_1 + M_2 + \cdots + M_j$ $SD_s = \sqrt{(SD_1)^2 + (SD_2)^2 + \cdots + (SD_j)^2}$ The Root Mean Squared (RMS) value of the standard deviations.
For two or more independent normal distributions in parallel: M_1, SD_1 M_2, SD_2 M_j, SD_j	M_p = Largest of $(M_1, M_2, \ldots, M_j)$ SD_p = Largest of $(SD_1, SD_2, \ldots, SD_j)$
A 95.4% service level equals the mean plus two standard deviations:	M + 2SD
A 99.7% service level equals the mean plus three standard deviations:	M + 3SD

- Rank order the process step standard deviations and minimize variability by determining the root cause of the largest standard deviation and either eliminating or significantly reducing it.
- Continue to minimize variability by determining the root cause of the next largest standard deviation and either eliminating or significantly reducing it.
- Analyze and minimize each network subcycle in turn.

Iterate the integration of nominal trading partners back to Step 4, as required.

NETWORK BLUEPRINT SHEET #2: THE COMPOSITE BOM

Sheet #2 of the network blueprint is the plan for integrating the bills of materials with both the network design and network operations, see Figure A-3. It defines the composite BOM, the dominant BOM type, and the network operating mode. The network's length and width, its delivery performance, and its flexibility are each influenced by decisions made from sheet #2.

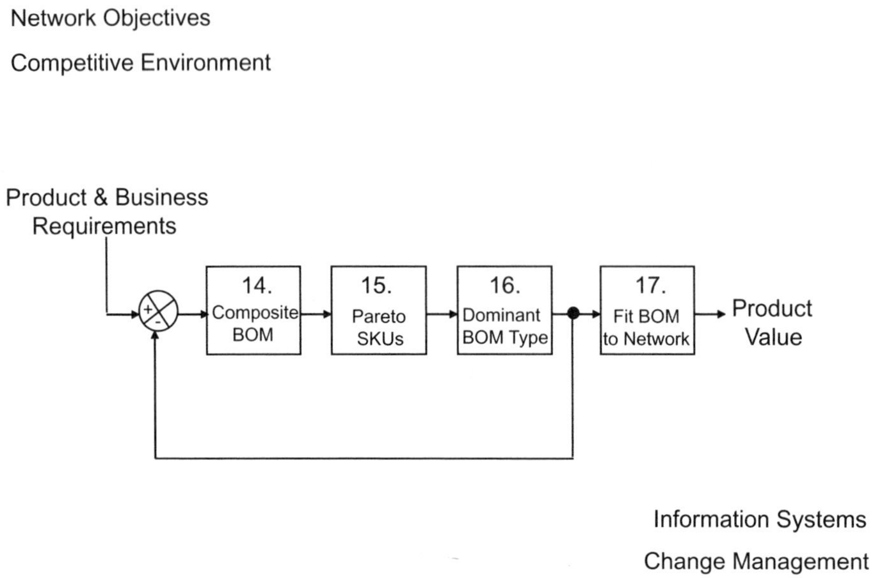

FIGURE A-3 Network blueprint sheet #2: the composite BOM.

The Product BOM Specification

The product BOM specification in Table A-4 documents key aspects of the fit between the network and the composite BOM. A composite BOM integrates the bills of materials required to build every product and product option that passes through the network. The specification table helps to differentiate the fit of this particular composite BOM from competing designs and modifications. The product BOM specification should be updated each time the composite BOM is iterated.

TABLE A-4
The Product BOM Specification

Specification	Qualifier—Circle one qualifier per row
Demand Requirements	
Dominant SKUs	[By revenue] [By contribution margin]
Operating mode	[CF] [BTS] [ATO] [BTO] [ETO]
Dominant product life cycle	[New product ramp] [Maturity] [Old product obsolescence]
Product Structure	
Composite BOM-type	[A] [I] [T] [V] [Combination]
Postponement opportunity	[At reseller] [In distribution] [at factory]
Risk pooling opportunity	BOM Level [2] [3] [4] [5] [Other]

Step 14: Generate a Composite BOM (Chapter 7)

- Align each BOM so that Level 0, Level 1, Level 2, etc. of Product A corresponds to Level 0, Level 1, Level 2, etc. of Product B and corresponds to Level 0, Level 1, Level 2, etc. of Product C, and so on.
- Pick two products to start.
- Work from the highest-level parent to the lowest-level child.
- For each product structure level, combine all the items at that level for both products. List only new and unique items. If an item is already listed for that level, then skip over it.
- Continue working down the product structure until the last levels of both products are exhausted.
- Combine the next product with the earlier combination by repeating the process. Stop the process when every applicable level of every product has been combined into the composite BOM.
- When completed, the composite BOM lists every "child" item from every supplier required to manufacture a complete set of "parent" products.

Step 15: List All SKUs and Pareto the List by Revenue and by Contribution Margin (Chapter 9)

- Create a master list of SKUs delivered through the supply chain network.
- Rank order the SKUs in the descending order of the revenue each one generates.
- Rank order the SKUs in the descending order of the Contribution Margin each one generates, where contribution margin = [price – variable costs].
- Which SKUs are in the top 20%? Where are these SKUs in their product life cycles? Are there any other SKUs that are growing so fast that they will enter the top 20% within a year?
- Optimize the network design and the network operation around the SKUs in the top 20%.

Step 16: Determine a Predominant BOM Type from the Composite BOM (Chapters 7, 9)

- What is the predominant BOM type of the composite BOM? (A) (I) (T) (V) (Combination)
- Is more than one BOM type required to manufacture all products? (Yes) (No)
- Eliminate product combinations that require noncompetitive BOM type combinations.
- Eliminate products that will soon be discontinued.
- Identify BOM product structure breakpoints to outsource upstream.
- Identify BOM product structure breakpoints to postpone downstream.

Iterate the composite BOM back to Step 14, as required.

Step 17: Fit the BOM to the Network and Decide the Network Operating Mode (Chapter 7)

- Match the composite BOM type with the corresponding operating mode. The operating mode should allow the product to be built only to the extent to which its options are customer defined.
- [I] goes with [CF].
- [A] goes with [BTS].
- [T] goes with [ATO].
- [V] goes with [BTO].
- [ETO] can be used for all BOM-types but requires a project planning methodology.

NETWORK BLUEPRINT SHEET #3: NETWORK OPERATIONS

Sheet #3 of the network blueprint is the plan for operating a competitive network, see Figure A-4. It locates the push/pull boundary, identifies the network constraint, differentiates pull from push planning, maximizes network vocalization and visualization, and defines a set of global performance measures. The network's asset investment, inventory placement, cash synchronization, and product delivery availability are each determined by decisions made from sheet #3.

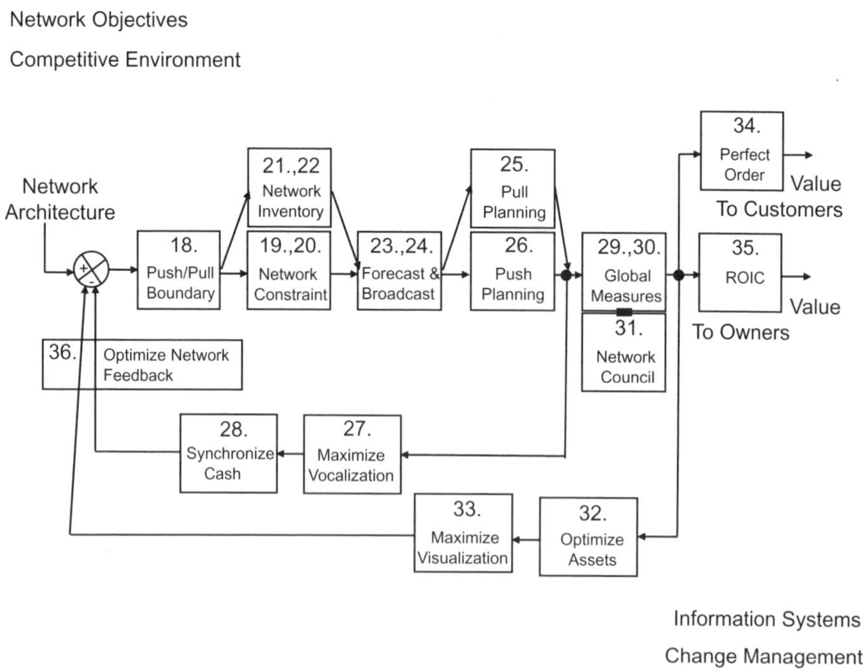

FIGURE A-4 Network blueprint sheet #3: network operation.

The Network Operation Specification

The network operation specification in Table A-5 documents key aspects of network operations. The specification table helps to differentiate this particular network operation from competing network operations and modifications. The network operations specification should be updated each time the network operation is iterated.

TABLE A-5
The Network Operation Specification

Specification	Qualifier—Circle one qualifier per row
Demand Requirements	
Demand pattern	[Continuous] [Seasonal] [Promotional] [New Product Introduction]
Demand distortion	[Amplification factor] [No bullwhip effect]
Competitive lead-time	[CF] [BTS] [ATO] [BTO] [ETO] Competitive data
Forecast	[Inventory rate] [Inventory mix] [Capacity rate] [Capacity mix] [Combination by operating zone]
Demand signal	[Point-of-sale demand] [Demand broadcast] [Sequential demand communication]
Push/pull boundary	Define the echelon containing the push/pull boundary
Zone Operations	
Product availability	BTS service level greater than [99.7%][95.5%] delivered from stock BTO service level greater than [99.7%][95.4%] delivered to first date
Operational control	[Pull-synchronized] [Pull-kanban] [Push-MRP II] [Push-VMI]
Network throughput	[Minimum rate] [Maximum rate]
Network constraint	[Skilled workforce] [Machine capacity] [Transportation capacity] [Management policy] [Inventory] [Cash]
Constraint movement	[Constraint moves with mix] [Constraint doesn't move with mix]
Time to ramp capacity	[+10%] [+20%] [+50%] [+100%] [+200%] [–10%] [–20%] [–50%] [–100%] [–200%]
Cash flow requirements	[Synchronized cash flow by cash buffer location] [Min/Max cash levels established by cash buffer location]
Network inventory placement	[Shipping buffer] [Postponement] [Constraint buffer] [Assembly buffer] [Preload] [Push/pull boundary] [Risk pooling] [Combinations]
Time to ramp inventory	[+10%] [+20%] [+50%] [+100%] [+200%] [–10%] [–20%] [–50%] [–100%] [–200%]
Maximize Vocalization	
Number of echelons connected	[2] [3] [4] [5] [6] [More]
Maximize Visualization	
Number of echelons connected	[2] [3] [4] [5] [6] [More]

Step 18: Locate the Push/Pull Boundary of Inventory Buffers and Cash Buffers Based on Customer Expectations and Competitive Delivery (Chapter 7)

- Locate the push/pull boundary such that the order-to-delivery cycle time to the customer is faster than the competition.
- Avoid locating the push/pull boundary where the BOM widens with great complexity.
- Recognize that the push/pull boundary is a set of inventory buffers and cash buffers all within the same echelon that cut across the entire network width.

Step 19: Determine Network Capability Over the Expected Demand Uncertainty (Chapters 7, 8)

- Use four to six months of order history to determine the sum of the means and the RMS value of the standard deviations of SKU demand. Use the BOM quantity per relationships to calculate the equivalent throughput in each echelon per unit delivered to the end-customer.
- To achieve a 99.7% service level, the network constraint should have the daily capacity to process the sum of the means plus three times the RMS value of the standard deviations of the equivalent throughputs of each independent demand. Two times the RMS value of the standard deviations drops the service level to 95.4%. All nonconstraint capacities are larger by definition.
- To achieve a 99.7% service level, a time buffer should have a safety time level equal to three times the RMS value of the standard deviations of the relevant value-added cycle times plus transit times. Two times the RMS value of the standard deviations drops the service level to 95.4%.
- To achieve a 99.7% service level, a quantity buffer should have a safety stock level equal to three times the RMS value of the standard deviations of the BOM equivalence of each independent demand. Two times the RMS value of the standard deviations drops the service level to 95.4%.
- To achieve a 99.7% service level, a cash buffer should have a safety cash level equal to three times the RMS value of the standard deviations of the mean accounts payable related to equivalent throughput in that echelon. Two times the RMS value of the standard deviations drops the service level to 95.4%.

Step 20: Identify the Network Constraint and the Network Orchestrator (Chapters 3, 8)

- Determine which trading partner is the network constraint. If the network constraint is a nominal trading partner, invest to shift the network constraint over to one of the trading partners.

- Which of the subcycles is the constraint? (Order-to-deliver) (Order-to-stock) (Invoice-to-pay) (Invoice-to-cash)
- If the network constraint is either information or cash, invest to subordinate an information or a cash constraint to a physical distribution constraint.
- Does network capacity constraint move with a shift in the demand mix? (Yes) (No)

Step 21: Position and Size the Inventory Buffers (Chapters 7, 8)

- *Shipping Buffer (downstream)*—Finished goods inventory held at a customer-facing node, such as a retail store, is the first product delivered to fulfill the customer's order. This inventory provides an immediate response; it is the most competitive delivery in terms of response time. When the demand quantity exceeds the shipping buffer, additional product is drop shipped from a warehouse or the remaining shipments are spread out over time until the store is replenished. The shipping buffer is sized to protect against variability in the fulfillment cycle times and transit times from the network location of the network constraint to the shipping buffer.
- *Postponement inventory (downstream)*—Nearly finished product is completed to customer order from a predefined set of options. Postponement is not customization. This inventory holds a safety stock of all the remaining items necessary to complete every option BOM. Sometimes postponement inventory doubles as a shipping buffer. Postponement is positioned close to the end-customer.
- *Preload inventory (typically downstream)*—This inventory is stocked at each node in a synchronized supply chain before synchronized operations can begin. Preload inventory establishes the maximum rate of throughput ramp up that can be achieved in one synchronization cycle after the start of synchronized operations.
- *Constraint buffer (any zone)*—The constraint buffer is a time buffer used to resolve upstream problems before the network constraint is halted, causing an unrecoverable loss in throughput. The constraint buffer is sized to protect against variability in the manufacturing cycle times and transit times from the source of raw materials to the network location of the network constraint. Material should not be allowed to enter the constraint buffer with components missing or with a known quality defect. Material should enter the constraint buffer when it is tied to a shippable order.
- *Assembly buffer (any zone)*—An assembly point occurs where constrained material and nonconstrained material come together. An assembly point can occur either upstream or downstream from the network constraint. The assembly buffer is sized to protect against variability in the transformation cycle times and transit times from the source of the constrained materials to the network location of the assembly buffer.
- *Push/pull boundary (any zone)*—This inventory location acts as the shock absorber between relatively smooth forecast-driven operations and relatively

erratic order-driven operations. Sometimes the push/pull boundary doubles as the constraint buffer or as risk-pooled safety stock.

- *Risk pooling inventory (upstream)*—Safety stock inventory locations that are far enough upstream that they can pool the risks of parallel, statistically independent demands. Risk pooling inventory is typically used to protect service level performance against unexpected swings in product mix. This safety stock is sized to cover the RMS of standard deviations of independent demand.

Step 22: Analyze the Composite BOM for Opportunities to Postpone and to Risk Pool Inventory. Use Statistical Safety Stock on Unique Materials to Support Mix Variation (Chapters 7, 8)

- Identify lower level common items in the composite BOM for risk pooling.
- Identify upper level unique items in the composite BOM for postponement.
- To achieve (99.7%) (95.4%) service level of safety stock, an inventory buffer should have a safety stock level equal to (3×) (2×) the RMS value of the standard deviations of the BOM equivalent of each independent demand.

Step 23: Forecast the Right Things and Forecast Things Right (Chapter 8)

- The demand for independent products is forecast, whereas the demand for lower level dependent items is calculated.
- Divide the standard deviation by the mean for each product forecast. Separate the list of products into volatile products where the standard deviation exceeds the mean and non-volatile products where the mean exceeds the standard deviation.
- Forecast demand and supply independently.
- Work the forecast in units, and dollarize the unit forecast as required.
- Subtract out the historical rate of returns from the historical demand pattern.
- Adjust the number of units in the demand forecast to include customer support requirements.
- Adjust the number of units in the forecast to compensate for any known process yields.
- Forecast inventory rate and capacity mix for a BTS business. Forecast inventory rate, inventory mix, capacity rate, and capacity mix for an ATO business. Forecast inventory mix and capacity rate for a BTO business. Forecast capacity rate and capacity mix for an ETO business.
- Both inventory levels and cash levels need to be forecast so that neither one constrains throughput.
- Use simple forecasting models. Level is simpler than trend; trend is simpler than seasonal.
- If the right forecasting model is being used, the forecast error should be statistically random and without bias. If non-random, change the forecast model. If biased, adjust the forecast by the [+/–] mean of the forecast error.

Step 24: Broadcast Demand in Parallel to Minimize the Bullwhip Effect (Chapter 7)

- *Rule 1*—The customer-facing end of the supply chain delivers the ordered rate and mix from its shipping buffer.
- *Rule 2A*—If the network constraint has the daily capacity to meet the rate and mix of the actual demand, then the rate and mix in the broadcast demand is identical to the actual demand.
- *Rule 2B*—If the network constraint does not have the daily capacity to meet the rate and mix of the actual demand, then the broadcast demand signal contains a constrained rate or mix. The network constraint manages the order backlog for the network.
- *Rule 3*—All other nodes produce an equivalent throughput of products, assemblies, or components that will satisfy the rate and mix of the broadcast demand signal.
- *Rule 4*—The supplier end of the network orders raw materials to match the cumulative daily rate of the actual demand.

Step 25: Use Collaborative Pull Planning in the Pull Zone (Chapter 8)

- There should be only one collaborative plan across the network for pull zone operations.
- The pull zone precedes the push zone.
- The highest levels of the product BOM may fall into the pull zone.
- Break the number of echelons between the end-customer and the push/pull boundary into one or more subzones. Use pull-synchronize when all trading partners can act in parallel and pull to an actual customer order. Use pull-kanban when the demand side (nominal) trading partner controls the pull to a stocking level.
- The network capability, preload inventory buffers, and synchronized cash buffers are re-centered against the mean demand once a month.

Step 26: Use Collaborative Push Planning in the Push Zone (Chapter 8)

- There should be only one collaborative plan across the network for push zone operations.
- The push zone succeeds the pull zone.
- The lower levels of the product BOM will fall into the push zone.
- Break the number of echelons between the push/pull boundary and raw materials into one or more subzones. Use push-MRP II when the push is from the buyer. Use push-VMI when the push is from the seller.
- Use push-rate when the push is to a stocking date. Use push-mix when the push is to a stocking level.
- The pull demand at the push/pull boundary becomes the demand forecast for push planning.

- The planning horizon must drive demand down through the lowest levels of the composite BOM.
- Push planning methods include the demand forecast, the supply forecast, S&OP, DRP, MPS, MRP, and CRP.

Step 27: Maximize the Vocalization of Demand Across the Network (Chapter 7)

- Connect all the trading partners and strategic nominal trading partners with actual point of sale demand information.
- Connect all the trading partners and strategic nominal trading partners with the daily broadcast demand originating from the network constraint.

Step 28: Synchronize Flows in the Pull Zone of the Network (Chapters 5, 8)

- Use a Bill Of Cash to break down revenue dollars by (nominal) trading partner.
- Plan for the downstream cash buffers to cover the cost of the preload inventory.
- Establish management policies that preauthorize cash flows for inventory.
- Define a set of inventory to cash triggers that synchronize cash flows across the pull echelons.
- Synchronize the flows of cash upstream with the logistics of moving material downstream.

Iterate network vocalization back to Step 18, as required.

Step 29: Plot the Principle Axes on the Value Circle (Chapters 4, 7); See Figure A-5

- The Velocity Principle:

$$\frac{\text{Design Velocity}}{\text{Baseline Network}} =$$

$$\frac{\text{\# Days to complete one subcycle in the new network design}}{\text{\# Days to complete one subcycle in the baseline network}}$$

  Where the #Days is the sum of each process step mean. Velocity increases toward the origin of the Value Circle.
- The Visualize Principle:

$$\frac{\text{\% of Network Visualizing}}{\text{Baseline Network}} =$$

$$\frac{\text{Actual number of nodes connected to global performance measures} \times 100\%}{\text{Total number of relevant nodes}}$$

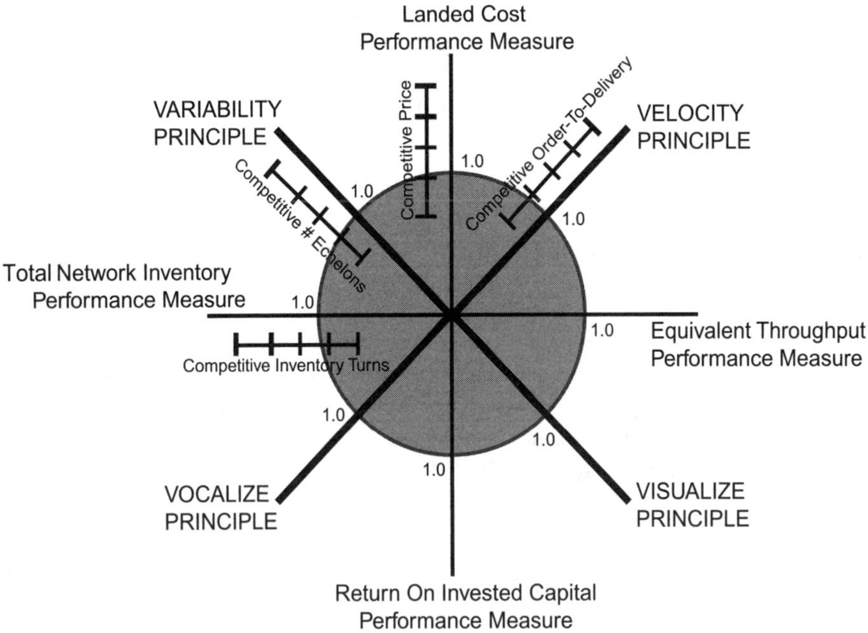

FIGURE A-5 The value circle.

Where the term relevant node includes all trading partners plus strategic nominal trading partners essential to the network's material flow. Visualization improves toward the origin of the value circle.

- The Vocalize Principle:

$$\frac{\text{\% of Network Vocalizing}}{\text{Baseline Network}} =$$

$$\frac{\text{Actual number of nodes connected to the broadcast demand} \times 100\%}{\text{Total number of relevant nodes}}$$

Where the term relevant node includes all trading partners plus strategic nominal trading partners essential to the network's material flow. Vocalization improves toward the origin of the value circle.

- The Variability Principle:

$$\frac{\text{Design Variability}}{\text{Baseline Network}} =$$

$$\frac{\text{\# Days of subcycle variability in the new network design}}{\text{\# Days of subcycle variability in the baseline network}}$$

Where the #Days is the root mean square value of the standard deviations for each of the process steps. Variability decreases toward the origin of the Value Circle.

Step 30: Plot the Global Performance Measures Axes on the Value Circle (Chapters 4, 6, 7, 9); See Figure A-5

- The Landed Costs Performance Measure:

$$\frac{\text{Design Landed Cost}}{\text{Baseline Landed Cost}} =$$

$$\frac{\text{\$ Cost of Goods Sold in the new network design}}{\text{\$ Cost of Goods Sold in the baseline network}}$$

See Chapter 4 for details of relevant labor, overhead, material, packaging materials, outsourced "material," freight, duty and the cost of quality. Use the mean throughput for the unit volume. Landed Cost deceases toward the origin of the Value Circle.

- The Equivalent Throughput Performance Measure:

$$\frac{\text{Operating throughput}}{\text{Baseline Network}} =$$

$$\frac{\text{Units of Operating Equivalent Throughput}}{\text{Units of Baseline Equivalent Throughput}}$$

See Chapter 6 for equivalent throughput details. Equivalent throughput increases toward the origin of the Value Circle.

- The Return On Invested Capital Performance Measure:

$$\frac{\text{Operating ROIC}}{\text{Baseline Network}} =$$

$$\frac{\text{\% Operating[Profit After Tax/[Capacity Asset + Inventory Asset + Receivables − Payables]]}}{\text{\% Baseline[Profit After Tax/[Capacity Asset + Inventory Asset + Receivables − Payables]]}}$$

% ROIC can be calculated for a single trading partner or for the whole network, see Chapter 9. % ROIC increases toward the origin of the Value Circle.

- The Total Network Inventory Performance Measure:

$$\frac{\text{Operating Total Network Inventory}}{\text{Baseline Network}} =$$

$$\frac{\text{Actual Inventory \$-Days}}{\text{Throughput Inventory \$-Days}}$$

See Chapter 7 for the inventory $-Days to sweep one unit of the composite BOM end-to-end plus the incremental inventory $-Days driven by network uncertainty and variability. Total network inventory decreases toward the origin of the value circle.

Step 31: Maintain Network Alignment with the Business Strategy (Chapter 9)

- Hold periodic (monthly) (quarterly) operations meetings of the Network Operations Council of upstream, midstream, and downstream trading partner representatives to resolve operational issues.
- Reach consensus on the right set of global performance measures.
- Define a common dashboard around these performance measures.
- Expand the percentage of (nominal) trading partners using these measures.

Step 32: Optimize the Inventory and Cash Assets in the Nodes and Pipelines (Chapters 7, 9)

- Insist on operating from only one plan in the pull zone and only one plan in the push zone for all trading partners. Follow the lead of the network orchestrator.
- Ensure the network constraint is a physical capacity constraint rather than an information constraint, a financial constraint, or a policy constraint.
- Plan the level of inventory in the inventory buffers and the level of cash in the cash buffers.
- Minimize variability and drive excess inventory out of the network.
- Use forward auctions to sell excess inventory.
- Use the customer's cash to finance network inventory by synchronizing the cash flow with a Bill Of Cash.

Step 33: Maximize Visualization Throughout the Network (Chapters 6, 7)

- Connect all the trading partners to information supporting a global performance measures dashboard.
- Monitor equivalent throughput in each echelon to gauge changes in network capacity relative to demand. Take action on network capacity where appropriate.
- Monitor total network inventory across the network to gauge changes in the inventory investment relative to demand. Take action on network inventory where appropriate.

Iterate network visualization back to Step 18, as required.

Step 34: Use the Perfect Order As a Measure of Value and Quality to the Customer (Chapter 9)

- Arrange a periodic sampling of the perfect order to be measured by key customers.
- The right product complete with all its ordered options? (Yes) (No)
- Delivered to the right place? (Yes) (No)

- Delivered at exactly the right time? (Not early) (Time window) (Not late)
- Delivered in the right quantity? (Exact quantity or weight) (No overage) (No underage)
- Invoiced with perfect pricing and discount information accuracy? (Yes) (No)
- Delivered with no returns? (Yes) (No)
- Delivered with no hassles? (Yes) (No)

Step 35: Use ROIC to Measure Owner Value (Chapter 9)

- Grow bottom line after tax profit from reduced landed cost and reduced income tax as related by the income statement.
- Grow top line revenue by matching supply with demand.
- Grow top line revenue by matching demand with supply.
- Reduce working capital requirements for smaller capacity, inventory and accounts receivable assets, and smaller accounts payable liabilities as related through the balance sheet.
- ROIC measures the (improvement)(deterioration) of both the income statement and the balance sheet.
- Improvement in ROIC correlates with (improvement)(deterioration) in a trading partner's common stock price.

Step 36: Optimize Network Planning and Performance Measurement Feedback (Chapter 9)

Closing a planning feedback path, Table A-6, or a performance measurement feedback path, Table A-7, around a network can cause an underdamped, overdamped, or oscillatory response.

- *Overdamped*—Delayed or late in making capacity, inventory, and cash adjustments. Late in adjusting to a performance measurement. Network performance can be improved from here.

TABLE A-6
Network Planning Feedback Loops

Inner loop definition The "pull" loop	Input = Forecast × Transform × Manufacture	Forward path = Fulfill Feedback path = Actual demand	Output = Throughput mix and rate
Middle loop definition The "push$_1$" loop	Input = Forecast × Transform	Forward path = Manufacture × Fulfill Feedback path = Actual demand + Planned demand	Output = Throughput mix and rate
Outer loop definition The "push$_2$" loop	Input = Forecast	Forward path = Transform × Manufacture × Fulfill Feedback path = Actual demand + Planned demand	Output = Throughput mix and rate

TABLE A-7
Network Performance Measurement Feedback Loops

First loop definition The fulfill loop	Input = Forecast × Transform × Manufacture	Forward path = Fulfill Feedback path = Fulfill performance measures	Output = Throughput mix and rate
Second loop definition The manufacture loop	Input = Forecast × Transform	Forward path = Manufacture × Fulfill Feedback path = Manufacture perform measures + Fulfill performance measures	Output = Throughput mix and rate
Third loop definition The transform loop	Input = Forecast	Forward pat = Transform × Manufacture × Fulfill Feedback path = Transform perform measures + Manufacture perform measures + Fulfill performance measures	Output = Throughput mix and rate

- *Underdamped*—Nervous response with excessive capacity, inventory, and cash readjustments. Excessive number of readjustments to a performance measurement. Network performance is past its optimal point.
- *Oscillatory*—Eliminate the bullwhip effect and any other sustained network instability in planning and measuring network capacity or the inventory and cash buffers.

FINAL STEPS

Having completed the journey from Step 1 through Step 36, it is time to fit an information system to the network. Finally, changing behavior from being internally focused and cost driven to becoming externally focused and network throughput driven requires explicit change management.

STEP 37: FIT AN INFORMATION SYSTEM TO THE NETWORK (CHAPTER 5)

- Work only within the context of the trading partners. The set of nominal trading partners is unstable.
- Map the required data elements to a minimum number of databases.
- Define the business rules within each software application to mirror each subcycle process loop.
- Minimize the partitioning of information caused by organizational boundaries, import/export boundaries, cultural boundaries, and information system boundaries.
- Drive toward parallelism for order cash interconnections.
- Put a process in place to continuously monitor data element accuracy.
- Pay strict attention to information security within the network.
- Work within industry standards and best practices.

Step 38: Manage Change Continuously (Chapters 6, 10)

- Share a compelling vision of what the new supply chain network offers to customers, owners, employees and suppliers.
- Acknowledge the enormity of the change, and communicate What's In It For Me (WIIFM) to each of the stakeholder groups.
- Staff for change with full time people.
- Employ program management tools.
- Change the performance measures in order to change people's behaviors.
- Communicate, communicate, communicate.
- Use a common, industry standard vocabulary when educating employee and trading partner teams about the principles of supply chain management.
- Provide employee cross-functional training on the use of the specific information systems to perform their work.
- Invest in network simulation practice for the operations management team with representation from each of the trading partners.
- Reward personal commitment, and celebrate small successes across organizational boundaries.

The network blueprint is now complete.

Appendix B: Bibliography

The following titles have had a profound influence on the author and this book:

Alber, K. L., and Walker, W. T., *Supply Chain Management Principles and Techniques for the Practitioner*, APICS E&R Foundation, Alexandria, VA, 1998.

Boeckerstette, J. A., and Shell, R. L., *Time Based Manufacturing*, McGraw-Hill, Norcross, GA, 1993.

Dell, M., *Direct From Dell: Strategies That Revolutionized an Industry*, HarperCollinsBusiness, London, 1999.

Goldratt, E. M., and Cox, J., *The Goal: Excellence In Manufacturing*, North River Press, Croton-on-Hudson, NY, 1984.

Goldratt, E. M., *It's Not Luck*, North River Press, Great Barrington, MA, 1994.

Handfield, R. B., and Nichols, E. L., Jr., *Supply Chain Redesign: Transforming Supply Chains into Integrated Value Systems*, Prentice Hall, Upper Saddle River, NJ, 2002.

Helfert, E. A., *Techniques of Financial Analysis: A Practical Guide to Measuring Business Performance*, 9th ed., McGraw-Hill, New York, 1996.

Hickman, T. K., and Hickman, W. M., Jr., *Global Purchasing: How To Buy Foreign Market Goods And Services*, Business One Irwin, Homewood, IL, 1992.

Kaplan, R. S., and Norton, D. P., *The Balanced Scorecard*, Harvard Business Press, Boston, MA, 1996.

Locke, D., *Global Supply Management: A Guide To International Purchasing*, Irwin Professional Publishing, Chicago, IL, 1996.

McCormack, K. P., and Johnson, W. C., with Walker, W. T., *Supply Chain Networks and Business Process Orientation: Advanced Strategies and Best Practices*, St. Lucie Press, Boca Raton, FL, 2003.

Nagle, T. T., and Holden, R. K., *The Strategy and Tactics of Pricing: Guide to Profitable Decision Making*, 3rd ed., Prentice Hall, Upper Saddle River, NJ, 2002.

Nelson, C. A., *Import Export: How to Get Started in International Trade*, 3rd ed., McGraw-Hill, New York, NY, 2000.

Noreen, E., Smith, D., and Mackey, J. T., *The Theory Of Constraints and Its Implications For Management Accounting*, North River Press, Great Barrington, MA, 1995.

Packard, D., *The HP Way: How Bill Hewlett and I Built Our Company*, Harper Business, New York, 1995.

Preiss, K., Goldman, S. L., and Nagel, R.N., *Cooperate to Compete: Building Agile Business Relationships*, Van Nostrand Reinhold, New York, 1996.

Rummler, G. A., and Brache, A. P., *Improving Performance: How To Manage The White Space On The Organization Chart*, Jossey-Bass, San Francisco, 1990.

Schragenheim, E., and Dettmer, H. W., *Manufacturing at Warp Speed: Optimizing Supply Chain Financial Performance*, St. Lucie Press, Boca Raton, FL, 2001.

Senge, P. M., *The Fifth Discipline: The Art & Practice of The Learning Organization*, Doubleday/Currency, New York, 1990.

Simchi-Levi, D., Kaminsky, P., and Simchi-Levi, E., *Designing and Managing the Supply Chain*, Irwin McGraw-Hill, Boston, MA, 2000.

Smith, D., *The Measurement Nightmare: How the Theory of Constraints Can Resolve Conflicting Strategies, Policies, and Measures*, St. Lucie Press, Boca Raton, FL, 2000.

Treacy, M., and Wiersema, F., *Discipline Of Market Leaders: Choose Your Customers, Narrow Your Focus, Dominate Your Market*, Addison-Wesley Publishing Co., Reading, MA, 1995.

TABLE B-1
Supply Chain Related Web Sites

Organization		URL
AME	The Association for Manufacturing Excellence	www.ame.org
APICS	The Educational Society for Resource Management	www.apics.org
ASCET	Achieving Supply Chain Excellence through Technology	www.ascet.com
ASQ	American Society for Quality	www.asq.org
CSCMP	Council of Supply Chain Management Professionals (formerly CLM)	www.cscmp.org
ICC	International Chamber of Commerce Including INCOTERMS	www.iccwbo.org www.iccbooks.com
IMA	Institute of Management Accountants	www.imanet.org
IOPP	Institute Of Packaging Professionals	www.iopp.org
ISM	Institute of Supply Management	www.ism.ws
MSI	Marketing Science Institute	www.msi.org
RLEC	Reverse Logistics Executive Council	www.rlec.org
SCC	The Supply-Chain Council Including the SCOR Model	www.supply-chain.org
	US Customs Service	www.customs.ustreas.gov
VICS	Voluntary Interindustry Commerce Standards Including CPFR®	www.vics.org www.cpfr.org
WERC	Warehousing Education and Research Council	www.werc.org
WTO	World Trade Organization	www.wto.org

Index

N

O

P

Index

D

E

F

M

N

Q

R

S

T